COGNITIVE
PSYCHOLOGY

About the Author

E. Bruce Goldstein is a member of the cognitive psychology program in the Department of Psychology at the University of Pittsburgh and is Adjunct Professor of Psychology at the University of Arizona. He has received the Chancellor's Distinguished Teaching Award for his classroom teaching and textbook writing. He received his PhD in experimental psychology from Brown University and was a post-doctoral fellow in the Biology Department at Harvard University before joining the faculty at the University of Pittsburgh. Bruce has published papers on retinal and cortical physiology, visual attention, and the perception of pictures. He is the author of *Sensation & Perception* (7th edition, Wadsworth, 2007) and the editor of the *Blackwell Handbook of Perception* (Blackwell, 2001) and the forthcoming two-volume *Encyclopedia of Perception* (Sage). He teaches undergraduate courses in cognitive psychology and sensation and perception and a graduate course in the teaching of psychology.

E. BRUCE GOLDSTEIN

University of Pittsburgh
University of Arizona

SECOND EDITION

COGNITIVE PSYCHOLOGY

Connecting Mind, Research, and Everyday Experience

 WADSWORTH
CENGAGE Learning

Australia • Brazil • Japan • Korea • Mexico • Singapore • Spain •
United Kingdom • United States

WADSWORTH
CENGAGE Learning™

Cognitive Psychology: Connecting Mind, Research, and Everyday Experience, Second Edition
E. Bruce Goldstein

Publisher: Michele Sordi

Senior Development Editor: Kate Barnes

Assistant Editor: Magnolia Molcan

Editorial Assistant: Rachel Guzman

Senior Technology Project Manager: Bessie Weiss

Marketing Manager: Sara Swangard

Marketing Communications Manager: Linda Yip

Project Manager, Editorial Production: Mary Noel

Creative Director: Rob Hugel

Art Director: Vernon T. Boes

Print Buyer: Karen Hunt

Permissions Editor: Bob Kauser

Production Service: Anne Draus, Scratchgravel Publishing Services

Text Designer: Cheryl Carrington

Art Editor: Lisa Torri

Photo Researcher: Laura Molmud

Copy Editors: Mary Anne Shahidi, Elizabeth Kittrell

Illustrator: Precision Graphics

Cover Designer: Cheryl Carrington

Cover Image: Brian Ross/IPN

Compositor: Newgen

For product information and technology assistance, contact us at
Cengage Learning Customer & Sales Support, 1-800-354-9706

For permission to use material from this text or product, submit all requests online at **www.cengage.com/permissions**
Further permissions questions can be emailed to
permissionrequest@cengage.com

ExamView® and ExamView Pro® are registered trademarks of FSCreations, Inc. Windows is a registered trademark of the Microsoft Corporation used herein under license. Macintosh and Power Macintosh are registered trademarks of Apple Computer, Inc. Used herein under license.

Library of Congress Control Number: 2007920373

ISBN-13: 978-0-495-09557-6

ISBN-10: 0-495-09557-5

Wadsworth
10 Davis Drive
Belmont, CA 94002-3098
USA

Cengage Learning is a leading provider of customized learning solutions with office locations around the globe, including Singapore, the United Kingdom, Australia, Mexico, Brazil, and Japan. Locate your local office at:
www.cengage.com/global

Cengage Learning products are represented in Canada by Nelson Education, Ltd.

To learn more about Wadsworth, visit **www.cengage.com/Wadsworth**

Purchase any of our products at your local college store or at our preferred online store **www.ichapters.com**

Printed in the United States of America
5 6 7 11 10 09

To Barbara

Brief Contents

Chapter 1   Introduction to Cognitive Psychology   1

Chapter 2   Cognition and the Brain: Basic Principles   27

Chapter 3   Perception   55

Chapter 4   Attention   99

Chapter 5   Short-Term and Working Memory   135

Chapter 6   Long-Term Memory: Basic Principles   176

Chapter 7   Everyday Memory and Memory Errors   235

Chapter 8   Knowledge   283

Chapter 9   Visual Imagery   322

Chapter 10   Language   356

Chapter 11   Problem Solving   395

Chapter 12   Reasoning and Decision Making   434

Glossary   485

References   507

Name Index   539

Subject Index   544

Contents

Chapter 1   Introduction to Cognitive Psychology   1

The Challenge of Cognitive Psychology   3
     The Complexity of Cognition   3
     The First Cognitive Psychologists   5
     ⊏⊐ Method: Reaction Time   6
The Decline and Rebirth of Cognitive Psychology   10
     The Rise of Behaviorism   11
     The Decline of Behaviorism   12
     The Cognitive Revolution   13
How Do Cognitive Psychologists Study the Mind?   16
     Behavioral and Physiological Approaches to Cognition   16
     The Behavioral Approach: Measuring Mental Rotation   17
     🖿 Demonstration: Comparing Objects   17
     The Physiological Approach: The Relationship Between Brain Activity and Memory   19
     Models in Cognitive Psychology   19
Something to Consider: Studying Cognition Across Many Disciplines   21
Test Yourself 1.1   22
Chapter Summary   23
Think About It   24
If You Want to Know More   24
Key Terms   25
CogLab: Mental Rotation   25

Chapter 2   Cognition and the Brain: Basic Principles   27

Neurons: The Building Blocks of the Nervous System   30
     Neurons Transform Environmental Energy Into Electrical Energy   30
     ⊏⊐ Method: Recording From Single Neurons   32
How Neurons Communicate   34
     Communication Between Neurons Occurs at the Synapse   34
     Excitation and Inhibition Interact at the Synapse   35
How Neurons Process Information   36
     Neurons Process Information by Interacting With Each Other   36
     Neural Processing Creates Neurons That Respond to Specific Types of Stimuli   38

Test Yourself 2.1   40

How Stimuli Are Represented by the Firing of Neurons   40

The Neural Code for Perceiving Faces   41

The Neural Code for Other Cognitive Capacities   42

Cognitive Processes and the Brain   42

Layout of the Brain   43

Different Areas of the Brain Serve Specific Functions   43

◄► Method: Neuropsychology   43

Cognitive Processes Are Signaled by Activity in Many Areas of the Brain   45

◄► Method: Brain Imaging   45

Interacting With the Environment Affects Operation of the Nervous System   48

Something to Consider: Are There Grandmother Cells After All?   50

Test Yourself 2.2   51

Chapter Summary   52

Think About It   52

If You Want to Know More   53

Key Terms   53

CogLab: Receptive Fields; Brain Asymmetry   54

Chapter 3   Perception   55

Bottom-Up and Top-Down Processing in Perception   57

▶ Demonstration: Perceiving a Picture   59

Recognizing Letters and Objects   61

Template Matching   61

Interactive Activation Model   62

◄► Method: Word Superiority Effect   64

Feature Integration Theory (FIT)   66

Recognition-by-Components Theory   69

Test Yourself 3.1   72

Perceptual Organization: Putting Together an Organized World   72

The Gestalt Laws of Perceptual Organization   74

▶ Demonstration: Finding Faces in a Landscape   78

The Gestalt Laws Provide "Best Guess" Predictions About What Is Out There   78

Why Computers Have Trouble Perceiving Objects   80

The Stimulus on the Receptors Is Ambiguous   81

Objects Need to Be Distinguished From Their Surroundings and From Each Other   81

Objects Can Be Hidden or Blurred   82

The Reasons for Changes of Lightness and Darkness Can Be Unclear   83

How Experience and Knowledge Create "Perceptual Intelligence"   84

Heuristics for Perceiving   84

▶ Demonstration: Shape From Shading   86

Knowledge Helps Us Perceive Words in Conversational Speech   87

▶ Demonstration: Organizing Strings of Sounds   87

Neurons Contain Information About the Environment   90

Something to Consider: Perception Depends on Attention   91

🐦 Demonstration: Change Detection   92
Test Yourself 3.2   94
Chapter Summary   94
Think About It   95
If You Want to Know More   96
Key Terms   97
CogLab: Change Detection; Apparent Motion; Blind Spot; Metacontrast Masking; Muller-Lyer Illusion; Signal Detection; Visual Search; Garner Interference   97

Chapter 4   Attention   99

Selective Attention: When Does Selection Occur?   101
🐦 Demonstration: Hearing Two Messages at Once   102
▭ Method: Dichotic Listening   102
Early Selection: Broadbent's Filter Model   103
Intermediate Selection: Treisman's Attenuation Theory   106
Late-Selection Models   109
How Does Task Load Affect Selective Attention?   110
▭ Method: Flanker-Compatibility Task   111
Test Yourself 4.1   113
Divided Attention: Paying Attention to More Than One Thing   114
Practice Can Lead to Automatic Processing   114
🐦 Demonstration: Stroop Effect   117
Automatic Processing Is Not Possible for Difficult Tasks   117
Divided Attention in the Real World: Inattention and Driving   118
Attention and Visual Processing   120
Directing Visual Attention With the Eyes   120
▭ Method: Measuring Eye Movements   120
Directing Visual Attention Without Eye Movements   122
▭ Method: Precueing   123
Object-Based Visual Attention   125
Something to Consider: Attention in Social Situations–The Case of Autism   127
Test Yourself 4.2   130
Chapter Summary   130
Think About It   131
If You Want to Know More   132
Key Terms   133
CogLab: Stroop Effect; Spatial Cueing; Attentional Blink; Change Detection; Simon Effect; Von Restorff Effect   134

Chapter 5   Short-Term and Working Memory   135

What Is Memory?   136
The Purposes of Memory   136
The Modal Model of Memory   138
Sensory Memory   141
The Sparkler's Trail and the Projector's Shutter   141

Sperling's Experiment: Measuring the Visual Icon   142

Short-Term Memory   145

What Is the Duration of Short-Term Memory?   146

Demonstration: Remembering Three Letters   146

What Is the Capacity of Short-Term Memory?   148

Demonstration: Digit Span   148

How Is Information Coded in Short-Term Memory?   150

Test Yourself 5.1   153

Working Memory: The Modern Approach to Short-Term Memory   154

Demonstration: Reading Text and Remembering Numbers   154

The Phonological Loop   156

Demonstration: Phonological Similarity Effect   157

Demonstration: Word-Length Effect   157

Demonstration: Articulatory Suppression   158

The Visuospatial Sketch Pad   159

Demonstration: Holding a Verbal Stimulus in the Mind   160

Demonstration: Holding a Spatial Stimulus in the Mind   160

The Central Executive   162

Update on the Working Memory Model: Addition of the Episodic Buffer   163

Working Memory and the Brain   164

The Delayed-Response Task in Monkeys   165

Neurons That Hold Information   166

Brain Imaging in Humans   167

Something to Consider: Working Memory in American Sign Language   168

Test Yourself 5.2   170

Chapter Summary   171

Think About It   172

If You Want to Know More   173

Key Terms   174

CogLab: Partial Report; Brown-Peterson; Memory Span; Phonological Similarity Effect;
Apparent Movement; Irrelevant Speech Effect; Modality Effect; Operation Span; Position Error;
Sternberg Search   174

Chapter 6   **Long-Term Memory: Basic Principles   176**

Introduction to Long-Term Memory   179

Distinctions Between LTM and STM   181

Demonstration: Serial Position   182

Demonstration: Reading a Passage   186

Types of Long-Term Memory   186

Declarative Memory   187

Episodic and Semantic Memory   187

The Separation of Episodic and Semantic Memories   188

Connections Between Episodic and Semantic Memories   189

Implicit Memory   191

Repetition Priming   192

◻ Method: Repetition Priming   192

◻ Method: Recognition and Recall   193

Procedural Memory   195

An Example of Implicit Memory in Everyday Experience   196

How Does Information Become Stored in Long-Term Memory?   196

Maintenance Rehearsal and Elaborative Rehearsal   197

Levels-of-Processing Theory   197

▶ Demonstration: Remembering Lists   198

◻ Method: Varying Depth of Processing   199

Transfer-Appropriate Processing   200

Additional Factors That Aid Encoding   202

▶ Demonstration: Reading a List   204

Test Yourself 6.1   207

How Are Memories Stored in the Brain?   207

Information Storage at the Synapse   208

Forming Memories in the Brain: The Fragility of New Memories   208

Forming Memories in the Brain: The Process of Consolidation   210

Memory for Emotional Stimuli   213

How Do We Retrieve Information From Long-Term Memory?   215

Retrieval Cues   215

◻ Method: Cued Recall   216

Encoding Specificity   218

State-Dependent Learning   220

What Memory Research Tells Us About Studying   221

Elaborate and Generate   221

Organize   222

Associate   223

Take Breaks   223

Match Learning and Testing Conditions   224

Something to Consider: Are Memories Ever "Permanent"?   225

◻ Method: Fear Conditioning   225

Test Yourself 6.2   228

Chapter Summary   229

Think About It   231

If You Want to Know More   231

Key Terms   233

CogLab: Serial Position; Implicit Learning; Levels of Processing; Encoding Specificity; Suffix Effect;
Von Restorff Effect   233

Chapter 7   Everyday Memory and Memory Errors   235

Prospective Memory: What I'm Going to Do Later   237

Autobiographical Memory: What Has Happened in My Life   238

The Multidimensional Nature of Autobiographical Memory   239

Memory Over the Life Span   240

Flashbulb Memories   242

◻ Method: Repeated Recall   244

The Constructive Nature of Memory   249
    Bartlett's "War of the Ghosts" Experiment   250
    Educated Guesses About High School Grades   251
    Source Monitoring and Source Monitoring Errors   252
Test Yourself 7.1   253
    Making Inferences   254
    Demonstration: Reading Sentences   254
    Schemas and Scripts   256
    Remembering a List of Words   258
    Demonstration: Memory for a List   258
    The Advantages and Disadvantages of Construction   259
Memory Can Be Modified or Created by Suggestion   260
    The Misinformation Effect   261
    Method: Presenting Misleading Postevent Information   261
    Creating False Memories for Early Events in People's Lives   264
Why Do People Make Errors in Eyewitness Testimony?   266
    Errors of Eyewitness Identification   267
    The Crime Scene and Afterward   268
    What Is Being Done?   272
Something to Consider: Memories of Childhood Abuse   275
Test Yourself 7.2   276
Chapter Summary   276
Think About It   279
If You Want to Know More   279
Key Terms   281
CogLab: Remember/Know; False Memory; Forgot It All Along Effect   281

Chapter 8   Knowledge   283

Categories Are Essential, but Definitions Don't Work   284
    Why Categories Are Useful   284
    Why Definitions Don't Work for Categories   286
Determining Categories by Similarity: Using Prototypes or Exemplars   288
    The Prototype Approach: Finding the Average Case   288
    Demonstration: Family Resemblance   290
    Method: Sentence Verification Technique   291
    The Exemplar Approach: Thinking About Examples   293
    Which Approach Works Best: Prototypes or Exemplars?   294
Is There a Psychologically "Privileged" Level of Categories?   295
    Rosch's Approach: What's Special About Basic-Level Categories?   295
    Demonstration: Listing Common Features   296
    Demonstration: Naming Things   297
    How Knowledge Can Affect Categorization   297
Test Yourself 8.1   298
Representing Relationships Between Categories: Semantic Networks   299

Introduction to Semantic Networks: Collins and Quillian's Model   299
◄► Method: Lexical Decision Task   303
Criticism of the Collins and Quillian Model   304
Collins and Loftus Answer the Critics   305
Assessment of Semantic Network Theories   306
Representing Concepts in Networks: The Connectionist Approach   307
Categories in the Brain   314
Something to Consider: The Effect of Culture on "Basic" Levels for Categorization and for Inference   315
Test Yourself 8.2   318
Chapter Summary   318
Think About It   320
If You Want to Know More   320
Key Terms   320
CogLab: Prototypes; Lexical Decision; Absolute Identification   321

Chapter 9   Visual Imagery   322

What Is Imagery, and What Is It For?   323
The Uses of Visual Imagery   323
The Plan of This Chapter   324
Imagery in the History of Psychology   325
Early Ideas About Imagery   325
Imagery and the Cognitive Revolution   325
◄► Method: Paired-Associate Learning   326
Imagery and Perception: Do They Share the Same Mechanisms?   327
Kosslyn's Mental-Scanning Experiments   327
◄► Method/Demonstration: Mental Scanning   328
The Imagery Debate: Is Imagery Spatial or Propositional?   328
Comparing Imagery and Perception   332
Is There a Way to Resolve the Imagery Debate?   336
Test Yourself 9.1   336
Imagery and the Brain   337
Imagery Neurons in the Brain   337
Brain Imaging   338
Transcranial Magnetic Stimulation   340
◄► Method: Transcranial Magnetic Stimulation (TMS)   340
Neuropsychological Case Studies   341
Conclusions From the Imagery Debate   346
Using Imagery to Improve Memory   347
Visualizing Interacting Images   347
Placing Images at Locations   348
▣ Demonstration: Method of Loci   348
Associating Images With Words   349
Something to Consider: Mental Representation of Mechanical Systems   350
▣ Demonstration: Mechanical Problems   350

Test Yourself 9.2   352
Chapter Summary   352
Think About It   353
If You Want to Know More   354
Key Terms   355
CogLab: Mental Rotation; Link Word   355

Chapter 10   **Language**   356

What Is Language?   357
    The Creativity of Human Language   357
    The Universality of Language   358
    Studying Language in Cognitive Psychology   358
Perceiving and Understanding Words   360
    Components of Words   361
    Perceiving Words   361
    Understanding Words   363
    Demonstration: Lexical Decision Task   364
    Method: Lexical Priming   365
    Summary: Words Alone and in Sentences   367
Understanding Sentences   368
    Semantics and Syntax   368
    Method: Event-Related Potential   368
    Parsing a Sentence   370
Test Yourself 10.1   376
Understanding Text and Stories   377
    How Inference Creates Coherence   377
    Situation Models   379
Producing Language: Speech Errors   381
    Method: Identifying Speech Errors   382
    Speech Errors and Language Mechanisms   382
Producing Language: Conversations   383
    Semantic Coordination   383
    Syntactic Coordination   384
    Method: Syntactic Priming   385
Something to Consider: Culture, Language, and Cognition   387
    Method: Categorical Perception   387
Test Yourself 10.2   388
Chapter Summary   389
Think About It   390
If You Want to Know More   391
Key Terms   393
CogLab: Word Superiority; Lexical Decision; Categorical Perception–Identification;
    Categorical Perception–Discrimination   394

Chapter 11   Problem Solving   395

What Is a Problem?   396
The Gestalt Approach: Problem Solving as Representation and Restructuring   397
    Representing a Problem in the Mind   398
    Insight in Problem Solving   398
    Demonstration: Two Insight Problems   399
    Obstacles to Problem Solving   401
    Demonstration: The Candle Problem   401
Modern Research on Problem Solving: The Information-Processing Approach   404
    Newell and Simon's Approach   405
    Demonstration: Tower of Hanoi Problem   405
    The Importance of How a Problem Is Stated   408
    Demonstration: The Mutilated-Checkerboard Problem   409
    Method: Think-Aloud Protocol   412
Test Yourself 11.1   413
Using Analogies to Solve Problems   413
    Method: Analogical Transfer   414
    Analogical Problem Solving and the Duncker Radiation Problem   414
    Demonstration: Duncker's Radiation Problem   414
    Analogical Encoding   419
    Analogy in the Real World   420
    Method: In-vivo Problem-Solving Research   420
How Experts Solve Problems   421
    Some Differences Between How Experts and Novices Solve Problems   421
Creative Problem Solving   423
    Demonstration: Creating an Object   426
Something to Consider: Sleep Inspires Insight   428
Test Yourself 11.2   429
Chapter Summary   430
Think About It   431
If You Want to Know More   432
Key Terms   432

Chapter 12   Reasoning and Decision Making   434

Deductive Reasoning: Thinking Categorically   437
    Validity and Truth in Syllogisms   437
    How Well Can People Judge Validity?   438
    Mental Models of Deductive Reasoning   440
Deductive Reasoning: Thinking Conditionally   443
    Forms of Conditional Syllogisms   443
    Why People Make Errors in Conditional Reasoning: The Wason Four-Card Problem   445
    Demonstration: Wason Four-Card Problem   445
Test Yourself 12.1   452

Inductive Reasoning: Reaching Conclusions From Evidence   452

    The Nature of Inductive Reasoning   452

    The Availability Heuristic   456

    Demonstration: Which Is More Prevalent?   456

    The Representativeness Heuristic   459

    Demonstration: Judging Occupations   459

    Demonstration: Description of a Person   460

    Demonstration: Male and Female Births   461

    The Confirmation Bias   462

Culture, Cognition, and Inductive Reasoning   463

    Demonstration: Questions About Animals   463

Decision Making: Choosing Among Alternatives   466

    The Utility Approach to Decisions   466

    Decisions Can Depend on How Choices Are Presented   469

    Demonstration: What Would You Do?   469

    Justification in Decision Making   471

The Physiology of Thinking   472

    The Prefrontal Cortex   473

    Neuroeconomics: The Neural Basis of Decision Making   475

Something to Consider: Is What Is Good for You Also Good for Me?   476

    Demonstration: A Personal Health Decision   477

Test Yourself 12.2   478

Chapter Summary   479

Think About It   481

If You Want to Know More   481

Key Terms   483

CogLab: Wason Selection Task; Typical Reasoning; Risky Decisions; Decision Making; Monty Hall   484

Glossary   485

References   507

Name Index   539

Subject Index   544

CogLab Experiments

Chapter 1   Introduction to Cognitive Psychology
  Mental Rotation   25
Chapter 2   Cognition and the Brain: Basic Principles
  Receptive Fields   54
  Brain Asymmetry   54
Chapter 3   Perception
  Change Detection   97
  Apparent Motion   98
  Blind Spot   98
  Metacontrast Masking   98
  Muller-Lyer Illusion   98
  Signal Detection   98
  Visual Search   98
  Garner Interference   98
Chapter 4   Attention
  Stroop Effect   134
  Spatial Cueing   134
  Attentional Blink   134
  Change Detection   134
  Simon Effect   134
  Von Restorff Effect   134
Chapter 5   Short-Term Memory and Working Memory
  Partial Report   174
  Brown-Peterson   174
  Memory Span   174
  Phonological Similarity Effect   174
  Apparent Movement   174
  Irrelevant Speech Effect   174
  Modality Effect   175
  Operation Span   175
  Position Error   175
  Sternberg Search   175

Chapter 6   Long-Term Memory: Basic Principles
  Serial Position   233
  Implicit Learning   233
  Levels of Processing   234
  Encoding Specificity   234
  Suffix Effect   234
  Von Restorff Effect   234
Chapter 7   Everyday Memory and Memory Errors
  Remember/Know   281
  False Memory   281
  Forgot It All Along Effect   281
Chapter 8   Knowledge
  Prototypes   321
  Lexical Decision   321
  Absolute Identification   321
Chapter 9   Visual Imagery
  Mental Rotation   355
  Link Word   355
Chapter 10   Language
  Word Superiority   394
  Lexical Decision   394
  Categorical Perception—Identification   394
  Categorical Perception—Discrimination   394
Chapter 12   Reasoning and Decision Making
  Wason Selection Task   484
  Typical Reasoning   484
  Risky Decisions   484
  Decision Making   484
  Monty Hall   484

Demonstrations

Chapter 1   Comparing Objects   17
Chapter 3   Perceiving a Picture   59
             Finding Faces in a Landscape   78
             Shape From Shading   86
             Organizing Strings of Sounds   87
             Change Detection   92
Chapter 4   Hearing Two Messages at Once   102
             Stroop Effect   117
Chapter 5   Remembering Three Letters   146
             Digit Span   148
             Reading Text and Remembering
                 Numbers   154
             Phonological Similarity Effect   157
             Word-Length Effect   157
             Articulatory Suppression   158
             Holding a Verbal Stimulus in the Mind   160
             Holding a Spatial Stimulus in the Mind   160
Chapter 6   Serial Position   182
             Reading a Passage   186
             Remembering Lists   198
             Reading a List   204
Chapter 7   Reading Sentences   254
             Memory for a List   258
Chapter 8   Family Resemblance   290
             Listing Common Features   296
             Naming Things   297
Chapter 9   Mental Scanning   328
             Method of Loci   348
             Mechanical Problems   350
Chapter 10   Lexical Decision Task   364
Chapter 11   Two Insight Problems   399
             The Candle Problem   401
             Tower of Hanoi Problem   405
             The Mutilated-Checkerboard Problem   409
             Duncker's Radiation Problem   414
             Creating an Object   426
Chapter 12   Wason Four-Card Problem   445
             Which Is More Prevalent?   456
             Judging Occupations   459
             Description of a Person   460
             Male and Female Births   461
             Questions About Animals   463
             What Would You Do?   469
             A Personal Health Decision   477

Methods

Chapter 1   Reaction Time   6
Chapter 2   Recording From Single Neurons   32
             Neuropsychology   43
             Brain Imaging   45
Chapter 3   Word Superiority Effect   64
Chapter 4   Dichotic Listening   102
             Flanker-Compatibility Task   111
             Measuring Eye Movements   120
             Precueing   123
Chapter 6   Repetition Priming   192
             Recognition and Recall   193
             Varying Depth of Processing   199
             Cued Recall   216
             Fear Conditioning   225
Chapter 7   Repeated Recall   244
             Presenting Misleading Postevent
                 Information   261
Chapter 8   Sentence Verification Technique   291
             Lexical Decision Task   303
Chapter 9   Paired-Associate Learning   326
             Mental Scanning   328
             Transcranial Magnetic Stimulation
                 (TMS)   340
Chapter 10   Lexical Priming   365
             Event-Related Potential   368
             Identifying Speech Errors   382
             Syntactic Priming   385
             Categorical Perception   387
Chapter 11   Think-Aloud Protocol   412
             Analogical Transfer   414
             In-vivo Problem-Solving Research   420

Preface to Instructors

The Rationale Behind the First Edition

The first edition of this book was shaped by feedback from teachers and students. From a survey of over 500 teachers and my conversations with colleagues, it became apparent that many teachers were looking for a text that not only covers the field of cognitive psychology but is also accessible to students. From my teaching of cognitive psychology, it also became apparent that many students perceive cognitive psychology as being too abstract and theoretical, and not connected to everyday experience. With this information in hand, I set out to write a book that would tell the story of cognitive psychology in a concrete way that would help students appreciate the connections between empirical research, the principles of cognitive psychology, and everyday experience.

I did a number of things to achieve this result. I started by including about a dozen **real-life examples** per chapter, and neuropsychological case studies where appropriate. To provide students with firsthand experience with the phenomena of cognitive psychology, I included over 40 **Demonstrations**—easy-to-do mini-experiments that were contained within the narrative of the text—as well as 20 additional suggestions of things to try. The demonstrations in this edition are listed on page xx.

Students also received access to over 45 online **CogLab experiments** that they could run themselves, and then compare their data to the class average and to the results of the original experiments from the literature. In order to ensure that students not only know the results of experiments but also appreciate how these results were obtained, I **described experiments in detail,** so students would understand what the experimenter and participants were doing. In addition, most of these descriptions were supported by illustrations such as pictures of stimuli, diagrams of the experimental design, or graphs of the results.

The first edition therefore combined many elements designed to achieve the goal of covering the basic principles of cognitive psychology in a way that students would find interesting and easy to understand. The popularity of the text (it was adopted at over 160 schools) indicates that this approach apparently struck a chord with both teachers and students. A recurring theme in the many e-mails I received about the book was that students found the text interesting and accessible, and came away feeling excited about the field of cognitive psychology.

The acceptance of the first edition was gratifying, but one thing I've learned from years of teaching and textbook writing is that there are always explanations that can be clarified, new pedagogical techniques to try, and new research and ideas to describe. I therefore welcomed the opportunity to write this new edition. If you have used the first edition, you will find much that is familiar and also some things that are new.

What Is the Same and What Is New in the Second Edition?

The second edition includes the features described above, plus two pedagogical features from the first edition: **Test Yourself** sections, which help students review the material, and **Think About It** questions, which ask students to consider questions that go beyond the material. Two additional pedagogical features, *If You Want to Know More* and *Chapter Summaries*, have been added for this edition.

If You Want to Know More includes brief descriptions of interesting topics related to the chapter, but which could not be discussed in detail in the text for space reasons. A few references are provided to help students begin exploring this additional material. **Chapter Summaries** provide succinct outlines of the chapters, without serving as a substitute for reading the chapters.

My first step in determining what changes to make in the text was to elicit feedback from students in my classes. I asked students to indicate one thing in each chapter that they had trouble with or that could have been stated more clearly. I used the more than 1,500 responses to pinpoint areas that needed work, and rewrote and reorganized parts of every chapter to provide clearer explanations.

One of the reasons cognitive psychology is such a successful science is that cognitive psychologists have devised ingenious methods to study the mind. Yet these methods are often ignored or are lost in the text. To remedy this, I have included over two dozen highlighted **Methods** sections that are integrated into the text, and which describe each method when it is first introduced. This not only highlights the importance of the method, but makes it easier to return to its description when it is referred to later in the text. Here are a few examples (see page xx for a complete list):

- Brain imaging
- Flanker-compatibility task
- Repetition priming
- Sentence verification technique
- Mental scanning
- Think-aloud protocol

The second edition also contains a great deal of **new content.** There are over 100 new glossary terms, and over 25 percent of the references are new to this edition. Most of these new references reflect research published since 2000, but some older research that helps tell the story of cognitive psychology has also been added. Much of this new material appears in a new end-of-chapter feature called **Something to**

Consider, which describes cutting-edge or controversial research. See the chapter-by-chapter list that follows for a summary of all of the content that is new to this edition.

In summary, this new edition has kept what worked in the first edition and made changes to improve clarity, update content, and provide more student-friendly features. Of course, the real test of a book is how it works in the classroom. I invite your feedback at bruceg@email.arizona.edu.

Chapter-by-Chapter List of New Content in This Edition

The following list indicates the major new content in this edition. Numbers in parentheses are page numbers.

Chapter 1: Introduction to Cognitive Psychology

- Methods now appear in Methods sections when they are introduced. The method of reaction time is described in this chapter. (6)
- Ebbinghaus's memory experiment is added to the history of cognitive psychology. (8)
- A new discussion of the role of models in cognitive psychology is included to make clear what models are, how they are related (or not related) to physiological mechanisms, and what they contribute to our understanding of cognition. (19)

Chapter 2: Cognition and the Brain: Basic Principles

- The methods of single unit recording, neuropsychology, and brain imaging are introduced in this chapter. Other physiological methods (such as evoked brain potentials and transcranial magnetic stimulation) are introduced when the first experiments involving these methods appear in later chapters. (32)
- The discussion of dissociations in neuropsychology has been revised to start with human examples that students can relate to. (43)
- A new section on experience-dependent plasticity has been added at the end of the chapter. Blakemore and Cooper's (1970) "selective rearing for orientation" experiment and Gauthier and coworkers' (1999) Greeble experiment, both of which were described in the first edition, have been moved to this section. (48)
- The Something to Consider section describes Quiroga and coworkers' (2005) research on "grandmother-like" cells in the hippocampus. This is a follow-up to the discussion, early in the chapter, of selective versus distributed mechanisms of neural coding. (50)

Chapter 3: Perception

- Material on template matching has been added, and the treatment of McClelland and Rummelhart's interactive activation model has been expanded. Bottom-up and top-down processing, which was introduced in the first chapter, is illustrated by showing how the interactive activation model can explain the word-superiority effect. (61)
- The description of Treisman's (1986) feature integration theory has been revised to focus on what illusory conjunctions tell us about the role of attention on binding. Robertson and coworkers' (1997) research on a patient with Balint's syndrome is described to show how a deficit in attention increases the perception of illusory conjunctions. (66)
- A discussion of statistical learning of transitional probabilities in speech sounds in 8-month-olds (Saffran et al., 1996) has been added to the discussion of how knowledge helps people perceive words in conversational speech. (88)
- The Something to Consider section describes change blindness, which was formerly in the attention chapter, to demonstrate the connection between perception and attention and to provide a lead-in to the attention chapter. (91)

Chapter 4: Attention

- The Stroop effect is presented here to demonstrate automatic processing. (117)
- A discussion of the "100-Car Naturalistic Driving Study" has been added to the section on cell phone use and driving accidents. This study, by the National Highway Traffic Safety Administration (2006), used videotaped records of people in actual driving situations to demonstrate how distractions increase driving accidents. (118)
- The section on visual attention has been expanded by describing how eye movements are measured, and how scanning patterns are determined by both bottom-up and top-down factors (Henderson, 2003; Land & Hayhoe, 2001). (120)
- The Something to Consider section describes Klin and coworkers' (2003) research on autistic observers' visual scanning patterns as they view the film *Who's Afraid of Virginia Woolf?* (127)

Chapter 5: Short-Term and Working Memory

- The discussion of the central executive has been expanded by describing Gazzaley and coworkers' (2005) experiment that demonstrates a link between suppression (a central executive function) and working memory performance. (162)
- The discussion of working memory has been updated by describing the episodic buffer (Baddeley, 2000). (163)
- The Something to Consider section describes research that compares working memory for spoken English to working memory for ASL. This discussion is

not only relevant to the nature of working memory, but also provides insight into the nature of scientific research by describing the implications of the fact that two laboratories have reported conflicting results (Boutla et al., 2004; Emmorey & Wilson, 2004) (168)

Chapter 6: Long-Term Memory: Basic Principles

- A boxed feature, "Memory in the Movies," discusses how memory loss has been depicted in movies and suggests a number of movies that are worth seeing. (178)
- The discussion of declarative memory now includes an expended consideration of the distinction between semantic and episodic memory, and a description of Tulving's (1985) definition of episodic and semantic memory in terms of consciousness. (187)
- The discussion of semantic and episodic memory in everyday experience has been revised to more fully consider connections between episodic and semantic memory, including a discussion of personal semantic memory (Westmacott & Moscovitch, 2003). (189)
- Morris and coworkers' (1977) transfer-appropriate processing experiment is now described immediately after levels of processing and has been rewritten to make it easier to understand. (200)
- The generation effect (Slameka & Graf, 1978) has been added to the section "Additional Factors That Aid Encoding" and is also included in the section "What Memory Tells Us About Studying" at the end of the chapter. (204)
- The discussion of brain processes in memory has been updated by describing the exciting new research that is reshaping our conception of the nature of memory consolidation. This section considers the controversy about the role of the hippocampus in retrieving long-term episodic memories (Frankland & Bontempi, 2005; Moskovitch et al., 2005). (210)
- New material on memory for emotional stimuli follows the discussion of consolidation. This section considers both behavioral evidence indicating that emotion generally enhances memory and physiological evidence that the amygdala and hippocampus are the major structures involved in memory for emotional stimuli or events (Dolcos et al., 2005). (213)
- The section on links between encoding and retrieval summarizes material on encoding from the first edition and includes a revised treatment of encoding specificity and state-depending learning. (218)
- Material on sleep and consolidation has been added to the section on memory and studying. (224)
- The Something to Consider section builds on the earlier discussion of consolidation by considering new research on memory reconsolidation that calls into question the idea that once a memory is consolidated it is "permanent." (Nader et al., 2000b; Sara, 2006). (225)

Chapter 7: Everyday Memory and Memory Errors

- Material on prospective memory has been added to emphasize that we use memory not only to remember the past, but to remember what we need to do in the future (Einstein & McDaniel, 1990; Schacter, 2001). (237)
- Autobiographical memory is defined more clearly and has been modified to include both episodic memory and the contribution of personal semantic memories (Rosenbaum et al., 2005). (238)
- Descriptions of the multimodal nature of memory (Cabeza et al., 2004; Greenberg & Rubin, 2003) and the cultural life-script explanation of the reminiscence bump (Berntsen & Rubin, 2004) have been added. (239)
- The discussion of flashbulb memories has been updated, considering both the Talicaro and Rubin (2003) research, which provides evidence for similarities between 9/11 memories and memories for "everyday" events, and Davidson and coworkers' (2006) research, which provides evidence for differences between 9/11 memories and memories for everyday events. (242)
- The McDermott and Chan (2006) pragmatic inference experiment now introduces the section on the role of inference in memory. (254)
- A new section on the advantages and disadvantages of construction has been added to the end of the section on constructive memory. (259)
- The section on suggestion in memory now describes three proposed mechanisms for the effect of misleading postevent information—memory-trace replacement, retroactive interference, and source monitoring errors. (262)
- The discussion of the creation of false memories now includes Lindsay and coworkers' (2004) experiment, which demonstrates that presenting photographs can increase the false memory effect. (265)
- A description of Shaw's (1996) research on how eyewitness confidence can be increased by postevent questioning has been added to the section on eyewitness memory. (271)

Chapter 8: Knowledge

- The section on connectionism has been revised to clarify the processes that occur as a connectionist network learns about a number of concepts simultaneously. This learning process is made more real to students by comparing it to how young children learn to differentiate between different concepts (McClelland & Rogers, 2003). (307)
- The Something to Consider section describes research on the "basic" category for concepts in two cultures (American and Itza; Medin & Atran, 2004). This cross-cultural research, which was originally described in the first edition, has been rewritten to simplify the discussion and make the conclusions easier to understand. (315)

Chapter 9: Visual Imagery

- The section on imagery and the brain now includes Kosslyn and coworkers' (1999) transcranial magnetic stimulation experiment and new fMRI research comparing brain activation to visual stimulation and imagery (Amedi et al., 2005; Ganis et al., 2004). (339)
- The Something to Consider section describes research on how imagery is used to solve mechanical problems (Hegarty, 2004). The results of this research are discussed both in relation to the imagery-perception debate and how people solve problems. (350)

Chapter 10: Language

- A description of morphemes has been added to the section on perceiving words, and the word superiority effect (which now appears in Chapter 3, Perception) has been replaced with the phonemic restoration effect (Warren, 1970). In addition, the material on the word-frequency effect has been expanded. (361)
- The description of Swinney's (1979) experiment on how people access meanings of ambiguous words when reading sentences now begins with a Methods section that describes the rationale behind lexical priming. This clarifies the description of Swinney's experiment that follows. (365)
- The description of parsing has been streamlined and simplified, with special attention to rewriting the Tanenhaus and coworkers' (1995) experiment to make the procedure and implications of the results clearer to students. (370)
- In the section on situation models, the Morrow and coworkers' (1987) experiment has been replaced by a more recent experiment by Horton and Rapp (2003). (379)
- A new section on language production has been added. This section focuses on what speech errors tell us about production mechanisms (Bock, 1995; Dell, 1995). (381)
- The discussion on conversation has been updated to include new material on syntactic coordination and syntactic priming (Branigan et al., 2000). (383)
- The material on the Sapir-Whorf hypothesis from the first edition, which included a description of the Roberson and coworkers' (2000) color perception experiment, has been updated by considering Regier and coworkers' (2005) work. (387)

Chapter 11: Problem Solving

- The description of Newell and Simon's concept of the problem space has been rewritten in response to student feedback, using a new example based on the Tower of Hanoi problem. (405)

- A description of Kotovsky's (1985) research on the acrobat problem has been added to the section on how problem difficulty can be influenced by the way a problem is stated. (408)
- The section on analogical problem solving has been rewritten to highlight research on the role of surface features and structural features. In connection with this, the Gentner and coworkers' (2003) experiment investigating analogical encoding has been added. (413)
- The idea of the analogical paradox (participants in psychological experiments tend to focus on surface features in analogy problems, whereas people in the real world frequently use deeper, more structural features; Dunbar, 2001) is introduced as part of a new discussion of real-world applications in analogical problem solving. In connection with this, the results of in-vivo problem solving research are described (Dunbar & Blanchette, 2001). (420)
- The section on creative problem solving has been rewritten, with a new emphasis on creative problem solving in applied settings, such as engineering and industrial product development (Jansson & Smith, 1991). (423)
- The Something to Consider section returns to principles introduced in the discussion of consolidation in Chapter 6, to consider research showing that sleep improves insightful problem solving (U. Wagner et al., 2004). (428)

Chapter 12: Reasoning and Decision Making

- The discussion of syllogisms has been rewritten in response to student feedback regarding the difficulty of this section. In addition to streamlining the discussion of the basic types of syllogisms, the idea of the difference between truth and validity, which often poses problems for students, has been rewritten. (437)
- Description of the mental model approach to determining validity (Johnson-Laird, 1999a, 1999b) has been rewritten, including a new description of the "Artists, Beekeepers, and Chemists" problem. (440)
- The discussion of conditional reasoning has been rewritten using new examples, which make it easier to understand the difference between truth and validity. (443)
- The section on how decisions can be influenced by the way choices are presented is now introduced by describing how opt-in and opt-out procedures result in different outcomes for identifying potential organ donors (Johnson & Goldstein, 2003). (469)
- The Something to Consider section describes the neuroeconomic approach to decision making, which combines approaches from the fields of psychology, neuroscience, and economics (Lee, 2006). Sanfey's (2006) experiment on the "ultimatum game" is used to illustrate this approach. (475)

▶▶▶ Ancillaries to Support Your Teaching

CogLab 2.0 for *Goldstein's Cognitive Psychology: Connecting Mind, Research, and Everyday Experience*

Free with every new copy of this book, CogLab 2.0 lets your students do more than just think about cognition . . . and now it is newly updated and easier to use! CogLab 2.0 is based on the original CogLab, which uses the power of the web to teach concepts using important classic and current experiments that demonstrate how the mind works. Nothing is more powerful for students than seeing for themselves the effects of these experiments! CogLab 2.0 includes exciting new features, such as simplified student registration, a global database that combines data from students all around the world, between-subject designs that allow for new kinds of experiments, and a "quick display" of student summaries. Also new are trial-by-trial data, standard deviations, and improved instructions.

Instructor Manual/Test Bank (ISBN 049510356X)

Written by Lisa Maxfield of California State University, Long Beach, this supplement contains chapter outlines, discussion questions, in-class demonstrations, term projects, and references to relevant websites. The test bank has approximately 65 multiple-choice questions and 5–7 essay questions per chapter. Each chapter has a section dedicated to CogLab online, providing discussion questions, experiments, and activities.

Multimedia Manager Instructor's Resource CD (ISBN 0495103543)

The Multimedia Manager helps you to enhance your Microsoft® PowerPoint® lecture with art from this textbook, videos, animations, and your own materials! This one-stop lecture and course preparation tool makes it easy for you to assemble, edit, publish, and present custom lectures for your course, using PowerPoint. Includes lecture outlines written by Jennifer Zapf of Indiana University.

ExamView® Computerized Testing (ISBN 0495103551)

Create, deliver, and customize tests and study guides (both print and online) in minutes with this easy-to-use assessment and tutorial system. ExamView offers both a Quick Test Wizard and an Online Test Wizard that guide you step by step through the process of creating tests—you can even see the test you are creating on the screen exactly as it will print or display online.

JoinIn on TurningPoint (ISBN 0495103578)

The easiest audience response system to use, JoinIn features instant classroom assessment and learning.

Website (www.cengage.com/psychology/goldstein)

When you adopt *Cognitive Psychology: Connecting Mind, Research, and Everyday Experience*, Second Edition, you and your students will have access to a rich array of teaching and learning resources that you won't find anywhere else. This outstanding site features critical thinking exercises, multiple-choice questions, short essay questions, flash cards, web links, and a glossary.

Preface to Students

As you begin reading this book, you probably have some ideas about how the mind works from things you have read, from other media, and from your own experiences. In this book, you will learn what we actually do and do not know about the mind, as determined from the results of controlled scientific research. Thus, if you thought that there is a system called "short-term memory" that can hold information for short periods of time, then you are right, and when you read the chapters on memory you will learn more about this system and how it interacts with other parts of your memory system. If you thought that some people can accurately remember things that happened to them as very young infants, you will see that there is a good chance that these reports are inaccurate. In fact, you may be surprised to learn that even more recent memories that seem extremely clear and vivid may not be entirely accurate due to basic characteristics of the way the memory system works.

But what you will learn from this book goes much deeper than simply adding more accurate information to what you already know about the mind. You will learn that there is much more going on in your mind than you are conscious of. You are aware of experiences such as seeing something, remembering a past event, or thinking about how to solve a problem—but behind each of these experiences are a myriad of complex and largely invisible processes. Reading this book will help you appreciate some of the "behind the scenes" activity in your mind that is responsible for everyday experiences such as perceiving, remembering, and thinking.

Another thing you will become aware of as you read this book is that there are many practical connections between the results of cognitive psychology research and everyday life. You will see examples of these connections throughout the book. But for now I want to focus on one especially important connection—what research in cognitive psychology can contribute to improving your studying. This discussion appears on pages 221–224 of Chapter 6, so you might want to look at this material now, rather than waiting until later in the course. But I invite you to also consider the following two principles, which are designed to help you get more out of this book.

Principle 1: It is important to know what you know.

A lament that professors often hear from students is, "I came to the lecture, read the chapters a number of times, and still didn't do well on the exam." Sometimes this statement is followed by ". . . and when I walked out of the exam, I thought I had done pretty well." If this is something that you have experienced, then the root of the problem may be that you didn't have a good awareness of what you knew about the material and what you didn't know. The problem is that if you think you know the material but actually don't, you might stop studying or might continue studying in an ineffective way, with the net result being a poor understanding of the material and an inability to remember it accurately, come exam time. Thus, it is important to test yourself on the material you have read by writing or saying the answers to the Test Yourself questions in the chapter and also by taking advantage of the sample test questions that are available on the publisher's website. To access these questions, go to www.cengage.com/highered. Under *Humanities and Social Sciences*, click on *Psychology*. Under *Select a Course* click on *Cognitive Psychology*. You will see a picture of the book. Under *Students*, click *Companion Site*. This takes you to the book's companion site, where you will find sample exam questions and other valuable learning aids. If you are using your own computer, bookmark the address.

Principle 2: Don't mistake ease and familiarity for knowing.

One of the main reasons that students may think they know the material, even when they don't, is that they mistake familiarity for understanding. Here is how it works: You read the chapter once, perhaps highlighting as you go. Then later, you read the chapter again, perhaps focusing on the highlighted material. As you read it over, the material is familiar because you remember it from before, and this familiarity might lead you to think, "Okay, I know that." The problem is that this feeling of familiarity is not necessarily equivalent to knowing the material and may be of no help when you have to come up with an answer on the exam. In fact, familiarity can often lead to errors on multiple-choice exams because you might pick a choice that looks familiar, only to find later that it was something you had read, but it wasn't really the best answer to the question.

This again brings us back to the idea of testing yourself. One finding of cognitive psychology is that the very act of *trying* to answer a question increases the chances you will be able to answer it when you try again later. The reason answering questions works is that *generating* material is a more effective way of getting information into memory than simply *reviewing* it. Thus you may find it effective to test yourself before rereading the chapter or going over your highlighted text.

Whichever study tactic you find works best for you, keep in mind that an effective strategy is to rest (take a break or study something else) before studying more and then retesting yourself. Research has shown that memory is better when studying is spaced out over time, rather than being done all at once. Repeating this process a number of times—testing yourself, checking back to see whether you were right, waiting, testing yourself again, and so on—is a more effective way of learning the material than simply looking at it and getting that warm, fuzzy feeling of familiarity, which may not translate into actually knowing the material when you are faced with questions about it on the exam.

• • •

I hope you will find this book to be clear and interesting and that you will sometimes be fascinated or perhaps even surprised by some of the things you read. I also hope that your introduction to cognitive psychology extends beyond just "learning the material." Cognitive psychology is endlessly interesting because it is about one of the most fascinating of all topics—the human mind. Thus, once your course is over I hope you will take away an appreciation for what cognitive psychologists have discovered about the mind and what still remains to be learned. I also hope that you will become a more critical consumer of information about the mind that you may encounter on the Internet or in movies, magazines, or other media. Finally, if you have any questions or comments about anything in the book, please feel free to contact me at **bruceg@email.arizona.edu.**

# Acknowledgments

The starting point for a textbook like this one is an author who has an idea for a book, but other people soon become part of the process. Editors first provide guidance regarding the kind of book teachers want and, along with outside reviewers, provide feedback about chapters as they are written. When the manuscript is completed, the production process begins, and a new group of people take over to turn the manuscript into a book. This means that this book has been a group effort and that I had lots of help, both during the process of writing and after submitting the final manuscript. I would therefore like to thank the following people for their extraordinary efforts in support of this book.

- MARIANNE TAFLINGER, my editor, for her encouragement at the beginning of this project and for her support as I wrote it; for appreciating my work; and for contributing many creative ideas at many points along the way. I also appreciate Marianne for our long and continuing relationship.
- KATE BARNES, my developmental editor. Kate was the person who made sure everything was right, through the process of writing and revising, and then as production unfolded. By both focusing on details and zooming out to consider the big picture, she made me feel that everything was under control. I am grateful for her help and enjoyed our collaboration in creating this book over the last year. Thank you, Kate.
- MICHELLE SORDI, psychology publisher, for all of her help and support.
- ANNE DRAUS of Scratchgravel Publishing Services, for being the ultimate professional. Having worked with Anne on the first edition of the book, I knew she would be wonderful to work with again, and I have not been disappointed. She made the complex process of assembling all of the various components of this book seem easy, even though it surely wasn't.
- VERNON BOES, for demonstrating that Nashville is the home not only of great music, but of excellent book design, the noon stagecoach, and the Abalone Bowling Alley. Thanks, Vernon, for lightening things up and for being open to feedback from all directions.
- CHERYL CARRINGTON for her elegant and functional interior design and beautiful cover.
- LISA TORRI, art editor, for yet again directing the art program for one of my books.
- MARY NOEL, content project manager, for making sure everything was done correctly and on time during the production process.
- LISA MAXFIELD, of California State University, Long Beach, for her work on the demanding and essential task of creating the test bank and instructor's manual.
- JENNIFER ZAPF, of Indiana University, for creating PowerPoint lectures for the book.
- LUCY FARIDANY, who as an editorial assistant during the early stages of creating this book took care of obtaining reviews and much else, which I wasn't even aware of, with graceful ease.

- Rachel Guzman, for taking over for Lucy for the second half of this project.
- Mary Anne Shahidi and Elizabeth Kittrell for their expert and meticulous copy editing.
- Laura Molmud for her photo research and for patiently waiting for my answers to her questions.
- Bob Kauser, for being sure all of the permissions were in order.
- Magnolia Molcan, assistant editor, for coordinating the supplements for the book.

In addition to the help I received from the above people on the editorial and production side, I received a great deal of help from teachers and researchers who gave me feedback on what I wrote and made suggestions regarding new work in the field. I thank the following people for their help:

Reviewers

Tom Alley
Clemson University

Marie Balaban
Eastern Oregon State College

Michael Beran
Georgia State University

Martin Bink
Western Kentucky University

Cynthia Clark
University of Northern Colorado

Paul Cunningham
Rivier College

Darryl Dietrich
College of St. Scholastica

Thomas Dunn
University of Northern Colorado

Deborah K. Eakin
Mississippi State University

Kara Federmeir
University of Illinois at Urbana–Champaign

Danielle D. Gagne
Alfred University

Veronica Galvan
University of San Diego

Lawrence Gottlob
University of Kentucky

Gary Heiman
Buffalo State College

Robert J. Hines
University of Arkansas at Little Rock

Mark S. Hoyert
Indiana University Northwest

Eve Isham
California State University–Fullerton

Kathy E. Johnson
Indiana University–Purdue University

Roger Kreuz
University of Memphis

Max Louwerse
University of Memphis

Patrick Monnier
Colorado State University

Brian Parry
San Juan College

Christy Porter
College of William and Mary

Jianjian Qin
California State University, Sacramento

James Rafferty
Bemidji State University

Carrie Rosengart
California University of Pennsylvania

Darrell Rudmann
Indiana University East

Mark Runco
Calfornia State University–Fullerton

Laura Seligman
University of Toronto

Jeri Thompson
Mount Union College

Wythe Whiting
Washington and Lee University

Robert Youmans
University of Illinois–Chicago

Jennifer Zapf
Indiana University

Specialist Reviewers

Daphne Bavelier
University of Rochester

Marlene Behrmann
Carnegie-Mellon University

Laurie Cunningham
Pittsburgh, Pennsylvania

Nancy Emmorey
San Diego State University

Merrill Garrett
University of Arizona

Betty Glisky
University of Arizona

Mary Hegerty
University of California, Santa Barbara

Tiago Maia
Carnegie-Mellon University

Jay McClelland
Stanford University

Lynn Nadel
University of Arizona

Janet Nicol
University of Arizona

Erik Reichle
University of Pittsburgh

Alan Sanfey
University of Arizona

Christian Schunn
University of Pittsburgh

Raymond Shaw
Merrimack College

Natasha Tokowitz
University of Pittsburgh

Previous Edition Reviewers

Thank you also to those who reviewed the manuscript, made suggestions, and provided illustrations for the first edition: Thomas Alley, Clemson University; Gerry Altmann, University of York; Cheryl Anagnopoulos, Black Hills State University; Chris Ball, College of William & Mary; Ute Bayen, University of North Carolina; Sheila Black, University of Alabama; James Brewer, Johns Hopkins University; Richard Catrambone, Georgia Tech; Steven Christman, University of Toledo; James Chumbley, University of Massachusetts; William Collins, University of Michigan; Brian Crabb, Western Washington University; Tim Curran, University of Colorado; Lila Davachi, New York

University; Robert Durham, University of Colorado–Colorado Springs; Martha Farah, University of Pennsylvania; Julie Fiez, University of Pittsburgh; Ira Fischler, University of Florida; Greg Francis, Purdue University; Jane Gaultney, University of North Carolina, Charlotte; Isabel Gauthier, Vanderbilt University; Gabriel Kreiman, California Institute of Technology; Linda Henkel, Fairfield University; Robert Hines, University of Arkansas at Little Rock; Audrey Holland, University of Arizona; Keith Holyoak, University of California, Los Angeles; Peter Howell, University College London; Kathy Johnson, Indiana University–Purdue University Indianapolis; Beena Khurana, Cornell University; Derek Mace, Pennsylvania State University, Behrend; Barbara Malt, Lehigh University; Lisa Maxfield, California State University, Long Beach; Richard Mayer, University of California, Santa Barbara; James L. McClelland, Carnegie-Mellon University; Jeff Mio, Cal Poly Pomona; Kristy Neilson, Marquette University; Charles Perfetti, University of Pittsburgh; John Philbeck, George Washington University; Gabriel Radvansky, University of Notre Dame; Eric Reichle, University of Pittsburgh; Lisa Saunders, University of Oregon; Christian Schunn, University of Pittsburgh; Bennett Schwartz, Florida International University; Carl Scott, University of St. Thomas; Aimée Surprenant, Purdue University; Greg Simpson, University of Kansas; Annette Taylor, University of San Diego; Natasha Tokowicz, University of Pittsburgh; Jyotsna Vaid, Texas A&M; Douglas Waring, Appalachian State University; Tessa Warren, University of Pittsburgh.

Introduction to Cognitive Psychology

1

The Challenge of Cognitive Psychology
  The Complexity of Cognition
  The First Cognitive Psychologists
  ◖◗ Method: Reaction Time

The Decline and Rebirth of Cognitive Psychology
  The Rise of Behaviorism
  The Decline of Behaviorism
  The Cognitive Revolution

How Do Cognitive Psychologists Study the Mind?
  Behavioral and Physiological Approaches to Cognition
  The Behavioral Approach: Measuring Mental Rotation
  ▶ Demonstration: Comparing Objects
  The Physiological Approach: The Relationship Between
    Brain Activity and Memory
  Models in Cognitive Psychology

Something to Consider: Studying Cognition Across
Many Disciplines

Test Yourself 1.1

Chapter Summary

Think About It

If You Want to Know More

Key Terms

CogLab: Mental Rotation

Some Questions We Will Consider

- How is cognitive psychology relevant to everyday experience? (2)
- Are there practical applications of cognitive psychology? (2)
- How is it possible to study the inner workings of the mind, when we can't really see the mind directly? (7)
- What is the field of cognitive psychology? (16)

Sarah is walking across campus. She stops for a moment to talk with a friend about the movie they saw last night. She can't talk for long because she has an appointment to plan her schedule for next term, so she says good-bye and heads off toward her advisor's office.

This minor event in Sarah's life is just one occurrence on a typical day. But if we stop for a moment to consider what's involved in this simple sequence of events, we see that beneath the simplicity lies mental processes such as the following:

- *Perception.* Sarah is able to find her way through campus, recognize her friend, and hear her speak.
- *Attention.* As she walks across campus, she focuses on only a portion of her environment, but seeing her friend captures her attention.
- *Memory.* Sarah remembers her friend's name, that she has an appointment, and how to find her way to her advisor's office. She finds it interesting that although she and her friend saw the same movie, they remember different things about it.
- *Language.* She talks with her friend about the movie they saw last night.
- *Reasoning and decision making.* Sarah needs to decide which courses to take and, soon, what to do after graduation. Should she go to graduate school or start looking for a job?

Not only is it easy to provide examples of cognition in everyday experience, but it is also easy to find examples in the news.

- *Perception.* Thousands of deaf people have had a cochlear implant operation that enables them to hear. Researchers are also working to develop devices that would provide sight to the blind.
- *Attention.* Researchers testify at a hearing of the New York State legislature that cell phones distract attention from driving. The legislature agrees and bans the use of cell phones while driving in New York (see http://www .nysgtsc.state.ny.us/ts-place.htm).
- *Memory.* Memory researchers search for ways to prevent the memory losses that are associated with aging. Also, research studies show that a large number of innocent people have been convicted of crimes based on faulty memory by eyewitnesses at crime scenes.
- *Problem solving and reasoning.* Experts ponder evidence to determine the cause of the disintegration of the space shuttle *Columbia* as it reentered the atmosphere on February 1, 2003.

Each of the items on the preceding lists are aspects of **cognition**—the mental processes that are involved in perception, attention, memory, problem solving, reasoning, and making decisions. **Cognitive psychology** is the branch of psychology concerned with the scientific study of cognition.

▶▶▶ The Challenge of Cognitive Psychology

How can we go beyond simply labeling different aspects of cognition, as we did for Sarah's walk across campus and the examples of cognition in the news? One approach would be to apply common sense and everyday observation to cognitive phenomena. This might lead to observations about things such as techniques that work for studying, for remembering what to do later in the day, or for solving certain types of problems. It might also lead us to conclude that cognitive tasks that we carry out almost effortlessly, such as perceiving forms or colors or paying attention to important things in the environment, are so straightforward and simple that there is little to study about how they operate. But before we decide that cognition is either obvious or simple, we should consider the following observation by memory researcher Endel Tulving (2001): "Much of science begins as exploration of common sense, and much of science, if successful, ends if not in rejecting it, then at least going far beyond it" (p. 1505).

Tulving's statement is what this book is about—how science has refined and expanded on our everyday explanations of cognition based on common sense. As we explore this idea, we will see that many of the processes involved in cognition are complex and often hidden from view.

The Complexity of Cognition

Many of the cognitions we listed to describe Sarah's behavior occurred without much effort on her part. She easily perceived the scene around her and recognized her friend. It took a little more effort to remember some of the details of the movie she saw the night before, but she also accomplished this without much difficulty. However, when cognitive psychologists look more closely at processes such as these, they find that beneath this ease and apparent simplicity lie complexities that may not be initially obvious.

To illustrate some of these complexities, let's consider attention. As Sarah walked through campus, her eyes were flooded with images, but she attended closely to just a few. Thus, as she waved to her friend (Figure 1.1), she was hardly aware of the woman with the scarf, even though she was clearly visible. This situation enables us to pose the following question: Even though both people are clearly present in Sarah's field of view, what causes her to be very aware of her friend, but hardly aware of the other person?

Here's another example from everyday experience: Have you ever returned to a place after many years away, and remembered things you hadn't thought about for years? When I asked students in my class to write about an experience that involved memory, one of my students related the following experience.

> When I was eight years old, both of my grandparents passed away. Their house was sold, and that chapter of my life was closed. Since then I can remember general things about being there as a child, but not the details. One day I decided to go for a drive. I went to my grandparents' old house, and I pulled around to the alley and parked. As

■ **Figure 1.1** As Sarah waves to her friend, she is only slightly aware of the woman wearing the scarf, even though that woman is clearly visible.

Bruce Goldstein

I sat there and stared at the house, the most amazing thing happened. I experienced a vivid recollection. All of a sudden, I was eight years old again. I could see myself in the backyard, learning to ride a bike for the first time. I could see the inside of the house. I remembered exactly what every detail looked like. I could even remember the distinct smell. So many times I tried to remember these things, but never so vividly did I remember such detail. (Angela Paidousis)

Angela's experience demonstrates that although it is sometimes difficult to remember things, returning to the place where the memories were originally formed can reveal memories that were there all along. These examples illustrate that experiences such as attention and memory (and other cognitions, as well) involve "hidden" processes we may not be aware of. One way of thinking about these hidden processes is to draw an analogy between what happens as an audience watches a play at the theater and how the mind works. At a play, the audience's attention is focused on the drama being created by the actors, but there is a great deal of activity backstage that the audience is unaware of. Some actors are changing costumes, others are listening for their cues, and stagehands are moving sets into place for the next scene change. Just as a great deal of activity occurs backstage in a play, a great deal of "backstage" activity occurs in your mind.

One of the goals of this book is to show you how cognitive psychologists have revealed the hidden processes that occur "behind the scenes." This chapter tells the beginning of a story of cognitive psychology research that began over 100 years ago, even before the field of psychology was formally founded. To give us perspective on where cognitive psychology is today, it is important to see where it came from, and so we will begin by describing some of the pioneering research on the mind that began in the 19th

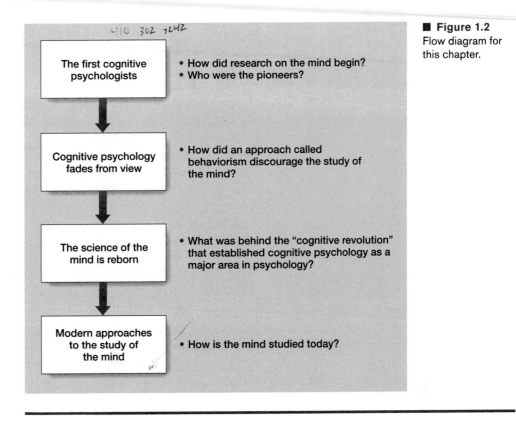

century (Figure 1.2). We then consider the first half of the 20th century, when studying the mind became unfashionable; the second half of the 20th century, when the study of the mind began to flourish again; and how psychologists and researchers in other fields approach present-day research on the mind.

The First Cognitive Psychologists

Cognitive psychology research began in the 19th century before there was a field called cognitive psychology—or even, for that matter, psychology. In 1868, eleven years before the founding of the first laboratory of scientific psychology, Franciscus Donders, a Dutch physiologist, did one of the first cognitive psychology experiments.

Donders' Reaction-Time Experiment Donders conducted research on what today would be called **mental chronometry**, measuring how long a cognitive processes takes. Specifically, he was interested in how long it took for a person to make a decision. He determined this by using a measure called *reaction time.*

◄► Method

Reaction Time

Reaction time—the interval between presentation of a stimulus and a person's response to the stimulus—is one of the most widely used measures in cognitive psychology. One reason for its importance is that measuring the speed of a person's reaction can provide information about extremely rapid processes that occur in the mind.

Reaction time is typically measured by presenting a stimulus and having a participant respond by pressing a button or a key on a computer keyboard as soon as the participant has completed a task. Tasks can range from simply indicating that the stimulus was presented ("Press the button when you see the light"), to making a decision about stimuli ("Press the key if the letters you see form a word" or "Press Key #1 if the statement is true and Key #2 if it is false"). In each of these cases, reaction time can provide insights into the nature of mental processing involved in these tasks. ◆

Donders measured the reaction time to perceiving a light. In the **simple reaction-time** task there was one location for the light, and participants pushed a button as quickly as possible after the light was illuminated (Figure 1.3a). In the **choice reaction-time** task, the light could appear on the left or on the right, and the participants were to push one button if the light was illuminated on the left, and the other button if the light was illuminated on the right (Figure 1.3b).

The rationale behind the simple reaction-time experiment is shown in Figure 1.4a. Presenting the stimulus (the light) causes a mental response (perceiving the light), which leads to a behavioral response (pushing the button). The reaction time (dashed line) is the time between presentation of the stimulus and the behavioral response.

(a) Press J when light goes on.   (b) Press J for left light, K for right.

■ **Figure 1.3** A modern version of Donders' (1868) reaction-time experiment: (a) the simple reaction-time task; and (b) the choice reaction-time task. For the simple reaction-time task, the participant pushes the J key when the light goes on. For the choice reaction-time task, the participant pushes the J key if the left light goes on, and the K key if the right light goes on. The purpose of Donders' experiment was to determine the time it took to decide which key to press for the choice reaction-time task.

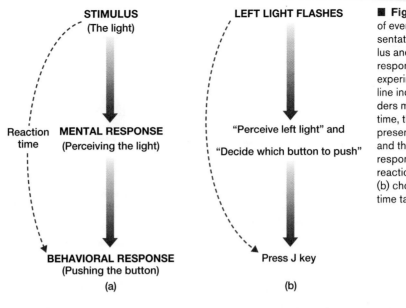

STIMULUS
(The light)

Reaction time

MENTAL RESPONSE
(Perceiving the light)

BEHAVIORAL RESPONSE
(Pushing the button)

(a)

LEFT LIGHT FLASHES

"Perceive left light" and

"Decide which button to push"

Press J key

(b)

■ **Figure 1.4** Sequence of events between presentation of the stimulus and the behavioral response in Donders' experiment. The dashed line indicates that Donders measured reaction time, the time between presentation of the light and the participant's response. (a) Simple reaction-time task; (b) choice reaction-time task.

In Figure 1.4b, a similar diagram for the choice reaction-time experiment, the mental response includes not only perceiving the light but also deciding which light was illuminated and then which button to push. Donders reasoned that choice reaction time would be longer than simple reaction time because of the time it takes to make the decision. Thus, the difference in reaction time between the simple and choice conditions would indicate how long it took to make the decision. Because the choice reaction time took one-tenth of a second longer than simple reaction time, Donders concluded that it took one-tenth of a second to decide which button to push.

Donders' experiment is important both because it was one of the first cognitive psychology experiments, and because it illustrates something extremely important about studying the mind—mental responses (perceiving the light and deciding which button to push, in this example) cannot be measured directly, but must be inferred from the participants' behavior. We can see why this is so by noting the dashed lines in Figure 1.4. These lines indicate that when Donders measured the reaction time, he was measuring the relationship between the presentation of the stimulus and the participant's response. He did not measure the mental response directly, but inferred how long it took from the reaction times. The fact that mental responses can't be measured directly, but must be inferred from observing behavior, is a principle that holds not only for Donders' experiment, but for all research in cognitive psychology.

Helmholtz's Unconscious Inference Hermann von Helmholtz was another 19th-century researcher who was concerned with studying the mind. Helmholtz, who was professor of physiology at the University of Heidelberg (1858) and professor of physics at the

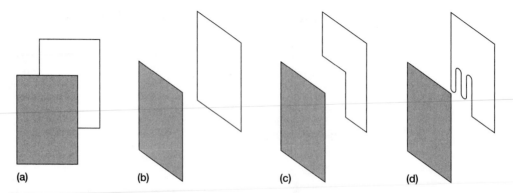

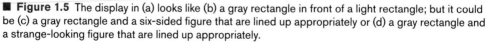

■ Figure 1.5 The display in (a) looks like (b) a gray rectangle in front of a light rectangle; but it could be (c) a gray rectangle and a six-sided figure that are lined up appropriately or (d) a gray rectangle and a strange-looking figure that are lined up appropriately.

University of Berlin (1871), was one of the preeminent physiologists and physicists of his day. He made basic discoveries in physiology and physics, and also developed the ophthalmoscope (the device that an optometrist or ophthalmologist uses to look into your eye) and proposed theories of object perception, color vision, and hearing.

One of the conclusions Helmholtz reached from his research on perception is a principle called the theory of **unconscious inference**, which states that some of our perceptions are the result of unconscious assumptions that we make about the environment. For example, consider Figure 1.5a. This display could be caused by one rectangle overlapping another (Figure 1.5b), or by a six-sided shape positioned to line up with the upper-right corner of the gray rectangle (Figure 1.5c), or a rectangle overlapping a strange shape (Figure 1.5d). However, according to the theory of unconscious inference, we infer that we are seeing a rectangle covering another rectangle because of experiences we have had with similar situations in the past. This inference is called unconscious because it occurs without our awareness or any conscious effort. Helmholtz's idea that we infer much of what we know about the world was an early statement of what is now considered to be a central principle of modern cognitive psychology.

Ebbinghaus's Memory Experiments Hermann Ebbinghaus (1885) performed his classic experiments on memory by learning lists of nonsense syllables like DAX, QEH, LUH, and ZIF. He used nonsense syllables so that his memory would not be influenced by the meaning of a particular word. He read lists of these syllables out loud to himself over and over and determined how many repetitions it took to repeat the lists with no errors. This initial learning is the first step in the **savings method**.

Ebbinghaus then waited a period of time and relearned the list using the same procedure. For short intervals between initial learning and relearning, it usually took fewer repetitions to relearn the list than it had taken him to initially learn it. For example, if Ebbinghaus had to repeat the list 9 times to initially learn it, it might take only 3 repeti-

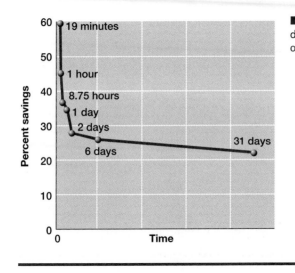

tions to relearn the list after a short interval. Based on this data, he calculated a savings score, using the following formula:

Savings = [(Initial repetitions) − (Relearning repetitions)] / Initial repetitions.

Multiplying the result by 100 converts the savings to a percentage, so for the example above,

Savings = [(9 − 3) / 9] × 100 = 67 percent.

By learning many different lists at retention intervals ranging from 19 minutes to 31 days, Ebbinghaus was able to plot the "forgetting curve" in Figure 1.6, which shows savings as a function of retention interval. Ebbinghaus's experiments were important because they provided a way to quantify memory and therefore plot functions like the forgetting curve that describe the operation of the mind. Notice that although Ebbinghaus's savings method was very different from Donders' reaction-time method, they have something in common: They both measure *behavior* to determine a property of the *mind*.

The First Psychology Laboratories People like Donders, Helmholtz, and Ebbinghaus, who were investigating the mind in the 19th century, were usually based in departments of physiology, physics, or philosophy, because there were no psychology departments at the time. But in 1879 Wilhelm Wundt founded the first laboratory of scientific psychology at the University of Leipzig, with the goal of studying the mind scientifically. He and his students carried out reaction-time experiments and measured basic properties of the senses, particularly vision and hearing.

The theoretical approach that dominated psychology in the late 1800s and early 1900s was called **structuralism**. According to structuralism, our overall experience is determined by combining basic elements of experience called sensations. Thus, just as

Table 1.1 Early Cognitive Psychologists

Donders	1868	Experiment: Simple vs. choice reaction time
		Idea: Mental processes cannot be observed directly, but must be inferred from behavior
Helmholtz	1860–80	Principle: Unconscious inference
Ebbinghaus	1885	Experiment: Memory for nonsense syllables
		Method: Savings technique
		Result: Forgetting curve
Wundt	1879	Established the first laboratory of scientific psychology
		Theory: Structuralism
		Method: Analytic introspection

chemistry had developed a periodic table of the elements, which organized elements on the basis of their molecular weights and chemical properties, Wundt wanted to create a "periodic table of the mind," which would include all of the basic sensations involved in creating experience. Wundt thought he could achieve this by using **analytic introspection**, a technique in which trained participants described their experiences and thought processes in response to stimuli. For example, in one experiment, Wundt asked participants to describe their experience of hearing a five-note chord played on the piano. Wundt was interested in whether they heard the five notes as a single unit or if they were able to hear the individual notes.

Although Wundt never achieved his goal of explaining behavior in terms of sensations, he had a major impact on psychology by establishing the first laboratory of scientific psychology and training PhDs who established psychology departments at other universities. By the beginning of the 20th century, psychology was taking hold in the United States, and much of the research was inspired by the work of the early cognitive psychologists mentioned in this chapter, who were interested in understanding mental functioning (Table 1.1). As we will see, however, events early in the 20th century would shift the focus of psychology away from the study of mental processes and toward the study of observable behavior. One of the major forces that caused psychology to reject the study of mental processes was a negative reaction to the technique of analytic introspection.

The Decline and Rebirth of Cognitive Psychology

Research in most early departments of psychology was conducted in the tradition of Wundt's laboratory, with its emphasis on using analytic introspection to reveal hidden mental processes. This emphasis on studying the mind was to change, however, because of the efforts of John Watson, who received his PhD in psychology in 1904 from the University of Chicago.

The Rise of Behaviorism

The story of how John Watson founded an approach to psychology called behaviorism is well known to introductory psychology students. We will briefly review it here because of its importance to the story of cognitive psychology.

Watson Founds Behaviorism

As a graduate student at the University of Chicago, Watson became dissatisfied with the method of analytic introspection. His problems with this method were (1) it produced extremely variable results from person to person, and (2) these results were difficult to verify because they were interpreted in terms of invisible inner mental processes.

In response to what Watson perceived to be deficiencies in analytic introspection, he proposed a new approach called **behaviorism**. One of Watson's papers, "Psychology as the Behaviorist Views It," set forth the goals of this approach to psychology in this famous quote:

> Psychology as the Behaviorist sees it is a purely objective, experimental branch of natural science. Its theoretical goal is the prediction and control of behavior. Introspection forms no essential part of its methods, nor is the scientific value of its data dependent upon the readiness with which they lend themselves to interpretation in terms of consciousness. . . . What we need to do is start work upon psychology making behavior, not consciousness, the objective point of our attack. (Watson, 1913, pp. 158, 176)

There are three key parts of this quote: (1) Watson rejects introspection as a method, (2) he eliminates consciousness as a topic for study, and (3) he suggests that psychology's main topic for study should be behavior. In another part of this paper, Watson also proclaims that "psychology . . . need no longer delude itself into thinking that it is making mental states the object of observation" (p. 163). Watson's goal was to eliminate the mind as a topic of study in psychology, and to replace it with the study of directly observable behavior.

As behaviorism became the dominant force in American psychology, psychologists' attention shifted from understanding the mind by inferring mental processes from behavior, to understanding behavior in terms of stimulus-response relationships, without any reference to the mind. Watson's most famous experiment was the "little Albert" experiment, in which Watson and Rosalie Rayner (1920) caused a 9-month-old boy named Albert to become frightened of a rat by presenting a loud noise every time the rat (which Albert had originally liked) came close to Albert.

Watson's ideas are associated with classical conditioning, which focused on how pairing one stimulus (such as the loud noise presented to Albert) with another, previously neutral stimulus (such as the rat) causes changes in the response to the neutral stimulus (Pavlov, 1927). Watson used the conditioning of little Albert to argue that behavior can be analyzed without any reference to the mind. For Watson, what was going on inside little Albert's head, either physiologically or mentally, was irrelevant. He cared only about how pairing one stimulus with another affected behavior.

Skinner's Operant Conditioning In the midst of behaviorism's dominance of American psychology, a young graduate student at Harvard named B. F. Skinner provided another tool for behaviorism, which insured this approach would dominate psychology for decades to come. Skinner introduced operant conditioning, which focused on how behavior is strengthened by presentation of positive reinforcers, such as food or social approval, or withdrawal of negative reinforcers, such as a shock or social rejection. For example, Skinner showed that reinforcing a rat with food for pressing a bar maintained or increased the rat's rate of bar pressing. Like Watson, Skinner was not interested in what was happening in the mind, but focused solely on determining the relationship between stimuli and responding (Skinner, 1938).

The Decline of Behaviorism

The behaviorists' idea that behavior can be understood by studying stimulus-response relationships influenced an entire generation of psychologists and dominated psychology in the United States during the 1940s, 1950s, and into the 1960s. Psychologists applied the techniques of conditioning to things like classroom teaching, treating psychological disorders, and testing the effects of drugs on animals. However, beginning in the 1950s, changes began to occur in psychology, which would eventually lead to a decline in the influence of behaviorism. One of the important events that led to the decline of behaviorism was the publication of Skinner's book *Verbal Behavior*, in 1957.

Noam Chomsky's Critique of Skinner's *Verbal Behavior* In his book *Verbal Behavior*, Skinner explained the development of language in children in terms of operant conditioning. Skinner argued that children learn language through operant conditioning. They imitate speech that they hear, and repeat correct speech because it is rewarded. But in 1959 Chomsky, a linguist from the Massachusetts Institute of Technology, published a scathing review of Skinner's book, in which he pointed out that children say many sentences that they have never heard ("I hate you, Mommy," for example), and that during the normal course of language development, they go through a stage in which they use incorrect grammar, such as "the boy hitted the ball," even though this incorrect grammar may never have been reinforced.

Chomsky saw language development as being determined not by imitation or reinforcement, but by an inborn biological program that holds across cultures. Chomsky's analysis led psychologists to reconsider the idea that language and other complex behaviors such as problem solving and reasoning can be explained by operant conditioning, and they began to realize that to understand complex cognitive behaviors it is necessary not only to measure observable behavior, but to consider what this behavior tells us about how the mind works.

The Misbehavior of Organisms Another event that led people to question behaviorism was the publication in 1961 of a paper titled "The Misbehavior of Organisms" by two of Skinner's students, Keller Breland and Marian Breland (1961). The title of their paper was, significantly, a takeoff on the title of Skinner's 1938 book *The Behavior of Organisms*, in which Skinner described how behavior can be controlled by reinforcements.

Drawing on their experience in using operant conditioning to train animals for circuses, TV, and film stunts, the Brelands described a number of situations in which their attempts to condition an animal's behavior ran head-on into the animal's built-in instincts. For example, according to the theory of operant conditioning, rewarding a behavior should increase its frequency. However, when the Brelands attempted to train a raccoon to drop two coins in a piggy bank by rewarding this response with food, the raccoon did not cooperate. After the raccoon was rewarded with food for dropping two coins into the bank, it took the next two coins and began rubbing them together, just as they do to remove the shells of newly caught crayfish. Eventually, the coin-rubbing response overpowered the coin-dropping response, and the Brelands had to abandon their attempt to condition the raccoon. The Brelands used this and other examples to emphasize the importance of biologically programmed behavior.

Although some researchers were questioning the ability of reinforcement to explain complex behavior like language in humans and the "coin rubbing" of Breland's raccoons, other researchers were developing an alternative approach to studying behavior, based on the idea that the mind is a processor of information.

The Cognitive Revolution

A number of events occurred in the 1950s that resulted in what has been called the **cognitive revolution**—a shift in psychology from the behaviorist's stimulus-response relationships to an approach in which the main thrust was to explain behavior in terms of the mind. These events provided a new way to study the mind, called the **information-processing approach**. One of the events that inspired psychologists to think of the mind in terms of information processing was a newly introduced information-processing device called the digital computer.

Introduction of the Digital Computer The first digital computers, which were developed in the late 1940s, were huge machines that took up entire buildings. But in 1954 IBM introduced a computer that was available to the general public. These computers were still extremely large compared to the laptops of today, but they found their way to university research laboratories, where they were used both to analyze data and, most important for our purposes, to suggest a new way to think about the mind.

One of the characteristics of computers that captured the attention of cognitive psychologists in the 1950s was that they processed information in stages. For example, the diagram in Figure 1.7a shows the layout of a computer in which information is received by an "input processor" and is then stored in a "memory unit" before it is processed by an "arithmetic unit," which then creates the computer's output. Applying this stage

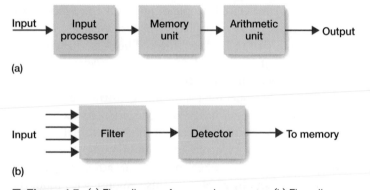

(a)

(b)

■ **Figure 1.7** (a) Flow diagram for an early computer. (b) Flow diagram for Broadbent's filter model of attention. This diagram shows that many messages enter a "filter" that selects the message to which the person is attending for further processing by a detector and then storage in memory. We will describe this diagram more fully in Chapter 4.

approach to the mind led psychologists to ask new questions and to frame their answers to these questions in new ways. British psychologists Colin Cherry and Donald Broadbent sought to answer two questions: "How much information can the mind take in?" and "Is it possible to attend to just some part of the incoming information?" These questions led to some pioneering work on attention.

Early Experiments on Attention To study how well people can pay attention to some information when other information is presented at the same time, Cherry (1953) asked participants to listen to two different messages, one presented to the left ear and the other presented to the right ear. To ensure that his participants were attending to one of the messages, Cherry asked them to repeat, out loud, the message presented to one of the ears. Cherry found that participants were able to focus on the message they were repeating, but could take in very little information from the other message.

Cherry's result was important because it showed both that people were able to focus their attention on one message among many, and also that there are limits to the amount of information that people can deal with. But what made this result even more important is what happened next: Donald Broadbent (1958) proposed a flow diagram (Figure 1.7b) to represent what happens in a person's mind as he or she directs attention to one stimulus in the environment, like Cherry's participants did when they focused their attention on the message presented to one ear.

This flow diagram, which we will describe in more detail in Chapter 4, is notable because it was the first to depict the mind as processing information in a sequence of stages. Applied to Cherry's experiment, "input" would be the sounds entering the person's ears; the "filter" lets through the part of the input to which the person is attending; and the "detector" records the information that gets through the filter. The important point for now is that the flow diagram provided a way to analyze the operation of the mind in terms of a sequence of processing stages. You will see many more flow diagrams like this throughout this book because they have become one of the standard ways of depicting the operation of the mind.

Two Historic Conferences At about the time Cherry and Broadbent were studying attention in England, two meetings were held in the United States that also played an important role in reintroducing the mind to psychology. In the summer of 1956, Dartmouth University held a research seminar on artificial intelligence. On September 10–12 of the same year, the Second Symposium on Information Theory was held at MIT. A notable paper presented at both conferences was Alan Newell and Herb Simon's (1956) description of their "logic theorist" computer program that enabled computers to solve logic problems. Both of these conferences brought together researchers from a number of fields, including psychology, linguistics, computer science, and anthropology.

All of the events we have described represented the beginning of a shift in psychology from behaviorism to the study of the mind. This shift has been called the cognitive revolution, but the word "revolution" should not be interpreted as meaning that the shift from behaviorism to cognitive approach occurred quickly. The scientists attending the conferences in 1956 had no idea that these conferences would, years later, be seen as historic events in the birth of a new way of thinking about the mind (Miller, 2003). In fact, the conferences were so influential that scientific historians have called 1956 "the birthday of cognitive science" (Bechtel et al., 1998; Neisser, 1988). But ten years after these meetings, a textbook on the history of psychology makes no mention of cognitive psychology (Misiak & Sexton, 1966), and it wasn't until 1967 that the first cognitive psychology textbook appeared (Neisser, 1967).

Nonetheless, events that began in the 1950s resulted in a new generation of psychologists who began conducting experiments in perception, attention, memory, language, and problem solving, and were interpreting their results in terms of the flow of information within the mind. It soon became evident that the information-processing approach worked, and so more and more psychologists became interested in using it, and by the 1980s, American psychology had evolved from being a behaviorist world to a cognitive one. It happened gradually, more like an *evolution* than a *revolution*, but the overall result was revolutionary (Figure 1.8).

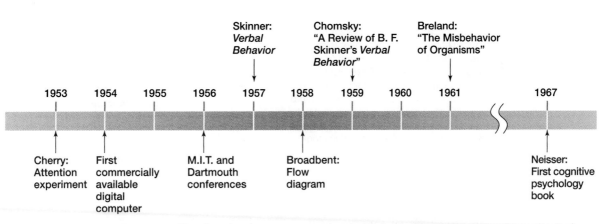

■ **Figure 1.8** Time line showing events associated with the decline of behaviorism (above the line) and events that led to the development of the information-processing approach to cognitive psychology (below the line).

◆◆◆ How Do Cognitive Psychologists Study the Mind?

Now that we have described the history of cognitive psychology, let's consider how cognitive psychology is studied today. The basic principle of using behavior to infer mental processes, as Donders did, still guides present-day research. In addition, modern researchers can also measure physiological responding.

Behavioral and Physiological Approaches to Cognition

An important characteristic of the present-day study of cognition is the use of both behavioral and physiological approaches to the study of the mind. The **behavioral approach** involves measuring the relationship between stimuli and behavior. For example, Donders used the behavioral approach because he measured the relationship between presentation of the light and the reaction time to respond to the light.

The **physiological approach** involves measuring the relationship between physiology and behavior. For example, let's assume we decide to repeat Donders' experiment in a modern laboratory so we can measure the time it takes to respond to presentation of the light *and* the brain activity that occurs in response to the light. Figure 1.9 updates the diagram of Figure 1.4, taking these physiological measurements into account. The diagram still includes the purely behavioral relationship between the stimulus and behavior from Figure 1.4 (A), but the physiological response creates another relationship: the relationship between the physiological response and behavior (B).

To understand what these relationships mean, let's consider how they might be measured if we repeated Donders' reaction-time experiment in a modern laboratory, which has a brain scanner that can indicate which areas of the brain are activated. (We will describe this technique in Chapter 2). We measure the stimulus-behavior relation-

■ **Figure 1.9** Updated sequence of events between stimulus and response, taking into account the physiological response. The mental response must be inferred from relationships that can be measured: A: relationship between the stimulus and behavior; B: relationship between the physiological response and behavior. It is also possible to measure the relationship between the stimulus and the physiological response.

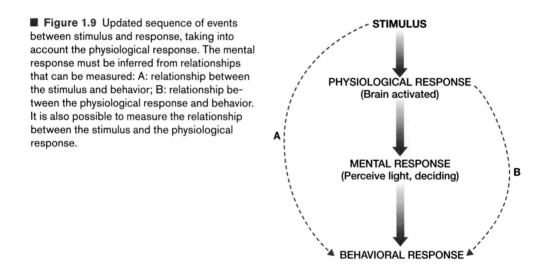

STIMULUS

PHYSIOLOGICAL RESPONSE
(Brain activated)

A

MENTAL RESPONSE
(Perceive light, deciding)

B

BEHAVIORAL RESPONSE

ship for simple and choice reaction-time tasks, as Donders did. In addition, we measure the physiology-behavior relationship at the same time by noting which brain areas are activated during the simple and choice reaction-time tasks.

Comparing the brain activation that occurred during the choice reaction-time task to the results in the simple reaction-time task might enable us to conclude that "making a choice between two lights activates an area of the brain that is not activated when a person is responding to just one light." This might lead to the hypothesis that this brain area may be involved in the process of making a decision between the two lights.

Although we have distinguished between the behavioral and physiological approaches for studying the mind, it is important to realize that the goal of both approaches is to understand how the mind operates. The behavioral approach makes inferences about the mind based on measurements of behavior, whereas the physiological approach makes inferences based on measurements of physiological responding. We will see that using both behavioral and physiological approaches results in a more complete understanding of how the mind operates than using either one alone.

To provide specific examples of how the behavioral and physiological approaches have been used by modern cognitive psychologists, we will describe two experiments that have used these approaches to study the processes involved in memory.

The Behavioral Approach: Measuring Mental Rotation

The following demonstration is based on an experiment by Roger Shepard and J. Metzler (1971) that was designed to study the properties of images people form in their minds.

 Demonstration

Comparing Objects

CogLab

**Mental
Rotation**

Look at the two pictures in Figure 1.10a and decide, as quickly as possible, whether they represent two different views of the same object ("same") or two different objects ("different"). Also make the same judgment for the two objects in Figure 1.10b. 🌶

When Shepard and Metzler measured participants' reaction time to decide whether pairs of objects were the same or different, they obtained the relationship shown in Figure 1.11 for objects that were the same. It took longer to compare two objects that were separated by a large angle, like the ones in Figure 1.10b, than it did to compare two objects that were separated by a smaller angle, like the ones in Figure 1.10a.

From this relationship between reaction time and difference in orientation, Shepard and Metzler inferred that participants were rotating an image of one of the objects in their mind, a phenomenon they called **mental rotation**. From the data in Figure 1.11 we can see that for an orientation difference of 40 degrees, it took 2 seconds to decide a pair was the same shape, but for a difference of 140 degrees, it took 4 seconds. Because it took 2 seconds to accomplish a rotation of 100 degrees, this means that participants

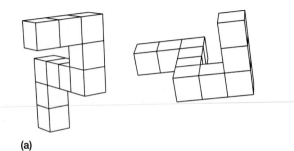

■ **Figure 1.10** Stimuli for the "Comparing Objects" demonstration. (Excerpted with permission from "Mental Rotation of Three-Dimensional Objects," by R. N. Shepard & J. Metzler. From *Science, 171,* pp. 701–703, Fig. 1A & B. Copyright © 1971 AAAS.)

(a)

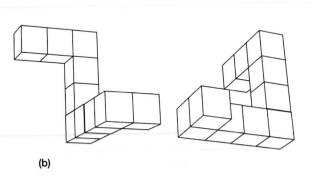

(b)

■ **Figure 1.11** Results of Shepard and Metzler's (1971) mental-rotation experiment. (Excerpted with permission from "Mental Rotation of Three-Dimensional Objects," by R. N. Shepard & J. Metzler. From *Science, 171,* pp. 701–703, Fig. 2A. Copyright © 1971 AAAS.)

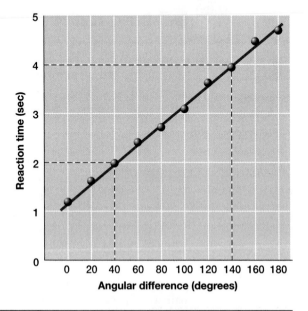

were rotating the images at a rate of 50 degrees per second. This experiment is considered a classic because it was one of the first to apply quantitative methods to the study of mental imagery.

The Physiological Approach: The Relationship Between Brain Activity and Memory

We are now going to describe a more recent experiment that used a technique called brain imaging, which we will describe in the next chapter. For our purposes it is simply necessary to know that this technique enables researchers to identify which areas of the brain are activated as a person carries out a specific task. In this experiment Lisa Davachi and coworkers (2003) showed participants a series of 200 words while monitoring participants' brain activity. Participants were instructed to create an image in their mind that went with each word. For example, if the word was "dirty," they could create an image of a garbage dump.

Twenty hours later, the participants were presented with the same 200 words they had seen earlier, along with 200 new words. During this part of the experiment, they were not in the brain scanner. Their task was to indicate which of the words they had seen before, so a correct answer would be "yes" when an old word was presented, and "no" when a new one was presented. Divachi found that participants remembered 54 percent of the old words (they said "yes" to an old word) and forgot the remaining 46 percent (they said "no" to an old word).

Divachi was interested in whether the remembered and forgotten words had elicited any difference in the brain activity when they were first presented. To answer this question, she looked at brain activity generated by the remembered and not remembered words in an area of the brain called the perirhinal cortex (an area located inside the brain that belongs to a cluster of areas that are involved in memory). The result, shown in Figure 1.12, was that brain activity was greater for the remembered words. Apparently, something was happening in the brain *as the participants were first exposed to the words* that led to better memory for some of the words later. Clearly, the physiological measurements in this experiment provide information about how the mind operates that could not be determined using the behavioral approach alone.

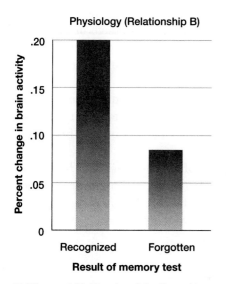

Figure 1.12 Results of the Davachi et al. (2003) experiment, showing the amount of brain activation that occurred during the learning part of the experiment for words that were recognized and for words that were forgotten during the test part of the experiment. This corresponds to Relationship B in Figure 1.9.

Models in Cognitive Psychology

What do cognitive psychologists do with the data they collect in their experiments? They analyze the data and attempt to draw conclusions about what the data mean, as we have seen in the Shepard and Meltzer and the Divachi and coworkers experiments. But cognitive psychologists are often interested in how their results fit into a bigger picture. How, for example, do the results of the experiments we have just described help us explain the processes involved in generating mental images and remembering words?

To understand the big picture, cognitive psychologists often create **models**. There are many kinds of models. For example, Newell and Simon's "logic theorist" was a computer model that simulated human behavior, but its inner workings bore little resemblance to the biology of the brain. However, there are other models that are closely linked to how information is processed by the brain.

The type of model you will see in this book, particularly in the first seven chapters, pictures information as flowing from one stage to the next, with these stages often being represented by boxes, as in Figure 1.13. This model, which is called the **modal model of memory**, was proposed in 1968 by Richard Atkinson and Richard Shiffrin to explain the basic processes that occur in memory. We will be describing this model in detail beginning in Chapter 5, but we will briefly describe how information flows through the three stages of the model now.

The first stage in this model is **sensory memory**. Sensory memory can take in a large amount of information, but most of it fades rapidly, within about half a second. Some of the information from sensory memory is then transferred into **short-term memory**, where information can be held for about 15–20 seconds, unless it is rehearsed, as when you repeat a telephone number you want to remember. Although much of the information that enters short-term memory is lost, some enters **long-term memory**, in which information can be stored for long periods of time, as when you remember some of the things you did yesterday, last summer, or many years ago.

Introduction of this model of memory stimulated thousands of experiments, which considered questions such as "How long is information held in each stage?" and "What causes some information to become stored in long-term memory and other information to be forgotten?"

The modal model illustrates an important property of models in general: They pose questions to be answered and organize data that has been generated by many different experiments into a common scheme. Another property of cognitive psychology models is that they are often revised based on the results of experiments. We will see in Chap-

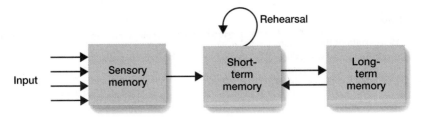

■ **Figure 1.13** Flow diagram of the modal model of memory proposed by Atkinson and Shiffrin (1968). This model will be described in detail in Chapter 5.

ter 5 that this is exactly what happened to the modal model. New results showed that memory is too complex to be described by just three stages, so new models that provide better explanations of the data have been proposed.

Students often wonder whether the boxes in these models stand for specific areas in the brain. Although in some models each box corresponds to a specific place in the brain, the boxes in most of the models we will be describing do not correspond to one brain area. We will see that a basic principle of the operation of the mind is that activity is distributed across many areas of the brain. Thus, although a model might represent long-term memory by a single box, the process of creating, storing, and retrieving memories involves a large number of separate brain areas, many of which interact with each other in complicated ways.

Something to Consider

Studying Cognition Across Many Disciplines

The historic 1956 meetings that are often taken as marking the beginning of the cognitive revolution were attended by researchers in many disciplines in addition to psychology. These conferences were therefore interdisciplinary, and so fall within the field of **cognitive science**, which is defined as the interdisciplinary study of the mind. Figure 1.14 shows the major fields that make up cognitive science (Miller, 2003). The lines connecting them represent the fact that studying the mind has involved interactions and collaborations between these different fields, with each field bringing its own perspective to understanding the mind.

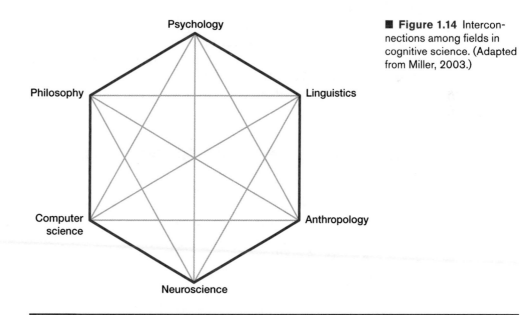

■ **Figure 1.14** Interconnections among fields in cognitive science. (Adapted from Miller, 2003.)

- *Psychology.* As we have described in this chapter, cognitive psychologists focus on using behavioral measures to understand the operation of the mind, and increasingly have also taken a physiological approach as well.
- *Computer science.* Computer scientists are concerned with artificial intelligence—creating computer programs that can duplicate intelligent behaviors such as perceiving and thinking. One application of artificial intelligence is designing computer-vision systems that enable computers to navigate vehicles over different terrains or to identify people as they pass through airport security.
- *Anthropology.* Cognitive anthropologists study the social and cognitive contexts of cognition. A cognitive anthropologist might, for example, study differences in thinking across different cultures.
- *Linguistics.* One of the most active areas of cognitive science research is the study of language. Linguists study how people use grammar and how people produce and understand language.
- *Neuroscience.* Neuroscientists study physiological processes involved in cognition, at levels ranging from single nerve cells to large areas of the brain.
- *Philosophy.* Philosophers are concerned with problems such as whether machines that can simulate human cognitions such as perceiving, thinking, or language can have *experiences* like those that humans report in connection with these activities.

Although many disciplines are concerned with studying the mind, researchers and theorists from different disciplines often work together, with some people using the methods from a number of disciplines. For example, much of the research you will read about in this book was carried out by psychologists who were trained both in the techniques of measuring behavior and in physiological methods such as recording from single neurons, measuring brain activation using a technique called brain imaging, and studying the behavior of patients with brain damage. Although researchers who study the mind may have their offices in different departments in the university, they are all connected by a single goal: finding ways to study and understand the inner workings of the mind.

Test Yourself 1.1

1. Why could we say that Donders, Helmholtz, and Ebbinghaus were cognitive psychologists, even though in the 19th century there was no field called cognitive psychology? Describe Donders' experiment and the rationale behind it, Helmholtz's theory of unconscious inference, and Ebbinghaus's memory experiments.
2. When was the first laboratory of scientific psychology founded, and how important was the study of mental functioning in psychology at the end of the 19th century and beginning of the 20th?
3. Describe the rise of behaviorism, especially the influence of Watson and Skinner. How did behaviorism affect research on the mind?

4. Describe the events that helped lead to the decline of behaviorism and the events that led to the "cognitive revolution."

5. Describe the behavioral and physiological approaches to the study of cognition. How are they different, and what do they have in common?

6. Describe Shepard and Metzler's mental-rotation experiment. What approach do these experiments illustrate?

7. Describe Divachi and coworkers' experiment that demonstrated a relationship between brain activation and memory.

8. Why are models important in cognitive psychology? Do the boxes in models like the modal model of memory correspond to structures in the brain?

9. What is cognitive science? Give some examples of how different disciplines would approach the study of the mind.

Chapter Summary

1. The complexity of cognition becomes apparent when we consider questions like "Why do we take in little information about a person we are not paying attention to, even though we can easily see them?" or "Why do memories suddenly reappear when we return to a specific location?"

2. The work of Donders (simple vs. choice reaction time), Helmholtz (unconscious inference), and Ebbinghaus (the forgetting curve for nonsense syllables) are examples of cognitive psychology from the 19th century.

3. Because the operation of the mind cannot be observed directly, its operation must be inferred from what we can measure, such as behavior or physiological responding. This is one of the basic principles of cognitive psychology.

4. The first laboratory of scientific psychology, founded by Wundt in 1879, was concerned largely with studying the mind. Structuralism was the dominant theoretical approach of this laboratory, and analytic introspection was one of the major methods used to collect data.

5. In the first decades of the 20th century, behaviorism was founded by John Watson, partly in reaction to structuralism and the method of analytic introspection. Its central tenet was that psychology was properly studied by measuring observable behavior, and that invisible mental processes were not valid topics for the study of psychology. Beginning in the 1930s and 40s, B. F. Skinner's work on operant conditioning assured that behaviorism would be the dominant force in psychology through the 1950s.

6. In the 1950s, a number of events occurred that led to what has been called the cognitive revolution—a decline in the influence of behaviorism and the reemergence of the study of the mind. These events included the following: (a) Chomsky's critique of Skinner's book *Verbal Behavior*; (b) reports by Breland and Breland that biological influences made it difficult to train some behaviors using operant conditioning; (c) the introduction of the digital computer and the idea that the mind processes information in stages, like computers; (d) Cherry's attention experiments and

Broadbent's introduction of flow diagrams to depict the processes involved in attention; (e) interdisciplinary conferences at MIT and Dartmouth in 1956.

7. Modern cognitive psychologists study the mind by using both behavioral and physiological approaches, which results in a more complete understanding of how the mind operates than using either one alone.

8. Two modern examples of the behavioral and physiological approaches are Shepard and Metzler's experiments studying mental rotation (behavioral approach) and Divachi and coworkers' experiment on the relationship between brain activity and memory (physiological approach).

9. Models play an essential role in cognitive psychology, by helping organize data from many experiments. The modal model of memory is an example of a particularly influential model. It is important to realize that models such as this one are constantly being revised in response to new data, and also that the boxes in these models often do not correspond to areas in the brain.

10. Cognitive science, the interdisciplinary study of the mind, includes researchers and theorists from psychology, computer science, anthropology, linguistics, neuroscience, and philosophy.

Think About It

1. Check the newspaper or newsmagazines for stories that are related to cognitive psychology, such as stories about memory research ("Scientists Race to Find Memory-Loss Cure"), those about memory in court testimony ("Defendant Says He Can't Remember What Happened"), and stories about decisions people make ("Survey Shows Many People Choose Not to Receive Flu Shots").

2. The idea that we have something called "the mind" that is responsible for our thoughts and behavior is reflected in the many ways that the word *mind* can be used. For example, consider "She is out of her mind" or "Do you mind if I borrow your notes?" See how many examples you can think of that illustrate different uses of the word *mind*, and decide how relevant each is to what you will be studying in cognitive psychology (as indicated by the table of contents of this book).

3. Donders compared the results of his simple and choice reaction-time experiments to infer how long it took to make the decision as to which button to push, when given a choice. But what about other kinds of decisions? Design an experiment to determine the time it takes to make a more complex decision. Then relate this experiment to the diagrams in Figures 1.4 or 1.9.

If You Want to Know More

1. *The birth of cognitive psychology.* To get a feel for the kinds of things cognitive psychologists were concerned with near the beginning of the "cognitive revolution," look at Ulrich Neisser's book, *Cognitive Psychology*. This was the first modern

textbook on the subject. Try comparing it to what's in this book. One thing you will notice is that the field of cognitive psychology is far more concerned with physiological processes now than it was at the beginning.

Neisser, U. (1967). *Cognitive psychology*. New York: Appleton-Century-Crofts.

Key Terms

Analytic introspection, 10
Behavioral approach, 16
Behaviorism, 11
Choice reaction time, 6
Cognition, 2
Cognitive psychology, 2
Cognitive revolution, 2
Cognitive science, 21
Information-processing approach, 13
Long-term memory, 20
Mental chronometry, 5

Mental rotation, 17
Modal model of memory, 20
Model, 20
Physiological approach, 16
Reaction time, 6
Savings method, 8
Sensory memory, 20
Short-term memory, 20
Simple reaction time, 6
Structuralism, 9
Unconscious inference, 8

CogLab   To experience these experiments for yourself, go to http://coglab.wadsworth.com. Be sure to read each experiment's setup instructions before you go to the experiment itself. Otherwise, you won't know which keys to press.

Primary Lab
Mental rotation   How a stimulus can be rotated in the mind to determine if its shape matches another stimulus (p. 17).

Cognition and the Brain: Basic Principles

2

Neurons: The Building Blocks of the Nervous System
  Neurons Transform Environmental Energy Into Electrical
    Energy
  ◄► Method: Recording From Single Neurons

How Neurons Communicate
  Communication Between Neurons Occurs at the Synapse
  Excitation and Inhibition Interact at the Synapse

How Neurons Process Information
  Neurons Process Information by Interacting With Each
    Other
  Neural Processing Creates Neurons That Respond to
    Specific Types of Stimuli

Test Yourself 2.1

How Stimuli Are Represented by the Firing of Neurons
  The Neural Code for Perceiving Faces
  The Neural Code for Other Cognitive Capacities

Cognitive Processes and the Brain
  Layout of the Brain
  Different Areas of the Brain Serve Specific Functions
  ◄► Method: Neuropsychology
  Cognitive Processes Are Signaled by Activity in Many
    Areas of the Brain
  ◄► Method: Brain Imaging

Interacting With the Environment Affects Operation of
the Nervous System

Something to Consider: Are There Grandmother Cells
After All?

Test Yourself 2.2

Chapter Summary

Think About It

If You Want to Know More

Key Terms

CogLab: Receptive Fields; Brain Asymmetry

Some Questions We Will Consider

- How do neurons process information? (36)
- How are faces represented by the firing of neurons? (41)
- How does the brain change its functioning to adapt to specific environmental conditions? (48)

At 7:00 AM, in response to hearing the familiar but irritating sound of his alarm clock, Juan swings his arm in a well-practiced arc, feels the contact of his hand with the snooze button, and in the silence he has created, turns over for 10 more minutes of sleep. How can we explain Juan's behavior in terms of physiology? What is happening inside Juan's brain that makes it possible for him to hear the alarm, take appropriate action to turn it off, and know that he can sleep a little longer and still get to his early-morning class on time?

We can give a general answer to this question by considering some of the steps involved in Juan's action of turning off the alarm. The first step in hearing the alarm occurs when sound waves from the alarm enter Juan's ears and stimulate receptors that change the sound energy into electrical signals (Figure 2.1a). These signals then reach the auditory area of Juan's brain, which causes him to hear the ringing of the bell (Figure 2.1b). Then signals are sent to the motor area of the brain, which controls movement. The motor area sends signals to the muscles of Juan's hand and arm (Figure 2.1c), which carry out the movement that turns off the alarm.

But there is more to the story than this sequence of events. For one thing, Juan's decision to hit the snooze button of his alarm is based on his knowledge that this will silence the alarm temporarily, and that the alarm will sound again in 10 minutes. He also knows that if he stays in bed for 10 more minutes, he will still have time to get to his class. A more complete picture of what's happening in Juan's brain when the alarm rings would, therefore, have to include processes involved in retrieving knowledge from memory and making decisions based on that knowledge. Thus, a seemingly simple behavior such as turning off an alarm in the morning involves a complex series of physiological events.

Students often wonder why they need to know about principles of nervous system functioning for a course in cognitive psychology. One answer to this question is that the development of brain scanning technology over the last few decades has placed the brain at the center of much present-day research in cognitive psychology. The study of cognitive psychology today consists of both purely behavioral experiments and experiments that consider links between behavior and the brain.

The purpose of this chapter is to give you the basic background you will need to understand the physiological material on perception, attention, memory, language, decision making, and problem solving that we will be covering in the chapters that follow. We will describe some basic principles of nervous system functioning by first considering the structure and functioning of cells called neurons, which are the building blocks and transmission lines of the nervous system. We then focus on the collection of 180 billion of these neurons that form the brain. As we do this you will see that to understand the brain, we need to understand how its neurons are organized and how they signal information about the environment and our actions within the environment (Figure 2.2).

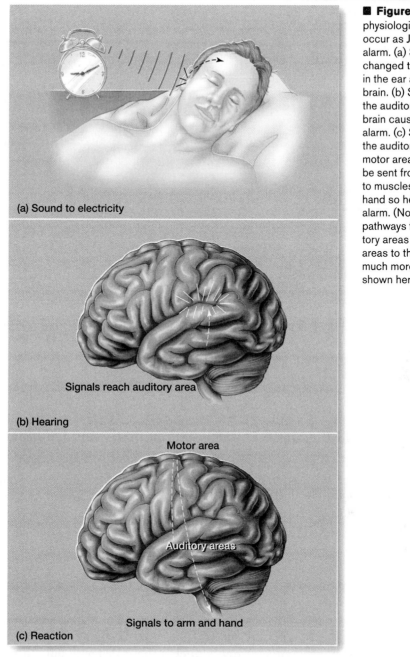

(a) Sound to electricity

Signals reach auditory area

(b) Hearing

Motor area

Auditory areas

Signals to arm and hand

(c) Reaction

■ Figure 2.1 Some of the physiological processes that occur as Juan turns off his alarm. (a) Sound waves are changed to electrical signals in the ear and are sent to the brain. (b) Signals reaching the auditory areas of the brain cause Juan to hear the alarm. (c) Signals sent from the auditory areas to the motor area cause signals to be sent from the motor area to muscles in Juan's arm and hand so he can turn off the alarm. (Note that the actual pathways from ear to auditory areas and from auditory areas to the motor area are much more complex than shown here.)

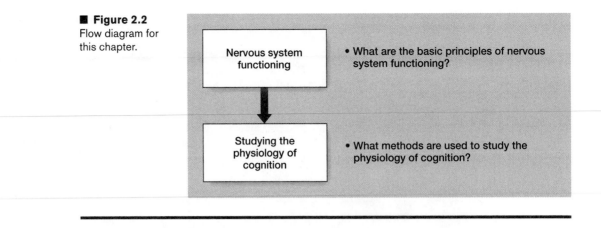

■ **Figure 2.2**
Flow diagram for this chapter.

| Nervous system functioning | • What are the basic principles of nervous system functioning? |
| Studying the physiology of cognition | • What methods are used to study the physiology of cognition? |

Neurons: The Building Blocks of the Nervous System

In the first American psychology textbook, Harvard psychologist William James (1890) described the brain as the "most mysterious thing in the world" because of the amazing feats it achieves and the intricacies of how it achieves them. One thing that contributes to the mysteriousness of the brain is its complexity. It is made up of billions of interconnected cells called neurons, which transmit electricity and communicate with each other.

Neurons Transform Environmental Energy Into Electrical Energy

For many years, the nature of the brain's tissue was a mystery. Looking at the interior of the brain with the unaided eye gave no indication that it is made up of billions of smaller units. The existence of these units was confirmed by the Italian anatomist Camillo Golgi (1844–1926), who developed a chemical technique that stained some neurons but left most unstained. This revealed the structure of single neurons in pictures like the one in Figure 2.3. **Neurons** are cells that are specialized to receive and transmit information in the nervous system.

Different parts of neurons are specialized to serve different functions (Figure 2.4). At the receiving end of the neuron is the cell body and its dendrites (Figure 2.4b). The **cell body** contains mechanisms to keep the cell alive; the **dendrites** that branch out from the cell body receive signals from other neurons. The transmitting structure of the neuron is the **axon**, or **nerve fiber**, a tube filled with fluid that conducts electrical signals. For some neurons, **sensory receptors** replace the cell body and dendrites at the receiving end (Figure 2.4a). These receptors are specialized structures that respond to light energy (vision), mechanical deformation (touch, pain), pressure changes in the air (to create hearing), molecules in the air (smell), and molecules in liquid (taste).

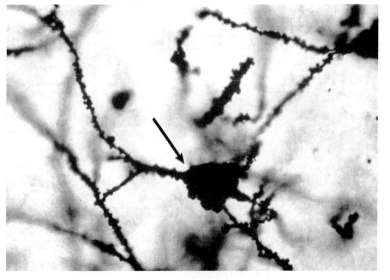

■ **Figure 2.3**
A portion of the brain that has been treated with Golgi stain shows the shapes of a few neurons. The arrow points to a neuron's cell body. The thin lines are dendrites or axons (see Figure 2.4).

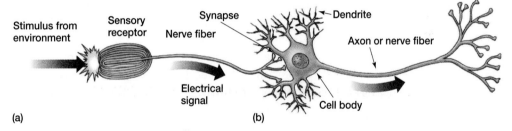

■ **Figure 2.4** Basic components of the neuron. (a) The neuron on the left contains a sensory receptor, which is specialized to receive information from the environment (in this case, pressure that would occur from being touched on the skin). (b) This neuron synapses on the neuron on the right, which has a cell body instead of a receptor.

The receptors achieve something quite amazing—they transform energy from the environment into electrical energy that represents the environment within our nervous system. The transformation of one form of energy into another form of energy is called **transduction**. An example of transduction is the sequence of events that occurs when you touch the "Withdrawal" button on the ATM screen at the bank. The pressure exerted by your finger, which is mechanical energy, is transduced by the ATM into electrical energy, which is then transduced back into mechanical energy to operate the mechanism that pushes your money out of the machine.

In the nervous system, transduction occurs when environmental energy is transformed into electrical energy. For example, in ● Color Plate 2.1 (see color insert) light energy that is reflected from the tree enters the eye through the pupil. This light energy activates receptors in the **retina**, a network of neurons that line the back of the eye, and these electrical signals exit the back of the eye in 1 million axons that make up the **optic nerve**.

What's important about the electrical signals in the optic nerve is that our perception of the tree—its dark, gnarled trunk, its green leaves fluttering in the wind, and the small bird nest nestled among its branches—is based on information contained within these electrical signals. The first step in understanding the nature of this information is to examine more closely what these electrical signals look like. This has been achieved by recording from individual neurons.

◪ Method

Recording From Single Neurons

Our goal in recording from single neurons is to detect the neuron's electrical signal and to relate these signals to cognitive processes such as perceiving the tree or remembering the tree later. We can appreciate why recording from individual neurons is important by considering the following situation: You walk into a large room in which there are thousands of people, all talking at once about a political speech they have just heard. The "crowd noise" you hear tells you little about what is going on in the room, other than perhaps the crowd's general level of excitement. However, listening to what individual people are saying provides more specific information about peoples' reactions to the speech.

Just as listening to individual voices provides valuable information about what is happening within a crowd, recording from single neurons provides valuable information about what is happening in the brain. These signals, called **action potentials**, are recorded by using tiny wires called **microelectrodes** that are placed in or near an axon, and that pick up the electrical signals that travel down the axon (Figure 2.5a). When the axon's electrical signals are displayed on a device called an oscilloscope, we see that the inside of the neuron becomes positive for about 1 millisecond and then returns to its original level (Figure 2.5b). Changing the time scale on our display creates a display like the one in Figure 2.5c in which the nerve impulses look like lines, or "spikes." Using this time scale makes it possible to display a number of action potentials as they pass by the electrode on their way down the axon. ◆

An example of how these action potentials can provide information about the environment is shown in Figure 2.6, which indicates how increasing the intensity of a light influences a neuron's firing. At low intensities, firing is slow (Figure 2.6a), but increasing the stimulus intensity causes an increase in the rate of nerve firing (Figures 2.6b and c). Notice that although the rate of nerve firing increases as stimulus intensity increases, the size of the action potentials remains the same. This is an important prop-

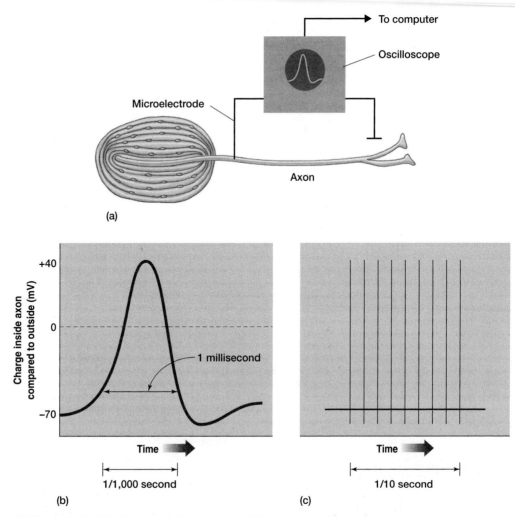

■ **Figure 2.5** (a) Action potentials are recorded from neurons with tiny microelectrodes that are positioned inside or right next to the neuron's axon. These potentials are displayed on the screen of an oscilloscope and are also sent to a computer for analysis. (b) An action potential recorded by a microelectrode looks like this. The inside of the axon becomes more positive, then goes back to the original level, all within 1 millisecond (1/1,000 second). (c) A number of action potentials displayed on an expanded time scale, so a single action potential appears as a "spike."

erty of action potentials because it means that information about stimulus intensity is represented not by the *size* of action potentials, but by their *rate of firing*.

But how do these action potential signals get from the eye to the brain? First, action potentials are **propagated**—once a signal is generated at one end of the axon it travels to the other end without decreasing in size. Second, signals can travel over long distances because individual neurons are linked together, as in Figure 2.4. We will now consider how the information in action potentials is transmitted from one neuron to the next.

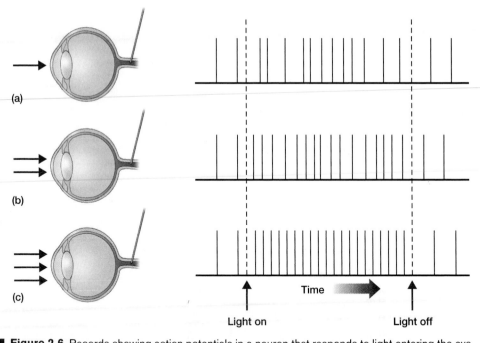

■ Figure 2.6 Records showing action potentials in a neuron that responds to light entering the eye. (a) Presenting light causes an increase in firing; (b) increasing the light intensity increases the rate of firing further; and (c) even more light results in a high rate of firing.

How Neurons Communicate

What happens once action potentials reach the end of an axon? The signal must somehow be transmitted to the next neuron, but how does this occur? One explanation, proposed by early physiologists, was that the end of one neuron makes direct contact with the receiving end of the next neuron. However, that turned out not to be the case, because for most neurons, there is a space, called the **synapse**, between the end of the axon and the next neuron (● Color Plate 2.2).

Communication Between Neurons Occurs at the Synapse

How are the electrical signals transmitted from one neuron to the next across the synapse? Early in the 1900s, it was discovered that the action potentials themselves do not travel across the synapse. Instead, they trigger a chemical process that bridges the gap between neurons. When the potentials reach the end of one neuron, they cause structures called synaptic vesicles to open and release chemicals called **neurotransmit-**

ters onto the next neuron (● Color Plate 2.2b). Neurotransmitters are chemicals that can affect the electrical signal of the neuron that receives the neurotransmitter.

The release of neurotransmitters onto the next neuron causes information to be transmitted from one neuron to another. But as we will see, more happens at the synapse than simply passing the baton from one neuron to the next. The transmission of information from one neuron to the next involves two different effects—excitation and inhibition—that interact at the synapse.

Excitation and Inhibition Interact at the Synapse

The two scenarios that can occur when neurotransmitters are released are shown in Figure 2.7. The release of an **excitatory neurotransmitter** from one of the neurons increases the chances that the next neuron will fire. This excitatory neurotransmitter is generally associated with increased nerve firing. The release of an **inhibitory neurotransmitter** decreases the chances that a neuron will fire, and is therefore associated with decreased nerve firing. Thus, some neurotransmitters cause **excitation**, which tends to increase the rate of nerve firing, and some neurotransmitters cause **inhibition**, which tends to decrease the rate of nerve firing. Although it may seem counterproductive for the nervous system to contain a mechanism like inhibition that decreases or stops nerve signals from being generated, we will see that inhibition is an essential part of the mechanism that enables neurons to process information.

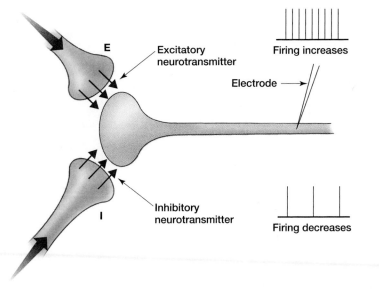

E — Excitatory neurotransmitter

Electrode

Firing increases

I — Inhibitory neurotransmitter

Firing decreases

■ **Figure 2.7**
Release of an excitatory neurotransmitter (top synapse) causes an increase in firing measured by the electrode in the axon of the postsynaptic neuron. Release of an inhibitory neurotransmitter (bottom synapse) causes a decrease in the firing. A given neuron can receive both excitatory and inhibitory inputs. The firing rate of the neuron is determined by the amount of excitatory and inhibitory transmitters it receives.

◆◆◆ How Neurons Process Information

Neurons do not operate alone. The brain contains 180 billion neurons, 80 billion of which are involved in cognitive processes (Kolb & Wishaw, 1990). Each of these billions of neurons receives signals from about 1,000 other neurons, so there are far more synapses in the brain than the 400 billion stars in the Milky Way! We will now consider how the processing of information by the nervous system is based on interactions between these neurons.

Neurons Process Information by Interacting With Each Other

To understand how the nervous system works, we need to understand how neurons interact with one another. These interactions take place at the synapses where one neuron releases its neurotransmitter onto another neuron and neural processing occurs. **Neural processing** occurs when a number of neurons synapse together to form a **neural circuit**—a group of interconnected neurons. Two simple circuits are shown in Figures 2.8 and 2.9. In these circuits we represent receptors by ellipses (◖), cell bodies by circles (●), nerve fibers by lines (———), excitatory synapses by Y's (Y), and inhibitory synapses by blue T's (⊣). Two basic properties of these circuits that contribute to neural processing are (1) **convergence**—a number of neurons sending signals to a single neuron—and (2) interaction of excitation and inhibition.

First, let's consider the circuit in Figure 2.8. This circuit contains convergence, but all of the synapses are excitatory. In this circuit, receptors 1 and 2 converge onto neuron

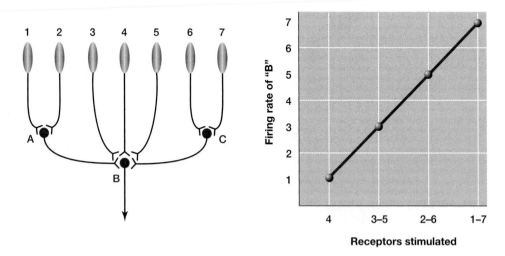

■ **Figure 2.8** Neural circuit in which signals from the seven receptors send signals to neuron B. The graph on the right indicates that as more receptors are stimulated, the response of neuron B increases.

A, 6 and 7 onto C, and 3, 4, and 5 onto B; and A and C converge onto B. We stimulate the circuit by first illuminating receptor 4 with a spot of light. This causes a small response in B, which is plotted on the graph to the right. We then change this spot into a bar of light by illuminating receptors 3, 4, and 5 (3 through 5), then receptors 2 through 6, and finally receptors 1 through 7. The graph shows that each time we increase the length of the stimulus, neuron B's firing rate increases. This occurs because stimulating more receptors increases the amount of excitatory transmitter released onto neuron B. Thus, in this circuit, neuron B's response provides information about the length of the stimulus. In this circuit, convergence is the main mechanism of neural processing.

We add another dimension to neural processing by making two of the synapses inhibitory to create the circuit in Figure 2.9, in which neurons A and C inhibit neuron B. Illuminating receptor 4 with a spot of light, as we did for the circuit in Figure 2.8, causes a small response in B, just as it did before. Extending the illumination to include receptors 3 through 5 adds the output of two more excitatory synapses to B and increases its firing. So far, this circuit is behaving similarly to the circuit in Figure 2.8. However, when we extend the illumination further to also include receptors 2 and 6, something different happens: Receptors 2 and 6 stimulate neurons A and C, which causes the release of inhibitory transmitter onto neuron B, decreasing its firing rate. Increasing the size of the stimulus again to illuminate receptors 1 and 7 increases the inhibition and further decreases the response of neuron B.

As shown in the graph to the right in Figure 2.9, this circuit results in weak firing of neuron B to small stimuli (a spot illuminating only receptor 4) or longer stimuli (illuminating receptors 1 through 7) and strong firing to a stimulus of medium length

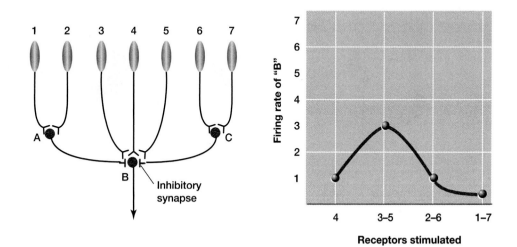

■ **Figure 2.9** The same circuit as in Figure 2.8 but the excitatory synapses from neurons A and C onto B are now inhibitory. The graph on the right indicates that as more receptors are stimulated, the response initially increases, but then decreases.

(illuminating receptors 3 through 5). The combination of convergence and inhibition has caused neuron B to respond best to a light stimulus of a specific size. The neurons that synapse with neuron B are therefore doing much more than simply transmitting electrical signals; they are acting as part of a neural circuit that enables the firing of neuron B to indicate the size of the stimulus falling on the receptors. The neural processing that occurs in our hypothetical circuit of Figure 2.9 shows how convergence, excitation, and inhibition can result in a neuron that responds best to a specific stimulus—in this case, a short bar of light.

Neural Processing Creates Neurons That Respond to Specific Types of Stimuli

Our discussion of neural processing has so far been based on the simple, hypothetical circuits in Figures 2.8 and 2.9. However, by recording from neurons in the visual system, researchers have shown that real neurons do, in fact, respond to specific stimuli. For example, neurons in the optic nerve of the cat have been found that respond similarly to neuron B in Figure 2.9. Figure 2.10 shows the response of a neuron that responds best to a small spot of light. Initially, the neuron's response increases as we increase the spot size (Figures 2.10a and b), but the response decreases once the spot gets too large (Figures 2.10c and d). This result—firing best to small spots of light—is similar to the result we obtained in our hypothetical circuit, which caused neuron B to respond best to a short bar of light.

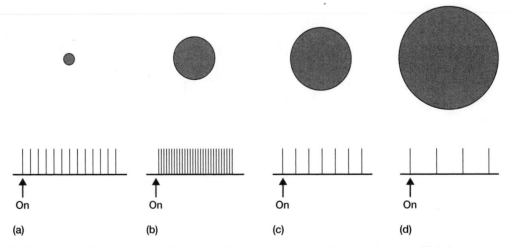

■ **Figure 2.10** How a neuron in the cat's optic nerve responds as the size of a spot of light increases. Notice that the best response occurs to the medium-sized spot of light in (b), but decreases when the spot is made larger, as in (c) and (d). (Adapted from Hubel & Wiesel, 1961.)

Even though many more receptors are involved for the cat's neuron than for our hypothetical circuit in Figure 2.9, the principle is the same: When the spot is small, mainly excitatory synapses are involved. Increasing the size of the stimulus slightly involves more excitatory synapses, so firing rate increases. However, increasing size further brings in inhibitory synapses, as in Figure 2.9, and the firing rate therefore decreases. Thus, increasing the size of the stimulus causes an increase in firing at first and then a decrease in firing as the stimulus becomes large enough to activate inhibitory synapses.

**Receptive
Fields**

Research on neurons in other areas of the visual system has revealed that as we move from the optic nerve to the brain and then to higher areas in the brain, neurons become even more specialized. David Hubel and Thorsten Wiesel (1965) won the Nobel Prize for their research on the visual system. They found neurons that respond best to a bar of light with a particular orientation, called **simple cells** (Figure 2.11a), neurons that respond best to bars of light of a particular orientation that were moving across the retina in a specific direction, called **complex cells** (Figure 2.11b), and neurons that respond best to an oriented bar of light with a specific length, or shaped like a corner, called **end-stopped cells** (Figure 2.11c). Neurons such as simple, complex, and end-stopped cells, which fire in response to specific features of the stimuli, are called **feature detectors**.

Recent research has revealed neurons that respond best to more complex stimuli than those studied by Hubel and Wiesel. For example, there are neurons in the monkey's cortex that respond best to complex geometrical stimuli (Figure 2.12a), to common objects in the environment such as buildings (Figure 2.12b), and to faces (Figure 2.12c; Kremer et al., 2000; Perret et al., 1992; Tanaka, 1993). It may seem amazing that neural processing based just on convergence, excitation, and inhibition could result in neurons that respond best to stimuli as complex as houses or faces, but remember that the brain contains billions of neurons and huge numbers of interconnections. The existence of these neurons illustrates the power of the neural processing that occurs within the huge number of interconnected neurons in the brain.

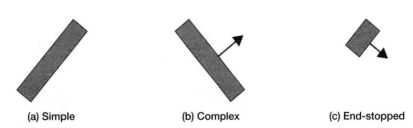

(a) Simple   (b) Complex   (c) End-stopped

■ **Figure 2.11** Stimuli that cause neurons in the cortex to fire. (a) Simple cells respond to bars of light with a particular orientation; (b) complex cells respond to oriented bars of light that are moving in a particular direction; (c) end-stopped cells respond best to moving bars of light of a particular length that are moving in a specific direction.

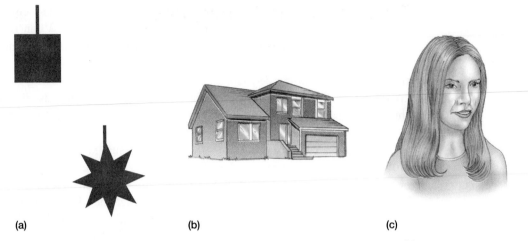

(a)   (b)   (c)

■ **Figure 2.12** Neurons have been found in the temporal cortex that respond to (a) complex geometrical figures; (b) common objects in the environment; and (c) faces.

Test Yourself 2.1

1. How does the example of Juan turning off his alarm clock support the idea that even simple behaviors involve a complex series of physiological events?
2. Describe the following: neuron structure, receptors, and transduction. What is the relationship between electrical signals in the nervous system and perception?
3. Why is it important to record from single neurons? How is this accomplished?
4. What are the properties of the action potentials that occur in nerve axons?
5. What is a synapse, and how do neurons communicate with each other by releasing excitatory and inhibitory neurotransmitters at the synapse?
6. How do convergence, excitation, and inhibition work to create neural processing that can cause a particular neuron to respond best to a small spot of light? Describe neurons in the cat's visual system that respond to small spots of light and neurons in the monkey visual system that respond to more complex stimuli.

How Stimuli Are Represented by the Firing of Neurons

We have seen that there are neurons that respond to specific types of stimuli such as houses and faces. We would expect that looking at a person's face would activate many face-selective neurons. But how does neural firing enable us to recognize a specific person's face? The firing of neurons in the cortex must contain information that stands for, or *represents*, this person's face. The information contained in the neural firing to that face (or to any other object or experience) is called the **neural code** for that object or experience.

The Neural Code for Perceiving Faces

Exactly what is the nature of the information transmitted by the neural code? To answer this, we will consider how a particular face can be represented by the firing of neurons in the temporal cortex. Although we will use faces as an example, our answer applies to all experiences, not just seeing faces.

One possible way that faces could be represented is by **specificity coding**—the representation of a specific stimulus, like a specific person's face, by the firing of very specifically tuned neurons that are specialized to respond just to a specific face. This is illustrated in Figure 2.13a, which shows that Bill's face would be signaled by the firing of neuron 1, which responds only to his face, Samantha's face is signaled by the firing of neuron 2, and Roger's face by the firing of neuron 3. Thus, specificity coding proposes that there are neurons that are tuned to respond just to one specific stimulus.

The idea that there might be single neurons that respond only to specific stimuli was proposed in the 1960s by Jerzy Konorski (1967) and Jerry Lettvin (see Barlow, 1995; Gross, 2002; Rose, 1996). Lettvin coined the term *grandmother cell* to describe this highly specific type of cell. A **grandmother cell**, according to Lettvin, is a neuron that responds only to a specific stimulus. This stimulus could be a specific image, such as a

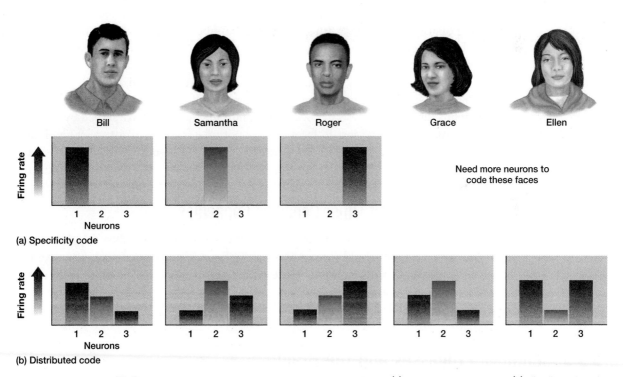

■ **Figure 2.13** How faces could be coded according to (a) specificity coding and (b) distributed coding. The height of the bars indicates the responses of neurons 1, 2, and 3 to each stimulus face. See text for explanation.

picture of your grandmother, or a concept, such as the idea of grandmothers in general, or your real-life grandmother (Gross, 2002).

But there are problems with this idea: (1) There are just too many different faces and other objects in the environment to assign specific neurons to each one; and (2) although there are neurons that respond only to specific types of stimuli, like faces, even these neurons respond to a number of different faces. Thus, a neuron that responds to Bill's face would also respond to Roger's and Samantha's faces as well. Because of these problems, the idea of a highly specific grandmother-type neuron has not been accepted by researchers. (But see Something to Consider on page 50 for a recent development.)

The generally accepted solution to the problem of sensory coding is that a particular object is represented not by the firing of a single neuron, but by the firing of *groups* of neurons. For example, let's consider how the three neurons in Figure 2.13b fire to a number of different faces. Bill's face causes all three neurons to fire, with neuron 1 responding the most and neuron 3 responding the least. Roger's face also causes firing in all three neurons, but the pattern is different, with neuron 3 responding the most and neuron 1 the least. All three neurons also fire to Samantha's face, but with a pattern that differs from the firing to either Bill's or Roger's faces. Thus, each face is represented by a pattern of firing across a number of neurons. This solution to the problem of sensory coding is called **distributed coding** because the code that indicates a specific face is *distributed* across a number of neurons. One of the advantages of distributed coding is that the firing of just a few neurons can signal a large number of stimuli. In our example, the firing of three neurons signals three faces, but these three neurons could signal other faces as well, such as Grace's and Ellen's, which would have their own pattern of firing.

What all of this means is that our ability to identify and recognize the huge number of different objects in our environment is the end result of distributed cooperation between many neurons. This occurs even for stimuli like faces that are served by specialized neurons that respond just to faces. It may not take many neurons to let you know that you are seeing a face, but it takes a number of neurons working together to signal the presence of one particular face.

The Neural Code for Other Cognitive Capacities

Although we used perceiving faces to illustrate the idea of distributed coding, it is likely that the same principles hold for other cognitive capacities. For example, when we remember something, that memory is represented by the pattern of firing of large numbers of neurons. We are now ready to move from neurons and neural circuits to consider the brain as a whole.

▶▶▶ Cognitive Processes and the Brain

One of the keys to understanding how the brain handles cognitive processes is to look at the functions of different areas of the brain. The brain is organized into different areas, each of which is associated with specific functions.

Layout of the Brain

The picture of the brain in ● Color Plate 2.3 shows the surface of its outer covering, which is called the **cerebral cortex**. The cerebral cortex is only 3 mm thick, but this thin layer of neurons contains the mechanisms responsible for most of our higher mental functions, such as perception, memory, language, thinking, and problem solving. The cerebral cortex is divided into four lobes: the **temporal lobe** (important for language, memory, hearing, and perceiving forms), the **occipital lobe** (the first place in the cerebral cortex where visual information is received), the **parietal lobe** (where signals are received from the touch system and which is also important for vision and attention), and the **frontal lobe** (which serves higher functions such as language, thought, memory, and motor functioning).

Beneath the cerebral cortex are **subcortical structures**, which also play important roles in cognition, especially in the processing of information for memories and the creation of emotions (● Color Plate 2.4). Some of the important subcortical structures are the **hippocampus**, which is important for forming memories, the **amygdala**, which is important for emotions and emotional memories, and the **thalamus**, which is important for processing information from the senses of vision, hearing, and touch.

Different Areas of the Brain Serve Specific Functions

The idea that different brain areas serve different functions is called **localization of function**. This localization, which we have already described for the four lobes of the brain and some of its subcortical structures, has been demonstrated using a number of different methods. Recording from single neurons has shown that neurons that respond to specific types of stimuli are often clustered in specific areas. For example, shape-selective neurons, like the ones that respond to stimuli like those shown in Figure 2.12, are found in the temporal lobe. This has led to the conclusion that there are areas in the temporal lobe that are specialized for the perception of shapes. One area in the temporal lobe, called the **fusiform face area (FFA)**, is rich in neurons that respond best to faces.

Research on the effects of brain damage in humans also provides evidence for localization of function. Brain damage is generally caused by accidents or by a stroke in which the blood supply to an area of the brain is disrupted. The study of the behavior of humans with brain damage is called **neuropsychology**.

◄► Method

Neuropsychology

The basic idea behind neuropsychology is that cognitive functioning breaks down in specific ways when specific areas of the brain are damaged (Feinberg & Farah, 2001). The major method of neuropsychology is the determination of **dissociations**—situations in which one function is absent while another function is present. There are two kinds of dissociations, **single dissociations**, which can be studied in a single person, and **double dissociations**, which require two or more people.

To illustrate a single dissociation, let's consider Alice, who has suffered damage to her temporal lobe. Testing Alice shows that she has a serious memory problem—she can remember things that have just happened, so her short-term memory (STM) is intact, but she can't hold on to these memories, so she can't form new long-term memories (LTM). For example, immediately after she has crossed the street, she can remember crossing the street, but a minute or two later she has no memory of that experience. Alice demonstrates a single dissociation—one function is present (STM) and another is absent (LTM). From a single dissociation, in which one function is lost while another function remains, we can conclude that two functions (in this example, STM and LTM) involve different mechanisms, although they may not operate totally independently of one another.

We can illustrate a double dissociation by finding another person who has one function present and another absent, but in a way opposite to Alice. For example, Bert, who has had damage to his frontal lobe, can't remember what has just happened (his STM is deficient), but he can form new long-term memories. The cases of Alice and Bert, taken together, are a double dissociation. Establishing a double dissociation enables us to conclude that two functions are served by different mechanisms *and* that these mechanisms operate independently of one another (Table 2.1). ◆

An example of how localization of function has been supported by neuropsychological research is the finding that some patients with damage to an area of the temporal lobe have difficulty naming human-made things like tools and furniture but can name living things (Table 2.2). Other patients, with damage in nearby areas of the temporal

Table 2.1 Double Dissociation: Two People With Brain Damage

	Function 1: Short-Term Memory	Function 2: New Long-Term Memories
Alice (temporal lobe damage)	OK	No
Bert (frontal lobe damage)	No	OK

Table 2.2 Neuropsychology of Categories

Cases	Naming	
	Living Things	**Nonliving Things**
Nonliving things deficient[†]	OK	Deficient
Living things deficient[*]	Deficient	OK

[*]Caramazza & Shelton, 1998; Farah & Wallace, 1992; Hart & Gordon, 1992; Hart et al., 1985; Hills & Caramazza, 1991; Silveri & Gainotti, 1988; Warrington & Shallice, 1984.

[†]Sheridan & Humphries, 1993; Warrington & McCarthy, 1983.

Source: Caramazza, 2000.

lobe, have the opposite problem: they can name nonliving things such as tools but have difficulty naming living things (Caramazza, 2000). This double dissociation—the existence of opposite problems in two different groups of people—supports the idea that the mechanisms for recognizing living things and tools and furniture are located in different areas of the brain and that these mechanisms operate independently from one another.

Cognitive Processes Are Signaled by Activity in Many Areas of the Brain

Although specific areas of the brain are specialized for specific functions, activities such as perceiving, remembering, and thinking activate a number of areas. One way this has been demonstrated is by a technique called brain imaging.

◄► Method

Brain Imaging

One of the most widely used techniques for measuring brain activity in humans is **brain imaging**, which allows researchers to create images that show which areas of the brain are activated as awake humans carry out various cognitive tasks. One of these techniques, **positron emission tomography (PET)**, was introduced in the 1970s (Hoffman et al., 1976; Ter-Pogossian et al., 1975). PET takes advantage of the fact that blood flow increases in areas of the brain that are activated by a cognitive task. To measure blood flow, a low dose of a radioactive tracer is injected into a person's bloodstream. (The dose is low enough that it is not harmful to the person.) The person's brain is then scanned by the PET apparatus, which measures the signal from the tracer at each location in the brain. Higher signals indicate higher levels of brain activity (● Color Plate 2.5).

PET enabled researchers to track changes in blood flow, in order to determine which brain areas were being activated. To use this tool, researchers developed the **subtraction technique**. Brain activity is first measured in a "control state" before stimulation is presented and is then measured while the stimulus is presented. For example, in a study designed to determine which areas of the brain are activated when a person manipulates an object in their hand, activity generated by simply placing the object in the hand would be measured first. This is the control state (Figure 2.14a). Then activity is measured as the person manipulates the object. This is the stimulation state (Figure 2.14b). Finally, the activity due to manipulation is determined by subtracting the control activity from the stimulation activity (Figure 2.14c).

Recently, another neuroimaging technique, called **functional magnetic resonance imaging (fMRI)**, has been introduced. Like PET, fMRI is based on the measurement of blood flow. An advantage of fMRI is that blood flow can be measured without radioactive tracers. fMRI takes advantage of the fact that hemoglobin, which carries oxygen in the blood, contains a ferrous (iron) molecule and therefore has magnetic properties. Thus,

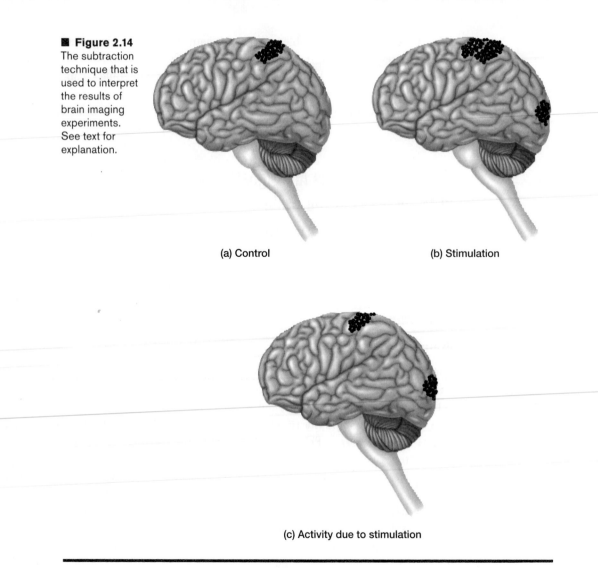

■ Figure 2.14
The subtraction technique that is used to interpret the results of brain imaging experiments. See text for explanation.

(a) Control

(b) Stimulation

(c) Activity due to stimulation

if a magnetic field is presented to the brain, the hemoglobin molecules line up, like tiny magnets.

fMRI indicates the presence of brain activity because the hemoglobin molecules in areas of high brain activity lose some of the oxygen they are transporting. This makes the hemoglobin more magnetic, so these molecules respond more strongly to the magnetic field. The fMRI apparatus determines the relative activity of various areas of the brain by detecting changes in the magnetic response of the hemoglobin. The subtraction technique described above for PET is also used for the fMRI, and because fMRI doesn't require radioactive tracers and is more accurate, this technique has become the main method for localizing brain activity in humans. ◆

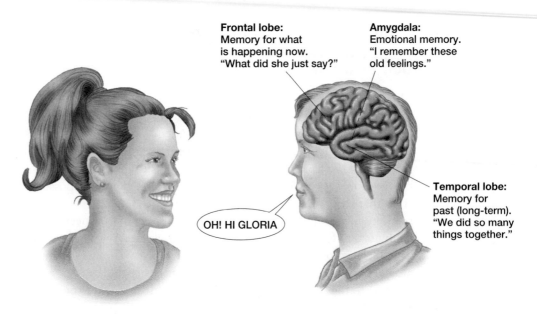

Frontal lobe:
Memory for what
is happening now.
"What did she just say?"

Amygdala:
Emotional memory.
"I remember these
old feelings."

Temporal lobe:
Memory for
past (long-term).
"We did so many
things together."

OH! HI GLORIA

■ **Figure 2.15** When Roger unexpectedly encounters his old girlfriend Gloria, different types of memories cause activation of a number of different areas of Roger's brain.

Brain imaging has made it possible to determine which areas of the brain are involved in different cognitive processes. For example, brain imaging has shown that memories that last only a short time, as when you look up a phone number and then forget it right after making your call, involve the prefrontal cortex (Courtney et al., 1998; Fiez, 2001). Memories that last a longer time involve a number of structures in the medial temporal lobe (Brewer et al., 1998; Wagner et al., 1998). Emotional memories activate the amygdala (Harmann, 1999; see ● Color Plate 2.4). Thus, when Roger unexpectedly encounters his old girlfriend Gloria, the memories triggered by this encounter activate a number of areas that are distributed across his brain (Figure 2.15).

This example illustrates a basic principle of brain functioning—cognitive processes usually involve activity that is distributed throughout a number of different areas of the brain. Although this may appear to contradict the idea of localization of function we discussed earlier, localization of function and distributed brain activity work together, because most cognitive processes involve a number of different functions. Thus, Roger's encounter with Gloria not only activates areas that are specialized for different types of memory, but also areas that are activated as he initially perceives Gloria and recognizes her face. Just as a symphony is created by many different instruments, all working together in an orchestra to create the harmonies and melodies of a particular composition, cognitive processes are created by many specialized brain areas, all working together to create a distributed pattern of activity that creates all of the different components of that particular cognition.

▶▶▶ Interacting With the Environment Affects Operation of the Nervous System

Although we can associate specific parts of the brain with specific functions, this does not mean that the functioning of different parts of the brain is rigid and fixed. One of the brain's properties that enables it to adapt to the environment is its ability to change, so that it responds best to what is commonly encountered in the environment.

The ability to adapt to the environment was a central feature of Charles Darwin's theory of evolution. According to this theory, animals that possess survival characteristics that enable them to survive pass their characteristics to the next generation, and so eventually these characteristics become typical of the species. Thus, although it may be important for parts of the brain to be specialized to carry out specific functions, the brain must also be able to adapt to the specific environment within which a person or animal lives. There is a great deal of evidence that the nervous system achieves this adaptation to the environment through a mechanism called **experience-dependent plasticity**, which causes neurons to develop so they respond best to the types of stimulation to which a person or animal has been exposed.

The idea of experience-dependent plasticity was first suggested by experiments on animals. For example, if we record from direction-selective neurons in the adult cat's cortex, we find that there are neurons that respond to a wide range of orientations. However, if kittens are raised in an environment that contains only verticals (Figure 2.16a), most of the neurons in their visual cortex become transformed so that they all respond best to verticals (Figure 2.16b; Blakemore & Cooper, 1970). Since this early demonstration of experience-dependent plasticity, many more experiments have demonstrated this effect in animals (Freedman et al., 2001; Merzenich et al., 1998).

Experience-dependent plasticity has also been demonstrated in humans using the brain imaging technique of fMRI. The starting point for this research is the finding that there is an area in the temporal lobe called the fusiform face area that contains many neurons that respond best to faces. Isabel Gauthier and coworkers (1999) determined whether this response to faces might be due to experience-dependent plasticity by measuring the level of activity in the FFA in response to faces and to objects called Greebles (Figure 2.17a). Greebles are families of computer-generated "beings" that all have the same basic configuration but differ in the shapes of their parts (just like faces). The brain cross-sections in the left two columns in ● Color Plate 2.6 show the location of the FFA (white squares). The color inside the FFA on the left indicates that faces activate neurons in the FFA. The lack of color on the right indicates that Greebles do not activate the FFA. The left pair of bars in Figure 2.17b represents the greater response to faces.

Gauthier then gave her participants extensive training in "Greeble recognition" over a 4-day period. These training sessions, which required that each configuration of Greeble be labeled with a specific name, turned the participants into "Greeble experts." The brain pictures on the right in ● Color Plate 2.6 and the right pair of bars in

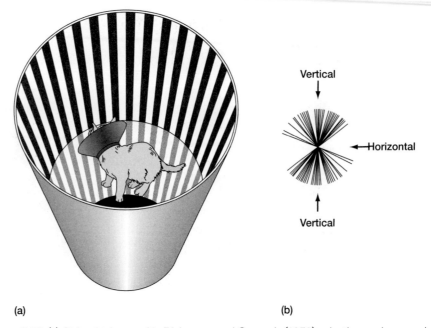

■ **Figure 2.16** (a) Striped tube used in Blakemore and Cooper's (1970) selective rearing experiments. The cat is wearing the ruff to prevent it from turning the verticals into horizontals by tilting its head. (b) Distribution of optimal orientations for a number of neurons recorded from a kitten that was raised in a vertical environment. Each line represents the best orientation for a single neuron. Notice that there are no neurons that respond to horizontal orientations. (Reprinted from "Development of the Brain Depends on the Visual Environment," by C. Blakemore & G. G. Cooper, 1970, *Nature, London, 228,* pp. 477–478, Copyright © 1970 with permission from Nature Publishing Group.)

Figure 2.17b show that after the training, the FFA responded almost as well to Greebles as to faces. Apparently, the FFA contains neurons that respond not just to faces, but to other complex objects as well. The particular objects to which the neurons respond best are established by experience with the objects. In fact, Gauthier has also shown that neurons in the FFA of people who are experts in recognizing cars and birds respond well not only to human faces, but to cars (for the car experts) and to birds (for the bird experts; Gauthier et al., 2000).

The property of experience-dependent plasticity, which has been demonstrated both in animals and in humans, means that although the brain is organized so that specific areas process specific kinds of information, its functioning can also be "tuned" to operate best within a specific environment. The Greeble example is for perception, but experience-dependent plasticity has also been demonstrated for other cognitive capacities as well. For example, Eleanor Maguire and coworkers (2000) showed that London taxi drivers have a larger-than-normal area in the part of the hippocampus associated with memory for aspects of the environment that are important for navigation. In fact, drivers with more years of experience in finding their way around the streets of London

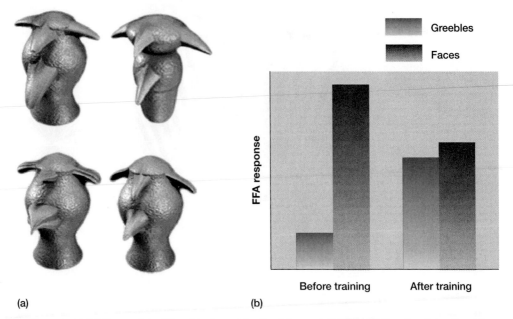

(a)   (b)

■ **Figure 2.17** (a) Some of the "Greebles" used by Gauthier et al. (1999). (b) Results of the Greeble experiment. The FFA response is the brain activity in the fusiform face area as measured by fMRI as participants view Greebles (dark bars) or faces (colored bars). The left pair of bars indicate that before training, the faces cause a large response in the FFA, and the Greebles cause a very small response. The right pair of bars indicate that after training, the FFA is activated both by faces and by Greebles.

had larger hippocampal "navigation" areas. In the chapters to come we will see how the brain's flexibility comes into play to determine cognitive capacities such as attention, perception, memory, and language.

Something to Consider

Are There Grandmother Cells After All?

Although the idea of a highly specific "grandmother cell" has generally not been accepted by researchers, a new development has brought this idea back to life. R. Quian Quiroga and coworkers (2005) recorded from neurons in the brains of eight patients with epilepsy. These patients had electrodes implanted in their hippocampus to help precisely localize where their seizures originated, in preparation for surgery (● Color Plate 2.7).

Patients viewed a number of different views of specific individuals and objects plus random pictures of other things, such as faces, buildings, and animals. Not surprisingly, a number of neurons responded to some of these stimuli. What was surprising, however, was that some neurons responded to a number of different views of just one person or building. For example, one neuron responded to all pictures of the actress Jennifer Aniston alone, but did not respond to other faces of famous people, nonfamous people, landmarks, animals, or other objects. Another unit responded to pictures of the actress Halle Berry. This neuron responded not only to photographs of Halle Berry, but to drawings of her, pictures of her dressed as the Catwoman character she played in a recent film, and also to the words "Halle Berry" (● Color Plate 2.7b). A third neuron responded to numerous views of the Sydney Opera House.

Do these neurons qualify as grandmother cells? Quiroga and coworkers are careful to note that presenting more pictures might have revealed additional stimuli that would cause these neurons to respond. But what is amazing about these neurons is how they respond to many different views of stimulus, different modes of depiction, and even words signifying the stimulus. These neurons are therefore not responding to visual features of the pictures, but to *concepts*—"Jennifer Aniston," "Halle Berry," "Sydney Opera House"—that the stimuli represent.

It is important to note that these neurons were in the hippocampus—an area associated not with vision, but with the storage of memories. Thus, perhaps the highly specialized nature of these neurons depends on the processing that occurs when information about the visual characteristics of objects is transformed into the abstract representation of these objects that are stored in memory. This illustrates a central principle of cognitive psychology: Although we can separate topics into chapters, as we have in this book, the brain is concerned not with dealing with processes such as perception, attention, and memory separately, but with the interaction between these processes that occurs as we interact with the environment.

Test Yourself 2.2

1. How is the brain organized into lobes? Subcortical structures?
2. What is neuropsychology? What are the basic principles behind determining single and double dissociations? What have dissociations told us about the mechanisms responsible for recognizing living and nonliving things?
3. Describe how neural coding could explain how we recognize a specific person's face. Be sure you understand specificity coding, grandmother cells, and distributed coding.
4. What are the basic principles of brain imaging, specifically PET scans and fMRI scans? How has brain imaging been used to show that memory results in activity that is distributed throughout the brain?
5. Why is it correct to say that the brain contains areas specialized for specific functions, while also saying that cognition results in activity that is distributed throughout many areas of the brain?
6. Describe experiments that support the idea of experience-dependent plasticity in cats and humans. Why is this property of the brain important?
7. What is the evidence that there might be grandmother-like neurons in the brain?

Chapter Summary

1. Neurons, the basic units of the nervous system, both generate and transmit electrical signals. Signals are generated in neurons containing receptors by a process called transduction. The resulting electrical signals represent properties of the environment.

2. Signals are recorded from single neurons using microelectrodes. This recording reveals propagated action potentials that remain the same size but increase their rate of firing in response to increases in stimulus intensity.

3. Neurons communicate with each other by their release of excitatory and inhibitory neurotransmitters at the synapse. Neural processing, which is caused by the interaction between inhibition and excitation in neural circuits, results in individual neurons that respond to specific stimuli such as small spots, oriented lines, geometrical objects, faces, and common objects in the environment.

4. The environment is represented in the nervous system by a neural code. Specificity coding—neurons that respond selectively to only one stimulus—is possible, but the most likely type of coding is distributed coding, in which properties of the environment are represented by the pattern of firing of groups of neurons.

5. The brain is organized into lobes and subcortical structures. Recordings from single neurons in animals and neuropsychological research in humans have shown that these areas have specialized functions.

6. The technique of brain imaging—PET scans and fMRI scans—has made it possible to determine the activity of the brain as a person carries out cognitive tasks. One finding is that most cognitive tasks activate many different areas of the brain.

7. Experiments on both animals and humans have demonstrated the property of experience-dependent plasticity, which causes neurons to become tuned to respond best to stimuli that are commonly found in the environment.

8. Recent research has discovered neurons in the hippocampus that respond best to specific concepts such as Halle Berry or the Sydney Opera House. These neurons appear to be associated with higher-order processes such as memory.

Think About It

1. In this chapter, we call the brain the mind's computer. What are computers good at, that the brain is not? How do you think the brain and the mind compare in terms of complexity? What advantage does the brain have over a computer?

2. People generally feel that they are experiencing their environment directly, especially when it comes to sensory experiences such as seeing, hearing, or feeling the texture of a surface. However, our knowledge of how the nervous system operates indicates that this is not the case. Why would a physiologist say that all of our experiences are indirect?

3. When brain activity is being measured in an fMRI scanner, the person's head is surrounded by an array of magnets and must be kept perfectly still. In addition, the operation of the machine is very noisy. How do these characteristics of brain scanners limit the types of behaviors that can be studied using brain scanning?

4. It has been argued that we will never be able to fully understand how the brain operates because doing this involves using the brain to study itself. What do you think of this argument?

If You Want to Know More

1. Mirror neurons. There are neurons in the brain that respond when a person or animal observes another person or animal carrying out an action. These same neurons also respond when the observer carries out the same action him- or herself. It has been suggested that these neurons may be involved in imitating another person's actions or taking another person's point of view.

Kohler, E., Keysers, C., Umita, M. A., Fogassi, L., Gallese, V., & Rizzolatti, G. (2002). Hearing sounds, understanding actions: Action representation in mirror neurons. *Science, 297,* 846–848.

2. Brain damage and behavior. There are numerous books that describe fascinating case studies of people whose behavior has been affected by brain damage.

Farah, M. J., & Feinberg, T. E. (2003). *Behavioral neurology and neuropsychology* (2nd ed.). New York: McGraw-Hill.

Ramachandran, V. S., & Blakeslee, S. (1998). *Phantoms of the mind: Probing the mysteries of the human mind.* New York: HarperCollins.

Sacks, O. (1985). *The man who mistook his wife for a hat.* New York: Touchstone.

Key Terms

Action potential, 32
Amygdala, 43
Axon, 30
Brain imaging, 45
Cell body, 30
Cerebral cortex, 43
Complex cells, 39
Convergence, 36
Dendrites, 30
Dissociations, 43
Distributed coding, 42

Double dissociation, 43
End-stopped cells, 39
Excitation, 35
Excitatory neurotransmitter, 35
Experience-dependent plasticity, 48
Feature detectors, 39
Frontal lobe, 43
Functional magnetic resonance
    imaging (fMRI), 45
Fusiform face area (FFA), 43
Grandmother cell, 41

Hippocampus, 43
Inhibition, 35
Inhibitory neurotransmitter, 35
Localization of function, 43
Microelectrodes, 32
Nerve fiber, 30
Neural circuit, 36
Neural code, 40
Neural processing, 36
Neuron, 30
Neuropsychology, 43
Neurotransmitter, 34–35
Occipital lobe, 43
Optic nerve, 32

Parietal lobe, 43
Positron emission tomography (PET), 45
Propagated, 33
Retina, 32
Sensory receptors, 30
Simple cells, 39
Single dissociation, 43
Specificity coding, 41
Subcortical structures, 43
Subtraction technique, 45
Synapse, 34
Temporal lobe, 43
Thalamus, 43
Transduction, 31

CogLab

To experience these experiments for yourself, go to http://coglab.wadsworth.com. Be sure to read each experiment's setup instructions before you go to the experiment itself. Otherwise, you won't know which keys to press.

Primary Lab

Receptive fields A receptive field of a visual neuron is the area on the retina that influences the activity of that neuron. In this lab, you can map the receptive fields of some neurons (p. 39).

Related Lab

Brain asymmetry How speed of processing for shapes and words may be different in the left and right hemispheres.

Perception

3

Bottom-Up and Top-Down Processing in Perception
　▶ Demonstration: Perceiving a Picture

Recognizing Letters and Objects
　Template Matching
　Interactive Activation Model
　◀▶ Method: Word Superiority Effect
　Feature Integration Theory (FIT)
　Recognition-by-Components Theory

Test Yourself 3.1

Perceptual Organization: Putting Together an Organized World
　The Gestalt Laws of Perceptual Organization
　▶ Demonstration: Finding Faces in a Landscape
　The Gestalt Laws Provide "Best Guess" Predictions
　　About What Is Out There

Why Computers Have Trouble Perceiving Objects
　The Stimulus on the Receptors Is Ambiguous
　Objects Need to Be Distinguished From Their
　　Surroundings and From Each Other
　Objects Can Be Hidden or Blurred
　The Reasons for Changes of Lightness and Darkness
　　Can Be Unclear

How Experience and Knowledge Create "Perceptual Intelligence"
　Heuristics for Perceiving
　▶ Demonstration: Shape From Shading
　Knowledge Helps Us Perceive Words
　　in Conversational Speech
　▶ Demonstration: Organizing Strings of Sounds
　Neurons Contain Information About the Environment

Something to Consider: Perception Depends on Attention
　▶ Demonstration: Change Detection

Test Yourself 3.2

Chapter Summary

Think About It

If You Want to Know More

Key Terms

CogLab: Change Detection; Apparent Motion; Blind Spot; Metacontrast Masking; Muller-Lyer Illusion; Signal Detection; Visual Search; Garner Interference

Some Questions We Will Consider

- Why does something that is so easy, like looking at a scene and seeing what is out there, become so complicated when we look at the mechanisms involved? (57)

- Why is recognizing an object so easy for humans, but so difficult for computers? (80)

- How is our knowledge of the world, which we use for perceiving, stored in the brain? (90)

Because of the ease with which we perceive, many people don't see the feats achieved by our senses as complex or amazing. "After all," the skeptic might say, "for vision, a picture of the environment is focused on the back of my eye, and that picture provides all the information my brain needs to duplicate the environment in my consciousness." But the erroneous idea that perception is not that complex is exactly what misled computer scientists in the 1950s and 1960s into proposing that it would take only about a decade or so to create "perceiving machines" that could negotiate the environment with humanlike ease. As it turned out, it took over 50 years to create computer-controlled robots capable of finding their way through the environment, and even these computers fall far short of humans' ability to perceive (Sinha, 2002).

In this chapter, we will explain why **perception** is so complex and why people still outperform computers by a wide margin. We begin by describing how the process of perception depends both on the incoming stimulation and the knowledge we bring to the situation. Following this introduction, we will devote the rest of the chapter to answering the question, "How do we perceive objects?" As we do this, we will see that one reason humans are better at perceiving objects than computers is that humans use perceptual intelligence—knowledge they have gained from their experience in perceiving (Figure 3.1).

One reason we will focus on object perception is that perceiving objects is central to our everyday experience. Consider, for example, what you would say if you were asked to look up and describe what you are perceiving right now. Your answer would, of course, depend on where you are, but it is likely that a large part of your answer would include naming the objects that you see. ("I see a book. There's a chair against the wall. . . .")

We also focus on object perception in this chapter because concentrating on one aspect of perception provides more in-depth understanding of the basic principles of

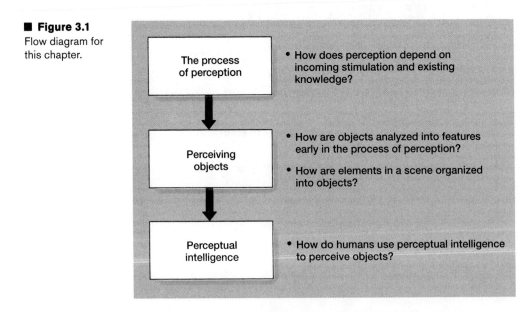

■ **Figure 3.1**
Flow diagram for this chapter.

The process of perception
- How does perception depend on incoming stimulation and existing knowledge?

Perceiving objects
- How are objects analyzed into features early in the process of perception?
- How are elements in a scene organized into objects?

Perceptual intelligence
- How do humans use perceptual intelligence to perceive objects?

perception than we could achieve by covering a number of different types of perception more superficially. After describing a number of mechanisms of object perception, we will consider "perceptual intelligence"—the idea that the knowledge we bring to a situation plays an important role in perception.

Bottom-Up and Top-Down Processing in Perception

Although perception seems to just "happen," it is actually the end result of a complex process. We can appreciate the complexity involved in seemingly simple behaviors by returning to our example of Juan and the alarm clock from the beginning of Chapter 2. We saw that one way to describe Juan's situation was to consider how neurons in his ear and brain respond to the ringing of his alarm. But we also saw that things become more complicated when we consider that Juan's response to his alarm (hitting the snooze button and going back to sleep) is determined by knowledge that he brings to the situation. His behavior is determined both by the stimulation provided by the ringing alarm clock and his knowledge that he can sleep longer and still get to class on time. We will now consider how behavior is determined both by the energy reaching a person's receptors and by the knowledge the person brings to a situation.

To illustrate this cooperation between stimulus energy and knowledge, we will consider Ellen, who is taking a walk in the woods. As she walks along the trail she is confronted with a large number of stimuli (Figure 3.2a). When she looks at a particularly distinctive tree off to the right, she doesn't notice the interesting pattern on the

(a) (b)

■ **Figure 3.2** (a) Ellen taking a walk in the woods, which contains a large number of stimuli; (b) the moth, which she sees and then recognizes, using a combination of bottom-up and top-down processing.

tree trunk at first, but then realizes that what she had at first taken to be a patch of moss was actually a moth (Figure 3.2b).

Let's stop for a moment to consider what has happened. Ellen perceived the moth because light reflected from the moth created an image in her eye (Figure 3.3a). This image triggered the process of transduction we discussed in Chapter 2 (page 31) and resulted in electrical signals, which traveled from the eye to Ellen's brain. This sequence of events, which started with stimulation of the receptors, is called **bottom-up processing**. Bottom-up processing—processing that begins with stimulation of the receptors—is crucial for determining Ellen's experience because if her receptors aren't stimulated, she won't see anything.

But bottom-up processing is not the whole story, because perception involves more than just registering energy on the receptors. We can appreciate this by considering Ellen's problem. Looking at the moth creates a pattern of light and dark on her retina, but it may not be obvious which of the light and dark areas belong to the moth and which belong to the textures of the tree trunk. To help achieve this, Ellen uses her knowledge of moths, not only to detect its presence on the tree, but also to determine that it is a moth, not a butterfly, and to identify what kind of moth it is. Knowledge that Ellen brings to bear on the perceptual problem of seeing and recognizing the moth represents **top-down processing**—processing that involves a person's knowledge (Figure 3.3b). Knowledge doesn't have to be involved in perception but, as we will see, it of-

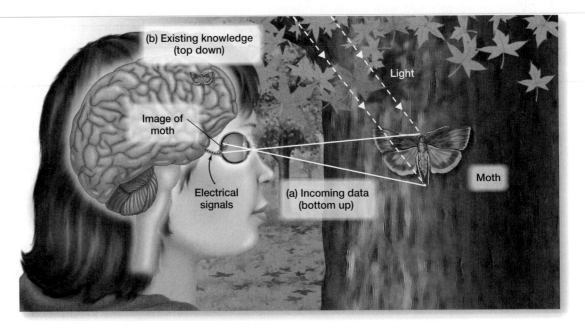

■ **Figure 3.3** Ellen's perception of the moth is determined by a combination of (a) incoming data (bottom-up information) and (b) existing knowledge (top-down information).

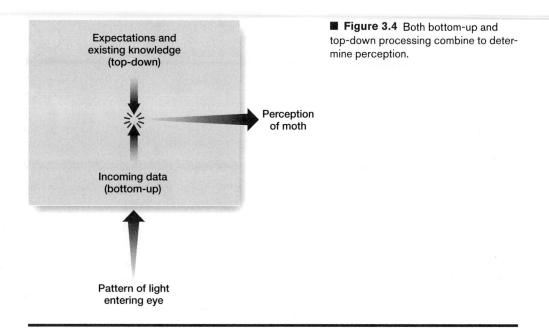

■ **Figure 3.4** Both bottom-up and top-down processing combine to determine perception.

ten is—with bottom-up and top-down processing collaborating to result in perception (Figure 3.4).

In our example, Ellen uses knowledge about moths she had learned much earlier. The following demonstration illustrates that incoming data can be affected by knowledge that has been provided just moments earlier.

 Demonstration

Perceiving a Picture

After looking at the drawing in Figure 3.5, close your eyes, then turn to the next page in the book without looking at the page. Then open and shut your eyes to briefly expose the picture in Figure 3.6 at the top of the page. Decide what the picture is based on this brief exposure. Do this now, before reading further.

■ **Figure 3.5** Picture for "perceiving a picture" demonstration. (Adapted from "The Role of Frequency in Developing Perceptual Sets," by B. R. Bugelski and D. A. Alampay, 1961, *Canadian Journal of Psychology, 15,* pp. 205–211, Copyright © 1961 by the Canadian Psychological Association.)

■ **Figure 3.6** (Adapted from "The Role of Frequency in Developing Perceptual Sets," by B. R. Bugelski et al., 1961, *Canadian Journal of Psychology, 15,* pp. 205–211, Copyright © 1961 by the Canadian Psychological Association.)

What did you see when you looked at Figure 3.6 above? Did it look like a rat (or a mouse)? If it did, you were influenced by the clearly rat- or mouselike figure you saw in Figure 3.5. But people who first observe Figure 3.10 (on page 63) usually identify Figure 3.6 as a man. (Try this demonstration on someone else.) This demonstration, which is called the **rat–man demonstration**, shows how recently acquired knowledge ("that pattern is a rat") can influence perception.

Another example of an effect of top-down processing is provided by an experiment by Stephen Palmer (1975), in which he presented a context scene such as the one on the left of Figure 3.7 and then briefly flashed one of the target pictures on the right. One of the targets was appropriate to the scene (the loaf of bread), one was inappropriate (the drum), and one was misleading (the mailbox, which was shaped like the loaf of bread). When the participants reported what the target picture was, they were correct 83 percent of the time for the appropriate object, 50 percent for the inappropriate object, and

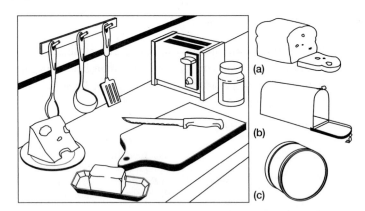

■ **Figure 3.7** Stimuli like those used in Palmer's (1975) experiment, which showed how context can influence perception. (Reprinted from "The Effects of Contextual Scenes on the Identification of Objects," by S. E. Palmer, 1975, *Memory and Cognition, 3,* pp. 519–526, Copyright © 1975 with permission of the author and the Psychodynamic Society Publishers.)

40 percent for the misleading object. This experiment shows how a person's knowledge of the context provided by a particular scene can influence perception.

As you will see in later chapters, there are numerous situations in which incoming data interacts with a person's knowledge. This occurs for attention, memory, language, and most of the other types of cognition we will be discussing. In this chapter, we will focus on perception by looking at what cognitive psychologists have discovered about how both bottom-up and top-down processes operate as we perceive objects. We start by describing how incoming stimuli are analyzed by the visual system. This analysis occurs rapidly and without our awareness and provides an example of how bottom-up and top-down processing can interact.

Recognizing Letters and Objects

As a first step in determining how we perceive objects, we will follow the lead of early cognitive psychologists, who focused on the simple case of perceiving letters of the alphabet. We begin with an idea called **template matching**, which turned out to be too simple to explain how we perceive letters, but which led to the idea of perception based on features, which is part of present-day explanations of object perception.

Template Matching

We begin with a simple example—how we recognize the letter *K* in Figure 3.8. One way the perceptual system could achieve this would be to compare the pattern *K* to a model or template of the letter *K* that is stored in the system. According to this idea, when

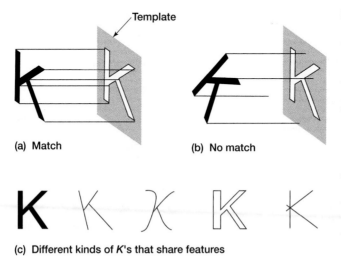

(a) Match (b) No match

(c) Different kinds of *K*'s that share features

■ **Figure 3.8** According to the idea of template matching, we can identify an object when it matches a template. Thus, in (a), in which the stimulus matches the template, the perceiver identifies it as a *K*. A problem arises, however, when the stimulus is tilted, as in (b), because then it no longer matches the template, and so the perceiver would not be able to identify it. (c) Each of these *K*'s would require different templates, but because they share features, they can be identified by a mechanism that takes these features into account.

the pattern matches the template, the perceiver recognizes the letter as a *K*. But this idea runs into problems when we consider what happens when the *K* is tilted, as in Figure 3.8b. Tilting the *K* poses no problem for a perceiver, who can still recognize it. However, template-matching theory would require a template for every orientation of the *K*. People also have no trouble identifying different forms of the same letter, like the *K*'s in Figure 3.8c. It is apparent that the template-matching model won't work, because a huge number of different templates would be needed just to recognize one letter. When we multiply this by how many objects there are in the environment, the number becomes astronomical. To deal with this problem, psychologists developed models of letter perception based on the idea that letters can be broken down into features.

Interactive Activation Model

We saw in Chapter 2 that there are cortical neurons called feature detectors that respond to oriented lines (Hubel & Wiesel, 1965). The discovery of feature detectors in the 1960s suggested that perhaps the perceptual system constructs letters and other objects in the environment from simple features, like oriented lines. Features help solve some of the problems associated with template matching, because although letters like the ones in Figure 3.8c look different, they all have features in common, such as vertical and slanted lines.

This idea led James McClelland and David Rumelhart (1981; also Rumelhart & McClelland, 1982) to propose the model of letter recognition shown in Figure 3.9. This model, which is called the **interactive activation model**, proposes that activation is sent through three levels: The **feature level** contains **feature units**—mainly straight and curved lines; the **letter level** contains **letter units**—one for each letter in the alphabet; and the **word level** contains **word units**—all the words a person knows. The simplified model in Figure 3.9 contains 6 feature units and 4 letter units. The complete model has 12 feature units and 26 letter units. We will use our simplified model to dem-

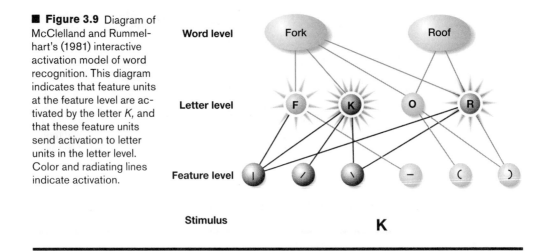

■ **Figure 3.9** Diagram of McClelland and Rummelhart's (1981) interactive activation model of word recognition. This diagram indicates that feature units at the feature level are activated by the letter *K*, and that these feature units send activation to letter units in the letter level. Color and radiating lines indicate activation.

Word level Fork Roof

Letter level F K O R

Feature level | / \ — ( )

Stimulus **K**

■ **Figure 3.10** The "man" stimulus for the rat–man demonstration. (Adapted from "The Role of Frequency in Developing Perceptual Sets," by B. R. Bugelski et al., 1961, *Canadian Journal of Psychology, 15,* pp. 205–211, Copyright © 1961 by the Canadian Psychological Association.)

onstrate how interactive activation handles the following three situations: (1) recognizing a single letter; (2) recognizing a single word; and (3) recognizing a letter within a word.

Recognizing a Single Letter Presenting the letter *K* activates feature units for *K*'s features—a straight line and two slanted lines (Figure 3.9). These feature units then send activation to each letter unit that contains these features—the *F, K, O,* and *R* in our example (in the full model, with all 26 letters, other letters would also be activated). According to the interactive activation model, the letter unit that is activated the most indicates which letter was presented. In our example, the *K* is activated the most, indicating that the *K* was, in fact, the letter that was presented.

Recognizing a Word We now consider how the model responds to the word *FORK*. In Figure 3.11 we have added a characteristic to the model that enables it to deal with words. Now, in the letter stage there is a letter unit for each letter's *position* in a word. For

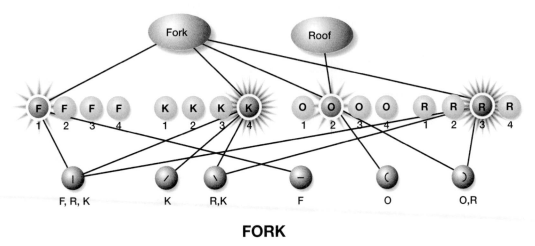

FORK

■ **Figure 3.11** How the word *FORK* activates the components of the interactive activation model. See text for explanation.

example, presenting *FORK* activates the features for the *F*, and each of these features send activation to letter unit F1—which is for *F* in the first position in a word. Similarly, the features for *O* activate the O2 letter unit (the *O* in the second position), *R*'s features activate the R3 unit, and *K*'s features activate the K4 unit.

These letter units then send activation to all words that contain letters in the correct positions. In our example, the word *FORK* receives signals from the F1, O2, R3, and K4 letter units. Notice that the word *ROOF* receives signals only from the O2 letter unit. In this word, the *R* and the *F* are in the wrong position to receive activation from the *R* and *F* letter units that are activated by *FORK*. Because *FORK* is more highly activated than *ROOF*, the model recognizes *FORK* as the word that was presented. Of course, in the full model, many more words would be involved, but the general result is that the word that is presented causes the most activation.

The Word Superiority Effect Next we consider how the model deals with recognizing a letter that is contained in a word, but first we will describe the **word superiority effect**— letters are easier to recognize when they are contained in a word, compared to when they appear alone or are contained in a nonword. This effect was first demonstrated by G. M. Reicher in 1969 using the following procedure.

◄► Method

Word Superiority Effect

A stimulus that is either (a) a word, like *FORK;* (b) a single letter, like *K;* or (c) a nonword, such as *RFOK,* is flashed briefly and is followed immediately by a masking stimulus, indicated in Figure 3.12 by XXXX, that stops further processing of the original stimulus. Following the mask, two letters are briefly presented, one that appeared in the original stimulus, and another that did not. The participants' task is to pick the letter that was presented in the original stimulus. In the example in Figure 3.12a, the word *FORK* was presented, so *K* would

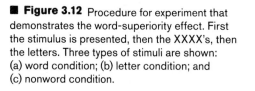

■ **Figure 3.12** Procedure for experiment that demonstrates the word-superiority effect. First the stimulus is presented, then the XXXX's, then the letters. Three types of stimuli are shown: (a) word condition; (b) letter condition; and (c) nonword condition.

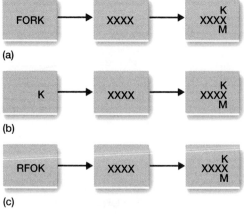

be the correct answer. *K* would also be the correct answer if the *K* were originally presented alone (Figure 3.12b), or if it were presented in a nonword like *RFOK* (Figure 3.12c). ◆

When Reicher's participants were asked to choose which of the two letters they saw in the original stimulus, they did so more quickly and accurately when the letter was part of the original word, as in Figure 3.12a, than when the letter was presented alone, as in Figure 3.12b, or was part of a nonword, as in Figure 3.12c. This more rapid processing of letters when in a word—the word superiority effect—means that letters in words are not processed letter by letter but that each letter is affected by its surroundings. With this experimental finding in hand, let's consider how the interactive activation model would explain the recognition of a letter within a word.

Recognizing a Letter Within a Word Figure 3.13 shows the letter level and word level from Figure 3.11, but with one added feature—**feedback activation**, indicated by the dashed arrows that extend from the word units back to the letter units. Feedback activation is activation that is sent from word units back to each of the letter units for that word. For example, the unit for *FORK* sends activation back to the K4 letter unit. This enhances the activation of the K4 unit.

The enhanced activity of the letter units caused by feedback activation explains the word superiority effect, because feedback activation does not occur when a letter is presented alone (note that the activation for K4 is greater than the activation for the *K* in Figure 3.9). Notice that some feedback activation would occur when a nonword such as *RFOK* is presented (because the K4 letter unit is activated and sends its activation to the *FORK* unit), but much less than for when *FORK* is presented. Thus, the letter *K* and each of the other letters in *FORK* are more highly activated when they appear in the word than when they appear alone or in a nonword.

The model in Figure 3.11 is important for a number of reasons. First, it proposes a mechanism that is consistent with what we know about neural firing. Excitation is sent from one level to another in the model, just as excitation is sent from one neuron to another in the nervous system. The model also contains another characteristic that corresponds to neural firing. It proposes a role for inhibition, which is sent between the letter units and between the word units. We didn't include inhibition in our example

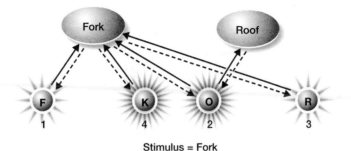

Stimulus = Fork

■ **Figure 3.13** The letter and word levels of the interactive activation model, showing how feedback activation from the word level to the letter level (dashed lines) increases activation of the letter units.

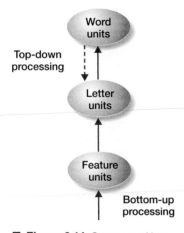

■ **Figure 3.14** Summary of how activation flows in the interactive activation model. Activation flowing from the feature units toward the word units represents bottom-up processing. Activation flowing from the word units to the letter units represents top-down processing.

above, but the net effect of inhibition is to enhance the activation of units corresponding to stimulus letters or words, compared to units that do not correspond to other letters or words.

The model is also important because it takes top-down processing into account. Remember that bottom-up processing is initiated by stimulation of the receptors, and top-down processing occurs when a person's knowledge affects processing. Thus, in this model, bottom-up processing occurs when letter or word stimuli activate the receptors, which then activate feature units. Top-down processing is also involved because the existence of word units is based on the person's knowledge of which strings of letters form words, and the feedback activation that is sent back from the words to the letter units reflects top-down processing (Figure 3.14).

This is an early version of a type of model called a *connectionist model*. Connectionist models involve networks that look like the ones in Figures 3.11 and 3.13. As we will see in Chapter 8, networks like this have been used to explain not only how we recognize letters and words, but how we learn to recognize stimuli we have never experienced before.

Considering how letters are recognized provides a good way to show how bottom-up and top-down processing interact with one another. But we are interested not just in how we recognize letters, but in how we recognize other types of objects as well. This step in our story takes us to Anne Treisman's *feature integration theory* of perception.

Feature Integration Theory (FIT)

Figure 3.15 shows the basic idea behind **feature integration theory** (**FIT**; Treisman, 1986). According to this theory, the first stage of perception is the **preattentive stage**, so named because it happens automatically and doesn't require any effort or attention by the perceiver. In this stage, an object is analyzed into its features.

The idea that an object is automatically broken into features may seem counterintuitive because when we look at an object, we see the whole object, not an object that

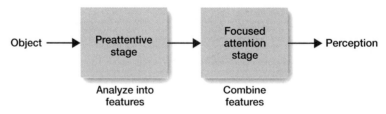

■ **Figure 3.15** Flow diagram for Treisman's (1986) feature integration theory (FIT). According to this theory, objects are first analyzed into features in the preattentive stage, and then these features are combined into an object that can be perceived in the focused attention stage.

has been divided into its individual features. The reason we aren't aware of this process of feature analysis is that it occurs early in the perceptual process, before we have become conscious of the object. Thus, when you see this book, you are conscious of its rectangular shape, but you are not aware that before you saw this rectangular shape, your perceptual system analyzed the book into individual features such as lines with different orientations.

To provide some perceptual evidence that objects are, in fact, analyzed into features, Treisman and H. Schmidt (1982) did an ingenious experiment to show that early in the perceptual process, features may exist independently of one another. Treisman and Schmidt's display consisted of four objects flanked by two black numbers (● Color Plate 3.1). They flashed this display onto a screen for one-fifth of a second, followed by a random-dot masking field designed to eliminate any residual perception that might remain after the stimuli were turned off. Participants were told to report the black numbers first and then to report what they saw at each of the four locations where the shapes had been.

In 18 percent of the trials, participants reported seeing objects that were made up of a combination of features from two different stimuli. For example, after being presented with the display in ● Color Plate 3.1, in which the small triangle was red and the small circle was green, they might report seeing a small red circle and a small green triangle. These combinations of features from different stimuli are called **illusory conjunctions**. Illusory conjunctions can occur even if the stimuli differ greatly in shape and size. For example, a small blue circle and a large green square might be seen as a large blue square and a small green circle.

According to Treisman, these illusory conjunctions occur because at the beginning of the perceptual process each feature exists independently of the others. That is, features such as "redness," "curvature," or "tilted line" are, at this early stage of processing, not associated with a specific object (Figure 3.16). They are, in Treisman's (1986) words,

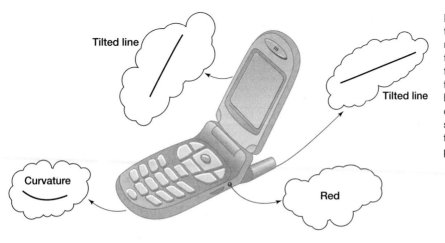

■ **Figure 3.16** The results of the illusory conjunction experiment suggest that very early in the perceptual process, features that make up an object are "free floating." This is symbolized here by showing some of the features of a cell phone as existing separately from one another at the beginning of the perceptual process.

"free floating" and can therefore be incorrectly combined in laboratory situations when briefly flashed stimuli are followed by a masking field.

You can think about these features as components of a visual "alphabet." At the very beginning of the process, perceptions of each of these components exist independently of one another, just as the individual letter tiles in a game of Scrabble exist as individual units when the tiles are scattered at the beginning of the game. However, just as the individual Scrabble tiles are combined to form words, the individual features combine to form perceptions of whole objects. According to Treisman's model, these features are combined in the second stage, which is called the **focused attention stage**. Once the features have been combined in this stage, we perceive the object.

During the focused attention stage, the observer's attention plays an important role in combining the features to create the perception of whole objects. To illustrate the importance of attention for combining the features, Treisman repeated the illusory conjunction experiment using the stimuli in ● Color Plate 3.1, but she instructed her participants to ignore the black numbers and to focus all of their attention on the four target items. This focusing of attention eliminated illusory conjunctions so that all of the shapes were paired with their correct colors.

When I describe this process in class, some students aren't convinced. One student said, "I think that when people look at an object, they don't break it into parts. They just see what they see." To convince this student (and the many others who, at the beginning of the course, are still not comfortable with the idea that cognition sometimes involves rapid processes we aren't aware of), I describe the case of R.M., a patient who had parietal lobe damage that resulted in a condition called **Balint's syndrome**. The crucial characteristic of Balint's syndrome is an inability to focus attention on individual objects.

According to feature integration theory, lack of focused attention would make it difficult for R.M. to combine features correctly, and this is exactly what happened. When R.M. was presented with two different letters of different colors, such as a red *T* and a blue *O*, he reported illusory conjunctions such as "blue *T*" on 23 percent of the trials, even when he was able to view the letters for as long as 10 seconds (Friedman-Hill et al., 1995; Robertson et al., 1997). The case of R.M. illustrates how a breakdown in the brain can reveal processes that are not obvious when the brain is functioning normally.

The feature analysis approach involves mostly bottom-up processing because knowledge is usually not involved. In some situations, however, top-down processing can come into play. For example, when Treisman did an illusory conjunction experiment using stimuli such as the ones in ● Color Plate 3.2 and asked participants to identify the objects, the usual illusory conjunctions occurred, so the orange triangle would, for example, sometimes be perceived to be black. However, when she told participants that they were being shown a carrot, a lake, and a tire, illusory conjunctions were less likely to occur, so participants were more likely to perceive the triangular "carrot" as being orange. Thus, in this situation, the participants' knowledge of the usual colors of objects influenced their ability to correctly combine the features of each object. In our everyday experience, in which we are often perceiving familiar objects, top-down processing combines with feature analysis to help us perceive things accurately.

The features in Treisman's model are things like lines, curves, and colors. But these types of features don't explain how we perceive the three-dimensional objects we routinely encounter in our environment. Another feature-based theory, called *recognition-by-components theory*, proposes three-dimensional features to deal with this situation.

Recognition-by-Components Theory

In the **recognition-by-components (RBC) theory** of perception, the features are not lines, curves, or colors, but are three-dimensional volumes called **geons**. Figure 3.17a shows a number of geons, which are shapes such as cylinders, rectangular solids, and pyramids. Irving Biederman (1987), who developed the recognition-by-components theory, has proposed that there are 36 different geons, which is enough to construct a large proportion of the objects that exist in the environment. Figure 3.17b shows a few objects that have been constructed from geons.

An important property of geons is that they can be identified when viewed from different angles. This property, which is called **view invariance**, occurs because geons contain **view invariant properties**—properties such as the three parallel edges of the rectangular solid in Figure 3.17 that remain visible even when the geon is viewed from many different angles.

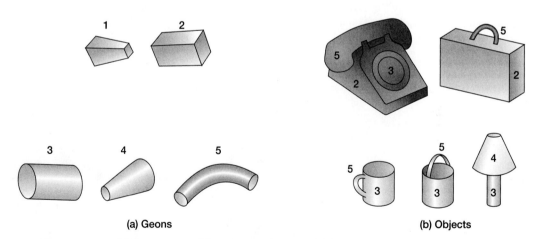

(a) Geons   (b) Objects

■ **Figure 3.17** (a) Some geons; (b) some objects created from the geons on the left. The numbers on the objects indicate which geons are present. (Adapted from "Recognition-by-Components: A Theory of Human Image Understanding," by I. Biederman, 1987, *Psychological Review, 24*, 2, pp. 115–147, Figures 3, 6, 7, and 11, Copyright © 1987 with permission from the author and the American Psychological Association.)

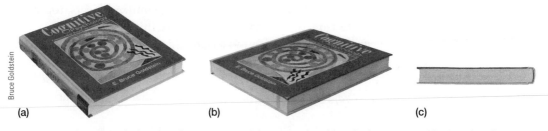

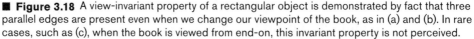

(a)   (b)   (c)

■ **Figure 3.18** A view-invariant property of a rectangular object is demonstrated by fact that three parallel edges are present even when we change our viewpoint of the book, as in (a) and (b). In rare cases, such as (c), when the book is viewed from end-on, this invariant property is not perceived.

You can test the view-invariant properties of a rectangular solid yourself by picking up a book and moving it around, so you are looking at it from many different viewpoints. As you do this, notice what percentage of the time you are seeing the three parallel edges. Also notice that occasionally, as when you look at the book end-on, you do not see all three edges (Figure 3.18c). However, these situations occur only rarely, and when they do occur, it becomes more difficult to recognize the object. For example, when we view the object in Figure 3.19a from the rarely encountered unusual perspective in Figure 3.19b, we see fewer basic geons and therefore have difficulty identifying it.

Two other properties of geons are *discriminability* and *resistance to visual noise*. **Discriminability** means that each geon can be distinguished from the others from almost all viewpoints. **Resistance to visual noise** means we can still perceive geons under "noisy" conditions such as might occur under conditions of low light or fog. For example, look at Figure 3.20. The reason you can identify this object (what is it?)—even though over half of its contour is obscured—is because you can still identify its geons.

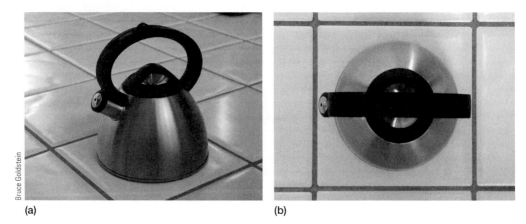

(a)   (b)

■ **Figure 3.19** (a) A familiar object; (b) the same object seen from a viewpoint that obscures most of its geons. This makes it harder to recognize the object.

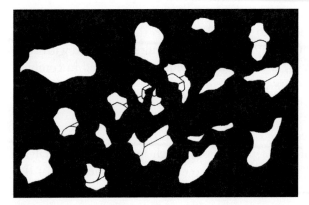

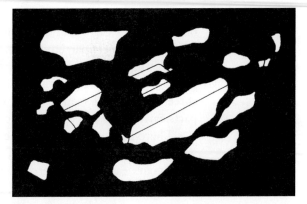

■ **Figure 3.20** What is the object behind the mask? (Adapted from "Recognition-by-Components: A Theory of Human Image Understanding," by I. Biederman, 1987, *Psychological Review, 24,* 2, pp. 115–147, Figure 26, Copyright © 1987 with permission from the author and the American Psychological Association.)

■ **Figure 3.21** The same object as in Figure 3.20 (a flashlight) with the geons obscured. (Adapted from "Recognition-by-Components: A Theory of Human Image Understanding," by I. Biederman, 1987, *Psychological Review, 24,* 2, pp. 115–147, Figure 25, Copyright © 1987 with permission from the author and the American Psychological Association.)

However, in Figure 3.21, in which the visual noise is arranged so the geons cannot be identified, it becomes impossible to recognize that the object is a flashlight.

The basic message of recognition-by-components theory is that if enough information is available to enable us to identify an object's basic geons, we will be able to identify the object (also see Biederman, 2001; Biederman & Cooper, 1991; Biederman et al., 1993). A strength of Biederman's theory is that it shows that we can recognize objects based on a relatively small number of basic shapes. For example, we easily recognize Figure 3.22a, which has nine geons, as an airplane, but even when only three geons are present, as in Figure 3.22b, we can still identify an airplane.

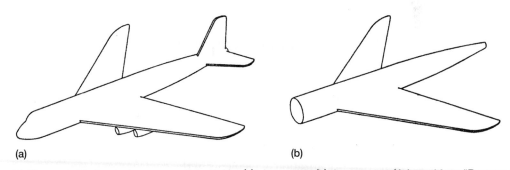

(a)   (b)

■ **Figure 3.22** An airplane, as represented by (a) nine geons; (b) three geons. (Adapted from "Recognition-by-Components: A Theory of Human Image Understanding," by I. Biederman, 1987, *Psychological Review, 24,* 2, pp. 115–147, Figure 13, Copyright © 1987 with permission from the author and the American Psychological Association.)

Both feature integration theory and recognition-by-components theory are based on the idea of early analysis of objects into parts. These two theories explain different facets of object perception. Feature integration theory is more concerned with very basic features like lines, curves, colors, and with how attention is involved in combining them, whereas recognition-by-components theory is more about how we perceive three-dimensional shapes. Thus, both theories explain how objects are analyzed into parts early in the perceptual process.

There is, however, more to perceiving objects than analyzing them into parts. We will now consider another aspect of object perception, which focuses not on analysis that occurs early in the perceptual process, but on how we organize elements of the environment into separate objects.

 Test Yourself 3.1

1. Describe the role of bottom-up and top-down processing as applied to Ellen seeing the moth on the tree, to the rat–man demonstration, and to Palmer's kitchen experiment.

2. What is the basic idea behind the feature analysis approach to perception? Describe the integrative activation model for recognizing letters. How do parts of this model relate to what we know about physiology? How do the word units help explain the word superiority effect?

3. Describe Treisman's feature integration theory. How do her experiments on illusory conjunctions support the idea that features are "free floating" in the preattentive stage? What is the focused attention stage, and what is the evidence that attention is important for combining the features?

4. Describe Biederman's recognition-by-components theory. How is it similar to Treisman's theory, and how is it different?

Perceptual Organization: Putting Together an Organized World

What do you see in Figure 3.23? Take a moment and decide before reading further.

If you have never seen this picture before, you may just see a bunch of black splotches on a white background. However, if you look closely you can see that the picture is a Dalmatian facing to the left, with its nose to the ground. Once you have seen the Dalmatian, it is hard to not to see it. Your mind has achieved **perceptual organization**—the organization of elements of the environment into objects—and has perceptually organized the black areas into a Dalmatian. But what is behind this process? The first psychologists to study this question were the **Gestalt psychologists**, who were active in Europe beginning in the 1920s.

R. C. Jones

■ **Figure 3.23** What is this? The process of grouping the elements of this scene together to form a perception of an object is called perceptual organization. (The object is a Dalmatian.)

In Chapter 1, we described how, early in the 1900s, perception was explained by an approach called **structuralism**, which involved adding up small, elementary units called **sensations**. According to this idea, we see the two glasses in Figure 3.24a because hundreds of tiny sensations, indicated by the dots in Figure 3.24b, add up to create our perception of the glasses. But the Gestalt psychologists took a different approach. Instead of looking at the glasses as a collection of tiny sensations, they considered the overall pattern created by the glasses. According to the Gestalt approach, the pattern in Figure 3.24a can potentially be perceived as representing a number of different objects, as shown in Figures 3.25a, b, and c. But even though many different objects could have created the pattern in Figure 3.24a, the fact that we automatically see the picture as two separate glasses, as in Figure 3.25a, caused the Gestalt psychologists to ask what causes us to organize our perception in this way. They answered this question by proposing that the mind groups patterns according to rules that they called the *laws of perceptual organization.*

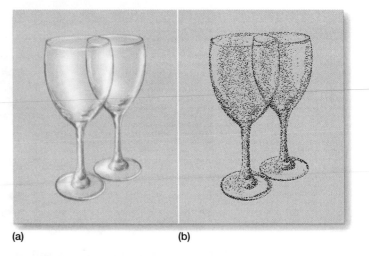

Figure 3.24 (a) Two overlapping wine glasses; (b) each dot represents a sensation. According to the structuralist approach, these individual sensations are combined to result in our perception of the glasses.

(a)　　　　　　　　(b)

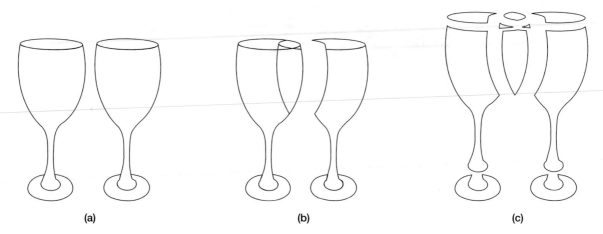

(a)　　　　　　　　(b)　　　　　　　　(c)

Figure 3.25 Each of the objects in (a), (b), and (c) could have resulted in the perception in Figure 3.24a if arranged appropriately in relation to one another. The Gestalt psychologists pointed out that we see the pattern as two glasses, as in (a), and proposed "laws of perceptual organization" to explain why certain perceptions are more likely than others.

The Gestalt Laws of Perceptual Organization

The **laws of perceptual organization** are a series of rules that specify how we perceptually organize parts into wholes. Let's look at six of the Gestalt laws.

Pragnanz *Pragnanz*, roughly translated from the German, means "good figure." The **law of Pragnanz**, the central law of Gestalt psychology, which is also called the **law of good figure** or the **law of simplicity**, states: *Every stimulus pattern is seen in such a*

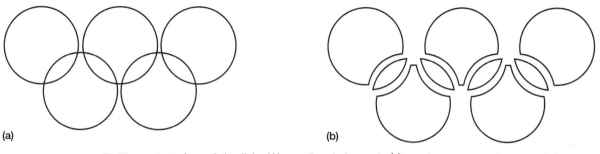

(a)　　　　　　　　　　　　　　　(b)

■ **Figure 3.26** Law of simplicity. We see five circles, as in (a), not the more complex array of nine objects, as in (b).

way that the resulting structure is as simple as possible. The familiar Olympic symbol in Figure 3.26a is an example of the law of simplicity at work. We see this display as five circles and not as other, more complicated shapes such as the ones in Figure 3.26b. We can also apply this law to the wine glasses in Figure 3.25. Seeing the pattern as two glasses as in Figure 3.25a is much simpler than seeing it as the more complex objects in Figures 3.25b and c.

Similarity Most people perceive Figure 3.27a as either horizontal rows of circles, vertical columns of circles, or both. But when we change some of the circles to squares, as in Figure 3.27b, most people perceive vertical columns of squares and circles. This perception illustrates the **law of similarity**: *Similar things appear to be grouped together.* This law causes the circles to be grouped with other circles and the squares to be grouped with other squares. Grouping can also occur because of similarity of lightness (Figure 3.27c), hue, size, or orientation.

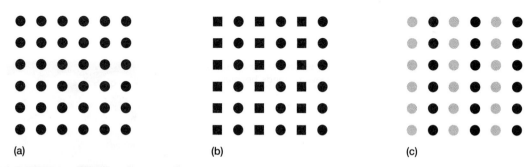

(a)　　　　　　　　　　(b)　　　　　　　　　　(c)

■ **Figure 3.27** Law of similarity. (a) This display can be perceived as either vertical columns or horizontal rows; (b) this is more likely perceived as columns of squares alternating with columns of circles, due to similarity of shape; (c) this is perceived as columns because of similarity of lightness.

Good Continuation We see wire starting at A in Figure 3.28 as flowing smoothly to B. It does not go to C or D because that path would involve making sharp turns and would violate the **law of good continuation**: *Points that, when connected, result in straight or smoothly curving lines, are seen as belonging together, and the lines tend to be seen as following the smoothest path.* Another effect of good continuation is shown in the Celtic knot pattern in Figure 3.29. In this case, good continuation assures that we see a continuous interweaved pattern that does not appear to be broken into little pieces every time one strand overlaps another strand. Good continuation also helped us to perceive the smoothly curving Olympic circles in Figure 3.26.

■ **Figure 3.28** Good continuation helps us perceive two separate wires, even though they overlap.

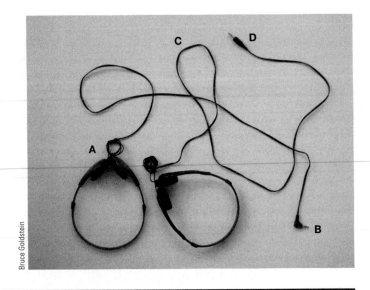

Bruce Goldstein

■ **Figure 3.29** We perceive this pattern as continuous interwoven strands because of good continuation.

Proximity or Nearness Figure 3.30a is the pattern from Figure 3.27a that can be seen as either horizontal rows or vertical columns or both. By moving the circles closer together, as in Figure 3.30b, we increase the likelihood that the circles will be seen in horizontal rows. This illustrates the **law of proximity** or **law of nearness**: *Things that are near to each other appear to be grouped together.*

Common Fate The **law of common fate** states: *Things that are moving in the same direction appear to be grouped together.* Thus, when you see a flock of hundreds of birds all flying together, you tend to see the flock as a unit, and if some birds start flying in another direction, this creates a new unit (Figure 3.31).

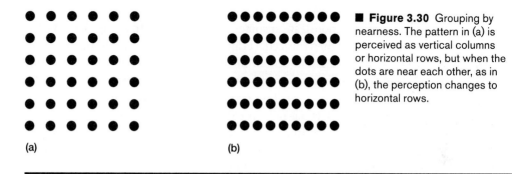

(a) (b)

■ **Figure 3.30** Grouping by nearness. The pattern in (a) is perceived as vertical columns or horizontal rows, but when the dots are near each other, as in (b), the perception changes to horizontal rows.

■ **Figure 3.31** A flock of birds that are moving in the same direction are seen as grouped together. When a portion of the flock changes direction, their movement creates a new group. This illustrates the law of common fate.

Familiarity According to the **law of familiarity**, *things are more likely to form groups if the groups appear familiar or meaningful* (Helson, 1933; Hochberg, 1971). You can appreciate how meaningfulness determines perceptual organization by doing the following demonstration.

Demonstration

Finding Faces in a Landscape

Consider the picture in ● Color Plate 3.3. At first glance this scene appears to contain mainly trees, rocks, and water. But on closer inspection you can see some faces in the trees in the background, and if you look more closely, you can see that a number of faces are formed by various groups of rocks. See if you can find all 12 faces that are hidden in this picture. ●

In this demonstration some people find it difficult to perceive the faces at first, but then suddenly they succeed. (Hint: The group of rocks at the bottom of the picture, just slightly to the right of center, forms a face.) The change in perception from "rocks in a stream" or "trees in a forest" into "faces" is a change in the perceptual organization of the rocks and the trees. The two shapes that you at first perceive as two separate rocks in the stream become perceptually grouped together when they become the left and right eyes of a face. In fact, once you perceive a particular grouping of rocks as a face, it is often difficult *not* to perceive them in this way—they have become permanently organized into a face. This effect of meaning on perceptual organization is an example of the operation of top-down processing in perception.

The Gestalt Laws Provide "Best Guess" Predictions About What Is Out There

The purpose of perception is to provide accurate information about the properties of the environment. The Gestalt laws help provide this information because they reflect things we know from long experience in our environment and because we are using them unconsciously all the time. For example, the law of good continuation reflects our understanding that many objects in the environment have straight or smoothly curving contours, so when we see smoothly curving contours, such as the wires in Figure 3.28, we correctly perceive the two wires.

The Gestalt laws usually result in accurate perceptions of the environment, but not always. We can illustrate a situation in which the Gestalt laws might cause an incorrect perception by imagining the following: As you are hiking in the woods, you stop cold in your tracks because, not too far ahead, you see what appears to be an animal lurking behind a tree (Figure 3.32a). The Gestalt laws of organization play a role in creating this perception. You see the two dark shapes to the left and right of the tree as a single object because of the Gestalt law of similarity (because both shapes are dark, it is likely that

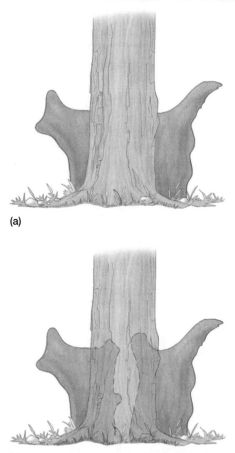

(a)

(b)

■ **Figure 3.32** (a) What lurks behind the tree? (b) It is two strangely shaped tree stumps, not an animal!

they are part of the same object). Also, good continuation links these two parts into one, because the line along the top of the object extends smoothly from one side of the tree to another. Finally, the image resembles animals you've seen before. For all of these reasons, it is not surprising that you perceive the two dark objects as part of one animal.

Because you fear that the animal might be dangerous, you take a different path, and as your detour takes you around the tree, you notice that the dark shapes aren't an animal after all, but are two oddly shaped tree stumps (Figure 3.32b). So in this case, the Gestalt laws have misled you.

Because the Gestalt laws do not always result in accurate perceptions of the environment, it is more correct to call them *heuristics* rather than *laws*. A **heuristic** is a "rule of thumb" that provides a best-guess solution to a problem. Another way of solving a problem, an **algorithm**, is a procedure guaranteed to solve a problem. An example of an algorithm is the procedures we learn for addition, subtraction, and long division. If we apply these procedures correctly, we get the right answer every time. In contrast, a heuristic may not result in a correct solution every time.

To illustrate the difference between a heuristic and an algorithm, let's consider two different ways of finding a cat hiding somewhere in the house. An algorithm for doing this would be to systematically search every room in the house (being careful not to let the cat sneak past you!). If you do this, you will eventually find the cat, although it may take a while. A heuristic for finding the cat would be to first look in the places where the cat likes to hide. So you check under the bed and in the hall closet. This may not always lead to finding the cat, but if it does, it has the advantage of being faster than the algorithm.

The fact that heuristics are usually faster than algorithms helps explain why the perceptual system is designed in a way that sometimes produces errors. Consider, for example, what the algorithm would be for determining what the shape in Figure 3.32a really is. The algorithm would involve walking around the tree so you can see the shape from different angles, perhaps taking a more close-up look at the objects behind the tree and maybe even poking them to see if they move. Although this may result in an accurate determination of what the shapes are, it is potentially risky (what if the shape actually *is* a dangerous animal?), and slow. The advantage of our Gestalt-based heuristics is that they are fast and are correct most of the time.

The influence of knowledge and the top-down processing that accompanies knowledge means that it is accurate to describe perception as being "intelligent." This intelligence becomes apparent when we bring our knowledge of faces to bear on the creation of faces in the rocks and trees of ● Color Plate 3.3. However, we could argue that there is a certain intelligence behind even simpler processes, such as grouping by similarity and nearness. The idea that these simple grouping processes could involve intelligence is perhaps not obvious because they seem so automatic. In fact, people often react to some of the Gestalt laws as if they are simply common sense. Our skeptic from the beginning of the chapter, who thought perception was simple, might say, "Of course things that are close to each other will become grouped. I don't think there's much intelligence involved in that."

It is easy to understand why someone might say this because these groupings usually happen so easily and naturally that it doesn't appear that much of anything is going on. It is a case of perception appearing to just "happen." But in reality there is a lot going on, because the Gestalt laws are based on characteristics of our environment. Grouping is easy because our perceptual system is tuned to respond, so when we encounter things that commonly occur in the environment, we will be likely to perceive them accurately. The need for perceptual intelligence becomes more obvious when we consider some of the problems both computers and humans must solve in order to perceive objects.

▶▶▶ Why Computers Have Trouble Perceiving Objects

At the beginning of the chapter, we noted that in the 1960s computer scientists predicted the problem of perception would be easily solved. As it turned out it wasn't easy at all, and although a chess-playing computer beat the world chess champion in 1997, it wasn't until 2005 that computer-controlled vehicles were able to successfully navigate a course that involved avoiding obstacles while traveling over varied types of terrain (Figure 3.33).

■ **Figure 3.33** On October 8, 2005, four robotic vehicles successfully navigated a 132-mile course through the desert. This vehicle, Carnegie-Mellon University's "Sandstorm," finished second to a vehicle from Stanford University. All of the vehicles operated without human intervention, after information about the course was loaded into their computers.

Evan Tahler, Red Team/Carnegie Mellon University

But even today, cases like Ellen's perception of a moth on a tree pose problems for even the most sophisticated computers. Although computer-controlled robots can navigate between two points, they still have trouble identifying specific objects. We can understand why it has been difficult to program computers to perceive, by considering a few of the problems that both computers and humans must deal with in order to accurately perceive objects in a scene.

The Stimulus on the Receptors Is Ambiguous

Objects seen from just one viewpoint result in ambiguous information on the receptors. For example, you might think the scene in ● Color Plate 3.4a is a circle of rocks, but viewing it from another angle reveals its true configuration (● Color Plate 3.4b). This ambiguity occurs because a particular image on the retina can be caused by an infinite number of different objects. This fact, called the **inverse projection problem**, is illustrated by Figure 3.34. In this figure, a square stimulus (solid lines) creates a square image on the retina. It also shows, however, that there are a number of other stimuli (dashed lines) that could create exactly the same image on the retina. A larger square that is farther away, a trapezoid that is tilted, as well as an infinite number of other objects, can create the same retinal image as the square. This creates problems for a computer, but humans usually perceive the correct object and not any of the other potential objects that might cast the same image on the retina.

Objects Need to Be Distinguished From Their Surroundings and From Each Other

It is often difficult to determine where one object ends and another begins. For example, look at ● Color Plate 3.5 and follow the directions in the caption below it. The problems posed by the scene illustrate that of the major tasks facing any perceiving

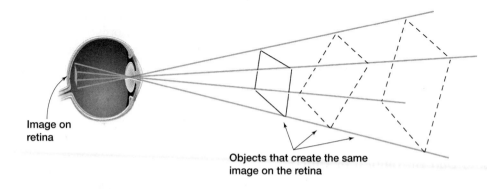

Image on retina

Objects that create the same image on the retina

■ **Figure 3.34** The principle behind the inverse projection problem. The small rectangular stimulus (solid lines) creates a rectangular image on the retina. However, this image could also have been created by the larger, more distant rectangle, by the tilted trapezoid (dashed lines), or many other stimuli. This is why we say that the image on the retina is ambiguous.

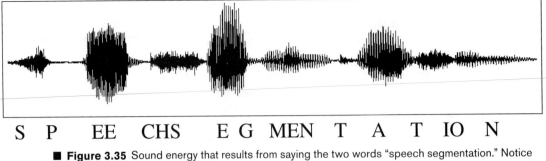

S   P   EE   CHS   E G MEN   T   A   T   IO   N

■ **Figure 3.35** Sound energy that results from saying the two words "speech segmentation." Notice that it is difficult to tell from this record where one word ends and the other begins. (Speech signal courtesy of Lisa Saunders.)

device is perceptually organizing parts of the scene so objects are perceived as separated from one another.

This problem of separating an overall stimulus into components also occurs in hearing. For example, when someone is talking to you, and you hear one word after another, you are solving the problem of **speech segmentation**—the organization of speech into individual words. You may wonder why this is a "problem," because it seems as if you are hearing individual words because there are spaces between them. However, when we look at the pattern of sounds produced by normal conversational speech, we see there are either no physical breaks in the sound or the breaks that do occur don't necessarily correspond to the breaks we perceive between words (Figure 3.35). The fact that the speech signal is continuous becomes obvious when you listen to someone speaking a foreign language. To someone unfamiliar with that language, the words seem to speed by in an unbroken string. However, to a speaker of that language who understands what the words mean, the words seem separate, just as the words of your native language seem separate to you.

If you have ever had a computerized voice tell you on the phone that "I can't understand you," you have an idea of the difficulty computers have in understanding speech. Computer speech recognition can be excellent when the number of words to be recognized is small, when the person speaks distinctly, with pauses between words, and when there is no background noise. Understanding rapid conversational speech is, however, much more difficult for computers than for humans, and adding background noise or other conversations, which humans can usually deal with, can cause a complete breakdown in the computer's ability to understand what is being said.

Objects Can Be Hidden or Blurred

Can you find the hidden objects in ● Color Plate 3.7? Although it might take a little searching, people can find the pencil and the glasses frame, even though only a small portion of these objects are visible. (See page 98 if you need a hint.) People also easily perceive the book, scissors, and paper as single objects, even though they are partially hidden by other objects.

This problem of hidden objects occurs not only when a pencil is covered by a notebook, but any time one object obscures part of another object. These occlusions of one object by another are extremely common in the environment. However, people easily understand that the covered object continues behind the object in front.

People are also able to recognize objects that are not in sharp focus, such as the faces in ● Color Plate 3.6. See how many of these people you can identify, and then consult the answer on page 98. Despite the degraded nature of these images, people can often identify many of them, whereas computers perform poorly on this task (Sinha, 2002).

The Reasons for Changes in Lightness and Darkness Can Be Unclear

In a scene such as the one in Figure 3.36, it is necessary to determine which changes in lightness and darkness are due to the physical properties of objects and which are due to changes in illumination. It is easy for us to tell that the border between area (a) and area (b) is due to a change in the illumination, caused by the shadow. We can

■ **Figure 3.36** For this scene, it would be difficult for a computer to sort out which changes are due to properties of different parts of the scene and which are due to changes in illumination.

also tell that the border between (a) and (c) occurs because the panel at (a) is made of lighter material than the one at (c). These judgments, which we make with ease, would not be easy for a computer, because it is difficult for the computer to tell which borders are caused by shadows and which are caused by other differences between parts of a scene.

These are only a few of the problems people routinely solve in everyday perception but which can pose difficulties for computers. Even the most powerful computers have great difficulty translating images from a scene into correct perceptions, and things get even more difficult for computers if we ask them to *identify* an object. A computer might be able to determine that the big blob in a scene is an object and not a shadow. But the computer might find it difficult to determine whether the object is a rock or a Volkswagen. In contrast, humans have no trouble dealing with this "What is it?" problem. The explanation for how humans can perceive more easily than computers is provided by two words: *perceptual intelligence*. Humans perceive by using both the information that stimulates their receptors and knowledge they bring to a situation.

How Experience and Knowledge Create "Perceptual Intelligence"

In this section we will focus on the knowledge that creates our perceptual intelligence. We will begin by describing a few more heuristics for perceiving, which, like the Gestalt heuristics, reflect commonly experienced aspects of the environment. We will then consider experiments showing that young infants can use knowledge they have obtained from past interactions with the environment to help them perceive. Finally, we will consider the idea that neurons contain knowledge, because they become tuned to respond best to commonly experienced aspects of the environment.

Heuristics for Perceiving

We have already noted that the Gestalt laws of organization are most accurately described as heuristics. We can also describe some additional heuristics. For example, most people see Figure 3.37a as a bunch of meaningless fragments, but perceive Figure 3.37b as five *B*'s, even though the colored shapes in (b) are identical to the ones in (a). The addition of the inkblot in (b) activates a perceptual heuristic called the **occlusion heuristic**, which states that when a large object is partially covered by a smaller occluding object, we see the larger one as continuing behind the smaller occluder. This rule, which is similar to the Gestalt principle of good continuation, prevents us from seeing things in our environment as being chopped into pieces when they are partially obscured by other objects (Figure 3.38).

The following demonstration illustrates another perceptual heuristic.

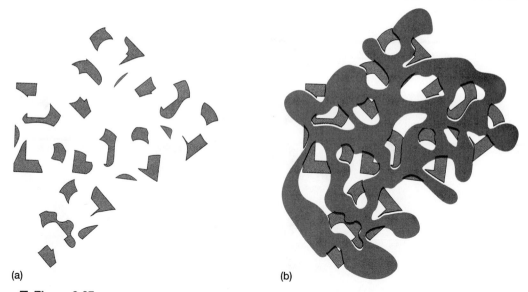

(a)   (b)

■ **Figure 3.37** (a) What is this? (b) Adding the ink blot, which covers only the open areas in the other pattern, reveals the presence of five *B*'s. (Reprinted from "Asking the 'What for' Question in Auditory Perception," by A. Bregman, in *Perceptual Organization,* M. Kubovy & J. R. Pomerantz, Eds., 1981, pp. 99–119. Copyright © 1981 with permission from Lawrence Erlbaum Associates, Inc.)

■ **Figure 3.38** Three men whose bodies are occluded by the two boards. Good continuation causes each man to be perceived as a single object that continues behind the boards.

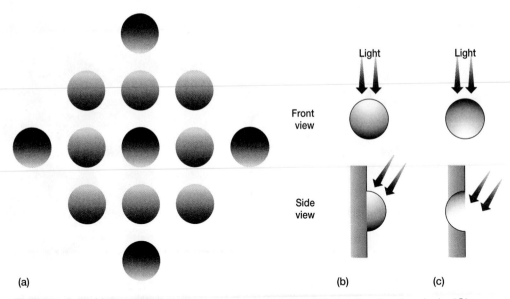

■ Figure 3.39 (a) Rounded shapes jutting out or indentations? Follow the directions in the "Shape From Shading" demonstration. (b) Light coming from above will illuminate the top of a shape that is jutting out, and (c) the bottom of an indentation.

 **Demonstration**

Shape From Shading

What do you perceive in Figure 3.39a? Do some of the discs look like they are sticking out, like parts of three-dimensional spheres, and do others appear to be indentations? If you do see the discs in this way, notice that the ones that appear to be sticking out are arranged in a square. After observing this, turn the page upside down so the black dot is on the bottom. Does this change your perception? ●

You can see from the explanation in Figure 3.39b and c that if we are assuming that light is coming from above (which is usually the case in the environment), then patterns like the circles that are light on the top would be created by an object that bulges out, but a pattern like the circles that are light on the bottom would be created by an indentation in a surface. The assumption that light is coming from above has been called the **light-from-above heuristic** (Kleffner & Ramachandran, 1992). Apparently, people make the light-from-above assumption because most light in our environment comes from above. This includes the sun as well as most artificial light sources.

Another example of an effect of the light-from-above heuristic is provided by the two pictures in Figure 3.40. You may perceive the picture in Figure 3.40a as a series of indentations in the sand and the picture in Figure 3.40b as bumps in the sand, but Fig-

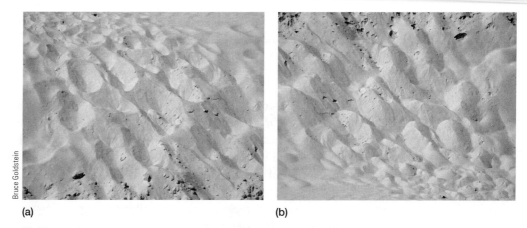

Bruce Goldstein

(a)   (b)

■ **Figure 3.40** Why does (a) look like indentations in the sand and (b) look like mounds of sand? See text for explanation.

ure 3.40b is simply Figure 3.40a turned upside down. Turn the book upside down, and see how your perception of the two pictures switches. What is happening here is that the light-from-above heuristic is determining your perception.

The heuristics people use for perception reflect knowledge about the environment (like "light usually comes from above"). People possess knowledge about many aspects of the environment—in addition to the direction of light and what happens when something is occluded. For example, humans know about the configurations of common objects such as faces; they know that the same object can look different when viewed from different angles; and they know about rules that govern language. We will now consider how information contained in the rules for language can be used to achieve perception by returning to the phenomenon of speech segmentation—determining when breaks occur between words in conversational speech—which we introduced on page 82.

Knowledge Helps Us Perceive Words in Conversational Speech

The fact that we can perceive individual words in conversational speech, even when there are no breaks in the speech signal (see Figure 3.35), means perception is based on more than the energy stimulating the receptors. One thing that helps us tell when one word ends and the other begins is knowledge of the meanings of words. The link between speech segmentation and meaning is illustrated by the following demonstration.

Demonstration

Organizing Strings of Sounds

Read the following words: Anna Mary Candy Lights Since Imp Pulp Lay Things. Now that you've read the words, what do they mean? ●

If you think this is a list of unconnected words beginning with the names of two women, Anna and Mary, you're right; but read this series of words out loud speaking rapidly and ignoring the spaces between the words on the page. When you do this can you hear a connected sentence that does *not* begin with the names Anna and Mary? (For the answer, see page 98—but don't peek until you've tried reading the words rapidly.)

If you succeeded in creating a new sentence from the series of words, you did so by changing the *perceptual organization* of the sounds, and this change was achieved by your knowledge of the *meaning* of the sounds. Just as the perceptual organization of the forest scene in ● Color Plate 3.3 depended on seeing the rocks as meaningful patterns (faces), your perception of the new sentence depended on knowing the meanings of the sounds you created when you said these words rapidly.

Another example of how meaning is responsible for organizing sounds into words is provided by these two sentences.

- Jamie's mother said, "Be a *big girl* and eat your vegetables."
- The thing *Big Earl* loved most in the world was his car.

"Big girl" and "Big Earl" are both pronounced the same way, so hearing them differently depends on the overall meaning of the sentence in which these words appear. This example is similar to the familiar "I scream, you scream, we all scream for ice cream" that many people learn as children. The sound stimuli for "I scream" and "ice cream" are identical, so the different organizations must be achieved by the meaning of the sentence in which these words appear.

Although segmentation is aided by knowing the meanings of words and being aware of the context in which these words occur, listeners use other information, as well, to achieve segmentation. As we learn a language, we learn that certain sounds are more likely to follow one another within a word, and other sounds are more likely to be separated by the space between two words. For example, consider the words *pretty baby*. In English it is likely that *pre* and *ty* will be in the same word (**pre-tty**) and that *ty* and *ba* will be separated by a space so will be in two different words (pre*ty ba*by). Thus, the space in the phrase *prettybaby* is most likely to be between *pretty* and *baby*.

Psychologists describe the way sounds follow one another in language in terms of **transitional probabilities**—the chances that one sound will follow another sound. Every language has transitional probabilities for different sounds, and as we learn a language we are learning not only how to say and understand words and sentences, but we are also learning about the transitional probabilities in that language. The process of learning about transitional probabilities and about other characteristics of language is called **statistical learning**. Research has shown that statistical learning is present in infants as young as 8 months of age.

Jenny Saffran and coworkers (1996) carried out an early experiment that demonstrated statistical learning in young infants. Figure 3.41a shows the design of this experiment. During the learning phase of the experiment, the infants heard four nonsense "words" such as *bidaku*, *padoti*, *golabu*, and *tupiro*, which were combined in random order to create two minutes of continuous sound. An example of part of a string created by combining these words is *bidaku**padoti**golabu**tupiro**padoti**bidaku*. . . . In this string,

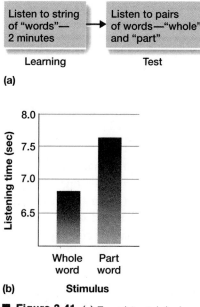

Listen to string of "words"— 2 minutes → Listen to pairs of words—"whole" and "part"

Learning

Test

(a)

(b) Stimulus

■ **Figure 3.41** (a) Experimental design of the experiment by Saffran and coworkers (1996), in which infants listened to a continuous string of nonsense syllables and were then tested to see which sounds they perceived as belonging together. (b) The results indicated that infants listened longer to the "part-word" stimuli. See text for explanation.

every other word is printed in boldface in order to help you pick out the words. However, when the infants heard these strings, all the words were pronounced with the same intonation, and there were no breaks between the words to indicate where one word ended and the other began.

Because the words were presented in random order and with no spaces between them, the infants heard what sounded like a jumble of random sounds. However, there was information within the string of words in the form of transitional probabilities, which the infants could potentially use to determine which groups of sounds were words. The transitional probabilities between two syllables that appeared *within* a word was always 1.0. For example, for the word *bidaku*, when *bi* was presented, *da* always followed it. Similarly, when *da* was presented, *ku* always followed it. In other words, these three sounds always occurred together and in the same order, to form the word *bidaku*. However, the transitional probabilities between the end of one word and the beginning of another was only 0.33. For example, there was only a 33 percent chance that the last sound, *ku*, from *bidaku*, would be followed by the first sound, *pa*, from *padoti*.

If Saffran's infants were sensitive to transitional probabilities, they would perceive stimuli like *bidaku* or *padoti* as words, because the three syllables in these words are linked by transitional probabilities of 1.0. In contrast, stimuli like *tibida* (the end of *padoti* plus the beginning of *bidaku*) would not be perceived as words, because the components were not linked.

To determine whether the infants did, in fact, perceive stimuli like *bidaku* and *padoti* as words, the infants were presented with pairs of three-syllable stimuli. One of the stimuli was a "word" that had been presented before, such as *padoti*. This was the "whole-word" test stimulus. The other stimulus was created from the end of one word and the beginning of another, such as *tibida*. This was the "part-word" test stimulus.

The prediction was that the infants would choose to listen to the part-word test stimuli longer than to the whole-word stimuli. This prediction was based on previous research that showed that infants tend to lose interest in stimuli that are repeated, and so become familiar, but pay more attention to novel stimuli that they haven't experienced before. Thus, if the infants had perceived the whole-word stimuli as words that were repeated over and over during the 2-minute learning session, they would pay less attention to these familiar stimuli than to the part-word stimuli that they had not perceived as being words.

Saffran measured how long the infants listened to each sound by presenting a blinking light near the speaker where the sound was coming from. When the light attracted the infant's attention, the sound began, and it continued until the infant looked away.

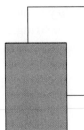

■ Figure 3.42
We usually perceive the white area as a rectangle, even though we can't see the whole stimulus. One reason for this is that we have learned from past experience that it is highly likely that in this situation the back shape is a rectangle.

Thus, the infant controlled how long they heard each sound by how long they looked at the light.

The result, shown in Figure 3.41b, indicates that the infants did, as predicted, listen longer to the part-word stimuli. These results are impressive, especially because the infants had never heard the words before, they heard no pauses between words, and they had only listened to the strings of words for 2 minutes. Apparently, infants are able to use the information provided by transitional probabilities to segment sounds into words.

This is important because it means infants are sensitive to things that occur together regularly in the environment, and can use this information to make sense of the world. Statistical learning is therefore an important mechanism for learning about the world. It is likely involved not only in speech segmentation but in other things as well, such as learning that objects usually continue behind an occluder, and when we see a display like the one in Figure 3.42 that the object in back is probably a rectangle, even though we can't see the whole object.

Neurons Contain Information About the Environment

All the knowledge we accumulate about the environment is stored in neurons. To appreciate what this means for perception, we need to realize that the experiences we have as we interact with the environment shape the way neurons function. This affects our ability to perceive because over time these neurons become tuned to respond to the types of stimuli we commonly encounter in the environment.

How do these neurons gain their properties? We answered this question when we described experience-dependent plasticity in Chapter 2 (see page 48). Remember that training people to become "Greeble experts" caused them to have more neurons that responded best to Greebles. Apparently, our experience in perceiving the environment shapes neurons, so they respond more efficiently to things we commonly experience.

The fact that neurons become tuned to respond best to what we commonly experience means that these neurons contain knowledge about the environment. Some examples, in addition to the neurons that become tuned to respond to Greebles, are the neurons in the fusiform face area (FFA) of the temporal lobe that respond best to faces (Figure 2.17). Other specialized neurons have been identified in the temporal cortex. Neurons in the **parahippocampal place area (PPA)** are activated by pictures indicating indoor and outdoor scenes like those shown in Figure 3.43a (Aguirre et al., 1998; Epstein et al., 1999; Epstein & Kanwisher, 1998). Apparently information about spatial layout is important for this area, because increased activation occurs both to empty rooms and rooms that are completely furnished (Kanwisher, 2003). These neurons must have gained their properties through experience, because human-made objects like houses have only existed for a few thousand years—far too short a time for evolution to have had any effect on the perceptual system. Another specialized area, called the **extrastriate body area (EBA)**, is activated by pictures of bodies and parts of bodies (but not by faces), as shown in Figure 3.43b (Downing et al., 2001).

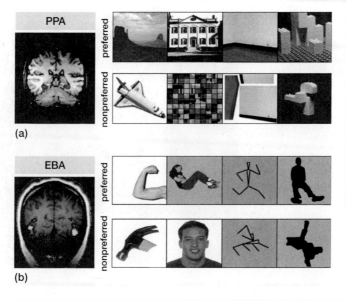

■ **Figure 3.43** (a) The parahippocampal place area is activated by places (top row), but not other stimuli (bottom row). (b) Extrastriate body area is activated by bodies (top), but not by other stimuli (bottom). (Reprinted with permission from N. Kanwisher, 2003. "The Ventral Visual Object Pathway in Humans: Evidence From fMRI." In L. M. Chalupa & J. S. Werner, Eds., *The Visual Neurosciences,* pp. 1179–1190. Cambridge, MA: MIT Press.)

We can conclude from all of this that both behavioral and physiological evidence supports the idea that the human brain is more than just a very complex computer. It is a very complex computer that is full of information about the world in which it functions. This information, which we often use without even being aware we are using it, is what makes humans "intelligent perceivers," and what gives humans a big advantage over present-day computers. To make computers as smart as people, it will be necessary to supply them with much of the built-in information that is stored in our brains.

Something to Consider

Perception Depends on Attention

What do we miss if we aren't paying attention? Daniel Simons and Christopher Chabris (1999) demonstrated we can miss a lot, by showing a 75-second film in which there were two teams of three players each, one passing a basketball around, and the other "guarding" them by following them around and putting their arms up as in a basketball game (Figure 3.44). The observers were told to count the number of passes, a task that focused their attention on the ball. After about 45 seconds, one of two events occurred. Either a woman carrying an umbrella or a person in a gorilla suit walked through the "game," an event that took 5 seconds.

After seeing the video, when observers were asked whether they saw anything unusual happen or whether they saw anything other than the six players, 46 percent of the observers failed to report that they saw the woman or the gorilla. In another experiment, when the gorilla stopped in the middle of the action, turned to face the camera, and thumped its chest, half of the observers still failed to notice it. These experiments

■ Figure 3.44 Frame from Simons and Chabris's (1999) "gorilla" film. (From "Gorillas in Our Midst: Sustained Inattentional Blindness for Dynamic Events," by D. J. Simons & C. F. Chabris, 1999. *Perception, 28,* pp. 1059–1074. Pion Limited, London. Figure provided by Daniel Simons.)

demonstrate that when observers are attending to one sequence of events, they can fail to notice another event, even when it is right in front of them (also see Goldstein & Fink, 1981; Neisser & Becklen, 1975).

The following demonstration provides another illustration of the difficulty in perceiving things that are not attended to.

Demonstration

Change Detection

When you are finished reading these instructions, look at the picture in ● Color Plate 3.8 for just a moment, and then turn the page and see whether you can determine what is different about ● Color Plate 3.9. Do this now. ●

Were you able to see what was different in the second picture? People often have trouble detecting the change even though it is obvious when you know where to look. (Try again, paying attention to the lower left portion of the picture.) Ronald Rensink and coworkers (1997) did a similar experiment in which they presented one picture, followed by a blank field, followed by the same picture, but with an item missing, followed by the blank field, then by the original picture, and so on. The pictures were alternated in this way until observers were able to determine what was different about the two pictures. Rensink found that the pictures had to be alternated back and forth a number of times before the difference was detected.

This difficulty in detecting changes in scenes is called **change blindness** (Rensink, 2002). The importance of attention (or lack of it) in determining change blindness was demonstrated by adding a cue indicating which part of a scene had been changed.

When Rensink did this, participants detected the changes much more quickly (also see Henderson & Hollingworth, 2003; Rensink, 2002).

The change-blindness effect also occurs when the scene changes in different shots of a film. Figure 3.45 shows successive frames from a video of a brief conversation between two women. The noteworthy aspect of this video is that changes take place in each new shot. In Shot B, the woman's scarf has disappeared; in Shot C, the other woman's hand is on her chin, although moments later, in Shot D, both arms are on the table. Also, the plates change color from red in the initial views to white in Shot D.

Although participants who viewed this video were told to pay close attention to the film, only 1 of 10 participants claimed to notice any changes. Even when the participants were shown the video again and were warned that there would be changes in "objects, body position, or clothing," they noticed fewer than a quarter of the changes that occurred (Levin & Simons, 1997).

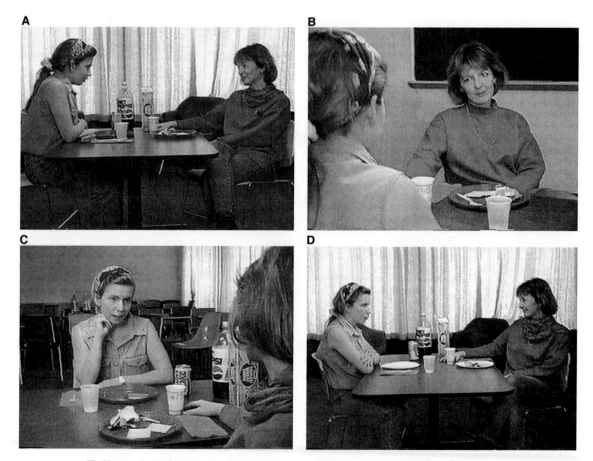

■ **Figure 3.45** Successive shots in a film used in Levin and Simons's (1997) change-blindness experiment. (From "Failure to Detect Changes in Attended Objects in Motion Pictures," by D. Levin & D. Simons, 1997, *Psychodynamic Bulletin and Review, 4*, pp. 501–506. Figures provided by Daniel Simons.)

Change blindness is interesting not only because it illustrates the importance of attention for perception, but also because it is a counterintuitive result. When Daniel Levin and coworkers (2000) told a group of observers about the changes that occurred in film sequences like the ones in Figure 3.45 and also showed them still shots from the film, 83 percent of the observers predicted that they would notice the changes. However, when these observers did not know which changes were going to occur, only 11 percent of the observers noticed the changes. Thus, even though people feel that they would detect such obvious changes, they fail to do so when actually tested. Levin coined the term **change blindness blindness** to describe the fact that people are "blind" to the fact that change blindness will occur.

One reason people might think they would see the changes is because they know that abrupt changes rarely occur in real life, and when they do occur, they are usually noticed. However, changes that occur in real life are often accompanied by motion, which creates a signal that attracts our attention to where the change will occur. But in change-blindness experiments, the change signal is eliminated by presenting a blank field, or a different film shot, between the two almost-identical stimuli. Thus, attention is not directed to the change, and we miss it (Rensink, 2000). When we discuss visual attention in the next chapter, we will consider some more examples of how attention can affect perception of the kinds of scenes we experience in our everyday environment.

CogLab

Change Detection

 Test Yourself 3.2

1. What idea about perception that was popular early in the 1900s did the Gestalt psychologists disagree with? What are the Gestalt laws of organization?
2. Why is it suggested that the Gestalt laws should be called heuristics rather than laws? What is a heuristic? An algorithm? What are the advantages of heuristics for perception?
3. Describe four reasons that perception is difficult for computers.
4. What is the occlusion heuristic? The light-from-above heuristic? How are these heuristics relevant to the "intelligence" of perception?
5. What is statistical learning, and how is it connected with the idea that human perception is intelligent?
6. What does it mean to say that "neurons contain information about the environment"?
7. What do change-blindness experiments tell us about the connection between perception and attention?

Chapter Summary

1. Perception begins with bottom-up processing, but top-down processing becomes involved when the perceptual process is influenced by a person's knowledge.
2. The template-matching model cannot explain letter recognition. Models based on features can explain a number of things about letter recognition, including

the word-superiority effect. The McClelland and Rummelhart model illustrates a model in which processing begins with features and occurs in stages, and which also takes into account how top-down processing can influence our ability to recognize letters.

3. Feature integration theory describes rapid processes that occur at the beginning of object perception, in which objects are broken down into features, and then these features create the perception of objects. Recognition-by-components theory describes how a feature analysis approach can be applied to the perception of three-dimensional objects.

4. The Gestalt approach to perception proposes laws of organization to explain how we perceptually organize parts into wholes. Because these laws provide "best guess" predictions of what is out there, they can be called heuristics. The Gestalt heuristics are just one example of the way our perceptual system is designed to deal with our environment.

5. It has been difficult to develop computer programs for perceiving objects because the stimulus on the receptors is ambiguous, objects need to be distinguished from their surroundings and from each other, objects can be hidden or blurred, and the reasons for changes in lightness and darkness can be unclear.

6. Humans solve the problems that are difficult for computers because humans possess built-in knowledge, which we can call perceptual intelligence. Examples of this knowledge are heuristics for perception, such as the Gestalt laws and other heuristics that reflect characteristics of the environment, and knowledge of word meanings and transitional probabilities between sounds that helps us achieve speech segmentation.

7. Statistical learning experiments have shown that very young infants can learn about characteristics of the environment that enable them to achieve speech segmentation.

8. Perceptual knowledge is stored in neurons through experience-dependent plasticity, which shapes neurons so they become tuned to fire best to specific characteristics of the environment.

9. Experiments involving simultaneous events and change detection demonstrate a close link between perception and attention.

Think About It

1. Describe a situation in which you initially thought you saw or heard something, but then realized that your initial perception was in error. What was the role of bottom-up and top-down processing in this process of first having an incorrect perception and then realizing what was actually there?

2. According to the feature analysis approach, our perceptual system analyzes objects into simple features. Look around in your environment, and see whether you can

describe objects in terms of their features. How well do you think objects can be described by their features? In addition to oriented lines and curves, what features might be needed to fully describe objects? How well do you think the feature analysis approach would work if you went out into the woods, where there are more natural objects and fewer objects made by humans?

3. Try observing the world as though there were no such thing as top-down processing. For example, without the aid of top-down processing, seeing a restaurant's restroom sign that says "Employees must wash hands" could be taken to mean that we should wait for an employee to wash our hands! If you try this exercise, be warned that it is extremely difficult because top-down processing is so pervasive in our environment that we usually take it for granted.

If You Want to Know More

1. Gestalt psychology. The ideas of the Gestalt psychologists dominated the field of perception in the mid-20th century and are still important today. Wolfgang Kohler was one of the founders of the Gestalt school.

Kohler, W. (1929). *Gestalt psychology*. New York: Liveright.

2. Features and visual search. The technique of visual search, in which participants search for a target stimulus in a display that contains many other stimuli as well, has been used to identify features for feature integration theory.

Treisman, A. (1986). Features and objects in visual processing. *Scientific American, 255,* 144B–125B.

Treisman, A. (1998). The perception of features and objects. In R. D. Wright (Ed.), *Visual attention* (pp. 26–54). New York: Oxford University Press.

3. Organization in hearing. The process of perceptual organization is usually illustrated using visual examples, but it occurs in hearing as well.

Deutsch, D. (1996). The perception of auditory patterns. In W. Prinz & B. Bridgeman (Eds.), *Handbook of perception and action* (Vol. 1, pp. 253–296). San Diego, CA: Academic Press.

4. Perception as problem solving. A number of modern researchers have proposed that perceptual mechanisms are similar to the mechanisms involved in cognitive processes like thinking and problem solving.

Ramachandran, V. S., & Anstis, S. M. (1986, May). The perception of apparent motion. *Scientific American*, 102–109.

Rock, I. (1983). *The logic of perception*. Cambridge, MA: MIT Press.

5. *Eye movements and visual perception.* In the next chapter, we discuss the role of eye movements in visual attention. They also play a major role in determining what we perceive.

Martinez-Conde, S., Macknick, S. L., & Hubel, D. H. (2004). The role of fixational eye movements in visual perception. *Nature Neuroscience, 5,* 229–240.

Key Terms

Algorithm, 79
Balint's syndrome, 68
Bottom-up processing, 58
Change blindness, 92
Change blindness blindness, 94
Common fate, law of, 77
Discriminability, 70
Extrastriate body area (EBA), 90
Familiarity, law of, 78
Feature integration theory (FIT), 66
Feature level, 62
Feature units, 62
Feedback activation, 65
Focused attention stage, 68
Geon, 69
Gestalt psychologists, 72
Good continuation, law of, 76
Good figure, law of, 74
Heuristic, 79
Illusory conjunctions, 67
Interactive activation model, 62
Inverse projection problem, 81
Laws of perceptual organization, 74
Letter level, 62
Letter units, 62
Light-from-above heuristic, 86

Nearness, law of, 77
Occlusion heuristic, 84
Parahippocampal place area (PPA), 90
Perception, 56
Perceptual organization, 72
Pragnanz, law of, 74
Preattentive stage, 66
Proximity, law of, 77
Rat–man demonstration, 60
Recognition-by-components (RBC) theory, 69
Resistance to visual noise, 70
Sensations, 73
Similarity, law of, 75
Simplicity, law of, 74
Speech segmentation, 82
Statistical learning, 88
Structuralism, 73
Template matching, 61
Top-down processing, 58
Transitional probabilities, 88
View invariance, 69
View invariant properties, 69
Word level, 62
Word superiority effect, 64
Word units, 62

CogLab
To experience these experiments for yourself, go to http://coglab.wadsworth.com. Be sure to read each experiment's setup instructions before you go to the experiment itself. Otherwise, you won't know which keys to press.

Primary Lab
Change detection A task involving detecting changes in alternating scenes (page 94).

Related Labs

Apparent motion How flashing two dots one after another can result in an illusion of motion.

Blind spot Map the blind spot in your visual field that is caused by the fact that there are no receptors where the optic nerve leaves the eye.

Metacontrast masking How presentation of one stimulus can impair perception of another stimulus.

Muller-Lyer illusion Measure the size of a visual illusion.

Signal detection Collect data that demonstrate the principle behind the theory of signal detection, which explains the processes behind detecting hard-to-detect stimuli.

Visual search Visual searching for targets that are accompanied by different numbers of distractors (page 96).

Garner interference An experiment about making perceptual judgments based on different dimensions of a stimulus.

Hint for Page 82 (Regarding Color Plate 3.7)

The pencil is in the foreground next to the corner of the computer. The glasses frame is peeking out from behind the computer, next to the scissors.

Answer to Question About Faces on Page 83 (Regarding Color Plate 3.6)

Prince Charles, Woody Allen, Bill Clinton, Saddam Hussein, Richard Nixon, Princess Diana.

Answer to Demonstration on Page 87

An American delights in simple play things.

Attention

4

Selective Attention: When Does Selection Occur?
  Demonstration: Hearing Two Messages at Once
  Method: Dichotic Listening
  Early Selection: Broadbent's Filter Model
  Intermediate Selection: Treisman's Attenuation Theory
  Late-Selection Models

How Does Task Load Affect Selective Attention?
  Method: Flanker-Compatibility Task

Test Yourself 4.1

Divided Attention: Paying Attention to More Than One Thing
  Practice Can Lead to Automatic Processing
  Demonstration: Stroop Effect
  Automatic Processing Is Not Possible for Difficult Tasks
  Divided Attention in the Real World:
    Inattention and Driving

Attention and Visual Processing
  Directing Visual Attention With the Eyes
  Method: Measuring Eye Movements
  Directing Visual Attention Without Eye Movements
  Method: Precueing
  Object-Based Visual Attention

Something to Consider: Attention in Social Situations—
The Case of Autism

Test Yourself 4.2

Chapter Summary

Think About It

If You Want to Know More

Key Terms

CogLab: Stroop Effect; Spatial Cueing; Attentional Blink; Change Detection; Simon Effect; Von Restorff Effect

Some Questions We Will Consider

- Is it possible to focus attention on just one thing, even when there are lots of other things going on at the same time? (101)

- Under what conditions can we pay attention to more than one thing at a time? (114)

- What does attention research tell us about the effect of talking on cell phones while driving a car? (118)

Sam is driving down the street toward his goal: a lunch date with his friend Susan. As he thinks about meeting Susan, he is listening to a talk show on satellite radio, but isn't thinking much about driving. However, just as he is passing the movie theater, something startling appears—a red ball approaches from the right, followed by a small boy chasing it. Sam's next actions are almost automatic: He glances quickly to the left, sees that the lane is open, swerves, hits his brakes, and miraculously avoids hitting the boy. "That was a close call," he thinks.

When he arrives at lunch, the restaurant is crowded and noisy. "Did you see the *Star Wars* promotion in front of the theater?" Susan asks. "Two guys fighting with light sabers." "Must have missed it," Sam says, and realizes that the boy had run out in front of his car just as he was passing the theater.

Attention is the process of concentrating on specific features of the environment, or on certain thoughts or activities. This focusing on specific features of the environment usually leads to the exclusion of other features of the environment (Colman, 2001; Reber, 1995). We can see how this applies to Sam's experience by noting that as he drives, his attention is directed to his lunch date. He also pays some attention to the radio and to what is happening in the street, but his driving is on "automatic." When the boy runs in front of the car, things change. The emergency captures Sam's attention, and he concentrates exclusively on his driving in order to avoid the boy. He becomes unaware of the radio and the street scene, and therefore misses the *Star Wars* promotion entirely.

Attention has a large effect on what we are aware of. This is obvious from Sam's experience and from Ellen's walk in the woods we described at the beginning of Chapter 3. Attention caused Ellen to focus on the tree in the first place, and then on the interesting pattern on the tree trunk, which turned out to be a moth. These examples illustrate how attention involves engagement of the mind and how this engagement affects our experience. This connection between attention and what is happening in the mind was described over 100 years ago by William James (1890) in his textbook *Principles of Psychology*:

> Millions of items . . . are present to my senses which never properly enter my experience. Why? Because they have no interest for me. My experience is what I agree to attend to. . . . Everyone knows what attention is. It is the taking possession by the mind, in clear and vivid form, of one out of what seem several simultaneously possible objects or trains of thought. . . . It implies withdrawal from some things in order to deal effectively with others.

Thus, according to James, we focus on some things to the exclusion of others. As you walk down the street, the things that you pay attention to—a classmate you recognize, the "Don't Walk" sign at a busy intersection, and the fact that just about everyone, except you, seems to be carrying an umbrella—stand out more than many other things in the environment.

As we will see in this chapter, attention is central to many aspects of cognition. Attention has an effect on perception (paying attention to something increases the chances

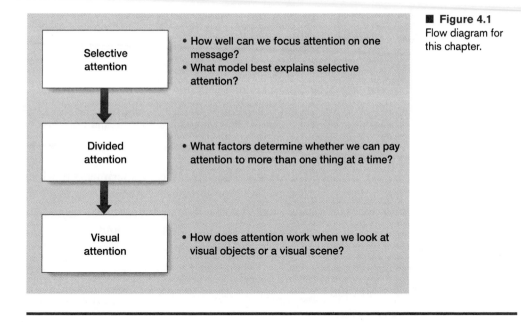

■ **Figure 4.1**
Flow diagram for
this chapter.

Selective
attention

- How well can we focus attention on one message?
- What model best explains selective attention?

Divided
attention

- What factors determine whether we can pay attention to more than one thing at a time?

Visual
attention

- How does attention work when we look at visual objects or a visual scene?

you will perceive it), on memory (you are more likely to remember something later if you were paying attention to it when it first occurred), on language (reading a sentence involves paying momentary attention to the words in the sentence, one after the other), and on solving problems (your success in solving the problem may depend on what aspect of the problem captures your attention).

In this chapter, we will consider a number of aspects of attention in approximately the order they have concerned attention researchers (Figure 4.1). We begin by considering the process of selective attention—our ability to attend to one message and ignore other, competing messages (as when Sam listens to Susan in the restaurant and ignores other people's conversations). In addition to focusing on one thing, we often want to pay attention to a few things at once, as Sam was doing just before the boy appeared. This is called divided attention. We will consider when divided attention is possible, and when it is not. Finally, we will examine recent research on how attention operates as we look at a visual scene.

Selective Attention: When Does Selection Occur?

Much of the early research on attention used auditory stimuli and focused on the process of **selective attention**—the ability to focus on one message and ignore all others. This research began with experiments indicating that if we are paying attention to one message, it is difficult or impossible to take in the information in another message presented at the same time. You can demonstrate this to yourself as follows.

Demonstration

Hearing Two Messages at Once

Enlist the help of another person. Select two books on different topics that you have not read before. Your task is to read one of these selections to yourself while the person reads the other selection out loud. Do this for about a minute, and note how well you are able to remember both passages. 🌑

Were you able to understand both passages? Experiments in which people are asked to pay attention to one of two simultaneously presented messages show that it is possible to focus on one message, but that not much information is obtained from the other message. One of the first of these experiments was done by Colin Cherry (1953), who used a procedure called **dichotic listening**.

◀▶ Method

Dichotic Listening

For dichotic listening, one message is presented to the left ear and another message is presented to the right ear. Participants are instructed to pay attention to one message (the attended message) and to ignore the other one (the unattended message) and to repeat the attended message out loud, as they are hearing it. This procedure of repeating a message out loud is called **shadowing**. The shadowing procedure is used to ensure that the participants are focusing their attention on the attended message (Figure 4.2). ◆

Cherry's participants shadowed the attended message while receiving the other message in the unattended ear. However, when they were asked what they heard in the

■ **Figure 4.2** In the shadowing procedure, a person repeats out loud words they have just heard.

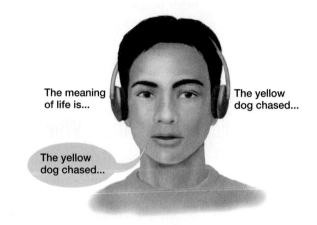

unattended ear, participants could say only that they could tell there was a message and could identify it as a male or female voice. They could not report the content of the message. Other dichotic listening experiments have confirmed this lack of awareness of most of the information being presented to the unattended ear. For example, Neville Moray (1959) showed that participants were unaware of a word that was repeated 35 times in the unattended ear.

Cherry's experiment is often described as a demonstration of the **cocktail party phenomenon**—the ability to pay attention to one message and ignore all other messages—because it resembles what people routinely achieve in a noisy party when they focus on one message and ignore all the others.

Cherry showed that a listener can select one message, but how is this selection achieved? One answer to this question, the **filter model of attention**, was proposed by Donald Broadbent (1958).

Early Selection: Broadbent's Filter Model

Donald Broadbent's (1958) filter model is a classic in psychology because it was one of the first to describe the human as an information processor, and it was the first to depict the course of this information processing with a flow diagram. Broadbent's model, which was designed to explain selective attention, states that information passes through the following stages (Figure 4.3).

1. *Sensory memory*, which holds all of the incoming information for a fraction of a second and then transfers all of it to the next stage. We will discuss sensory memory in more detail in Chapter 5.
2. The *filter* identifies the attended message based on its physical characteristics—things like the speaker's tone of voice, pitch, speed of talking, and accent—and lets only this message pass through to the detector in the next stage. All other messages are filtered out.
3. The *detector* processes information to determine higher-level characteristics of the message such as its meaning. Because only the important, attended information has been let through the filter, the detector processes all of the information that enters it.

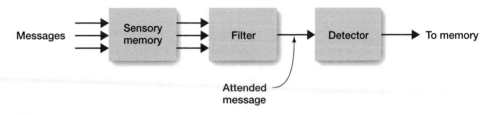

■ **Figure 4.3** Flow diagram of Broadbent's filter model of attention.

4. *Short-term memory* receives the output of the detector. Short-term memory holds information for 10–15 seconds and also transfers information into long-term memory, which can hold information indefinitely. We will describe short- and long-term memory in Chapters 5 and 6.

Broadbent's model is called an **early-selection model**, because the filtering step occurs before the incoming information is analyzed to determine its meaning. One way to think about the filter is to consider a sieve at use at the beach, trapping the coarse grains of sand and letting through the small grains (Figure 4.4a). The filter in Broadbent's model filters messages in a similar way, but instead of filtering based on the size of particles, it filters based on physical characteristics of the message, such as the speaker's pitch or rate of speaking (Figure 4.4b).

Most of the early research on selective attention used auditory stimuli such as stories, letters, or words. Also, because we have two ears, researchers were able to present one message to the left ear and another message to the right ear. As we will see, researchers thought of the left and right ears as separate *channels*, and they were concerned with how people take in information from these two channels under different conditions.

An example of this dual-channel research is Broadbent's (1958) "split-scan" experiment (Figure 4.5). Letters were presented to the left and right ears in pairs. For example, *M* was presented to the right ear and *H* was simultaneously presented to the left ear, then *R* and *S*, then *W* and *P*. The participant's task was to repeat the six letters immediately after hearing all six.

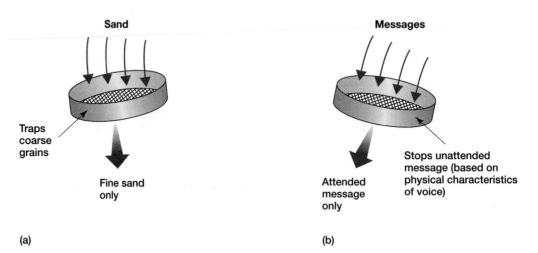

(a)　　　　　　　　　　　　　　(b)

■ **Figure 4.4** (a) A sieve that lets through small grains of sand and keeps coarse sand from getting through, based on the physical characteristic of the size of the sand particles; (b) Broadbent's model of attention lets through the attended message and keeps the unattended message from getting through, based on physical characteristics of the message, such as the pitch of a person's voice.

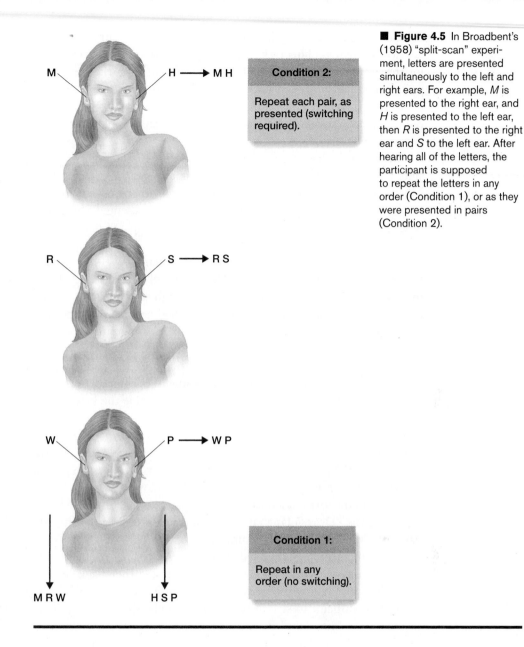

Figure 4.5 In Broadbent's (1958) "split-scan" experiment, letters are presented simultaneously to the left and right ears. For example, *M* is presented to the right ear, and *H* is presented to the left ear, then *R* is presented to the right ear and *S* to the left ear. After hearing all of the letters, the participant is supposed to repeat the letters in any order (Condition 1), or as they were presented in pairs (Condition 2).

Condition 2:

Repeat each pair, as presented (switching required).

Condition 1:

Repeat in any order (no switching).

In Condition 1, participants were asked to report the letters in any order. When given these instructions, they tended to report all the letters that were presented to one ear (*MRW*) and then all the letters that were presented to the other ear (*HSP*). The reason they did this, according to Broadbent, is because it is difficult to switch back and forth between channels, but it is easier to first report all the information from one channel and then repeat all of the information from the other. In this condition, participants reported 65 percent of the letters correctly.

In Condition 2, participants were told to report pairs of letters in the order each *pair* was presented. This task, which required participants to respond "MH; RS; WP" for the example in Figure 4.5, was more difficult than the other task because to do it, participants had to switch back and forth between channels as the letters were being presented. In this condition, participants reported only 20 percent of the letters correctly. Broadbent concluded from this result that it is difficult to switch attention between channels.

Broadbent's theory stimulated a great deal of research on attention, but the results of some of this research posed problems for his theory. For example, Neville Moray (1959) used the dichotic listening procedure and had his participants shadow the message from one ear. But when Moray presented the listener's name to the other, unattended ear, about a third of the participants detected it (also see Wood & Cowan, 1995).

Moray's participants had recognized their names even though, according to Broadbent's theory, the name should have been filtered out before reaching the detector. (Remember that the filter is supposed to let through only one message, based on its physical characteristics.) Clearly, the person's name had not been filtered out and, most important, it had been analyzed enough to determine its meaning. You may have had an experience similar to Moray's laboratory demonstration if, as you were talking to someone in a noisy room, you have suddenly heard someone else saying your name.

Following Moray's lead, other experimenters showed that information presented to the unattended ear is processed enough to provide the listener with some awareness of its meaning. For example, J. A. Gray and A. I. Wedderburn (1960) did the following experiment, which is sometimes called the "Dear Aunt Jane" experiment, as an undergraduate research project at the University of Oxford. As in Cherry's dichotic listening experiment, the participants were told to shadow the message presented to one ear. As you can see from Figure 4.6, the attended (shadowed) ear received the message "Dear 7 Jane," and the unattended ear received the message "9 Aunt 6." However, rather than reporting the "Dear 7 Jane" message that was presented to the attended ear, participants reported hearing "Dear Aunt Jane."

Switching to the unattended channel to say "Aunt" means that the participant's attention had jumped from one ear to the other and then back again. This occurred because they were taking the *meaning* of the words into account. Although Broadbent had shown it is difficult to switch between channels, the meaning of the words presented in the "Dear Aunt Jane" experiment caused participants to switch channels anyway. Because results such as these could not be explained by Broadbent's filter theory, Anne Treisman (1964a) proposed another theory, which she called the **attenuation theory of attention**.

Intermediate Selection: Treisman's Attenuation Theory

Treisman proposed that selection occurs in two stages, and she replaced Broadbent's filter with an *attenuator* (Figure 4.7). The **attenuator** analyzes the incoming message in terms of (1) its physical characteristics—whether it is high-pitched or low-pitched,

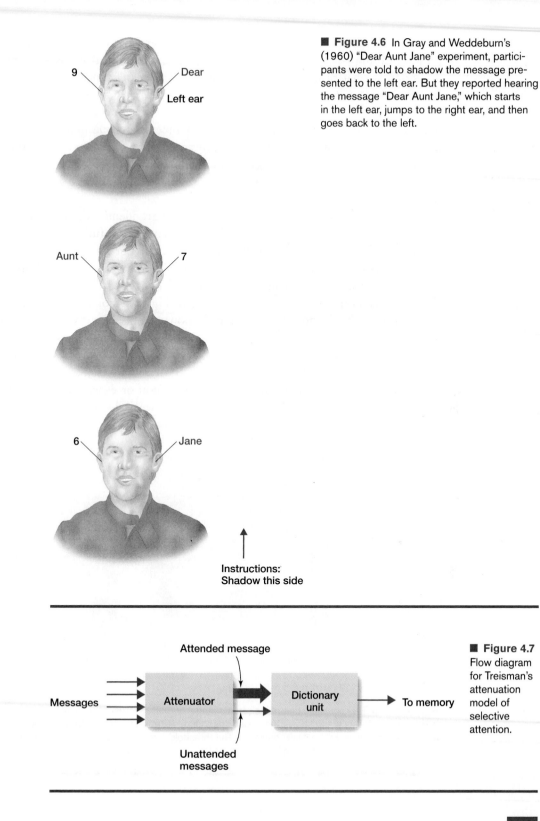

■ **Figure 4.6** In Gray and Weddeburn's (1960) "Dear Aunt Jane" experiment, participants were told to shadow the message presented to the left ear. But they reported hearing the message "Dear Aunt Jane," which starts in the left ear, jumps to the right ear, and then goes back to the left.

9 — Dear
Left ear

Aunt — 7

6 — Jane

Instructions:
Shadow this side

■ **Figure 4.7** Flow diagram for Treisman's attenuation model of selective attention.

Attended message

Messages → Attenuator → Dictionary unit → To memory

Unattended messages

fast or slow, (2) its language—how the message groups into syllables or words, and (3) its meaning—how sequences of words create meaningful phrases. Note that this is similar to what Broadbent proposed, but in Treisman's model, language and meaning can also be used to separate the messages. Treisman proposed, however, that the analysis of the message proceeds only as far as is necessary to identify the attended message. For example, if there are two messages, one in a male voice and one in a female voice, then analysis at the physical level is adequate to separate the low-pitched male voice from the higher-pitched female voice. If, however, the voices are similar, then it might be necessary to use the message's meaning to separate the two messages.

Once the attended and unattended messages are identified, both messages are let though the attenuator, but the attended message emerges at full strength, and the unattended messages are attenuated—they are still present, but are weaker than the attended message. Because at least some of the unattended message gets through the attenuator, Treisman's model has been called a "leaky filter" model.

The final output of the system is determined in the second stage when the message is analyzed by the **dictionary unit**. The dictionary unit contains stored words, each of which have thresholds for being activated (Figure 4.8). A threshold is the smallest signal strength that can barely be detected. Thus, a word with a low threshold might be detected even when it is presented softly or is obscured by other words.

According to Treisman, words that are common or especially important, such as the listener's name, have low thresholds, so even a weak signal in the unattended channel can activate that word, and we hear our name from across the room. Uncommon

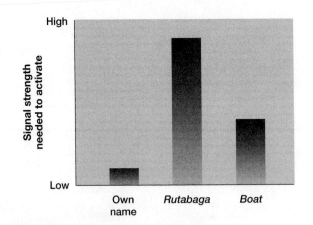

■ **Figure 4.8** The dictionary unit of Treisman's model contains words, each of which has a threshold for being detected. This graph shows the thresholds that might exist for three words. The person's name has a low threshold, so it will be easily detected. The thresholds for the words *rutabaga* and *boat* are higher, because they are used less or are less important to this particular listener.

words or words that are unimportant to the listener have higher thresholds, so it takes the strong signal of the attended message to activate these words. Thus, according to Treisman, the attended message gets through, *plus* some parts of the weaker unattended message. Treisman's model, like Broadbent's, is often called an early-selection model because the attended message can be separated from the unattended message early in the information-processing system. However, because further selection can also occur later, we have called Treisman's model an *intermediate-selection model*.

Late-Selection Models

Some researchers proposed **late-selection models,** which state that selection of stimuli for final processing doesn't occur until after the information has been analyzed for its meaning (Deutsch & Deutsch, 1963; Norman, 1968).

An experiment by Donald MacKay (1973) supports this idea of late selection. He had participants listen to ambiguous sentences, such as "They were throwing stones at the bank," that could be taken more than one way. (In this example, "bank" can refer to a riverbank or to a financial institution.) These ambiguous sentences were presented to the attended ear, while biasing words were presented to the other, un-attended ear. For example, as the participants were shadowing "They were throwing stones at the bank," either the word "river" or "money" was being presented to the un-attended ear.

After hearing a number of the ambiguous sentences, participants were presented with pairs of sentences such as the following:

> They threw stones toward the side of the river yesterday.
> They threw stones at the savings and loan association yesterday.

When they indicated which of these two sentences was closest in meaning to one of the sentences they had heard previously, MacKay found that the meaning of the bi-asing word had affected the participants' choice. For example, if the biasing word was "money," participants were more likely to pick the second sentence. This occurred even though participants reported that they were unaware of the biasing words that were pre-sented to the unattended ear. Because the meaning of the unattended word ("money") was affecting the participant's judgment, this word must have been processed to the level of meaning.

Figure 4.9 symbolizes the differences between the early- and late-selection ap-proaches to selective attention in terms of what characteristics of messages are pro-cessed. According to the early-selection view, only the physical characteristics of the message are processed before selection occurs. According to the late-selection view, both the physical characteristics and the meaning are processed before selection occurs. Because there is evidence to support both views, how can we choose between them? One idea that has been proposed is that the information that gets processed during a selective-attention task is determined by the nature of the task (Kahaneman, 1973;

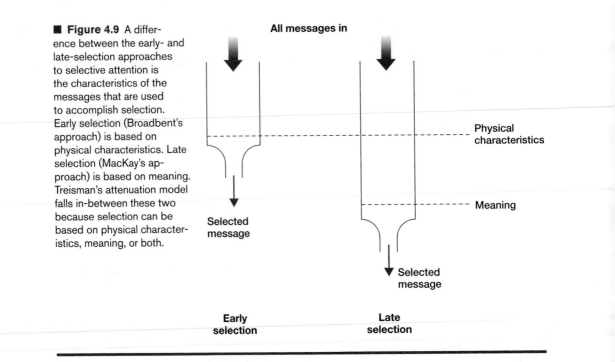

■ **Figure 4.9** A difference between the early- and late-selection approaches to selective attention is the characteristics of the messages that are used to accomplish selection. Early selection (Broadbent's approach) is based on physical characteristics. Late selection (MacKay's approach) is based on meaning. Treisman's attenuation model falls in-between these two because selection can be based on physical characteristics, meaning, or both.

Lavie, 1995). Nilli Lavie (1995) proposed that the crucial variable is **task load**—how much of a person's cognitive resources are used to accomplish a task.

How Does Task Load Affect Selective Attention?

Lavie describes a **high-load task** as one that uses most or all of a person's resources and so leaves no capacity to handle other tasks. A **low-load task** uses few resources, leaving some to handle other tasks. These two situations are illustrated by the following examples:

High load: Samantha is practicing for her piano recital. She is working on a particularly difficult part, repeating it over and over, and is so intent that nothing can distract her.

Low load: Ragu is quickly scanning a celebrity gossip magazine that he has little interest in. He is easily distracted, especially when someone he knows enters the room.

Samantha's task is high load because she had to focus all of her resources on mastering the piano passage. No resources remained to deal with other stimuli, so nothing distracted her. In contrast, Ragu's task was low load and left him with enough resources to notice and perhaps even interact with people entering the room. The effect of task load on the processing of other stimuli has been studied in the laboratory using a technique called the flanker-compatibility task.

◄► Method

Flanker-Compatibility Task

In the flanker-compatibility task, a participant is presented with a central display, that may contain a target, and a "flanker" distractor stimulus off to the side (Figure 4.10a). The participant's task is to detect the target in the central display as rapidly as possible, while ignoring the distractor stimulus. For example, if participants are told that the target is the square, they would push a key as quickly as possible as soon as they detect the square.

The question posed by this task is "Can the participant so totally focus their attention on detecting the target in the central display that the identity of the distractor will not affect their performance?" You might think it would be easy to do this. After all, the distractor is off to the side, so it is just a matter of focusing attention on the central display and ignoring the distractor. Nonetheless, the distractor can affect detection of the target. This is demonstrated by using two types of distractors: (1) A compatible distractor, which is the same as the target (Figure 4.10a) and (2) an incompatible distractor, which is different from the target (Figure 4.10b).

The task in Figure 4.10 is called the *low-load condition,* because there is only one potential target. The participants' task is therefore easy—they just have to determine whether or not the shape that is present is the target. When Shawn Green and Daphne Bavelier (2003) measured reaction times for detecting targets in displays like the ones in Figure 4.10, they found that the reaction time was longer for the incompatible distractor (Figure 4.10c). Thus, even though the participant was instructed to focus attention on the circular display that contained the target, some information from the distractor was being processed. Appar-

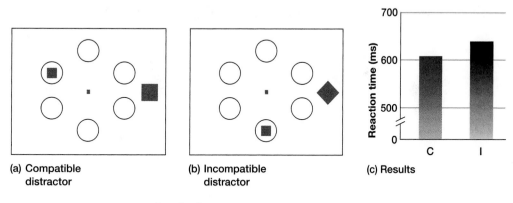

(a) Compatible distractor

(b) Incompatible distractor

(c) Results

Low load

■ **Figure 4.10** Flanker-compatibility task. (a) Display in which the small square is the target, and the large square on the right is the distractor. This distractor is "compatible" because it is the same as the target. (b) Display in which the distractor is "incompatible" because it is different from the target. (c) Results of Green and Bevelier's (2003) experiment, which found that the reaction time to indicate the presence of a target is longer for the incompatible distractor (bar I) than for the compatible distractor (bar C).

ently, this task was so easy that the participant still had resources available to process information in the flanker stimuli. ◆

What happens when task load is increased? Figure 4.11 shows the high-load condition, in which the target is still the square, but there are five additional shapes. The results for this condition are shown in Figure 4.11c. In this condition, the longer incompatible reaction time does not occur. (The difference between the compatible and incompatible reaction times is not statistically significant.) When the load is high, the type of distractor does not affect reaction time. This occurs because the participant needs to use all of his or her resources to deal with the more complex display, so there are no resources left to process the distractor.

The results in Figures 4.10 and 4.11 demonstrate differences between performance on low-load and high-load tasks, but you might be wondering whether a task that is high load for one person might be low load for another person. For example, although mastering the piano passage is a high-load task for Samantha, it may be a relatively easy, low-load task for a master concert pianist. In fact, Green and Bavelier showed that the results in Figure 4.11—in which increasing load eliminates the longer reaction time for the incompatible distractor condition—do not occur for people who, through many hours of practice, have become experts at playing video games.

The results for the video-game experts are shown in Figure 4.12. The results for the low-load condition (Figure 4.12a) are similar to the results for the non-video-game participants (compare to Figure 4.10c), in which reaction times were larger for the incompatible distractors. However, Figure 4.12b shows that increasing the load for the video-game experts did not eliminate the performance difference for compatible and incompatible distractors. Even at high loads, the video-game players still had enough

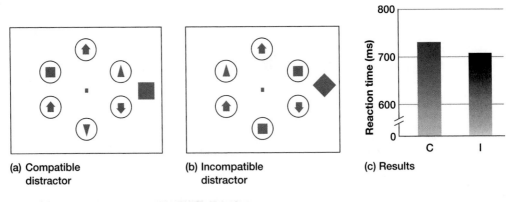

(a) Compatible distractor

(b) Incompatible distractor

(c) Results

High load

■ **Figure 4.11** Stimuli for the flanker-compatibility task in which the load is increased by adding additional stimuli to the display. The target is still the square, as in Figure 4.10, so the distractor is compatible in (a) and incompatible in (b). The results, shown in (c), indicate that under this high-load condition, the reaction times are the same for both compatible and incompatible distractors. (From Green & Bavelier, 2003.)

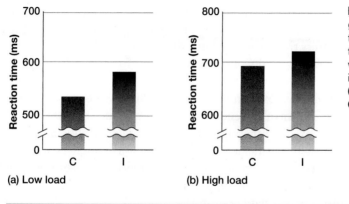

Figure 4.12 When video-game experts are tested using the flanker-compatibility task, their reaction times are higher when the distractor is incompatible under both (a) low-load and (b) high-load conditions. (From Green & Bevelier, 2003.)

resources left to process the distractors. What this means, according to Green and Bavelier, is that playing video games can enhance the ability to process visual information (Green & Bavelier, 2006). What is particularly interesting about this result is that the effects of video-game practice generalized to the flanker-compatibility task, which the video-game players had never seen.

The flanker-compatibility experiments show that our ability to selectively attend is determined by load, and that training, as in the example of the video-game players, can affect this ability. Nelli Lavie (1995, 2005) suggests that the effect of load on selective attention can explain the differences between some of the results that were used to support the idea of early selection and late selection. According to Lavie, experiments that support the idea of early selection involve high-load tasks, which involve processing complex messages. For example, Broadbent's dichotic listening experiments, which support early selection, involve a high-load task because complex messages are presented to the left and right ears. Because this high-load task requires most of the participant's resources, the attended message is processed and the unattended one isn't.

Experiments that support the idea of late selection involve low-load tasks that require less of the participant's resources, so both the attended message and some of the unattended message can be processed. MacKay's experiments, which support late selection, involve a low-load task because while the participants are listening to a sentence presented to one ear, just single words are being presented to the other ear. Apparently, the answer to the question "When does selection occur?" depends on the type of task involved, with complex, high-load tasks favoring early selection, and easier, low-load tasks favoring late selection.

Test Yourself 4.1

1. How has the dichotic listening procedure been used to demonstrate the cocktail party phenomenon? What did this procedure tell us in Colin Cherry's experiment about how well people can focus on the attended message and how much information can be taken in from the unattended message?

2. Describe Broadbent's model of attention. Why is it called an early-selection model? What was the purpose of the split-scan experiment, in which participants had to repeat letters that they heard in a dichotic listening task?

3. What were the results of experiments by Moray (words in the unattended ear) and Gray and Wedderburn ("Dear Aunt Jane")? Why are the results of these experiments difficult to explain based on Broadbent's filter model of attention?

4. Describe Treisman's attenuation theory. How does it deal with the fact that we are sometimes aware of messages that are presented to the unattended channel?

5. Describe the experiment in which ambiguous sentences were used to provide evidence for the late-selection model of attention. Be sure you understand why the result of this experiment supports late-selection theory.

6. Describe how the flanker-compatibility task has been used to test participants on low-load and high-load conditions. What is the evidence that training can increase a person's ability to deal with high-load tasks?

7. How has the early- versus late-selection debate been recast by Lavie's ideas about how task load affects selective attention?

Divided Attention: Paying Attention to More Than One Thing

Our emphasis so far has been on attention as a mechanism for focusing on one task. We have seen that sometimes we take in information from an "unattended" task, even when we are trying to focus on one task, as in the low-load condition in the flanker-compatibility experiments. But what if you want to consciously distribute your attention to a few tasks? Can we focus on more than one thing at a time? Although you might be tempted to answer "no" based on the fact that it is difficult to listen to two conversations at once, there are many situations in which **divided attention**—the distribution of attention to two or more tasks—can occur. For example, people can simultaneously drive, have conversations, listen to music, and think about what they're going to be doing later that day. The ability to divide attention depends on a number of factors, including practice and the difficulty of the task.

Practice Can Lead to Automatic Processing

Recently, as I was standing on the curb waiting for the "walk" signal, I observed a woman driving a car marked "AAA Driving School." I was impressed both by how slowly she was driving and by the intense look of concentration on her face. She was paying very close attention to her task, and it clearly was not easy for her. Many people have had this experience when learning to drive, but later, with practice, they find that driving becomes much easier.

Research on divided attention has shown that with practice, people can learn to simultaneously do two things that at first may have seemed fairly difficult. For example, when two college students first arrived at Elizabeth Spelke's laboratory to be participants in an attention experiment, they could easily read short stories and take dictation (writing words that were spoken to them), but couldn't do both at the same time (Spelke et al., 1976). However, after 85 hours of practice spread over 17 weeks, they were able to read a story rapidly and with good comprehension while simultaneously categorizing dictated words (for example, classifying "chair" as "furniture").

Divided attention was demonstrated in another way by Walter Schneider and Richard Shiffrin (1977) using the procedure illustrated in Figure 4.13, in which participants had to divide their attention between remembering target characters (letters or numbers) and monitoring a series of rapidly presented stimuli. At the beginning of a trial, participants saw a *memory set* that consisted of from 1 to 4 target characters (Figure 4.13a). They then saw a quick succession of 20 *test frames* (Figure 4.13b). Each frame had four positions, and at each position, there was either a random dot pattern, a target (one of the characters from the memory set) or a distractor (a character from the *distractor set*). The distractors were always from a different category than the characters in the memory set, so if the targets were numbers, the distractors were always letters. Schneider and Shiffrin called this way of presenting stimuli the *consistent mapping condition* because the participants always knew that the target would be numbers and the distractors would be letters.

As the 20 frames were being presented for a particular trial, the participants' task was to detect and identify a target, if one was presented in one of the frames (Figure 4.13c). In half of the trials, a single target was presented in one of the 20 frames. In the other half, no target was presented. (We can see from the example that the target *3* did appear in one of the frames on this particular trial.)

At the beginning of the experiment, the participants' performance was only 55 percent correct, and it took 900 trials for performance to reach 90 percent (Figure 4.14).

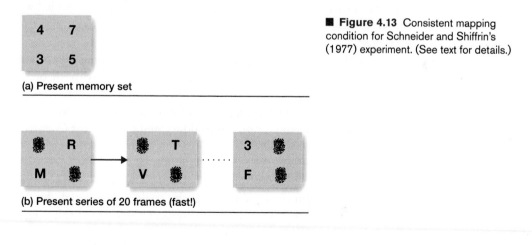

(a) Present memory set

■ Figure 4.13 Consistent mapping condition for Schneider and Shiffrin's (1977) experiment. (See text for details.)

(b) Present series of 20 frames (fast!)

(c) Was target from memory set present in a frame?

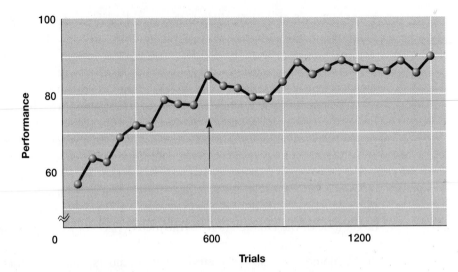

■ Figure 4.14 Improvement in performance with practice in Schneider and Schiffrin's experiment. The arrow indicates the point at which participants reported that the task had become automatic. (Reprinted from "Controlled and Automatic Human Information Processing: Perceptual Learning, Automatic Attending, and a General Theory," by R. M. Shiffrin & W. Schneider, *Psychological Review, 84*, pp. 127–190. Copyright © 1977 with permission of the American Psychological Association.)

Participants reported that for the first 600 trials, they had to keep repeating the target items in the memory set in order to remember them. (Although targets were always numbers and distractors letters, the actual targets and distractors changed from trial to trial). However, participants reported that after about 600 trials, the task had become automatic: The frames appeared and participants responded without consciously thinking about it. They would do this even when as many as four targets had been presented.

What this means, according to Schneider and Shiffrin, is that practice made it possible for participants to divide their attention to deal with all of the target and test items simultaneously. Furthermore, the many trials of practice resulted in **automatic processing**, a type of processing that occurs (1) without intention (it automatically happens without the person intending to do it), and (2) at a cost of only some of a person's cognitive resources.

One of my students described a situation in which she used automatic processing during her summer job working as a mail sorter at the post office. She found the job to be boring but became so good at it that she could listen to audiobooks as she sorted the mail. She said she was able to do so "unconsciously, without thinking about it," which is one of the properties of automatic processing.

Another demonstration of automatic processing is the Stroop effect, which is illustrated in the following demonstration.

 **Demonstration**

Stroop Effect

Turn to ● Color Plate 4.1. Your task is to name, as quickly as possible, the color of ink used to print each of the circles. For example, starting in the upper left corner, and going across, you would say, "red, blue, . . ." and so on. Time yourself (or a friend, whom you have enlisted to do this task), and determine how many seconds it takes to report the colors of all of the circles. Then repeat the same task for ● Color Plate 4.2, remembering that your task is to specify the color of the *ink,* not the color name that is spelled out. ●

CogLab

Stroop Effect

If you found it harder to name the colors of the words than the colors of the circles, then you were experiencing the **Stroop effect**, which was first described by J. R. Stroop in 1935. This effect, in which the names of the words interfere with the ability to name the colors of the ink, is caused by people's inability to avoid paying attention to the meanings of the words, even though they are instructed to ignore them. Reading words is so highly practiced and has become so automatic that it is difficult *not* to read them. Note that although reading the words uses few cognitive resources, it does use enough resources to slow down the speed of saying the colors.

Automatic Processing Is Not Possible for Difficult Tasks

Let's now return to the laboratory and again consider Shiffrin and Schneider's participants, who after a great deal of practice were able to perform their task automatically with 90 percent accuracy. We can relate this result to my student's mail-sorting experience and also to the example from the beginning of the chapter, in which Sam was able to simultaneously drive, listen to his radio, and perhaps do other things as well. He was able to do this because he had so much practice driving that it had become automatic.

But what about the situation that occurred when the boy ran out in front of Sam's car? As soon as that happened, being on "automatic" no longer worked. Sam had to devote all of his attention to dealing with the emergency, and so was no longer able to divide his attention among a number of tasks. Schneider and Schiffrin considered how divided attention is affected when task difficulty is increased.

To make the task more difficult, Schneider and Shiffrin used only letters for both targets and distractors, and changed the targets and distractors on each trial so that a target on one trial could be a distractor on another trial. In this condition, which was called the *varied mapping condition,* the rules kept changing from trial to trial. For example, Figure 4.15 shows a situation in which the target on Trial 1 is a *P,* and one of the distractors is a *T.* But on Trial 2, the *T* has now become the target, and the *P* is a distractor.

The varied mapping condition was so difficult that the participants never achieved the automatic processing that they had achieved in the consistent mapping condition. Schneider and Shiffrin describe the processing used in the varied mapping condition as

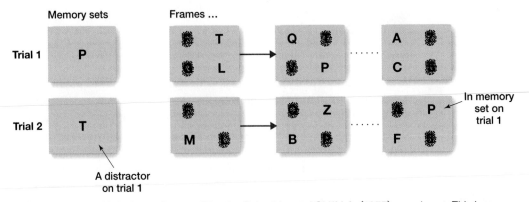

Figure 4.15 Varied mapping condition for Schneider and Shiffrin's (1977) experiment. This is more difficult than the consistent mapping condition because all the characters are letters and also because a character that was a distractor on one trial (like the *T*) can become a target on another trial, and a character that was in the memory set on one trial (like the *P*) can become a distractor on another trial.

controlled processing, because the participants had to pay close attention at all times and had to search for the target among the distractors in a much slower and more controlled way than in the consistent mapping condition.

Let's summarize the results of the experiments we have discussed in this section: Divided attention is possible if tasks are easy or well-practiced. Divided attention becomes difficult or impossible, however, when even one of the tasks is made too hard. For example, you may find it easy to talk and drive at the same time if traffic is light on a familiar road. But as traffic increases and then you see a flashing "Construction Ahead" sign, you might have to stop your conversation to devote all of your cognitive resources to driving.

Divided Attention in the Real World: Inattention and Driving

Driving is one of those tasks that demand constant attention. Not paying attention due to drowsiness or involvement in other tasks can have disastrous consequences. The seriousness of driver inattention has recently been verified by a research project called the "100-Car Naturalistic Driving Study" (National Highway Traffic Safety Administration, 2006). In this study, video recorders in 100 vehicles created records of both what the drivers were doing and the view out the front and rear windows.

The records obtained from these recordings documented 82 crashes and 771 near crashes in over 2 million miles of driving. For 80 percent of the crashes and 67 percent of the near crashes, the driver was inattentive in some way 3 seconds beforehand. One middle-aged man kept glancing down and to the right, apparently sorting through papers in a stop-and-go driving situation, until he slammed into an SUV. A woman eating a hamburger dropped her head below the dashboard just before she hit the car in front of her. One of the most distracting activities was pushing buttons on a cell phone or a similar device. Over 22 percent of near crashes involved that kind of distraction.

This naturalistic research confirms earlier findings, which demonstrated a connection between cell phone use and traffic accidents. A survey of accidents and cell phone use in Toronto showed that the risk of a collision when using a cell phone was four times higher than when a cell phone was not being used (Redelmeier & Tibshirani, 1997). Perhaps the most significant result of the Toronto study is that hands-free cell phone units offered no safety advantage.

In a laboratory experiment on the effects of cell phones, David Strayer and William Johnston (2001) placed participants in a simulated driving task that required them to apply the brakes as quickly as possible in response to a red light (Figure 4.16a). Doing this task while talking on a cell phone caused the participants to miss twice as many of the red lights compared to when they weren't talking on the phone, and increased the time it took to apply the brakes (Figure 4.16b). In agreement with the results of the Toronto study, the same decrease in performance occurred regardless of whether participants used a "hands-free" cell phone device or a handheld model. Strayer and Johnston concluded from this result that the cognitive task of talking on the phone uses resources that would otherwise be used for driving the car (also see Haigney & Westerman, 2001; Lamble et al., 1999; Spence & Read, 2003; Violanti, 1998).

The main message here is that distracting attention can degrade performance. And cell phones aren't the only attention-grabbing device found in cars. An article in the *New York Times* titled "Hi, I'm Your Car. Don't Let Me Distract You," notes that many new cars have distraction-producing devices such as GPS navigation systems and menu screens for high-tech computer controls (Peters, 2004). Because these devices require attention and time (an average of 5.4 seconds to read and process electronic maps, for example), these distractions could, like cell phone use, also be contributing to unsafe driving by using cognitive resources that might be needed in high-load driving situations.

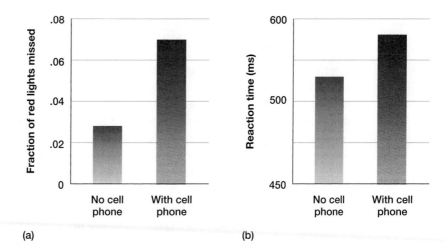

(a)　　　　　　　　(b)

■ **Figure 4.16** Result of Strayer and Johnston's (2001) cell phone experiment. When the person was talking on a cell phone, they (a) missed more red lights, and (b) took longer to apply the brakes.

▶▶▶ Attention and Visual Processing

Much of the early research on attention was done using auditory stimuli, as in the shadowing tasks we described at the beginning of the chapter. But more and more research has used visual displays. For example, in the change-blindness experiments we described at the end of Chapter 3, the participants observed two slightly different pictures that were flashed one after another (p. 92). The key finding of these studies was that participants initially found it difficult to detect the differences between the pictures. However, when their attention was directed to the area of the picture that was different, they detected the difference immediately.

In this chapter, we have described a number experiments that used visual stimuli—including the flanker-compatibility experiments, which illustrated the role of load in visual processing (p. 111), and Schneider and Shiffrin's experiments in which they investigated the conditions that resulted in automatic or controlled processing (p. 115). In this section, we will look more closely at how we direct our attention to things in the visual environment.

Directing Visual Attention With the Eyes

One of the most consistent activities we engage in is moving our eyes to perceive the environment. We look at a scene by carrying out **saccades**—rapid movements of the eyes from one place to another—and **fixations**—short pauses on points of interest. When freely viewing a scene, we make an average of three fixations per second. Psychologists measure and study these eye movements using a device called an **eye tracker**.

◆▷ Method

Measuring Eye Movements

Early researchers measured eye movements by attaching small mirrors and lenses to the eyes, which meant that the cornea had to be anesthetized (Yarbus, 1967). However, modern researchers use camera-based eye trackers like the one in Figure 4.17. These units create a record of the position of the eyes superimposed on a picture of the stimulus or scene that the person is observing (Henderson, 2003; Morimoto & Mimica, 2005). ● Color Plate 4.3 shows an eye movement record for a person looking at a picture of a fountain. The saccades are indicated by lines and the fixations by dots. ◆

What determines where we fixate in a scene? The answer to this question is complicated because our looking behavior depends on a number of factors, including characteristics of the scene and the knowledge and goals of the observer. In ● Color Plate 4.4a, certain areas stand out because they are brightly colored, have high contrast, or have highly visible orientations. These areas are described as having high **stimulus salience**—they are conspicuous and therefore attract attention based on their stimulus properties.

■ **Figure 4.17** A person looking at a stimulus picture in a camera-based eye tracker. (Reprinted from "Human Gaze Control During Real-World Scene Perception," by J. M. Henderson, *Trends in Cognitive Sciences, 7,* pp. 498–503. Copyright 2003. With permission from Elsevier.)

Capturing attention by stimulus salience is a bottom-up process—it depends solely on the pattern of stimulation falling on the receptors, as opposed to the meaningfulness of the images. By taking into account the color, contrast, and orientations in the display in ● Color Plate 4.4a, Derrick Parkhurst and coworkers (2002) created the **saliency map** in ● Color Plate 4.4b. To determine whether observers' fixations were controlled by the stimulus saliency indicated by the map, Parkhurst measured where people fixated when presented with various pictures. He found that the initial fixations were closely associated with the saliency map, with fixations being more likely on high-saliency areas.

But where we look is not determined solely by the bottom-up processes triggered by stimulus salience. Parkhurst found that as people continued to view the pictures, other factors, such as the meanings of the objects in the pictures, apparently begin influencing scanning, especially for meaningful pictures such as the ones in ● Color Plates 4.3 and 4.4a. Influences such as this, which depend on the observer's knowledge and interests, involve top-down processing.

If a scene is familiar, eye movements may be influenced by a perceiver's **scene schema**—knowledge about what is contained in typical scenes. An example of a scene schema is an "office schema," which includes the knowledge that a computer and telephone will probably be on a desk, books will be in a bookcase, and there may be some file cabinets along the wall. This knowledge can help guide fixations from one area of a scene to another. In addition, particularly meaningful stimuli, such as human faces, often receive many fixations.

Attention occurs not only as we view static scenes, but as we carry out actions. The development of lightweight head-mounted eye trackers make it possible to track a person's eye movements as they perform tasks in the environment. This research shows that when a person is carrying out a task, the demands of the task override factors such

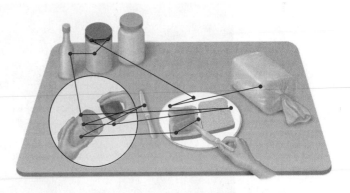

■ **Figure 4.18** Sequence of fixations of a person making a peanut butter sandwich. The first fixation is on the loaf of bread. (From Land & Hayhoe, 2001.)

as stimulus saliency. Figure 4.18 shows the fixations and eye movements that occurred as a person was making a peanut butter sandwich. The process of making the sandwich begins with the movement of a slice of bread from the bag to the plate. Notice that this operation is accompanied by an eye movement, from the bread to the plate. The peanut butter jar is then fixated on, lifted, and moved to the front as its lid is removed. The knife is then fixated on, picked up, and used to scoop the peanut butter, which is then spread on the bread (Land & Hayhoe, 2001).

The key finding of these measurements, and also of another experiment in which eye movements were measured as a person prepared tea (Land et al., 1999), was that the person's eye movements were determined primarily by the task. Few objects or areas that were irrelevant to the task were fixated. Furthermore, the eye movement usually preceded a motor action by a fraction of a second. For example, the person first fixated the peanut butter jar and then reached over to pick it up.

Because a number of factors are involved in determining where a person looks, it isn't surprising that there is a good deal of individual variation in the way pictures are scanned. Although it is often possible to predict *where* in a particular picture people will fixate, it is more difficult to predict the *order* in which things will be fixated because of this variability from person to person.

Directing Visual Attention Without Eye Movements

It has been said that eye movements are windows into the mind, because where people look reveals what environmental information they are attending to. However, there is more to attention than just moving the eyes to look at objects. We can pay attention to things that are not directly in our line of vision, as evidenced by the basketball player who dribbles down court while paying attention to a teammate off to the side, just before she throws a dead-on pass without looking. We can also look directly at something without paying attention to it. You may have had this experience if you have been reading a book and then suddenly become aware that although you were moving your eyes across the page and "reading" the words, you had no idea what you had just read. Even

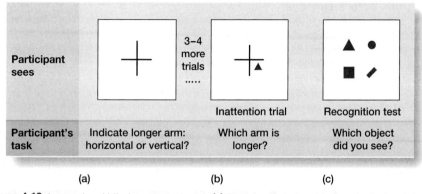

Participant sees		3-4 more trials			
			Inattention trial		Recognition test
Participant's task	Indicate longer arm: horizontal or vertical?		Which arm is longer?		Which object did you see?
	(a)		(b)		(c)

■ **Figure 4.19** Inattentional blindness experiment. (a) Participants judge whether the horizontal or vertical arm is longer on each trial. (b) After a few trials, the inattention trial occurs, in which a geometrical object is flashed, along with the arms. (c) In the recognition test, the participant is asked to indicate which geometrical object was presented.

though you were *looking* at the words, you apparently were not *paying attention*. There is a mental aspect of attention that involves processing that can occur independently of eye movements.

Looking right at something without paying attention, as happens when you are scanning a sentence with your eyes while thinking about something else, results in **inattentional blindness**. A stimulus that is not attended is not perceived, even though a person might be looking directly at it. Arien Mack and Irvin Rock (1998) demonstrated this effect using the procedure shown in Figure 4.19. The observer's task was to indicate which arm of the cross was longer, the horizontal or the vertical. Then, on the inattention trial of the series, a small test object, which was within the observer's field of clear vision, is added to the display. When observers were then given a recognition test in which they are asked to pick the object that was presented, they were unable to do so. Paying attention to the vertical and horizontal arms apparently made observers "blind" to the unattended test object.

Just as we can look right at something without paying attention to it, we can also look at something while directing our attention off to the side. The effect of directing attention to a location without moving the eyes has been studied using a procedure called precueing, in which the participant is presented with a "cue" that indicates where a stimulus is most likely to appear.

◧ **Method**

Precueing

Figure 4.20 shows the stimuli used in a **precueing** experiment done by Michael Posner and coworkers (1980). Participants looked at a small square that was flanked by two lights on each side. Initially none of the lights were turned on, but at the beginning of a trial, the participants saw a cue signal inside the square that indicated which light was going to be

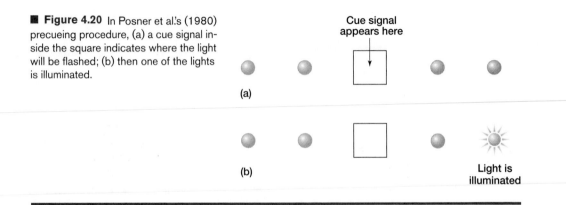

Figure 4.20 In Posner et al.'s (1980) precueing procedure, (a) a cue signal inside the square indicates where the light will be flashed; (b) then one of the lights is illuminated.

turned on (Figure 4.20a). One second later, one of the lights was illuminated (usually the one that was indicated by the cueing signal, but occasionally a light at another position was illuminated). The participants' task was to push a button as rapidly as possible when they saw the light—either in its "predicted" position, or in another position (Figure 4.20b). ◆

The result of Posner and coworkers' (1980) experiment was that participants responded faster when the light appeared at the location indicated by the cueing signal than when it appeared at different locations, even though they had always kept their eyes fixed steadily on the small box. This shows that paying attention off to the side can affect information processing at the place where attention is directed.

This effect of directing attention to the side has been studied physiologically by Carol Colby and coworkers (1995). They trained a monkey to keep its eyes fixated on a dot marked *Fix* (see Figure 4.21) while a peripheral light was flashed at a location off to the right. In the "fixation only" condition (Figure 4.21a), the monkey's task was to continue looking at the fixation light and to release its hand from a bar when the *fixation* light dimmed. In the "fixation and attention" condition (Figure 4.21b), the monkey also kept looking at the fixation light but released the bar when the *peripheral* light dimmed. Thus, in the fixation and attention condition, the monkey had to pay attention to what was happening off to the side.

As the monkey was performing these tasks, Colby recorded from a neuron in the parietal cortex that fired to the peripheral light. The records in Figure 4.21 show that this neuron responded poorly when the monkey was not paying attention to the light but that the response increased when the monkey shifted its attention to the light—even though it was always looking directly at the fixation point. This means that the image of the light and fixation point on the monkey's retina was always the same. Thus, the greater response when the monkey was paying attention to the peripheral light must have been caused not by any change of the stimulus on the monkey's retina, but by the monkey's attention to the light. What do you think this result says about the role of top-down processing in attention?

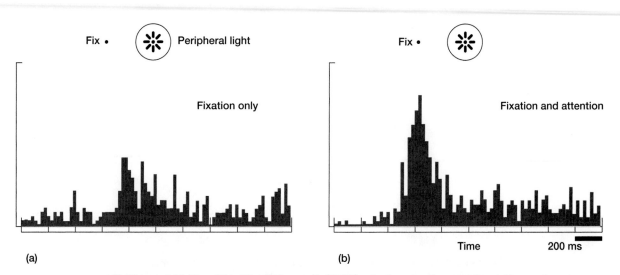

Figure 4.21 Top: Stimuli for Colby et al.'s (1995) selective-attention experiment. The monkey always looked at the dot marked *Fix*. A light was flashed off to the side, inside the circle. Bottom: (a) Nerve firing when the monkey was not paying attention to the light; (b) firing when the monkey was paying attention. (Reprinted from "Oculocentric Spatial Representation in Parietal Cortex," by C. L. Colby et al., *Cerebral Cortex, 5,* pp. 470–481. Copyright © 1995, with permission from Oxford University Press.)

Object-Based Visual Attention

Attention, as studied using the precueing procedure, considers how people move their attention from one place to another. This is called **location-based attention**. But other experiments have shown that attention can also be associated with specific objects, a situation called **object-based attention**. Experiments studying object-based attention have shown that when attention is directed to one *place* on an object, the enhancing effect of this attention spreads throughout the object.

Consider, for example, the experiment diagrammed in Figure 4.22 (Egly et al., 1994). The participant first saw two side-by-side rectangles, followed by a cue signal that indicated where the target would probably appear (Figure 4.22a). After the cue, the participant pressed a button when the target appeared anywhere in the display (Figure 4.22b). Reaction time was fastest when the target appeared at A, where the cue signal predicted it would appear. However, the most important result of this experiment is that participants responded faster when the target appeared at B than when it appeared at C. Note that B is in the same rectangle as A, and C is in the neighboring rectangle, but that B and C are the same distance from A. Apparently, the enhancing effect of attention had spread within the rectangle on the right, so even though the cue was at A, some enhancement occurred at B, as well.

The same result occurs even when the rectangles are occluded by a horizontal bar, as shown in Figure 4.23a (Moore et al., 1998). The fact that attention can affect the

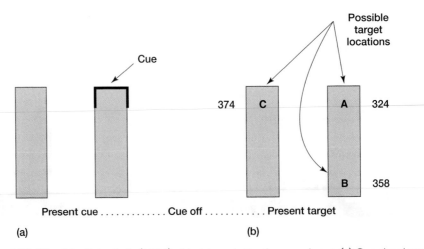

Cue

Possible target locations

374   C   A   324

B   358

Present cue . . . . Cue off . . . . Present target

(a)   (b)

■ **Figure 4.22** Stimuli for Egly et al.'s (1994) object-based attention experiment. (a) Cue signal appears at the top or bottom of one of the rectangles to indicate where the target will probably appear; (b) target appears at one of the ends of the rectangle. Numbers indicate reaction times in microseconds for when the cue appeared at the top of the right rectangle.

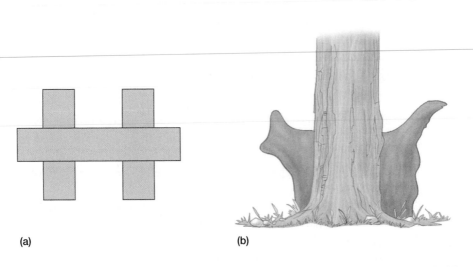

(a)   (b)

■ **Figure 4.23** (a) Stimuli in Figure 4.22 but with a horizontal bar added (Moore et al., 1998). (b) The "creature" lurking behind the tree from Chapter 3 (Figure 3.32a).

whole object, even when it is occluded by other objects, is important because occlusion such as this occurs in the real world all the time. For example, remember our "creature" lurking behind the tree, shown again in Figure 4.23b. Because attention spreads behind the tree, our awareness spreads throughout the object, thereby enhancing the chances we will recognize the interrupted shape as an animal. (Also see Baylis & Driver, 1993;

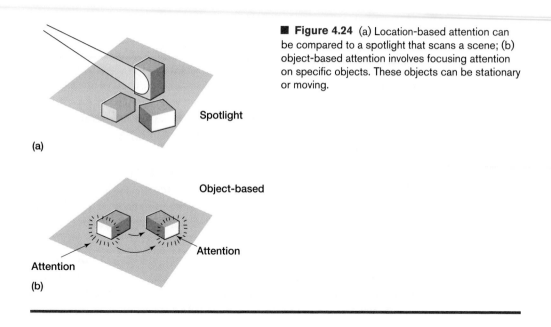

Figure 4.24 (a) Location-based attention can be compared to a spotlight that scans a scene; (b) object-based attention involves focusing attention on specific objects. These objects can be stationary or moving.

Driver & Baylis, 1989, 1998; and Lavie & Driver, 1996, for more demonstrations of how attention spreads throughout objects.)

We have seen that attention can be based both on where a person is looking in the *environment* (that is, it can be location-based) and on where a person is looking on a *specific object* (object-based). We can think of these two modes of visual attention as involving two different mechanisms that operate under different conditions. For static scenes or scenes that contain few objects, location-based visual attention can be likened to a spotlight that scans different locations (Figure 4.24a). For dynamic environments, object-based visual attention can involve a mechanism that locks onto objects and follows them as they move (Figure 4.24b; Behrmann & Tipper, 1999; Luck & Vecera, 2002). Recent physiological evidence has shown that location-based and object-based attention activate different areas of the brain (Shomstein & Behrmann, 2006).

Something to Consider

Attention in Social Situations—The Case of Autism

Attention is a crucial component of social situations. We pay attention not only to what others are saying, but also to facial expressions and body language that provide information about the person's thoughts, emotions, and feelings. The link between attention and social interactions becomes especially evident when we consider a situation in which that link is disturbed, as occurs in people with **autism**. Autism is a serious developmental disorder in which one of the major symptoms is the withdrawal of contact from other people. People with autism typically do not make eye contact with others and have difficulty telling what emotions others are experiencing in social situations.

Research has revealed many differences in both behavior and brain processes between autistic and nonautistic people (Grelotti et al., 2002). Ami Klin and coworkers (2003) point out the following paradox: Even though people with autism can often solve reasoning problems that involve social situations, they cannot function when placed in an actual social situation. One possible reason for this is differences in the way autistic people observe what is happening. This was demonstrated by Klin and coworkers (2003), by comparing eye fixations of autistic and nonautistic people as they watched the film *Who's Afraid of Virginia Woolf?*

Figure 4.25 shows fixations on a shot of George Segal's and Sandy Dennis's faces. The shot occurred just after another character in the film, played by Richard Burton, has smashed a bottle. The nonautistic observers fixated on Segal's eyes in order to access his emotional reaction, but the autistic observers looked near Sandy Dennis's mouth or off to the side.

Another difference between how autistic and nonautistic observers direct their attention is related to the tendency to direct their eyes to the place where a person is pointing. Figure 4.26 compares the fixations of a nonautistic person (shown in white) and an autistic person (shown in black). In this scene, Segal points to the painting and

■ **Figure 4.25** Where people look when viewing this image from the film *Who's Afraid of Virginia Woolf?* Nonautistic viewers: white crosses; autistic viewers: black crosses. (From "The Enactive Mind, or From Actions to Cognition: Lessons From Autism," by A. Klin, W. Jones, R. Schultz, & F. Volkmar, *Philosophical Transactions of the Royal Society of London B*, pp. 345–360. Copyright 2003 The Royal Society. Published online.)

Viewer with Autism

Typically Developing Viewer

■ **Figure 4.26** Scan paths for nonautistic viewers (white path) and autistic viewers (black path) in response to the picture and dialogue while viewing this shot from *Who's Afraid of Virginia Woolf?* (From "The Enactive Mind, or From Actions to Cognition: Lessons From Autism," by A. Klin, W. Jones, R. Schultz, & F. Volkmar, *Philosophical Transactions of the Royal Society of London B*, pp. 345–360. Copyright 2003 The Royal Society. Published online.)

asks Burton's character, "Who did the painting?" The nonautistic person follows the pointing movement from Segal's finger to the painting to Burton's face to await a reply. In contrast, the autistic observer looks elsewhere first, then back and forth between the pictures.

All of these results indicate that because of the way autistic people attend or don't attend to events as they unfold in a social situation, they see different things in the environment than nonautistic observers. Autistic people look more at things, whereas nonautistic observers look at other people's actions and especially at their faces and eyes. Autistic observers therefore create a mental representation of a situation that does not include much of the information that nonautistic observers usually use in interacting with others.

However, the eye movement patterns we have described are probably not the *cause* of autistic people's difficulties in social situations. Their difficulties may have more to do with negative emotional reactions they experience when looking at or interacting with other people. These negative emotions influence where they look, which influences how well they can understand what is happening, which, in turn, makes it even more difficult to function in social situations.

Test Yourself 4.2

1. How did the results of Spelke's experiment and Schneider and Shiffrin's experiment provide support for the idea that divided attention is possible, and that it can be accomplished through automatic processing? What is the Stroop effect, and how does it demonstrate automatic processing?

2. What changes did Schneider and Shiffrin make in their experiment that decreased their participants' ability to divide their attention so that controlled processing occurred rather than automatic processing?

3. What is the evidence linking inattention and traffic accidents? How has cell phone use while driving been related to increased accidents and decreased performance on driving-related tasks?

4. How do eye movements direct attention in a visual scene? How are eye movements influenced by bottom-up and top-down processing?

5. Describe the idea that there is more to attention than directing the eyes toward objects.

6. How has physiological research shown that focusing attention off to the side can affect neural firing to that stimulus?

7. What is the evidence for object-based attention? When would location-based attention be most important? When would object-based attention be more important?

8. Compare how autistic and nonautistic people attend to visual stimuli in social situations.

Chapter Summary

1. Selective attention, the ability to focus on one message while ignoring all others, has been demonstrated using the dichotic listening procedure.

2. A number of models have been proposed to explain the process of selective attention. Broadbent's filter model proposes that the attended message is separated from the incoming signal early in the analysis of the signal. Treisman's model proposes later separation and adds a dictionary unit to explain how the unattended message can sometimes get through. Late selection models propose that selection doesn't occur until messages are processed enough to determine their meaning.

3. The ability to selectively attend is affected by task load. Flanker-compatibility experiments have shown that when attentional tasks involve low load, some cognitive capacity remains, so some processing of unattended signals can occur. When attentional tasks involve high load, processing of unattended material is prevented. Lavie suggests that the results of experiments supporting early and late selection can be explained in terms of the effect of task load.

4. Results of experiments using the flanker-compatibility task show that video-game players are not as affected by high task load as nonplayers.

5. Divided attention is possible for easy tasks, or for highly practiced difficult tasks. In these situations, automatic processing is possible. Divided attention is not, however, possible for highly demanding tasks, which require controlled processing.

6. Driver inattention is one of the major causes of automobile accidents. There is evidence that using cell phones during driving is associated with increases in traffic accidents and decreases in performance of driving-related tasks.

7. Eye movements are a basic mechanism for determining attention to different parts of a visual scene. Both bottom-up processes, like stimulus salience, and top-down processes, such as scene schemas, influence how eye movements are directed to parts of a scene.

8. Visual attention can be directed to different places in a scene even without eye movements. This has been demonstrated by precueing experiments, which have shown that paying attention to a location enhances processing at that location. This is called location-based attention.

9. Object-based attention occurs when attention is directed toward specific objects. The enhancing effects of attention spread throughout an object.

10. People with autism do not direct their attention in social situations in the same way as nonautistic observers. Autistic people attend to things, where nonautistic people attend more to other people.

Think About It

1. Pick two items from the following list, and decide how difficult it would be to do both at the same time. Some things are difficult to do simultaneously because of physical limitations. For example, it is not possible (or at least extremely dangerous) to type on your computer and drive at the same time. Others things are difficult to do simultaneously because of cognitive limitations. For each pair of activities that you pick, decide why it would be easy or difficult to do them simultaneously. Be sure to take the idea of cognitive load into account.

Driving a car	Talking on a cell phone
Reading a book for pleasure	Flying a kite
Doing math problems	Walking in the woods
Talking to a friend	Listening to a story
Thinking about tomorrow	Writing a paper for class
Rock climbing	Dancing

2. Find someone who is willing to participate in a brief "observation exercise." Cover a picture (preferably one that contains a number of objects or details) with a piece of paper, and tell the person that you are going to uncover the picture and that their task is to report everything that they see. Then uncover the picture very briefly (less than a second), and have the person write down, or tell you, what they saw.

Then repeat this procedure, increasing the exposure of the picture to a few seconds, so the person can direct his or her attention to different parts of the picture. Perhaps try this a third time, allowing even more time to observe the picture. From the person's responses, what can you conclude about the role of attention in determining what people are aware of in their environment?

3. Art composition books often state that it is possible to arrange elements in a painting in a way that controls both *what* a person looks at in a picture and the *order* in which a person looks at things. What would the results of research on visual attention have to say about this idea?

4. How does the attention involved in carrying out actions in the environment differ from the attention involved in scanning a picture for details, as in the previous "observation exercise"?

5. As you sit in a stadium watching a football game, there is a lot going on in the game, in the stands, and on the sidelines. Which things that you might look at would involve object-based attention, and which would involve location-based attention?

6. As the quarterback steps back to pass, the offensive line blocks out the defense, so the quarterback has plenty of time to check out what is happening downfield and hits an open receiver. Later in the game, two 300-pound linemen get through to the quarterback. While he scrambles for safety, he fails to see the open receiver downfield and instead throws a pass toward another receiver that is almost intercepted. How can these two situations be related to the way selective attention is affected by task load?

7. It has been argued that talking on a cell phone while driving is really not that different from listening to the radio or talking to a passenger in the car. What arguments can you think of that (a) support this idea, and (b) argue against it?

If You Want to Know More

1. Losing a sense. Loss of one sense can cause changes both in a person's ability to perceive with the other senses, and in the physiological mechanisms of the remaining senses.

Proksch, J. & Bavelier, D. (2002). Changes in the spatial distribution of visual attention after early deafness. *Journal of Cognitive Neuroscience, 14,* 687–701.

2. Attention and load. Perceptual load plays an important role in our ability to attend to more than one thing at a time as well as our ability to focus our attention on just one thing at a time.

Lavie, N. (2005). Distracted and confused? Selective attention under load. *Trends in Cognitive Sciences, 2,* 75–82.

3. Video games. It has been shown that practice with video games can improve a person's ability to process visual information. The study described in the chapter has been followed by further research.

Green, C. S. & Bavelier, D. (2006). Effect of action video games on the spatial distribution of visuo-spatial attention. *Journal of Experimental Psychology: Human Perception & Performance, 32,* 1465–1478.

4. Eye movements. The role of eye movements in determining attention is often studied by measuring the sequence of fixations that a person makes when freely viewing a picture. However, another important variable is how long a person looks at particular areas of a picture. Factors that determine the length of fixation may not be the same as factors that determine the sequence of fixations.

Henderson, J. M. (2003). Human gaze control during real-world scene perception. *Trends in Cognitive Sciences, 7,* 498–503.

5. Visual neglect. An effect of brain damage called visual neglect causes a person to pay attention to only half of their visual field.

Behrmann, M., & Tipper, S. P. (1999). Attention accesses multiple reference frames: Evidence from visual neglect. *Journal of Experimental Psychology: Human Perception and Performance, 25,* 83–101.

Halligan, P. W., Fink, G. R., Marshall, J. C., & Vallar, G. (2003). Spatial cognition: Evidence from visual neglect. *Trends in Cognitive Sciences, 7,* 125–133.

Tipper, S. P., & Behrmann, M. (1996). Object-centered not scene-based visual neglect. *Journal of Experimental Psychology: Human Perception and Performance, 22,* 1261–1278.

Key Terms

Attention, 100

Attenuation theory of attention, 106

Attenuator, 106

Autism, 127

Automatic processing, 116

Cocktail party phenomenon, 103

Controlled processing, 118

Dichotic listening, 102

Dictionary unit, 108

Divided attention, 114

Early-selection model, 104

Eye tracker, 120

Filter model of attention, 103

Fixation, 120

Flanker-compatibility task, 111

High-load task, 110

Inattentional blindness, 123

Late-selection model, 109

Location-based attention, 125

Low-load task, 110

Object-based attention, 125

Precueing, 123

Saccades, 120

Saliency map, 121

Scene schema, 121

Selective attention, 101

Shadowing, 102

Stimulus salience, 120

Stroop effect, 117

Task load, 110

CogLab

To experience these experiments for yourself, go to http://coglab.wadsworth.com. Be sure to read each experiment's setup instructions before you go to the experiment itself. Otherwise, you won't know which keys to press.

Primary Labs

Stroop effect How reaction time to naming font colors is affected by the presence of conflicting information from words (p. 117).

Spatial cueing How cueing attention affects reaction time to the cued area. Evidence for the spotlight model of attention (p. 125).

Related Labs

Attentional blink How paying attention to one stimulus affects the ability to attend to a subsequent stimulus.

Change detection A task involving detecting changes in alternating scenes (described in Chapter 3, p. 94)

Simon effect How speed and accuracy of responding is affected by the location of the response to a stimulus.

Von Restorff effect How the distinctiveness of a stimulus can influence memory.

Short-Term and Working Memory

5

What Is Memory?
  The Purposes of Memory
  The Modal Model of Memory

Sensory Memory
  The Sparkler's Trail and the Projector's Shutter
  Sperling's Experiment: Measuring the Visual Icon

Short-Term Memory
  What Is the Duration of Short-Term Memory?
  ☛ Demonstration: Remembering Three Letters
  What Is the Capacity of Short-Term Memory?
  ☛ Demonstration: Digit Span
  How Is Information Coded in Short-Term Memory?

Test Yourself 5.1

Working Memory: The Modern Approach
to Short-Term Memory
  ☛ Demonstration: Reading Text and Remembering Numbers
  The Phonological Loop
  ☛ Demonstration: Phonological Similarity Effect
  ☛ Demonstration: Word-Length Effect
  ☛ Demonstration: Articulatory Suppression
  The Visuospatial Sketch Pad
  ☛ Demonstration: Holding a Verbal Stimulus in the Mind
  ☛ Demonstration: Holding a Spatial Stimulus in the Mind
  The Central Executive
  Update on the Working Memory Model: Addition
    of the Episodic Buffer

Working Memory and the Brain
  The Delayed-Response Task in Monkeys
  Neurons That Hold Information
  Brain Imaging in Humans

Something to Consider: Working Memory
in American Sign Language

Test Yourself 5.2

Chapter Summary

Think About It

If You Want to Know More

Key Terms

CogLab: Partial Report; Brown-Peterson; Memory
Span; Phonological Similarity Effect; Apparent
Movement; Irrelevant Speech Effect; Modality Effect;
Operation Span; Position Error; Sternberg Search

Some Questions We Will Consider

- Why can we remember a telephone number long enough to place a call, but then we forget it almost immediately? (139)

- Is there a way to increase the ability to remember things that have just happened? (149)

- Do we use the same memory system to remember things we have seen and things we have heard? (155)

Everything in life is memory, save for the thin edge of the present.
—Gazzaniga (2000)

The thin edge of the present is what is happening right at this moment, but a moment from now the present will become the past, and some of the past will become stored in memory. What you will read in this chapter and the two that follow supports the idea that "everything in life is memory" and shows how our memory of the past not only provides a record of a lifetime of events we have experienced and knowledge we have learned, but can also affect our experience of what is happening right at this moment.

What Is Memory?

The definition of memory provides the first indication of its importance in our lives: **Memory** is the processes involved in retaining, retrieving, and using information about stimuli, images, events, ideas, and skills after the original information is no longer present.

The Purposes of Memory

The fact that memory retains information that is no longer present means that we can use our memory as a "time machine" to go back just a moment—to the words you read at the beginning of this sentence—or many years—to events as early as a childhood birthday party. This "mental time travel" afforded by memory can place you back in a situation, so you feel as though you are reliving it, even to the extent of experiencing feelings that were occurring long ago. But memory goes beyond reexperiencing events. We also use memory to remember what we need to do later in the day, to remember facts we have learned, and to use skills we have acquired.

If you were asked to create a "Top 10" list of what you use memory for, what would you include? When I ask my students to do this, most of their items relate to day-to-day activities. The top five items on their list involved remembering the following things.

1. Material for exams
2. Their daily schedule
3. Names
4. Phone numbers
5. Directions to places

Remembering material for exams is probably high on most students' lists, but it is likely that people from different walks of life, such as business executives, construction workers, homemakers, or politicians, would create lists that differ from the ones created by college students in ways that reflect the demands of their particular lives. Remembering the material that will be on the next cognitive psychology exam would be an unlikely entry on a construction worker's list, but remembering the procedure for framing a house might be on that list.

One reason I ask students to create a "memory list" is to get them to think about how important memory is in their day-to-day lives. But the main reason is to make them aware of how they *don't* include many important functions on their lists, because they take them for granted. A few of these things include labeling familiar objects (you know you are reading a "book" because of your past experience with books), having conversations (you need memory to keep track of the flow of a conversation), knowing what to do in a restaurant (you need to remember a sequence of events, starting with being seated and ending with paying the check), and finding your way to class.

The list of things that depend on memory is an extremely long one because just about everything we do depends on remembering what we have experienced in the past. But perhaps the most powerful way to demonstrate the importance of memory is to consider what happens to people's lives when they lose their memory. Consider, for example, the case of Clive Wearing (Annenberg, 2000; D. Wearing, 2005).

Wearing was a highly respected musician and choral director in England who, in his 40s, contracted viral encephalitis, which destroyed parts of his temporal lobe that are important for forming new memories. Because of his brain damage, Wearing lives totally within the most recent one or two minutes of his life. He remembers what just happened and forgets everything else. When he meets someone, and the person leaves the room and returns three minutes later, Wearing reacts as if he hadn't met the person earlier. Because of his inability to form new memories, he constantly feels he has just become conscious for the first time.

This feeling is made poignantly clear by Wearing's diary, which contains hundreds of entries like "I have woken up for the first time" and "I am alive" (Figure 5.1). But Wearing has no memory of ever writing anything except for the sentence he has just written. When questioned about previous entries, Wearing acknowledges that they are in his handwriting, but because he has no memory for writing them, he denies that they are his. It is no wonder that he is confused, and not surprising that he describes his life as being "like death." His loss of memory has robbed him of his ability to participate in life in any meaningful way, and he needs to be constantly cared for by others.

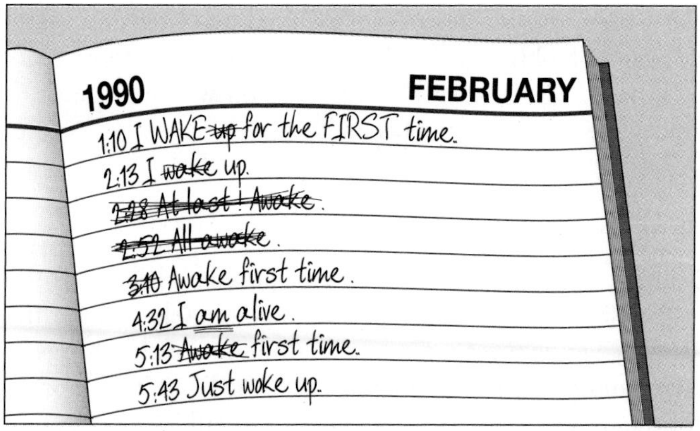

Figure 5.1 Clive Wearing's diary looked like this. Sometimes he would cross out previous entries because he could only remember writing the most recent entry.

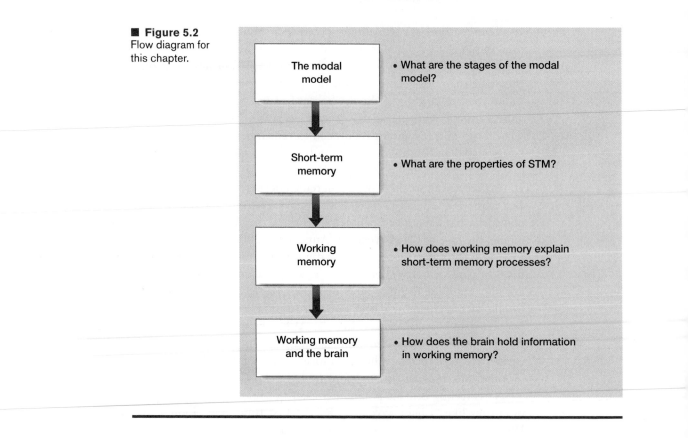

■ **Figure 5.2**
Flow diagram for this chapter.

In this chapter we will begin describing the basic principles of memory so we can understand both cases like Clive Wearing's and also the basic principles behind normal memory processes (Figure 5.2). We begin by describing a model of memory we introduced in Chapter 1 called the modal model (see p. 20). After describing the modal model, we will focus on the short-term components of the model, first looking at properties of sensory memory and short-term memory and then at research that has led to a more modern way of looking at the short-term stage of memory, which is called working memory. Finally, we will describe research on where some of the mechanisms of working memory are located in the brain.

The Modal Model of Memory

The **modal model of memory**, which was proposed by Richard Atkinson and Richard Shiffrin (1968), is shown in Figure 5.3. As we noted in Chapter 1, this model, which was proposed 40 years ago, is too simple to explain many of the things that have been discovered about memory since the model was proposed, but it does provide a way to introduce many of the basic principles of memory. We will, therefore, use the modal model as our starting point, and will update the model later in this and subsequent chapters.

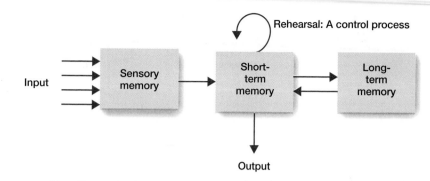

■ **Figure 5.3** Flow diagram for Atkinson and Shiffrin's (1968) model of memory. This model, which is described in the text, is called the modal model because of the huge influence it has had on memory research.

The stages of the modal model are called the **structural features** of the model. There are three major structural features:

1. **Sensory memory** is an initial stage that holds all incoming information for seconds or fractions of a second.
2. **Short-term memory (STM)** holds 5–7 items for about 15–30 seconds. We will be describing the characteristics of short-term memory in this chapter.
3. **Long-term memory (LTM)** can hold a large amount of information for years or even decades. We will describe long-term memory in Chapters 6 and 7.

Atkinson and Shiffrin also describe the memory system as including **control processes,** which are active processes that can be controlled by the person and may differ from one task to another. An example of a control process is **rehearsal**—repeating a stimulus over and over, as you might repeat a telephone number in order to hold it in your mind after looking it up in the phone book. Other examples of control processes are (1) strategies you might use to help make a stimulus more memorable, such as relating the numbers in a phone number to a familiar date in history, and (2) strategies of attention that help you selectively focus on other information you want to remember.

To illustrate how the structural features and control processes operate, let's consider what happens as Rachel looks up the number for Mineo's Pizza in the phone book (Figure 5.4). When she first looks at the book, all of the information that enters her eyes is registered in sensory memory (Figure 5.4a). But Rachel focuses on the number for Mineo's using the control process of selective attention, so the number enters STM (Figure 5.4b), and Rachel uses the control process of rehearsal to keep it there (Figure 5.4c).

After Rachel has dialed the phone number, she may forget it because it has not been transferred into long-term memory. However, she decides to memorize the number so next time she won't have to look it up in the phone book. The process she uses to memorize the number, a control process we will discuss in Chapter 6, transfers the number

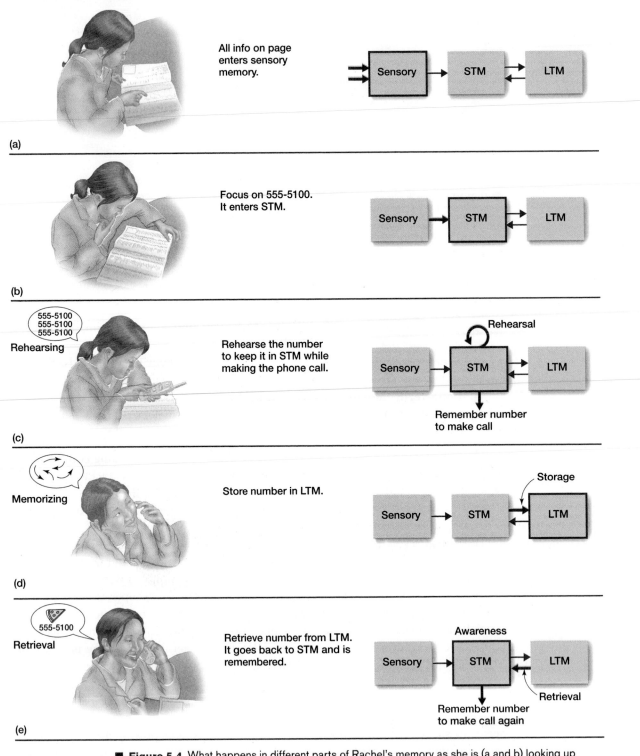

Figure 5.4 What happens in different parts of Rachel's memory as she is (a and b) looking up the phone number, (c) calling the pizza shop, and (d) memorizing the number. A few days later, (e) she retrieves the number from long-term memory to order pizza again. Darkened parts of the modal model indicate which processes are activated for each action that Rachel takes.

into long-term memory, where it is stored (Figure 5.4d). A few days later, when Rachel's urge for pizza returns, she remembers the number. This process of remembering information that is stored in long-term memory is called retrieval because the information must be retrieved from LTM so it can reenter STM to be used (Figure 5.4e).

One thing that becomes apparent from our example is that the components of memory do not act in isolation. Long-term memory is essential for storing information, but before we can become aware of this stored information, it must be moved back into STM. We will now consider each component of the model, beginning with sensory memory.

Sensory Memory

Sensory memory is the retention, for brief periods of time, of the effects of sensory stimulation. We can demonstrate this brief retention for the effects of visual stimulation with two familiar examples: the trail left by a moving sparkler and the experience of seeing a film.

The Sparkler's Trail and the Projector's Shutter

It is dark, sometime around the Fourth of July, and you place a match to the tip of a sparkler. As sparks begin radiating from the hot spot at the tip, you sweep the sparkler through the air, and create a trail of light (Figure 5.5). Although it appears that this trail is created by light left by the sparkler as you wave it through the air, there is, in fact, no light along this trail. The lighted trail is a creation of your mind, which retains a

■ **Figure 5.5** (a) A sparkler can cause a trail of light when it is moved rapidly. (b) This trail occurs because the perception of the light is briefly held in the mind.

Table 5.1 Persistence of Vision in Film

What Happens?	What Is on the Screen?	What Do You Perceive?
Film frame 1 is projected.	Picture 1	Picture 1
Shutter closes and film moves to the next frame.	Darkness	Picture 1 (persistence of vision)
Shutter opens and film frame 2 is projected.	Picture 2	Picture 2*

*Note that the images appear so rapidly (24 per second) that you don't see individual images, but see a moving image created by the rapid sequence of images.

perception of the sparkler's light for a fraction of a second. This retention of the perception of light in your mind is called the **persistence of vision.**

Something similar happens while you are watching a film in a darkened movie theater. You may see actions moving smoothly across the screen, but what is actually projected is quite different. We can appreciate what is happening on the screen by considering the sequence of events that occur as a film is projected. First, a single film frame is positioned in front of the projector lens, and when the projector's shutter opens, the image on the film frame is projected onto the screen. The shutter then closes, so the film can move to the next frame without causing a blurred image, and during that time, the screen is dark. When the next frame has arrived in front of the lens, the shutter opens again, flashing the next image onto the screen. This process is repeated rapidly, 24 times per second, so 24 still images are flashed on the screen every second, with each image separated by a brief period of darkness (see Table 5.1).

A person viewing the film sees the progression of still images as movement and doesn't see the dark intervals between the images because the persistence of vision fills in the darkness by retaining the image of the previous frame. If the period between the images is too long, the mind can't fill in the darkness completely, and you perceive a flickering effect. This is what happened in the early movies when the projectors flashed images more slowly, causing longer dark intervals. This is why these early films were called "flickers," a term that remains today, when we talk about going to the "flicks."

Sperling's Experiment: Measuring the Visual Icon

The persistence of vision effect that adds a trail to our perception of moving sparklers and fills in the dark spaces between frames in a film has been known since the early days of psychology (Boring, 1942). This lingering of the visual stimulus in our mind was studied by Sperling (1960) in a famous experiment in which he flashed an array of letters, like the one in Figure 5.6a, on the screen for 50 milliseconds (ms; 50/1,000 second) and asked his participants to report as many of the letters as possible. This part of the

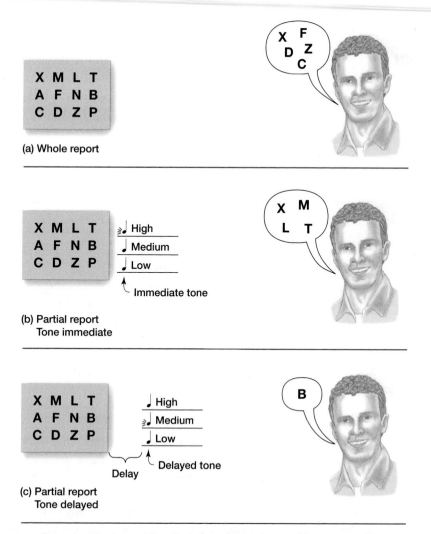

(a) Whole report

(b) Partial report
Tone immediate

High
Medium
Low
Immediate tone

(c) Partial report
Tone delayed

High
Medium
Low
Delayed tone
Delay

■ **Figure 5.6** Procedure for three of Sperling's (1960) experiments. (a) Whole report method: Person saw all 12 letters at once for 50 ms and reported as many as he or she could remember. (b) Partial report: Person saw all 12 letters, as before, but immediately after they were turned off, a tone indicated which row the person was to report. (c) Delayed partial report: Same as (b), but with a short delay between extinguishing the letters and presentation of the tone.

experiment used the **whole report method** because participants were asked to report as many letters as possible from the whole matrix. When they did this they were able to report an average of 4.5 out of the 12 letters.

At this point Sperling could have concluded that because the exposure was brief, participants saw only an average of 4.5 of the 12 letters. However, there is another possibility: Perhaps participants saw most of the letters immediately after they were presented, but their perception faded rapidly as they were reporting the letters, so by the time they had reported 4–5 letters, they could no longer see the matrix or remember what had been there.

Sperling devised the **partial report method** to determine which of these two possibilities is correct. In this technique, he flashed the matrix for 50 ms, as before, but immediately after it was flashed, he sounded one of the following cue tones, to indicate which row of letters the participants were to report (Figure 5.6b):

High-pitched:	Top row
Medium-pitched:	Middle row
Low-pitched:	Bottom row

Note that because the tones were presented *after* the letters were turned off, the participant's attention was directed not to the actual letters, which were no longer present, but to whatever trace remained in the participant's mind after the letters were turned off.

When the cue tones directed participants to focus their attention onto one of the rows, they correctly reported an average of about 3.3 of the 4 letters (82 percent) in that row. Because participants saw an average of 82 percent of the letters no matter which row was cued, Sperling concluded that the correct description of what was happening was that immediately after the display was presented, participants saw an average of 82 percent of the letters in the whole display, but were not able to report all of these letters because they rapidly faded as the initial letters were being reported.

Sperling then did an additional experiment to determine the time course of this fading. For this experiment, Sperling devised a **delayed partial report method** in which the presentation of cue tones was delayed for a fraction of a second after the letters were extinguished (Figure 5.6c).

The result of the delayed partial report experiments was that when the cue tones were delayed for about half a second after the flash, participants were able to report only slightly more than 1 letter in a row, or a total of about 4 letters for all three rows—the same number of letters they reported using the whole-report technique. Figure 5.7 plots this result in terms of the number of letters available to the participants from the entire display, as a function of time following presentation of the display. This graph indicates that immediately after a stimulus is presented, all or most of the stimulus is available for perception. This is sensory memory. Then, over the next second, sensory memory fades, until by 1 second, less than 5 of the 12 letters in the matrix can be reported. Note that this corresponds to the number of letters that were reported in the whole report technique.

Sperling concluded from these results that a short-lived sensory memory registers all or most of the information that hits our visual receptors but that this information decays within less than a second. This brief sensory memory for visual stimuli is called **iconic memory** or the **visual icon** (icon means "image"), and corresponds to the sensory memory stage of Atkinson and Shiffrin's model. Other research, using auditory stimuli, has shown that sounds also persist in the mind. This persistence of sound, which is called **echoic memory**, lasts for a few seconds after presentation of the original stimulus (Darwin et al., 1972).

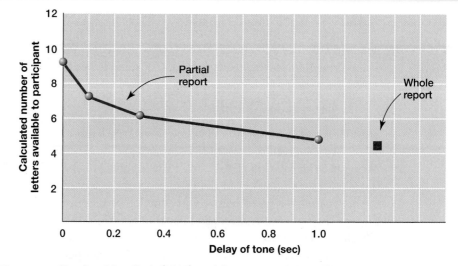

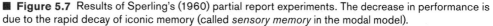

■ **Figure 5.7** Results of Sperling's (1960) partial report experiments. The decrease in performance is due to the rapid decay of iconic memory (called *sensory memory* in the modal model).

Thus, sensory memory can register huge amounts of information (perhaps all of the information that reaches the receptors), but it retains this information for only seconds or fractions of a second. There has been some debate regarding the purpose of this large but rapidly fading store (Haber, 1983), but many cognitive psychologists believe that the sensory store is important for (1) collecting information to be processed; (2) holding the information briefly while initial processing is going on; and (3) filling in the blanks when stimulation is intermittent.

Sperling's experiment is important not only because it reveals the capacity of sensory memory (large) and its duration (brief), but also because it provides yet another demonstration of how clever experimentation can reveal extremely rapid cognitive processes that we are usually unaware of. (See the discussion of illusory conjunctions in Chapter 3, page 67, for another example of how cognitive psychologists studied a rapid process that occurs without our awareness.)

Short-Term Memory

Whatever you are thinking about right now, or remember from what you have just read, is in your short-term memory. As we will see shortly, most of this information is eventually lost, with only some of it reaching the more permanent store of long-term memory. Because of the brief duration of STM, it is easy to downplay its importance compared to LTM. In my class survey of the uses of memory, my students focused almost entirely on how memory enables us to hold information for long periods, such as remembering directions, people's names, or material that might appear on an exam. Certainly, our ability to store information for long periods is important, as attested by cases such as Clive Wearing's, whose inability to form LTMs makes it impossible for him to function independently. But, as we will see, STM (and working memory, which we will describe later) is also crucial for normal functioning. Consider, for example, the following sentence.

The human brain is involved in everything we know about the important things in life, like music and dancing.

How do we understand this sentence? First, the beginning of the sentence is stored in STM. We then read the rest of the sentence and determine the overall meaning by comparing the information at the end of the sentence to the information at the beginning. But what if we couldn't hold the beginning of the sentence in STM? If the information in the first phrase faded before you completed the sentence, you might think that the topic of the sentence is music and dancing and wouldn't realize that the sentence is really about the brain.

Holding small amounts of information for brief periods is the basis of a great deal of our mental life. Everything we think about or know at a particular moment in time involves STM because short-term memory is our window on the present. (Remember from Figure 5.4e that Rachel became aware of the pizzeria's phone number by transferring it from LTM to STM.) Early research on STM focused on answering the following two questions: (1) What is the duration of STM? and (2) How much information can STM hold?

What Is the Duration of Short-Term Memory?

John Brown (1958) in England and Lloyd Peterson and Margaret Peterson (1959) in the United States carried out experiments to determine the duration of STM. In their experiments participants were given a task similar to the one in the following demonstration.

Demonstration

Remembering Three Letters

CogLab

Brown-Peterson

You will need another person to serve as a participant in this experiment. Tell the person that you are going to read three letters followed by a number. Once the person hears the number he or she should start counting backward by 3's from that number, and then when you say "Recall," the person should write down the three letters heard at the beginning. Once the person starts counting, time 20 seconds and say, "Recall." Note the accuracy and repeat this procedure for a few more trials, using a new set of letters and a new three-digit number on each trial. ◗

Peterson and Peterson found that their participants were able to remember about 80 percent of the letters after a 3-second delay (left bar in Figure 5.8a), but could remember an average of only 10 percent of the three-letter groups after an 18-second

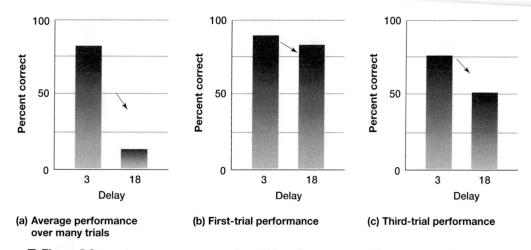

(a) Average performance over many trials

(b) First-trial performance

(c) Third-trial performance

■ **Figure 5.8** Results of Peterson and Peterson's (1959) duration of STM experiment. (a) The result originally presented by Peterson and Peterson, showing a large drop in memory for letters for a delay of 18 seconds between presentation and test; (b) analysis of Peterson and Peterson's results by Keppel and Underwood, showing little decrease in performance on Trial 1 and (c) more decrease by Trial 3.

delay (right bar in Figure 5.8a). Peterson and Peterson initially interpreted this result as demonstrating that participants forgot the letters because their memory trace decayed during the 18 seconds. However, when G. Keppel and Benton Underwood (1962) looked closely at Peterson and Peterson's results, they found that if they considered the participants' performance on just the first trial, there is little falloff between the 3-second and the 18-second delay (Figure 5.8b). However, when they analyzed the results for the third trial, they began seeing a drop-off in performance between the 3-second and the 18-second delay (Figure 5.8c).

Why would memory become worse after a few trials? Keppel and Underwood suggested that the drop-off in memory was due not to decay of the memory trace, as Peterson and Peterson had proposed, but to **proactive interference (PI)**—interference that occurs when information that was learned previously interferes with learning new information.

The effect of proactive interference is illustrated by what might happen when a frequently used phone number is changed. Consider, for example, what might happen when Rachel calls the number she had memorized for Mineo's Pizza, 521-5100, only to get a recording saying that the phone number has been changed to 522-4100. Although Rachel tries to remember the new number, she makes mistakes at first because proactive interference is causing her memory for the old number to interfere with her memory for the new number. The fact that the new number is similar to the old one adds to the interference and makes it harder to remember the new number.

What does it mean that the reason for the decrease in memory is proactive interference, rather than decay? From the point of view of understanding the basic mechanisms underlying memory, it is important to know that interference is a basic mechanism of forgetting. From the point of view of our everyday life experience, it is easy to see that interference is happening constantly, as one event follows the next (and even when nothing is "happening," we are usually thinking about something). The outcome of this constant interference is that the effective duration of STM, when rehearsal is prevented, is about 15–20 seconds.

What Is the Capacity of Short-Term Memory?

Information is not only lost rapidly from STM, but there is a limit to how much information can be held there. One measure of this capacity is provided by the **digit span**—the number of digits a person can remember.

CogLab

Memory
Span

Digit Span You can determine your digit span by doing the following demonstration.

Demonstration

Digit Span

Using an index card or piece of paper, cover all of the numbers below. Move the card down to uncover the first string of numbers. Read the numbers, cover them up, and then write them down in the correct order. Then move the card to the next string and repeat this procedure until you begin making errors. The longest string you are able to reproduce without error is your digit span.

    2 1 4 9
    3 9 6 7 8
    6 4 9 7 8 4
    7 3 8 2 0 1 5
    8 4 2 6 1 4 3 2
    4 8 2 3 9 2 8 0 7
    5 8 5 2 9 8 1 6 3 7

If you succeeded in remembering the longest string of digits, you have a digit span of 10. The typical span is between 5 and 8 digits.

According to measurements of digit span, the capacity of STM is 5–8 items. But what exactly is an item? George Miller (1956) considered this question in a famous paper titled "The Magical Number Seven, Plus or Minus Two." Miller expanded the definition of an item beyond digits by considering how we remember words and combinations of words. Consider, for example, trying to remember the following words: *monkey, child, wildly, zoo, jumped, city, ringtail, young.* How many units are there in this list? There are 8 words, but if we group them differently, they can form the following 4 pairs: *ringtail monkey, jumped wildly, young child, city zoo.* We can take this one step further by arranging these groups of words into one sentence: The *ringtail monkey jumped wildly* for the *young child* at the *city zoo.*

Chunking Is the sentence about the child watching a monkey at the zoo 8 items, 4 items, or 1 item? Miller introduced the concept of **chunking** to describe the fact that small units (like words) can be combined into larger meaningful units, like phrases, or even larger units, like sentences, paragraphs, or stories. A **chunk** has been defined as a collection of elements that are strongly associated with one another but are weakly associated with elements in other chunks (Gobet et al., 2001). In our example the word *ringtail* is strongly associated with the word *monkey* but is not as strongly associated with the other words, such as *child* or *jumped*.

Research has shown that chunking in terms of meaning can increase our ability to hold information in STM. Thus, we can recall a sequence of 5–8 unrelated words, but arranging the words to form a meaningful sentence so that the words become more strongly associated with one another increases the memory span to 20 words or more (Butterworth et al., 1990).

K. Anders Ericcson and coworkers (1980) demonstrated an effect of chunking by showing how a college student with average memory ability was able to achieve amazing feats of memory. Their participant, S.F., was asked to repeat strings of random digits that were read to him. Although S.F. had a typical memory span of 7 digits, after extensive training (230 one-hour sessions), he was able to repeat sequences of up to 79 digits without error. How did he do it? S.F. used chunking to recode the digits into larger units that formed meaningful sequences. For example, 3492 became "3 minutes and 49 point 2 seconds, near world-record mile time," and 893 became "89 point 3, very old man." This example illustrates an interaction between STM and LTM, because S.F., who was a runner, created some of his chunks based on his knowledge of running times that were stored in LTM.

Another example of chunking that is based on an interaction between STM and LTM is provided by an experiment by William Chase and Herbert Simon (1973a, 1973b) in which they showed chess players pictures of chess pieces on a chessboard for 5 seconds. The chess players were then asked to reproduce the positions they had seen. Chase and Simon compared the performance of a chess master who had played or studied chess for over 10,000 hours to the performance of a beginner who had less than 100 hours of experience. The results, shown in Figure 5.9a, show that the chess master placed 16 pieces out of 24 correctly on his first try, compared to just 4 out of 24 for the beginner. Moreover, the master required only four trials to reproduce all of the positions exactly, whereas even after seven trials the beginner was still making errors.

We know that the master's superior performance was caused by chunking because it occurred only when the chess pieces were arranged in positions from a real chess game. When the pieces were arranged randomly, the chess master performed as poorly as the begin-

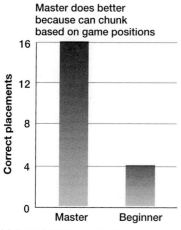

(a) **Actual game positions**

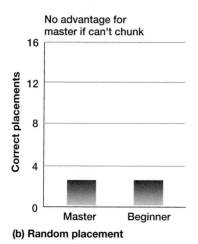

(b) **Random placement**

■ **Figure 5.9** Results of Chase and Simon's (1973a, 1973b) chess memory experiment. (a) The chess master is better at reproducing actual game positions. (b) Master's performance drops to level of beginner when pieces are arranged randomly.

ner (Figure 5.9b). Chase and Simon concluded that the chess master's advantage was due not to a more highly developed short-term memory, but to his ability to group the chess pieces into meaningful chunks. Because the chess master had stored many of the patterns that occur in real chess games in LTM, he saw the layout of chess pieces not in terms of individual pieces but in terms of 4 to 6 chunks, each made up of a group of pieces that formed familiar, meaningful patterns. When the pieces were arranged randomly, the familiar patterns were destroyed, and the chess master's advantage vanished (also see DeGroot, 1965; Gobet et al., 2001).

Chunking is an essential feature of STM because it expands the capacity of STM so it can handle 5–8 *chunks* rather than just 5–8 *items*. This enables the limited-capacity STM to deal with the large amount of information involved in many of the tasks we perform every day, such as chunking letters into words as you read this, remembering the first three numbers of familiar telephone exchanges as a unit, and transforming long conversations into smaller units of meaning.

How Is Information Coded in Short-Term Memory?

Coding refers to the way information is represented. Remember, for example, our discussion in Chapter 2 of how a person's face can be represented by the pattern of firing of a number of neurons. Determining how a stimulus is represented by the firing of neurons is a **physiological approach to coding**. We can also take a **mental approach to coding** by asking how a stimulus or an experience is represented in the mind. For example, imagine that you have just finished listening to your cognitive psychology professor give a lecture. We can describe different kinds of mental coding that occur for this experience by considering some of the ways you might remember what happened in class.

Remembering the sound of your professor's voice is an example of **auditory coding**. Imagining what your professor looks like, perhaps by conjuring up an image in your mind, is an example of **visual coding**. Finally, remembering what your professor was talking about is an example of coding in terms of meaning, which is called **semantic coding** (see Table 5.2).

Auditory Coding One of the early experiments that investigated coding in STM was done by R. Conrad in 1964. In Conrad's experiment, participants saw a number of target letters flashed briefly on a screen and were told to write down the letters in the order

Table 5.2 Types of Coding

Type of Coding	Example
Auditory	Sound of the person's voice
Visual	Image of a person
Semantic	Meaning of what the person is saying

they were presented. Conrad found that when participants made errors, they were most likely to misidentify the target letter as another letter that *sounded like* the target. For example, "F" was most often misidentified as "S" or "X," two letters that sound similar to "F." Thus, even though the participants *saw* the letters, the mistakes they made were based on the letters' *sounds*.

From these results Conrad concluded that the code for STM is auditory (based on the *sound* of the stimulus), rather than visual (based on the *visual appearance* of the stimulus). This conclusion fits with our common experience with telephone numbers. Even though our contact with them in the phone book is visual, we usually remember them by repeating their sound over and over rather than by visualizing what the numbers look like in the phone book (also see Wickelgren, 1965).

Visual Coding Some tasks, such as remembering the details of a diagram or an architectural floor plan, require visual codes (Kroll, 1970; Posner & Keele, 1967; Shepard & Metzler, 1971). This use of visual codes in STM was demonstrated in an experiment by Guojun Zhang and Herbert Simon (1985), who presented Chinese language symbols to native-speaking Chinese participants. The stimuli for this experiment were "radicals" and "characters" (Figure 5.10a). Radicals are symbols that are part of the Chinese language and that are not associated with any sound. Characters consist of a radical plus another symbol, and do have a sound.

When participants were asked to reproduce a series of radicals presented one after another, or a series of characters, they were able to reproduce a string of 2.7 radicals, on the average, and a string of 6.4 characters, on average (Figure 5.10b). The participants' ability to remember the radicals must be due to visual coding because the radicals have

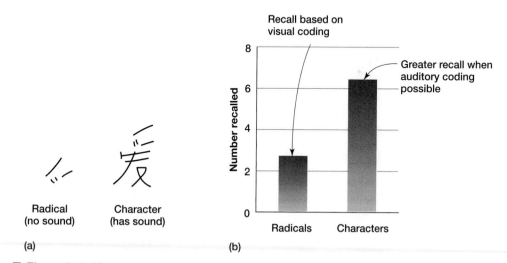

■ **Figure 5.10** (a) Examples of radical and character stimuli for Zhang and Simon's (1985) coding experiment. (b) Results showing evidence for visual coding (left bar) and auditory coding (right bar).

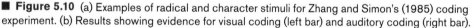

no sound or meaning. The participants' superior memory for the characters is most likely due to the addition of auditory coding because each character is associated with a sound. Thus, both visual and auditory coding can be involved in STM.

Semantic Coding There is also evidence for semantic coding in STM. This is illustrated by an experiment by Delos Wickens and coworkers (1976). Table 5.3 shows the experimental design for Wickens' experiment. He used three different groups of participants—a "professions" group, a "meat" group, and a "fruit" group. Participants in each group listened to three words (for example, *banana, peach, apple* for the fruit group), counted backward for 15 seconds, and then attempted to recall the three words. They did this for a total of four trials, with different words presented on each trial.

The basic idea behind this experiment was to first create a decrease in memory for all three groups by starting Trials 2 and 3 with different words from the same category as was presented in Trial 1 (to cause proactive interference, which we discussed on page 147). This result is shown in Figure 5.11, which indicates that participants in all three groups remembered about 87 percent of the words on Trial 1 (Figure 5.11a), and the performance for all three groups dropped on Trials 2 and 3 (Figures 5.11b and c), so by Trial 3 they remembered only about 30 percent of the words.

The crucial trial in the experiment was Trial 4, because on this trial all three groups were presented with names of fruits. From Figure 5.11d we can see that performance remained low for the fruit group because proactive interference continued for that group. But something different happened for the other two groups. Performance increased for the meat group and the professions group because shifting to fruits eliminated the proactive interference that had built up on Trials 1–3 for the names of meats and professions. The resulting increase in performance is called **release from proactive interference**, or release from PI. Figure 5.11d also indicates that the release from PI is not as pronounced for the switch from meats to fruits because meats and fruits are more similar to each other than are professions and fruits.

What does release from PI tell us about coding in STM? The key to answering this question is to realize that the release from PI that occurs in the Wickens experiment

Table 5.3 Wickens' Experiment Demonstrating Semantic Coding in STM

		Groups	
	Fruit	**Meat**	**Profession**
Trial 1	banana, peach, apple	salami, pork, chicken	lawyer, firefighter, teacher
Trial 2	plum, apricot, lime	bacon, hot dog, beef	dancer, minister, executive
Trial 3	melon, lemon, grape	hamburger, turkey, veal	accountant, doctor, editor
Trial 4	orange, cherry, pineapple (same category)	**orange, cherry, pineapple** (switch category)	**orange, cherry, pineapple** (switch category)

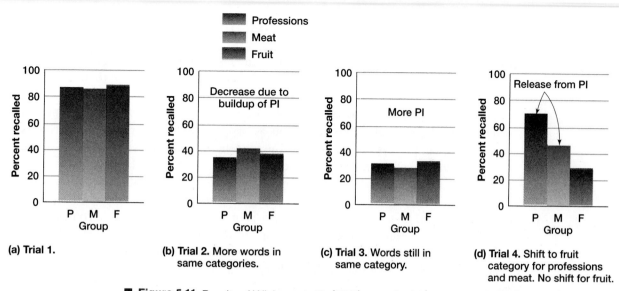

Figure 5.11 Results of Wickens et al.'s (1976) proactive inhibition experiment. (See Table 5.3 for design). (a) Initial performance on Trial 1. (b and c) On Trials 2 and 3, performance for all groups (professions, meat, and fruit) drops due to proactive interference. (d) On Trial 4, performance recovers for the professions and meat group due to release from proactive interference.

depends on the words' *categories* (fruits, meats, professions). Because placing words into categories involves the *meanings* of the words, the results of the Wickens experiment demonstrate the operation of *semantic coding* in STM.

Test Yourself 5.1

1. Why can we say that "memory is life"? Answer this question by considering what memory does for people with the ability to remember, and what happens when this ability is lost, as in cases like Clive Wearing's.
2. Describe Atkinson and Shiffrin's modal model of memory both in terms of its structure (the boxes connected by arrows) and the control processes. Then describe how each part of the model comes into play when you decide you want to order pizza but can't remember the pizzeria's phone number.
3. Describe sensory memory and Sperling's experiment in which he measured the capacity and duration of sensory memory.
4. Is memory lost from STM by decay or by interference? Be sure you understand the Peterson and Peterson experiment and Keppel and Underwood's interpretation of it. What is the time span of STM?
5. What is the capacity of STM, and how is it influenced by chunking?
6. Describe evidence supporting auditory, visual, and semantic coding of STM.

◆◆◆ Working Memory: The Modern Approach to Short-Term Memory

In Chapter 1 we noted that models are used in cognitive psychology to organize data that has been generated in many experiments and also to pose questions to be answered by additional experiments. By these criteria, the modal model has been one of the most useful models in cognitive psychology, because it explains a great deal of data and has resulted in thousands of experiments. But as happens with most models, new results emerge that can't be easily explained by the model. This leads either to revision of the model or proposal of an entirely new one.

In the case of the short-term memory components of the modal model, new results prompted Alan Baddeley and Graham Hitch (1974) to propose that STM be replaced by *working memory*—a mechanism that consists of a number of specialized components. One of the main results that led to the proposal of working memory was the observation that under some conditions participants could do two tasks at once. You can see this for yourself by doing the following demonstration.

▣ Demonstration

Reading Text and Remembering Numbers

Keep these numbers in your mind (7, 1, 4, 9) as you read the following passage.

> Baddeley reasoned that if STM had a limited storage capacity of about the length of a telephone number, filling up the storage capacity should make it difficult to do other tasks that depend on STM. But he found that participants could hold a short string of numbers in their memory while carrying out another task, such as reading or even solving a simple word problem. How are you doing with this task? What are the numbers? What is the gist of what you have just read? ◗

Because Baddeley's participants were able to read while simultaneously remembering numbers, he concluded that the short-term process must consist of a number of components that can function separately. In the demonstration, the digit span task in which you held numbers in your memory was handled by one component while comprehending the paragraph was handled by another component. Based on results such as this, Baddeley decided the name of the short-term process should be changed from short-term memory to *working memory*.

Baddeley (2000b) defines **working memory** as follows: Working memory is a limited-capacity system for temporary storage and manipulation of information for complex tasks such as comprehension, learning, and reasoning. From this definition we can see that working memory differs from STM in two ways:

1. Short-term memory is a single component, whereas working memory consists of a number of parts.
2. Short-term memory is concerned mainly with holding information for a brief period of time, whereas working memory is concerned with the manipulation of information that occurs during complex cognition.

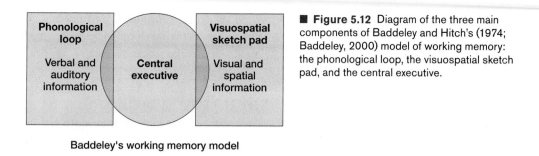

■ **Figure 5.12** Diagram of the three main components of Baddeley and Hitch's (1974; Baddeley, 2000) model of working memory: the phonological loop, the visuospatial sketch pad, and the central executive.

Baddeley's working memory model

Thus, working memory is concerned not just with how memory operates, but with how information is processed in the service of various forms of cognition, such as problem solving, thinking, attention, and language (Baddeley, 2000b).

Working memory accomplishes the manipulation of information through the action of three components: the *phonological loop*, the *visuospatial sketch pad*, and the *central executive* (Figure 5.12).

- The **phonological loop** holds verbal and auditory information. Thus, when you are trying to remember a telephone number or a person's name, or to understand what your cognitive psychology professor is talking about, you are using your phonological loop (Figure 5.13a).

■ **Figure 5.13** Tasks handled by components of working memory. (a) The phonological loop handles language. Reading is shown here, but the phonological loop also processes information that is received verbally, as when listening to someone speak. (b) The visuospatial sketch pad processes visual and spatial information.

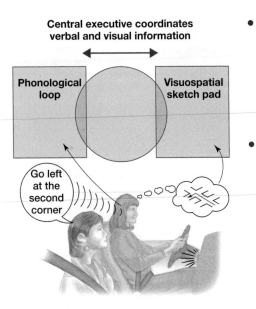

Central executive coordinates verbal and visual information

Phonological loop

Visuospatial sketch pad

Go left at the second corner

■ **Figure 5.14** Tasks processed by the phonological loop (hearing directions; listening to the radio) and visuospatial sketch pad (visualizing the route) being coordinated by the central executive.

- The **visuospatial sketch pad** holds visual and spatial information. When you form a picture in your mind or do tasks like solving a puzzle or finding your way around campus, you are using your visuospatial sketch pad (Figure 5.13b). As you can see from the diagram, the phonological loop and the visuospatial sketch pad are attached to the central executive.

- The **central executive** is where the major work of working memory occurs. The central executive pulls information from long-term memory and coordinates the activity of the phonological loop and visuospatial sketch pad by focusing on specific parts of a task and switching attention from one part to another. One of the main jobs of the central executive is to decide how to divide attention between different tasks. For example, imagine you are driving in a strange city, and a friend in the passenger seat is reading you directions to a restaurant while the news is being broadcast on the car radio. As your phonological loop takes in the verbal directions, your sketch pad is helping visualize a map of the streets leading to the restaurant (Figure 5.14), and the central executive is coordinating and combining these two kinds of information. In addition, the central executive might be helping you focus your attention on the directions and ignore the messages from the radio.

As we describe working memory, keep in mind that it is a hypothesis about how the mind works that needs to be tested by experiments. A number of experiments have been conducted to illustrate how the phonological loop and visuospatial sketch pad work in different situations.

The Phonological Loop

CogLab

Phonological Similarity Effect

Three phenomena support the idea of a system specialized for language: the phonological similarity effect, the word-length effect, and articulatory suppression.

Phonological Similarity Effect The **phonological similarity effect** occurs when letters or words that sound similar are confused. Remember Conrad's experiment in which he showed that people often confuse similar-sounding letters, such as "T" and "P." Conrad interpreted this result to support the idea of auditory coding in STM. In present-day terminology Conrad's result would be described as a demonstration of the phonological similarity effect, which occurs as words are processed in the phonological loop of working memory. Here is another demonstration of the phonological similarity effect:

Demonstration

Phonological Similarity Effect

Task 1: Slowly read the following letters. Look away and count to 15. Then write them down.

g, c, b, t, v, p

Task 2: Now do the same thing for these letters.

f, l, k, s, y, g ●

Which of the two tasks was more difficult? Many people find that they confuse the similar-sounding letters in Task 1 and sometimes report similar-sounding letters that weren't present, like *d, e,* or *z.* In contrast, it is easier to remember the different-sounding letters in Task 2. This confusion of the letters in Task 1 is an example of the phonological similarity effect.

Word-Length Effect The **word-length effect** occurs when memory for lists of words is better for short words than for long words.

Demonstration

Word-Length Effect

Task 1: Read the following words, look away, and then write down the words you remember.

beast, bronze, wife, golf, inn, limp, dirt, star

Task 2: Now do the same thing for the following list.

alcohol, property, amplifier, officer, gallery, mosquito, orchestra, brick-layer ●

Each list contains eight words, but according to the word-length effect the second list will be more difficult to remember because the words are longer. Results of an experiment by Baddeley and coworkers (1984) that illustrate this advantage for short words are shown in Figure 5.15. The word-length effect occurs because it takes longer to rehearse the long words and to produce them during recall.

The word-length effect explains the initially surprising finding that American children have a larger digit span than Welsh children. Before you conclude that American children are smarter than Welsh children, consider that the names of numbers in Welsh (un, dau, tri, pedwar, pump, chwech . . .) are longer than the names of the numbers in English (one, two, three, four, five, six . . .). Because it takes longer to pronounce

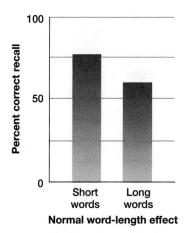

■ **Figure 5.15** How word length affects memory, showing that recall is better for short words (Baddeley et al., 1984).

Welsh numbers, fewer can be held in the phonological loop, and the memory span for these numbers is therefore less (Ellis & Hennelly, 1980).

In another study of memory for verbal material, Baddeley and coworkers (1975) found that people are able to remember the number of items that they can pronounce in about 1.5–2.0 seconds (also see Schweickert & Boruff, 1986). Try counting out loud, as fast as you can, for 2 seconds. According to Baddeley, the number of words you can say should be close to your digit span. (Note, however, that some researchers have proposed that the word-length effect does not occur under some conditions. See Lovatt et al., 2000, 2002).

Articulatory Suppression A phenomenon called **articulatory suppression** occurs when a person is prevented from rehearsing items to be remembered by repeating an irrelevant sound such as "the" ("the, the, the, . . .") (Baddeley, 2000b; Baddeley et al., 1984; Murray, 1968). Articulatory suppression has three effects: (1) it reduces the memory span; (2) it eliminates the word-length effect; and (3) it reduces the phonological similarity effect for reading words.

Articulatory suppression reduces memory span because speaking interferes with rehearsal. The following demonstration, which is based on an experiment by Baddeley and coworkers (1984), illustrates this effect of articulatory suppression:

Demonstration

Articulatory Suppression

Task 1: Read following list. Then turn away and recall as many words as you can.

dishwasher, hummingbird, engineering, hospital, homelessness, reasoning

Task 2: Read the following list while repeating the word "the" out loud (i.e., "the, the, the . . ."). Then turn away and recall as many words as you can.

automobile, apartment, basketball, mathematics, syllogism, catholicism

Articulatory suppression occurs when remembering the second list becomes harder because repeating *the, the, the* overloads the phonological loop.

Baddeley and coworkers (1984) also found that repeating "the, the, the . . ." not only reduces the ability to remember lists of words, but it also eliminates the word-length effect (Figure 5.16a). According to the word-length effect, a list of one-syllable words should be easier to recall than a list of longer words because the shorter words leave more space in the phonological loop for rehearsal. However, eliminating rehearsal by saying "the, the, the . . ." eliminates this advantage for short words (Figure 5.16b).

Saying "the, the, the . . ." also reduces the phonological similarity effect for words that are read. Normally words that are read are initially represented in the visuospatial sketch pad, and then this information is transferred to the phonological loop. However, saying "the, the, the . . ." prevents this information from being transferred to the phonological loop because the phonological loop is engaged (Figure 5.17). Thus, similar-

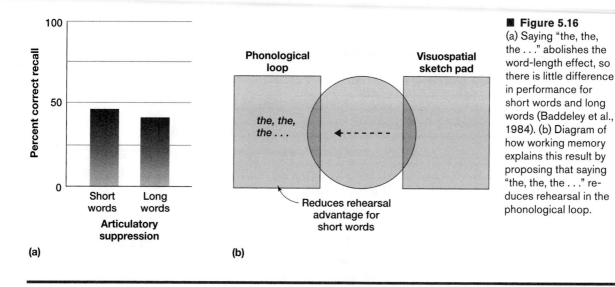

(a)

(b)

■ **Figure 5.16**
(a) Saying "the, the, the . . ." abolishes the word-length effect, so there is little difference in performance for short words and long words (Baddeley et al., 1984). (b) Diagram of how working memory explains this result by proposing that saying "the, the, the . . ." reduces rehearsal in the phonological loop.

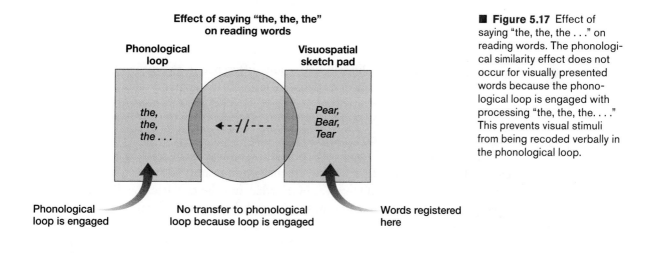

■ **Figure 5.17** Effect of saying "the, the, the . . ." on reading words. The phonological similarity effect does not occur for visually presented words because the phonological loop is engaged with processing "the, the, the. . . ." This prevents visual stimuli from being recoded verbally in the phonological loop.

sounding words can't be confused based on their sound, so the phonological similarity effect is eliminated.

The Visuospatial Sketch Pad

We have seen that operation of the phonological loop can explain performance on verbal tasks. We also saw, in the example that involved saying "the, the, the . . ." while reading words, that it is necessary to consider the visuospatial sketch pad to explain situations in which visual stimuli are involved. We will now consider a series of experiments by Lee Brooks (1968) involving tasks that either both depend on the phonological loop or

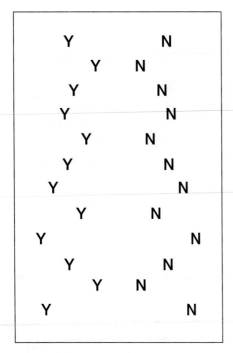

Figure 5.18 Response matrix for the "Holding a Verbal Stimulus in the Mind" demonstration. (From Brooks, 1968.)

that can be shared between the phonological loop and the visuo-spatial sketch pad. The following demonstration is based on one of Brooks' tasks:

Demonstration

Holding a Verbal Stimulus in the Mind

Task 1: Memorize the sentence below, and then without looking at it, consider each word in order and say "yes" if it is a noun and "no" if it isn't a noun.

John ran to the store to buy some oranges.

Task 2: Memorize the sentence below, and then use Figure 5.18 to indicate whether each word is a noun. As you remember each word in the order it appears in the sentence, point to the *Y* if the word is a noun and to the *N* if it isn't (move down a row in the display in Figure 5.18 for each new word).

The bird flew out the window to the tree.

Did you notice any difference in the difficulty of these two tasks? Participants in Brooks's (1968) experiment, on which this demonstration is based, found it easier when they pointed to *Y* or *N* than when they said *yes* or *no*. We can explain this result in terms of working memory and the visuospatial sketch pad by recognizing that verbal tasks depend on the phonological loop and spatial tasks depend on the visuospatial sketch pad. Thus, for the first task, when the stimulus and task were both verbal (Figure 5.19a), the phonological loop was overloaded and the task became difficult. But for the second task, when the stimulus was verbal and the task was spatial (Figure 5.19b), the processing was distributed between the loop and sketch pad, and the task became easier. We can also demonstrate the effect of distributing processing across the loop and sketch pad by asking a person to hold a spatial stimulus in his or her mind, as in the following demonstration:

Demonstration

Holding a Spatial Stimulus in the Mind

Task 3: Visualize the *F* in Figure 5.20. Then look away from the figure, and while visualizing the *F* in your mind, start at the upper left corner (the one marked with the *) and, moving around the outline of the *F* in a clockwise direction in your mind, point to *Y* in Figure 5.18 for an outside corner, and *N* for an inside corner.

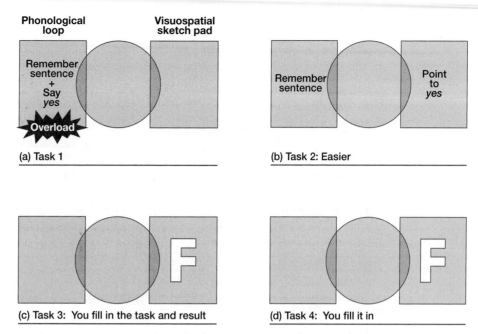

Phonological loop   **Visuospatial sketch pad**

Remember sentence + Say *yes*

Overload

(a) Task 1

Remember sentence   Point to *yes*

(b) Task 2: Easier

(c) Task 3: You fill in the task and result

(d) Task 4: You fill it in

■ **Figure 5.19** The results of Brooks's (1968) experiments, explained in terms of working memory. (a) When the stimulus is verbal, Task 1, which requires a verbal response, is difficult because the phonological loop has to process both the verbal stimulus and verbal response. (b) Task 2, which requires a visual response, is easier because processing is divided between the phonological loop and the visuospatial sketch pad. (c and d) Fill in these diagrams for Tasks 3 and 4 in the demonstration "Holding a Spatial Stimulus in the Mind."

■ **Figure 5.20** "F" stimulus for "Holding a Spatial Stimulus in the Mind" demonstration. (From Brooks, 1968.)

Task 4: Visualize the *F* again, but this time, as you move around the outline of the *F* in a clockwise direction in your mind, say *yes* if the corner is an outside corner (like the first one) or *no* if it is an inside corner.

Which was easier, pointing to *Y* or *N* or saying *yes* or *no*? ➤

Most people find that saying *yes* or *no* is easier for this task. Keeping in mind that pointing and holding the *F* in the mind are spatial tasks, and that saying *yes* or *no* is a verbal task, fill in the working memory diagrams for Task 3 (Figure 5.19c) and Task 4 (Figure 5.19d) to show why saying *yes* or *no* is easier.

The important result is that for both of these demonstrations the task is easier when the stimulus being held in the mind and the operation being performed on that stimulus involve *different* capacities. The tasks in these two demonstrations taken together demonstrate that working memory is set up so it can process different types of information simultaneously, but has trouble when similar types of information are presented at the same time.

The Central Executive

The central executive does most of the work of working memory because it coordinates the operation of the phonological loop and visuospatial sketch pad. Because of the complexity of this task, memory researchers are just beginning to understand the operation of the central executive.

One function of the central executive is controlling the suppression of irrelevant information. This can be important when carrying out a task that involves paying attention to relevant information while ignoring irrelevant information such as when the driver in Figure 5.14 had to ignore the car radio so she could listen to the directions.

In an experiment that considered this suppression function of working memory, Adam Gazzaley and coworkers (2005) showed participants stimuli like the ones in Figure 5.21. In the "face relevant" task, participants were told to remember the faces and ignore the scenes when the four cue stimuli (two faces and two scenes) were presented, and then, after a 9-second delay, to indicate whether the face presented during the test period matched one of the cue faces. In the "passive" task, participants just looked at

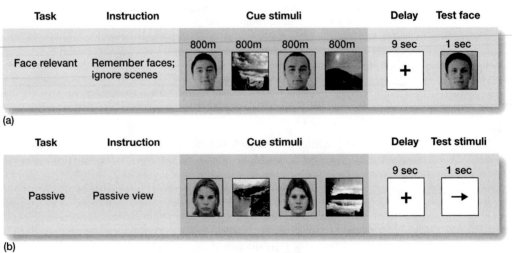

■ **Figure 5.21** Stimuli used in the Gazzaley et al. (2005) experiment. (a) In the first part of the "face relevant" task, cue stimuli (pictures of faces and scenes) are presented, and the participant is told to remember the faces and ignore the scenes. After a short delay, a test stimulus (face) is presented, and the participant decides whether this face matches one of the cue stimuli. (b) In the first part of the "passive" task, participants passively view the stimuli. After the delay, they indicate the direction of the arrow. The participant's fMRI is measured in both conditions while the cue stimuli are being presented.

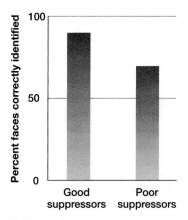

Figure 5.22 Results of the Gazzaley et al. (2005) experiment. Good suppressors (participants whose brain activity was low for scenes in the "face relevant" task compared to the passive task) identified more of the faces correctly than poor suppressors.

the pictures and pressed a button indicating the direction of the arrow during the test.

During the first part of the "face relevant" task, when participants were supposed to be ignoring the scene, Gazzaley measured the fMRI response of an area in the temporal cortex that responded to scenes. During the second part of the experiment, Gazzaley measured how accurately participants were able to indicate whether the test face matched the cue faces.

From the results of the fMRI measurements, Gazzaley was able to divide his participants into two groups. The "good suppressors" showed less brain activity when they were supposed to be ignoring the scenes than during the passive condition. The "poor suppressors" showed greater brain activity when they were supposed to be ignoring the scenes than during the passive condition.

Figure 5.22, which compares the two groups' performance in the test, shows that the good suppressors correctly identified 89 percent of the faces, whereas the poor suppressors correctly identified only 67 percent of the faces. This demonstrates that the ability to suppress irrelevant information, which is a central executive function, results in better memory for relevant information.

Update on the Working Memory Model: Addition of the Episodic Buffer

We have seen that the working memory model can explain a large number of results. However, just as new data led Baddeley to propose the working memory model to replace the STM component of the modal model, additional data led Baddeley to propose changes in the original working memory model.

As Baddeley and other researchers did experiments to test the working memory model, they noted that the model couldn't explain some results. For example, consider the phenomenon of articulatory suppression, in which saying "the, the, the . . ." decreases the memory span. The explanation for this decrease in memory span was that saying "the, the, the . . ." eliminated rehearsal in the phonological loop. The problem with the data, however, is that in most experiments the memory span decreased only slightly—from about 7 words to 5 words. Baddeley felt that the effect should be larger if saying "the, the, the . . ." was preventing rehearsal. Baddeley also noted that some patients with poor STM, so their digit span is only 1, could repeat back 5–6 words if they formed a sentence (Vallar & Baddeley, 1984; Wilson & Baddeley, 1988).

Both of these results indicate that performance is better than would be expected based on the working memory model. To deal with these results, Baddeley (2000a) has

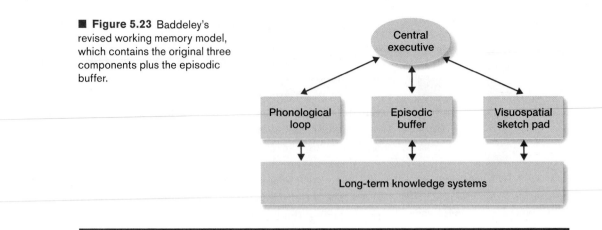

■ **Figure 5.23** Baddeley's revised working memory model, which contains the original three components plus the episodic buffer.

added an additional component to the model, called the **episodic buffer** (Figure 5.23). The episodic buffer is basically a "backup" store that communicates with both LTM and the components of working memory. An important property of the episodic buffer that helps explain the better-than-expected performance on some tasks is that it can hold information longer and has greater capacity than the phonological loop or visuo-spatial sketch pad.

If you think this description of the episodic buffer is a little vague, you're right. The episodic buffer is, like the STM and the original working memory model, a model that needs to be tested and revised based on further experiments (Repovs & Baddeley, 2006). The important message, for our purposes, is that models designed to explain mental functioning are constantly being refined and modified to explain new results.

Working Memory and the Brain

Early physiological studies of the short-term component of memory demonstrated that behaviors that depended on working memory can be disrupted by damage to specific areas of the brain, especially the prefrontal cortex (Figure 5.24). The prefrontal cortex receives input from the sensory areas, which are involved in processing incoming visual and auditory information. It also receives signals from areas involved in carrying out actions and is connected to areas in the temporal cortex that are important for forming long-term memories (see ● Color Plate 2.3 for location of the temporal lobe). Thus the "wiring diagram" of the prefrontal cortex is exactly what we would expect for the operation of a memory system like working memory that has to take incoming information from the environment and pass some of this information on to longer-term storage.

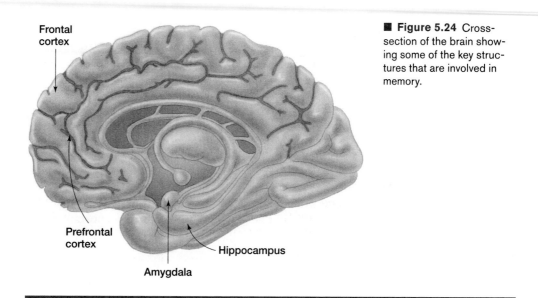

Frontal cortex

Prefrontal cortex

Amygdala

Hippocampus

■ **Figure 5.24** Cross-section of the brain showing some of the key structures that are involved in memory.

The Delayed-Response Task in Monkeys

Early work on the physiology of working memory used a task called the **delayed-response task**, which required a monkey to hold information in working memory during a delay period.

Figure 5.25 shows the setup for this task. The monkey sees a food reward in one of two food wells. Both wells are then covered, a screen is lowered, and then there

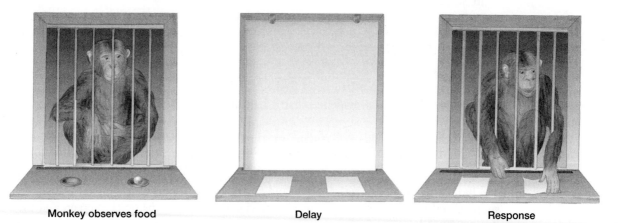

Monkey observes food   Delay   Response

■ **Figure 5.25** The delayed-response task being administered to a monkey.

is a delay before the screen is raised again. When the screen is raised, the monkeys must reach for the correct food well to obtain a reward. Monkeys can be trained to accomplish this task, but if their prefrontal cortex is removed, their performance drops to chance level, so they pick the correct food well only about half of the time.

This result supports the idea that the prefrontal (PF) cortex is important for holding information for brief periods of time. In fact, it has been suggested that one reason we can describe the memory behavior of very young infants (younger than about 8 months of age) as "out of sight, out of mind" (when an object that the infant can see is then hidden from view, the infant behaves as if the object no longer exists) is that their frontal and prefrontal cortex does not become developed until about 8 months (Goldman-Rakic, 1992). The idea that PF cortex is important for working memory is also supported by experiments that have looked at how single neurons in PF cortex respond during a brief delay.

Neurons That Hold Information

One of the requirements for any physiological system for memory is the ability to record and hold information after the original stimulus is no longer present. Shintaro Funahashi and coworkers (1989) conducted an experiment in which they recorded from neurons in a monkey's PF cortex while it carried out a delayed-response task. For the task, the monkey first looked steadily at a fixation point, X, while a square was flashed at one position on the screen (Figure 5.26a). In this example, the square was flashed in the upper left corner (on the other trials, the square would be flashed at different positions on the screen). This causes a small response in the neuron.

After the square went off, there was a delay of a few seconds. The nerve firing records in Figure 5.26b show that the neuron was firing during this delay. This firing is the neural record of the monkey's working memory for the position of the square. After the delay, the fixation X goes off. This is a signal for the monkey to move its eyes to where the square had been flashed (Figure 5.26c). The monkey's ability to do this provides behavioral evidence that it had, in fact, remembered the location of the square.

The key result of this experiment was that Funahashi found neurons that responded when the square was flashed in a *particular location* and that the neurons continued responding during the delay. For example, some neurons responded only when the square was flashed in the upper right corner and then during the delay, and other neurons responded only when the square was presented at other positions on the screen and then during the delay. The firing of these neurons indicates that an object was presented at a particular place, and this information remains available for as long as these neurons continue firing (also see Funahashi, 2006).

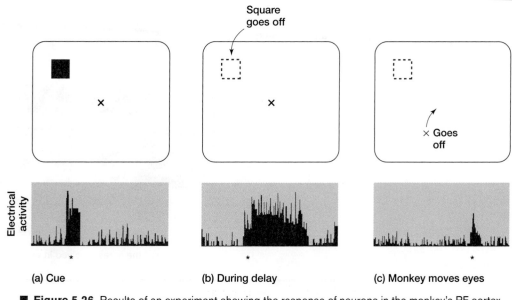

Square goes off

Electrical activity

(a) Cue

(b) During delay

(c) Monkey moves eyes

× Goes off

■ **Figure 5.26** Results of an experiment showing the response of neurons in the monkey's PF cortex during an attentional task. Neural responding is indicated by an asterisk (*). (a) A cue square is flashed at a particular position, causing the neuron to respond. (b) The square goes off, but the neuron continues to respond during the delay. (c) The fixation X goes off, and the monkey demonstrates its memory for the location of the square by moving its eyes to where the square was. (Adapted from "Mnemonic Coding of Visual Space in the Primate Dorsolateral Prefrontal Cortex," by S. Funahashi et al., *Journal of Neurophysiology, 61,* pp. 331–349. Copyright (c) 1989 with permission from the American Physiological Society.)

Research has also found neurons in other areas of the brain that respond during the delay in a working memory task. Neurons with these properties have been found in the primary visual cortex, which is the first area of the brain that receives visual signals (Super et al., 2001), and the inferotemporal cortex, which is a visual area responsible for perceiving complex forms (Desimone et al., 1995). Thus, although the PF cortex may be the brain area that is most closely associated with working memory, other areas are also involved.

Brain Imaging in Humans

The conclusion that many brain areas are involved in working memory has been confirmed by research using imaging techniques such as PET and fMRI to measure brain activity in humans. These studies show that as a person carries out a working memory task, activity occurs in the prefrontal cortex (Courtney et al., 1998) and in other areas

■ **Figure 5.27** Some of the areas in the cortex that have been shown by brain imaging research to be involved in working memory. (Adapted from Fiez, 2001.)

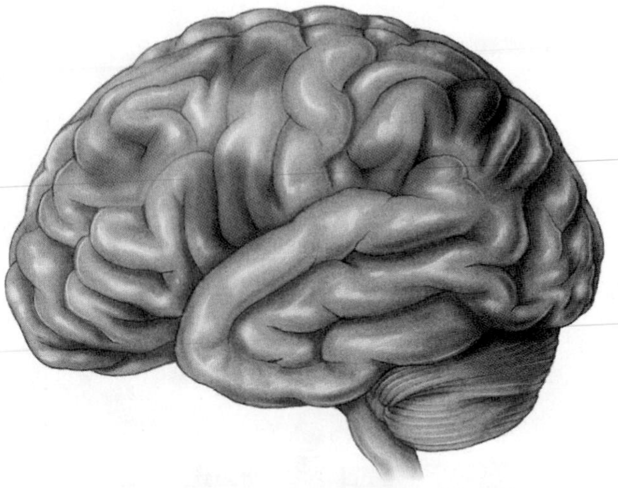

Some of the areas involved in working memory

as well (Fiez, 2001; Olesen et al., 2004). Figure 5.27, which summarizes the data from many experiments, shows that in addition to the prefrontal cortex, other areas in the frontal lobe and also areas in the parietal lobe and the cerebellum are involved in working memory. As we continue our study of the physiology of memory in the next chapter, we will see that a similar situation exists for long-term memory: One or two structures are especially important for long-term memory tasks, but many structures, distributed across the brain, are involved as well.

Something to Consider

Working Memory in American Sign Language

American Sign Language (ASL) is a language based on hand and arm gestures that is used by deaf people in the United States and parts of Canada. These gestures create a language that has the linguistic properties of spoken language. For example, ASL contains features (specific gestures) that make up words and rules for arranging words into sentences.

Because ASL is a visual language, we might expect that it would be processed not by the phonological loop, which processes spoken language, but by the visuospatial sketch pad, which processes visual and spatial information. Research has shown, however, that ASL shares many properties with spoken language, including many of the phenomena associated with the phonological loop.

Margaret Wilson and Karen Emmorey (1997) showed that the phonological similarity and word-length effects (see pages 156 and 157, respectively) occur for ASL. They demonstrated the phonological similarity effect by showing that memory for lists of words that are signed similarly (Figure 5.28a) is worse than memory for words that are signed differently (Figure 5.28b). They demonstrated the word-length effect (called the sign length effect for ASL) by showing that memory is worse for words that have signs that take longer to produce (Figure 5.28c). Based on these results, Wilson and Emmorey (1997) concluded that the phonological loop of signing is similar to the phonological loop for speech and that the phonological loop appears to process language input regardless of whether the language is created by sound or by gestures.

Speech and signing has also been compared by comparing the memory spans for signed and spoken material. On page 148 we discussed digit span, which is the number of digits a person can repeat back in the order in which they were presented. We also saw that the digit span can be influenced by the word-length effect—memory is better for lists of short words than for lists of longer words. This effect occurs because it takes longer to rehearse and produce longer words. (Remember that the digit span for Welsh

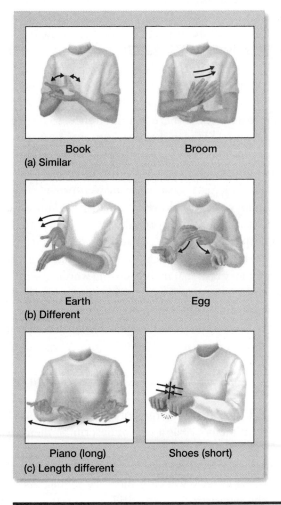

Book
(a) Similar
Broom

Earth
(b) Different
Egg

Piano (long)
(c) Length different
Shoes (short)

■ **Figure 5.28**
(a) *Book* and *broom* are signed similarly; (b) *earth* and *egg* are signed differently; (c) the sign for *piano* takes longer to produce than the sign for *shoes*. (From Wilson & Emmorey, 1997.)

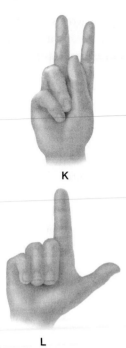

K

L

■ **Figure 5.29** Finger signs for the letters *A* and *B*. These signs, which are used to spell out words, can be produced as rapidly as spoken letters.

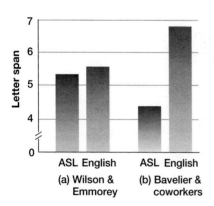

■ **Figure 5.30** Letter spans for ASL and English reported by (a) Wilson and Emmorey (2006, in press) and (b) Bavelier and coworkers (in press).

speakers is smaller than for English speakers because the names of Welsh numbers take longer to pronounce.)

The word-length effect poses a problem when comparing memory for speech and signing because signed words take longer to produce than spoken words. However, this problem can be eliminated by using letters as stimuli and comparing spoken letters with letters that are signed using a technique called finger spelling, which enables signers to produce letters as quickly as they can be spoken (Figure 5.29). When this experiment was done by two different laboratories, with both taking measures to match duration of spoken letters and finger-spelled letters, they reported the results shown in Figure 5.30—one lab reported similar letter spans for speaking and signing (Wilson & Emmorey, 2006, in press), and the other reported differences (Bavelier et al., in press).

Why are these results different? This situation—when two laboratories considering the same question report different results—is not unusual in cognitive psychology or science in general. The reason for differences can lie in small differences in procedures, stimuli, or participants. Presently, it is not clear what has caused the differences shown in Figure 5.30, but we can state the following conclusions from each result: (1) If there is no difference in letter span for speaking and signing when duration and other factors are equated, then this suggests that working memory capacity for English and ASL is the same, so modality (auditory vs. visual) does not matter. (2) If there is a difference, this suggests that working memory for English and ASL may differ in capacity, perhaps due to differences between the memory mechanisms for auditory and visual stimuli.

The question of how memory functions for different modalities is of great interest to cognitive psychologists because the answers provide insights into the basic operation of the memory system. However, what about language usage in the real world? In everyday usage, signing words does take longer than speaking words. But despite this apparent disadvantage for ASL, the performance of signers is the same as speakers when tested on a more complex working memory task that involves using words in sentences (Boutla et al., 2004). Whatever researchers eventually conclude about the basic mechanisms involved in remembering signs and speech, it appears that real-world language usage is similar for ASL and for English.

Test Yourself 5.2

1. Why has "working memory" replaced the modal model's "short-term memory" as a way of describing memory that lasts only a short time? How does working memory differ from STM?
2. Describe the characteristics of each of the three components of Baddeley's working memory model. As you describe these characteristics, also consider the following: the phonological similarity effect; the word-length effect; articulatory suppres-

sion; how verbal and spatial information is processed by the phonological loop and visuospatial sketch pad (Brooks's experiments); and the link between central executive functioning and memory performance (Gazzaley et al. experiment).

3. What were some of the reasons that Baddeley proposed adding the episodic buffer to the working memory model?

4. The physiology of working memory has been studied using (1) brain lesions in monkeys, (2) neural recording from monkeys, and (3) brain imaging in humans. What do the results of each of these procedures tell us about working memory and the brain?

5. Describe similarities and differences in the working memory of signers using ASL and speakers of English.

Chapter Summary

1. Memory is the process involved in retaining, retrieving, and using information about stimuli, images, events, ideas, and skills after the original information is no longer present. It is important for dealing with day-to-day events, and cases such as Clive Wearing's illustrate the importance of memory for normal functioning.

2. Atkinson and Shiffrin's modal model of memory consists of three structural features—sensory memory, short-term memory, and long-term memory. Another feature of the model is control process such as rehearsal and attentional strategies.

3. Sperling used two methods, whole report and partial report, to determine the capacity and time course of visual sensory memory. The duration of visual sensory memory (iconic memory) is less than 1 second, and of auditory sensory memory (echoic memory) is about 2–4 seconds.

4. Short-term memory is our window on the present. Brown, and Peterson and Peterson, determined that the duration of STM is about 15–20 seconds. They interpreted the short duration of STM as being caused by decay, but a later reanalysis of their data indicated it was due to proactive interference.

5. The capacity of STM is 5–8 items, as measured by digit span. This capacity can be expanded by chunking, so that it is possible to remember 5–8 chunks rather than 5–8 digits. Examples of chunking are the memory performance of the runner S.F. and how chess masters use their knowledge of chess to remember chess piece positions.

6. Information can be coded in STM in terms of sound (auditory coding), vision (visual coding), and meaning (semantic coding). Auditory coding was illustrated by Conrad's experiment that analyzed the type of errors made in memory for letters. Visual coding was illustrated by Zhang and Simon's experiment with Chinese characters, and semantic coding by Wickens' release from proactive interference experiment.

7. The short-term memory component of the modal model was revised by Baddeley in order to deal with results that couldn't be explained by a single short-term process. In this new model, working memory replaces STM.

8. Working memory is a limited-capacity system for storage and manipulation of information in complex tasks. It consists of three components—the phonological loop, which holds auditory or verbal information, the visuospatial sketch pad, which holds visual and spatial information, and the central executive, which coordinates the action of the phonological loop and visuospatial sketch pad.

9. The following effects can be explained in terms of operation of the phonological loop: (a) phonological similarity effect; (b) word-length effect; and (c) articulatory suppression.

10. Brooks did some experiments that indicated that two tasks can be handled simultaneously if one involves the visuospatial sketch pad and the other involves the phonological loop. Performance decreases if one component of working memory is called on to deal with two tasks simultaneously.

11. Researchers are just beginning to understand the functioning of the central executive. One function, the suppression of irrelevant information, was studied by Gazzaley by measuring brain activity and memory performance during a memory task that involved suppression. The results of this experiment showed that greater suppression, measured by brain activity, was associated with better performance in the memory task.

12. The working memory model has been updated to include an additional component called the episodic buffer, which has a greater capacity and can hold information longer than the phonological loop or visuospatial sketch pad.

13. Behaviors that depend on working memory can be disrupted by damage to the prefrontal cortex. This has been demonstrated by testing monkeys on the delayed-response task.

14. There are neurons in the prefrontal cortex that fire to presentation of a stimulus and continue firing as this stimulus is held in memory.

15. Brain imaging experiments in humans reveal that a large number of brain areas are involved in working memory.

16. Comparisons of working memory for signers who use ASL and speakers of English show that the phonological similarity effect and word-length effect occur for both. There is controversy regarding whether digit span is different for speakers and signers, but tests of more complex language abilities indicate no difference between signers and speakers.

Think About It

1. Analyze the following in terms of how the various stages of the modal model are activated, using Rachel's pizza-ordering experience in Figure 5.4 as a guide: (1) listening to a lecture in class, taking notes, or reviewing the notes later as you study for an exam; (2) watching a scene in a James Bond movie in which Bond captures the female enemy agent whom he had slept with the night before.

2. Adam has just tested a woman who has brain damage, and he is having difficulty understanding the results. She can't remember any words from a list when she is

tested immediately after hearing the words, but her memory gets better when she is tested after a delay. Interestingly enough, when the woman reads the list herself, she remembers well at first, so in that case the delay is not necessary. Can you explain these observations using the modal model? The working memory model? Can you think of a new model that might explain this result better than those two?

If You Want to Know More

1. Physiology of visual working memory. Recent physiological research has studied how long visual information is held in working memory, individual differences in visual working memory capacity, and where different types of stimuli are processed in the brain.

Cowan, N., & Morey, C. C. (2006). Visual working memory depends on attentional filtering. *Trends in Cognitive Sciences, 10,* 139–141.

Mecklinger, A., Gruenwald, C., Besson, M., Magnie, M., & Von Cramon, D. Y. (2002). Separable neuronal circuits for manipulable and non-manipulable objects in working memory. *Cerebral Cortex, 12,* 1115–1123.

Todd, J. J., & Marios, R. (2004). Capacity limit of visual short-term memory in human posterior parietal cortex. *Nature, 428,* 751–754.

2. Working memory and language. Working memory is important for many language functions, including reading ability and second language learning.

Bayliss, D. M., Jarrold, C., Baddeley, A. D., & Leigh, E. (2005). Differential constraints on the working memory and reading abilities of individuals with learning difficulties and typically developing children. *Journal of Experimental Child Psychology, 92,* 76–99.

Perani, D. (2005). The neural basis of language talent in bilinguals. *Trends in Cognitive Sciences, 9,* 211–213.

3. Working memory and intelligence. There is evidence that the working memory function of monitoring one task while doing something else is related to intelligence.

Conway, A. R. A., Kane, M. J., & Engle, R. W. (2003). Working memory capacity and its relation to general intelligence. *Trends in Cognitive Sciences, 7,* 547–552.

4. Cognitive neuroscience of working memory. A recent special issue of the journal *Neuroscience* contains 35 papers that survey current knowledge about the neuroscience of working memory. The paper below leads off the issue.

Repovs, G., & Bresjanac, M. (2006). Cognitive neuroscience of working memory. *Neuroscience, 139,* 1–3.

Key Terms

American Sign Language (ASL), 168
Articulatory suppression, 158
Auditory coding, 150
Central executive, 156
Chunk, 149
Chunking, 149
Coding, 150
Control processes, 139
Delayed partial report method (Sperling), 144
Delayed-response task, 165
Digit span, 148
Echoic memory, 144
Episodic buffer, 164
Iconic memory, 144
Long-term memory, 139
Memory, 136
Mental approach to coding, 150
Modal model of memory, 138

Partial report method (Sperling), 144
Persistence of vision, 142
Phonological loop, 155
Phonological similarity effect, 156
Physiological approach to coding, 150
Proactive interference (PI), 147
Rehearsal, 139
Release from proactive interference, 152
Semantic coding, 150
Sensory memory, 139
Short-term memory, 139
Structural features, 139
Visual coding, 150
Visual icon, 144
Visuospatial sketch pad, 156
Whole report method (Sperling), 143
Word-length effect, 157
Working memory, 154

CogLab   To experience these experiments for yourself, go to http://coglab.wadsworth.com. Be sure to read each experiment's setup instructions before you go to the experiment itself. Otherwise, you won't know which keys to press.

Primary Labs

Partial report   The partial report condition of Sperling's iconic memory experiment (p. 144).

Brown-Peterson   How memory for trigrams fades (p. 146).

Memory span   How memory span depends on the nature of stimuli that are presented (p. 148).

Phonological similarity effect   How recall for items on a list is affected by how similar the items sound (p. 156).

Related Labs

Apparent movement   How the perception of movement can be achieved by flashing still images (p. 142).

Irrelevant speech effect   How recall for items on a list is affected by the presence of irrelevant speech.

Modality effect How memory for the last one or two items in a list depends on whether the list is heard or read.

Operation span Measuring the operation-word span, a measure of working memory.

Position error What happens when trying to remember the order of a series of letters.

Sternberg search A method to determine how information is retrieved from short-term memory.

Long-Term Memory: Basic Principles

6

Introduction to Long-Term Memory
  Distinctions Between LTM and STM
    Demonstration: Serial Position
    Demonstration: Reading a Passage
  Types of Long-Term Memory

Declarative Memory
  Episodic and Semantic Memory
  The Separation of Episodic and Semantic Memories
  Connections Between Episodic and Semantic Memories

Implicit Memory
  Repetition Priming
    Method: Repetition Priming
    Method: Recognition and Recall
  Procedural Memory
  An Example of Implicit Memory in Everyday Experience

How Does Information Become Stored
in Long-Term Memory?
  Maintenance Rehearsal and Elaborative Rehearsal
  Levels-of-Processing Theory
    Demonstration: Remembering Lists
    Method: Varying Depth of Processing
  Transfer-Appropriate Processing
  Additional Factors That Aid Encoding
    Demonstration: Reading a List

Test Yourself 6.1

How Are Memories Stored in the Brain?
  Information Storage at the Synapse
  Forming Memories in the Brain: The Fragility
    of New Memories
  Forming Memories in the Brain: The Process
    of Consolidation
  Memory for Emotional Stimuli

How Do We Retrieve Information
From Long-Term Memory?
  Retrieval Cues
    Method: Cued Recall
  Encoding Specificity
  State-Dependent Learning

What Memory Research Tells Us About Studying
  Elaborate and Generate
  Organize
  Associate
  Take Breaks
  Match Learning and Testing Conditions

Something to Consider: Are Memories Ever
"Permanent"?
    Method: Fear Conditioning

Test Yourself 6.2

Chapter Summary

Think About It

If You Want to Know More

Key Terms

CogLab: Serial Position; Implicit Learning; Levels of
Processing; Encoding Specificity; Suffix Effect; Von
Restorff Effect

Some Questions We Will Consider

- What is the best way to store information in long-term memory? (196)

- How is it possible that a lifetime of experiences and accumulated knowledge can be stored in neurons? (207)

- What are some techniques we can use to help us get information out of long-term memory when we need it? (215)

Jimmy G. had been admitted to the Home for the Aged, accompanied by a transfer note that described him as "helpless, demented, confused, and disoriented." As neurologist Oliver Sacks talked with Jimmy about events of his childhood, his experiences in school, and his days in the Navy, Sacks noticed that Jimmy was talking as if he were still in the Navy, even though he had been discharged 10 years earlier. Sacks (1985) recounts the rest of his conversation with Jimmy as follows:

"What year is this, Mr. G?" I asked, concealing my perplexity under a casual manner.

"Forty-five, man. What do you mean?" He went on, "We've won the war, FDR's dead, Truman's at the helm. There are great times ahead."

"And you, Jimmy, how old would you be?" Oddly, uncertainly, he hesitated a moment, as if engaged in calculation. "Why, I guess I'm nineteen, Doc. I'll be twenty next birthday." Looking at the gray-haired man before me, I had an impulse for which I have never forgiven myself—it was, or would have been, the height of cruelty had there been any possibility of Jimmy's remembering it.

"Here," I said, and thrust a mirror toward him. "Look in the mirror and tell me what you see. Is that a nineteen-year-old looking out from the mirror?"

He suddenly turned ashen and gripped the sides of the chair. "Jesus Christ," he whispered. "Christ, what's going on? What's happened to me? Is this a nightmare? Am I crazy? Is this a joke?"—and he became frantic, panicky.

"It's okay, Jim," I said soothingly. "It's just a mistake. Nothing to worry about. Hey!" I took him to the window. "Isn't this a lovely spring day. See the kids there playing baseball?" He regained his color and started to smile, and I stole away, taking the hateful mirror with me.

Two minutes later I reentered the room. Jimmy was still standing by the window, gazing with pleasure at the kids playing baseball below. He wheeled around as I opened the door, and his face assumed a cheery expression.

"Hiya, Doc!" he said. "Nice morning! You want to talk to me—do I take this chair here?" There was no sign of recognition on his frank, open face.

"Haven't we met before, Mr. G?" I said casually.

"No, I can't say we have. Quite a beard you got there. I wouldn't forget you, Doc!"

. . .

"You remember telling me about your childhood, growing up in Pennsylvania, working as a radio operator in a submarine? And how your brother is engaged to a girl from California?"

"Hey, you're right. But I didn't tell you that. I never met you before in my life. You must have read all about me in my chart."

"Okay," I said. "I'll tell you a story. A man went to his doctor complaining of memory lapses. The doctor asked him some routine questions, and then said, 'These lapses. What about them?' 'What lapses?' the patient replied."

"So that's my problem," Jimmy laughed. "I kinda thought it was. I do find myself forgetting things, once in a while things that have just happened. The past is clear, though." (Sacks, 1985, p. 14)

Jimmy G. suffers from **Korsakoff's syndrome**, a condition caused by a prolonged deficiency of vitamin B1, usually as a result of chronic alcoholism. The deficiency leads

Memory Loss in the Movies

There are countless movies that feature a character with memory loss. In some movies, a character loses his or her memory for everything in their past, including their identity, but is able to form new memories. This is what happened to Gregory Peck's character in the 1945 classic *Spellbound*, which was directed by Alfred Hitchcock. In other movies, the main character has trouble forming new memories. For example, Lenny, the fictional character played by Guy Pearce in *Memento* (2000), had a problem like Clive Wearing's and Jimmy G's, but it was apparently not as severe, because he was able to function in the outside world, although with some difficulty. To compensate for his inability to form new memories, Lenny recorded his experiences with a Polaroid camera and had key facts tattooed onto his body (Figure 6.1). Although Lenny's problem was identified in the movie as a loss of short-term memory, his short-term memory was fine, because he could remember what had just happened to him. His problem was that he couldn't form new long-term memories.

In *50 First Dates*, Drew Barrymore plays a woman who has a memory problem that occurs only in the movies—she remembers what is happening to her on a given day, but when she wakes up the next morning she can't remember anything that happened on that day. The fact that her memory "resets" every morning seems not to bother Adam Sandler, who falls in love with her, either in spite of or because of her memory problems.

The following are some other movies in which memory loss plays a crucial role: *Anastasia* (1956; Ingrid Bergman); *Dead Again* (1991; Emma Thompson); *Goundhog Day* (1993; Bill Murray); *The Long Kiss Goodnight* (1996; Geena Davis); *Who Am I?* (1998; Jackie Chan); *The Bourne Identity* (2002; Matt Damon); *Paycheck* (2003; Ben Affleck); *Eternal Sunshine of the Spotless Mind* (2004; Jim Carrey/Kate Winslet). (See Think About It on page 231 for more on memory loss in the movies.)

© CORBIS SYGMA

■ **Figure 6.1** Guy Pearce's character, Lenny, from the film *Memento*. To deal with his memory problem, he had key facts he wanted to remember tattooed on his body.

to the destruction of areas in the frontal and temporal lobes, which causes severe impairments in memory. The damage to Jimmy G.'s memory makes it impossible for him to assimilate or retain new knowledge. He cannot recognize people he has just met, follow a story in a book, find his way to the corner drugstore, or solve problems that take more than a few moments to figure out. Jimmy's problem is similar to Clive Wearing's, from Chapter 5. He is unable to form new long-term memories, and his reality therefore consists of some memories from long ago plus what has happened within the last 30–60 seconds.

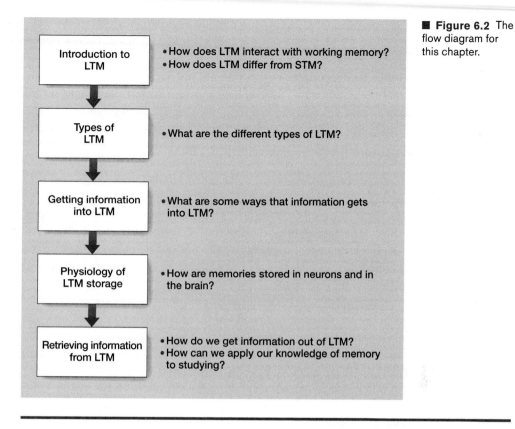

Figure 6.2 The flow diagram for this chapter.

The severe disabilities suffered by Jimmy G. and Clive Wearing illustrate the importance of being able to retain information about what has happened in the past. The purpose of this chapter is to begin looking at how long-term memory operates. We will do this by following the plan shown in Figure 6.2. First we introduce LTM by looking at how it interacts with STM/working memory, and how it differs from STM. We then describe the types of LTM, how information becomes stored in LTM, and the physiological mechanisms responsible for this storage. Finally, we will describe some of the factors involved in retrieving information from LTM. The principles introduced in this chapter lay the groundwork for the next chapter, in which we will continue our discussion of LTM by considering everyday applications of memory and why we make errors of memory.

Introduction to Long-Term Memory

One way to describe LTM is as an "archive" of information about past events in our lives and knowledge we have learned. What is particularly amazing about this storage is how it stretches from just a few moments ago to as far back as we can remember. The large time span of LTM is illustrated in Figure 6.3, which shows what a student who has just taken a seat in class might be remembering about events that occurred at various times in the past.

His first recollection—that he has just sat down—would be contained in his short-term/working memory because it happened within the last 30 seconds. But everything before that—from his recent memory that 5 minutes ago he was walking to class, to a memory from 10 years earlier of the elementary school he had attended in the third grade—is part of long-term memory.

Although all of these memories are contained in LTM, they aren't all the same. More-recent memories tend to be more detailed, and much of this detail and often the specific memories themselves fade with the passage of time and as other experiences accumulate. Thus, on October 1, 2006, this person would probably not remember the details of what happened while walking to class on October 1, 2005, but would remember some of the general experiences from around that time. One of the things that we will be concerned with in this chapter and the next one is why we retain some information and lose other information.

But simply considering LTM as an "archive" that retains information from the past leaves out an important function of LTM. LTM works closely with working memory to help create our ongoing experience. Consider, for example, what happens when Tony's friend Cindy says, "Jim and I saw the new James Bond movie last night" (Figure 6.4). As Tony's working memory is holding the exact wording of that statement in his mind, it is simultaneously accessing information from long-term memory, which helps him understand what Cindy is saying. Tony's ability to understand the sentence depends on retrieving, from LTM, the meanings of each of the words that make up the sentence. His

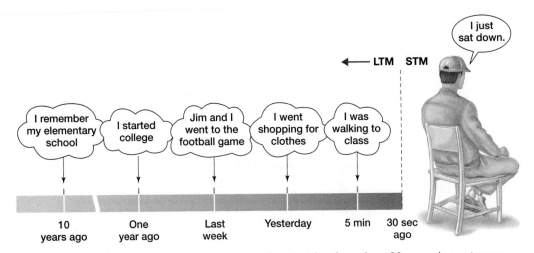

■ **Figure 6.3** Long-term memory covers a span that stretches from about 30 seconds ago to your earliest memories. Thus, all of this student's memories, except the memory "I just sat down," would be classified as long-term memories.

■ **Figure 6.4** Tony's STM, which is dealing with the present, and his LTM, which contains knowledge relevant to what is happening, work together as Cindy tells him something.

LTM also contains a great deal of additional information about movies, James Bond, and Cindy. Although Tony might not consciously think about all of this information (after all, he has to pay attention to the next thing that Cindy is going to tell him), it is all there in his LTM and adds to his understanding of what he is hearing and his interpretation of what that might mean.

LTM therefore provides both an archive that we can refer to when we want to remember events from the past, and a wealth of background information that we are constantly consulting as we use working memory to make contact with what is happening at a particular moment.

Distinctions Between LTM and STM

The interplay between what is happening in the present and information from the past, which we described in the interaction between Tony and Cindy, is based on the distinction between STM and LTM that was the centerpiece of the modal model of memory (see p. 138). Beginning in the 1960s, a great deal of research was conducted that was designed to distinguish between short-term processes (called short-term memory at the time) and long-term memory. This distinction was studied in a classic experiment by B. B. Murdoch, Jr. (1962), which is illustrated by the following demonstration:

Serial Position

Get someone to read the stimulus list (see end of chapter, on p. 234) to you at a rate of about one word every 2 seconds. Right after the last word, write down all of the words you can remember. ●

You can analyze your results by noting how many words you remembered from the first five entries on the list, the middle five, and the last five. Did you remember more words from the first or last five than from the middle? Individual results vary widely, but when Murdoch did this experiment on a large number of participants and plotted the percentage recall for each word versus the word's position on the list, he obtained a function called the **serial-position curve**.

Serial-Position Curve Murdoch's serial-position curve, shown in Figure 6.5, indicates that memory is better for words at the beginning of the list and at the end of the list. Superior memory for stimuli presented at the beginning of a sequence is called the **primacy effect**. A possible explanation of the primacy effect is that participants had time to rehearse these words and transfer them to LTM. According to this idea, participants begin rehearsing the first word right after it is presented, and because no other words

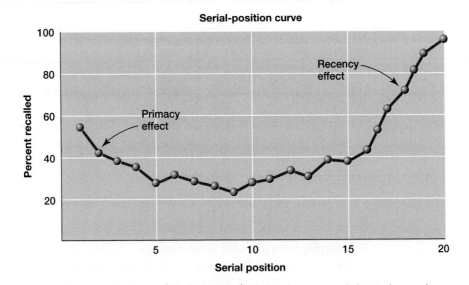

■ **Figure 6.5** Serial-position curve (Murdoch, 1962). Notice that memory is better for words presented at the beginning of the list (primacy effect) and at the end (recency effect). (Reprinted from "The Serial Position Effect in Free Recall," by B. B. Murdoch, Jr., *Journal of Experimental Psychology, 64,* pp. 482–488. Copyright © 1962 with permission from the American Psychological Association.)

have been presented, it receives 100 percent of the person's attention. When the second word is presented, attention becomes spread over two words, and so on, so as additional words are presented less rehearsal is possible for later words.

Murray Glanzer and Anita Cunitz (1966) tested the idea that rehearsal of the early words might lead to better memory by presenting the list at a slower pace, so there was more time between each word and participants had more time to rehearse. Just as we would expect if the primacy effect is due to rehearsal, increasing the time between each word increased memory for the early words (see dashed curve in Figure 6.6a). (Addi-

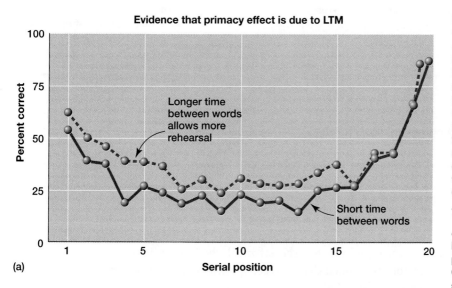

(a)

Figure 6.6 Result of Glanzer and Cunitz's (1966) experiment. (a) The solid curve is the serial position curve from Figure 6.5. The dashed curve occurred when the words were presented more slowly. (b) The serial-position curve has a normal recency effect when the memory test is immediate (solid line), but no recency effect occurs if the memory test is delayed for 30 seconds (dashed line). (Reprinted from *Journal of Verbal Learning and Verbal Behavior, 5,* M. Glanzer & A. R. Cunitz, "Two Storage Mechanisms in Free Recall," pp. 351–360, Figures 1 & 3, Copyright © 1966, with permission from Elsevier.)

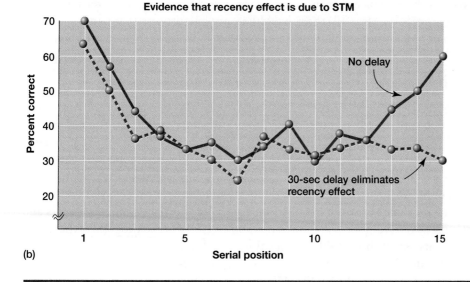

(b)

Table 6.1 Primacy and Recency Effects

Effect	Why Does It Occur?	How Can It Be Changed?
Primacy Effect		
Better memory for words at the beginning of the serial-position curve.	Words are rehearsed during presentation of the list, so they get into LTM.	To increase, present the list more slowly, so there is more time for rehearsal (see Figure 6.6a).
Recency Effect		
Better memory for words at the end of the serial-position curve.	Words are still in STM.	To decrease, test after waiting 30 seconds after end of the list, so information is lost from STM (see Figure 6.6b).

tional explanations have been proposed to explain memory for the middle words. See Neath & Suprenant, 2003, for details.)

Superior memory for stimuli presented at the end of a sequence is called the recency effect. One possible explanation for the better memory for words at the end of the list is that the most recently presented words are still in STM. To test this idea, Glanzer and Cunitz had their participants count backward for 30 seconds right after hearing the last word of a list. This counting prevented rehearsal and allowed time for information to be lost from STM. The result was what we would predict: The delay caused by the counting eliminated the effect (dashed curve in Figure 6.6b). Glanzer and Cunitz therefore concluded that the recency effect is due to storage of recently presented items in STM (Table 6.1).

But what is the evidence that short-term/working memory and long-term memory are separate processes? After all, there could be only one process that handles memories for both recent events and later events. We will now see how neuropsychological evidence has shown that STM/working memory and LTM are, in fact, two separate processes.

Neuropsychological Evidence In Chapter 2 we introduced the technique of determining dissociations, which is used to draw conclusions from case studies of brain-damaged patients (see Method: Neuropsychology, p. 43). This technique has been used in memory research to differentiate between STM and LTM by identifying people with brain damage that has affected one of these functions while sparing the other. We will see that studies of patients have established a double dissociation between STM and LTM. That is, there are some patients with functioning STM who can't form new LTMs and other patients who have poor STM but functioning LTM. Taken together, these two types of patients establish a double dissociation, which indicates that STM and LTM operate independently and are served by different mechanisms.

In Chapter 5 we described Clive Wearing, the musician who lost his memory due to viral encephalitis and who has a functioning STM but is unable to form new

Table 6.2 A Double Dissociation for STM and LTM

	STM	LTM
Clive Wearing and H.M.	OK	Impaired
K.F.	Impaired	OK

LTMs. Another case of functioning STM but absent LTM is the case of H.M., who became one of the most famous cases in neuropsychology when surgeons removed his hippocampus (see Figure 5.24) in an attempt to eliminate epileptic seizures that had not responded to other treatments (Scoville & Milner, 1957).

The operation eliminated H.M.'s seizures, but unfortunately also eliminated his ability to form new LTMs. Thus, the outcome of H.M.'s case is similar to that of Clive Wearing's, except Clive Wearing's brain damage was caused by disease, and H.M.'s was caused by surgery. H.M.'s unfortunate situation occurred because in 1953 the surgeons did not realize that the hippocampus is crucial for the formation of LTMs. Once they realized the devastating effects of removing the hippocampus, H.M.'s operation was never repeated. However, H.M. has been studied for over 50 years and has taught us a great deal about memory. The property of H.M.'s memory that is important for distinguishing between STM and LTM is the demonstration that it is possible to lose the ability to form new LTMs while still retaining STM.

There are also people with the opposite problem: normal LTM but poor STM. Patient K.F.'s problem with STM was indicated by her reduced digit span—the number of digits she could remember (see p. 148; Shallice & Warrington, 1970). Whereas the typical span is between 5 and 8 digits, K.F. had a digit span of 2 and, in addition, the recency effect in her serial-position curve, which is associated with STM, was reduced. Even though K.F.'s STM was greatly impaired, she had a functioning LTM, as indicated by her ability to form and hold new memories of events in her life. (See Think About It on page 231 for more on K.F.)

Table 6.2, which indicates which aspects of memory are impaired and which are intact for Clive Wearing, H.M., and K.F., demonstrates that a double dissociation exists for STM and LTM. We can conclude, therefore, that STM and LTM are caused by different mechanisms, which can act independently.

Coding in Long-Term Memory We can also distinguish between STM and LTM by comparing the way information is coded by the two systems. In Chapter 5 we saw that auditory, visual, and semantic coding can occur for STM. LTM can also involve each of these types of coding. For example, you use visual coding in LTM when you recognize someone based on his or her appearance, auditory coding when you recognize a person based on the sound of his or her voice, and semantic coding when you remember the general gist or meaning of something that happened in the past.

Although *some* semantic coding does occur in STM, semantic coding is the *predominant* type of coding in LTM. Semantic encoding is illustrated by the kinds of errors that people make in tasks that involve LTM. For example, remembering the word "tree" as "bush" would indicate that the meaning of the word "tree" (rather than its visual appearance or the sound of saying "tree") is what was registered in LTM.

Jacqueline Sachs (1967) demonstrated the importance of meaning in LTM by having participants listen to a tape recording of a passage like the one in the following demonstration.

 **Demonstration**

Reading a Passage

Read the following passage:

> There is an interesting story about the telescope. In Holland, a man named Lippershey was an eyeglass maker. One day his children were playing with some lenses. They discovered that things seemed very close if two lenses were held about a foot apart. Lippershey began experimenting and his "spyglass" attracted much attention. He sent a letter about it to Galileo, the great Italian scientist. Galileo at once realized the importance of the discovery and set about to build an instrument of his own.

Now cover up the passage and indicate which of the following sentences is identical to a sentence in the passage and which sentences are changed.

1. He sent a letter about it to Galileo, the great Italian scientist.
2. Galileo, the great Italian scientist, sent him a letter about it.
3. A letter about it was sent to Galileo, the great Italian scientist.
4. He sent Galileo, the great Italian scientist, a letter about it.

Which sentence did you pick? Sentence 1 is the only one that is identical to one in the passage. Many of Sachs's participants (who heard a passage about two times as long as the one you read) correctly identified (1) as being identical and knew that (2) was changed. However, a number of people identified (3) and (4) as matching one in the passage, even though the wording was different. These participants apparently remembered the sentence's meaning and not its exact wording. The finding that specific wording is forgotten but the general meaning can be remembered for a long time has been confirmed in many experiments. Semantic coding in LTM is important not only for remembering stories, but events from the past as well.

Types of Long-Term Memory

So far, we have been discussing LTM in general. But researchers have found it useful to distinguish between different types of LTM. The most basic division of LTM is between *declarative memory* and *implicit memory*. **Declarative memory** is our conscious recollection of events we have experienced or facts we have learned. **Implicit (or nondeclarative) memory** is memory that occurs when a past experience influences behavior, but we are not aware of the experience that is influencing the behavior (Figure 6.7).

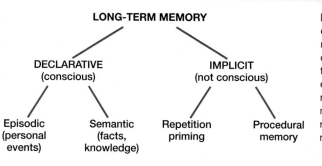

■ Figure 6.7 Long-term memory can be divided into declarative memory and implicit memory. We can also distinguish between two types of declarative memory, episodic and semantic. There are a number of different types of implicit memory. Two of the main types are repetition priming and procedural memory.

Declarative Memory

Most memory researchers distinguish between two types of declarative memory. **Episodic memory** is memory for personal events in our lives. For example, remembering visiting your grandfather's house when you were 10 is an example of episodic memory. **Semantic memory** involves facts and knowledge, such as knowledge about how an automobile engine works or the names of famous modern painters.

Episodic and Semantic Memory

When we say that episodic memory is memory for events and semantic memory is memory for facts, we are distinguishing between these two types of memory based on the types of *information* remembered. Endel Tulving (1985) has, however, suggested that episodic and semantic memory can also be distinguished based on the type of *experience* associated with each (also see Gardiner, 2001; Wheeler et al., 1997).

The defining property of the *experience* of episodic memory is that it involves **mental time travel**. When we are having an episodic memory we are traveling back in time to reconnect with events that happened in the past. For example, I can travel back in my mind to 1996 to remember cresting the top of a mountain near the California coast for the first time and seeing the Pacific Ocean far below, stretching into the distance. I remember sitting in the car, seeing the ocean, saying "Wow!" to my wife who was sitting next to me, and some of the emotions I was experiencing. Tulving describes this experience of episodic memory as **self-knowing** or **remembering**, with the idea that *remembering* always involves mental time travel. Note, however, that putting oneself back in a situation through mental time travel does not guarantee that the memory is accurate. As we will see in the next chapter, memories of events from our past do not always correspond to what actually happened.

In contrast to the mental time travel property of episodic memory, the experience of semantic memory involves accessing knowledge about the world that does not have to be tied to any specific personal experience. This knowledge can be things like facts, vocabulary, numbers, and concepts. When we experience semantic memory, we are not traveling

Table 6.3 Episodic and Semantic Memory

Type of Memory	Information	Characteristics	Consciousness (Tulving)
Episodic	Personally experienced events	"Mental time travel" that revisits past experiences	Self-knowing
Semantic	Facts, knowledge about the world	Knowledge, without mental time travel	Knowing

back to a specific experience in our past, but we are experiencing things we are familiar with and know about. For example, I know many facts about the Pacific Ocean—where it is located, that it is big, that if you travel west from San Francisco you end up in Japan. All of these things are semantic memories. Tulving describes the experience of semantic memory as **knowing**, with the idea that *knowing* does not involve mental time travel.

The distinctions between episodic and semantic memory are summarized in Table 6.3. We will now consider the evidence that supports the idea that episodic and semantic memories are served by different mechanisms.

The Separation of Episodic and Semantic Memories

It is possible to classify some memories as episodic and others as semantic, but is there any evidence to support the idea that there are two types of long-term memory that are served by different mechanisms? Neuropsychological research on people with different kinds of brain damage provides evidence for these differences.

Neuropsychological Evidence We first consider the case of K.C., who at the age of 30 rode his motorcycle off a freeway exit ramp and suffered severe damage to his hippocampus and surrounding structures (Rosenbaum et al., 2005). Because of this injury, K.C. lost his episodic memory—he can no longer relive any of the events of his past. He can, however, remember that certain things happened. For example, K.C. knows that his brother died—an event that occurred 2 years before the accident. He is not, however, aware of experiencing things such as hearing about the circumstances of his brother's death, where he was when he heard about it, or what happened at the funeral. K.C. also remembers facts like where the eating utensils are located in the kitchen and the difference between a strike and a spare in bowling. Thus, K.C. has lost the episodic part of his memory, but his semantic memory is largely intact.

A person whose brain damage resulted in symptoms opposite to those experienced by K.C. is an Italian woman who was in normal health until she suffered an attack of encephalitis at the age of 44 (DeRenzi et al., 1987). The first signs of a problem were headaches and a fever, which were later followed by hallucinations lasting for 5 days. When she returned home after a 6-week stay in the hospital, she had difficulty recog-

Table 6.4 Dissociations of
Episodic and Semantic Memory

	Semantic	Episodic
K.C.	OK	Poor
Italian woman	Poor	OK

nizing familiar people; she had trouble shopping because she couldn't remember the meaning of words on the shopping list or where things were in the store; and she could no longer recognize famous people or recall facts such as the identity of Beethoven or the fact that Italy was involved in World War II. All of these are semantic memories.

Despite this severe impairment of memory for semantic information, the woman's episodic memory for events in her life was preserved. She could remember what she had done during the day and things that had happened weeks or months before. Table 6.4 summarizes the two cases we have described. These cases, taken together, demonstrate a double dissociation between episodic and semantic memory, which supports the idea that memory for these two different types of information probably involves different mechanisms.

Although the double dissociation shown in Table 6.4 supports the idea of separate mechanisms for semantic and episodic memory, not all researchers agree that a double dissociation has been demonstrated, and so research continues on how brain damage affects LTM. (See Squire & Zola-Morgan, 1998, and Tulving & Markowitsch, 1998, for further discussion of this evidence.) There is, however, evidence from brain imaging experiments that retrieving episodic and semantic memories activates different areas of the brain.

Brain Imaging Evidence Evidence for separate mechanisms has also been provided by the results of brain imaging experiments. Brian Levine and coworkers (2004) had participants keep diaries of audiotaped descriptions of everyday events (example: "It was the last night of our Salsa dance class. . . . People were dancing all different styles of Salsa. . . ."), and facts drawn from their world knowledge ("By 1947, there were 5,000 Japanese Canadians living in Toronto").

When the participants later listened to these descriptions while in an MRI scanner, the everyday experiences elicited retrieval of episodic memories, and the facts elicited retrieval of semantic memories. The results were complicated, because many brain areas were involved, but the overall conclusion of this study was that retrieving episodic and semantic memories causes overlapping but different patterns of brain activity. Other research comparing brain activity during episodic and semantic retrieval has also found differences between the areas activated by episodic and semantic memory (Cabeza & Nyberg, 2000; Duzel et al., 1999; Nyberg et al., 1996).

Connections Between Episodic and Semantic Memories

The distinctions between episodic and semantic memories have been extremely useful for understanding memory mechanisms. But although we can distinguish between episodic and semantic memory, we can also show that there are connections between them.

Episodic Memories Can Be Lost, Leaving Only Semantic First consider how we acquire the knowledge that makes up our semantic memories. Sitting in the sixth grade, you learn about how the U.S. government works. Then in the seventh grade you look back and remember what was going on in class as you were learning about U.S. government. Placing yourself back in the class and remembering what was happening is episodic memory. Later, in college, you still remember the information you learned in the sixth grade and may even know that you learned about U.S. government in the sixth grade. However, if you have lost the episodic component of this memory and can no longer remember the specific day you were sitting there in class, you are experiencing a semantic memory. This example illustrates that the knowledge that makes up semantic memories is initially attained through a personal experience that could be the basis of an episodic memory, but that memory for this experience often fades, leaving only semantic memory.

This kind of "morphing" from episodic to semantic memory can also occur for personal experiences. For example, consider graduating from high school. This is an important event in many people's lives, and one that they may remember for many years. It is likely that many of the readers of this book can clearly place themselves at their high school graduation. Memory for many of the details of this event may, however, fade over the years, until many years later, not enough of the details remain to achieve the mental time travel required for episodic memory. Nonetheless, semantic memory remains, if the person knows the year they graduated, the high school they graduated from, and other facts associated with their graduation.

Semantic Memory Can Be Enhanced If Associated With Episodic Memory Semantic memories that have personal significance, which are called **personal semantic memories**, are easier to remember than semantic memories that are not personally significant. For example, knowledge about the facts associated with your high school graduation would be personal semantic memories because your high school graduation has personal significance for you. Robyn Westmacott and Morris Moscovitch (2003) showed that participants have better recall for names of public figures such as actors, singers, and politicians whom they associated with personal experiences. For example, you would be more likely to recall the name of a popular singer in a memory test if you had attended one of his or her concerts than if you had just read about the singer in magazines.

Semantic Memory Can Influence Our Experience by Influencing Attention Consider this situation: Steven and Seth are watching a football game. The quarterback takes the snap, is rushed hard, and flips the ball over the oncoming linemen for a completion. Later, Seth remembers the details of the play, which was a pass over the left side, but the play doesn't stand out for Stephen. Seth remembers the play because his semantic memory, which contains knowledge about football, caused him to direct his attention to what various players were doing as the play unfolded. Thus, Seth's semantic memory helped direct his attention, so he formed memories about specific plays, but Stephen just remembered that there were running plays and passing plays (Figure 6.8).

Semantic knowledge can influence formation of episodic memory

Low knowledge of football — "I remember a football game."

High knowledge of football — "I remember the pass Roethlisberger threw over the left side on third and 10!"

They both saw the same game!

■ **Figure 6.8** How a person's knowledge can influence their episodic memory. Even though two people have seen the same football game, they remember different things about it because of their differing knowledge of football.

●●● Implicit Memory

CogLab

Implicit Learning

When we access our declarative memory, we are conscious of doing so. We know we are thinking back to relive an earlier experience (episodic memory—Tulving's "self-knowing" or "remembering") or that we are retrieving knowledge about past events or about facts we have learned (semantic memory—Tulving's "knowing"). But the defining characteristic of implicit memory is that we are not conscious we are using it (see right side of Figure 6.7). Implicit memory occurs when some previous experience improves our performance on a task, even though we do not consciously remember the experience (Roediger, 1990; Schacter, 1987; Tulving, 1985). Tulving describes implicit memory as **nonknowing**. There are a number of types of implicit memory. We will focus on **repetition priming** and **procedural memory**.

- *Repetition priming:* when the response to an item increases in speed or accuracy because it has been encountered recently. For example, seeing the word *bird* may cause you to respond more quickly to it than to another word you had not seen, even if you may not remember seeing *bird* earlier.
- *Procedural memory:* memory for how to do things, such as riding a bike, typing, or playing a musical instrument. In this case, the skill involved in doing these things remains even after there is no memory for learning the skill.

Long-Term Memory: Basic Principles

Repetition Priming

To demonstrate repetition priming, it is necessary to show that presentation of one stimulus affects performance on that stimulus when it is presented again later.

◄► Method

Repetition Priming

The basic rationale behind priming is that if one presentation of a stimulus has an effect that continues after it is no longer present, this continuing effect will facilitate the response to the next presentation of the stimulus. In a typical experiment, the first stimulus, which is called the **priming stimulus**, is presented, followed by a time interval, and then the test stimulus is presented. The test stimulus can be the same as the priming stimulus or can be different but related in some way. For example, the priming stimulus could be the word *cabaret*, and the test stimulus could be the word fragment C _ _ A R _ T. The participant's task is to fill in the spaces to create a word.

If repetition priming occurs, the participant will be more likely to successfully complete this fragment than another fragment that did not correspond to a priming stimulus. This test would involve measuring how many word fragments the participant was able to complete. Another measure of performance used in repetition priming experiments is how quickly the participant responds. Whatever the measure, the question is, "Did the priming stimulus affect the response to the test stimulus?" ◆

Tulving (1962) demonstrated repetition priming by presenting participants with 96 words and then giving them a word-completion test like the one described above. For this test, half of the fragments corresponded to words the participants saw in the learning part of the experiment, and half were based on new words. The results of this experiment, shown in Figure 6.9, indicate that participants completed 47 percent of the fragments that corresponded to words they had previously seen, but completed only 30 percent of fragments that corresponded to the new words.

At this point, you might agree that repetition priming has occurred, because previously seeing the words improved performance on the word-fragment test. But you might wonder whether this is an example of implicit memory. Remember that for implicit memory to be involved, participants should not be consciously aware that they had seen the words before. One way this is accomplished in this experiment is by not using a memory test ("Have you seen this word before?"), but instead, asking participants to solve a problem ("Create a word from these letters"). Another technique that helps ensure that implicit memory is involved is to instruct participants to respond as

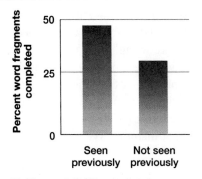

■ Figure 6.9 The results of Tulving et al.'s (1982) repetition priming experiment. Participants completed more word fragments for words they had seen before than for words they hadn't seen before. (Adapted from Tulving et al., 1982.)

quickly as possible, by saying the first answer that comes to mind. This decreases the chances they will take time to consciously remember whether or not they had previously seen the word.

Tulving was, of course, aware of the possibility that participants could consciously remember words from the list as they were carrying out the word-completion task. To show that performance on the word-completion task did not depend on conscious remembering of the words, Tulving measured participants' memory using a recognition memory test.

◄► Method

Recognition and Recall

Most of the experiments we have described so far have used a **recall test**, in which participants are presented with stimuli and then, after a delay, are asked to remember as many of the stimuli as possible. All of the STM experiments we described in Chapter 5 tested participants' recall. Recall is also involved when a person is asked to recollect things that have happened in his or her life, such as graduating from high school, or facts they have learned, such as the capital of Nebraska.

Memory can also be tested by using a **recognition test**. The typical procedure is to present stimuli during a study period and then, later, to present the same stimuli plus other stimuli that were not presented. The participants' task is to pick the stimuli that were originally presented. Sach's (1967) experiment, which we described on page 186, was a recognition test. She had participants read a paragraph about Galileo and then pick the sentence that had appeared in the story from four possibilities, three of which did not appear in the story. A multiple-choice exam, in which the task is to pick the correct answer from a number of alternatives, is another example of a recognition test. ◆

Tulving used a recognition procedure by presenting his participants with a list that contained both words they had seen before and new words. Their task was to indicate which of the words they had seen before. When Tulving tested recognition 1 hour after presenting the original list and 7 days after presenting the original list, he found that recognition was much lower after 7 days (solid line in Figure 6.10). However, performance on the word-completion test remained the same at 1 hour or 7 days (dashed line). This suggests that performance on the word-completion test did not depend on conscious memory for recognized words.

Although it is possible to question the potential influence of conscious memories in experiments such as Tulving's (see Butler & Berry, 2001), testing patients with brain damage, who have lost the ability to retain long-term memories, provides a demonstration of "pure" implicit memory. For example, Elizabeth Warrington and Lawrence Weiskrantz (1968) tested five patients with Korsakoff's syndrome (like Jimmy G., whom

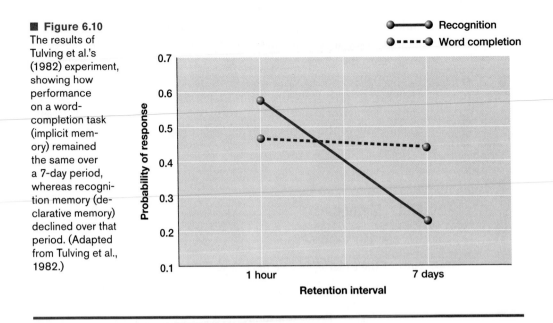

■ **Figure 6.10**
The results of Tulving et al.'s (1982) experiment, showing how performance on a word-completion task (implicit memory) remained the same over a 7-day period, whereas recognition memory (declarative memory) declined over that period. (Adapted from Tulving et al., 1982.)

we described at the beginning of the chapter), by presenting incomplete pictures such as the ones in Figure 6.11 (Gollin, 1960). The participant's task was to identify the picture. The fragmented version in Figure 6.11a was presented first, and then participants were shown more and more complete versions (b, c, d, and e) until they were able to identify the picture.

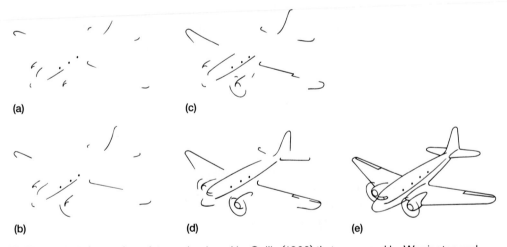

■ **Figure 6.11** Incomplete pictures developed by Gollin (1960) that were used by Warrington and Weiskrantz (1968) to study implicit memory in patients with amnesia. (Reprinted from *Nature, London, 217,* March 9, 1968, E. K. Warrington, & L. Weiskrantz, "New Method of Testing Long-Term Retention With Special Reference to Amnesic Patients," pp. 972–974, Fig. 1. Copyright © 1968 with permission from Nature Publishing Group.)

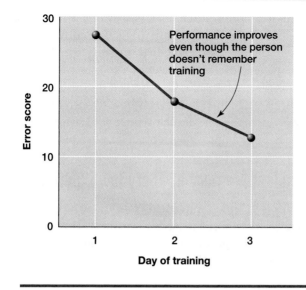

Figure 6.12 Results of Warrington and Weiskrantz's (1968) experiment.

The results, shown in Figure 6.12, indicate that by the third day of testing these participants made fewer errors before they were able to identify the pictures than they did at the beginning of training, even though they had no memory for any of the previous day's training. The improvement of performance represents an effect of implicit memory because the patients learned from experience but couldn't remember having had the experience.

Procedural Memory

We do not remember where or when we learned many of our basic skills, but nonetheless, we usually have little trouble doing them. This occurs to me as I write these sentences (yes, I write things out longhand before typing them into the computer). I can't remember learning to write, but I can do it. This is procedural memory. Another aspect of procedural memory is that people can do things without being consciously aware of *how* they do them. Consider, for example, riding a bike. Can you explain how you keep your balance? Or how about tying your shoes? Tying shoes is so easy for most people that they do it without even thinking about it. If you think you are aware of how you do it, describe which lace you loop over the other one, and then what you do next. Most people have to either tie their shoes or visualize tying their shoes before they can answer this question.

Riding a bike and tying your shoes are both motor skills that involve movement and muscle action. But you have also developed many purely cognitive skills that qualify as involving procedural memory. Consider, for example, your ability to read the sentences in this book. Can you describe the rules you are following for creating sentences from the words and creating meaningful thoughts from the sentences? Unless you've studied linguistics, you probably don't know these rules, but that doesn't stop you from being a skilled reader.

One characteristic of procedural memory is that it is often present in people like Jimmy G. and Clive Wearing who have lost the ability to retain episodic memories. Thus, Jimmy G. can still tie his shoes, and Clive Wearing, who was a professional musician, can still play the piano. In fact, people who can't form new long-term memories can still learn new skills. For example, K.C., who had lost his episodic memory because of a motorcycle accident (see page 188), learned how to sort and stack books in the library after his injury. Even though he doesn't remember learning to do this, he can still do it, and his performance can improve with practice.

An Example of Implicit Memory in Everyday Experience

An example of a situation in which implicit memory may affect our behavior without our awareness is when we are exposed to advertisements that extol the virtues of a product or perhaps just present the product's name. Although we may believe that we are unaffected by some advertisements, they can have an effect just because we are exposed to them.

This idea is supported by the results of an experiment by T. J. Perfect and C. Askew (1994), who had participants scan articles in a magazine. Each page of print was faced by an advertisement, but participants were not told to pay attention to the advertisements. However, when they were asked to rate the advertisements on a number of dimensions such as how appealing, eye-catching, distinctive, and memorable they were, they gave higher ratings to the ones they had been exposed to than to other advertisements that they had never seen. This result qualifies as an effect of implicit learning because when the participants were asked to indicate which advertisements had been presented at the beginning of the experiment, they recognized only an average of 2.8 of the original 25 advertisements.

This result is related to the **propaganda effect**, in which participants are more likely to rate statements they may have read or heard before as being true, simply because they have been exposed to them before. This effect can occur even when the person is told that the statements are false when they first read or hear them (Begg et al., 1992). The propaganda effect involves implicit memory because it can operate even when people are not aware that they have heard or seen the statements before, or they may have even thought they were false when they first heard them. Later in our discussion of LTM, especially in Chapter 7, we will see how implicit memory can lead to errors of memory. We will see, for example, how eyewitnesses to crimes have identified people as having been at the crime scene not because they were actually there, but because the eyewitnesses had seen them somewhere else at another time, so they seemed familiar.

How Does Information Become Stored in Long-Term Memory?

One of your goals in reading this chapter is probably to transfer the information you are reading into long-term memory, so you can remember it later, for an exam. The process of acquiring information and transforming it into memory is called **encoding**.

Notice that the term *encoding* is similar to the term *coding* that we discussed in relation to STM in Chapter 5 and LTM in this chapter. Some authors use these terms interchangeably. We will use the term *coding* to refer to the *form* with which information is represented. For example, a word can be coded visually or by its sound or by its meaning. We will use the term *encoding* to refer to the *process* used to get information into LTM. For example, a word can be encoded by repeating it over and over, by thinking of other words that rhyme with it, or by using it in a sentence. One of the main messages in this chapter is that some methods of encoding are more effective than others.

Encoding goes hand in hand with **retrieval**—the process of transferring information from LTM back into working memory, where it becomes accessible to consciousness (that is, we remember it!). When we consider retrieval later in this chapter, we will see that how we encode information can affect our ability to retrieve it. We will now focus on how information is encoded and then describe the brain processes involved in forming memories. After that, we will consider retrieval and how it relates to encoding.

Maintenance Rehearsal and Elaborative Rehearsal

One of the central concerns of early cognitive psychologists was determining the relationship between encoding and rehearsal. We saw in Chapter 5 that rehearsal can be used to keep information in STM or in working memory, as when you repeat a phone number you have just looked up in the phone book. Although rehearsal can keep information in working memory, rehearsal doesn't guarantee that information will be transferred into LTM. You know this from your experience in rehearsing a telephone number and then forgetting it right after you place the call. When you rehearse a telephone number in this way you are usually just repeating the numbers without any consideration of meaning or making connections with other information. This kind of rehearsal, called **maintenance rehearsal**, helps *maintain* information in memory, but it is not an effective way of *transferring* information into long-term memory.

Another kind of rehearsal, **elaborative rehearsal**, occurs when you think about the meaning of an item or make connections between the item and something you know. We can demonstrate that elaborative rehearsal is a good way to establish long-term memories by describing an approach to memory called *levels-of-processing theory*.

Levels-of-Processing Theory

CogLab

Levels of Processing

In 1972 Fergus Craik and Robert Lockhart proposed the idea of **levels of processing (LOP)**. According to **levels-of-processing theory**, memory depends on how information is encoded. In other words, memory depends on how information is programmed into the mind. The following demonstration introduces the idea that there are different ways to program information into the mind.

 **Demonstration**

Remembering Lists

Part 1. Cover up the list below and then uncover each word one by one. Count the number of vowels in each word and then go right on to the next one.

> chair
> mathematics
> elephant
> lamp
> car
> elevator
> thoughtful
> cactus

Now cover the list, and then count backward by 3's from 100. When you get to 76, write down the words you remember. Do that now.

Part 2. Cover up the list below and uncover each word one by one as you did in the previous part. This time, visualize how useful the item might be if you were stranded on an uninhabited island.

> umbrella
> exercise
> forgiveness
> rock
> hamburger
> sunlight
> coffee
> bottle

Cover the list and count backward by 3's from 99. When you reach 75, write down the words you remember. Do that now. ●

Which procedure resulted in better memory, counting the number of vowels or visualizing an item's function? Most of the experiments that have asked this kind of question have found memory to be superior when a meaningful connection has been made between an item and something else. Thus, memory for words is better when the words are processed by relating them to other knowledge, such as how useful an object might be on an uninhabited island, than when processed based on a nonmeaningful characteristic such as the number of vowels. Craik and Lockhart's levels-of-processing theory states that memory depends on the **depth of processing** that an item receives. They describe depth of processing by distinguishing between shallow processing and deep processing.

Shallow processing involves little attention to meaning. Shallow processing occurs when attention is focused on physical features such as the number of vowels in a

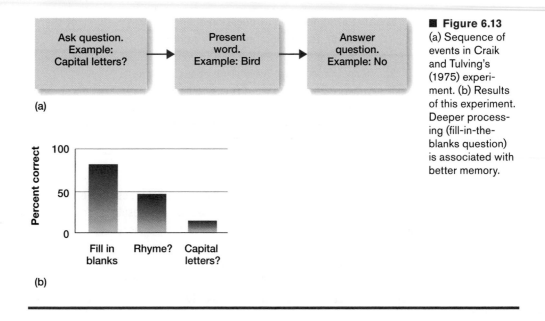

■ **Figure 6.13**
(a) Sequence of events in Craik and Tulving's (1975) experiment. (b) Results of this experiment. Deeper processing (fill-in-the-blanks question) is associated with better memory.

word or whether the word is printed in lowercase or capital letters. It also occurs during maintenance rehearsal, in which an item is repeated to keep it in memory but without considering its meaning or its connection with anything else.

Deep processing involves close attention, focusing on an item's meaning and relating it to something else. Considering how an item might be useful in a particular situation or creating an image of the item in relation to another item would create deep processing. This way of processing an item occurs during elaborative rehearsal and, according to levels-of-processing theory, results in better memory than shallow processing.

The prediction of better memory for deep processing has been confirmed in a number of experiments in which memory for words is measured after the words are encoded, using methods that involve different depths of processing.

◄► Method

Varying Depth of Processing

The procedure diagrammed in Figure 6.13a, which was used by Fergus Craik and Endel Tulving (1975), illustrates how depth of processing can be varied by asking different kinds of questions about a word. A question is presented, followed by a word, and then the participant's response. Shallow processing is achieved by asking questions about the word's physical characteristics. Deeper processing is achieved by asking about the word's sound, and the deepest processing is achieved by a task that involves the word's meaning. The following are examples like those used in Craik and Tulving's experiment.

1. Shallow processing: A question about physical features of the word
   Question: Is the word printed in capital letters?
   Word: bird
2. Deeper processing: A question about rhyming
   Question: Does the word rhyme with *train*?
   Word: pain
3. Deepest processing: A fill-in-the-blanks question
   Question: Does the word fit into the sentence "He saw a _____ on the street"?
   Word: car.

After participants responded to questions like the ones above, they were given a memory test to see how well they recalled the words. The results, shown in Figure 6.13b, indicate that deeper processing is associated with better memory. ◆

Levels-of-processing theory generated a great deal of research when it was first introduced, but the theory's popularity decreased because many researchers felt that "depth of processing" was not adequately defined. They pointed out that saying a particular task involves deep processing because it results in better memory defines deep processing based on the *result* to be expected from deep processing. For example, we could conclude that a task involving meaning results in deep processing because it results in better memory. Depth of processing, these researchers argue, needs to be defined independently from its result. Also, experiments studying a phenomenon called *transfer-appropriate processing* show that memory performance is sometimes determined not by depth of processing but by the relationship between how information is encoded and how it is retrieved later.

Transfer-Appropriate Processing

The phenomenon of **transfer-appropriate processing** shows that memory performance is enhanced if the type of task at encoding matches the type of task at retrieval. A transfer-appropriate processing experiment varies the type of task used for encoding and the type used for retrieval. We can understand what this means by considering an experiment by Donald Morris and coworkers (1977).

Participants in Morris's experiment were presented with 32 sentences during the encoding part of the experiment. There were two tasks during encoding: the meaning task and the rhyming task (Figure 6.14), which used the following procedures.

1. *Meaning-task encoding.* Participants heard fill-in-the-blanks sentences in which the word *blank* replaced the target word. Following this sentence, the participants heard the target word and had to respond "yes" if they thought it fit into the sentence and "no" if they thought it didn't fit into the sentence. For example, for the sentence "The *blank* rode the bicycle," followed by the target word *boy*, the answer would be "yes."

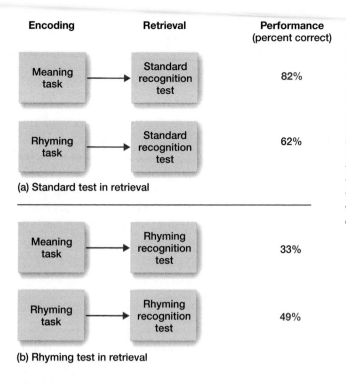

Encoding	Retrieval	Performance (percent correct)
Meaning task	Standard recognition test	82%
Rhyming task	Standard recognition test	62%

(a) Standard test in retrieval

Meaning task	Rhyming recognition test	33%
Rhyming task	Rhyming recognition test	49%

(b) Rhyming test in retrieval

■ **Figure 6.14** Design and results for transfer-appropriate processing experiment (Morris et al., 1977). (a) On a standard recognition test, participants who carried out the meaning task performed better than participants who carried out the rhyming task. (b) On a test that involved rhyming, participants who carried out the rhyming task performed better than participants who carried out the meaning task. These results would not be predicted by levels-of-processing theory.

2. *Rhyming-task encoding.* Participants heard a statement involving rhyming, in which the word *blank* replaced the target word. Following this statement, the participants heard the target word and had to respond "yes" if the statement was correct and "no" if it wasn't. For example, for the sentence "*Blank* rhymes with toy," followed by the target word *boy*, the answer would be "yes."

In the retrieval part of the experiment, participants from both the meaning and rhyming groups were given a recognition test in which they were presented with the 32 target words from acquisition and 32 new words. One group of participants was given a standard recognition test in which their task was to indicate whether a word had been one of the target words during acquisition (Figure 6.14a). For example, when presented with the word *boy*, the correct answer would be "yes." The results shown in the right-hand column indicate that performance was better for participants who had carried out the meaning task during encoding. This is what levels-of-processing theory would predict because during encoding the meaning task would result in deeper processing than the rhyming task.

Having provided evidence that was consistent with levels-of-processing theory, Morris proceeded to present evidence that cannot be explained by levels-of-processing theory. To do this he used a rhyming recognition test during retrieval (Figure 6.14b). Participants were presented with the same words that were used in the standard recognition test, but their task was to indicate whether each word *rhymed* with one of the words they had heard during acquisition. For example, when presented with the word *joy*, the answer would be "yes," because *joy* rhymes with *boy*, which was presented during acquisition.

The result of this experiment, shown in the right-hand column, was that participants in the rhyming group, who had done the rhyming task and so were encouraged to focus on the words' sounds during encoding, were able to remember more words than participants in the meaning group. This is not the result that levels-of-processing theory would predict because the meaning group, which processed the stimuli most deeply during encoding, did not perform as well as the rhyming group, which used "shallower" processing during encoding. The key to the better performance of the rhyming group was transfer-appropriate processing—both encoding and retrieval were based on sound. This experiment, therefore, demonstrated that memory depends not just on levels of processing, but also on how well the conditions at encoding and retrieval match.

Additional Factors That Aid Encoding

Although levels-of-processing theory is no longer the central focus of memory research that it was in the 1970s, its enduring contribution is the idea that memory is affected by the way information is programmed into the mind. This is illustrated by (1) how memory is affected by forming connections with other information, (2) whether information to be remembered is generated by the person, and (3) how information to be remembered is organized.

Forming Connections With Other Information If you were given the task of remembering the word *chicken*, which sentence do you think would result in the best memory?

1. She cooked the chicken.
2. The great bird swooped down and carried off the struggling chicken.

Craik and Tulving (1975) found that memory is much better when the word is presented within the complex sentence. Their explanation for this result is that the complex sentence creates more connections between the word to be remembered and other things, and these other things act as *cues* that help us retrieve the word when we are trying to remember it. Consider, for example, your response to each of the sentences about the chicken. If reading them resulted in images in your mind, which image was more vivid—a woman cooking, or a giant bird carrying a struggling chicken?

Apparently, most of the participants in Craik and Tulving's experiment found the giant-bird sentence to be more memorable, although this wasn't true for one student in my class, who reported that because her mother cooks a lot of chicken, she thought of her mother when reading the shorter sentence. Thus, for this student, the image of her mother cooking formed a stronger connection than the image of the swooping bird.

Gordon Bower and David Winzenz (1970) decided to test whether or not imagery can help create connections that will enhance memory. They presented a list of 15 pairs

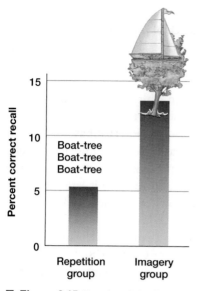

Figure 6.15 Results of the Bower and Winzenz (1970) experiment. Participants in the repetition group repeated word pairs. Participants in the imagery group formed images representing the pairs.

of nouns, such as *boat* and *tree*, to participants for 5 seconds each. One group was told to silently repeat the pairs as they were presented, and another group was told to form a mental picture in which the two items were interacting. When participants were later asked to recall as many of the words as possible, the participants who created the images remembered more than twice as many words as the participants who just repeated the word pairs (Figure 6.15).

Another example of how memory is improved by connections is provided by the **self-reference effect**: Memory is better if you are asked to relate a word to yourself. T. B. Rogers and coworkers (1979) demonstrated this by using the same procedure Craik and Tulving had used in their depth-of-processing experiment. Just as in Craik and Tulving's experiment, Rogers' participants were presented with a cue question and then a word, and were asked to apply the cue question to the word and answer "yes" or "no" (Figure 6.16a).

For example, one of the questions in the Rogers experiment was "Is the word long?" and another was "Does the word describe you?" The words were adjectives such as *shy* and *outgoing*. When Rogers then tested his participants' recall, he obtained the results shown in Figure 6.16b for words that resulted in a "yes" response. Participants were almost three times more likely to remember words that they rated as describing themselves than they were to remember words that they rated for length.

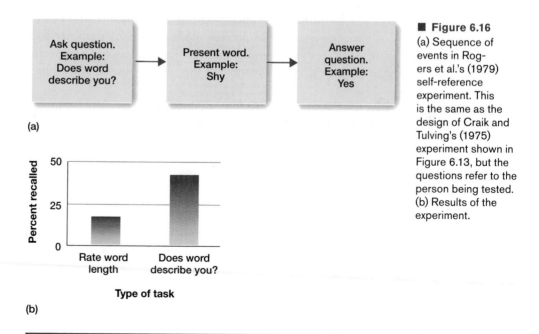

(a)

(b)

Figure 6.16 (a) Sequence of events in Rogers et al.'s (1979) self-reference experiment. This is the same as the design of Craik and Tulving's (1975) experiment shown in Figure 6.13, but the questions refer to the person being tested. (b) Results of the experiment.

Why were participants more likely to remember words they had connected to themselves? We can answer this question in terms of depth of processing by saying that making a judgment about whether the word describes you results in deeper processing than judging whether the word is long or short. But another possible explanation is that the self provides information, or *cues*, that become linked to the word and that make it easier to remember later. This is similar to the example in which the information provided by the giant swooping bird provided a cue that helped participants remember the word *chicken*. Cues such as this, that help us remember information that has been stored in memory, are called **retrieval cues**. The fact that the way we encode information can create retrieval cues that help us remember the information later illustrates the close link between how information is encoded and our ability to retrieve it later. Another example of the link between encoding and retrieval is provided by the *generation effect*.

Generating Information Generating material yourself, rather than passively receiving it, enhances learning and retention. Norman Slameka and Peter Graf (1978) demonstrated this effect, which is called the **generation effect**, by having participants study a list of word pairs in two different ways:

1. Read group: Read these pairs of related words.
   king–crown; horse–saddle; lamp–shade; etc.
2. Generate group: Fill in the blank with a word that is related to the first word.
   king–cr_____ ; horse–sa_____ ; lamp–sh_____ ; etc.

After either reading or generating the list of word pairs, they were presented with the first word in each pair and were told to indicate the word that went with it.

The results of this experiment were that participants who had *generated* the second word in each pair learned 28 percent more word pairs than participants who just *read* the word pairs. You might guess that this finding has some important implications for studying for exams. We will return to this idea at the end of the chapter.

Organizing Information File folders, computerized library catalogs, and tabs that separate different subjects in your notebook are all designed to organize information, so it can be accessed more efficiently. The memory system also uses organization to access information. This has been shown in a number of ways.

 Demonstration

Reading a List

Get paper and pen ready. Read the following words, then cover them and write down as many as possible.

apple, desk, shoe, sofa, plum, chair, cherry, coat, lamp, pants, grape, hat, melon, table, gloves

STOP! Do this now, before reading further.

Look at the list you created and notice whether similar items (for example, apple, plum, cherry; shoe, coat, pants) are grouped together. If they are, your result is similar to the result of research that shows that participants spontaneously organize items as they recall them (Jenkins & Russell, 1952). One reason for this result is that remembering words in a particular category may serve as a retrieval cue for other words in that category. So, remembering the word "apple" helps you retrieve "grape" or "plum" and therefore creates a recall list that is more organized than the original list that you read.

If words presented randomly become organized in the mind, what happens when words are presented in an organized way from the beginning, during encoding? Gordon Bower and coworkers (1969) answered this question by presenting material to be learned in a "tree," which organized a number of words according to categories. For example, one tree organized the names of different minerals by grouping together precious stones, rare metals, and so on (Figure 6.17).

One group of participants studied trees for "minerals," "animals," "clothing," and "transportation" for 1 minute each and were then asked to recall as many words as they could from all four trees. In the recall test, participants tended to organize their responses in the same way that the trees were organized, first saying "minerals," then "metals," then "common," and so on. Participants in this group recalled an average of 73 words from all four trees.

Another group of participants also saw four trees, but the words were randomized, so that each tree contained a random assortment of minerals, animals, clothing, and transportation. These participants were able to remember only 21 words from all four trees. Thus, organizing material to be remembered results in substantially better recall. Perhaps this is something to keep in mind when creating study materials for an exam.

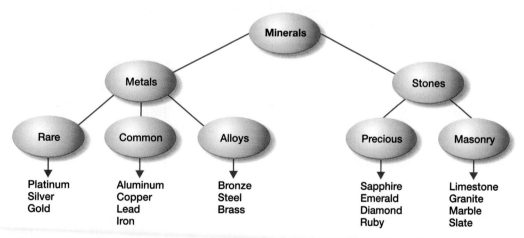

■ **Figure 6.17** The organized tree for "minerals" used in Bower et al.'s (1969) experiment on the effect of organization on memory. (Reprinted from *Journal of Verbal Learning and Verbal Behavior, 8,* Bower et al., "Hierarchical Retrieval Schemes in Recall of Categorized Word Lists," pp. 323–343, Copyright © 1969, with permission from Elsevier.)

You might, for example, find it useful to organize material you are studying for your cognitive psychology exam in trees like the one in Figure 6.18.

If presenting material in an organized way improves memory, we might expect that preventing organization from happening would reduce the ability to remember. This effect was illustrated by John Bransford and Marcia Johnson (1972), who asked their participants to read the following passage:

> If the balloons popped, the sound wouldn't be able to carry since everything would be too far away from the correct floor. A closed window would also prevent the sound from carrying, since most buildings tend to be well insulated. Since the whole operation depends on the steady flow of electricity, a break in the middle of the wire would also cause problems. Of course, the fellow could shout, but the human voice is not loud enough to carry that far. An additional problem is that the string could break on the instrument. Then there would be no accompaniment to the message. It is clear that the best situation would involve less distance. Then there would be fewer potential problems. With face to face contact, the least number of things could go wrong. (p. 719)

What was that all about? If you had a problem understanding the passage, you're not alone, because so did Bransford and Johnson's participants. But most important, their participants also found it extremely difficult to *remember* this passage.

To make sense of this passage, look at Figure 6.19 on page 208 and then reread the passage. When you do this, the passage makes more sense. Because of this, Bransford and Johnson's (1972) participants who saw this picture *before* they read the passage remembered twice as much from the passage as participants who did not see the picture or participants who saw the picture *after* they read the passage. The key here is *organization*. The picture provides a framework that helps the reader link one sentence to the next to create a meaningful story. The resulting organization makes this passage easier to comprehend and much easier to remember later. This is, therefore, another example

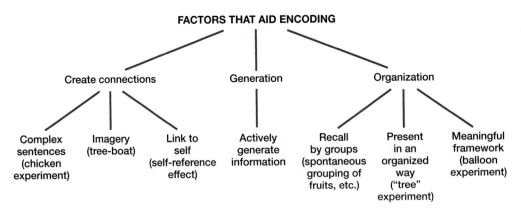

FACTORS THAT AID ENCODING

Create connections
- Complex sentences (chicken experiment)
- Imagery (tree-boat)
- Link to self (self-reference effect)

Generation
- Actively generate information

Organization
- Recall by groups (spontaneous grouping of fruits, etc.)
- Present in an organized way ("tree" experiment)
- Meaningful framework (balloon experiment)

■ **Figure 6.18** The organized tree for the material about encoding presented in this chapter.

that illustrates how the ability to remember material depends on how that material is programmed into the mind.

✎ Test Yourself 6.1

1. Why is it incorrect to simply consider LTM to be an archive for storing information?
2. What is the relation between the primacy and recency effects in the serial position curve and STM and LTM? Be sure you understand how these relationships were determined.
3. How have neuropsychological case studies distinguished between STM and LTM? Also, compare coding in STM and LTM.
4. What is the difference between declarative memory and implicit memory?
5. What are the distinctions between episodic memory and semantic memory, in terms of the type of *information* involved and the person's *experience*?
6. How has research with participants with and without brain damage supported the idea that episodic memory and semantic memory are served by different mechanisms? Also, describe three ways in which episodic and semantic memory are related.
7. What is implicit memory, and how has this type of memory been studied using priming and neuropsychological case studies? How might this type of memory influence our response to advertisements and political speeches?
8. What is procedural memory, and how have neuropsychological case studies been used to distinguish it from episodic and semantic memory?
9. What is the difference between elaborative rehearsal and maintenance rehearsal in terms of (a) the procedures associated with each type of rehearsal, and (b) their effectiveness for creating long-term memories?
10. What is levels-of-processing theory? How has it been tested? How does it relate to the difference between maintenance and elaborative rehearsal? What are some criticisms of the theory?
11. Describe Morris's transfer-appropriate processing experiment. What implications do the results of this experiment have for levels-of-processing theory?
12. Give examples of how memory for a word can be increased by (a) using it in a sentence, (b) generating the word during acquisition, and (c) organizing information.

▶▶▶ How Are Memories Stored in the Brain?

When you use your memory to travel back in time to earlier this morning, or last New Year's Eve, or to your early days in grade school, you are accessing information about these events that is stored in your brain. What form does this storage take? How can a record of what happened to you in the fifth grade be stored in neurons? One way researchers answer these questions is by looking at what happens at synapses in the brain.

Information Storage at the Synapse

Remember from Chapter 2 that synapses are the small spaces between the end of one neuron and the cell body or dendrite of another neuron (Figure 2.4), and that when signals reach the end of a neuron, they cause neurotransmitters to be released onto the next neuron. It is here, at the synapse, that the physiology of memory begins, according to an idea first proposed by the Canadian psychologist Donald Hebb.

Hebb (1948) introduced the idea that learning and memory are represented in the brain by physiological changes that take place at the synapse. Let's assume that a particular experience causes nerve impulses to travel down the axon of neuron A in Figure 6.20a, and when these impulses reach the synapse, neurotransmitter is released onto neuron B. Hebb's idea was that this activity strengthens the synapse by causing structural changes, greater transmitter release, and increased firing (Figures 6.20b and c). Hebb also proposed that all of these changes at the synapse, plus the many other synapses that are activated by a particular experience, provide a neural record of the experience. Memory, according to this idea, is represented by changes at the synapse.

Hebb's proposal that synaptic changes provide a record of experiences is still the starting point for modern research on the physiology of memory. Researchers who followed Hebb's lead determined that activity at the synapse causes a sequence of chemical reactions, which result in the synthesis of new proteins, which cause structural changes at the synapse like those shown in Figure 6.20c (Kida et al., 2002; Chklovskii et al., 2004).

One outcome of these changes at the synapse is a phenomenon called **long-term potentiation (LTP)**—enhanced firing of neurons after repeated stimulation (Bliss & Lomo, 1973; Bliss et al., 2003; Kandel, 2001). Long-term potentiation is illustrated by the firing records in Figure 6.20. The first time neuron A is stimulated, neuron B fires slowly (Figure 6.20a). However, after repeated stimulation (Figure 6.20b), B fires much more rapidly to the same stimulus (Figure 6.20c). LTP is important because it shows that repeated stimulation causes not only structural changes but also enhanced responding.

Forming Memories in the Brain: The Fragility of New Memories

We now move from considering how experience affects the structure and activity at synapses to how memories are stored in the brain. Researchers have studied failures of memory caused by trauma that results in a concussion or in permanent brain damage. There are numerous examples of situations in which people have been unable to remem-

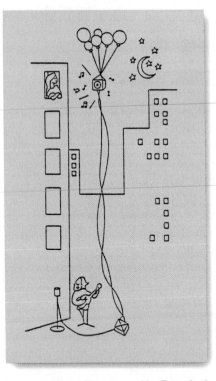

■ **Figure 6.19** Picture used by Bransford and Johnson (1972) to illustrate the effect of organization on memory. (Reprinted from *Journal of Verbal Learning and Verbal Behavior, 11*, J. D. Bransford & M. K. Johnson, "Contextual Prerequisites for Understanding: Some Investigations of Comprehension and Recall," pp. 717–726, Copyright © 1972, with permission from Elsevier.)

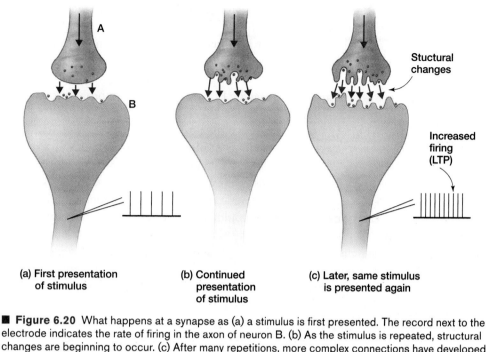

(a) First presentation of stimulus

(b) Continued presentation of stimulus

(c) Later, same stimulus is presented again

■ **Figure 6.20** What happens at a synapse as (a) a stimulus is first presented. The record next to the electrode indicates the rate of firing in the axon of neuron B. (b) As the stimulus is repeated, structural changes are beginning to occur. (c) After many repetitions, more complex connections have developed between the two neurons, which causes an increase in the firing rate, even though the stimulus is the same one that was presented in (a).

ber experiences that occurred just before a trauma. These examples are easy to find in football. As a player runs downfield on a kickoff, he is hit hard enough to suffer a concussion. Sitting on the sidelines after the play, he remembers lining up for the kickoff but doesn't remember running down the field or getting hit. The loss of memory for what has happened prior to the trauma is called **retrograde amnesia** (Figure 6.21).

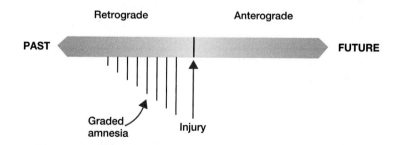

■ **Figure 6.21** Anterograde amnesia is amnesia for events that occur after an injury (the inability to form new memories). Retrograde amnesia is amnesia for events that happened before the injury (the inability to remember information from the past). The vertical lines, which symbolize the amount of retrograde amnesia, indicate that amnesia is more severe for events or learning that was closer in time to the injury. This is the graded nature of retrograde amnesia.

Retrograde amnesia also occurs in people who receive shock treatments, called *electroconvulsive therapy (ECT)*, to help relieve severe depression. In these treatments, a brief electrical current is passed through the brain, causing loss of consciousness for a few minutes. These patients typically suffer from retrograde amnesia upon awakening—they can't remember things that happened just before the shock (Squire, 1986). (However, amnesia caused by ECT is generally temporary, so most of the lost memories are eventually regained.)

One of the most famous cases of retrograde amnesia is H.M., whom we described on page 185. Remember that removal of H.M.'s hippocampus made it impossible for him to form new memories, a condition called **anterograde amnesia**. But H.M. also suffered from retrograde amnesia. H.M.'s retrograde amnesia extended back for about 10–15 years prior to his operation, but he could remember events that occurred before then. Thus, although he couldn't remember what had happened in the decade before his operation, he could remember events from his childhood, but apparently not with as much clarity and detail as a person without brain damage. H.M.'s retrograde amnesia is an example of **graded amnesia**—amnesia is most severe for events that occurred just prior to the injury and becomes less severe for earlier, more remote events (Frankland & Bontempi, 2005; Figure 6.21).

All of these examples show that memory for recent events is more fragile than memory for remote events. This means that a process must occur before memories become resistant to being disrupted. This process is called *consolidation*.

Forming Memories in the Brain: The Process of Consolidation

Consolidation transforms new memories from a fragile state, in which they can be disrupted, to a more permanent state, in which they are resistant to disruption (Frankland & Bontempi, 2005). This process involves a reorganization in the nervous system, which occurs at two levels. **Synaptic consolidation** occurs at synapses and happens rapidly, over a period of minutes. The structural changes shown in Figure 6.20 are an example of synaptic consolidation. **Systems consolidation** involves the gradual reorganization of circuits within brain regions and takes place on a longer time scale, lasting weeks, months, or even years.

Early research on consolidation, which focused on synaptic consolidation, discovered molecular processes involved in synthesizing the proteins that result in structural changes at the synapse. More recent research has focused on systems consolidation by investigating the role of different brain areas in consolidation. The case of H.M., who lost his ability to form new memories after his hippocampus was removed, indicates the importance of the hippocampus in consolidation. The graded property of retrograde amnesia, in which amnesia is worse for memories formed just before the brain injury, plus other evidence, led to the proposal of the **standard model of consolidation**. The standard model proposes that memory retrieval depends on the hippocampus during consolidation, and then once consolidation is complete, retrieval no longer depends on the hippocampus. Figure 6.22 shows the steps in this process (Frankland & Bontempi, 2005; Nadel & Moscovitch, 1997).

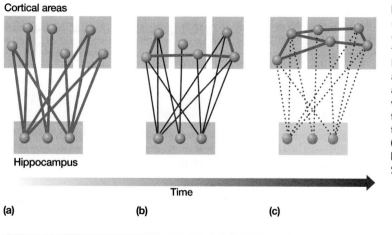

■ **Figure 6.22** Sequence of events that occur in consolidation. Connections between the cortex and the hippocampus are initially strong but weaken as connections within the cortex are established. (Adapted from Frankland & Bontempi, 2005.)

Incoming information activates a number of areas in the cortex (Figure 6.22a). Activation is distributed across the cortex because memories typically involve many sensory and cognitive areas. For example, your memory for last New Year's Eve could include sights, sounds, and possibly smells, as well as emotions you were feeling and thoughts you were thinking at the stroke of midnight. To deal with the fact that this experience results in activity that is distributed across many cortical areas, the cortex communicates with the hippocampus, as indicated by the color lines in Figure 6.22a. The hippocampus coordinates the activity of the different cortical areas, which, at this point, are not yet connected in the cortex.

The major mechanism of consolidation is **reactivation**, a process during which the hippocampus replays the neural activity associated with a memory. During reactivation, activity occurs in the network connecting the hippocampus and the cortex. This activity results in the formation of connections between the cortical areas (Figure 6.22b). This reactivation process occurs during sleep or during periods of relaxed wakefulness, and can also be enhanced if a person consciously rehearses a memory (Frankland & Bontempi, 2005; Huber et al., 2004; Nadel & Moscovitch, 1997; Peigneux et al., 2004). The idea that consolidation occurs during sleep is supported by the finding that memory for learning is enhanced when the learning is immediately followed by a period of sleep (Peigneux et al., 2004; Walker & Stickgold, 2004).

Eventually, the cortical connections become strong enough so that the different sites in the cortex become directly linked, and the hippocampus is no longer necessary (Figure 6.22c). Thus, according to this model, the hippocampus is strongly active when memories are first formed (Figure 6.23a), but become less active as memories

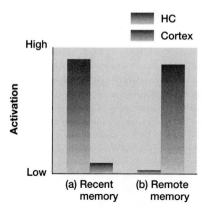

■ **Figure 6.23** According to the standard model of consolidation, retrieval of recent memories depends on the hippocampus, and cortical connections have not yet formed. (a) Thus, for retrieval of recent memories, hippocampal activation is high and cortical activation is low. Once consolidation has occurred, cortical connections have formed, and the hippocampus is no longer needed. (b) Thus, for retrieval of remote memories, cortical activation is high, and there is no hippocampal activation.

are consolidated, until eventually only cortical activity is necessary for **remote memories**—memories for events that occurred long ago (Figure 6.23b).

Most researchers accept that both the hippocampus and the cortex are involved in consolidation. There is, however, some disagreement regarding whether the hippocampus is important only at the beginning of consolidation, as depicted in Figure 6.23, or whether the hippocampus continues to be important, even for remote memories. The idea that the hippocampus is involved only at the beginning of consolidation is supported by experiments that show that recently learned memories cause activity in the **medial temporal lobe (MTL)** (which includes the hippocampus, or HC, and associated structures), but remote memories do not activate the MTL (Haist et al., 2001; Wiltgen et al., 2004; see Figure 6.24).

It is important to note that most of the evidence that the MTL is not activated for remote memories has involved *semantic* memories. There is, however, evidence that something different happens for *episodic* memories. When participants are instructed to engage in "mental time travel," so they become aware of the details of things that happened in the past, then MTL is activated both when recent episodic memories are retrieved *and* when remote episodic memories are retrieved. This is illustrated in Figure 6.25, which shows that the response of the hippocampus, measured with fMRI, is the same as people remember recent events and as they remember remote events (Ryan et al., 2001).

Another experiment, by Asaf Gilboa and coworkers (2004), elicited recent and remote episodic memories by showing participants photographs of themselves engaging

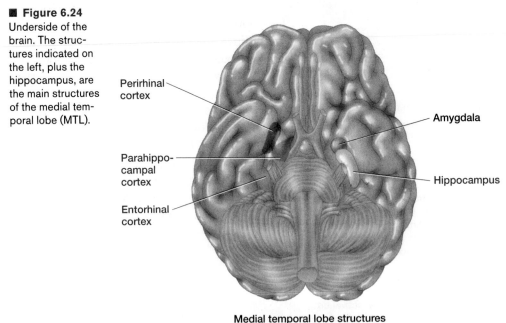

■ **Figure 6.24**
Underside of the brain. The structures indicated on the left, plus the hippocampus, are the main structures of the medial temporal lobe (MTL).

Perirhinal cortex

Parahippo-campal cortex

Entorhinal cortex

Amygdala

Hippocampus

Medial temporal lobe structures
(labelled in blue)

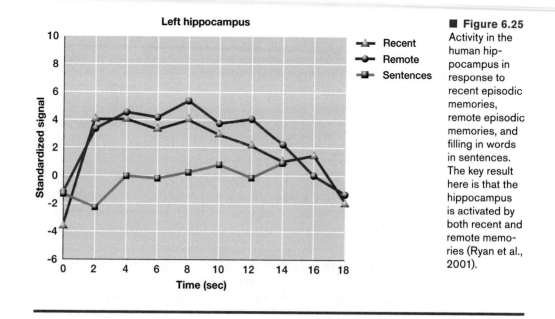

Figure 6.25
Activity in the human hippocampus in response to recent episodic memories, remote episodic memories, and filling in words in sentences. The key result here is that the hippocampus is activated by both recent and remote memories (Ryan et al., 2001).

in various activities that were taken at times ranging from very recently, to when they were 5 years old. The results of this experiment also showed that the hippocampus was activated during retrieval of both recent and remote memories.

The experiments that demonstrate MTL and HC activation when retrieving remote episodic memories support the idea that the hippocampus and MTL are *always* important when accessing the details of episodic memories (Moscovitch et al., 2005; Nadel & Moscovitch, 1997). This result, if confirmed, would call for revision of the standard model of consolidation, illustrated in Figures 6.22 and 6.23.

But not all of the evidence supports the idea that the standard model needs to be revised. For example, Peter Bayley and coworkers (2005) describe patients with damage to the MTL who were still able to remember the details of remote episodic memories. This result fits the standard model.

What these conflicting results tell us is that more research is needed to determine whether or not the hippocampus is involved in remote memories. One thing that can, however, be stated is that memories are not simply "stamped in." They involve changes at the synapse and a consolidation process involving both the hippocampus and the cortex, which can be influenced by activity in both the waking state and sleep. Memory is also influenced by characteristics of the stimuli that people experience. One of these characteristics is the emotional content of experiences.

Memory for Emotional Stimuli

When you think back to memorable events in your life, you might notice that highly emotional events stand out. Personal events such as beginning or ending relationships or events experienced by many people simultaneously, like the 9/11 terrorist attacks, seem to be remembered more easily and vividly than less emotionally charged events. This feeling that emotionally charged events are easier to remember has been confirmed by laboratory research. For example, when Kevin LaBar and Elizabeth Phelps (1998) tested participants' ability to recall arousing words (for example, profanity and sexually explicit words) and neutral words (like *street* and *store*) immediately after they were presented, they observed better memory for the arousing words (Figure 6.26a). Additionally, Florin Dolcos and coworkers (2005) tested participants' ability to recognize emotional and neutral pictures 1 year after they were initially presented and observed better memory for the emotional pictures (Figure 6.26b).

When we look at what is happening physiologically, one structure stands out—the amygdala. The importance of the amygdala has been demonstrated in a number of ways. For example, in the experiment by Dolcos described above, he measured fMRI as people were remembering and found that amygdala activity was higher for the emotional words (also see Cahill et al., 1996; Hamann et al., 1999).

The link between emotions and the amygdala has also been demonstrated by testing a patient, B.P., who had suffered damage to his amygdala. When participants without brain damage viewed a slide show about a boy and his mother in which the boy is injured halfway through the show, these participants had enhanced memory for the emotional part of the story (when the boy is injured). In contrast, B.P.'s memory was the same as that of the non–brain-damaged participants for the first part of the story but was not enhanced for the emotional part (Cahill et al., 1995). It appears, therefore, that emotions may trigger mechanisms in the amygdala that help us remember the event associated with the emotions.

Interestingly, emotion not only improves memory, but the advantage for emotional stimuli compared to neutral becomes even greater with time (Dolcos et al., 2005; LaBar & Phelps, 1998). It has therefore been suggested that emotions may enhance the process of consolidation (LaBar & Phelps, 1998). We will have more to say about this in Chapter 7, when we look at how people remember specific emotional events like the 9/11 terrorist attack.

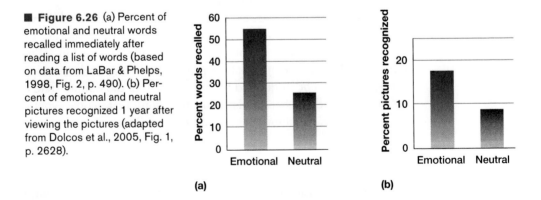

■ **Figure 6.26** (a) Percent of emotional and neutral words recalled immediately after reading a list of words (based on data from LaBar & Phelps, 1998, Fig. 2, p. 490). (b) Percent of emotional and neutral pictures recognized 1 year after viewing the pictures (adapted from Dolcos et al., 2005, Fig. 1, p. 2628).

How Do We Retrieve Information From Long-Term Memory?

Our emphasis so far has been on how information gets into LTM. We have described experiments that demonstrate the importance of elaborative encoding, forming connections with other information, generating material, and how material is organized. We have also seen that the consolidation of memories involves changes both at the synapses and in the hippocampus and cortex and that emotions may aid encoding.

Once memories have been created by effective encoding and physiological storage, we need to be able to retrieve them. The process of retrieval is extremely important because most of our failures of memory are failures of retrieval. These retrieval failures occur when the information is "in there," but we can't get it out. For example, you've studied hard for an exam but can't come up with the answer when you're taking the exam, only to remember it later when the exam is over. Or you can't remember a person's name when you unexpectedly see him or her, but it suddenly comes to you as the two of you are talking (or worse, after the person leaves). In both of these examples, the information you needed had been encoded, but you couldn't retrieve it when you needed it.

Retrieval Cues

Research on retrieval has focused on ways to get information out of storage and into consciousness. One of the most powerful ways to achieve this is to provide retrieval cues for that information. When we introduced retrieval cues on page 204, we defined them as cues that help us remember information stored in our memory. As we now consider these cues in more detail, we will see that this information can come from a number of different sources.

An experience I had as I was preparing to leave home to go to class illustrates how *location* can serve as a retrieval cue. While I was in my office at home, I had made a mental note to be sure to take the DVD on amnesia to school for my cognitive psychology class. A short while later, as I was leaving the house, I had a nagging feeling that I was forgetting something, but I couldn't remember what it was. This wasn't the first time I've had this problem, so I knew exactly what to do. I returned to my office, and as soon as I got there, I remembered that I was supposed to take the DVD. Returning to the place where I had originally thought about taking the disk helped me to retrieve my original thought. My office provided a retrieval cue for remembering what I wanted to take to class.

You may have had similar experiences in which returning to a particular place stimulated memories associated with that place. The following description by one of my students, which appeared in Chapter 1, illustrates retrieval of memories of childhood experiences.

> When I was 8 years old, both of my grandparents passed away. Their house was sold, and that chapter of my life was closed. Since then I can remember general things

about being there as a child, but not the details. One day I decided to go for a drive. I went to my grandparents' old house and I pulled around to the alley and parked. As I sat there and stared at the house, the most amazing thing happened. I experienced a vivid recollection. All of a sudden, I was 8 years old again. I could see myself in the backyard, learning to ride a bike for the first time. I could see the inside of the house. I remembered exactly what every detail looked like. I could even remember the distinct smell. So many times I tried to remember these things, but never so vividly did I remember such detail. (Angela Paidousis)

My experience in my office and Angela's experience outside her grandparents' house are examples of retrieval cues that are provided by returning to the location where memories were initially formed. There are many other things besides location that can provide retrieval cues. Hearing a particular song can bring back memories for events you might not have thought about for years. Or consider smell. I once experienced a musty smell like the stairwell of my grandparents' house and was instantly transported back many decades to the experience of climbing those stairs as a child.

The operation of retrieval cues has also been demonstrated in the laboratory using a technique called cued recall.

◖◗ Method

Cued Recall

We can distinguish two types of recall procedures. In **free recall** a participant is simply asked to recall stimuli. These stimuli could be a list of words presented by the experimenter or events experienced earlier in the participant's life. In **cued recall**, the participant is presented with cues to aid in recall of the previously experienced stimuli. These cues are typically a word or a phrase. For example, Endel Tulving and Zena Pearlstone (1966) did an experiment in which they presented participants with a list of words to remember. The words were drawn from specific categories such as "birds" (*pigeon, sparrow*), "furniture" (*chair, dresser*), and "professions" (*engineer, lawyer*), although the categories were not specifically indicated in the original list. For the memory test, participants in the free-recall group were asked to write down as many words as possible. Participants in the cued-recall group were also asked to recall the words, but were provided with the names of the categories, "birds," "furniture," and "professions" (Figure 6.27). ◆

The results of Tulving and Pearlstone's experiment demonstrate that retrieval cues aid memory. Participants in the free-recall group recalled 40 percent of the words, whereas participants in the cued-recall group recalled 75 percent of the words.

One of the most impressive demonstrations of the power of retrieval cues is provided by Timo Mantyla (1986), who presented his participants with a list of 600 nouns, such as *banana, freedom,* and *tree.* During learning, the participants were told to write down three words they associated with each noun. For example, three words for *banana* might be *yellow, bunches,* and *edible.* When the participants took a surprise memory test, in which they were presented with the three words they had created and were asked to

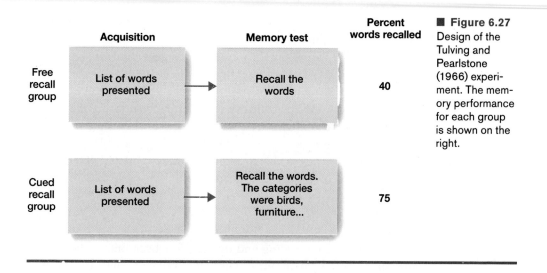

	Acquisition	Memory test	Percent words recalled
Free recall group	List of words presented	Recall the words	40
Cued recall group	List of words presented	Recall the words. The categories were birds, furniture...	75

Figure 6.27 Design of the Tulving and Pearlstone (1966) experiment. The memory performance for each group is shown on the right.

produce the original word, they were able to remember 90 percent of the 600 words (top bar in Figure 6.28).

Mantyla also ran another group of participants who did not create the three cues on their own. Rather, they were provided with three cues for each word that had been generated by someone else. When participants in this condition were later presented with the three cue words in a memory test, they were able to remember 55 percent of the nouns (second bar in Figure 6.28). You might think that it might be possible to

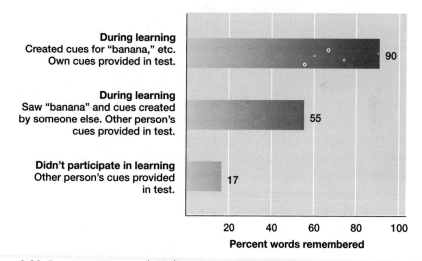

Figure 6.28 Results of Mantyla's (1986) experiment. Memory was best when retrieval cues were created by the person (top bar), not as good when retrieval cues were created by someone else (middle bar), and worst when the cues were created by someone else and the person had never seen them associated with the word (bottom bar).

guess "banana" from the three properties, *yellow*, *bunches*, and *edible*, even if you had never been presented with the word *banana*. But when Mantyla ran another control group in which he presented the cue words generated by someone else to participants who had never seen the original nouns, these participants were able to determine only 17 percent of the nouns. Thus, the result of this experiment demonstrates that retrieval cues (the three words) provide extremely effective information for retrieving memories, but that the retrieval cues were more effective when they were created by the person whose memory was being tested. (Also see Wagenaar, 1986, for a description of a study in which Wagenaar was able to remember almost all of 2,400 diary entries he kept over a 5-year period by using retrieval cues.)

Encoding Specificity

CogLab

**Encoding
Specificity**

The link between encoding and retrieval has been one of the recurring themes of this chapter. For example, in our discussion of retrieval cues, we saw that memory is better when a cue that was associated with an event is reinstated when the event is to be remembered. A principle that is closely related to retrieval cues is **encoding specificity**, which states that we learn information together with its context. Returning to our example of how Angela experienced a vivid recollection of experiences from her childhood, we can appreciate that she originally had these experiences within the context of her grandparent's house. Thus, when she returned to the house later, she remembered many of her past experiences.

A classic experiment that demonstrates encoding specificity is D. R. Godden and Alan Baddeley's (1975) "diving experiment." In this experiment, one group of participants put on diving equipment and studied a list of words underwater, and another group studied the words on land (Figure 6.29a). Each of these groups was then divided, so half of the participants were tested for recall on land and half were tested underwater. The results, shown in Figure 6.29b, indicate that the best recall occurred when encoding and retrieval occurred in the same location.

The results of the diving study, and many others, suggest that a good strategy for test taking would be to study in an environment similar to the environment in which you will be tested. Although this doesn't mean you necessarily have to do all of your studying in the classroom where you will be taking the exam, you might want to duplicate, in your study situation, some of the conditions that will occur during the exam.

This conclusion about studying is supported by an experiment by Harry Grant and coworkers (1998), using the design in Figure 6.30a. Participants read an article on psychoimmunology while wearing headphones. The participants in the "silent" condition heard nothing in the headphones. Participants in the "noisy" condition heard a tape of background noise recorded during lunchtime in a university cafeteria (which they were told to ignore). Half the participants in each group were then given a short-answer test on the article under the silent condition, and the other half were tested under the noisy condition.

The results, shown in Figure 6.30b, indicate that participants did better when the testing condition matched the study condition. Because your next cognitive psychology

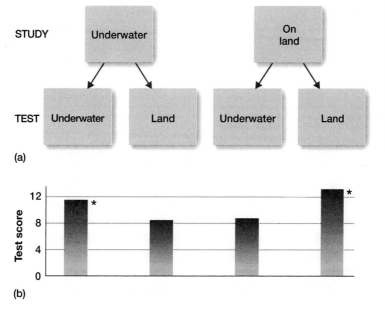

■ Figure 6.29
(a) Design for Godden and Baddeley's (1975) "diving" experiment. (b) Results for each test condition are indicated by the bar directly under that condition. Asterisks indicate situations in which study and test conditions matched.

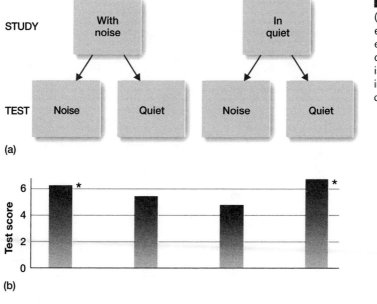

■ Figure 6.30
(a) Design for Grant et al.'s (1998) "studying" experiment. (b) Results of the experiment. Asterisks indicate situations in which study and test conditions matched.

Long-Term Memory: Basic Principles

exam will take place under silent conditions, it might make sense to study under silent conditions. (Interestingly, a number of my students report that having outside stimulation such as music or television present helps them study. This idea clearly violates the principle of state-dependent learning. Can you think of some other reasons that students might nonetheless say this?)

State-Dependent Learning

Another example of how the relationship between encoding and retrieval can influence memory is **state-dependent learning**—learning that is associated with a particular *internal state*, such as mood or state of awareness. According to the principle of state-dependent learning, memory will be better when a person's state during retrieval matches his or her internal state during encoding. For example, Eric Eich and Janet Metcalfe (1989) demonstrated that memory is better when a person's mood during retrieval matches his or her mood during encoding. They did this by asking participants to think positive thoughts while listening to "merry" music or depressing thoughts while listening to "melancholic" music (Figure 6.31a). Participants rated their mood while listening to the music, and the encoding part of the experiment began when their rating reached "very pleasant" or "very unpleasant." Once this occurred, usually within 15–20 minutes, participants studied lists of words while in their positive or negative mood.

After the study session ended, the participants were told to return in 2 days (although those in the sad group stayed in the lab a little longer, snacking on cookies and chatting with the experimenter while happy music played in the background, so they

■ **Figure 6.31**
(a) Design for Eich and Metcalfe's (1989) "mood" experiment.
(b) Results of the experiment.

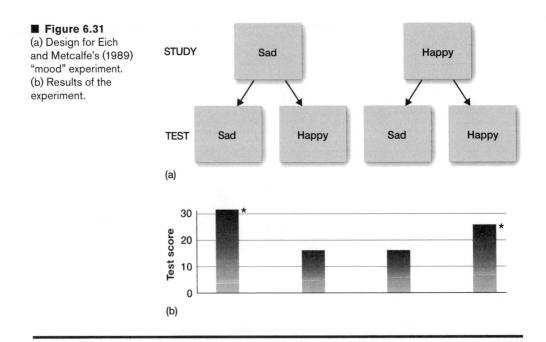

wouldn't leave the laboratory in a bad mood). Two days later, the participants returned, and the same procedure was used to put them in a positive or negative mood. When they reached the mood, they were given a memory test for the words they had studied 2 days earlier. The results, shown in Figure 6.31b, show that they did best when their mood at retrieval matched their mood during encoding (also see Eich, 1995).

▶▶▶ What Memory Research Tells Us About Studying

Although the laboratory research we have been describing is interesting, you may be more concerned with how to remember all this material about memory for the next exam! Luckily, many of the principles that have been discovered in the laboratory work outside the laboratory as well, and you can use some of them to increase the effectiveness of your studying.

The ideas in this section are presented as suggestions for you to consider. I say this because people's learning styles differ, and what might work for one person might be impractical or ineffective for another. Also, different types of material may require different techniques. One method of studying may work best for memorizing lists or definitions, and another method may be better for learning concepts or basic principles. We will consider the following five ways of improving learning and memory.

1. Elaborate and generate
2. Organize
3. Associate
4. Take breaks
5. Match learning and testing conditions

Elaborate and Generate

Because elaboration is one of the themes of this chapter, it should be no surprise that elaboration is an important part of effective studying. The step that helps transfer the material you are reading into long-term memory is elaboration—thinking about what you are reading and giving it meaning by relating it to other things that you know. Of course, it is easy to say this, but how can you actually do it?

One of the mistakes that many students make is that they study using maintenance rehearsal rather than elaborative rehearsal. I have talked with students who have spent many hours studying without achieving positive results because their method was just to read and reread the book and their lecture notes. (See the Preface to Students, pages xxxi–xxxii, for two principles related to the idea that just reading and rereading the material is often not an effective study technique.)

Reading the material is just the first step toward remembering the material. One of the most effective ways to achieve elaborative studying is to make up questions about the material. Research has shown that students who read a text with the idea of *making up* questions did as well on an exam as students who read a text with the idea of *answer-*

ing questions later, and both groups did better than a group who did not create or answer questions (Frase, 1975).

One way to create questions is to start with general questions and then get more specific. So the question "What is episodic memory?" might be followed by "How does episodic memory differ from semantic memory?" Making up questions is itself a form of elaborative processing, and so is attempting to answer the questions. Once you answer the questions, be sure to get feedback to see whether you were correct. Feedback helps track your progress and is also a form of elaborative processing.

The techniques we are describing work not only because they involve elaborative processing, but because of the generation effect, which we described on page 204. According to the generation effect, memory is better when you generate the material yourself than when you simply review information that is already present.

In the first edition of this book I invited students to send me e-mails describing study techniques they found effective. The following response, from Mahya Tavakkoli of the University of Toronto, is relevant to the idea of elaboration and generation:

> My study technique is to talk out loud and explain everything that I know. Sometimes when you read the material, you think "Yeah! I know this!" and move on. But when you get to the exam, you get stuck! This is because the material is not in front of you. So by explaining everything out loud, it makes much more sense. It's a good method to pretend that you're the professor trying to teach a class of 500 students. Then you really get excited about studying!

Mahya's method of "pretending you are the professor" is an excellent way of using both elaboration and generation to both encode material and ensure that you can retrieve it when you need it. The method of talking out loud may seem strange (do it where no one will hear you!) but is often used by teachers (the author of this book, included) to ensure that they know the material well enough to present it to a class.

Finally, beware of highlighting. A survey by S. W. Peterson (1992) found that 82 percent of students highlight, and most of them do so while they are reading the material for the first time. The problem with highlighting is that it seems like elaborative processing (you're taking an active role in your reading by highlighting important points), but it often becomes automatic behavior that involves moving the hand, but little deep thinking about the material. When Peterson (1992) compared comprehension for a group who highlighted and a group who didn't, he found no difference between the performance of the two groups when they were tested on the material. Highlighting may be a good first step for some people, but it is usually important to go back over what you highlighted using techniques such as elaborative rehearsal or generating questions in order to get that information into your memory.

Organize

We've seen that memory is better when the material is organized. Organization creates a framework that helps relate some information to other information and therefore makes the material more meaningful. Organization can be achieved by making "trees," as in Figure 6.18, or outlines or lists that group similar facts or principles together.

Organization also helps reduce the load on your memory. We can illustrate this by looking at a perceptual example. If you see the black and white pattern in Figure 3.23 as a bunch of black and white areas, it is extremely difficult to describe what it is. However, once you've seen this pattern as a Dalmatian it becomes meaningful and becomes much easier to describe and to remember (Wiseman & Neisser, 1974). This relates to the phenomenon of chunking that we discussed in Chapter 5. Grouping small elements into larger, more meaningful ones increases memory. Organizing material is one way to achieve this. (Also see page 348 in Chapter 9 for a discussion of how using images to create organization can be used to improve memory.)

Associate

An important aspect of elaborative processing is associating what you are learning to what you already know. This becomes easier as you learn more because your prior learning creates a structure on which to hang new information.

Techniques based on association, such as creating images that link two things, as in Figure 6.15, often prove useful for learning individual words or definitions. For example, when I was first learning the difference between proactive interference (old information interferes with learning new information; see page 147) and retroactive interference (new information interferes with remembering old information), I thought of a "PRO" football player smashing everything in his path as he runs forward in time. I no longer need this image to remember what proactive interference is, but it was helpful when I was first learning this concept.

Take Breaks

Saying "take breaks" is another way of saying, "study in a number of shorter study sessions rather than trying to learn everything at once," or "don't cram." There are good reasons to say these things. The main reason is that research has shown that memory is better when studying the material is broken into a number of short sessions with breaks in between than when studying occurs in one long session, even if study time is the same in both groups. This advantage for short study sessions is called the **distributed versus massed practice effect** (Reder & Anderson, 1982; Smith & Rothkopf, 1984).

The distributed versus massed practice effect occurs for a number of reasons, including the following:

1. It is difficult to maintain close attention to material throughout a long study session.
2. Studying after a break gives better feedback about what you actually know. Although it may be easy to read over something and to then remember it a few moments later, the real test is whether you remember it a few hours or days later.

Another angle on taking breaks is provided by the research we described on consolidation. Remember that consolidation is enhanced during sleep. Thus, one of the most effective breaks you can take from studying involves going to sleep. Not only does sleep have a restorative effect that improves your ability to concentrate and pay attention, but it helps consolidate what you were studying before you went to sleep.

Matching Learning and Testing Conditions

From what we know about encoding specificity and state-dependent learning, memory should be better when study (encoding) and testing (retrieval) conditions match as closely as possible. To strictly follow this procedure, you would have to do all of your studying in the classroom in which you will be taking the exam. This might be an impractical strategy, however, not only because of the logistics involved in studying in a room where there are other classes, but also because your classroom might not be a comfortable place to study, and you might not be highly motivated to spend even more time in your classroom. A solution to this problem is to study in a number of different places. Research has shown that people remember material better when they have learned it in a number of different locations, compared to spending the same amount of time studying in one location (Smith et al., 1978).

Looking at all of these techniques, we can see that many of them involve using more effective encoding strategies. Elaborating, generating, organizing, and associating all encourage deeper processing of the material you are trying to learn. But these techniques can also involve retrieval. Making up questions about the material helps encoding, but answering the questions, which involves retrieval, not only provides feedback about how well you know the material but helps achieve better encoding as well. Thus, as you try remembering something that you've studied, the very act of trying to remember creates stronger encoding of that material (Figure 6.32; see Buckner and Wheeler, 2001).

You may be using some of the study techniques we have described already, or you may benefit from trying them if you aren't. Do you have a study technique that isn't mentioned here, but that works for you and that you can relate to the memory principles we have discussed in this chapter? If so, I invite you to send a description of your technique to me at bruceg@email.arizona.edu.

■ **Figure 6.32** Attempting to retrieve information by answering questions about what you have studied can strengthen encoding. This strengthened encoding then increases the likelihood that retrieval will be successful.

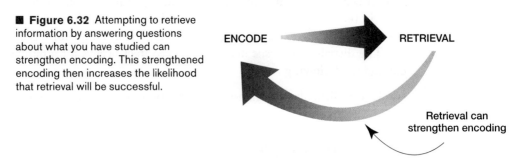

ENCODE   RETRIEVAL

Retrieval can strengthen encoding

Something to Consider

"These are exciting times in memory research. What once seemed simple and settled now seems complex and open to new ideas" (Nadel & Land, 2000). The "simple and settled" part of memory research that Lynn Nadel and Cantey Land are referring to are the following two ideas, which we discussed on page 210:

1. Memory is initially fragile, so a disrupting event that occurs shortly after a memory is formed can disrupt formation of the memory.
2. Once consolidation has occurred, then the same disrupting event cannot affect the memory.

What has changed in memory research so that now what seemed settled has become complex and open to new ideas? The answer to this question is that new experiments have caused many memory researchers to question the idea that once memory is consolidated, it cannot be disrupted (Lewis & Maher, 1965; Sara & Hars, 2006). One of these experiments, by Karim Nader and coworkers (2000a), used a procedure called fear conditioning.

◆▷ Method

Fear Conditioning

Conditioning is a procedure in which pairing a neutral stimulus with a stimulus that elicits a response causes the neutral stimulus to elicit that response. The classic example of conditioning is Pavlov's (1927) experiment in which he presented a ringing bell (the neutral stimulus) to a dog, followed by presentation of food (which causes the dog to salivate). This pairing eventually caused the dog to salivate when it heard the bell. **Fear conditioning** operates on the same principle, but the stimulus that initially causes a response is unpleasant and is therefore usually avoided. For example, if a rat hears a tone and then receives a shock to its foot, the shock causes the rat to freeze in place. This pairing of tone and shock causes the tone to take on properties of the shock, so when the rat is tested later, the previously neutral tone causes the fear response of freezing (Figure 6.33). ◆

Nader's experiments investigated how injection of the chemical *anisomycin* would affect fear conditioning in the rat. Anisomycin is an antibiotic that inhibits protein synthesis, which causes the structural changes at the synapse that are responsible for the formation of new memories (see page 209). Nader injected the anisomycin under three different conditions. The first two conditions produced results that fit the "simple" model of consolidation we described above.

Condition 1: Immediate presentation of anisomycin prevents conditioning. Inject anisomycin during initial conditioning. This disrupts memory formation because

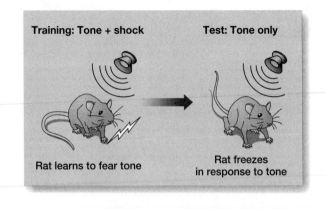

Training: Tone + shock

Test: Tone only

Rat learns to fear tone

Rat freezes
in response to tone

the anisomycin disrupts protein synthesis before consolidation can occur. This disruption is indicated by the fact that the rat does not freeze when the tone is presented on Day 3 (Figure 6.34a).

Condition 2: Later presentation of anisomycin alone has no effect. Inject anisomycin on Day 2, 24 hours after the pairing of the tone and shock. This does not disrupt the rat's memory for the tone-shock pairing, as indicated by the fact that the rat freezes when the tone is presented on Day 3. The ineffectiveness of the anisomycin in this condition means that by Day 2 consolidation has occurred. (Figure 6.34b). This is consistent with the principle that once memory is consolidated it can't be disrupted. However, the results of Nader's Condition 3 have caused many memory researchers to question this idea.

Condition 3: Later presentation of anisomycin with the tone eliminates conditioning. Re-present the tone on Day 2 and then inject anisomycin. Re-presenting the tone reactivates memory for the tone-shock pairing and causes the rat to freeze. Injecting the anisomycin shortly after memory is reactivated eliminates the rat's memory for the shock-tone pairing, as indicated by the fact that the rat does not freeze when the tone is presented on Day 3 (Figure 6.34c). This is the same result on Day 3 that occurred for Condition 1, except in this case the anisomycin was injected on Day 2, *after* the memory had been consolidated. Thus, by reactivating the memory on Day 2, Nader set up a situation in which the memory became vulnerable to disruption, and injecting the anisomycin eliminated the memory.

The result in Condition 3 shows that when a memory is reactivated, it becomes fragile, just as it was immediately after it was first formed. Nader and other researchers have proposed that after a memory is reactivated, the memory must undergo a process called **reconsolidation**, which is similar to the consolidation that occurred after the initial learning, although it apparently occurs more rapidly (Dudai, 2006; Dudai & Eisenberg, 2004; Nader, 2003; Nader & Land, 2000; Sara, 2000).

Looked at in this way, memory becomes susceptible to being changed or disrupted every time it is retrieved. You might think that this is not necessarily a good thing. Af-

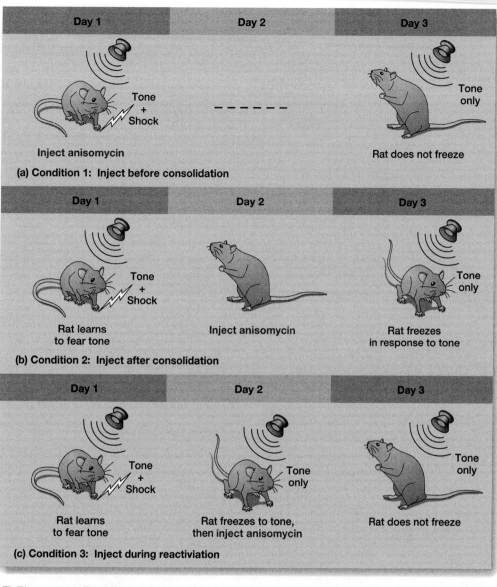

Figure 6.34 The effect on fear conditioning of injecting anisomycin. This is based on an experiment by Nader et al. (2000a). See text for details.

ter all, putting your memory at risk for disruption every time you use it doesn't sound particularly useful. However, everyday memory retrieval isn't usually accompanied by situations such as getting hit on the head, or being injected with a protein synthesis inhibitor, which would eliminate the memory. It is therefore unlikely that, in everyday experience, reactivation and subsequent reconsolidation would necessarily eliminate memories after they have been retrieved.

Reconsolidation might, however, provide an opportunity for reinforcing or updating memories. For example, consider an animal that returns to the location of a food source and finds that the food has been moved to a new nearby location. Returning to the original location reactivates the original memory, new information about the change in location updates the memory, and the updated memory is then reconsolidated. Looked at in this way, memory becomes a more dynamic and adaptable process. Rather than being fixed, memories can evolve to deal with new situations.

One of the questions facing memory researchers is whether a similar process occurs in humans. Most of the evidence for the idea of reactivation followed by reconsolidation comes from research on animals, and even this evidence indicates that reconsolidation may occur only under certain conditions. There is some suggestive evidence that reconsolidation may occur in humans (Nader, 2003), but more research needs to be done to determine if this does occur and, if so, under what conditions.

Based on psychological research on human memory, we know our memory is not static or fixed, but is a "work in progress" that is constantly being constructed and remodeled in response to new learning and changing conditions. We will be describing this aspect of memory in detail in the next chapter, when we consider the creative, constructive properties of memory.

Test Yourself 6.2

1. What is the idea behind the statement "Memories are stored at synapses"? What evidence supports this idea?
2. Why can we say that new memories are "fragile"?
3. According to the "standard model" of consolidation, what happens during systems consolidation? What modification to the standard model has been proposed? (Hint: It involves the hippocampus.)
4. How does the memory of emotional stimuli differ from memory for nonemotional stimuli? What happens physiologically when emotional stimuli are remembered?
5. Retrieval cues are a powerful way to improve the chances that we will remember something. Why can we say that memory performance is better when you use a word in a sentence, create an image, or relate it to yourself, all techniques involving retrieval cues? What further evidence for the effectiveness of retrieval cues has been provided by Tulving and Pearlstone and by Mantyla?
6. Describe all of the ways to demonstrate links between encoding and retrieval. Which of these specifically involve the relationship between encoding and retrieval? Be sure you understand encoding specificity and the experiments that demonstrate state-dependent learning.
7. Describe five ways of improving learning and memory that are relevant to achieving effective studying. Give examples for each.
8. What is reconsolidation? What are the implications of the results of experiments that demonstrate reconsolidation?

Chapter Summary

1. Long-term memory is an "archive" of information about past experiences in our lives and knowledge we have learned. LTM coordinates with working memory to help create our ongoing experience.

2. The primacy and recency effects that occur in the serial position curve have been linked to long-term memory and short-term memory, respectively.

3. The following evidence supports the idea that STM and LTM are two separate processes: (1) double dissociation between STM and LTM in patients with brain damage; (2) differences in the primary mode of coding, with LTM more likely to be coded semantically than STM.

4. Declarative memory is our conscious recollection of events we have experienced or facts we have learned. There are two types of declarative memory: Episodic memory is memory for personal events in our lives; semantic memory is memory for facts and knowledge.

5. According to Tulving, the defining property of the experience of episodic memory is that it involves mental time travel (self-knowing or remembering). The experience of semantic memory (knowing) does not involve mental time travel.

6. The following evidence supports the idea that episodic and semantic memory involve different mechanisms: (1) double dissociation of episodic and semantic memory in patients with brain damage; (2) brain imaging, which indicates that overlapping but different areas are activated by episodic and semantic memories.

7. Even though episodic and semantic memories are served by different mechanisms, they are connected in the following ways: (1) Episodic memories can be lost, leaving semantic; (2) semantic memory can be enhanced by association with episodic memory; (3) semantic memory can influence attention, and therefore what information we take in and potentially remember later.

8. Implicit memory occurs when previous experience improves our performance on a task, even though we do not remember the experience. Tulving calls implicit memory nonknowing.

9. Two types of implicit memory are repetition priming—when presenting a stimulus affects the response to the same stimulus or a similar stimulus when presented later—and procedural memory—memory for how to do things. The propaganda effect is an example of implicit memory.

10. The process of acquiring information and transferring it into memory is called encoding. Encoding therefore refers to the process used to get information into LTM.

11. Some mechanisms of encoding are more effective than others in transferring information into LTM. Maintenance rehearsal helps maintain information in STM but is not an effective way of transferring information into LTM. Elaborative rehearsal is a good way to establish LTMs.

12. Levels-of-processing theory states that memory depends on how information is encoded or programmed into the mind. According to this theory, shallow process-

ing is not as effective as deep processing. An experiment by Craik and Tulving showed that memory was better following deep processing than following shallow processing.

13. Transfer-appropriate processing refers to the finding that memory performance is enhanced when the type of coding that occurs during acquisition matches the type of retrieval that occurs during a memory test. The results of an experiment by Morris support this idea.

14. Additional factors that aid encoding are (1) finding connections with other information (the "chicken" sentence experiment; creating images; the self-reference effect); (2) generating information (the generation effect); and (3) organizing information (spontaneous organization during recall; Bower's "tree" experiment; the "balloon experiment" illustrating what happens when organization is difficult).

15. Research on the physiological basis of memory indicates that the formation of memories is associated with structural changes at the synapse. These structural changes are then translated into enhanced nerve firing, as indicated by long-term potentiation.

16. Concussions and electroconvulsive therapy can cause retrograde amnesia. This retrograde amnesia is graded, so that memory loss is greatest for events that happened closest in time to the trauma. This indicates that newly formed memories are fragile.

17. Consolidation transforms new memories into a state in which they are more resistant to disruption. Synaptic consolidation occurs at synapses and is rapid. Systems consolidation involves the reorganization of cortical circuits and is slower.

18. The standard model of consolidation proposes that memory retrieval depends on the hippocampus during consolidation and that after consolidation is complete, retrieval involves the cortex, and the hippocampus is no longer involved. There is evidence supporting the standard model, and also evidence supporting the idea that retrieval of episodic memories always involves the hippocampus.

19. Memory for emotional stimuli is generally enhanced compared to memory for neutral stimuli. The results of brain scanning and neuropsychological experiments indicate that the amygdala is involved in emotional memory.

20. Retrieving long-term memories is aided by retrieval cues. This has been determined by cued-recall experiments and experiments in which participants created retrieval cues that later helped them retrieve memories.

21. The principle of encoding specificity states that we learn information along with its context. Godden and Baddeley's "diving experiment" and Grant's studying experiment illustrate the effectiveness of encoding and retrieving information under the same conditions.

22. According to the principle of state-dependent learning, a person's memory will be better when his or her internal state during retrieval matches the state during encoding. Eich's mood experiment supports this idea.

23. Five memory principles that can be applied to studying are (1) elaborate and generate, (2) organize, (3) associate, (4) take breaks, and (5) match learning and test conditions.

24. Recent research on memory, based largely on fear conditioning in rats, indicates that memories can become susceptible to disruption when they are reactivated by retrieval. After reactivation these memories must be reconsolidated. This process may be a mechanism for refining and updating memories.

Think About It

1. What do you remember about the last 5 minutes? How much of what you are remembering is in your STM while you are remembering it? Were any of these memories ever in LTM?

2. On page 185, we described the case of K.F., who had normal LTM but poor STM. What problem does K.F.'s condition pose for the modal model of memory? Can you think of a way to modify the model that would handle K.F.'s condition?

3. Not all long-term memories are alike. There is a difference between remembering what you did 10 minutes ago, 1 year ago, and 10 years ago, even though all of these memories are called "long-term memories." What kinds of investigations could you carry out to demonstrate the properties of these different long-term memories?

4. Describe an experience in which retrieval cues led you to remember something. This experience could include things like returning to a place where your memory was initially formed, being somewhere that reminds you of an experience you had in the past, having someone else provide a "hint" to help you remember something, or reading about something that triggers a memory.

5. How do you study? Which study techniques that you use should be effective, according to the results of memory research? How could you improve your study techniques by taking into account the results of memory research? (Also see Preface to Students, pages xxxi–xxxii.)

6. Rent movies like *Memento, 50 First Dates*, or the ones listed in the Box "Memory Loss in the Movies" (see page 178). Describe the memory loss depicted in these movies, and compare their problem with the cases of memory loss described in this chapter. Determine how accurately depictions of memory loss in movies correspond to memory loss that occurs in actual cases of trauma or brain damage. You may have to do some additional research on memory loss to answer this question (for example, start by doing a Google search for "memory loss" or "amnesia").

If You Want to Know More

1. Top-down processing and the suffix effect. The suffix effect occurs when a sound presented at the end of a list of words decreases the recency effect in the serial-position curve. This effect can depend on the participant's interpretation of the meaning of the sound, which means that top-down processing can be involved in this effect.

Neath, I., Surprenant, A. M., & Crowder, R. G. (1993). The context-dependent stimulus suffix effect. *Journal of Experimental Psychology: Learning, Memory and Cognition, 19*, 698–703.

2. Superior memory. What distinguishes people who have superior memory capabilities from people with "normal" memory capabilities? Apparently, in some cases, the answer has to do with the strategies that these people use.

Maguire, E. A., Valentine, E. R., Wilding, J. M., & Kapur, N. (2003). Routes to remembering: The brains behind superior memory. *Nature Neuroscience, 6*, 90–95.

Wilding, J., & Valentine, E. R. (1997). *Superior memory.* Hove, UK: Psychology Press.

3. Memory loss in Alzheimer's disease. Patients with Alzheimer's disease experience progressive loss of memory as different structures are attacked by the disease.

Fleischman, D. A., & Gabrieli, J. (1999). Long-term memory in Alzheimer's disease. *Current Opinion in Neurobiology, 9*, 240–244.

Fleischman, D. A., Wilson, R. S., Gabrieli, J. D. E., Schneider, J. A., Bienias, J. L., & Bennett, D. A. (2005). Implicit memory and Alzheimer's disease: Neuropathology. *Brain, 128*, 2006–2015.

Gilboa, A., Ramirex, J., Kohler, S., Westmacott, R., Black, S. E., & Moscovitch, M. (2005). Retrieval of autobiographical memory in Alzheimer's disease: Relation to volumes of medial temporal lobe and other structures. *Hippocampus, 15*, 535–550.

4. Cognitive changes in normal aging. Cognitive changes occur normally, as people age. Some of these changes have been related to changes in the brain.

Cabeza, R., Anderson, N. D., Locantore, J. K., & McIntosh, A. R. (2002). Aging gracefully: Compensatory brain activity in high-performing older adults. *Neuroimage, 17*, 1394–1402.

Hedden, T., & Gabrieli, J. D. E. (2004). Insights into the ageing mind: A view from cognitive neuroscience. *Nature Reviews Neuroscience, 5*, 87–97.

5. Reconsolidation and therapy. The idea of reconsolidation has led to speculation about new ways to treat problems such as obsessive-compulsive disorder and drug dependency.

Lee, J. L. C., DiCiano, P., Thomas, K. L., & Everitt, B. J. (2005). Disrupting reconsolidation of drug memories reduces cocaine-seeking behavior. *Neuron, 47*, 795–801.

Nader, K. (2003). Memory traces unbound. *Trends in Neurosciences, 26*, 65–70.

6. Tip-of-the-tongue phenomenon. The tip-of-the-tongue (TOT) experience occurs when a person can't retrieve a memory but has a strong feeling that he or she will be able to retrieve it sooner or later.

Brown, R., & McNeil, D. (1966). The "tip of the tongue" phenomenon. *Journal of Verbal Learning and Verbal Behavior, 5,* 325–337.

Schwartz, B. I., Travis, D. M., Castro, A. M., & Smith, S. S. (2000). The phenomenology of real and illusory tip-of-the-tongue states. *Memory & Cognition, 28,* 18–27.

Key Terms

Anterograde amnesia, 210

Conditioning, 225

Consolidation, 210

Cued recall, 216

Declarative memory, 186

Deep processing, 199

Depth of processing, 198

Distributed versus massed practice effect, 223

Elaborative rehearsal, 197

Encoding, 196

Encoding specificity, 218

Episodic memory, 187

Fear conditioning, 225

Free recall, 216

Generation effect, 204

Graded amnesia, 210

Implicit (nondeclarative) memory, 186

Knowing, 188

Korsakoff's syndrome, 177

Levels of processing (LOP), 197

Levels-of-processing theory, 197

Long-term potentiation (LTP), 208

Maintenance rehearsal, 197

Medial temporal lobe (MTL), 212

Mental time travel, 187

Nonknowing, 191

Personal semantic memory, 190

Primacy effect, 182

Priming stimulus, 192

Procedural memory, 191

Propaganda effect, 196

Reactivation, 211

Recall test, 193

Recency effect, 184

Recognition test, 193

Reconsolidation, 226

Remembering, 187

Remote memory, 212

Repetition priming, 191

Retrieval, 197

Retrieval cues, 204

Retrograde amnesia, 209

Self-knowing, 187

Self-reference effect, 203

Semantic memory, 187

Serial-position curve, 182

Shallow processing, 198

Standard model of consolidation, 210

State-dependent learning, 220

Synaptic consolidation, 210

Systems consolidation, 210

Transfer-appropriate processing, 200

CogLab

To experience these experiments for yourself, go to http://coglab.wadsworth.com. Be sure to read each experiment's setup instructions before you go to the experiment itself. Otherwise, you won't know which keys to press.

Primary Labs

Serial position How memory for a list depends on an item's position on the list (p. 182).

Implicit learning How we can learn something without being aware of the learning (p. 191).

Levels of processing How memory is influenced by depth of processing (p. 197).

Encoding specificity How memory is affected by both conditions at encoding and retrieval, and the relation between them (p. 218).

Related Labs

Suffix effect How adding an irrelevant item to the end of a list affects recall for the final items on a list in a serial-position experiment.

Von Restorff effect How the distinctiveness of a stimulus can influence memory.

Stimulus List for "Serial Position" Demonstration on Page 182

1. barricade
2. children
3. diet
4. gourd
5. folio
6. meter
7. journey
8. mohair
9. phoenix
10. crossbow
11. doorbell
12. muffler
13. mouse
14. menu
15. airplane

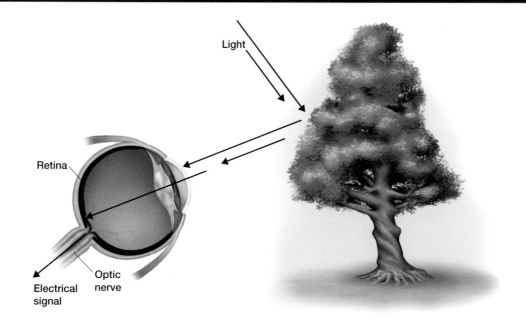

Light

Retina

Optic nerve

Electrical signal

● **Color Plate 2.1** Light reflected from the tree enters the eye through the pupil, and electrical signals leave the back of the eye in the optic nerve. Our perception of the tree is based on the information contained in these electrical signals. (p. 32)

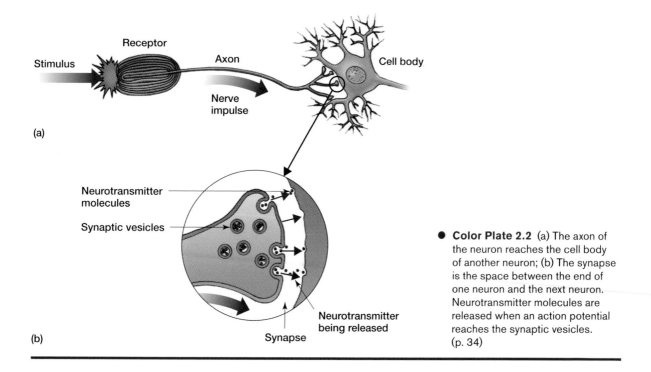

Receptor

Stimulus

Axon

Cell body

Nerve impulse

(a)

Neurotransmitter molecules

Synaptic vesicles

Neurotransmitter being released

Synapse

(b)

● **Color Plate 2.2** (a) The axon of the neuron reaches the cell body of another neuron; (b) The synapse is the space between the end of one neuron and the next neuron. Neurotransmitter molecules are released when an action potential reaches the synaptic vesicles. (p. 34)

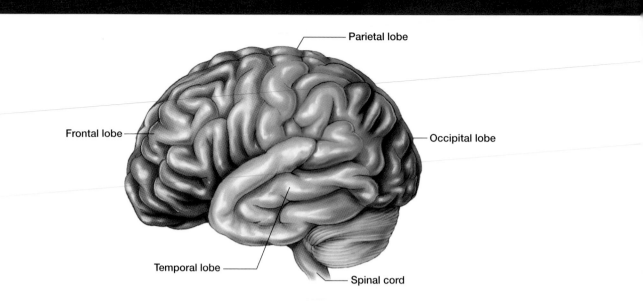

Parietal lobe

Frontal lobe

Occipital lobe

Temporal lobe

Spinal cord

● **Color Plate 2.3** The human brain, showing the four major lobes. (p. 43)

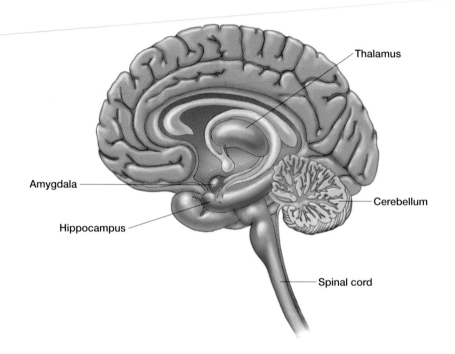

Thalamus

Amygdala

Cerebellum

Hippocampus

Spinal cord

● **Color Plate 2.4** Cross-section of the human brain, showing a number of the subcortical areas that are important for cognition. (p. 43)

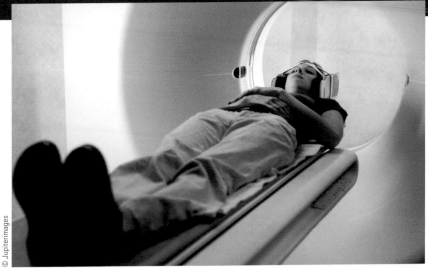

(a)

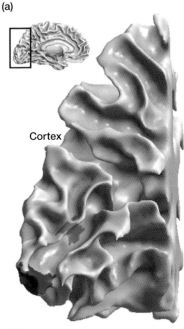

Cortex

(b)

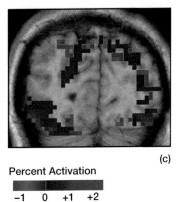

(c)

Percent Activation

−1   0   +1   +2

● **Color Plate 2.5** (a) Person in a brain scanner. (b) Results of measurements made by PET and fMRI are displayed by using colors to indicate areas of the brain that are activated. The colored areas in this three-dimensional picture of the brain indicate areas that were activated by visual stimuli presented at two different locations in space. The area colored violet was activated by stimuli directly in front of the person. The area colored blue was activated by stimuli off to the side. (c) The colored areas in this brain cross-section were activated by viewing pictures of faces. The amount of activation is indicated by the specific color. Yellow and red indicate increases in activation. Blue and green indicate decreases in activation. (p. 45)

(Part b: From "Visual Field Representations and Locations of Visual Areas V1/2/3 in Human Visual Cortex," by R. F. Dougherty, V. M. Koch, A. A. Brewer, B. Fischer, J. Modersitzki, & B. A. Wandell, *Journal of Vision, 3,* pp. 586–598. Part c: From "The Representation of Objects in the Human Occipital and Temporal Cortex," by Alumit Ishai, Leslie G. Ungerleider, Alex Martin, & James V. Haxby, *Journal of Cognitive Neuroscience, 12:*2, pp. 35–51. © 2000 by the Massachusetts Institute of Technology.)

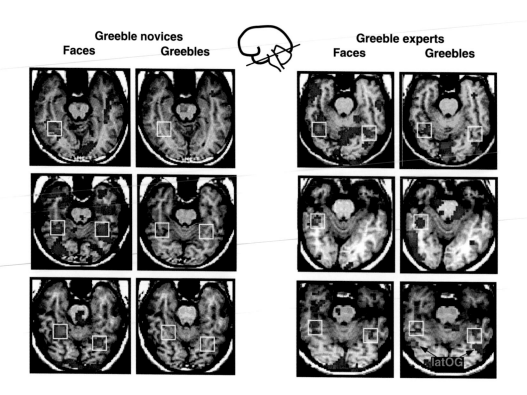

● **Color Plate 2.6** Brain activation caused by seeing faces and Greebles for Greeble novices (left two columns) and Greeble experts (right two columns). Records for three different participants are shown. The location of the fusiform face area (FFA) is indicated by the white squares. Comparing the right column for Greeble experts to the right column for Greeble novices show that becoming a Greeble expert causes an increase in FFA activation for Greebles. (p. 48)

(From "Activation of the Middle Fusiform 'Face Area' Increases With Expertise in Recognizing Novel Objects," by I. Gauthier, M. J. Tarr, A. W. Anderson, P. Skudlarski, & J. C. Gore, *Nature Neuroscience, 2*, pp. 568–573. Copyright 1999. Reprinted by permission from Macmillian Publishers Ltd.)

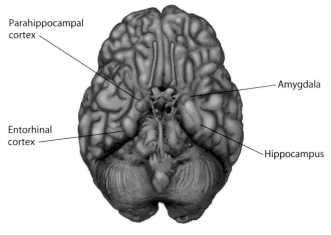

Parahippocampal cortex

Amygdala

Entorhinal cortex

Hippocampus

(a)

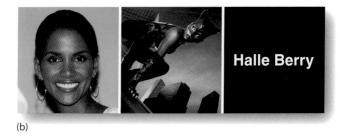

Halle Berry

(b)

● **Color Plate 2.7** (a) Location of the hippocampus and some of the other structures that were studied by Quiroga and coworkers (2005). (b) Some of the stimuli that caused a neuron in the hippocampus to fire. (p. 50)

(Part b, from left: Evan Agostini/Getty Images; © Doane Gregory/Warner Bros./Bureau L.A. Collection/CORBIS.)

1 8

Color Plate 3.1 Stimuli for Treisman and Schmidt's (1982) illusory conjunction experiment. (p. 67)

(From "Illusory Conjunctions in the Perception of Objects," by A. M. Treisman & H. Schmidt, *Cognitive Psychology, 14,* pp. 107–141. Copyright 1982. With permission from Elsevier.)

Color Plate 3.2 Three stimuli used by Treisman to illustrate how top-down processing can influence the combining of features. (p. 68)

(From "Illusory Conjunctions in the Perception of Objects," by A. M. Treisman & H. Schmidt, *Cognitive Psychology, 14,* pp. 107–141. Copyright 1982. With permission from Elsevier.)

● **Color Plate 3.3** *The Forest Has Eyes* by Bev Doolittle (1985). Can you find 12 faces in this picture? (p. 78)

(a)

(b)

● **Color Plate 3.4** An environmental sculpture by Thomas Macaulay. (a) When viewed from exactly the right vantage point, the stones appear to be arranged in a circle. (b) Viewing the stones from another angle reveals a truer picture of their configuration. (p. 81)

● **Color Plate 3.5** Try separating each of the buildings at A and at B in this skyline of Pittsburgh. Most people can do this easily. For example, they can tell that there are two separate buildings to the right of B, a square-shaped, smaller building in front of a much taller building, with a spire sticking up into the clouds. However, separating these buildings is not easy for a computer. There are many other places in this scene that would pose problems for a computer. For example, is the dark cloud at C attached to the spire? Is the yellow band at D part of the stands in the baseball field, or is it across the river? (p. 81)

● **Color Plate 3.6** Who are these people? See page 98 for the answers. (p. 83)

(From "Recognizing Complex Patterns," by P. Sinha, *Nature Neuroscience Supplement, 5*, pp. 1094–1097. Copyright 2002. Reprinted by permission from Macmillan Publishers Ltd.)

Bruce Goldstein

● **Color Plate 3.7** A portion of the mess on the author's desk. Can you locate the hidden pencil (easy) and the author's glasses (hard)? (p. 82)

Bruce Goldstein

● **Color Plate 3.8** Stimulus for change-blindness demonstration. See text. (p. 92)

Bruce Goldstein

● **Color Plate 4.1** Stimulus for Stroop demonstration. See text. (p. 117)

YELLOW   **RED**   **BLUE**   **PURPLE**   **GREEN**

ORANGE   **YELLOW**   **GREEN**   **BLUE**   **RED**

GREEN   **PURPLE**   **ORANGE**   **RED**   **BLUE**

● **Color Plate 4.2** Stimulus for Stroop demonstration. See text. (p. 117)

Courtesy of John M. Henderson, University of Edinburgh

First fixation

● **Color Plate 4.3** Scan path of a person viewing a picture of a fountain in Bordeaux, France. Fixations are indicated by the yellow dots, and eye movements (saccades) by the red lines. This person looked at high-interest areas, such as the statues and lights, but ignored areas such as the fence and the sky. (p. 120)

(a) Visual scene

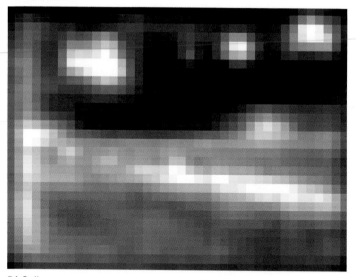

(b) Saliency map

● **Color Plate 4.4** (a) Visual scene; (b) saliency map of the scene determined by analyzing the color, contrast, and orientations in the scene. Lighter areas indicate greater salience. (p. 120)

(Reprinted from "Modeling the Role of Salience in the Allocation of Overt Visual Attention," by D. Parkhurst, K. Law, & E. Niebur, *Vision Research, 42,* pp. 107–123. Copyright 2002. With permission from Elsevier.)

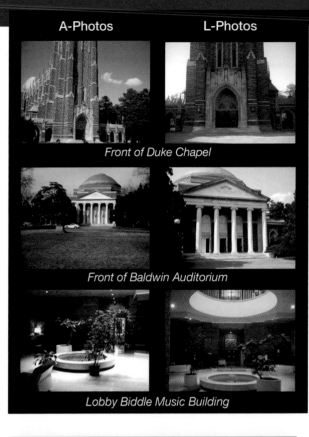

A-Photos | L-Photos

Front of Duke Chapel

Front of Baldwin Auditorium

Lobby Biddle Music Building

● **Color Plate 7.1** Photographs from Cabeza and coworkers' (2004) experiment. A-photos ("autobiographical") were taken by the participant. L-photos ("laboratory") were taken by someone else. These photos were used in the memory experiment described in the text. (p. 239)

(From "Brain Activity During Episodic Retrieval of Autobiographical and Laboratory Events: An fMRI Study Using Novel Photo Paradigm," by R. Cabeza, S. E. Prince, S. M. Daselaar, D. L. Greenberg, M. Budde, F. Dolcos, K. S. LaBar, & D. C. Rubin, *Journal of Cognitive Neuroscience, 16*, pp. 1583–1594. Copyright 2004.)

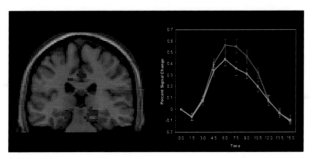

(a) Parietal cortex

(b) Parahippocampal gyrus

A photos = more activation

● **Color Plate 7.2** (a) fMRI response of an area in the parietal cortex showing areas activated by both the A-photos and the L-photos during the memory test. The graph on the right indicates that activation was the same for the A-photos and L-photos. (b) Areas in the parahippocampal gyrus that were activated by the A-photos and the L-photos. The graph indicates that for this area of the brain, activation was greater for the A-photos. (p. 240)

(From "Brain Activity During Episodic Retrieval of Autobiographical and Laboratory Events: An fMRI Study Using Novel Photo Paradigm," by R. Cabeza, S. E. Prince, S. M. Daselaar, D. L. Greenberg, M. Budde, F. Dolcos, K. S. LaBar, & D. C. Rubin, *Journal of Cognitive Neuroscience, 16*, pp. 1583–1594. Copyright 2004.)

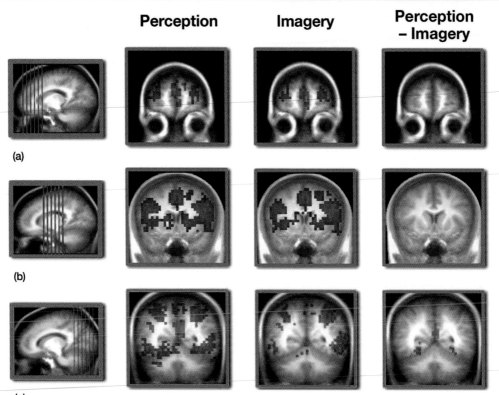

| | Perception | Imagery | Perception – Imagery |

(a)

(b)

(c)

● **Color Plate 9.1** Brain scan results from Ganis et al. (2004). The vertical lines through the brains in the far left column indicate where activity was being recorded. (a) The columns labeled "Perception" and "Imagery" indicate the response of areas in the frontal lobe in the perception and imagery conditions. "Perception − Imagery" indicates the difference between activation in these two conditions. The absence of color in this record indicates that activation was the same. (b) Responses farther back in the brain. Activation was the same in this area as well. (c) Responses from the back of the brain, including the primary visual area. The color in the far right record indicates that there was a greater response in the perception condition. (p. 339)

(Reprinted from "Brain Areas Underlying Visual Mental Imagery and Visual Perception: An fMRI Study," by G. Ganis, W. L. Thompson, & S. M. Kosslyn, *Cognitive Brain Research, 20,* pp. 226–241. Copyright 2004.)

● **Color Plate 10.1 (facing page)** (a) Results of Roberson et al.'s (2000) color-naming experiment for the British participants. The identity of the colored Munsell chip located at any place on a diagram can be determined by referring to the notations along the top and left sides of the diagrams. For example, the Munsell name of the chip indicated by the dot is Chip 5B-9. British participants call this chip "blue." (b) Results for the Berinmo participants. The Berinmo call Chip 5B-9 "wap." (c) The results of Regier et al.'s (2005) analysis of "best color" judgments for over 100 different languages, using the color stimuli shown in Color Plate 10.3. The circular areas indicate colors that were judged to be the best examples of colors in each language. Although there is some variability, there is also general agreement across cultures regarding which colors are "best." (p. 387)

(Part a: Reprinted from "Color Categories Are Not Universal: Replications and New Evidence From a Stone-Age Culture," by D. Roberson et al., 2000, *Journal of Experimental Psychology: General, 129,* pp. 369–398, Figures 1 and 2. Copyright © 2000 with permission from the American Psychological Association. Part b: "Language, Thought, and Color: Recent Developments," by P. Kay & T. Regier, *Trends in Cognitive Sciences, 10,* pp. 51–54. Copyright 2006. Part c: "Focal Colors Are Universal After All," by T. Regier, P. Kay, & R. S. Cook, *Proceedings of the National Academy of Sciences, 102,* pp. 8386–8391. Copyright 2005.)

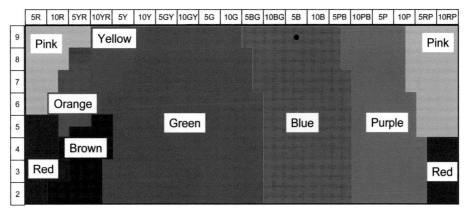

(a)

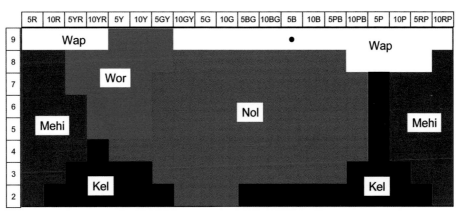

(b)

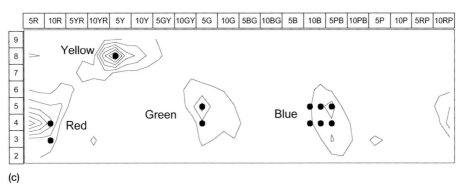

(c)

● **Color Plate 10.1**

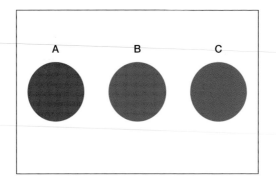

A   B   C

● **Color Plate 10.2** Color chips like those used in Roberson's categorical perception experiment. Participants were asked to indicate whether two chips are the same or different. For example, a participant would be asked to respond "same" or "different" when shown chips A and B, or when shown chips B and C. For the British participants, chips B and C are more likely to be judged to be different because they have different color names. (p. 387)

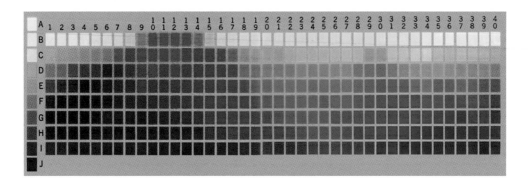

● **Color Plate 10.3** Munsell chips that Reiger et al. (2005) used in their color naming experiment. The results of this experiment are shown in Color Plate 10.1c. (p. 388)

(Courtesy, Richard Cook, University of California at Berkeley; Paul Kay, International Computer Science Institute, Berkeley, California; Terry Regier, University of Chicago. http://www.icsi.berkeley/edu/wcs/data.html)

Everyday Memory and Memory Errors

7

Prospective Memory: What I'm Going to Do Later

Autobiographical Memory: What Has Happened in My Life
   The Multidimensional Nature of Autobiographical
     Memory
   Memory Over the Life Span
   Flashbulb Memories
   ◄► Method: Repeated Recall

The Constructive Nature of Memory
   Bartlett's "War of the Ghosts" Experiment
   Educated Guesses About High School Grades
   Source Monitoring and Source Monitoring Errors

Test Yourself 7.1
   Making Inferences
   🖝 Demonstration: Reading Sentences
   Schemas and Scripts
   Remembering a List of Words
   🖝 Demonstration: Memory for a List
   The Advantages and Disadvantages of Construction

Memory Can Be Modified or Created by Suggestion
   The Misinformation Effect
   ◄► Method: Presenting Misleading Postevent Information
   Creating False Memories for Early Events in People's Lives

Why Do People Make Errors in Eyewitness Testimony?
   Errors of Eyewitness Identification
   The Crime Scene and Afterward
   What Is Being Done?

Something to Consider: Memories of Childhood Abuse

Test Yourself 7.2

Chapter Summary

Think About It

If You Want to Know More

Key Terms

CogLab: Remember/Know; False Memory;
Forgot It All Along Effect

Some Questions We Will Consider

- What kinds of events from their lives are people most likely to remember? (240)
- What properties of the memory system make it both highly functional and also prone to error? (249)
- Why is eyewitness testimony often cited as the cause of wrongful convictions? (266)

It should be clear by now that memory is not just a "stamp pad of experience"—a place where information comes in and is automatically stored for future reference. Experiences become encoded, manipulated by a short-term process called working memory, admitted or not admitted to long-term memory, solidified over a period of time through the process of consolidation, and transferred back to working memory when needed.

Chapters 5 and 6 introduced the idea that the process of memory is complex. We saw that working memory has a number of components and that there are different types of long-term memory. We also saw that our ability to remember depends not only on the structure of the memory system, but on how we program information into the system. But to truly understand memory, we need to consider how memory operates in the environment. Think about what this means. How much of what happens to you in a typical day do you remember a few hours later, a few days later, a year later? It is clear that we remember only a few of the multitude of things that happen to us every day.

Our main focus in this chapter will be to ask why we remember certain things, and why what we remember sometimes does not correspond to what actually happened. We will see that studying the errors we make when remembering leads to the conclusion that what we remember is determined by creative mental processes (Figure 7.1). We will see that this creativity is a gift that helps us determine what happened when we

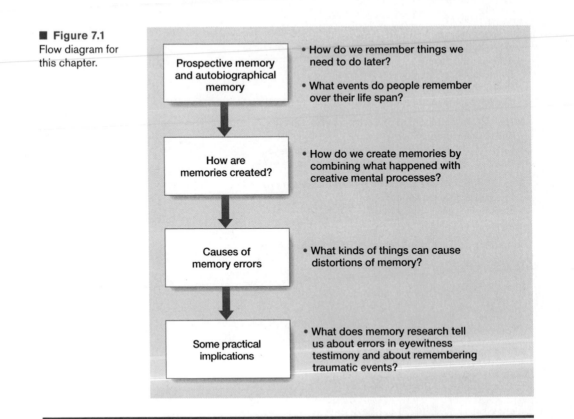

■ **Figure 7.1**
Flow diagram for this chapter.

Prospective memory and autobiographical memory
- How do we remember things we need to do later?
- What events do people remember over their life span?

How are memories created?
- How do we create memories by combining what happened with creative mental processes?

Causes of memory errors
- What kinds of things can cause distortions of memory?

Some practical implications
- What does memory research tell us about errors in eyewitness testimony and about remembering traumatic events?

have incomplete information, but that this creativity can also affect the accuracy of our memory. To begin our consideration of memory in the environment, we will first consider how we remember what needs to be done in the future.

◆◆◆ Prospective Memory: What I'm Going to Do Later

What does your "To Do" list look like for today? Remembering what you need to do and then doing these things involves **prospective memory**—remembering to perform intended actions, like going to class, taking your books to school, keeping an evening appointment, or taking medications. Two components are necessary for successful prospective memory performance: (1) remembering what you want to do, and (2) remembering to do it at the right time. These two things are easy for events that occur on a regular basis, like brushing your teeth in the morning or being at your cognitive psychology class at the same time every Tuesday and Thursday. But for things that occur just occasionally, cues to remind you to do something can be important.

Giles Einstein and Mark McDaniel (1990) hypothesized that prospective memory might be better when these cues are distinctive than when they are familiar. Consider, for example, the task of delivering a message to your friend Ralph. Seeing Ralph later in the day might function as a cue to remind you to deliver the message. However, Einstein and McDaniel propose that distinctive cues are more effective than familiar cues. If this is so, remembering to deliver the message to Ralph might be harder than remembering to deliver a message to a stranger. This would occur both because the stranger provides a distinctive cue, which stands out more than Ralph, who you see every day, and because seeing Ralph might trigger associations—such as talking about the movie your saw last night—which could distract you from remembering to deliver the message.

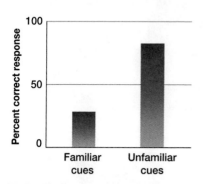

■ **Figure 7.2** Results of Einstein and McDaniel's (1990) prospective memory experiment, showing that correct responses are more likely for unfamiliar cue words.

Einstein and McDaniel devised a procedure to study the effect of cue familiarity on prospective memory. Their participants were told that they would see a list of words on a computer screen and that they should press a key when a cue word was presented. In the "familiar" condition, cue words like *rake* and *method* were used. In the unfamiliar condition, cue words like *sone* and *monad* were used. The results, shown in Figure 7.2, confirm the idea that unfamiliar cues result in better prospective memory: Correct responses were three times more likely for unfamiliar cue words than for familiar cue words.

Einstein and McDaniel were studying an *event-based task*—the task (pushing a button) is triggered when an external event occurs (presentation of the cue word). The example of delivering a message when seeing Ralph is also an event-based task. Another type of prospective memory task is a *time-based task*. In this case, the task is to remember to do something at a particular time. For example, your doctor tells you that you need to take a pill every morning for the next

2 weeks. This type of task is potentially more difficult than an event-based task, because there is no cue. Daniel Schacter (2001) suggests that a solution to this problem is to create cues that turn the time-based task into an event-based task. Schacter suggests, for example, that one way to remember to take a pill in the morning would be to place the medication next to your toothbrush, so when you brush your teeth in the morning you will remember to take the pill.

Prospective memory is clearly important and complicated (see Einstein & Mc-Daniel, 2005; Kliegel et al., 2004; Penningroth, 2005, for further research on prospective memory). But most memory research has focused on how we retrieve memories from our past. When we retrieve memories from our past, we are usually dealing with autobiographical memory—memory for events we have experienced.

◆◆◆ Autobiographical Memory: What Has Happened in My Life

Autobiographical memory has been defined as recollected events that belong to a person's past (Rubin, 2005). When we remember the events that make up the stories of our life by using "mental time travel" to place ourselves back into a specific situation, we are experiencing autobiographical memory. As we saw in Chapter 6, experiencing a memory by using mental time travel is episodic memory. These autobiographical episodic memories can be experienced in two ways: (1) from a **field perspective**, which is remembering an event as if you are seeing it (Figure 7.3a), and (2) from an **observer**

(a) Field perspective   (b) Observer perspective

■ **Figure 7.3** (a) Field perspective—you remember the event as you would see it. (b) Observer perspective—seeing yourself in the event.

perspective, which is remembering an event as observed from the outside, so you see yourself in the event (Figure 7.3b). We are more likely to experience recent memories from a field perspective and more-remote memories from an observer perspective (Nigro & Neisser, 1983).

Although autobiographical memories are usually considered to be episodic memories, the connections between episodic and semantic memory that we discussed in Chapter 6 (p. 189) mean that autobiographical memory can have semantic components as well. We noted, for example, that we have many personal semantic memories—facts we know about our lives, such as where we lived at various times, the schools we went to, or the name of a childhood friend. Note that these are facts, which we can remember without actually reexperiencing events, and therefore are semantic memories. Taking into account personal semantic memories such as these, we can define autobiographical memory as episodic memory for events in our lives *plus* personal semantic memories of facts about our lives.

The Multidimensional Nature of Autobiographical Memory

Autobiographical memories are far more complex than memory that might be measured in the laboratory by asking a person to remember a list of words. Autobiographical memories are multidimensional because they consist of spatial, emotional, and sensory components. The memory of patients who have suffered brain damage that has caused a loss of visual memory, but without causing blindness, provides an example of the importance of the sensory component of autobiographical memory. Daniel Greenberg and David Rubin (2003) found that patients who had lost their ability to recognize objects or to visualize objects, because of damage to visual areas of the cortex, also experienced a loss of autobiographical memory. This may have occurred because visual stimuli were not available to serve as retrieval cues for memories. But even memories not based on visual information are lost in these patients. Apparently, visual experience plays an important role in forming autobiographical memories. (It would seem reasonable that for blind people, auditory experience might take over this role.)

A brain-scanning study that illustrates a difference between autobiographical memory and laboratory memory was done by Roberto Cabeza and coworkers (2004). Cabeza measured the brain activation caused by two sets of stimulus photographs—one set that the participant took and another set was taken by someone else (● Color Plate 7.1). We will call the photos taken by the participant A-photos, to stand for "autobiographical" photographs, and the ones taken by someone else as L-photos, to stand for "laboratory" photographs.

The stimulus photographs were created by giving 12 Duke University students digital cameras and telling them to take pictures of 40 specified campus locations over a 10-day period. After taking the photographs, each participant was shown their own photos (A-photos) and photos taken by other participants (L-photos). Then a few days later they saw their own photos, the L-photos they had seen before, and some new L-photos they had never seen. As the participant indicated whether each stimulus was an A-photo, an L-photo that they had seen, or a new L-photo, their brain activity was measured in an MRI scanner.

The brain scans showed that A-photos and L-photos both activated many of the same structures in the brain—mainly ones like the MTL that are associated with episodic memory, as well as an area in the parietal cortex that is involved in processing scenes (● Color Plate 7.2a). However, the A-photos also activated regions associated with processing information about the self, with memory for visual space, and with recollection (memory associated with "mental time travel" that we discussed in Chapter 6). ● Color Plate 7.2b shows the greater A-photo activation compared to L-photo activation in the hippocampus. Thus, when viewing pictures of a particular location, the pictures people took themselves elicited memories associated with taking the picture, and therefore activated a more extensive network of brain areas than pictures that were taken by someone else. This activation reflects the richness of experiencing autobiographical memories, as compared to laboratory memories.

One way to think about the richness of autobiographical memory is to think of a person's life as a story that consists of a large number of events, ranging from small and inconsequential (eating fast food last Thursday) to much larger and meaningful (going to college; getting a job). Just as certain parts of a story you might read in a book stand out later, certain events in the story of a person's life stand out. We now consider why some events stand out more than others.

Memory Over the Life Span

What determines which particular life events we will remember years later? Personal milestones such as graduating from college or receiving a marriage proposal stand out, as do highly emotional events such as surviving a car accident (Pillemer, 1998). Events that become significant parts of a person's life story tend to be remembered well. For example, going out to dinner with someone for the first time might stand out if you ended up having a long-term relationship with that person, but the same dinner date might be far less memorable if you never saw the person again.

Transition points in people's lives appear to be particularly memorable. This is illustrated by what Wellesley College juniors and seniors said when they were asked to recall the most influential event that happened during their freshman year. Most of the responses to this question were descriptions of events that occurred in September. When alumni were asked the same question, they remembered more events from September of their freshman year *and* from the end of their senior year—another transition point (Pillemer et al., 1996).

A particularly interesting result occurs when participants over 40 are asked to remember events in their lives. For these participants, memory is high for recent events and for events experienced from adolescence and early adulthood (between 10 and 30 years of age; Figure 7.4; Conway, 1996; Rubin et al., 1998). This enhanced memory for adolescence and young adulthood that can be demonstrated in people over 40 years old is called the **reminiscence bump**.

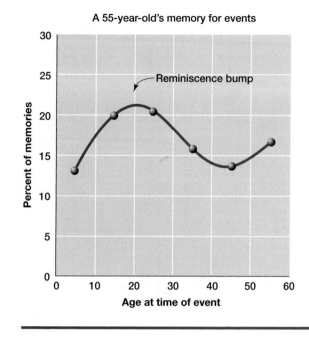

A 55-year-old's memory for events

■ **Figure 7.4** Percentage of memories from different ages, recalled by a 55-year-old, showing the reminiscence bump. (Reprinted from *Journal of Memory and Language, 39,* R. W. Schrauf & D. C. Rubin, "Bilingual Autobiographical Memory in Older Adult Immigrants: A Test of Cognitive Explanations of the Reminiscence Bump and the Linguistic Encoding of Memories," pp. 437–457, Fig. 1, Copyright © 1998 with permission from Elsevier.)

Why are adolescence and young adulthood special times for encoding memories? The **life-narrative hypothesis** states that people assume their life identities during that time. It is the time of "our" generation and the time people return to when they become nostalgic for the "good old days." In addition, it is a time when lots of "firsts" occur—going to college, committing to a partner, starting a career.

Another explanation for the reminiscence bump, called the **cognitive hypothesis,** is that encoding is better during periods of rapid change that are followed by stability. Adolescence and young adulthood fit this description because the rapid changes that occur during these periods are followed by the relative stability of adult life.

One way to test this hypothesis is to find people who have experienced rapid changes in their lives that occurred at a time past adolescence or young adulthood. The cognitive hypothesis would predict that the reminiscence bump should occur later for these people. To test this idea, Robert Schrauf and David Rubin (1998) determined the recollections of people who had emigrated to the United States in their 20s and in their mid-30s. Figure 7.5, which shows the memory curves for two groups of immigrants, indicates that the reminiscence bump occurs at the normal age for people who emigrated early, but is shifted to 15 years later for those who emigrated later, just as the cognitive hypothesis would predict.

Finally, another explanation is the **cultural life script hypothesis.** This explanation distinguishes between a person's life story, which is all of the events that have occurred in a person's life, and a **cultural life script,** which is the events that *commonly* occur in a particular culture. For example, when Dorthe Berntsen and David Rubin (2004) asked people to list when important events in a typical person's life usu-

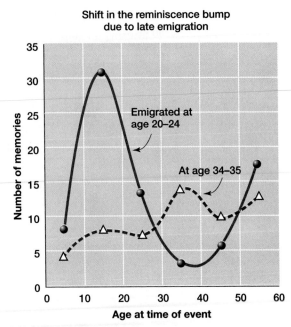

Figure 7.5 The reminiscence bump for people who emigrated at age 34 to 35 is shifted toward older ages, compared to the bump for people who emigrated between the ages of 20 to 24. (Reprinted from *Journal of Memory and Language, 39,* R. W. Schrauf & D. C. Rubin, "Bilingual Autobiographical Memory in Older Adult Immigrants: A Test of Cognitive Explanations of the Reminiscence Bump and the Linguistic Encoding of Memories," pp. 437–457, Fig. 2, Copyright © 1998 with permission from Elsevier.)

Table 7.1 Explanations for the Reminiscence Bump

Explanation	Basic Characteristic
Life narrative	Period of assuming person's life identity.
Cognitive	Encoding is better during periods of rapid change.
Cultural life script	Culturally shared expectations structure recall.

ally occur, some of the more common responses were falling in love (16 years), college (22 years), marriage (27 years), and having children (28 years). Interestingly, a large number of the most commonly mentioned events occur during the period associated with the reminiscence bump. This doesn't mean that events in a *specific* person's life always occur at those times, but according to the cultural life script hypothesis, events in a person's life story become easier to recall when they fit the cultural life script for that person's culture. It is likely that each of the explanations we have described (see Table 7.1) makes some contribution to creating the reminiscence bump.

Flashbulb Memories

What about events that are brief but highly memorable? Everyone reading this book probably has vivid memories of the terrorist attacks of September 11, 2001 (Figure 7.6). Do you remember when you first heard about the attacks? How you found out? Where

■ **Figure 7.6** Posters like this one are just one of the many reminders of the terrorist attacks of September 11, 2001.

you were? Your initial reaction? What you did next? I remember walking into the psychology department office and hearing from a secretary that someone had crashed a plane into the World Trade Center. At the time, I pictured a small private plane that had gone off course, but a short while later, when I called my wife from a pay phone near my classroom, she told me that the first tower of the World Trade Center had just collapsed. Shortly after that, in class, my students and I discussed what we knew about the situation and decided to cancel class for the day.

The memories I have described about how I heard about the 9/11 attack, and the people and events directly associated with finding out about the attack, are still vivid in my mind, more than 5 years later. Is there something special about memories that are associated with unexpected, emotionally charged events? According to Roger Brown and James Kulik (1977), there is. They proposed that memories for the circumstances surrounding learning about events such as 9/11 are special. Their proposal was based on an earlier event—the assassination of President John F. Kennedy on November 22, 1963.

In referring to the day Kennedy's assassination occurred, Brown and Kulik stated that "for an instant, the entire nation and perhaps much of the world stopped still to have its picture taken." This description, which likened the process of forming a memory to the taking of a photograph, led them to coin the term **flashbulb memory** to refer to a person's memory for the circumstances surrounding hearing about shocking, highly charged important events. It is important to emphasize that the term *flashbulb memory* refers to memory for the circumstances surrounding how a person *heard about* an event, not memory for the event itself. Thus, a flashbulb memory for 9/11 would be memory for where you were and what you were doing when you found out about the terrorist attack.

Brown and Kulik argue that there is something special about the mechanisms responsible for flashbulb memories. They not only occur under highly emotional circumstances, but they are remembered for long periods of time and are especially vivid and detailed. Brown and Kulik describe the mechanism responsible for these vivid and detailed memories as a "Now Print" mechanism, as if these memories are created like a photograph that resists fading.

Brown and Kulik's idea that flashbulb memories are like a photograph was based on people's descriptions of what they remembered about how they heard about events like the assassinations of John F. Kennedy and Martin Luther King, Jr. From these descriptions, Brown and Kulik concluded that people could often describe in some detail what they were doing when they had heard about these highly emotional events. But the procedure Brown and Kulik used was flawed because the only data they collected was what people remembered years after the events had occurred. The problem with this procedure is that there was no way to determine whether the reported memories were accurate. The only way to check for accuracy is to compare the persons memory to reports collected immediately after the event. This technique, called **repeated recall**, was used by later researchers.

◄► Method

Repeated Recall

The idea behind repeated recall is to determine whether memory changes over time, by testing participants a number of times after an event. The person's memory is first measured immediately after a stimulus is presented or something happens. Even though there is some possibility for errors or omissions immediately after the event, this report is taken as being the most accurate representation of what happened and is used as a baseline. Days, months, or years later, when participants are asked to remember what had happened, their reports are compared to the baseline. This use of a baseline provides a way to check the accuracy of later reports. ◆

Over the years since Brown and Kulik's "Now Print" proposal, research using the repeated recall task has shown that flashbulb memories are not like photographs. Unlike photographs, which remain the same for many years, people's memories for how they heard about flashbulb events change over time. In fact, one of the main findings of research on flashbulb memories is that although people report that memories surrounding flashbulb events are especially vivid, they are often inaccurate or lacking in detail. For example, Ulric Neisser and N. Harsch (1992) did a study in which they asked participants how they heard about the explosion of the space shuttle *Challenger* that occurred in 1986 (Figure 7.7). Participants filled out a questionnaire within a day after the explosion, and then filled out the same questionnaire 2½ to 3 years later. One participant's response, a day after the explosion, indicated that she had heard about it in class:

I was in my religion class and some people walked in and started talking about [it]. I didn't know any details except that it had exploded and the schoolteacher's students had all been watching, which I thought was so sad. Then after class I went to my room and watched the TV program talking about it, and I got all the details from that.

But 2½ years later, her memory had changed to the following:

When I first heard about the explosion I was sitting in my freshman dorm room with my roommate, and we were watching TV. It came on a news flash, and we were both totally shocked. I was really upset, and I went upstairs to talk to a friend of mine, and then I called my parents.

Responses like these, in which participants reported first hearing about the explosion in one place, such as a classroom, and then later remembered that they first heard about it on TV, were common. Right after the explosion, 21 percent of the participants indicated that they first heard about it on TV, but 2½ years later, 45 percent of the participants reported that they first heard about it on TV. Reasons for the increase in TV memories could be that the TV reports become more memorable through repetition and that TV is a major source of news. Thus, memory for hearing about the *Challenger* explosion had a property that is also a characteristic of memory for less dramatic, ev-

© Bettmann/CORBIS

■ **Figure 7.7** Neisser and Harsch (1992) studied people's memories for the day they heard about the explosion of the space shuttle *Challenger.*

eryday events: It was affected by peoples' experiences following the event (people may have seen accounts of the explosion) and their general knowledge (people often first hear about important news on TV).

The announcement of the O. J. Simpson murder trial verdict, which occurred on October 3, 1995, provides another example of how memories for an event can be influenced by other experiences. Heike Schmolck and coworkers (2000) determined accuracy of memory by comparing participants' reports long after the event to their reports shortly after the event. They found that many of the responses at 32 months were inaccurate. For example, compare the 3-day and 32-month responses below:

Response at 3 days: I was in the commuter lounge at college and saw it on TV. As 10:00 approached, more and more people came into the room.

Response at 32 months: I first heard it while I was watching TV at home in my living room. My sister and father were with me. . . .

The large number of inaccurate responses in the *Challenger* and the O. J. Simpson studies suggests that perhaps memories that are supposed to be flashbulb memories may decay just like regular memories. In fact, the authors of the O. J. Simpson study conclude that "it seems unlikely that so-called flashbulb memories differ from ordinary episodic memories in any fundamental way" (Schmolck et al., 2000, p. 44).

This conclusion is supported by an experiment in which a group of college students was asked a number of questions on September 12, 2001, the day after the terrorist attacks on the World Trade Center and the Pentagon (Talarico & Rubin, 2003). Some of these questions were about the terrorist attacks ("When did you first hear the news?"). Others were similar questions about an everyday event in the person's life that occurred in the days just preceding the attacks. After picking the everyday event, the participant created a two- or three-word description that could serve as a cue for that event in the future. Some participants were retested 1 week later, some 6 weeks later, and some 32 weeks later by asking them the same questions about the attack and the everyday event.

One result of this experiment was that the participants remembered fewer details and made more errors at longer intervals after the events, with little difference between the results for the flashbulb and everyday memories (Figure 7.8a). This result supports the idea that there is nothing special about flashbulb memories. However, another result, shown in Figure 7.8b, did indicate a difference between flashbulb and everyday memories: People's belief that their memories were accurate stayed high over the entire 32-week period for the flashbulb memories, but dropped for the everyday memories. Ratings of vividness and how well they could "relive" the events also stayed high and constant for the flashbulb memories but dropped for the everyday memories. Thus, the idea that flashbulb memories are special appears to be based at least partially on the fact that people *think* the memories are stronger and more accurate; however, this study found that, *in reality*, there was little or no difference between flashbulb and everyday memories in terms of the amount remembered and the accuracy of what is remembered.

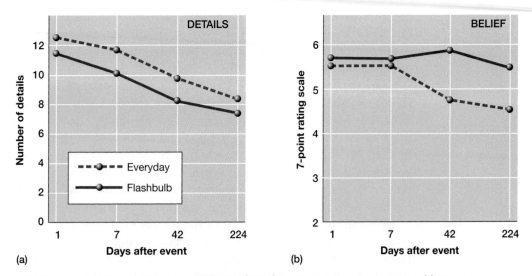

■ Figure 7.8 Results of Talarico and Rubin's (2003) flashbulb memory experiment. (a) The decrease in the number of details remembered was similar for memories of 9/11 and for memories of an everyday event. (b) Participants' belief that their memory was accurate remained high for 9/11, but decreased for memories of the everyday event. (Extracted from "Consistency and Key Properties of Flashbulb and Everyday Memories," by J. M. Talarico & D. C. Rubin, *Psychological Science, 14,* 5, Fig. 1. Copyright © 2003 with permission from the American Psychological Society.)

Although Talarico and Rubin found that people's memories for hearing about 9/11 decreased in accuracy in the same way as memories for everyday events that just preceded 9/11, another experiment, by Patrick Davidson and coworkers (2006), found that memories for events associated with hearing about 9/11 were more resistant to fading than memories for other events that took place at that time. Davidson and coworkers asked participants questions such as "How did you hear the news?" "Where were you when you heard about the attack?" and "Who was present?" shortly after the 9/11 attack. They also had the participants answer the same questions for an everyday event—the most interesting event (as picked by the participant) that had occurred in the few days preceding 9/11.

One year later, the participants were contacted for a surprise memory test in which they were asked the same questions as before. If they weren't able to remember the everyday event, they were given a cue, such as "party" or "movie," to help them remember the event. The participants' response to each of the questions was scored by assigning 0 points if they couldn't remember or remembered it very inaccurately, 1 point if their memory was partially correct or less specific than the original memory, and 2 points if their memory was very similar to their original report. The resulting "congruence score" was determined by adding the points for all of the questions and scaling the total so that 1.0 was the maximum possible. Congruence for 9/11 memories were fairly high 1 year later (0.77), but the score for the everyday events was much lower (0.33;

Figure 7.9a). A particularly striking difference between memory for the two events was that whereas all of the participants had no trouble remembering 9/11, only 65 percent of the participants were able to remember what the everyday event was, even after being prompted with a cue (Figure 7.9b).

The results of both the Talarico and Rubin (2003) and Davidson and coworkers (2006) experiments showed that memory for the flashbulb event declined with time. This agrees with the idea that a stamped-in "flashbulb" memory that is like a photograph is not correct. However, Davidson and coworkers' participants found it more difficult to remember their everyday event. It is not clear why this occurred, although one possibility is that Davidson's participants were not aware that they would be tested later (the 1-year test was a surprise) and also because the retrieval cue they were given may not have been as effective as the one provided to Talarico and Rubin's participants.

We can understand why the retrieval cues may have differed in effectiveness by returning to the results of Timo Mantyla's experiment that we described in Chapter 6 (page 216). The results of that experiment showed that retrieval cues are more effective when they are created by the participant than when they are created by someone else. The fact that Talarico and Rubin's participants created their own retrieval cues, whereas Davidson's participants did not, may be why Davidson's participants remembered less about their everyday events, and why the results of this experiment demonstrated a large difference in the memories associated with flashbulb and everyday events.

Davidson suggests that better memory for 9/11 is probably due to two characteristics of memories surrounding flashbulb events. First, they involve high emotions. Most people associate finding out about 9/11 not just with the event itself but also with intense emotions such as surprise, disbelief, anger, and fear. As we saw in Chapter 6, high

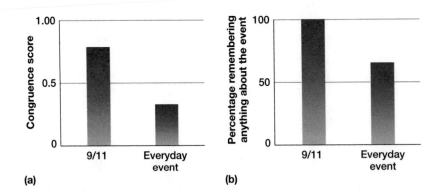

■ **Figure 7.9** Results of Davidson et al.'s (2006) flashbulb memory experiment. (a) Congruence score for 9/11 memories and memories for the everyday event, measured 1 year after the events. (b) Percent of participants who were able to remember at least something about the 9/11 and everyday events. Note that 35 percent of the participants could not remember anything about the everyday event. (Based on data from Davidson et al., 2006, and personal communication.)

emotions trigger physiological processes, especially in the amygdala, that are associated with better memory for emotional events (see p. 213). It would not be surprising, therefore, if memory for hearing about flashbulb events was somewhat better than memory for less emotional, "everyday" events (Davidson & Glisky, 2002).

A second factor that can potentially enhance memory for flashbulb events is added rehearsal. Ulric Neisser (2000) feels we may remember events like those that happened on 9/11 not because of a special mechanism, but because we rehearse these events after they occur. This idea is called the **narrative rehearsal hypothesis.**

The narrative rehearsal hypothesis makes sense when we consider the events that followed 9/11. How many times did you see the planes crashing into the World Trade Center replayed on TV? How much did you read about events surrounding 9/11 or talk about them with other people? Neisser argues that if rehearsal is the reason for our memories of significant events, then the term "flashbulb" is misleading. Remember, however, that the memory we are concerned with is the characteristics surrounding how you *heard about* 9/11. But much of the "rehearsal" associated with this event was rehearsal for events that occurred after hearing about it. Seeing TV replays of the planes crashing into the towers, for example, might result in people focusing more on that than on who told them about it or where they were. This would explain the intrusion of the TV errors such as those that occurred in the *Challenger* and O. J. Simpson studies.

Although the exact mechanism responsible for memory of flashbulb events is still being discussed by memory researchers, perhaps the most important outcome of the flashbulb memory research is what it tells us about memory in general. It confirms that the specific context surrounding an event can influence memory. Both the emotional context of an event and things that happened after an event can potentially affect later reports about the event. The idea that people's memories for an event are determined by the event context and by things in addition to what happened at the time has led many researchers to propose that what people remember is a "construction" that is based on what actually happened plus additional influences.

The Constructive Nature of Memory

We have seen that we remember certain things better than others because of their special significance or because of when they happened in our lives. But we have also seen that what people remember may not match what actually happened. When people report memories for past events, they may not only omit things, but they may also distort or change things that happened, and in some cases they may even report things that never happened at all.

According to the **constructive approach to memory,** what people report as memories are constructed by the person based on what actually happened plus additional factors, such as the person's knowledge, experiences, and expectations. This approach is called *constructive* because the mind *constructs* memories based on a number of sources of information.[1] One of the first experiments to suggest that memory is constructive is Bartlett's "War of the Ghosts" experiment.

Bartlett's "War of the Ghosts" Experiment

The British psychologist Fredrick Bartlett conducted a classic study of the constructive nature of memory, which is known as the "War of the Ghosts" experiment. In this experiment, which Bartlett ran before World War I and published in 1932, his participants read the following story from Canadian Indian Folklore.

The War of the Ghosts

One night two young men from Egulac went down to the river to hunt seals, and while they were there it became foggy and calm. Then they heard war cries, and they thought: "Maybe this is a war party." They escaped to the shore and hid behind a log. Now canoes came up, and they heard the noise of paddles and saw one canoe coming up to them. There were five men in the canoe, and they said:

"What do you think? We wish to take you along. We are going up the river to make war on the people."

One of the young men said: "I have no arrows." "Arrows are in the canoe," they said. "I will not go along. I might be killed. My relatives do not know where I have gone. But you," he said, turning to the other, "may go with them."

So one of the young men went, but the other returned home. And the warriors went on up the river to a town on the other side of Kalama. The people came down to the water, and they began to fight, and many were killed. But presently the young man heard one of the warriors say: "Quick, let us go home; that Indian has been hit." Now he thought: "Oh, they are ghosts." He did not feel sick, but they said he had been shot.

So the canoes went back to Egulac, and the young man went ashore to his house and made a fire. And he told everybody and said: "Behold I accompanied the ghosts, and we went to fight. Many of our fellows were killed, and many of those who attacked us were killed. They said I was hit, and I did not feel sick."

He told it all, and then he became quiet. When the sun rose, he fell down. Something black came out of his mouth. His face became contorted. The people jumped up and cried. He was dead. (Bartlett, 1932, p. 65)

After his participants read this story, Bartlett asked them to recall it as accurately as possible. He then used the technique of **repeated reproduction**, in which the same participants came back a number of times to try to remember the story at longer and

---

[1]Some researchers use the term "constructive memory" to refer to constructive processes that influence memory during encoding and "reconstructive memory" to refer to constructive processes that influence memory during retrieval. The distinction between these two terms is, however, often subtle, and both refer to the idea that our memory reports are the result of processes in which we create memories based on what actually happened plus other factors, including inferences based on our previous experiences and knowledge of the world. In this book we will, therefore, follow the lead of those who use only the general term "constructive" (see Schacter et al., 1998).

longer intervals after they first read it. This is similar to the repeated recall technique used in the flashbulb memory experiments (see Methods: Repeated Recall, page 244).

Bartlett's experiment is considered important because it was one of the first to use the repeated reproduction technique. But the main reason the "War of the Ghosts" experiment is considered important is because of the nature of the errors Bartlett's participants made and how Bartlett interpreted these errors.

Not surprisingly, participants eventually forgot much of the information in the story. Most participants' reproductions of the story were shorter than the original and contained many omissions and inaccuracies. One thing that was related to these errors was the strangeness of the story—a myth from an unfamiliar culture. Remember the idea of organization in Chapter 6—especially the balloon experiment. It's hard to remember things that are difficult to organize. Bartlett used a story that was difficult to organize and which therefore resulted in errors, and the nature of the errors revealed something interesting about the process of memory.

Bartlett noticed that the changes that occurred in the remembered stories tended to reflect the participants' own culture. The original story, which came from Canadian folklore, was transformed by many of Bartlett's participants to make it more consistent with their own experience with the culture of Edwardian England. For example, one participant remembered the two men who were out hunting seals as being involved in a sailing expedition, the "canoes" as "boats," and the man who joined the war party as a fighter that any good Englishman would be proud of—ignoring his wounds, he continued fighting and won the admiration of the natives. The original story, which was a folktale that seemed strange to Bartlett's English participants, was "constructed," or "reconstructed," into a story that reflected characteristics of the culture in which they were raised.

Although Bartlett's experiment was one of the first to consider how changes that occur in memory can be related to a constructive process, it had little impact on psychology in 1932 because behaviorism was gaining momentum. Eventually, however, the "War of the Ghosts" experiment came to be considered a classic, and memory as a constructive process has been considered in many other experiments.

Educated Guesses About High School Grades

Another example of memory that appears to involve a constructive process is provided by a study in which college students were asked to remember their high school grades (Bahrick et al., 1996). Checking the students' reports against their high school transcripts indicated that the students had accurately remembered *A* grades 89 percent of the time, but accurately remembered *D* grades only 29 percent of the time. Seventy-nine of the 99 students inflated their grades by remembering some of them as being higher than what they actually received.

There are a number of possible reasons for this result. One reason could be that people tend to remember positive events more readily than negative events (Loftus, 1982). Thus, *A*'s or *B*'s would be remembered better than *C*'s or *D*'s. Another reason is that memory is constructive. Someone who is a good student, but who doesn't remember what grade they received in 10th grade geometry, might base their guess on the fact that most of their grades were *A*'s and *B*'s. Because a guess of *A* or *B* would have a good chance of being correct, they take a "best guess" approach and guess *A*. If this is, in fact, the reason for the inaccurate memories in this experiment, it would be correct to say that participants constructed their memory based on their general experience of receiving grades in the past. (Stop, for a moment, and consider how this is similar to the large number of TV responses observed in the flashbulb memory studies.)

We understand that memory can be constructed, but exactly how does this construction work? Some clues come from considering a process called **source monitoring**.

Remember/
know

Source Monitoring and Source Monitoring Errors

I recently overheard the following conversation:

"Did you hear about the new movie *Brokeback Mountain* that opened last week?"
"Yes, I read about it in the *Times*."
"Really? Sam told me about it, or maybe it was Bernita. I can't remember."

You might think this conversation is about a movie, but to a psychologist it is an example of **source memory**—the process of determining the origins of our memories, knowledge, or beliefs (Johnson et al., 1993). In this example, one person identified the newspaper as his source of information about the movie, and the other person seemed unsure of his source, thinking it was either Sam or Bernita. If he thought it was Sam, but it turned out to be Bernita, he would be committing a **source monitoring error**—misidentifying the source of a memory. Source monitoring errors are also called **source misattributions** because the memory is attributed to the wrong source. Source monitoring provides an example of the constructive nature of memory because when we remember something, we usually retrieve the memory first ("I heard about *Brokeback Mountain*"), and we then use a decision process to determine where that memory came from ("It must have been from reading that article in the paper"; Mitchell & Johnson, 2000).

An experiment by Larry Jacoby and coworkers (1989) demonstrates an effect of source monitoring errors by testing participants' ability to distinguish between famous and nonfamous names. In the acquisition part of the experiment, Jacoby had participants read a number of made-up nonfamous names like *Sebastian Weissdorf* and *Valerie Marsh* (Figure 7.10). In the *immediate test*, which was presented right after the participants saw the list of nonfamous names, participants were told to pick out the names of famous people from a list containing (1) the nonfamous names they had just seen, (2) new nonfamous names that they had never seen before, and (3) famous names, like Minnie Pearl (a country singer) or Roger Bannister (the first person to run a 4-minute mile), that many people might have recognized in 1988, when the experiment was done. Just before this test, participants were told that all of the names they had just seen in the first part of the experiment were nonfamous. Because the test was given shortly after the participants had seen the first list of nonfamous names, they correctly identified

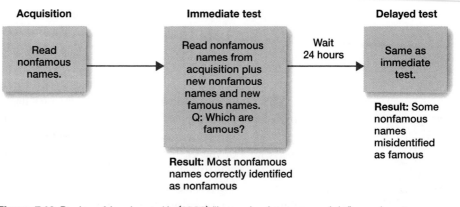

Figure 7.10 Design of Jacoby et al.'s (1989) "becoming famous overnight" experiment.

most of the old nonfamous names (like Sebastian Weissdorf and Valerie Marsh) as being nonfamous.

The interesting result occurred in the *delayed test*, which happened 24 hours later. When tested on the same list of names a day later, participants were more likely to identify the old nonfamous names as being famous. Thus, even though they may have identified Sebastian Weissdorf as not being famous in the immediate test, his name was more likely to be labeled as famous 24 hours later. Because of this result, Jacoby's paper is titled "Becoming Famous Overnight."

How did Sebastian Weissdorf become famous overnight? To answer this question, put yourself in the place of one of Jacoby's participants. It is 24 hours since you first saw the names, and you now have to decide whether Sebastian Weissdorf is famous or nonfamous. How do you make your decision? Sebastian Weissdorf doesn't pop out as someone you know of, but the name is familiar. You ask yourself the question: "Why is this name familiar?" This is a source monitoring problem, because to answer this question you need to determine the source of your familiarity. You could be familiar with the name Sebastian Weissdorf because you saw it 24 hours earlier, or because it is the name of a famous person. Apparently, some of Jacoby's participants decided that the familiarity was caused by fame, and so the previously unknown Sebastian Weissdorf became famous!

Test Yourself 7.1

1. What portions of autobiographical memories would be classified as episodic? What portions could be classified as semantic?
2. What is prospective memory? What conditions make it more difficult to remember things you need to do later?
3. What does it mean to say that autobiographical memories are "multidimensional"? How did the "photography" experiment provide evidence for this idea?

4. What would a plot of "events remembered" versus "age" look like for a 50-year-old person? What theories have been proposed to explain the peak that occurs in this function?

5. The idea of flashbulb memories has been debated by psychologists. What is behind the idea that some memories are "special" and are therefore labeled as "flashbulb" memories? What evidence indicates that memories for "flashbulb" experiences are not long-lived like photographs? What evidence suggests that there may, in fact, be something "special" about memory for flashbulb events?

6. How do the results of the O. J. Simpson study, Bartlett's "War of the Ghosts" experiment, and the "remembering high school grades" experiment all support the idea of the constructive nature of memory?

7. Source monitoring errors provide another example of the constructive nature of memory. Describe what source monitoring and source monitoring errors are and why they are considered "constructive."

Making Inferences

We introduced the idea of the constructive nature of memory by suggesting that memory reports can be created by inferences based on a person's experiences and knowledge. In this section, we will consider this idea further. But first, do this demonstration.

Demonstration

Reading Sentences

For this demonstration, read the following sentences, pausing for a few seconds between each one.

1. The children's snowman vanished when the temperature reached 80.
2. The flimsy shelf weakened under the weight of the books.
3. The absent-minded professor didn't have his car keys.
4. The karate champion hit the cinder block.
5. The new baby stayed awake all night.

Now that you have read the sentences, turn to "Reading Sentences" Demonstration on page 282 at the end of the chapter, and follow the directions.

Compare your answers in the fill-in-the-blank exercise you just completed to the words that you originally read above. When William Brewer (1977) and Kathleen McDermott and Jason Chan (2006) presented participants with a similar task, involving many more sentences than you read, they found that errors occurred for about a third of the sentences. For the sentences above, the most common errors were as follows: (1) *vanished* became *melted*; (2) *weakened* became *collapsed*; (3) *didn't have* became *lost*; (4) *hit* became *broke* or *smashed*; and (5) *stayed awake* became *cried*.

These wording changes illustrate a process called **pragmatic inference**, which occurs when reading a sentence leads a person to expect something that is not explicitly stated or necessarily implied by the sentence (Brewer, 1977). These inferences are based on knowledge gained through experience. Thus, although reading that a baby stayed awake all night does not include any information about crying, knowledge about babies might lead a person to infer that the baby was crying.

In a classic experiment that demonstrated how inference can affect memory, John Bransford and Marcia Johnson (1973) had participants read a number of action statements in the acquisition part of the experiment and then tested their memory for the statements later. Statement 1 below is an example of one of the action statements that was read during acquisition by participants in the experimental group, and statement 2 is an example of one of the action statements read by participants in the control group (Figure 7.11).

1. *Experimental Group:* John was trying to fix the birdhouse. He was pounding the nail when his father came out to watch him and help him do the work.
2. *Control Group:* John was trying to fix the birdhouse. He was looking for the nail when his father came out to watch him and help him do the work.

Both groups were then tested by presenting them with a number of test statements that they had not seen, and were asked to indicate whether they had seen them before. Statement 3 is an example of a test statement that went with statements 1 and 2. Notice

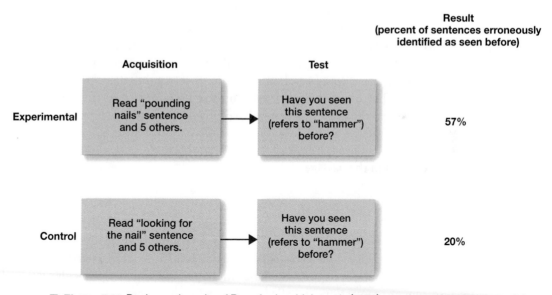

■ **Figure 7.11** Design and results of Bransford and Johnson's (1973) experiment that tested people's memory for the wording of action statements. More errors were made by participants in the experimental group because they identified more sentences as being originally presented, even though they were not.

that this statement contains the word *hammer*, which was not contained in either of the original statements.

3. *Experimental and Control Groups:* John was using a hammer to fix the birdhouse when his father came out to watch him and to help him do the work.

Participants in the experimental group said they had previously seen 57 percent of the test statements, but participants in the control group said they had previously seen only 20 percent of the test statements. For the example above, the participants in the experimental group, who had read the sentence that mentioned *pounding* the nail, were more likely to be misled into thinking that the original sentence had contained the word *hammer*. Apparently, the participants in the experimental group inferred, from the use of the word *pounding*, that a hammer had been used, even though it was never mentioned. This makes sense because we usually pound nails with hammers, but in this case, the participant's inference has caused an error of memory (also see McDermott & Chan, 2006).

Here is the scenario used in another memory experiment, which was designed specifically to elicit inferences based on the participants' past experiences (Arkes & Freedman, 1984):

In a baseball game, the score is tied 1 to 1. The home team has runners on first and third, with one out. A ground ball is hit to the shortstop. The shortstop throws to second base, attempting a double play. The runner who was on third scores, so it is now 2–1 in favor of the home team.

After hearing a story similar to this one, participants were asked to indicate whether the sentence "The batter was safe at first" was part of the passage. From looking at the story, you can see that this sentence was never presented, and most of the participants who didn't know much about baseball correctly indicated this. However, participants who knew the rules of baseball were more likely to say that the sentence had been presented. They based this judgment on their knowledge that if the runner on third had scored, then the double play must have failed, which means that the batter safely reached first. Knowledge, in this example, resulted in a correct inference about what probably happened in the ball game, but to an incorrect inference about the sentence that was presented in the passage.

Schemas and Scripts

The examples above illustrate how a person's memory reports can be influenced by their knowledge. Our knowledge about what is involved in a particular experience—be it things that can happen in a baseball game, working at a particular job, or being in a campus organization—is called a **schema** for that experience.

In an experiment that studied how memory is influenced by people's schemas about offices, participants were seated in an office waiting to be in an experiment (Figure 7.12). When the participants were called into another room, they were told that the experi-

■ **Figure 7.12** Office in which Brewer and Treyens' (1981) participants waited before being tested on their memory for what was present in the office. (From "Role of Schemata in Memory for Places," by W. F. Brewer & J. C. Treyens, *Cognitive Psychology, 13,* pp. 207–230. Copyright 1981. With permission from Elsevier.)

ment was actually a memory experiment, and their task was to write down what they saw while they were sitting in the office (Brewer & Treyens, 1981). The participants responded by writing down many of the things they remembered seeing, but also included some things that were not there but which fit into their "office schema." For example, although there were no books in the office, 30 percent of the participants reported that they saw books. Thus, the information in schemas can provide a guide for making inferences about what you remember. In this particular example, the inference turned out to be wrong. Other examples of how schemas have led to erroneous decisions in memory experiments have made use of a type of schema called a script.

A **script** is our conception of the *sequence* of actions that usually occur during a particular experience. For example, your script for the experience of going to class might include the following sequence: (1) get to class 10 minutes before it is scheduled to start, (2) wait for students from the previous class to leave, (3) enter class and find a seat, (4) take notes on the lecture, and (5) leave when the professor has finished the lecture.

Scripts can influence our memory by setting up expectations about what usually happens in a particular situation. To test the influence of scripts, Gordon Bower and coworkers (1979) did an experiment in which participants were asked to remember short passages like the following:

The Dentist

Bill had a bad toothache. It seemed like forever before he finally arrived at the dentist's office. Bill looked around at the various dental posters on the wall. Finally the dental hygienist checked and x-rayed his teeth. He wondered what the dentist was doing. The dentist said that Bill had a lot of cavities. As soon as he'd made another appointment, he left the dentist's office.

The participants read a number of passages like this one, all of which were about familiar activities like going to the dentist, going swimming, or going to a party. After a delay period, the participants were given the titles of the stories they had read and were told to write down what they remembered about each story as accurately as possible. The participants created stories that included much material that matched the original stories, but they also included material that wasn't presented in the original story but which is part of the script for the activity described. For example, for the dentist story some participants reported reading that "Bill checked in with the dentist's receptionist." This statement is part of most people's "going to the dentist" script, but was not included in the original story. Thus, knowledge of the dentist script caused the participants to add information that wasn't originally presented. Another example of a link between knowledge and memory is provided by the following demonstration.

Remembering a List of Words

Try the following demonstration.

Demonstration

Memory for a List

Read the following list at a rate of about one item per second, and then cover the list and write down as many of the words as possible. In order for this demonstration to work, it is important that you cover the words and complete the memory test before reading past the list of words.

bed, rest, awake, tired, dream
wake, night, blanket, doze, slumber
snore, pillow, peace, yawn, drowsy

Does your list of remembered words include any words that are not on the list above? This experiment was introduced by James Deese (1959) and studied further by

Henry Roediger and Kathleen McDermott (1995). When I present this list to my class, there are always a substantial number of students who report that they remember the word "sleep." Remembering *sleep* is a false memory because it isn't on the list. This false memory occurs because people associate *sleep* with other words on the list. This is similar to the effect of schemas, in which people create false memories for office furnishings that aren't present because they associate these office furnishings with what is usually found in offices. Again, constructive processes have created an error in memory.

The Advantages and Disadvantages of Construction

The constructive property of memory reflects the creative nature of our mental processes, which enables us to do things like understand language, solve problems, and make decisions. This creativity also helps us "fill in the blanks" when there is incomplete information. For example, remember the experiment in which some participants inferred that John was using a hammer after reading that "he was pounding the nail. . . ." Imagine how tiresome it would be if we had to explain everything in excruciating detail in order to know what was happening. After all, John *could* be pounding the nail into the birdhouse with a rock! Luckily, we know that a hammer is the tool that is usually used to pound nails.

Even though this creativity serves a good purpose, it sometimes results in errors of memory. These errors, plus the fact that we forget many of the things we have experienced, have led many people to wish that their memory was better—an idea that most students would agree with, especially around exam time. However, the case of the Russian memory expert Shereshevskii (S) shows that perhaps almost-perfect memory may not be advantageous after all. After extensively studying S, the Russian psychologist A. R. Luria (1968) concluded that S's memory was "virtually limitless" (but Wilding and Valentine, 1997, point out that he did occasionally make mistakes).

Although S's impressive memory made it possible for him to make a living by demonstrating his memory powers on stage, it made many aspects of his life difficult. For one thing, S had trouble forgetting things he no longer needed. His mind was like a blackboard on which everything that happened was written and couldn't be erased. There are many things that flit through our minds briefly, and then we don't need them again. Unfortunately for S, these things stayed there even when he wished they would go away.

S also was not good at reasoning that involved drawing inferences or "filling in the blanks" based on partial information. We do this so often that we take this ability for granted, but S's ability to record massive amounts of information, and his inability to erase it, may have hindered his ability to do this.

S's exceptional memory demonstrates that it may not be an advantage to remember everything perfectly. Storing everything that is experienced was apparently annoying to S, and it is also an inefficient way for a system to operate because storing everything that happens can overload the system. To avoid this "overload," our memory system is designed to selectively remember things that are particularly important to us or that

■ Figure 7.13 The "animal lurking behind a tree" picture from Chapter 3. This looks like an animal, but maybe it isn't one.

occur often in our environment (Anderson & Schooler, 1991). Although the resulting system does not exactly record everything we experience, it does operate well enough to have enabled humans to survive as a species.

One way to appreciate the survival value of the memory system is to remember our discussion in Chapter 3 of why we may erroneously perceive the object in Figure 3.32a (repeated here as Figure 7.13) as an animal lurking behind a tree. Our perceptual system, like our memory system, is designed to use partial information to arrive at a "best guess" solution to a perceptual problem, which is correct most of the time. Occasionally, this system comes up with an erroneous perception (see Figure 3.32b), but most of the time it provides the correct answer. The few errors we may experience are more than compensated for by a feature of our perceptual system that is essential for our survival—its great speed even when faced with incomplete information. Our memory system works the same way. Although it may not come up with the correct answers every time, it usually provides us with what we need to know to function rapidly and efficiently, even though we may not always have complete information.

Memory is clearly a highly functional system that serves us well. However, sometimes the requirements of modern life create situations that humans have not been designed to handle. Consider, for example, driving a car. Evolution has not equipped our perceptual and motor systems to deal with weaving in and out of heavy traffic or driving at high rates of speed. Of course, we do these things anyway, but accidents happen. Similarly, our perceptual and memory systems have not evolved to handle demands such as providing eyewitness testimony in court. In a situation such as this, memory should ideally be perfect. After all, another person's freedom or life might be at stake. And just as car accidents happen, memory accidents happen as well. We will shortly consider what can happen when memory is put to the test in the courtroom, but first we need to consider another aspect of memory that can potentially result in memory errors.

▶▶▶ Memory Can Be Modified or Created by Suggestion

People are suggestible. Advertisements pitching the virtues of different products influence what people purchase. Arguments put forth by politicians, opinion makers, and friends influence who people vote for. Advertisements and political arguments are examples of things that might influence a person's attitudes, beliefs, or behaviors. We will now see how information presented by others can also influence a person's memory for past events. We first consider a phenomenon called the misinformation effect, in which a person's memory for an event is modified by things that happen after the event has occurred.

The Misinformation Effect

In a typical memory experiment, a person sees or hears some stimulus, such as words, letters, or sentences, or observes pictures or a film of an event, and is asked to report what he or she experienced. But what if the experimenter were to add information that went beyond simply asking the person what he or she remembered? This is the question that Elizabeth Loftus and coworkers asked in a series of pioneering experiments that established the **misinformation effect**—misleading information presented after a person witnesses an event can change how that person describes that event later. This misleading information is referred to as **misleading postevent information**, or **MPI**.

◄► Method

Presenting Misleading Postevent Information

The usual procedure in an experiment in which misleading postevent information (MPI) is presented is to first present the stimulus to be remembered. For example, this stimulus could be a list of words read by the participant or a film of an event observed by the participant. The MPI is presented to one group of participants before their memory is tested and is not presented to a control group. As you will see below, MPI is often presented in a way that seems natural, so it does not occur to the participant that they are being misled. We will also see, however, that even when participants are told that postevent information may be incorrect, presenting this information can still affect their memory reports. The effect of MPI is determined by comparing the memory reports of participants who received this misleading information to the memory reports of participants who did not receive it. ◆

An experiment by Elizabeth Loftus and coworkers (1978) illustrates a typical MPI experiment. Participants saw a series of slides in which a car stops at a stop sign and then turns the corner and hits a pedestrian. Some of the participants then answered a number of questions, including "Did another car pass the red Datsun while it was stopped at the stop sign?" For another group of participants (the MPI group) the words "yield sign" replaced "stop sign" in the stop sign question. Participants were then shown pictures from the slide show plus some pictures they had never seen. Those in the MPI group were more likely to say they had seen the picture of the car stopped at the yield sign (which, in actuality, they had never seen) than were participants who were not exposed to MPI. This shift in memory caused by MPI demonstrates the misinformation effect.

Presentation of MPI can alter not only what participants report they saw, but their conclusions about other characteristics of the situation. For example, Loftus and Steven Palmer (1974) showed participants films of a car crash (Figure 7.14) and then asked either (1) "How fast were the cars going when they *smashed* into each other?" or (2) "How fast were the cars going when they *hit* each other?" Although both groups saw the same event, the average speed estimate by participants who heard the word "smashed" was 41 miles per hour, whereas the estimates for participants who heard "hit" was

■ **Figure 7.14** Participants in the Loftus and Palmer (1974) experiment saw a film of a car crash, with scenes similar to the picture shown here, and were then asked leading questions about the crash.

34 miles per hour. Even more interesting for the study of memory are the participants' responses to the question "Did you see any broken glass?" which Loftus asked 1 week after they had seen the slide show. Although there was no broken glass in the original presentation, 32 percent of the participants who heard "smashed" before estimating the speed reported seeing broken glass, whereas only 14 percent of the participants who heard "hit" reported seeing the glass (see Loftus, 1993, 1998).

The misinformation effect shows not only how false memories can be created by suggestion but also provides an example of how different researchers can interpret the same data in different ways. Remember that the goal of cognitive psychology is to study mental processes, but that these mental processes must be inferred from the results of behavioral or physiological experiments. The question posed by the misinformation effect is, "What is happening that changes the participants' memory reports?" Different researchers have proposed different answers to this question.

Loftus explains the misinformation effect by proposing the **memory-trace replacement hypothesis**, which states that MPI impairs or replaces memories that were formed during the original experiencing of an event. According to this idea, seeing a stop sign creates a memory trace for a stop sign, but presentation of MPI that a yield sign was present causes the memory for the stop sign to be replaced by a new memory for a yield sign. The process of reconsolidation, which we described on page 226, could provide a physiological mechanism for this replacement because according to the idea of reconsolidation, reactivating a memory can form new memory traces.

Another explanation proposes that the original information is not remembered because of **retroactive interference**, which occurs when more recent learning interferes with memory for something that happened in the past. For example, retroactive interference would be involved if studying for your Spanish exam made it more difficult to remember some of the vocabulary words you had studied for your French exam earlier in the day. This explanation is similar to the memory-trace replacement hypothesis in that the new information affects the old information. However, in this case, the old information isn't eliminated; it is simply interfered with.

Another explanation for the misinformation effect is based on the idea of source monitoring, which we discussed earlier in this chapter. According to source monitoring, a person incorrectly concludes that the source of their memory for the incorrect event (yield sign) was the slide show, even though the actual source was the experimenter's statement after the slide show. The following experiment by Stephen Lindsay (1990) investigated source monitoring and MPI by asking whether participants who are exposed to MPI really believe they saw something that was only suggested to them. The answer to this question would be "yes" if the participant is making a source monitoring error.

Lindsay's participants first saw a sequence of slides showing a maintenance man stealing money and a computer. This slide presentation was narrated by a female speaker, who simply described what was happening as the slides were being shown. Two days later, participants returned to the lab for a memory test. Just before the test, they listened to a story, without slides, by the same female speaker. This story was similar to the one they had heard and seen 2 days earlier, but with a few details changed. For example, a pack of Marlboro cigarettes in the original became Winstons in the retelling of the story, and a can of Maxwell House coffee became Folgers.

Before the participants heard the second telling of the story, they were informed that there were some incorrect details in it, and so they should ignore what they heard in the second story when taking the memory test. In the memory test, participants were asked questions such as "The man had a pack of cigarettes. What brand of cigarette was shown in the slides?" Three of the questions were about misled items, for which they had received incorrect information in the second story, and three were about control items, for which they had not received incorrect information.

The results, shown in Figure 7.15a, indicate that for the misled items, 27 percent of the responses corresponded to the incorrect information in the second story. This compares to only 9 percent of incorrect responses for the control items. These responses to the misled items were source monitoring errors because the participants were confusing the information from the second story with the information from the first story.

The results for another group of participants, who heard a male voice tell the second story, are shown in Figure 7.15b. In

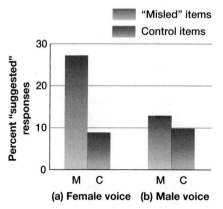

■ **Figure 7.15** Results of Lindsay's (1990) source monitoring experiment. (a) Effect of misleading information provided by the female voice on responses to misled (M) and control (C) items. (b) There was no difference, compared to control, when the male voice presented misleading information.

Table 7.2 Explanations for the Misinformation Effect

Explanation	Basic Principle
Memory-trace replacement (Loftus)	MPI replaces original memory.
Retroactive interference	MPI interferes with (but does not eliminate) original memory.
Source monitoring error	MPI is mistakenly identified as what was originally experienced.

this case, misled items received only 13 percent incorrect responses, which was not significantly different from the 10 percent incorrect responses for the control items. This lack of source monitoring errors occurred because the male voice was different from the female voice, so it was easier to distinguish which information came from which story. Thus, using the same female voice for both stories created source monitoring errors that led participants to believe they saw something that they didn't see.

Although the mechanism that causes the misinformation effect is still being discussed by researchers, there is no doubt that the effect is real and that experimenters' suggestions can influence participants' reports in memory experiments (Table 7.2). Some of the most dramatic demonstrations of the effect of experimenter suggestibility show that suggestion can cause people to believe that events had occurred early in their lives even though these events had never happened.

Creating False Memories for Early Events in People's Lives

Ira Hyman, Jr., and coworkers (1995) created false memories for long-ago events in an experiment in which they contacted the parents of their participants and asked them to provide descriptions of actual events that happened when the participants were children. The experimenters then also created descriptions of false events, ones that never happened, such as a birthday that included a clown and a pizza, and spilling a bowl of punch at a wedding reception.

Participants, who as college students were far removed from these childhood experiences, were given some of the information from the parents' descriptions and were told to elaborate on them. They were also given some of the information from the false events and were told to elaborate on them as well. The result was that 20 percent of the false events were "recalled" and described in some detail by the participants. For example, the following conversation occurred when an interviewer (I) asked a participant (P) what he remembered about the following false event.

> I: At age 6 you attended a wedding reception, and while you were running around with some other kids you bumped into a table and turned a punch bowl over on a parent of the bride.

P: I have no clue. I have never heard that one before. Age 6?

I: Uh-huh.

P: No clue.

I: Can you think of any details?

P: Six years old; we would have been in Spokane, um, not at all.

I: OK.

However, in a second interview that occurred 2 days later, the participant responded as follows:

I: The next one was when you were 6 years old and you were attending a wedding.

P: The wedding was my best friend in Spokane, T___. Her brother, older brother, was getting married, and it was over here in P___, Washington, cause that's where her family was from, and it was in the summer or the spring because it was really hot outside, and it was right on the water. It was an outdoor wedding, and I think we were running around and knocked something over like the punch bowl or something and um made a big mess and of course got yelled at for it.

I: Do you remember anything else?

P: No.

I: OK.

What is most interesting about this participant's response is that he didn't remember the wedding the first time, but did remember it the second time. Apparently, hearing about the event and then waiting caused the event to emerge as a false memory. This can be explained by familiarity. When questioned about the wedding the second time, the participant's familiarity with the wedding from the first exposure caused him to accept the wedding as having actually happened. This is like Jacoby's "becoming famous overnight" experiment, in which familiarity led participants to erroneously label Sebastian Weissdorf and other nonfamous people as being famous. Both of these cases illustrate source monitoring errors because the participants interpreted the source of their familiarity to something that never happened.

Recently, Stephen Lindsay and coworkers (2004) did an experiment that used the procedure described above, but with one additional twist. Participants were presented with descriptions of real childhood experiences supplied by their parents and another experience that never occurred (placing a toy called Slime, a brightly colored gelatinous compound, in their first-grade teacher's desk). Additionally, Lindsay had one group of participants look at a photograph of their first- or second-grade class, like the one in Figure 7.16, as they were being presented with the story about placing the slime toy in the teacher's desk. The result of this experiment was that the group of the participants who saw the picture experienced more than twice as many false memories than the group who did not see the picture. There are a number of reasons this might have occurred, but the important point for our purposes is that adding the picture enhanced the false

Figure 7.16 Photograph of a second-grade class like the ones shown to participants in Lindsay et al.'s (2004) experiment. (From "True Photographs and False Memories," by D. S. Lindsay, L. Hagen, J. D. Read, K. A. Wade, & M. Garry, *Psychological Science, 15,* pp. 149–154. Copyright 2004. With permission from the American Psychological Society.)

memory effect. We will return to this result in the Something to Consider section at the end of the chapter.

Suggestion has also succeeded in creating false memories for events that supposedly occurred early in infancy. Susan DuBreuil and coworkers (1998) told participants they had a personality profile that made it likely they could remember things from their childhood. They were also told that memories are permanent, and it's just a matter of getting them out of storage. After receiving this information, participants were told that "about the time you were born, hospitals in the United States were influenced by research on the effects of early visual stimulation and so began hanging mobiles over cribs." Participants were then hypnotized, were instructed to go to when they were 1 day old and lying in their crib, and were asked to describe what they were experiencing. Sixty-one percent of the participants reported seeing a mobile or described something that was consistent with the general characteristics of a mobile, and one-third of them believed their reports were probably or definitely real memories (DuBreuil et al., 1998).

Why Do People Make Errors in Eyewitness Testimony?

We have seen, from the results of numerous laboratory studies, that memory is fallible. But nowhere is this fallibility more evident and significant than in the area of **eyewitness testimony**—testimony by an eyewitness to a crime about what he or she saw during commission of the crime. Eyewitness testimony is one of the most convincing types of evidence to a jury, and the more confident the person giving the testimony, the more convincing it is (Cutler et al., 1990). Unfortunately, however, high confidence is a poor predictor of witness accuracy. This is indicated by the results of many studies that, taken together, indicate that the correlation between confidence and accuracy of eyewitness testimony is only 0.29 (Sporer et al., 1995).

Many innocent people have been incarcerated based on mistaken identification by eyewitnesses to a crime. These mistaken identifications occur for a number of reasons. Some errors are caused by difficulties in perceiving a person's face and others with inaccurate memory for what was perceived. We will first look at the evidence for errors of eyewitness identification, and we will then ask why these errors have occurred.

Errors of Eyewitness Identification

In the United States, 200 people per day become criminal defendants based on eyewitness testimony (Goldstein et al., 1989). Unfortunately, there are many instances in which errors of eyewitness testimony have resulted in the conviction of innocent people. For example, consider the case of David Webb, who was sentenced to up to 50 years in prison for rape, attempted rape, and attempted robbery based on eyewitness testimony. After serving 10 months he was released after another man confessed to the crimes. Charles Clark went to prison in 1938 for murder, based on eyewitness testimony, which, 30 years after his incarceration, was found to be inaccurate. He was released in 1968 (Loftus, 1979). Lenell Gertner served 16 months for robbing a restaurant based on five "positive" eyewitness identifications. Later, four of the five eyewitnesses identified a different person, and Gertner was released (Wells, 1985).

The disturbing thing about these examples is not only that they occurred, but that they suggest that many other innocent people are currently serving time for crimes they didn't commit. This conclusion has recently been confirmed by a number of cases in which innocent people have been exonerated based on DNA evidence that became available after they were convicted. In one survey of 40 such cases, 36 involved identification of innocent people by erroneous eyewitness testimony. In these cases, the innocent persons had served an average of 8.5 years in prison, and five had been sentenced to death (Wells et al., 2000). (Also see Junkin, 2004, for the story of Kirk Bloodworth, the first death row inmate exonerated by DNA evidence.)

These miscarriages of justice and many others, some of which have undoubtedly never been discovered, are based on the assumption, made by judges and jurors, that people see and report things accurately. In essence, many people in the criminal justice system have subscribed to the erroneous idea that memory is like a camera.

We have seen from laboratory research that memory is definitely not like a camera, and research using crime scene scenarios supports this idea. A number of experiments have presented participants with films of actual crimes or of staged crimes and then have asked them to pick the perpetrator from a photospread (photographs of a number of faces, one of which could be the perpetrator). In one study, participants viewed a security videotape in which a gunman was in view for 8 seconds and then were asked to pick the gunman from photographs. Every participant picked someone they thought was the gunman, even though his picture was not included in the photospread (Wells & Bradfield, 1998). In another study, using a similar experimental design, 61 percent of the participants picked someone from a photospread, even though the perpetrator's picture wasn't included (Kneller et al., 2001).

These studies show how difficult it is to accurately identify someone after viewing a videotape of a crime. But things become even more complicated when we consider some of the things that happen during actual crimes.

The Crime Scene and Afterward

Even under ideal conditions, identifying faces is a difficult task and errors occur (Henderson et al., 2001). But other factors can intervene to make the task even more difficult.

Errors Associated With Attention Emotions often run high during commission of a crime, and this can affect what a person pays attention to and what the person remembers later. One mechanism that may be operating during a crime has to do with how emotions may affect a person's field of attention. Easterbrook (1959) suggests that attention narrows as arousal increases. Thus, if arousal is very low, attention is spread over a broad area, resulting in attention to irrelevant information. Moderate arousal narrows attention, so more relevant information is attended, and very high arousal focuses attention too narrowly, so some relevant information may be missed. According to this idea, being in a state of moderate arousal will result in a focus of attention that is best suited to being aware of relevant information at a crime scene.

Weapons focus is related to this idea of how attention can affect a witness's access to relevant information. **Weapons focus**, the tendency to focus attention on a weapon, narrows attention, as in Easterbrook's high-arousal condition, and results in less attention to relevant information such as the perpetrator's face. Claudia Stanny and Thomas Johnson (2000) studied weapons focus by measuring how well participants remembered details of a filmed simulated crime. They found that participants were more likely to recall details of the perpetrator, the victim, and the weapon in the "no-shoot" condition (a gun was present but not fired) compared to the "shoot" condition (the gun was fired; Figure 7.17). Apparently, the presence of a weapon that was fired distracted attention from other things that were happening (also see Tooley et al., 1987).

Errors Due to Familiarity Crime scenes not only involve a perpetrator and a victim, but often include innocent bystanders. These bystanders add yet another dimension to the testimony of eyewitnesses because there is a chance that a bystander could mistakenly be identified as a perpetrator because of familiarity from some other context. A real-life example of misidentification based on familiarity is the case of Donald Thompson, a memory researcher who was talking about memory errors on a TV program at exactly

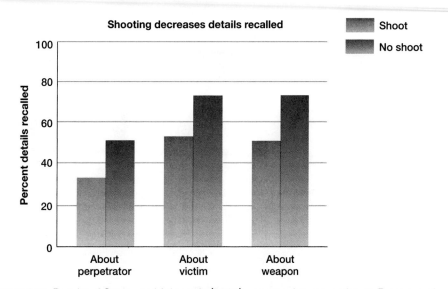

■ Figure 7.17 Results of Stanny and Johnson's (2000) weapons-focus experiment. Presence of a weapon that was fired is associated with a decrease in memory about the perpetrator, the victim, and the weapon.

the time that a woman was attacked in her home. The woman, who had been watching Thompson on the program, subsequently implicated Thompson as the person who had raped her, based on her memory for his face. Of course, Thompson had a perfect alibi because he was in the TV studio at the time of the crime (Schacter, 2001).

In another case, a ticket agent at a railway station was robbed and subsequently identified a sailor as being the robber. Luckily for the sailor, he was able to show that he was somewhere else at the time of the crime. When asked why he identified the sailor, the ticket agent said that he looked familiar. But the reason he looked familiar was not that he was the robber, but because he lived near the train station and had purchased train tickets from the agent on a number of occasions. This was therefore an example of a source monitoring error. The ticket agent thought the source of his familiarity with the sailor was seeing him during the holdup. In reality, however, the source of his familiarity was seeing him when he purchased tickets. The sailor had become transformed from a ticket buyer into a holdup man by a source monitoring error (Ross et al., 1994).

Figure 7.18a shows the design for a laboratory experiment on familiarity and eyewitness testimony (Ross et al., 1994). Participants in the experimental group saw a film of a male teacher reading to students, and participants in the control group saw a film of a female teacher reading to students. Participants in both groups then saw a film of the female teacher getting robbed and were asked to pick the robber from a photospread. The photographs did not include the actual robber, but did include the male teacher, who resembled the robber. The result indicates that the participants in the experimental group were three times more likely to pick the male teacher than participants in

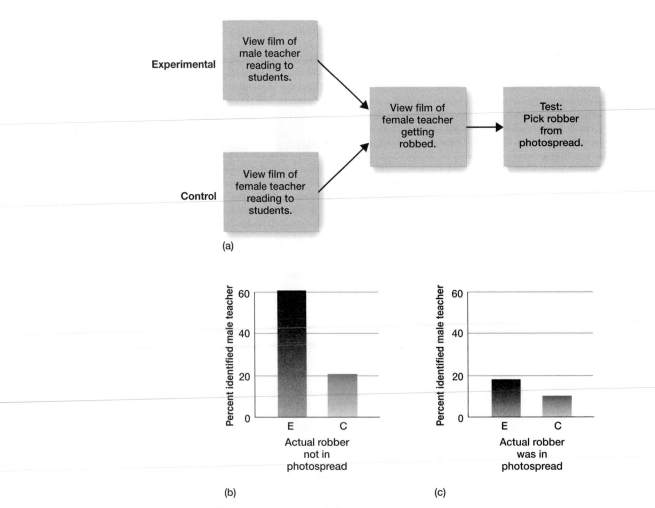

Figure 7.18 (a) Design of Ross et al.'s (1994) experiment on the effect of familiarity on eyewitness testimony. (b) When the actual robber was not in the photospread, the male teacher was erroneously identified as the robber 60 percent of the time. (c) When the actual robber was in the photospread, the male teacher was erroneously identified less than 20 percent of the time.

the control group (Figure 7.18b). Even when the actual robber's face was included in the photospread, 18 percent of the participants in the experimental group picked the teacher, compared to 10 percent in the control group (Figure 7.18c).

Errors Due to Suggestion From what we know about the misinformation effect, it is obvious that a police officer asking a witness "Did you see the white car? . . ." could influence the witness's later testimony about what he or she saw. But suggestibility can also operate on a more subtle level. Consider the following situation. A witness to a crime is looking through a one-way window at a lineup of six men standing on a stage. The police officer says, "Which one of these men did it?" What is wrong with this question?

The problem with the police officer's question is that it includes the implication that the crime perpetrator is in the lineup. This suggestion increases the chances that the witness will pick someone, perhaps using reasoning like, "Well, the guy with the beard looks more like the robber than any of the other men, so that's probably the one." Of course, looking *like* the robber and actually *being* the robber may be two different things, so the result may be identification of an innocent man. A better way of presenting the task is to let the witness know that the crime suspect may or may not be in the lineup.

Here is another situation, taken from a transcript from an actual criminal case, in which suggestion could have played a role.

> Eyewitness to a crime on viewing a lineup: "Oh, my God. . . . I don't know. . . . It's one of those two . . . but I don't know. . . . . Oh, man . . . the guy a little bit taller than number two. . . . It's one of those two, but I don't know."

> Eyewitness 30 minutes later, still viewing the lineup and having difficulty making a decision: "I don't know . . . number two?"

> Officer administering lineup: "Okay." Months later . . . at trial: "You were positive it was number two? It wasn't a maybe?"

> Answer from eyewitness: "There was no maybe about it. . . . I was absolutely positive." (Wells & Bradfield, 1998)

The problem with this scenario is that the police officer's response of "okay" may have influenced the witness to think that he or she had correctly identified the suspect. Thus, the witness's initially uncertain response turns into an "absolutely positive" response. In a paper titled "Good, You Identified the Suspect . . . ," Gary Wells and Amy Bradfield (1998) had participants view a video of an actual crime and then asked them to identify the perpetrator from a photospread that did not actually contain a picture of the perpetrator (Figure 7.19).

All of the participants picked one of the photographs, and following their choice, witnesses received either confirming feedback from the experimenter ("Good, you identified the suspect"), no feedback, or disconfirming feedback ("Actually, the suspect was number __"). A short time later, the participants were asked how confident they were about their identification. The results, shown at the bottom of the figure, indicate that participants who received the confirming feedback were more confident of their choice. Thus, this is another example of how postevent information can influence eyewitness testimony.

Increasing Confidence Due to Postevent Questioning John Shaw (1996) suggests that asking witnesses questions after they have described a crime scene can increase their confidence in their description. He bases this conclusion on an experiment in which he showed participants a series of slides showing objects in an apartment. They were then asked to identify the objects they saw by picking them from a number of pictures, some of which they had seen and some of which they had not seen. Each set of pictures was accompanied by a question, such as "Which of these magazines did you see in the apartment?"

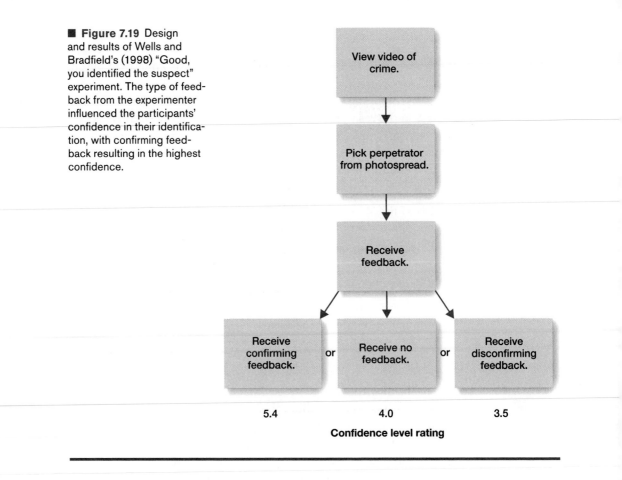

■ **Figure 7.19** Design and results of Wells and Bradfield's (1998) "Good, you identified the suspect" experiment. The type of feedback from the experimenter influenced the participants' confidence in their identification, with confirming feedback resulting in the highest confidence.

View video of crime.

Pick perpetrator from photospread.

Receive feedback.

Receive confirming feedback.   or   Receive no feedback.   or   Receive disconfirming feedback.

5.4   4.0   3.5

Confidence level rating

Following the test, one group of participants was asked questions about their choices. For example, they were asked to think about the magazine question and then to describe in detail the item they chose and to indicate specific characteristics such as its color and dimensions. Two days later, participants from both groups were asked to rate their confidence of their choices for each item. Figure 7.20a shows that for the items they had recognized correctly, the confidence of both the questioned and not-questioned groups was high. However, Figure 7.20b shows that for items that were incorrectly recognized, the confidence of the questioned group was over twice as high as the confidence of the not-questioned group. What may be happening here is that answering questions about an object makes it easier to retrieve memory for the objects later, and the participant mistakes ease of retrieval for accuracy of their report.

What Is Being Done?

The first step toward correcting problems caused by inaccurate eyewitness testimony is to realize that the problem exists. That has been achieved, largely through the efforts of memory researchers and attorneys and investigators for unjustly convicted people. The

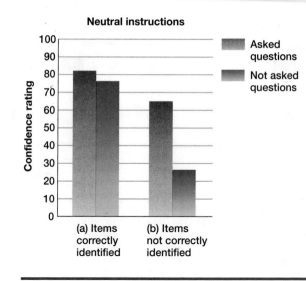

Neutral instructions

■ **Figure 7.20** Results of Shaw's (1996) experiment. (a) Asking questions about objects a person saw in a room had little effect on confidence for objects that were remembered correctly, but (b) increased confidence for objects that were remembered incorrectly.

next step is to propose specific solutions. Cognitive psychologists have made the following suggestions:

1. *When asking a witness to pick the perpetrator from a lineup, inform the witness that the perpetrator may not be in the particular lineup they are viewing.* As we have seen from the results of a number of studies, witnesses will usually pick a person from a lineup even when the perpetrator is not present. When a witness assumes the perpetrator is in the lineup, this increases the chances that an innocent person who looks similar to the perpetrator will be selected. In one experiment, telling participants that the perpetrator may not be present in a lineup caused a 42 percent decrease in false identifications of innocent people (Malpass & Devine, 1981).

2. *When constructing a lineup, use "fillers" who are similar to the suspect.* Police investigators are reluctant to increase the similarity of people in lineups because they are afraid this will decrease the chances of identifying the suspect. However, when R. C. L. Lindsay and Gary Wells (1980) had participants view a tape of a crime scene, and then tested them using high-similarity and low-similarity lineups, they obtained the results in Figure 7.21. Figure 7.21a shows that when the perpetrator was in the lineup, increasing similarity did decrease identification of the perpetrator, from 0.71 to 0.58. However, Figure 7.21b shows that when the perpetrator was not in the lineup, increasing similarity caused a large decrease in incorrect identification of an innocent person, from 0.70 to 0.31. Thus, increasing similarity does result in missed identification of some guilty suspects, but substantially reduces the erroneous identification of many innocent people, especially when the perpetrator is not in the lineup.

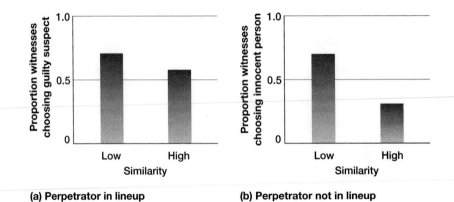

■ **Figure 7.21** Results of Lindsay and Wells' (1980) experiment, showing that (a) when the perpetrator is in the lineup, increasing similarity decreased identification of the perpetrator, but (b) when the perpetrator is not in the lineup, increasing similarity caused an even greater decrease in incorrect identification of innocent people.

3. *When presenting a lineup, use sequential rather than simultaneous presentation.* The usual depiction of lineups in movies—and the one most often used in police work—is 5 or 6 people standing in a line, facing the witness, who is hidden behind a one-way window. The problem with this way of presenting a lineup is that it increases the chances that the witness will make a relative judgment—comparing people in the lineup to each other, so the question is "Who is most like the person I saw?" However, when each person in the lineup is presented sequentially—one at a time—then the witness compares each person not to the other people, but to their memory of what they saw. Lindsay and Wells (1985) found that for lineups in which the perpetrator was not present, an innocent person was falsely identified 43 percent of the time in the simultaneous lineup, but only 17 percent of the time in the sequential lineup. The beauty of the sequential lineup is that it does not decrease the chances of identifying the suspect when he or she is included in the lineup.

4. *Improve interviewing techniques.* We have already seen that making suggestions to the witness ("Good, you identified the suspect") can cause errors. Cognitive psychologists have developed an interview procedure called the **cognitive interview**, which is based on what is known about memory retrieval. This interview procedure involves letting the witness talk with a minimum of interruption and also uses techniques that help the witness recreate the situation present at the crime scene by having them place themselves back in the scene and recreate things like emotions they were feeling, where they were looking, and how the scene may have appeared when viewed from different perspectives. Comparisons of the results of cognitive interviews to routine police questioning have shown that the cognitive interview results in 25–60 percent more information than the police interview (Fisher et al., 1989; Geiselman et al., 1985; Geiselman et al., 1986).

Recommendations like those described above have led to the publication of *Eyewitness Evidence: A Guide for Law Enforcement* by the U.S. Justice Department (available at http://www.ojp.usdoj.gov/nij/pubs-sum/178240.htm), which includes many of these suggestions, plus others. One thing that is striking about these recommendations is that they are the direct outcome of psychological research. Thus, whereas one goal of cognitive psychology research is to determine basic mechanisms of memory, this research often has practical implications as well.

Something to Consider

Memories of Childhood Abuse

Eileen Lipsker was 28 years old in 1989 when, as she watched her young red-haired daughter draw pictures in their family room, she suddenly remembered a similar scene from 20 years earlier when, as an 8-year-old, she was playing with her red-haired friend Susan. This memory ended with the image of Eileen's father, George Franklin, raping and murdering her friend. Later, during therapy, memories surfaced of her father sexually abusing her (Terr, 1994). Based on these reports, George Franklin was convicted of first-degree murder in 1990 and was sentenced to life in prison.

This case is just one of many that began surfacing in the 1980s that shared a common theme: A memory of being abused or witnessing abuse appeared after many years of having no memory of these events, and a family member is accused and convicted based solely on the reported memory. Later, in some of the cases, it was determined that the abuse did not, in fact, happen. This was the outcome for George Franklin, whose conviction was later overturned on appeal.

How could this happen? One answer is suggested by the following scenario: Patient X enters therapy for an eating disorder and depression. The therapist believes that symptoms such as eating disorders and depression are caused by childhood sexual abuse that has been pushed out of memory (Blume, 1990; Fredrickson, 1992). This therapist, who belongs to a group of therapists that memory researchers have identified as "trauma-memory oriented therapists," tells the patient that memories of abuse can be buried—pushed out of consciousness because of their painful nature—and suggests trying some visualization exercises to help the patient unlock this lost memory. In some cases, the therapist might ask the patient to obtain childhood family pictures because sometimes viewing them helps retrieve these memories.

From what you know about the possibility that memories can be created by suggestion, it is easy to see that the situation described above could provide powerful suggestions, which could lead the creation of a false memory for abuse. As we saw from the description of Lindsay et al.'s (2004) experiment on page 265, having the patient view pictures can further enhance the possibility of creating false memories.

Of course, it is also possible that the patient was abused, and that he or she is remembering something that actually happened. The incidence of childhood sexual abuse in the United States is shockingly high, with millions of people affected. Elizabeth Loftus (1993), a memory researcher who has extensively studied cases of memory of childhood sexual abuse, points out that the question is not whether or not childhood sexual abuse occurs, but how abuse is recalled by adults. "If we accept all allegations no matter how dubious," states Loftus, "this increases the likelihood that people will begin to disbelieve genuine cases of childhood sexual abuse that truly deserve sustained attention."

Unfortunately, there is no test or procedure that can accurately differentiate between real memories and false memories. But given what we do know about memory, it is important that we take into account the specific situations under which memories for long-ago events are elicited. Thus, it is important to keep in mind both the seriousness and high prevalence of abuse, while also not losing sight of the possibility that memory can be created by suggestion.

Test Yourself 7.2

1. There have been many experimental demonstrations of how knowledge we have gained from past experiences can result in memory errors. Describe how the studies that involved the following questions demonstrated this effect of knowledge, and consider the role of inference in each of these examples: (1) Was John pounding a nail? (2) Was the runner safe at first? (3) What was in the office? (Why is this an example of a schema?), (4) What happened at the dentist? (Why is this an example of a script?), and (5) What words did you remember from a list of words associated with "sleep"?

2. Why can we say that memory is highly functional but that it may not be perfectly suited to all situations?

3. Experiments that have shown that memory can be affected by suggestion have led to the proposal of the misinformation effect. How has the misinformation effect been demonstrated, and what mechanisms have been proposed to explain this effect?

4. How has it been shown that suggestion can influence people's memories for early childhood experiences?

5. What is the evidence both from "real life" and laboratory experiments that eyewitness testimony is not always accurate? Describe how the following factors have been shown to lead to errors in eyewitness testimony: weapons focus, familiarity, leading questions, and feedback from a police officer.

6. What procedures have cognitive psychologists proposed to increase the accuracy of eyewitness testimony?

7. How does the suggestibility of memory pose problems for situations in which adults remember, during therapy, that they were abused as children?

Chapter Summary

1. To truly understand memory we need to consider how memory operates in the environment. When we do this, we find that we make many errors in memory and that these errors have something to tell us about the basic mechanisms of memory.

2. Prospective memory is remembering to perform intended actions. Einstein and McDaniel showed that prospective memory is better when cues for remembering are distinctive. Time-based prospective memory tasks are more difficult to remember than event-based tasks. A solution is to turn a time-based task into an event-based task.

3. Autobiographical memory has been defined as recollected events that belong to a person's past. It can also be defined as episodic memory for events in our lives plus personal semantic memories of facts about our lives.

4. The multidimensional nature of autobiographical memory has been studied by showing that people who have lost their visual memory due to brain damage experience a loss of autobiographical memory. Also supporting the multidimensional nature of autobiographical memory is Cabeza's experiment, which showed that a person's brain is more extensively activated when viewing photographs he or she took him- or herself than when viewing photographs taken by another person.

5. When people are asked to remember events over their lifetime, transition points are particularly memorable. Also, people over 40 tend to have good memory for events they experienced from adolescence to early adulthood. This is called the reminiscence bump.

6. The following hypotheses have been proposed to explain the reminiscence bump: (1) life-narrative, (2) cognitive, and (3) cultural life script.

7. Brown and Kulik proposed the term flashbulb memory to refer to a person's memory for the circumstances surrounding hearing about shocking, highly charged, important events. They proposed that these flashbulb memories are vivid and detailed, like photographs.

8. A number of experiments indicate that it is not accurate to equate flashbulb memories with photographs because, as time passes, people make many errors when reporting flashbulb memories. Studies of memories for hearing about both the *Challenger* explosion and the announcement of the O. J. Simpson murder trial verdict showed that people's responses became more inaccurate with increasing time after the event.

9. Talarico and Rubin's study of people's memory for when they first heard about the 9/11 terrorist attack indicates that memory errors increased with time, just as for other memories, but that people remained more confident of the accuracy of their 9/11 memory. Another 9/11 study, by Davidson and coworkers, also showed that memory for 9/11 declined with time, but that people had better memory for the events surrounding 9/11 than for another more ordinary event that had occurred at the same time. The difference in these results might be explained by differences in the procedure in these two experiments.

10. According to the constructive approach to memory, what people report as memories are constructed by the person based on what actually happened plus additional factors such as the person's knowledge, experiences, and expectations. Bartlett's "War of the Ghosts" experiment and the experiment in which students were asked to remember their high school grades both resulted in many memory errors. These errors can be explained in terms of the constructive process of memory.

11. Source memory is the process of determining the origins of our memories, knowledge, or beliefs. A source monitoring error occurs when the source of a memory is misidentified. Jacoby's "becoming famous overnight" experiment illustrates an effect of source monitoring errors.

12. Inference is one of the mechanisms of the constructive process of memory. The following experiments show that inference can cause memory errors: (1) pragmatic inference, (2) Bransford and Johnson's "pounding nail," and (3) the baseball story.

13. Our knowledge about what is involved in a particular experience is a schema for that experience. The experiment in which participants were asked to remember what was in an office illustrates how schemas can cause errors in memory reports.

14. A script is our conception of the sequence of actions that usually occur during a particular experience. The "dentist experiment," in which a participant is asked to remember a paragraph about going to the dentist, illustrates how scripts can result in memory errors.

15. The experiment in which people were asked to recall a list of words related to sleep illustrates how our knowledge about things that belong together (for example, that *sleep* belongs with *bed*) can result in reporting words that were not on the original list.

16. Although people often think that it would be an advantage to have a photographic memory, the case of the memory expert S shows that it may not be an advantage to be able to remember everything perfectly. The fact that our memory system does not store everything may even add to the survival value of the system.

17. Experiments in which misleading postevent information is presented to participants in memory experiments indicate that memory can be influenced by suggestion. An example of such an experiment is Loftus's traffic-accident experiment. The following explanations have been proposed to explain the errors caused by misleading postevent information: (1) memory-trace hypothesis, (2) effect of retroactive interference, and (3) effect of source monitoring errors. Lindsay's experiment provides support for the source monitoring explanation, but the reasons for the effect of MPI are still being debated by memory researchers.

18. An experiment by Hyman showed that it is possible to create false memories for early events in a person's life. A similar experiment by Lindsay showed that this false-memory effect for early events can be made stronger by showing the participants a picture of their first- or second-grade class. DuBreuil was able to show that false memories can be created for events that supposedly occurred early in infancy.

19. There is a great deal of evidence that eyewitness testimony about crimes can be prone to memory errors. Some of the reasons for errors in eyewitness testimony are (1) not paying attention to all relevant details, due to the emotional situation during a crime (weapons focus is one example of such an attentional effect), (2) errors due to familiarity, which can result in misidentification of an innocent person due to source monitoring error, (3) errors due to suggestion during questioning about a crime (the "Good, you identified the suspect" experiment illustrates how a police officer's responses can cause memory errors), and (4) increased confidence due to postevent questioning.

20. Cognitive psychologists have made a number of suggestions of ways to decrease errors in eyewitness testimony.

21. The problem of childhood sexual abuse is serious and widespread. There is the potential, however, that false memories for abuse could be created by some of the techniques used by therapists to try to help their patients remember events in their past. The problem of differentiating between accurate memories of abuse and false memories created in the therapy situation is a serious one because there is no test or procedure that can accurately differentiate between real memories and false memories.

Think About It

1. What do you remember about how you heard about the terrorist attacks of September 11, 2001? How confident are you that your memory of these events is accurate? Given the results of experiments on flashbulb memories described in this chapter, what do you think the chances are that your memories might be in error? Are there any ways that you could check the accuracy of your memories?

2. What do you remember about what you did on the most recent major holiday (Thanksgiving, Christmas, New Year's, your birthday, etc.)? What do you remember about what you did on the same holiday 1 year earlier? How do these memories differ in terms of (a) how difficult they were to remember, (b) how much detail you can remember, and (c) the accuracy of your memory? (How would you know if your answer to part c is correct?)

3. There are a large number of reports of people who have been unjustly imprisoned due to errors of eyewitness testimony, and more cases are being reported every day based on DNA evidence. Given this fact, how would you react to the proposal that eyewitness testimony should no longer be admitted as evidence in courts of law?

4. Interview people of different ages regarding what they remember about their lives. How does the result you find fit with the results of autobiographical memory experiments, especially the data that support the idea of a reminiscence bump in older people?

5. The process of reconsolidation was discussed at the end of Chapter 6. How might this idea provide a physiological explanation for the effects of suggestibility on memory that we discussed in this chapter?

If You Want to Know More

1. True and false memories in the brain. Can we distinguish between true and false memories by looking at activity in the brain? One idea, called the sensory reactivation hypothesis, is that true memories involve activation of sensory areas that were activated when the original memory was formed.

Schacter, D. L., & Slotnick, S. D. (2004). The cognitive neuroscience of memory distortion. *Neuron, 44,* 149–160.

Wheeler, M. E., & Buckner, R. L. (2004). Functional-anatomic correlates of remembering and knowing. *NeuroImage, 21,* 1337–1349.

Wheeler, M. E., Petersen, S. E., & Buckner, R. L. (2000). Memory's echo: Vivid remembering reactivates sensory-specific cortex. *Proceedings of the National Academy of Sciences, 97,* 11125–11129.

2. Social influence, source-monitoring, and the misinformation effect.
Source monitoring and the misinformation effect can be influenced by social factors.

Assefi, S. L., & Garry, M. (2003). Absolut® memory distortions: Alcohol placebos influence the misinformation effect. *Psychological Science, 14,* 77–80.

Hoffman, H. G., Granhag, P. A., See, S. T. K., & Loftus, E. F. (2001). Social influences on reality-monitoring decisions. *Memory and Cognition, 29,* 394–404.

3. Memory distortions caused by personal bias.
In a very readable book, Daniel Schacter describes a number of ways that memory can be distorted. In one of the chapters he discusses how memory can be distorted by biases related to personal and social factors such as how people perceive themselves and how they think about events in their lives.

Schacter, D. L. (2001). *The seven sins of memory.* New York: Houghton Mifflin.

4. Confabulation.
People with damage to their frontal lobes often engage in a process called confabulation, which involves making outlandish false statements. One characteristic of confabulation is that the person believes that even the most impossible-sounding statements are true. It has been suggested that this may tell us something about the role of the frontal lobes in normal memory.

Moscovitch, M. (1995). Confabulation. In D. L. Schacter (Ed.), *Memory distortion* (pp. 226–251). Cambridge, MA: Harvard University Press.

5. Mechanisms of the misinformation effect.
The chapter you just read reviews three ideas about the mechanisms responsible for the misinformation effect. This paper presents another idea, which argues against the memory-trace impairment hypothesis.

McCloskey, M., & Zaragoza, Z. (1985). Misleading postevent information and memory for events: Arguments and evidence against memory impairment hypothesis. *Journal of Experimental Psychology: General, 114,* 3–18.

6. Suggestibility in children.
We have seen that adults can be influenced by suggestion. Young children pose additional problems, especially when they are called on to present testimony in court.

Bruck, M., Ceci, S. J., & Hembrooke, H. (2002). The nature of children's true and false narratives. *Developmental Review, 22,* 520–554.

Principe, G. F., Kanaya, T., Ceci, S. J., & Singh, M. (2006). Believing is seeing: How rumors can engender false memories in preschoolers. *Psychological Science, 17,* 243–248.

7. *The Moses illusion.* The Moses illusion occurs when people answer "two" to the question "How many animals of each kind did Moses take on the ark?" even though they know that Noah was the one with the ark. A number of different hypotheses have been proposed to explain this effect.

Park, H., & Reder, L. M. (2004). Moses illusion: Implications for human cognition. In R. F. Pohl (Ed.), *Cognitive illusions* (pp. 275–291). Hove, UK: Psychology Press.

Key Terms

Autobiographical memory, 238
Cognitive hypothesis, 241
Cognitive interview, 274
Constructive approach to memory, 249
Cultural life script, 241
Cultural life script hypothesis, 241
Eyewitness testimony, 266
Field perspective, 238
Flashbulb memory, 243
Life-narrative hypothesis, 241
Memory-trace replacement hypothesis, 262
Misinformation effect, 261
Misleading postevent information (MPI), 261
Narrative rehearsal hypothesis, 249

Observer perspective, 238
Pragmatic inference, 255
Prospective memory, 237
Reminiscence bump, 240
Repeated recall, 244
Repeated reproduction, 250
Retroactive interference, 262
Schema, 256
Script, 257
Source memory, 252
Source misattribution, 252
Source monitoring, 252
Source monitoring error, 252
Weapons focus, 268

CogLab

To experience these experiments for yourself, go to http://coglab.wadsworth.com. Be sure to read each experiment's setup instructions before you go to the experiment itself. Otherwise, you won't know which keys to press.

Primary Labs

Remember/know Distinguishing between remembered items in which there is memory for learning the item and items that just seem familiar (p. 252).

False memory How memory for words on a list sometimes occurs for words that were not presented (p. 258).

Forgot it all along effect How it is possible to remember something and also have the experience of having previously forgotten it (p. 275)?

"Reading Sentences" Demonstration (continued from page 254)

The sentences below are the ones you read in the demonstration on page 254 but with one or two words missing. Without looking back at the original sentences, fill in the blanks with the words that were in the sentence you initially read.

The flimsy shelf _____ under the weight of the books.
The children's snowman _____ when the temperature reached 80.
The absent-minded professor _____ his car keys.
The new baby _____ all night.
The karate champion _____ the cinder block.

After doing this, return to page 254 and read the text that follows the demonstration.

Knowledge

8

Categories Are Essential, but Definitions Don't Work
 Why Categories Are Useful
 Why Definitions Don't Work for Categories

Determining Categories by Similarity: Using Prototypes or Exemplars
 The Prototype Approach: Finding the Average Case
 ☛ Demonstration: Family Resemblance
 ◄► Method: Sentence Verification Technique
 The Exemplar Approach: Thinking About Examples
 Which Approach Works Best: Prototypes or Exemplars?

Is There a Psychologically "Privileged" Level of Categories?
 Rosch's Approach: What's Special About Basic-Level Categories?
 ☛ Demonstration: Listing Common Features
 ☛ Demonstration: Naming Things
 How Knowledge Can Affect Categorization

Test Yourself 8.1

Representing Relationships Between Categories: Semantic Networks
 Introduction to Semantic Networks: Collins and Quillian's Model
 ◄► Method: Lexical Decision Task
 Criticism of the Collins and Quillian Model
 Collins and Loftus Answer the Critics
 Assessment of Semantic Network Theories

Representing Concepts in Networks: The Connectionist Approach

Categories in the Brain

Something to Consider: The Effect of Culture on "Basic" Levels for Categorization and for Inference

Test Yourself 8.2

Chapter Summary

Think About It

If You Want to Know More

Key Terms

CogLab: Prototypes; Lexical Decision; Absolute Identification

Some Questions We Will Consider

- Why do we need to know about categories such as "cars," "people," "mountains," and "birds" in order to make sense of our experiences? (284)

- How are the relationships between various objects "filed away" in the mind? (295)

- How is information about different categories stored in the brain? (314)

- Do people in different cultures categorize objects in the same way? (315)

Imagine that you find yourself in another town, where you have never been before. As you walk down the street, you notice that there are many things that are not exactly the same as what you would encounter if you were in your own town. On the other hand, there are lots of things that seem familiar. Cars pass by, there are buildings on either side of the street and a gas station on the corner, and a cat dashes across the street and makes it safely to the other side. Luckily, you know a lot about cars, buildings, gas stations, and cats, so you have no trouble understanding what is going on.

You know about the various components of this street scene because your mind is full of concepts. A **concept** is a mental representation that is used for a variety of cognitive functions, including memory, reasoning, and using and understanding language (Solomon et al., 1999). Thus, when you think about cats, you are drawing on your concept, or mental representation, of cats, which includes information about what cats are, what they usually look like, how they behave, and so on.

By far the most commonly studied function of concepts is **categorization**, which is the process by which things are placed into groups called **categories**. For example, when you see vehicles in the street you can place them into categories such as cars, SUVs, Chevrolets, Fords, American cars, and foreign cars.

This chapter begins by describing why categories are important (Figure 8.1). We then explain why categorization can't be understood by simply looking up a definition. Most of the chapter is devoted to describing two approaches to categorization. The comparison approach is based on the idea that we decide whether something belongs in a category by comparing it to a standard. The network approach is based on the idea that knowledge about categories can be represented by networks, which are diagrams that indicate how information about categories is organized in the mind. The chapter concludes by describing how categories are represented in the brain and how categorization is influenced by culture.

▶▶▶ Categories Are Essential, but Definitions Don't Work

Categories are not simply convenient ways of sorting objects. They are tools that are essential for our understanding of the world.

Why Categories Are Useful

One of the most important functions of categories is to help us to understand individual cases we have never seen before. For example, being able to say that the furry animal across the street is a "cat" provides a great deal of information about it (Figure 8.2). Categories have therefore been called "pointers to knowledge" (Yamauchi & Markman, 2000), and so once you know something is in a category, whether it is *cat*, *gas station*, or *impressionist painting*, you know a lot of general things about it and can focus your energy on specifying what's special about this particular object (see Solomon et al., 1999; Spalding & Murphy, 1996).

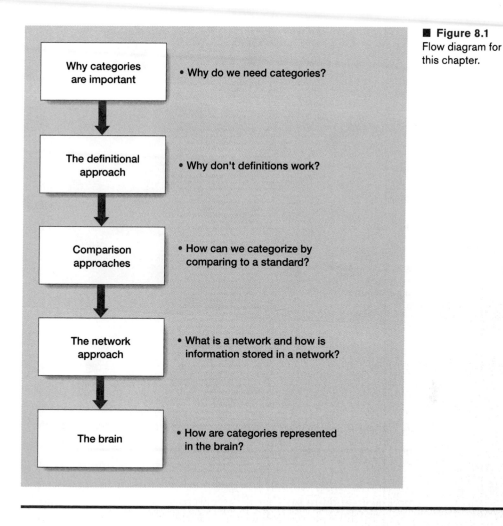

■ Figure 8.1
Flow diagram for this chapter.

As we will see later in this chapter, categories not only provide information about the basic properties of things that belong to that category, but also serve as a valuable tool for making inferences about things that belong to other categories. For example, if we know that field mice are being stricken by a particular disease, we might infer that there is a good chance that other rodents, especially those most closely related to field mice, may be carrying the disease as well.

Being able to place things in categories can also help us understand behaviors that we might otherwise find baffling. For example, if we see a man with the left side of his face painted black and the right side painted gold we might wonder what is going on. However, once we note that the person is heading toward the football stadium and it is Sunday afternoon, we can categorize the person as a "Pittsburgh Steelers fan." Placing him in that category explains his painted face and perhaps other strange behaviors that we might observe as well (Solomon et al., 1999).

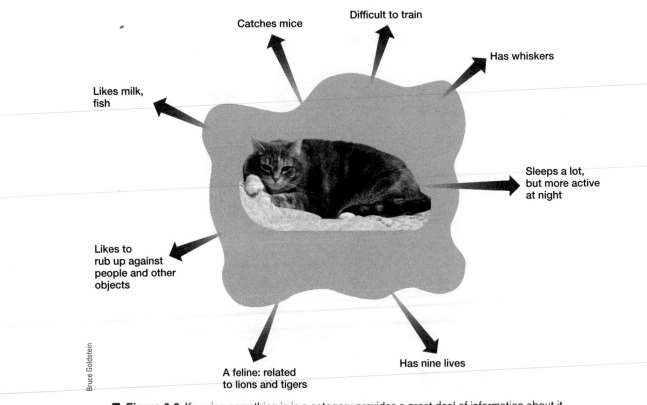

Catches mice

Difficult to train

Has whiskers

Likes milk, fish

Sleeps a lot, but more active at night

Likes to rub up against people and other objects

A feline: related to lions and tigers

Has nine lives

Bruce Goldstein

■ **Figure 8.2** Knowing something is in a category provides a great deal of information about it.

These various uses of categories testify to their importance in everyday life. It is no exaggeration to say that if there were no such thing as categories we would have a very difficult time dealing with the world. Consider what it would mean if every time you saw a different object, you knew nothing about it, other than what you could find out by investigating it individually. Clearly, life would become extremely complicated if we weren't able to rely on the knowledge provided to us by categories. Given the importance of categories, cognitive psychologists have been interested in answering the question "How are objects placed in categories?" We will now see that although we are constantly using categories to help us understand the world, we can't simply specify that something belongs to a particular category by looking up a definition.

Why Definitions Don't Work for Categories

According to the **definitional approach to categorization** we can decide whether something is a member of a category by determining whether a particular object meets the definition of the category. Definitions work well for some things, such as geometrical objects. Thus, defining a *square* as "a plane figure having four equal sides" works.

However, for most natural objects (such as birds, trees, and plants) and many human-made objects (like chairs), definitions do not work well at all.

The problem is that not all of the members of everyday categories have the same features. So, although the dictionary definition of *chair* as "a piece of furniture consisting of a seat, legs, back, and often arms, designed to accommodate one person" may sound reasonable, there are objects we call *chairs* that don't meet that definition. For example, although the objects in Figure 8.3a and b would be classified as chairs by this definition, the ones in Figures 8.3c and d would not. Most chairs may have legs and a back, as specified in the definition, but most people would still call the disc-shaped

(a)

(b)

(c)

(d)

■ **Figure 8.3** Different objects, all possible "chairs."

furniture in Figure 8.3c a chair, and might go so far as saying that the rock formation in Figure 8.3d is being used as a chair.

The philosopher Wittgenstein (1953) noted this problem with definitions and offered a solution:

> Consider for example the proceedings we call "games." I mean board-games, card-games, ball-games, Olympic games, and so on. For if you look at them you will not see something in common to *all*, but similarities, relationships, and a whole series of them at that. I can think of no better expression to characterize these similarities than "family resemblances."

Wittgenstein proposed the idea of **family resemblance** to deal with the fact that definitions often do not include all members of a category. Family resemblance refers to the fact that things in a particular category resemble one another in a number of ways. Thus, instead of setting definite criteria that every member of a category must meet, the family resemblance approach allows for some variation within a category. Chairs may come in many different sizes and shapes and be made of different materials, but every chair does resemble other chairs in some way. Looking at category membership in this way, it is possible to see how a kitchen chair and a beanbag chair could both be called chairs.

The definitional approach to categorization is based on determining whether the properties of a particular object match a definition. We will now consider two approaches that start with the idea that categorization is based on determining how similar the properties of an object are to standard representations of the category, the *prototype approach* and the *exemplar approach*.

Determining Categories by Similarity: Using Prototypes or Exemplars

The prototype and exemplar approaches to categorization are both based on the idea that membership in a category can be determined by comparing an object to a "standard" that represents the category. The two approaches differ, however, in their definition of the nature of the standard. The prototype approach states that the standard is determined by averaging category members. The exemplar approach states that the standard is created by considering a number of typical members of a category. We begin considering these approaches by describing a program of research on the prototype approach that Eleanor Rosch began in the 1970s.

The Prototype Approach: Finding the Average Case

CogLab

Prototypes

The basic idea behind the **prototype approach to categorization** is that we decide whether an object belongs to a category by determining whether it is similar to a standard representation of the category called a prototype. A **prototype** is formed by averaging

Figure 8.4 Three real birds—a sparrow, a robin, and a blue jay—and a "prototype" bird that is the average representation of the category "birds."

the category members we have encountered in the past (Rosch, 1973). For example, the prototype for the category *birds* might be based on some of the birds you usually see, such as sparrows, robins, and blue jays, but doesn't necessarily look exactly like a particular type of bird. Thus, the prototype is not an actual member of the category, but is an "average" representation of the category (Figure 8.4).

Of course, not all birds are like robins, blue jays, or sparrows. Owls, buzzards, and penguins are also birds. Rosch describes these variations within categories as representing differences in **prototypicality**. **High prototypicality** means that the category member closely resembles the category prototype (it is like a "typical" member of the category). **Low prototypicality** means that the category member does not resemble a typical member of the category. Rosch (1975a) quantified this idea by presenting participants with a category title, such as *bird* or *furniture*, and a list of about 50 members of the category. The participants' task was to rate the extent to which each member represented the category title on a 7-point scale, with a rating of 1 meaning that the member is a very good example of what the category is, and a rating of 7 meaning that the member fits poorly within the category or is not a member at all.

Results for some of the objects in two different categories are shown in Figure 8.5. The 1.18 rating for *sparrow* reflects the fact that most people would agree that a sparrow is a good example of a bird (Figure 8.5a). The 4.53 rating for *penguin* and 6.15 for *bat* reflects the fact that penguins and bats are not considered good examples of birds. Similarly, *chair* and *sofa* (1.04) are considered very good examples of furniture, but *mirror* (4.39) and *telephone* (6.68) are poor examples (Figure 8.5b). The idea that sparrows are a better example of "bird" than penguins or bats is not very surprising. But Rosch went beyond this obvious result by doing a series of experiments that demonstrated differences between good and bad examples of a category.

Prototypical Objects Have High Family Resemblance How well do good and poor examples of a category compare to other items within the category? The following demonstration is based on an experiment by Rosch and Carolyn Mervis (1975).

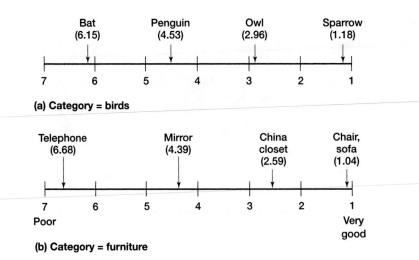

Bat
(6.15)

Penguin
(4.53)

Owl
(2.96)

Sparrow
(1.18)

7   6   5   4   3   2   1

(a) Category = birds

Telephone
(6.68)

Mirror
(4.39)

China
closet
(2.59)

Chair,
sofa
(1.04)

7   6   5   4   3   2   1
Poor   Very
                                  good

(b) Category = furniture

■ **Figure 8.5** Results of Rosch's (1975a) experiment in which participants judged objects on a scale of 1 (good example of a category) to 7 (poor example). (a) Ratings for birds; (b) ratings for furniture.

Demonstration

Family Resemblance

Rosch and Mervis's (1975) instructions were as follows: For each of the following common objects, list as many characteristics and attributes that you feel are common to these objects. For example, for *bicycles* you might think of things they have in common like *two wheels, pedals, handlebars, you ride on them, they don't use fuel,* and so on. For *dogs* you might think of things they have in common like *having four legs, barking, having fur,* and so on. Give yourself about a minute to write down the characteristics for each of the following items:

chair   sofa   mirror   telephone

If you responded like Rosch and Mervis's participants, you assigned many of the same characteristics to *chair* and *sofa.* For example, chairs and sofas share the characteristics of having legs, having backs, you sit on them, they can have cushions, and so on. It is likely, however, that your list contains far less overlap for *mirror* and *telephone,* which are also members of the category *furniture* (see Figure 8.5b). When an item's characteristics have a large amount of overlap with the characteristics of many other items in a category, this means that the family resemblance of these items is high. However, little overlap means the family resemblance is low.

Rosch and Mervis also showed that there was a strong relationship between family resemblance and prototypicality, because items high on prototypicality had high family resemblance. Thus, good examples of the category *furniture,* like chair and sofa, share many attributes with other members of this category, and poor examples, like mirror and telephone, do not. In addition to the connection between prototypicality and family resemblance, researchers have determined the following connections between prototypicality and behavior:

Statements About Prototypical Objects Are Verified Rapidly Edward Smith and coworkers (1974) used a procedure called the *sentence verification technique* to determine how rapidly people could answer questions about an object's category.

◧ Method

Sentence Verification Technique

The procedure for the **sentence verification technique** is simple. Participants are presented with statements and answer "yes" if they think the statement is true, and "no" if they think it isn't. Try this yourself, for the following two statements:

- An apple is a fruit.
- A pomegranate is a fruit. ◆

When Smith and coworkers (1974) used this technique, they found that participants responded faster for objects that are high in prototypicality (like *apple* for the category *fruit*), than they did to objects that are low in prototypicality (like *pomegranate;* Figure 8.6). This ability to judge highly prototypical objects more rapidly is called the **typicality effect.**

Prototypical Objects Are Named First When participants are asked to list as many objects as possible, they tend to list the most prototypical members of the category first (Mervis et al., 1976). Thus *sparrows* would be named before *penguins.*

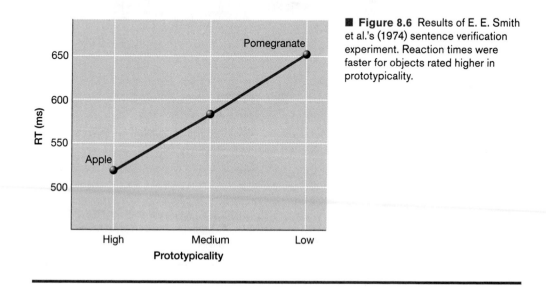

■ **Figure 8.6** Results of E. E. Smith et al.'s (1974) sentence verification experiment. Reaction times were faster for objects rated higher in prototypicality.

Prototypical Objects Are Affected More by Priming Priming occurs when presentation of one stimulus facilitates the response to another stimulus that usually follows closely in time (see Method: Repetition Priming, Chapter 6, p. 192). Rosch (1975b) demonstrated that prototypical members of a category are affected by a priming stimulus more than are nonprototypical members. The procedure for Rosch's experiment is shown in Figure 8.7. Participants first heard the prime, which was the name of a color, such as *green*. Two seconds later they saw a pair of colors side by side and indicated by pressing a key, as quickly as possible, whether the two colors were the same or different.

The side-by-side colors were paired in three different ways: (1) Colors were the same and were good examples of the category (primary reds, blues, greens, etc.; Figure 8.7a); (2) colors were the same, but were poor examples of the category (less rich versions of the good colors, such as light blue, light green, etc.; Figure 8.7b); (3) colors were different, with the two colors coming from different categories (for example, pairing red with blue; Figure 8.7c).

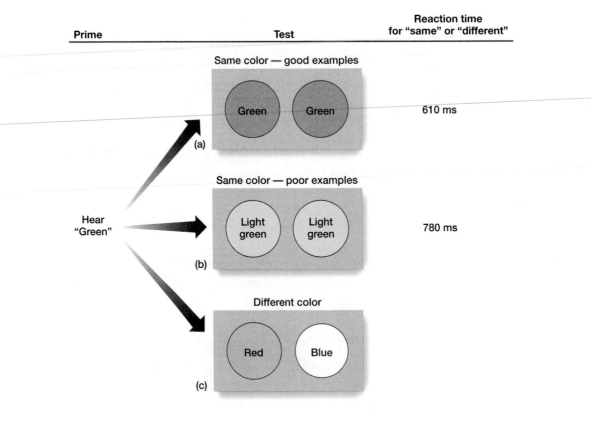

■ **Figure 8.7** Procedure for Rosch's (1975b) priming experiment. Results for the conditions when the test colors were the same are shown on the right. (a) The person's "green" prototype matches the good green, but (b) is a poor match for the light green.

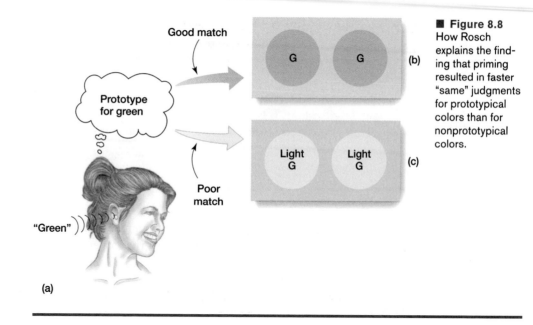

■ Figure 8.8
How Rosch
explains the find-
ing that priming
resulted in faster
"same" judgments
for prototypical
colors than for
nonprototypical
colors.

The most important result occurred when the colors were the same because in this condition, priming resulted in faster "same" judgments for the prototypical (good) colors (RT = 610 ms) than to the nonprototypical (poor) colors (RT = 780 ms). Thus, when participants heard the word *green*, they judged two patches of primary green as being the same more rapidly than two patches of light green.

Rosch explains this result as follows: When the participant hears the word *green* they imagine a "good" (highly prototypical) green (Figure 8.8a). The principle behind priming is that the prime will facilitate the participants' response to a stimulus if it contains some of the information needed to respond to the stimulus. This apparently occurs when the good greens are presented in the test (Figure 8.8b), but not when the poor greens are presented (Figure 8.8c). Thus, the results of the priming experiments support the idea that participants create images of good prototypes in response to color names. Table 8.1 summarizes the various ways, previously discussed, that prototypicality affects behavior.

The prototype approach to categorization, and in particular Rosch's pioneering research, represented a great advance over the definitional approach because it provided a wealth of experimental evidence that all items within a category are not the same. But another approach to categorization, called the *exemplar approach*, also takes into account the fact that there is a wide variation among items that belong to a particular category.

The Exemplar Approach: Thinking About Examples

The **exemplar approach to categorization**, like the prototype approach, involves determining whether an object is similar to a standard object. However, whereas the standard for the prototype approach is a single "average" member of the category, the stan-

Table 8.1 Some Effects of Prototypicality

Effect	Property of High-Prototypical Items
Family resemblance	Have more in common with other members of the category.
Typicality	Reaction time to statements like "A _____ is a bird" is faster to high-prototypical items (like robin) than to low-prototypical items (like ostrich).
Naming	Named first when people list examples of a category.
Priming	Facilitates making same–different color judgments for high-prototypical items.

dard for the exemplar approach involves many examples, each one called an exemplar. **Exemplars** are actual members of the category that a person has encountered in the past. Thus, deciding whether a particular animal is a dog involves comparing it to dogs that have been experienced in the past.

The exemplar approach can explain many of Rosch's results, which were used to support the prototype approach. For example, the exemplar approach explains the typicality effect (in which reaction times for the sentence verification task are faster for better examples of a category than for less-good examples) by proposing that objects that are like more of the exemplars are classified faster. Thus, a sparrow is similar to many exemplars, so it is classified faster than a penguin, which is similar to few exemplars. This is basically the same as the idea of family resemblance that we described for prototypes that states that "better" objects will have higher family resemblance.

Which Approach Works Best: Prototypes or Exemplars?

Which approach—prototypes or exemplars—best describes how people use categories? One advantage of the exemplar approach is that by using real examples, it can more easily take into account atypical cases such as flightless birds. Rather than comparing a penguin to an "average" bird, we remember that there are some birds that don't fly. This ability to take into account individual cases means that the exemplar approach doesn't discard information that might be useful later. Thus, penguins, ostriches, and other birds that are not typical can be represented as exemplars, rather than becoming lost in the overall average that creates a prototype. The exemplar approach can also deal more easily with variable categories like games. Although it is difficult to imagine what the prototype might be for a category that contains football, computer games, solitaire, marbles, and golf, the exemplar approach requires only that we remember some of these varying examples.

Based on the results of a number of research studies, some researchers have concluded that people may use both approaches. It has been proposed that as we initially learn about a category, we may average exemplars into a prototype and then, later in learning, some of the exemplar information becomes stronger (Keri et al., 2002; Malt, 1989). Thus, early in learning we would be poor at taking into account "exceptions," such as ostriches or penguins, but later, exemplars for these cases would be added to the category (Minda & Smith, 2001; Smith & Minda, 1998).

Other research indicates that the exemplar approach may work best for small categories such as "U.S. presidents" or "Mountains taller than 15,000 feet," and that the prototype approach may work best for larger categories, such as "birds" or "automobiles." We can describe this blending of prototypes and exemplars in commonsense terms by the following example: We know generally what cats are (the prototype), but we know specifically our own cat the best (an exemplar; Minda & Smith, 2001).

Is There a Psychologically "Privileged" Level of Categories?

As we have considered the prototype and exemplar approaches, we have used examples of categories such as *furniture*, which contains members such as *beds, chairs,* and *tables.* But, as you can see in Figure 8.9, the category *chairs* can contain smaller categories such as *kitchen chairs* and *dining room chairs.* This kind of organization, in which larger, more general categories are divided into smaller, more specific, categories to create a number of levels of categories, is called a **hierarchical organization**.

One question cognitive psychologists have asked about this organization is whether there is a "basic" level that is more psychologically important or "privileged" than other levels. The research we will describe indicates that there is a basic level of categories with special psychological properties but that, in some cases, the basic level may not be the same for everyone. We begin by describing Rosch's research, in which she introduced the idea of basic-level categories.

Rosch's Approach: What's Special About Basic-Level Categories?

Rosch's research starts with the observation that there are different levels of categories, ranging from general (like *furniture*) to specific (like *kitchen table*), as shown in Figure 8.9, and that when people use categories they tend to focus on one of these lev-

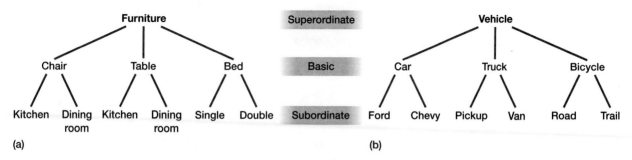

(a)

(b)

■ **Figure 8.9** Levels of categories for (a) furniture and (b) vehicles. Rosch provided evidence for the idea that the basic level is "psychologically privileged."

els. She distinguished three levels of categories: the **superordinate level** (for example, *furniture*), the **basic level** (for example, *table*), and the **subordinate level** (for example, *kitchen table*). She proposed that the basic level is psychologically special because it is the level above which much information is lost and below which little information is gained. Before reading further, do the following demonstration.

Demonstration

Listing Common Features

This demonstration is a repeat of the task you did in the Family Resemblance demonstration on page 290, but with different categories. For the following categories, list as many features that would be common to all or most of the objects in the category. For example, for *table* you might list "has legs."

1. furniture
2. table
3. kitchen table

If you responded like the participants in the Rosch, Mervis, and coworkers (1976) experiment, who were given the same task, you listed only a few common features for furniture, but many for table and kitchen table. Rosch's participants listed an average of 3 common features for the superordinate-level category *furniture*, 9 for basic-level categories such as *table*, and 10.3 for subordinate-level categories such as *kitchen table* (right column of Figure 8.10). Thus, we can see that when we start at the basic level and go up to the superordinate level, we lose a lot of information (9 features versus 3 features). However, when we go from basic to subordinate, we gain only a little information (9 features versus 10.3 features). Thus, the basic level meets Rosch's criterion for being special (going above the level results in a large loss of information; below results in hardly any gain). Here is another demonstration that is relevant to the idea of a basic level.

■ **Figure 8.10** *Left column:* category levels; *middle column:* examples of each level for furniture; *right column:* average number of common features, from Rosch, Mervis et al.'s (1976) experiment.

LEVEL	EXAMPLE	NUMBER OF COMMON FEATURES	
Superordinate	Furniture	3	*Lose a lot of information.*
Basic	Table	9	*Gain just a little information.*
Subordinate	Kitchen table	10.3	

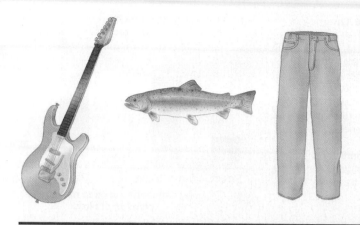

■ **Figure 8.11** Stimuli for the "naming things" demonstration.

Demonstration

Naming Things

Look at Figure 8.11 and, as quickly as possible, write down or say a word that identifies each picture. ●

What names did you assign to each object? When Rosch, Mervis, and coworkers (1976) did a similar experiment, they found that people tended to pick a basic-level name. So they picked *guitar* (basic level) rather than *musical instrument* (superordinate) or *rock guitar* (subordinate), *fish* rather than *animal* or *trout*, and *pants* rather than *clothing* or *Levi's*.

In another experiment, Rosch, Simpson, and coworkers (1976) showed participants a category label, like *car* or *vehicle*, and then after a brief delay, presented a picture. The participants' task was to indicate, as rapidly as possible, whether the picture was a member of the category. The results showed that they accomplished this task more rapidly for basic-level categories than for superordinate-level categories. Thus, they would respond "yes" more rapidly when the picture of an automobile was preceded by the word *car* than when the picture was preceded by the word *vehicle*.

How Knowledge Can Affect Categorization

Rosch's experiments, which were carried out on college undergraduates, showed that there is a level of category, which she called "basic," that reflects people's everyday experience. This has been demonstrated by many researchers in addition to Rosch. Thus, when J. D. Coley and coworkers (1997) asked Northwestern University undergraduates to name, as specifically as possible, 44 different plants on a walk around campus, 75 percent of the responses used labels like "tree," rather than more specific labels like "oak tree."

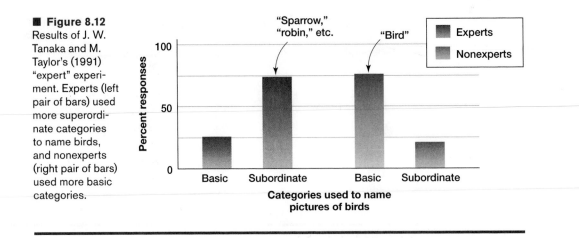

Figure 8.12
Results of J. W. Tanaka and M. Taylor's (1991) "expert" experiment. Experts (left pair of bars) used more superordinate categories to name birds, and nonexperts (right pair of bars) used more basic categories.

But instead of asking college undergraduate to name plants, what if Coley had taken a group of horticulturalists around campus? Do you think they would say "tree" or "oak tree"? An experiment by James Tanaka and Marjorie Taylor (1991) asked a similar question for birds. They asked bird experts and nonexperts to name pictures of objects. There were objects from many different categories (tools, clothing, flowers, etc.), but Tanaka and Taylor were interested in how the participants responded to the four bird pictures.

The results (Figure 8.12) show that the experts responded by saying the birds' names (*robin, sparrow, jay,* or *cardinal*), but the nonexperts responded by saying *bird.* Apparently the experts have learned to pay attention to features of birds that nonexperts are unaware of. Thus, in order to fully understand how people categorize objects, it is necessary to consider not only the properties of the objects, but the learning and experience of the people perceiving these objects (also see Johnson & Mervis, 1997).

From the result of Tanaka's bird experiment we can guess that it is likely that a horticulturist walking around campus would label plants more specifically than people who had little specific knowledge about plants. In fact, research we will describe in the Something to Consider section at the end of the chapter shows that members of the Guatemalan Itza culture, who live in close contact with their natural environment, call an oak tree an *oak tree,* not a *tree.*

Test Yourself 8.1

1. Why is the use of categories so important for our day-to-day functioning?
2. Describe the definitional approach to categories. Why does it initially seem like a good way of thinking about categories, but then become troublesome when we consider the kinds of objects that can make up a category?
3. What is the prototype approach, and what were the experiments that Rosch did that demonstrated connections between prototypicality and behavior?

4. What is the exemplar approach to categorization? How does it differ from the prototype approach, and how might the prototype approach and exemplar approach work together?

5. What does it mean to say that there are different levels within a category? What arguments did Rosch present to support the idea that one of these levels is "privileged"? How has research on how experts categorize led to modifications of Rosch's ideas about which category is "basic" or "privileged"?

Representing Relationships Between Categories: Semantic Networks

We have seen that categories can be arranged in a hierarchical organization that represents the levels of categories from general (at the top) to specific (at the bottom). Our main focus in the last section was on deciding which level of the hierarchy is psychologically privileged. In this section, our main concern is to explain how this hierarchical organization can represent how categories are *organized* in the mind. The approach we will be describing, called the **semantic network** approach, proposes that concepts are arranged in networks that represent the way concepts are organized in the mind.

Introduction to Semantic Networks: Collins and Quillian's Model

One of the first semantic network models was based on the pioneering work of Ross Quillian (1967, 1969), whose goal was to develop a computer model of human memory. We will describe Quillian's approach by looking at a simplified version of his model proposed by Allan Collins and Quillian (1969).

Figure 8.13 shows Collins and Quillian's network. Figure 8.13a, which shows the "skeleton" of Collins and Quillian's model, indicates that the network consists of nodes that are connected by links. Each node represents a category or concept, and concepts are placed in the network so that related concepts are connected.

In Figure 8.13b, some concept names have been added to the nodes. The fact that the nodes are connected by links means that they are related to each other in the mind. Thus, the model shown in Figure 8.13b indicates that there is an association in the mind between *canary* and *bird*, and between *bird* and *animal*.

In Figure 8.13c we have filled in the rest of the network by adding the concepts *fish*, *shark*, *salmon*, and *ostrich*, and also by including properties of each concept at the nodes. We can illustrate how this network works by considering how we would retrieve the properties of canaries from the network. We start by entering the network at the concept node for *canary*.

When we do this we obtain the information that a canary *can sing* and *is yellow*. To access more information about *canary*, we move up the link to *bird* and learn that a

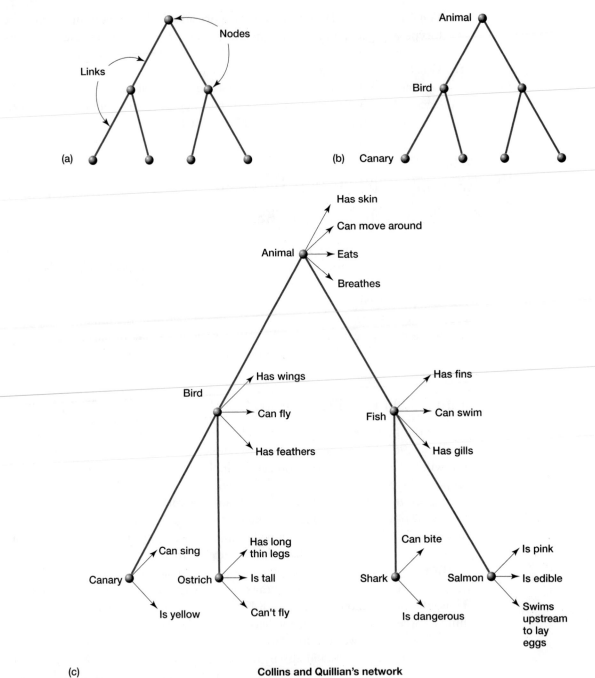

(a)

(b)

(c)   **Collins and Quillian's network**

■ **Figure 8.13** Building a semantic network. (a) The skeleton nodes connected by links. (b) Adding
concept names to the nodes, with more specific ones at the bottom and more general ones at the top.
(c) Adding properties of each concept. This is the network proposed by Collins and Quillian (1969). (Reprinted from *Journal of Verbal Learning and Verbal Behavior, 8,* A. M. Collins & M. R. Quillian, "Retrieval
Time From Semantic Memory," pp. 240–247, Fig. 1, Copyright © 1969, with permission from Elsevier.)

canary is a *bird* and that a *bird has wings, can fly,* and *has feathers.* Moving up another level to *animal,* we find that a *canary* is also an *animal,* which *has skin, can move around, eats,* and *breathes.*

You might wonder why we have to travel from *canary* to *bird* to find out that a canary can fly. After all, that information could have been placed at the canary node and then we would know it right away. But Collins and Quillian felt that including *can fly* at the node for every bird (*canary, robin, vulture,* etc.) was inefficient and would use up too much storage space. Thus, instead of indicating the properties *can fly* and *has feathers* for every kind of bird, these properties were placed at the node for *bird* because this property holds for most birds. This way of storing shared properties just once at a higher-level node is called **cognitive economy**.

Although cognitive economy makes the network more efficient, it does create a problem because not all birds fly. To deal with this problem while still achieving the advantages of cognitive economy, Collins and Quillian added exceptions at lower nodes. For example, to handle the fact that ostriches don't fly, the property *can't fly* is added to the node for *ostrich.*

How do the elements in this semantic network correspond to the actual operation of the brain? Remember from our discussion of models in cognitive psychology in Chapter 1 (p. 20) that elements of models do not necessarily correspond to specific structures in the brain. Thus, the links and nodes we have been describing do not necessarily correspond to specific nerve fibers or locations in the brain. This model, and other network models we will be describing, are concerned with how concepts and their properties are associated in the mind. Physiological findings relevant to these models, such as neurons that respond best to specific categories (see p. 314), were not available until many years after these models were proposed.

Putting aside any possible connection between the network and actual physiology, we can ask how accurately the model represents how concepts are organized in the mind. The beauty of the network's hierarchical organization, in which general concepts are at the top and specific ones are at the bottom, is that it results in the testable prediction that the time it takes for a person to retrieve information about a concept should be determined by the distance that must be traveled through the network. Thus, the model predicts that by using the sentence verification technique, in which participants are asked to answer "yes" or "no" to statements about concepts (see page 291), it should take longer to answer "yes" to the statement *a canary is an animal* than to *a canary is a bird.* This prediction follows from the fact that it is necessary to travel along two links to get from *canary* to *animal* but only one to get to *bird* (Figure 8.14).

Collins and Quillian (1969) tested this prediction by measuring the reaction time to a number of different statements and obtained the results

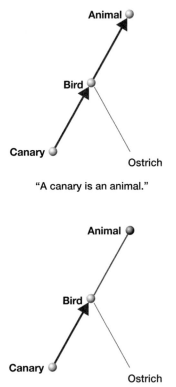

■ Figure 8.14 The distance between concepts predicts how long it takes to retrieve information about concepts as measured by the sentence verification technique. Because it is necessary to travel on two links to get from *canary* to *animal* (top), but on only one to get from *canary* to *bird* (bottom), it should take longer to verify the statement "a canary is an animal."

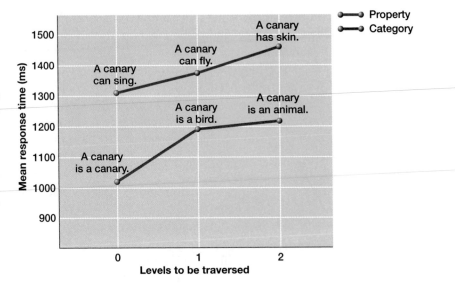

Figure 8.15 Results of Collins and Quillian's (1969) experiment that measured reaction times to statements that involved traversing different distances in the network. Greater distances are associated with longer reaction times, both when verifying statements about properties of canaries (top) and about categories of which the canary is a member (bottom). (Reprinted from *Journal of Verbal Learning and Verbal Behavior, 8,* A. M. Collins & M. R. Quillian, "Retrieval Time From Semantic Memory," pp. 240–247, Fig. 2, Copyright © 1969, with permission from Elsevier.)

shown in Figure 8.15. As predicted, statements that required further travel from *canary* resulted in longer reaction times.

Another property of the theory, which leads to further predictions, is spreading activation. **Spreading activation** is activity that spreads out along any link that is connected to an activated node. For example, if we move through the network from *canary* to *bird*, the node at *bird* and the link we use to get from *canary* to *bird* are activated, as indicated by the color arrow in Figure 8.16. This activation then spreads to other nodes

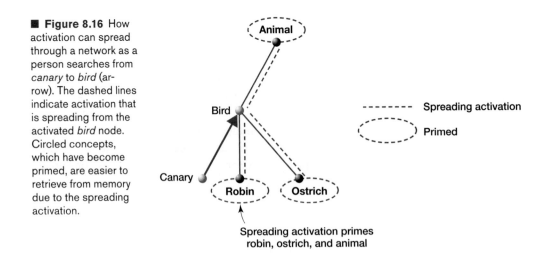

Figure 8.16 How activation can spread through a network as a person searches from *canary* to *bird* (arrow). The dashed lines indicate activation that is spreading from the activated *bird* node. Circled concepts, which have become primed, are easier to retrieve from memory due to the spreading activation.

in the network, as indicated by the dashed lines. Thus, if the pathway from *canary* to *bird* is activated, activation spreads to concepts that are connected to *bird*, such as *animal* and other types of birds. The result of this spread of activation is that the additional concepts that receive this activation become "primed" and so can be accessed more easily from memory.

The spreading activation explanation of priming was studied by David Meyer and Roger Schvaneveldt (1971) in a paper published shortly after Collins and Quillian's model was proposed. They used a method called the *lexical decision task*.

CogLab

Lexical Decision

◄► Method

Lexical Decision Task

In the **lexical decision task**, participants read stimuli, some of which are words and some of which are not words. Their task is to indicate as quickly as possible whether each entry is a word or a nonword. For example, the correct responses for *bloog* would be "no" and for *bloat* would be "yes." ◆

Myer and Schvaneveldt used a variation of the lexical decision task by presenting participants with two strings of letters, one above the other, as in Figure 8.17. The participants' task was to press the "yes" key when both strings were words or the "no" key when one or both were not words. Thus, the two nonwords shown in Figure 8.17a or the word and nonword in Figure 8.17b would require a "no" response, but the two stimuli in Figure 8.17c and d would require a "yes" response.

The key variable in this experiment was the association between the pairs of real words. In some trials the words were closely associated (like *bread* and *wheat*), and in some trials they were weakly associated (*chair* and *money*). The result, shown in

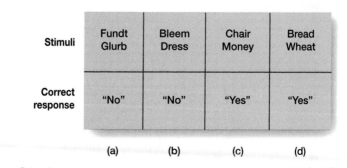

■ **Figure 8.17** Stimuli and correct responses for Meyer and Schvaneveldt's (1971) priming experiment.

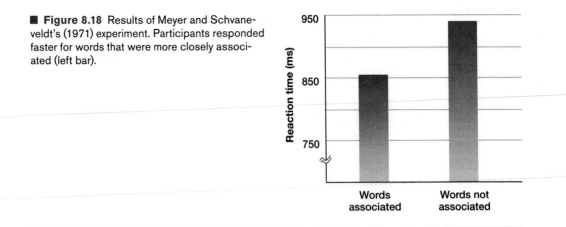

■ **Figure 8.18** Results of Meyer and Schvaneveldt's (1971) experiment. Participants responded faster for words that were more closely associated (left bar).

Figure 8.18, was that reaction time was faster when the two words were associated. Meyer and Schvaneveldt proposed that this might have occurred because retrieving one word from memory triggers a spread of activation to other nearby locations in a network, and that more activation will spread to words that are related so that the response to the related words will be faster than the response to unrelated words.

Criticism of the Collins and Quillian Model

Although Collins and Quillian's model was supported by the results of a number of experiments, it didn't take long for other researchers to call the theory into question. They pointed out that the theory couldn't explain the typicality effect, in which reaction times are faster for more typical members of a category than for less typical members (see page 291; Rips et al., 1973). Thus, the statement *a canary is a bird* is verified more quickly than the sentence *an ostrich is a bird*, but the model predicts equally fast reaction times because *canary* and *ostrich* are just one node away from *bird*.

Researchers also questioned the concept of cognitive economy because of evidence that people may, in fact, store specific properties of concepts (like *has wings* for *canary*) right at the node for that concept (Conrad, 1972). In addition, Lance Rips and coworkers (1973) obtained sentence verification results such as the following:

A pig is a mammal.   RT = 1,476 ms
A pig is an animal.   RT = 1,268 ms

A pig is an animal is verified more quickly, but as we can see from the network in Figure 8.19, the Collins and Quillian model predicts that *a pig is a mammal* should be verified more quickly because a link leads directly from pig to mammal,

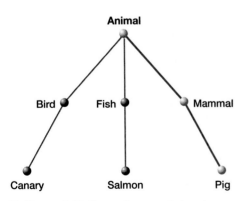

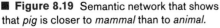

■ **Figure 8.19** Semantic network that shows that *pig* is closer to *mammal* than to *animal*.

but we need to travel one link past the mammal node to get to *animal*. Sentence verification results such as these, plus the other criticisms of the theory, led Collins and Elizabeth Loftus (1975) to propose a new semantic network model designed to handle the results that the Collins and Quillian model couldn't explain.

Collins and Loftus Answer the Critics

Collins and Loftus's (1975) model can deal with the typicality effect by using shorter links to connect concepts that are more closely related. For example, the network in Figure 8.20 indicates that *vehicle* is connected to *car*, *truck*, and *bus* by short links (because these are closely related concepts), but is connected to *fire engine* and *ambulance* (which are less typical vehicles than *car*, *truck*, or *bus*) with longer links.

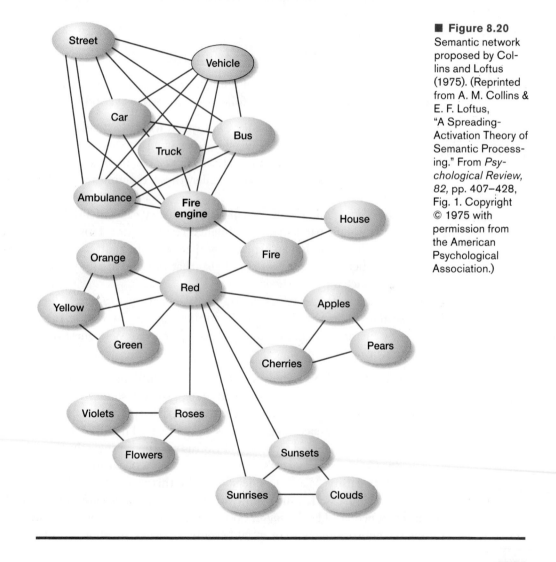

■ **Figure 8.20** Semantic network proposed by Collins and Loftus (1975). (Reprinted from A. M. Collins & E. F. Loftus, "A Spreading-Activation Theory of Semantic Processing." From *Psychological Review, 82*, pp. 407–428, Fig. 1. Copyright © 1975 with permission from the American Psychological Association.)

The Collins and Loftus model abandons the hierarchical structure used by Collins and Quillian in favor of a structure based on a person's experience. This means that the spacing between various concepts can differ for various people depending on their experience and knowledge about specific concepts.

In addition to proposing experientially based links between concepts, Collins and Loftus also proposed a number of additional modifications to the Collins and Quillian model to deal with problems like cognitive economy and the *pig/mammal* problem. The details of their proposed modifications aren't that important. What is important is that these modifications made it possible to explain just about any result of categorization experiments. Collins and Loftus describe their theory as "a fairly complicated theory with enough generality to apply to results from many different experimental paradigms" (1975, p. 427). Although you might think that being able to explain just about any result would be an advantage, this property of the model led some researchers to criticize it, as we will see in the next section.

Assessment of Semantic Network Theories

Why would a model be criticized if it can explain just about any result? We can answer this question by considering the following properties of good psychological theories:

1. *Explanatory power.* The theory can explain why a particular result occurred by making a statement like "Behavior A occurred because . . ."
2. *Predictive power.* The theory can predict the results of a particular experiment by making a statement like "Under these circumstances, Behavior B will occur."
3. *Falsifiability.* The theory or part of the theory can potentially be shown to be wrong when a particular experimental result occurs. This means that it should be possible to design an experiment that can potentially yield results that would be predicted by the theory, and also that can potentially yield results that are *not* predicted by the theory.
4. *Generation of experiments.* Good theories usually stimulate a great deal of research to test the theory, to determine ways of improving the theory, to use new methods suggested by the theory, or study new questions raised by the theory.

When we evaluate the original Collins and Quillian theory against these criteria, we find that although it does explain and predict some results (see the data in Figure 8.15), there are many results it can't explain, such as the typicality effect and the longer reaction times for sentences like "A pig is a mammal." These failures to accurately explain and predict are what led Collins and Loftus to propose their theory.

But Collins and Loftus's theory has been criticized for being so flexible that it is difficult to falsify. We can understand why this is a problem by considering the networks in Figure 8.21, which show the node for *fire engine* and some of its links for two different people. The *fire engine* node would be more easily activated by related concepts for the network in (b) than in (a) because the links are shorter in (b). But the lengths

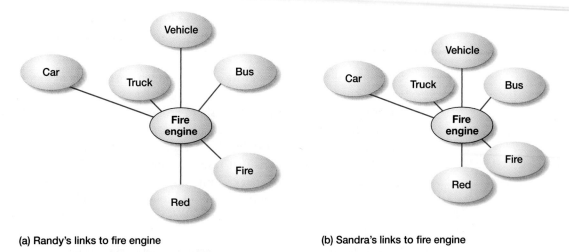

(a) Randy's links to fire engine   (b) Sandra's links to fire engine

■ **Figure 8.21** The node for *fire engine* and some of the concepts to which it is linked for two different people: (a) longer links, and (b) shorter links.

of the links can be determined by a number of factors, including a person's past experience with fire engines or other types of vehicles. Unfortunately, there are no definite rules for determining these lengths—or, for that matter, for determining things like how long activation remains after it spreads, or how much total activation is needed to trigger a node. This means that by appropriately adjusting things like the length of the links and how long activation lasts, the model can "explain" many different results.

But if a theory can explain almost any result by adjusting various properties of the model, what has it really explained? That question is what led P. N. Johnson-Laird and coworkers (1984) to criticize semantic network theories and to conclude that these theories are "too powerful to be refuted by empirical evidence." This is a way of saying that it is difficult to falsify the theories. (See Anderson & Bower, 1973; Glass & Holyoak, 1975, for additional semantic network theories.)

Although research on semantic network theories was declining by the 1980s, network theories began a resurgence with the publication of two volumes titled *Parallel Distributed Processing: Explorations in the Microstructure of Cognition* by James McClelland and David Rumelhart (McClelland & Rumelhart, 1986; Rumelhart & McClelland, 1986). These books proposed a network model of mental functioning called **connectionism.**

Representing Concepts in Networks: The Connectionist Approach

McClelland and Rumelhart proposed that concepts are represented in networks that contain nodes and links like semantic networks but that operate very differently from semantic networks. The idea of connectionist networks was partially inspired by the nervous system, in which neurons are connected to form neural networks (see Chapter 2). The basic characteristics of the **connectionist networks**, proposed by McClelland and Rumelhart, are:

- Connectionist networks consist of **units**, which are connected to form networks (McClelland & Rogers, 2003). McClelland describes these units as "neuron-like units" because they share properties with neurons. Like neurons, some units can be activated by stimuli from the environment, and some can be excited or inhibited by other units. Units are also connected with each other in circuits that resemble simple neural circuits (see Chapter 2). There are three types of units: **input units**, which are activated by stimulation from the environment; **hidden units**, which receive signals from the input units; and **output units**, which receive signals from hidden units (Figure 8.22).

- Knowledge is represented in connectionist networks by the distributed activity of many units (McClelland et al., 1995). Figure 8.23a shows how the concept *canary* might be represented by the pattern of activation in hidden and output units. What this means is that when a person thinks about what a canary is, the person's knowledge about the properties of canaries is represented in their mind by the pattern of activation in many units. Note that this is different from the situation in semantic networks, in which this knowledge about *canary* is represented by activity in individual nodes (Figure 8.23b).

- Because the processing in these networks, as in the nervous system, occurs in many parallel lines at the same time, and because the representation of concepts in these networks is distributed across many units, the connec-

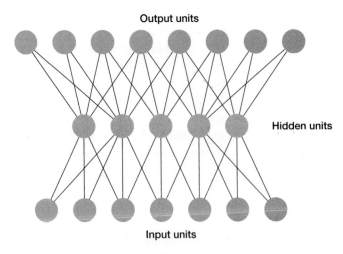

■ **Figure 8.22** A connectionist network showing input units, hidden units, and output units. Incoming stimuli activate the input units, and signals travel through network, activating the hidden and output units. Note that this is an extremely simplified version of a connectionist network. Networks used in research on connectionism contain many more units and more-complex connections between units.

Output units

Hidden units

Input units

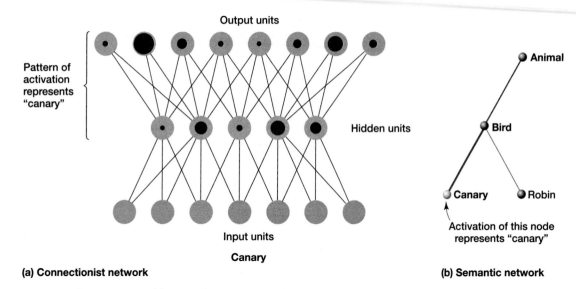

Output units

Pattern of activation represents "canary"

Hidden units

Input units

Canary

(a) Connectionist network

Animal

Bird

Canary　Robin

Activation of this node represents "canary"

(b) Semantic network

■ **Figure 8.23** (a) How information is represented in a connectionist network by the distributed pattern of activity in a number of units. Activation is indicated by the size of the dots inside the units, with large dots indicating more activation. In this example, *canary* is represented by the pattern of activation of hidden and output units. (b) In a semantic network like the one in Figure 8.13c, *canary* is represented by activation of the *canary* node.

tionist approach is also called the **parallel distributed processing (PDP) approach.**

- Processing in connectionist networks is achieved by **weights** at each connection. Weights, which can be positive (analogous to excitation in neural circuits) or negative (analogous to inhibition), determine how strongly an incoming signal will activate the next unit.

How does a pattern of activity in the hidden or output units become associated with a particular stimulus or concept? A number of different mechanisms have been proposed to explain how this occurs. We are going to focus on a mechanism called **supervised learning,** in which the network learns by a process that is analogous to the way a child gains knowledge about the world by making mistakes and being corrected. For example, a child learning language might point to a car and say *aumobile.* In response to this, the parent might provide the correct pronunciation—*auto-mobile.* The child usually continues to make mistakes, and may also mistakenly call a truck an *aumobile.* But eventually, with practice and continued guidance, the child learns how to say *automobile* and not to call trucks *automobiles.*

To see how a similar process occurs in a connectionist network, let's consider what happens when we present the input *canary* to the network in Figure 8.24. As you read this example, keep in mind that what we are describing is the response of a computer

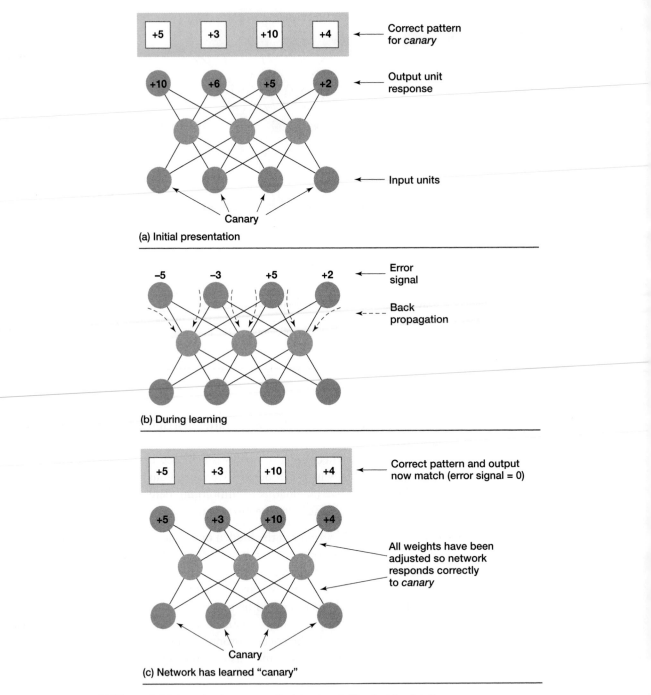

Canary

(a) Initial presentation

(b) During learning

Canary

(c) Network has learned "canary"

■ **Figure 8.24** Learning in a connectionist network. See text for details.

that has been programmed to simulate a connectionist network, with its input, hidden, and output units.

To start the process, the experimenter specifies a concept, such as *canary*. Presenting *canary* excites the input units for canary and causes activation to flow through the network through the hidden units and then to the output units. Before any learning has occurred, the weights in the network are random, so the pattern of activity in the output units does not correspond to the correct pattern for *canary*. The correct pattern, which has been programmed into the computer by the experimenter, is indicated above the output units in Figure 8.24a. Just as a child uses the parents' correct pronunciation as a model for his or her next attempt at saying a word, the network uses the correct pattern as a guide for its next attempt at producing the pattern for canary.

The network uses this pattern to calculate an **error signal**, which is the difference between the actual activity of each output unit and the correct activity. The error signal for our example, which is indicated by the numbers above the output units in Figure 8.24b, is −5, −3, +5 and +2. This error signal provides information that the network can use to learn how to create the correct output pattern for *canary*. This learning occurs through a process called **back propagation**, in which the error signal is transmitted backward through the circuit. This back propagation of the error signal is symbolized by the dashed arrows in Figure 8.24b.

Information provided by the back propagated error signal indicates how the network's weights need to be adjusted so that the output signal will match the correct signal. From the error signal in our example, we can see that the strength of the inputs to the units on the left need to be decreased, and the strength of the inputs to two units on the right need to be increased. This is achieved by changing the weights of the connections between the units.

After the weights are changed, the input *canary* results in a new output pattern. This new pattern is closer to the correct pattern, but doesn't match perfectly. The process then repeats, with a new error signal being sent back through the network, and new weights being created, to bring the output pattern even closer to the correct pattern. Eventually, when the input *canary* results in an error signal of zero, the output is correct, and the learning process is completed (Figure 8.24c).

Although this process seems straightforward, with the network using the error signal on each trial to modify the weights and bring the output signal closer to the correct pattern, there is one complication: The network also needs to be able to respond correctly not only to *canary*, but to *robin* and *oak tree* and many other concepts. Thus, during the learning process, the networks' weights must be adjusted so it generates the correct pattern not only for *canary*, but also for *robin* and *oak tree* and other concepts as well.

One way to deal with this problem is to train the network on a large number of words or concepts at once, first presenting *canary*, then *robin*, then *oak tree*, and so on. Remember that the correct pattern will be different for each concept, with each one generating a different error signal. Because the network has to respond correctly to many different concepts, it is important to design the network's learning process so changing the weights to get a better response to *canary* doesn't result in a worse response to *oak tree.* This is achieved by changing the weights very slowly on each trial, so changing the weights in response to one concept causes little disruption of the weights for the other concepts that are being learned at the same time. Eventually, after thousands of trials, the weights in the network become adjusted so the network generates the correct output pattern for many different concepts.

Figure 8.25 shows how eight hidden units in a complex connectionist network respond during a learning process in which the network is presented with a number of different concepts, one after another (McClelland & Rogers, 2003). Each bar represents the activation in each of eight hidden units in response to different inputs. At the beginning of the process, activity is about the same in each unit (Learning trials = 0). But as learning progresses, with each concept being presented one after another and the weights being changed just slightly after each trial, the patterns become adjusted, so by Trial 250 the patterns for *salmon* and *canary* begin to look different, and by Trial 2,500 it is easy to tell the difference between the patterns for *salmon* and *canary* or between *canary*

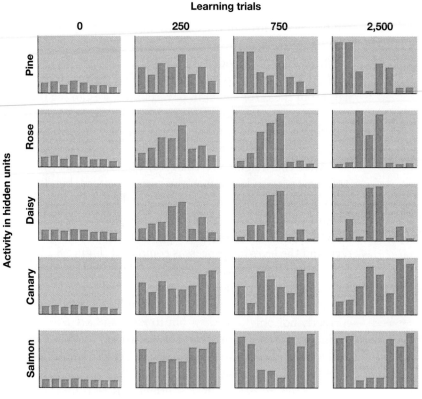

■ **Figure 8.25** Patterns of responding in eight hidden units during learning in a connectionist network. See text for details. (Adapted from McClelland & Rogers, 2003.)

and *daisy*. Also note that the two flowers, *rose* and *daisy*, have similar but slightly different patterns.

There are two important things to remember about the connectionist approach: (1) It proposes a slow learning process that eventually creates a network capable of handling a wide range of inputs, and (2) information about each input is contained in the *distributed* pattern of activity across a number of units. Thus, just as the nervous system represents different faces by different patterns of activity in neurons (see Figure 2.13b), the connectionist network represents different concepts by different patterns of activity in its units. Some other properties of connectionist networks are as follows:

- *The system is not totally disrupted by damage.* Because information in the network is distributed across many units, damage to the system does not completely disrupt its operation. This property, in which disruption of performance occurs only gradually as parts of the system are damaged, is called **graceful degradation** and is similar to what often happens in actual cases of brain damage.

- *Learning can be generalized.* Because similar concepts have similar patterns, training a system to recognize the properties of one concept (such as *automobile*) also provides information about other, related concepts (such as *truck* and *vehicle*). This is similar to the way we actually learn about concepts because learning about automobiles enables us to predict properties of different types of automobiles we've never seen. This ability to generalize is the basis of intelligent behavior and the constructive nature of memory (see McClelland et al., 1995).

- *Successful computer models have been developed.* Computer models based on connectionist networks have been created that respond to being damaged in ways similar to the response that occurs in actual cases of brain damage in humans. Some researchers have suggested that studying the way networks respond to damage may suggest strategies for rehabilitation of human patients (Farah et al., 1993; Hinton & Shallice, 1991; Olson & Humphreys, 1997). In addition, connectionist networks have been developed that simulate normal cognitive functioning for processes such as language processing, memory, and cognitive development (Rogers & McClelland, 2004; Seidenberg & Zevin, 2006).

Although connectionist networks have a number of features that enable them to reproduce many aspects of concept formation, opinion regarding connectionist networks is divided. Some researchers believe that this approach holds great promise and are especially attracted to working on a system that shares some properties with the nervous system. Other researchers think that there are limits to what connectionist networks can explain, and feel that even if these networks may explain some aspects of how we store knowledge, the best way to explain how knowledge is represented in the mind is to combine connectionism with some of the other approaches to semantic memory that we discussed at the beginning of the chapter.

▶▶▶ Categories in the Brain

The first indication that different areas of the brain may be specialized to process information about different categories came from neuropsychological research. Elizabeth Warrington and Tom Shallice (1984) summarized a number of papers that showed that people with damage to their inferior temporal (IT) lobe tend to lose ability to recognize living things, while retaining the ability to recognize human-made artifacts such as tools and furniture. (Remember from Chapter 3 that the IT cortex is associated with form perception and the perception of faces). Later research discovered some patients who had difficulty recognizing tools, but not living things. These are examples of a condition called **visual agnosia**, in which people can *see* objects perfectly well, but they cannot *name* these objects.

These cases, summarized in Table 8.2, indicate a double dissociation for living things versus nonliving things. Remember from Chapters 2 (page 43) and 6 (page 188) that a double dissociation means that two functions (in this case, categorizing living things and categorizing nonliving things) are served by different and independent mechanisms. However, just to make things interesting, Hills and Caramazza (1991) found a patient who was unable to name nonliving things and some living things, like and fruits and vegetables, but could name other living things, such as animals.

The idea that nonliving and living things are represented in different places in the brain has been confirmed by fMRI research, but there is a lot of overlap between activations for different categories (Chao et al., 1999). This has led to the idea that categories are represented by distributed activity, with categories with similar features causing more similar patterns of brain activity (Low et al., 2003; Martin & Chao, 2001).

Research on how single neurons in the brain respond to different stimuli has led to the discovery of **category-specific neurons** in the temporal lobe that respond best to objects like the ones shown in Figure 8.26 (Kreiman et al., 2000a). Keep in mind that these neurons respond not to just one particular object, but to a large number of objects that make up a particular category. Thus, the neuron that responds to the picture of the

Table 8.2 Neuropsychology of Categories

Cases	Naming	
	Living Things	**Nonliving Things**
Cases that result in an inability to name living things*	Deficient	OK
Cases that result in an inability to name nonliving things†	OK	Deficient

*Caramazza & Shelton, 1998; Farah & Wallace, 1992; Hart & Gordon, 1992; Hart et al., 1985; Hills & Caramazza, 1991; Silveri & Gainotti, 1988; Warrington & Shallice, 1984.

†Sheridan & Humphreys, 1993; Warrington & McCarthy, 1983.

Source: Caramazza, 2000.

■ **Figure 8.26** There are neurons in the temporal lobe, called category-specific neurons, that respond best to specific objects like the ones shown here. (Reprinted by permission from Macmillan Publishers Ltd from "Category-Specific Visual Responses of Single Neurons in the Human Medial Temporal Lobe," by G. Kreiman, C. Koch, & I. Fried, *Nature Neuroscience, 3,* pp. 946–953, September 1, 2000.)

house in Figure 8.26 will also respond to pictures of many other houses as well. Results such as this have led to the proposal that recognizing a particular house probably involves the firing of a large number of "house" neurons, with that particular house being represented by a specific pattern of "house neuron" firing. This is analogous to the idea we introduced in Chapter 2, that a particular person's face is represented by the pattern of firing of a number of neurons (see Figure 2.13).

But what about the face of a person who you know well, or a house or building you are very familiar with? The discovery of neurons like the ones we described in Chapter 2, which respond selectively to specific well-known people or buildings, such as Halle Berry or the Sydney Opera House, indicates that there may be neurons in the hippocampus that respond very specifically to a particular concept (see Something to Consider: Are There Grandmother Cells After All? on page 50).

▥ Something to Consider

The Effect of Culture on "Basic" Levels for Categorization and for Inference

When we described Rosch's research, we saw that she determined that the "basic" or "privileged" level of categories is one level below the superordinate level. Thus, for the superordinate-level concept *animal*, the basic level would be *bird* (Table 8.3). But later

Table 8.3 Basic Levels for Different Groups, Determined by Naming Objects

Rosch's Levels	Examples	Location of Basic Level for Different Groups
Superordinate	Animal	
Basic	Bird	U.S. college students
Subordinate	Sparrow	Itza and bird expert

research showed that for experts in an area, the basic level can be two levels below the superordinate level. Thus, "basic" for bird experts is not *bird* but is a more specific category such as *sparrow*.

Additional evidence that the level that is basic can be determined by expertise comes from cross-cultural studies of how members of a traditional village in Guatemala, the Maya Itza, categorize plants, birds, and animals. The Itza live in close contact with their natural environment and therefore have a great deal of knowledge about local plants and animals. They identify items in the environment at Rosch's subordinate level. That is, a sparrow would be classified a *sparrow* rather than as a bird (Coley et al., 1997).

The idea of a basic level for categories has also been studied in another way. Coley (Coley et al., 1997) and Douglas Medin and Scott Atran (2004), did a number of experiments that investigated how U.S. undergraduates and members of the Itza culture make *inferences* across categories. Participants in these experiments were presented with questions like the following:

If all *oak trees* are susceptible to the disease of the leaf called eta, are all other *trees* susceptible?

There were questions about various plants and animals, with each question always stating that a lower-level category had a disease (*oak tree*, in this example) and asking whether that means members of a higher-level category (*trees*) had the disease.

We will focus on the three questions below, each of which corresponds to a relationship indicated by the numbered arrows in Figure 8.27a.

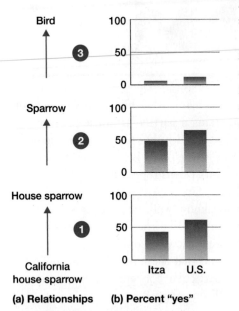

Figure 8.27 (a) Levels of categories. The numbers next to the arrows correspond to relationships 1, 2, and 3 from the text. (b) Percent "yes" responses to relationships 1, 2, and 3 for Itza and U.S. participants (Coley et al., 1997).

Relationship 1: If all *California house sparrows* are susceptible to disease eta, are all *house sparrows* susceptible?

Relationship 2: If all *house sparrows* are susceptible to disease eta, are all *sparrows* susceptible?

Relationship 3: If all *sparrows* are susceptible to disease eta, are all *birds* susceptible?

Figure 8.27b shows the percentage of "yes" responses for the Itza and U.S. participants averaged over all of the different animal and plant questions that were presented. For example, 44 percent of Itza responses and 63 percent of the U.S. responses were "yes" to statements like relationship 1 above.

These results show that when "basic" is measured in terms of making inferences, Itza and U.S. participants show a similar pattern of responses. For both cultures, "yes" responses were high for relationships 1 and 2, but dropped to a much lower percentage of "yes" responses for relationship 3. From this result, Coley and coworkers (1997) concluded that when making inferences, both Itza and U.S. participants treat the "sparrow" level as "basic."

What this tells us is that the two different ways of measuring "basic" result in different outcomes when comparing the two cultures. When "basic" is determined by naming objects (Rosch's procedure and the procedure we used in the demonstration on page 297), the Itza's basic level is more specific (for example, *sparrow*) than the basic level for U.S. participants (for example, *bird*). But when basic level is determined by asking participants to make inferences, the basic level for both Itza and U.S. participants is the same (*sparrow*).

One possible explanation for these results is that although it helps to be an expert for the naming task (it is necessary, for example, to know which birds are *sparrows*), it may not be necessary to be an expert for the inference task. This is because the names at the various levels are given in the task. It is, therefore, not necessary to be able to identify which birds are *sparrows*, or which sparrows are *California house sparrows*; it is just necessary to reason that "all birds with similar names (*sparrow*, in this case) will probably be susceptible to similar diseases." Whether this is how the U.S. and Itza participants are approaching this task remains to be determined by further experiments.

Another interesting question that also needs to be tested by more experiments is why the Itza seem to be less likely than the U.S. participants to infer that if one type of sparrow had *eta*, the next highest type would also have it. For example, 66 percent of U.S. participants—but only 49 percent of Itza participants—said "yes" to the statement that if house sparrows have eta then all sparrows would have it. Could it be that the U.S. participants, being nonexperts about plants and animals, are more prone to categorize all sparrows as being similar, but the Itza, with their greater knowledge, are more aware of possible differences between specific types of sparrows?

What all of this research tells us is that studying just American college students may not be giving us the full picture of how cognitive processes operate for humans in general. In fact, Medin and Atran's (2004) research on the Itza led them to propose that "standard populations may yield misleading results because they represent examples of especially impoverished experience with nature." In this statement, "standard populations" refers to American college students. When we consider reasoning in Chapter 12, we will look again at how culture can influence cognitive processes. (Also see Bailenson et al., 2002; Lopez et al., 1997; Medin et al., 2006; Proffitt et al., 2000; and Tang et al., 2006, for some other findings that demonstrate differences in cognition among cultures.)

Test Yourself 8.2

1. What is the basic idea behind the semantic network approach? What is the goal behind this approach, and how did the network created by Collins and Quillian accomplish this goal?
2. What is the evidence for and against the Collins and Quillian model? How did Collins and Loftus modify the model to deal with criticisms of the Collins and Quillian model, and how were these modifications received by other researchers?
3. What are some of the properties of a good psychological theory? How can we apply these properties to the semantic network theories?
4. What is the relationship between the properties of connectionist networks and the real networks that exist in the nervous system?
5. What is the goal of a connectionist network? Describe how a connectionist network would achieve this goal, beginning with the input of a stimulus and ending with the representation of that stimulus in the network. Also consider how the way information is represented in a connectionist network differs from the way it is represented in a semantic network.
6. What is the evidence about how categories are represented in the brain?
7. What has cross-cultural research taught us about how people from different cultures use categories as a way to make inferences?

Chapter Summary

1. Semantic memory is our memory for facts and knowledge.
2. Categories are "pointers to knowledge." Once you know something is in a category, you know a lot of general things about it and can focus your energy on specifying what is special about this particular object.
3. The definitional approach to categorization doesn't work because most categories contain members that do not conform to the definition. The philosopher Wittgenstein proposed the idea of family resemblances to deal with the fact that definitions do not include all members of a category.
4. The idea behind the prototypical approach to categorization is that we decide whether an object belongs to a category by deciding whether it is similar to a standard representative of the category—called a prototype. A prototype is formed by averaging category members a person has encountered in the past.
5. Prototypicality is a term used to describe how well an object resembles the prototype of a particular category.
6. The following is true of high-prototypical objects: (a) They have high family resemblance; (b) statements about them are verified rapidly; (c) they are named first; and (d) they are affected more by priming.

7. The exemplar approach to categorization involves determining whether an object is similar to an exemplar. An exemplar is an actual member of a category that a person has encountered in the past.

8. An advantage to the exemplar approach is that it doesn't discard information about atypical cases within a category, such *penguin* in the "bird" category. The exemplar approach can also deal more easily with categories that contain widely varying members, like games.

9. Researchers have concluded that people use both approaches to categorization. Prototypes may be more important as people initially learn about categories, and then later exemplar information may become more important. Exemplars may work best for small categories (U.S. presidents), and prototypes may work best for larger categories (birds).

10. The kind of organization in which larger, more general categories are divided into smaller, more specific categories is called hierarchical organization. Experiments by Rosch indicate that a "basic level" of categories (such as *guitar*, as opposed to *musical instrument* or *rock guitar*) is a "privileged" level of categorization that reflects people's everyday experience.

11. Experiments in which experts were tested show that the basic level of categorization can depend on a person's degree of expertise.

12. The semantic network approach proposes that concepts are arranged in networks that represent the way concepts are organized in the mind. Collins and Quillian's model is a network that consists of nodes that are connected by links. Concepts and properties of concepts are located at the nodes. Properties that hold for most members of a concept are stored at higher-level nodes. This is called cognitive economy.

13. Collins and Quillian's model is supported by the results of experiments using the sentence verification technique. The spreading activation feature of the model is supported by priming experiments.

14. The Collins and Quillian model has been criticized for several reasons: It can't explain the typicality effect, the idea of cognitive economy doesn't always hold, and it can't explain all results of sentence verification experiments.

15. Collins and Loftus proposed another semantic network model, designed to deal with criticisms of the Collins and Quillian model. This model was, in turn, criticized because it was so flexible that it could explain any result.

16. The connectionist approach proposes that concepts are represented in networks that consist of input units, hidden units, and output units, and that information about concepts is represented in these networks by a distributed activation of these units. This approach is therefore also called the parallel distributed processing (PDP) approach.

17. Connectionist networks learn the correct distributed pattern for a particular concept through a gradual learning process that involves adjusting the weights that determine how activation is transferred from one unit to another.

18. Connectionist networks have a number of features that enable them to reproduce many aspects of human concept formation.

19. The idea that concepts are represented by specialized brain areas has been supported by neuropsychological evidence and by the results of brain scanning experiments and experiments that have recorded from category-specific neurons and neurons that appear to respond to specific concepts.

20. Cross-cultural research on members of the Itza culture indicates that culture can affect which level of categories is considered basic. This research has shown that the Itza name natural objects at a more specific level than U.S. college students, but that the Itza and college students demonstrate similar patterns of response when making inferences involving categories.

Think About It

1. In this chapter we have seen how networks can be constructed that link different levels of concepts. In Chapter 6 we saw how networks can be constructed that organize knowledge about a particular topic (see Figures 6.17 and 6.18). Create a network that represents the material in this chapter by linking together things that are related. How is this network similar to or different from the semantic network in Figure 8.13? Is your network hierarchical? What information does it contain about each concept?

2. Do a survey to determine people's conception of "typical" members of various categories. For example, ask several people to name, as quickly as possible, three typical "birds" or "vehicles" or "beverages." What do the results of this survey tell you about what level is "basic" for different people? What do the results tell you about the variability of different people's conception of categories?

If You Want to Know More

1. More on concepts. If you want to read more about concepts, see *The Big Book of Concepts*, which starts by asserting that "concepts are the glue that holds our mental world together."

Murphy, G. (2004). *The big book of concepts.* Cambridge, MA: MIT Press.

Key Terms

Back propagation, 311
Basic level, 296
Categorization, 284
Category, 284

Category-specific neurons, 314
Cognitive economy, 301
Concept, 284
Connectionism, 307

Connectionist networks, 308
Definitional approach to categorization, 286
Error signal, 311
Exemplar, 294
Exemplar approach to categorization, 293
Family resemblance, 288
Graceful degradation, 313
Hidden units, 308
Hierarchical organization, 295
High prototypicality, 289
Input units, 308
Lexical decision task, 303
Low prototypicality, 289
Output units, 308
Parallel distributed processing (PDP)
    approach, 309

Prototype, 288
Prototype approach to categorization, 288
Prototypicality, 289
Semantic network approach, 299
Sentence verification technique, 291
Spreading activation, 302
Subordinate level, 296
Superordinate level, 296
Supervised learning, 309
Typicality effect, 291
Units, 308
Visual agnosia, 314
Weight, 309

CogLab To experience these experiments for yourself, go to http://coglab.wadsworth.com. Be sure to read each experiment's setup instructions before you go to the experiment itself. Otherwise, you won't know which keys to press.

Primary Labs

Prototypes A method for studying the effect of concepts on responding (p. 288).

Lexical decision Demonstration of the lexical decision task, which has been used to provide evidence for the concept of spreading activation (p. 303).

Related Lab

Absolute identification Remembering labels that have been associated with a stimulus.

Visual Imagery

9

What Is Imagery, and What Is It For?
  The Uses of Visual Imagery
  The Plan of This Chapter

Imagery in the History of Psychology
  Early Ideas About Imagery
  Imagery and the Cognitive Revolution
  ◘ Method: Paired-Associate Learning

Imagery and Perception: Do They Share the Same Mechanisms?
  Kosslyn's Mental-Scanning Experiments
  ▸ Method/Demonstration: Mental Scanning
  The Imagery Debate: Is Imagery Spatial or Propositional?
  Comparing Imagery and Perception
  Is There a Way to Resolve the Imagery Debate?

Test Yourself 9.1

Imagery and the Brain
  Imagery Neurons in the Brain
  Brain Imaging
  Transcranial Magnetic Stimulation
  ◘ Method: Transcranial Magnetic Stimulation (TMS)
  Neuropsychological Case Studies
  Conclusions From the Imagery Debate

Using Imagery to Improve Memory
  Visualizing Interacting Images
  Placing Images at Locations
  ▸ Demonstration: Method of Loci
  Associating Images With Words

Something to Consider: Mental Representation of Mechanical Systems
  ▸ Demonstration: Mechanical Problems

Test Yourself 9.2

Chapter Summary

Think About It

If You Want to Know More

Key Terms

CogLab: Mental Rotation; Link Word

Some Questions We Will Consider

- How do "pictures in your head" that you create by imagining an object compare to the experience you have when you see the actual object? (327)

- What happens in your brain when you create visual images with your eyes closed? (337)

- How can we use visual imagery to improve memory? (347)

As you look up to observe your surroundings, you experience images that are created by nerve impulses that are traveling from your retina to your brain and then to areas in your brain that are responsible for perception. But there is another way to experience images. Consider, for example, your experience as you answer the following questions:

- How many windows are there in front of the house or apartment where you live?
- How is the furniture arranged in your bedroom?
- Are an elephant's ears rounded or pointy?

People often report that they answer questions such as these by forming images in their mind. These images that you create in your mind, even though the actual stimuli you are imagining are not present, are the result of **mental imagery**—experiencing a sensory impression in the absence of sensory input.

What Is Imagery, and What Is It For?

The particular kind of mental imagery involved in the examples above is **visual imagery**—"seeing" in the absence of a visual stimulus. The ability to recreate the sensory world in the absence of physical stimuli occurs in other senses as well. People also have the ability to imagine tastes, smells, and tactile experiences, and because most people can imagine melodies of familiar songs in their head, it is not surprising that musicians often report strong auditory imagery and that the ability to imagine melodies has played an important role in musical composition. Paul McCartney says that the song "Yesterday" came to him as a mental image, when he woke up with the tune in his head. Another example of auditory imagery is when orchestra conductors use a technique called the "inner audition" to practice without their orchestras by imagining a musical score in their minds. When they do this, they not only imagine the sounds of the various instruments but their locations relative to the podium as well.

In this chapter we will consider visual imagery, because most of the research on mental imagery has focused on visual imagery and because understanding visual imagery provides connections to other cognitive phenomena such as perception, memory, and thinking.

The Uses of Visual Imagery

Just as auditory imagery has played an important role in the creative process of music, visual imagery has resulted in both scientific insights and practical applications. One of the most famous accounts of how visual imagery led to scientific discovery is the story related by the 19th-century chemist Kekule, about how the structure of benzene came to him in a dream in which he saw a writhing chain that formed a circle that resembled a snake, with its head swallowing its tail. This visual image gave Kekule the insight that the carbon atoms that make up the benzene molecule are arranged in a ring.

A more recent example of visual imagery leading to scientific discovery is Albert Einstein's description of how he developed the theory of relativity by imagining himself traveling beside a beam of light (Intons-Peterson, 1993). On a less cosmic level, the golfer Jack Nicklaus has described how he discovered an error in the way he gripped his club as he was practicing golf swings in a dream (Intons-Peterson, 1993).

One message of these examples is that visual imagery provides a way of thinking that adds another dimension to purely verbal techniques. But the thing that is most important about imagery is that it is associated not only with discoveries by famous people, but with most people's everyday experience. In this chapter, we will consider the basic characteristics of visual imagery and how it relates to other cognitive processes such as thinking, memory, and perception.

The Plan of This Chapter

We will begin our discussion of visual imagery by describing the history of imagery in psychology. We will see how the study of imagery has paralleled the rise, fall, and re-birth of the study of cognition in general (Figure 9.1). We then consider a debate about

■ **Figure 9.1**
Flow diagram for
this chapter.

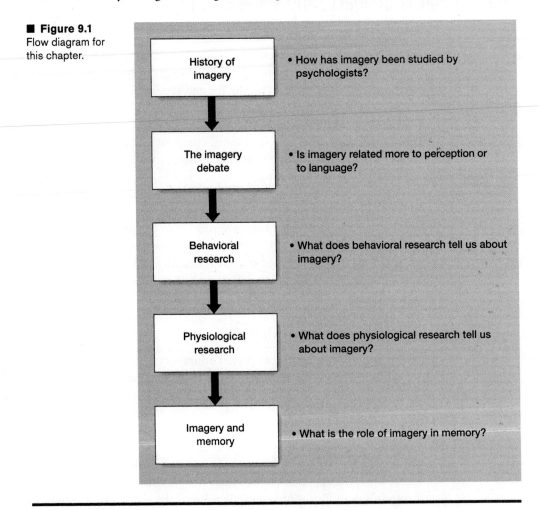

the mechanisms of imagery, which has grappled with the question, "Does visual imagery share mechanisms with perception, or is it created by mechanisms similar to those involved in language?" As we look at arguments for both sides, we will describe experiments involving both the behavioral and physiological approaches to studying imagery. We then consider the relationship between imagery and memory, which suggests how imagery can be used to improve memory.

Imagery in the History of Psychology

We can trace the history of imagery back to the first laboratory of psychology, which was founded by Wilhelm Wundt.

Early Ideas About Imagery

Wundt proposed that images were one of the three basic elements of consciousness, along with sensations and feelings, and he also proposed that because images accompany thought, studying images was a way of studying thinking. This idea of a link between imagery and thinking gave rise to the **imageless-thought debate**, with some psychologists taking up Aristotle's idea that "thought is impossible without an image," and others contending that thinking can occur without images.

Evidence supporting the idea that imagery was not required for thinking was Francis Galton's (1883) observation that people who have great difficulty forming visual images were still quite capable of thinking (also see Richardson, 1994, for more modern accounts of imagery differences between people). Other arguments both for and against the idea that images are necessary for thinking were proposed in the late 1800s and early 1900s, but these arguments and counterarguments ended when behaviorism toppled imagery from its central place in psychology (Watson, 1913; see Chapter 1, page 11). The behaviorists branded the study of imagery as being unproductive because visual images are invisible to everyone except the person experiencing them. This led the founder of behaviorism, John Watson, to describe images as "unproven" and "mythological" (1928), and therefore not worthy of study. The dominance of behaviorism from the 1920s through the 1950s pushed the study of imagery out of mainstream psychology. However, this situation changed when the study of cognition was reborn in the 1950s.

Imagery and the Cognitive Revolution

The history of cognitive psychology that we described in Chapter 1 recounts events in the 1950s and 1960s that came to be known as the cognitive revolution. One of the keys to the success of this "revolution" was that cognitive psychologists developed ways to measure behavior that could be used to infer cognitive processes. One example of a method that linked behavior and cognition is Alan Paivio's (1963) work on memory in which he showed that it was easier to remember concrete nouns, like *truck* or *tree*, that can be imaged, than it is to remember abstract nouns, like *truth* or *justice*, that are difficult to image. One technique Paivio used was *paired-associate learning*.

◀▷ Method

Paired-Associate Learning

In a **paired-associate learning** experiment participants are presented with pairs of words like *boat–hat* or *car–house* during a study period. They are then presented with the first word from each pair during the test period. Their task is to recall the word that was paired with it during the study period. Thus, if they were presented with the word *boat,* the correct response would be *hat.* ◆

Paivio (1963, 1965) found that memory for pairs of concrete nouns, such as *hotel–student*, which are likely to evoke mental images, is much better than memory for pairs of abstract nouns, such as *knowledge–honor*, which are less likely to evoke mental images. To explain this result, Paivio proposed the **conceptual-peg hypothesis**. According to this hypothesis, concrete nouns create images that other words can "hang onto." For example, if presenting the pair *boat–hat* creates an image of a boat, then presenting the word *boat* later will bring back the boat image, which provides a number of places on which participants can place the hat in their mind (See Paivio, 2006, for an updating of his ideas about memory.)

Mental Rotation

Whereas Paivio inferred cognitive processes by measuring memory, Roger Shepard and J. Meltzer (1971) inferred cognitive processes by using *mental chronometry*, the determination of the time needed to carry out various cognitive tasks. In Shepard and Meltzer's experiment, which we described in Chapter 1 (see page 17), participants saw pictures like the ones in Figure 9.2. Their task was to indicate, as rapidly as possible, whether the two pictures were of the same object or of different objects. This experiment showed that the time it took to decide that two views were of the same object was directly related to the angle between the two views (See Figure 1.11). This result was interpreted as showing that participants were mentally rotating one of the views to see

■ **Figure 9.2** Stimuli for Shepard and Metzler's (1971) mental rotation experiment. (Excerpted with permission from "Mental Rotation of Three-Dimensional Objects," by R. N. Shepard & J. Metzler. From *Science, 171,* pp. 701–703, Fig. 1A & B. Copyright © 1971 AAAS.)

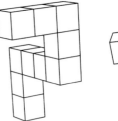 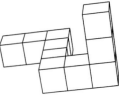

whether it matched the other one. What was important about this experiment was that it was one of the first to apply quantitative methods to the study of imagery and to suggest that imagery and perception may share the same mechanisms.

Imagery and Perception: Do They Share the Same Mechanisms?

The idea that imagery and perception may share the same mechanisms is based on the observation that although mental images are different from perception because they are not as vivid or long lasting, imagery shares many properties with perception. Shepard and Metzler's results showed that mental and perceptual images both involve spatial analogs of the stimulus. That is, the spatial experience for both imagery and perception match the layout of the actual stimulus. This idea, that there is a spatial correspondence between imagery and perception, is supported by a number of experiments by Stephen Kosslyn involving a task called **mental scanning**, in which participants create mental images and then scan them in their minds.

Kosslyn's Mental-Scanning Experiments

Stephen Kosslyn has done enough research on imagery to fill three books (Kosslyn, 1980, 1994, 2006), and he has proposed some influential theories of imagery based on parallels between imagery and perception. In one of his early experiments, Kosslyn (1973) asked participants to memorize a picture of an object such as the boat in Figure 9.3, and then to create an image of that object in their mind and to focus on one part of the boat, such as the anchor. They were then asked to look for another part of the boat, such as the motor, and to press the "true" button when they found this part or the "false" button when they couldn't find it.

Kosslyn reasoned that if imagery, like perception, is spatial, then it should take longer for the participants to find parts that are located farther from the initial point of focus because they would be scanning across the image of the object. This is actually what happened, so Kosslyn took this as evidence for the spatial nature of imagery. But, as often happens in science, another researcher proposed a different explanation.

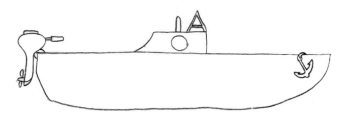

■ **Figure 9.3** Stimulus for Kosslyn's (1973) image-scanning experiment. (Reprinted from S. M. Kosslyn, "Scanning Visual Images: Some Structural Implications." From *Perception & Psychophysics, 14,* pp. 90–94, Fig. 1. Copyright © 1973 with permission from the Psychonomic Society Publications.)

G. Lea (1975) proposed that the longer reaction times observed by Kosslyn could have been caused by the fact that as participants scanned, they encountered other interesting parts, such as the cabin, which may have increased their reaction time.

To answer this concern, Kosslyn and coworkers (1978) did another scanning experiment, this time asking participants to scan between two places on a map. Before reading about Kosslyn's experiment, try the following demonstration.

Method/Demonstration

Mental Scanning

Imagine a map of your state that includes three locations, the place where you live, a city that is far away, and another city that is closer but which does not fall on a straight line connecting your location and the far city. For example, for my state, I imagine Pittsburgh, the place where I am now; Philadelphia, all the way across the state (contrary to some people's idea, Pittsburgh is not a suburb of Philadelphia!); and Erie, which is closer than Philadelphia but not in the same direction (Figure 9.4).

Your task is to create a mental image of your state and starting at your location, to form an image of a black speck moving along a straight line between your location and the closer city. Be aware of about how long it took to arrive at this city. Then repeat the same procedure for the far city, again noting about how long it took to arrive.

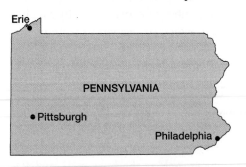

■ **Figure 9.4** Example of a state map for "mental travel across a state" demonstration. Use your own state for this demonstration.

Kosslyn's participants used the same procedure as you did for the demonstration, but were told to imagine an island like the one in Figure 9.5a, that contained seven different locations. By having participants scan between every possible location (a total of 21 trips), Kosslyn determined the relationship between reaction time and distance shown in Figure 9.5b. Just as for the boat experiment, it took longer to scan between greater distances on the image, a result that supports the idea that visual imagery is spatial in nature. However, as convincing as Kosslyn's results were, Zenon Pylyshyn (1973) proposed another explanation, which started what has been called the **imagery debate**—a debate about whether imagery is based on spatial mechanisms such as those involved in perception, or is based on mechanisms related to language, which are called *propositional mechanisms*.

The Imagery Debate: Is Imagery Spatial or Propositional?

Much of the research we have described so far in this book is about determining the nature of the mental representations that lie behind different cognitive experiences. For example, when we considered short-term memory in Chapter 5, we presented evidence that information in STM is often represented in auditory form, as when you rehearse a telephone number you have just looked up in the phone book.

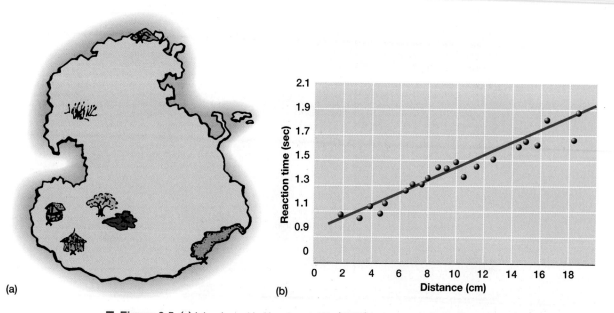

■ **Figure 9.5** (a) Island used in Kosslyn et al.'s (1978) image-scanning experiment. Participants mentally traveled between the various locations on the island. (b) Results of the island experiment. (S. M. Kosslyn, T. Ball, & B. J. Reiser, "Visual Images Preserve Metric Spatial Information: Evidence From Studies of Image Scanning." From *Journal of Experimental Psychology: Human Perception and Performance, 4,* pp. 47–60, Figs. 2 & 3. Copyright © 1978 with permission from the American Psychological Association.)

Kosslyn interpreted the results of his research on imagery as supporting the idea that the mechanism responsible for imagery involves a **spatial representation**, a representation in which different parts of an image can be described as corresponding to specific locations in space. But Pylyshyn (1973) disagreed, saying that just because we *experience* imagery as spatial, that doesn't mean that the *underlying representation* is spatial. After all, one thing that is clear from research in cognitive psychology is that we often aren't aware of what is going on in our mind. The spatial experience of mental images, argues Pylyshyn, is an **epiphenomenon**—something that accompanies the real mechanism but is not actually part of the mechanism.

An example of an epiphenomenon is lights flashing as a mainframe computer carries out its calculations. The lights may be indicating that *something* is going on inside the computer, but doesn't necessarily tell us what is actually happening. In fact, if all of the light bulbs blew out, the computer would continue operating just as before. Mental images, according to Pylyshyn, are similar—they indicate that *something* is happening in the mind, but don't tell us *how* it is happening.

Pylyshyn proposed that the mechanism underlying imagery is not spatial but is propositional. A **propositional representation** is one in which relationships can be represented by symbols, as when the words of language represent objects and relationships between objects. Thus, the propositional representation of a cat under a table

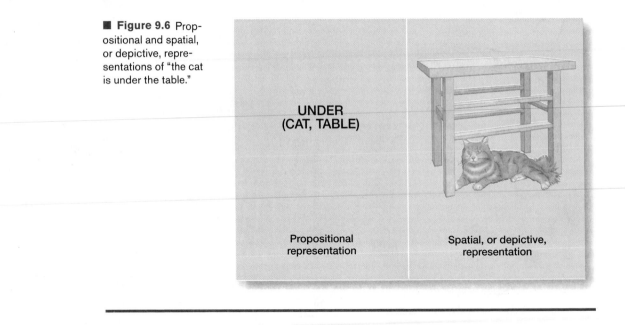

Figure 9.6 Propositional and spatial, or depictive, representations of "the cat is under the table."

UNDER
(CAT, TABLE)

Propositional
representation

Spatial, or depictive,
representation

would be the notation UNDER (CAT, TABLE). In contrast, a spatial representation would involve a spatial layout showing the cat and the table, as can be represented in a picture (Figure 9.6). Spatial relationships represented by pictures are called **depictive representations** because they are *depicted* by the picture.

We can understand the propositional approach better by returning to the depictive representation of Kosslyn's boat from Figure 9.3. Figure 9.7 shows how the visual

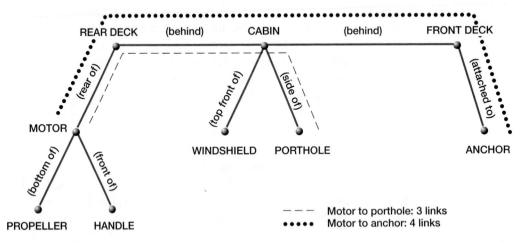

Figure 9.7 How the visual appearance of the boat in Figure 9.3 can be represented propositionally. Paths between motor and porthole (dashed line) and motor and anchor (dotted line) indicate the number of nodes that would be traversed between these parts of the boat. (Reprinted from S. M. Kosslyn, "Mental Imagery," in S. M. Kosslyn & D. N. Osherson, *An Invitation to Cognitive Science*, 2nd edition, volume 2: *Visual Cognition*, pp. 267–296, Fig. 7.6. Copyright © 1995 with permission from MIT Press.)

appearance of this boat can be represented propositionally. The words indicate parts of the boat, the length of the lines indicate the distances between the parts, and the words in parentheses indicate the spatial relations between the parts. A representation such as this would predict that when starting at the motor, it should take longer to find the anchor than to find the porthole because it is necessary to travel through three nodes to get to the porthole (dashed line) and four nodes to get to the anchor (dotted line). This kind of explanation proposes that imagery operates in a way similar to the semantic networks we described in Chapter 8 (see page 299).

In addition to suggesting that Kosslyn's results can be explained in terms of propositional representations, Pylyshyn also suggested that one reason that scanning time increases as the distance between two points on an image increases is that the participants are responding to Kosslyn's tasks based on what they know about what usually happens when they are looking at a real scene. According to Pylyshyn (2003), "When asked to imagine something, people ask themselves what it would look like to see it, and they then simulate as many aspects of this staged event as they can . . ." (p. 113). According to this idea, the results of Kosslyn's image-scanning experiments can be explained by the fact that people know that in the real world it takes longer to travel longer distances, so they simulate this result in Kosslyn's experiment. This is called the **tacit-knowledge explanation** because it states that participants unconsciously use knowledge about the world in making their judgments.

Although Pylyshyn was in the minority (most researchers accept the spatial representation explanation of visual imagery), his criticisms couldn't be ignored, and researchers from the "spatial" camp proceeded to gather more evidence. For example, to counter the tacit-knowledge explanation of Kosslyn's mental-scanning results, Ronald Finke and Stephen Pinker (1982) briefly presented a four-dot display, like the one in Figure 9.8a, and then after a 2-second delay, presented an arrow, as in Figure 9.8b. The

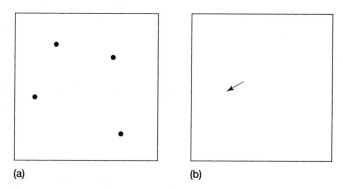

(a)   (b)

■ **Figure 9.8** Stimuli for Finke and Pinker's (1982) experiment. The display in (a) was presented first, followed, after a 2-second delay, by the arrow in (b). The participants' task was to determine whether the arrow pointed to any of the dots that had been presented in the first display. (Reprinted from "Spontaneous Imagery Scanning in Mental Extrapolation," by R. A. Finke & S. Pinker, 1982, *Journal of Experimental Psychology: Learning, Memory and Cognition, 8,* 2, pp. 142–147, Fig. 1, Copyright © 1982 with permission from the American Psychological Association.)

participants' task was to indicate whether the arrow was pointing to any of the dots they had just seen.

Although the participants were not told to use imagery or to scan outward from the arrow, they took longer to respond for greater distances between the arrow and the dot. In fact, the results look very similar to the results of other scanning experiments. Finke and Pinker argue that because their participants wouldn't have had time to memorize the distances between the arrow and the dot before making their judgments, it is unlikely that they used tacit knowledge about how long it should take to get from one point to another.

We've discussed both the spatial and the propositional approaches to imagery because these two explanations provide an excellent example of how data can be interpreted in different ways. Pylyshyn's criticisms stimulated a large number of experiments that have taught us a great deal about the nature of visual imagery (also see Intons-Peterson, 1983). The weight of the evidence supports the idea that imagery is served by a spatial mechanism, and that it shares mechanisms with perception. We will now look at additional evidence that supports the idea of a spatial representation.

Comparing Imagery and Perception

We begin by describing another experiment by Kosslyn. This one looks at how imagery is affected by the size of an object in a person's visual field.

Size in the Visual Field If you were to observe an automobile from far away, it would fill only a portion of your visual field, and it would be difficult to see small details such as the door handle. But as you move closer, it fills more of your visual field, and you can perceive details like the door handle more easily (Figure 9.9). With these observations about perception in mind, Kosslyn wondered whether this relationship between viewing distance and the ability to perceive details also occurs for mental images.

To answer this question, Kosslyn (1978) asked participants to imagine animals next to each other, such as an elephant and a rabbit, and told them to imagine that they

View from afar   Move closer

■ **Figure 9.9** Moving closer to an object, such as this car, has two effects: (1) The object fills more of the field of view; and (2) details are easier to see.

were standing close enough to the larger animal so that it filled most of their visual field (Figure 9.10a). He then posed questions such as "Does a rabbit have whiskers?" and asked his participants to find that part of the animal in their mental image and to answer as quickly as possible. When he repeated this procedure but told participants to imagine a rabbit and a fly next to each other, participants created larger images of the rabbit, as shown in Figure 9.10b. The result of these experiments, shown alongside the pictures, was that participants answered questions about the rabbit more rapidly when it filled more of the visual field.

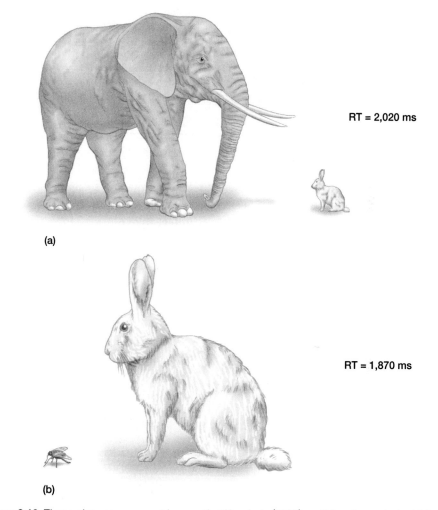

RT = 2,020 ms

(a)

RT = 1,870 ms

(b)

■ **Figure 9.10** These pictures represent images that Kosslyn's (1978) participants created, which filled different portions of their visual field. (a) Imagine elephant and rabbit, so elephant fills the field. (b) Imagine rabbit and fly, so rabbit fills the field. Reaction times indicate how long it took participants to answer questions about the rabbit.

In addition to asking participants to respond to details in visual images, Kosslyn also asked them to do a **mental-walk task,** in which they were to imagine that they were walking toward their mental image of an animal. Their task was to estimate how far away they were from the animal when they began to experience "overflow"—when the image filled the visual field or when its edges started becoming fuzzy. The result was that participants had to move closer for small animals (less than a foot for a mouse) than for larger animals (about 11 feet for an elephant), just as they would have to do if they were walking toward actual animals. This result therefore provides evidence for the idea that images are spatial, just like perception.

Interactions of Imagery and Perception Another way to demonstrate connections between imagery and perception is to show that they interact with one another. The basic rationale behind this approach is that if imagery affects perception, or perception affects imagery, this means that imagery and perception both have access to the same mechanisms.

The classic demonstration of interaction between perception and imagery dates back to 1910 when Cheves Perky did the experiment pictured in Figure 9.11. Perky asked her participants to "project" visual images of common objects onto a screen, and then to describe these images. Unbeknownst to the participants, Perky was back-projecting a very dim image of this object onto the screen. Thus, when participants were asked to create an image of a banana, Perky projected a dim image of a banana onto the screen. Interestingly, the participants' descriptions of their images matched the images that Perky was projecting. For example, they described the banana as being oriented vertically, just as was the projected image. Even more interesting, not one of Perky's 24 participants noticed that there was an actual picture on the screen. They had apparently mistaken an actual picture for a mental image.

■ **Figure 9.11** Participant in Perky's (1910) experiment. Unbeknownst to the participants, Perky was projecting dim images onto the screen.

Modern researchers have replicated Perky's result (see Craver-Lemley & Reeves, 1992; Segal & Fusella, 1970) and have demonstrated interactions between perception and imagery in a number of other ways. Martha Farah (1985) instructed her participants to imagine either the letter *H* or *T* on a screen (Figure 9.12a). Once they had formed clear images on the screen, they pressed a button that caused two squares

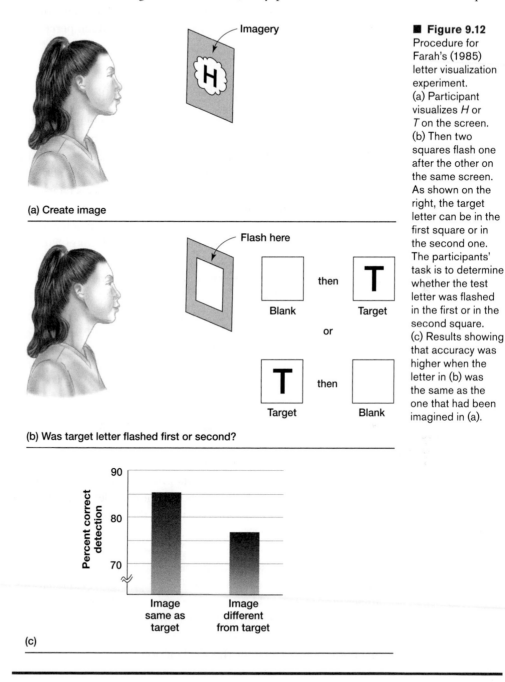

(a) Create image

Flash here

Blank   then   Target

or

Target   then   Blank

(b) Was target letter flashed first or second?

(c)

■ **Figure 9.12**
Procedure for Farah's (1985) letter visualization experiment. (a) Participant visualizes *H* or *T* on the screen. (b) Then two squares flash one after the other on the same screen. As shown on the right, the target letter can be in the first square or in the second one. The participants' task is to determine whether the test letter was flashed in the first or in the second square. (c) Results showing that accuracy was higher when the letter in (b) was the same as the one that had been imagined in (a).

to flash, one after the other (Figure 9.12b). One of the squares contained a target letter, which was either an *H* or a *T*. The participants' task was to indicate whether the letter was in the first square or the second one. The results, shown in Figure 9.12c, indicate that the target letter was detected more accurately when the participant had been imagining the same letter rather than the different letter. Farah interpreted this result as showing that perception and imagery share mechanisms, and many other experiments have demonstrated similar interactions between perception and imagery (see Kosslyn & Thompson, 2000).

Is There a Way to Resolve the Imagery Debate?

You might think, from the evidence of parallels between imagery and perception and of interactions between them, that the imagery debate would have been settled once and for all in favor of the spatial explanation. But John Anderson (1978) warned that despite this evidence, we still can't rule out the propositional explanation, and Martha Farah (1988) pointed out that it is difficult to rule out Pylyshyn's tacit-knowledge explanation just on the basis of the results of behavioral experiments like the ones we have been describing. She argued that it is always possible that participants can be influenced by their past experiences with perception, so they could unknowingly be simulating perceptual responses in imagery experiments.

But Farah suggested a way out of this problem: Instead of relying solely on behavioral experiments, we should investigate how the brain responds to visual imagery. The reason Farah was able to make this proposal was that by the 1980s, evidence about the physiology of imagery was becoming available from neuropsychology—the study of patients with brain damage—and from electrophysiological measurements. In addition, beginning in the 1990s, brain imaging experiments provided additional data regarding the physiology of imagery.

 Test Yourself 9.1

1. Is imagery just a "laboratory phenomenon," or does it occur in real life?
2. Make a list of the important events in the history of the study of imagery in psychology, beginning with the imageless-thought debate from the 1800s, through the studies of imagery that occurred early in the cognitive revolution in the 1960s.
3. How did Kosslyn use the technique of mental scanning to demonstrate similarities between perception and imagery? Why were Kosslyn's experiments criticized, and how did Kosslyn answer this criticism with additional experiments?
4. Describe the spatial (or depictive) and propositional explanations of the mechanism underlying imagery. How can the propositional explanation interpret the results of Kosslyn's boat and island image-scanning experiments?
5. What is the tacit-knowledge explanation of imagery experiments? What experiment was done to counter this explanation?

6. How have experiments demonstrated interactions between imagery and perception? What additional evidence is needed to help settle the imagery debate, according to Farah?

Imagery and the Brain

As we look at a number of types of physiological experiments, we will see that there is a great deal of evidence that points to a connection between imagery and perception, but that the overlap is not perfect. We begin by looking at the results of research that has measured the brain's response to imagery and will then consider how brain damage affects the ability to form visual images.

Imagery Neurons in the Brain

Studies in which activity is recorded from single neurons in humans are rare. But Gabriel Kreiman and coworkers (2000b) were able to study patients who had electrodes implanted in various areas in their medial temporal lobe (see Figure 6.24) in order to determine the source of severe epileptic seizures that could not be controlled by medication.

They found neurons that responded to some objects but not to others. For example, the records in Figure 9.13a show that the neuron responds to a picture of a baseball,

(a) Perception

(b) Imagery

■ **Figure 9.13** Responses of single neurons in a person's medial temporal lobe that (a) respond to perception of a baseball but not to a face, and (b) respond similarly when the person imagines a baseball or a face. (Reprinted by permission from Macmillan Publishers Ltd from "Category-Specific Visual Responses of Single Neurons in the Human Medial Temporal Lobe," by G. Kreiman, C. Koch, & I. Fried, *Nature Neuroscience, 3,* pp. 946–953, September 1, 2000.)

but does not respond to a picture of a face. Neurons that respond to specific objects are called category-specific neurons (see Chapter 8, p. 314; also see Freedman et al., 2001). This neuron is a special type of category-specific neuron because, as shown by the records in Figure 9.13b, it also fires in the same way when the person closes his eyes and imagines a baseball (good firing) or a face (no firing). Kreiman calls these neurons imagery neurons. What's especially significant about these imagery neurons is that they respond both to *perceiving* an object and to *imagining* it.

Brain Imaging

Beginning in the early 1990s, a large number of brain imaging experiments were carried out in which brain activity was measured, using either PET or fMRI, as participants were creating visual images or during a baseline condition in which they were not creating images. Subtracting the baseline response from the imagery response indicated which areas of the brain were activated by imagery (see Method: Brain Imaging, Chapter 2, page 45).

One of the early brain imaging experiments to study imagery was carried out by LeBihan and coworkers (1993), who demonstrated that both perception and imagery activate the visual cortex. Figure 9.14 shows how activity in the striate cortex increased both when a person observed presentations of actual visual stimuli (marked "Perception"), *and* when the person was imagining the stimulus ("Imagery"). In another brain imaging experiment, asking participants to think about questions that involve imag-

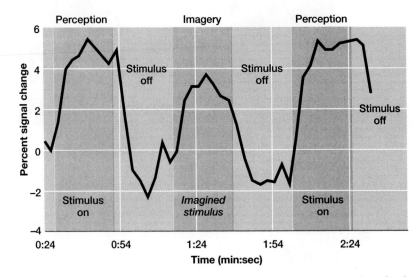

■ **Figure 9.14** Brain activity measured using fMRI. Activity increases to presentation of a visual stimulus (shaded area marked "Stimulus on") and also increases when participants were imagining the stimulus (area marked "Imagined stimulus"). In contrast, activity is low when there is no stimulus (LeBihan et al., 1993).

ery, such as "Is the green of the trees darker than the green of the grass?" generated a greater response in the visual cortex than the response generated to nonimagery questions, such as "Is the intensity of electrical current measured in amperes?" (Goldenberg et al., 1989).

A number of recent brain imaging experiments have demonstrated overlap between brain areas activated by perceiving an object and those activated by creating a mental image of the object, but along with this overlap, differences have also been observed between the areas activated by perception and by imagery. For example, Giorgio Ganis and coworkers (2004) used fMRI to measure activation under two conditions, perception and imagery. For the perception condition, participants observed a line drawing of an object, like the tree in Figure 9.15. For the imagery condition, participants were told to imagine a picture that they had studied before, when they heard a tone. For both the perception and imagery tasks, participants had to answer a question such as "Is the object higher than it is wide?"

Results of Ganis's experiment are shown in ● Color Plate 9.1. This shows brain activation at three different locations in the brain. ● Color Plate 9.1a shows activation in the frontal lobe for perception and imagery in the two center columns, and for the difference between perception and imagery in the right column. The absence of any color in the right column indicates there is no difference between the activation caused

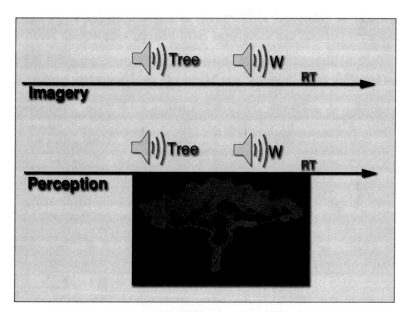

■ **Figure 9.15** Procedure for Ganis et al.'s (2004) experiment. A trial begins with the name of an object that was previously studied, in this case "tree." In the imagery condition, participants had their eyes closed and had to imagine the tree. In the perception condition, participants saw a faint picture of the object. Participants then heard instructions. The *W* in this example means they were to judge whether the object was "wider than tall."

by perception and by imagery. The same result also occurs for activation further back in the brain (● Color Plate 9.1b). However, in ● Color Plate 9.1c, which shows activity nearer the back of the brain, the color in the far right column indicates that there are some areas that respond more for perception than for imagery. This greater activity for perception isn't surprising because this is the location of the visual receiving area, where signals from the retina first reach the cortex. Thus, there is almost complete overlap of the activation caused by perception and imagery in the front of the brain, but some differences near the back of the brain.

Other experiments have also concluded that there are similarities but some differences between brain activation for perception and imagery. For example, an fMRI experiment by Amir Amedi and coworkers (2005) showed overlap, but also found that when participants were creating images, some areas associated with nonvisual areas such as hearing and touch were *deactivated*. That is, during imagery, their activation was decreased. Amedi suggests that the reason for this might be that visual mental images are more fragile than real perception, and so this deactivation helps to quiet down irrelevant activity that might interfere with the mental image.

The differences in activation that are observed when comparing perception and imagery are not that surprising. After all, seeing an object is different from imagining it. But what is most noteworthy in all of these experiments is the great degree of overlap between activation for perception and imagery (also see Slotnick et al., 2005). This overlap supports the idea that imagery and perception share some mechanisms.

Transcranial Magnetic Stimulation

Although the brain imaging experiments we have just described are consistent with the idea that imagery and perception share the same mechanisms, showing that an area of the brain is activated by imagery does not *prove* that this activity *causes* imagery. For example, Pylyshyn states that just as the spatial experience of mental images is an epiphenomenon (see page 329), brain activity can also be an epiphenomenon. According to Pylyshyn, brain activity in response to imagery may be indicating that *something* is happening, but may have nothing to do with *causing* imagery. To deal with this possibility, Stephen Kosslyn and coworkers (1999) did an experiment using a technique called **transcranial magnetic stimulation (TMS)**.

◄► Method

Transcranial Magnetic Stimulation (TMS)

One way to investigate whether an area of the brain is involved in determining a particular function is to remove that part of the brain in animals or study cases of brain damage in humans (see pp. 43–44). Of course, we cannot purposely remove a portion of a person's brain, but it is possible to temporarily disrupt the functioning of a particular area, by applying a

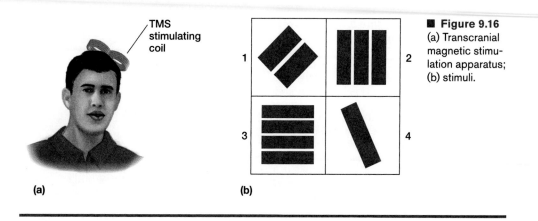

■ **Figure 9.16**
(a) Transcranial magnetic stimulation apparatus; (b) stimuli.

pulsating magnetic field to the skull using a stimulating coil, as shown in Figure 9.16a. A series of pulses presented to a particular area of the brain for a few seconds decreases or eliminates brain functioning in that area for seconds or minutes. A participant's behavior is tested while the brain area is deactivated. If the behavior is disrupted, it is concluded that the deactivated area of the brain is causing that behavior. ◆

Kossyln and coworkers (1999) presented transcranial magnetic stimulation to the visual area of the brain while participants were carrying out either a perception task or an imagery task. For the perception task, participants briefly viewed a display like the one in Figure 9.16b and were asked to make a judgment about the stripes in two of the quadrants. For example, they might be asked to indicate whether the stripes in quadrant 3 were longer than the stripes in quadrant 2. The imagery task was the same, but instead of seeing the stripes, the participants closed their eyes and based their judgments on their mental image of the display.

Kosslyn measured participants' reaction time to make the judgment, both when transcranial magnetic stimulation was being applied to the visual area of the brain and also during a control condition when the stimulation was directed to another part of the brain. The result indicated that stimulation caused participants to respond more slowly, and that this slowing effect occurred both for perception and for imagery. Based on this result, Kosslyn concluded that the brain activation that occurs in response to imagery is not an epiphenomenon and that brain activity in the visual cortex plays a causal role in both perception and imagery.

Neuropsychological Case Studies

How can we use studies of people with brain damage to help us understand imagery? One approach is to determine how brain damage affects imagery. Another approach is to determine how brain damage affects both imagery and perception, and to note whether both are affected in the same way.

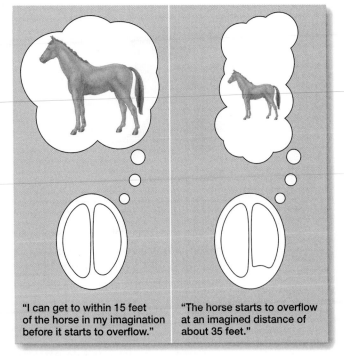

■ **Figure 9.17** Results of mental-walk task for patient M.G.S. Left: Before her operation, she could mentally "walk" to within 15 feet before the image of the horse overflowed her visual field. Right: After removal of the right occipital lobe, the size of the visual field was reduced, and she could mentally approach only to within 35 feet of the horse before it overflowed her visual field. (Reprinted from M. J. Farah, "The Neural Basis of Mental Imagery." In M. Gazzaniga (Ed.), *The Cognitive Neurosciences,* 2nd edition. Cambridge, MIT Press, pp. 965–974 (Fig. 66.2), Copyright © 2000, with permission of The MIT Press.)

"I can get to within 15 feet of the horse in my imagination before it starts to overflow."

"The horse starts to overflow at an imagined distance of about 35 feet."

Removing Part of the Visual Cortex Decreases Image Size Patient M.G.S. was a young woman who was about to have part of her right occipital lobe removed as treatment for a severe case of epilepsy. Before the operation, Martha Farah and coworkers (1992) had M.G.S. perform the mental-walk task that we described earlier, in which she imagined walking toward an animal and estimated how close she was when the image began to overflow her visual field. Figure 9.17 shows that before the operation, M.G.S. felt she was about 15 feet from an imaginary horse before its image overflowed. But when Farah had her repeat this task after her right occipital lobe was removed, the distance increased to 35 feet. This occurred because removing part of the visual cortex reduced the size of her field of view, so the horse filled up the field when she was farther away. This result supports the idea that the visual cortex is important for imagery.

Perceptual Problems Are Accompanied by Problems With Imagery A large number of cases have been studied in which a patient with brain damage has a perceptual problem and also has a similar problem in creating images. For example, people who have lost the ability to see color due to brain damage are also unable to create colors through imagery (DeRenzi & Spinnler, 1967; DeVreese, 1991).

Damage to the parietal lobes can cause a condition called **unilateral neglect,** in which the patient ignores objects in one half of their visual field, even to the extent of shaving just one side of his face, or eating only the food on one side of her plate.

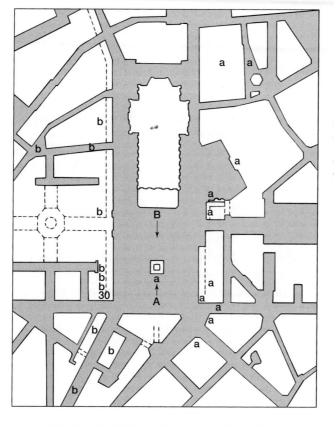

Figure 9.18 Piazza del Duomo in Milan. When Bisiach and Luzzatti's (1978) patient imagined himself standing at A, he could name objects indicated by *a*'s. When he imagined himself at B, he could name objects indicated by *b*'s. (Reprinted from "Unilateral Neglect of Representational Space," by E. Bisiach & G. Luzzatti, 1978, *Cortex, 14*, pp. 129–133. Copyright © 1978 with permission from Cortex.)

E. Bisiach and G. Luzzatti (1978) tested the imagery of a patient with neglect by asking him to describe things he saw when imagining himself standing at one end of the Piazza del Duomo in Milan, a place with which he had been familiar before his brain was damaged (Figure 9.18). The patient's responses showed that he neglected the left side of his mental image, just as he neglected the left side of his perceptions. Thus, when he imagined himself standing at A, he neglected the left side and named only objects to his right (small *a*'s). When he imagined himself standing at B, he continued to neglect the left side, this time naming only objects on his right (small *b*'s).

The correspondence between the physiology of mental imagery and the physiology of perception, as demonstrated by brain scans in normal participants and the effects of brain damage in participants with neglect, supports the idea that mental imagery and perception share physiological mechanisms. However, not all physiological results support a one-to-one correspondence between imagery and perception.

Dissociations Between Imagery and Perception When we discussed memory in Chapters 5 and 6, we described dissociations, in which people with brain damage had one memory function present and another function absent (see Method: Neuropsychology, Chapter 2, page 43). Cases have also been reported of dissociations between imagery and perception. For example, C. Guariglia and coworkers (1993) studied a patient whose brain damage had little effect on his ability to perceive but caused neglect in his mental images (his mental images were limited to just one side, as in the case just described).

Another case of normal perception but impaired imagery is the case of R.M., who had suffered damage to his occipital and parietal lobes (Farah et al., 1988). R.M. was able to recognize objects and to draw accurate pictures of objects that were placed before him. However, he was unable to draw objects from memory, a task that requires imagery. He also had trouble answering questions that depend on imagery, such as verifying whether the sentence "A grapefruit is larger than an orange" is correct.

Dissociations have also been reported with the opposite result, so that perception is impaired but imagery is relatively normal. For example, Marlene Behrmann and coworkers (1994) studied C.K., a 33-year-old graduate student who was struck by a car as he was jogging. C.K. suffered from visual agnosia, the inability to visually recognize objects. Thus, he labeled the pictures in Figure 9.19a as a "feather duster" (the dart), a "fencer's mask" (the tennis racquet), and a "rose twig with thorns" (the asparagus). These results show that C.K. could recognize parts of objects but couldn't integrate them into a meaningful whole. But despite his inability to name pictures of objects, C.K. was able to draw objects from memory in rich detail, a task that depends on imagery (Figure 9.19b). Interestingly, when he was shown his own drawings later, he was unable to identify them.

■ **Figure 9.19** (a) Pictures incorrectly labeled by C.K., who had visual agnosia. (b) Drawings from memory by C.K. (Reprinted from "Intact Visual Imagery and Impaired Visual Perception in a Patient With Visual Agnosia," by M. Behrmann et al., 1994, *Journal of Experimental Psychology: Human Perception and Performance, 30,* pp. 1068–1087, Figs. 1 & 6. Copyright © 1994 with permission from the American Psychological Association.)

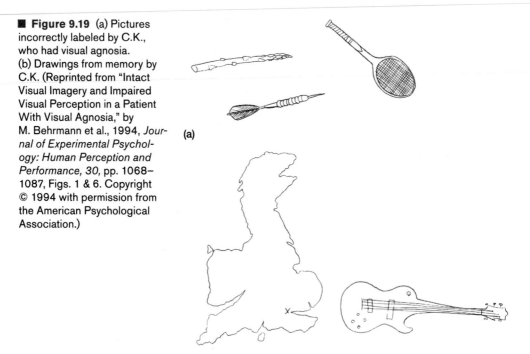

(a)

(b)

Table 9.1 Double Dissociation Between Imagery and Perception

	Imagery	Perception
R.M.	Poor	Good
C.K.	Good	Poor

Making Sense of the Neuropsychological Results The neuropsychological cases present a paradox: On one hand, there are many cases in which there are close parallels between perceptual deficits and deficits in imagery. On the other hand, there are a number of cases in which dissociations occur, so that perception is normal but imagery is poor (Guariglia's patient and R.M.), or perception is poor but imagery is normal (C.K.).

The cases in which imagery and perception are affected differently by brain damage provide evidence for a double dissociation between imagery and perception (Table 9.1). The presence of a double dissociation is usually interpreted to mean that the two functions (perception and imagery, in this case) are served by different mechanisms (see page 43), a conclusion that contradicts the other evidence we have presented that shows that imagery and perception share mechanisms.

One way to explain this paradox, according to Behrmann and coworkers (1994), is that the mechanisms of perception and imagery overlap only partially, with the mechanism for perception being located at both lower and higher visual centers and the mechanism for imagery being located mainly in higher visual centers (Figure 9.20). According to this idea, visual perception involves *bottom-up processing*, which starts when light enters the eye and an image is focused on the retina, and then continues as signals are sent along the visual pathways to the visual cortex and then to higher visual centers.

The visual cortex is crucial for perception because it is here that objects begin being analyzed into components like edges and orientations. This information is then sent to higher visual areas, where perception is "assembled" (see page 39). In contrast, imagery is a *top-down process*, which originates in higher brain areas that are responsible for

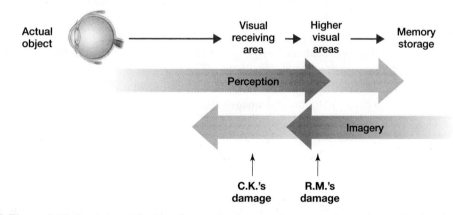

■ **Figure 9.20** Depiction of the idea that mechanisms serving perception are located both at lower and higher visual centers and that mechanisms serving imagery are located mainly at higher levels (Behrmann et al., 1994). The general locations of damage for C.K. and R.M. are indicated by the vertical arrows. These locations can explain why C.K. has a perceptual problem but can still create images, and why R.M. has trouble creating images but can still perceive.

memory. Mental images are therefore "preassembled," and do not depend on activation of cortical areas such as the visual cortex.

Based on this explanation, we can hypothesize that C.K.'s difficulty in perceiving is caused by damage early in the processing stream, but that he can still create images because higher-level areas of his brain are intact. Similarly, we can hypothesize that R.M.'s difficulty in creating mental images is caused by damage to higher-level areas, where mental images originate, but that he can perceive objects because areas earlier in the processing stream are still functioning.

Although this explanation works for C.K. and R.M., it can't explain the case of M.G.S., the woman who had part of her visual cortex removed (see Figure 9.17). Even though M.G.S.'s damage was earlier in the cortex, she experienced changes in both perception and imagery. Cases such as this emphasize the challenge of interpreting the results of neuropsychological research. It is likely that further research will lead to modifications in the explanation shown in Figure 9.20, or perhaps a new explanation altogether.

Conclusions From the Imagery Debate

The imagery debate provides an outstanding example of a situation in which a controversy motivated a large amount of research. Most psychologists, looking at the behavioral and physiological evidence, have concluded that imagery and perception are closely related and share some (but not all) mechanisms (but see Pylyshyn, 2001, 2003, who doesn't agree).

The idea of shared mechanisms follows from all of the parallels and interactions between perception and imagery. The idea that not all mechanisms are shared follows from some of the fMRI results, which show that the overlap between brain activation is not complete; some of the neuropsychological results, which show dissociations between imagery and perception; and also from differences between the experience of imagery and perception. For example, perception occurs automatically when we look at something, but imagery needs to be generated with some effort. Also, perception is stable—it continues as long as you are observing a stimulus—but imagery is fragile—it can vanish without continued effort.

Another example of a difference between imagery and perception is that it is harder to manipulate mental images than images that are created perceptually. This was demonstrated by Deborah Chalmers and Daniel Reisberg (1985), who asked their participants to create mental images of ambiguous figures such as the one in Figure 9.21, which can be seen as a rabbit or a duck. Perceptually, it is fairly easy to "flip" between these two perceptions. However, Chalmers and Reisberg found that participants who were holding a mental image of this figure were unable to flip from one perception to another. Later research has shown that people can manipulate simpler mental images (Finke et al., 1989) or can manipulate mental images when given extra information and "hints" (Mast & Kosslyn, 2002). So the experiments on manipulating images lead to the same conclusion as all of the other experiments we have de-

■ **Figure 9.21** What is this, a rabbit (facing right) or a duck (facing left)?

scribed: Imagery and perception have many features in common, but there are also differences between them.

♦♦♦ Using Imagery to Improve Memory

It is clear that imagery can play an important role in memory. But how can you harness the power of imagery to help you remember things better? To answer this question, let's return to our discussion in Chapter 6 of how information can be encoded in long-term memory.

Visualizing Interacting Images

When we showed, in Chapter 6, that encoding is aided by forming connections with other information, we introduced the idea that these connections can be enhanced by imagery. Participants who created images based on two paired words (like *boat* and *tree*) remembered over twice as many words as participants who just repeated the words (Figure 6.15).

Apparently, visualization is most effective when images of objects are paired in an interactive way, but it is not necessary that these interactions be bizarre, as has been suggested by some authors of books on memory improvement. Wollen and coworkers (1972) showed that bizarreness is not necessary by instructing participants to learn pairs of words that were accompanied by pictures such as those in Figure 9.22. Some

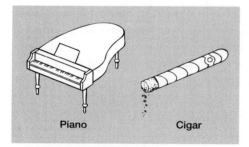
Piano   Cigar

(a) Noninteracting, nonbizarre

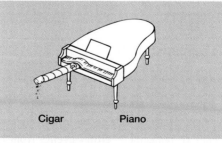
Piano   Cigar

(b) Noninteracting, bizarre

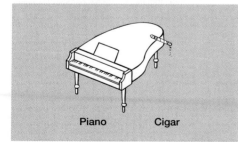
Piano   Cigar

(c) Interacting, nonbizarre

Cigar   Piano

(d) Interacting, bizarre

■ **Figure 9.22** Pictures used by Wollen et al. (1972) to study the role of creating bizarre images in memory. (Reprinted from *Cognitive Psychology,* Volume 3, K. A. Wollen et al., "Bizarreness Versus Interaction of Mental Images as Determinants of Learning," pp. 518–523, Figure 1, Copyright © 1972, with permission from Elsevier.)

of the pictures showed the two objects *separately*, in both (a) nonbizarre and (b) bizarre versions. Other picture showed the two objects *interacting* in both (c) nonbizarre and (d) bizarre versions. Memory was better for the interacting images compared to the noninteracting images, but bizarreness had no effect. Apparently, just creating images and having them interact is enough to improve memory (although creating bizarre images can be more fun!).

Placing Images at Locations

We also saw in Chapter 6 that organization improves encoding. The mind tends to spontaneously organize information that is initially unorganized, and presenting information that is organized improves memory performance.

The power of imagery to improve memory is tied to its ability to create organized locations upon which memories for specific items can be placed. An example of the organizational function of imagery from ancient history is provided by a story about the Greek poet Simonides. According to legend, 2,500 years ago Simonides presented an address at a banquet, and just after he left the banquet, the roof of the hall collapsed, killing most of the people inside. To compound this tragedy, many of the bodies were so severely mutilated that they couldn't be identified. But Simonides realized that as he had looked out over the audience during this address, he had created a mental picture of where each person had been seated at the banquet table. Based on this image of people's locations around the table, he was able to determine who had been killed.

What is important about this rather gory example is that Simonides realized that the technique he had used to help him remember who was at the banquet could also be used to remember other things as well. He found that he could remember things by imagining a physical space, like the banquet table, and by placing, in his mind, items to be remembered in the seats surrounding the table. This feat of mental organization enabled him to later "read out" the items by mentally scanning the locations around the table, just as he had done to identify the people's bodies. Simonides had invented what is now called the **method of loci**—a method in which things to be remembered are placed at different locations in a mental image of a spatial layout.

The following demonstration illustrates how to use the method of loci to remember something from your own experience.

 Demonstration

Method of Loci

Pick a place with a spatial layout that is very familiar to you, such as the rooms in your house or apartment, or the buildings on your college campus. Then pick 5–7 things that you want to remember—either events from the past or things you need to do later today. Create an image representing each event, and place each image at a location in the house.

If you need to remember the events in a particular order, decide on a path you would take while walking through the house or campus, and place the images representing each event along your walking path so they will be encountered in the correct order. After you have done this, retrace the path in your mind, and see if encountering the images helps you remember the events. To really test this method, try mentally "walking" this path a few hours from now. ●

Placing images at locations can help retrieve memories later. For example, to help me remember a dentist appointment later in the day, I could visually place a huge pair of teeth in my living room. To remind myself to go to the gym and work out, I could imagine an elliptical trainer on the stairs that lead from the living room to the second floor, and to represent the wild west TV program *Deadwood* that I want to watch later tonight, I could imagine a cowboy sitting on the landing at the top of the stairs.

Associating Images With Words

CogLab

Link Word

The **pegword technique** involves imagery, as in the method of loci, but instead of visualizing items in different locations, you associate them with concrete words. The first step is to create a list of nouns, like the following: one–bun; two–shoe; three–tree; four–door; five–hive; six–sticks; seven–heaven; eight–gate; nine–mine; ten–hen. It's easy to remember these words in order because they were created by rhyming them with the numbers. The next step is to pair each of these things to be remembered with each pegword by creating a vivid image of your item-to-be-remembered with the object represented by the word.

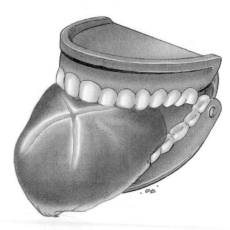

Figure 9.23 shows an image I created for the dentist appointment. For the other items I wanted to remember, I might picture an elliptical trainer inside a shoe, and a cowboy in a tree. The beauty of this system is that it makes it possible to immediately identify an item based on its order on the list. So if I want to identify the third thing I need to do today, I go straight to *tree*, which translates into my image of the cowboy in a tree, and this reminds me to watch *Deadwood* on TV.

Imagery techniques like the ones just mentioned are often the basis behind books that claim to provide the key to improving your memory (see Crook & Adderly, 1998; Lorayne & Lucas, 1996; Treadeau, 1997). Although these books do provide imagery-based techniques that work, people who purchase these books in the hope of discovering an easy way to develop "photographic memory" are often disappointed because although imagery techniques do work, they do not provide easy, "magical" improvements in memory, but rather require a great deal of practice and perseverance (Schacter, 2001).

■ **Figure 9.23** An image used by the author to remember a dentist appointment, using the pegword technique.

Something to Consider

Mental Representation of Mechanical Systems

Visual imagery, which has played an important role in scientific discoveries such as determining the structure of benzene and Einstein's theory of relativity (page 323), is also an important mechanism for solving mechanical problems (Hegarty, 2004). For example, consider the problems in the following demonstration:

Demonstration

Mechanical Problems

Try solving the three problems in Figure 9.24. (a) The five-gear problem: If each of these gears meshes with the one next to it, and gear #1 is turning clockwise, in what direction is gear #5 turning? (b) The water-pouring problem: The two glasses are the same height and are filled to the same level. When these two glasses are tilted, will the water begin pouring out of the glasses at the same angle of tilt or at different angles? If the angles are different, which glass will pour first? (c) The pulley problem: If you pull on the free end of the rope (at the arrow), will the lower pulley turn clockwise? 🔶

How did you solve these problems? One approach to solving mechanical problems is to use **mental simulation**, in which the operation of the mechanical system is mentally represented. If you used this procedure for the five-gear problem, you probably imagined gear #1 turning clockwise, gear #2 turning counterclockwise, gear #3 clockwise, and so on. Another way to solve the gear problem is by using a **rule-based approach**, which would involve applying a rule such as "when one gear turns, the one next to it rotates in the opposite direction" or "all odd numbered gears rotate in the same direction."

These two ways of solving the gear problem are analogous to the two sides of the visual imagery debate we have been discussing in this chapter. The *mental simulation*

■ **Figure 9.24** (a) The five-gear problem; (b) the water-pouring problem; (c) the pulley problem. See demonstration for details. (From Hegarty, 2004.)

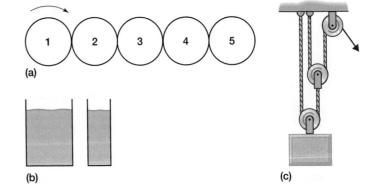

approach is analogous to the idea that visual imagery involves a *spatial representation*. The *rule-based approach* is analogous to the idea that visual imagery involves a *propositional representation*. In our discussion of the imagery debate, we presented a large amount of evidence favoring the spatial representation explanation of imagery. However, things are not as one-sided for solving mechanical problems. As we saw for the gear problem, both spatial representation and rule-based approaches can be used.

Let's now consider the water-pouring problem. The answer to this problem is that water will start pouring from the wide glass first. Figure 9.25a shows that this is the case, by superimposing the narrow and the wide glasses. From this diagram, you can see that whereas water is about to pour from the wide glass, it is still below the edge of the narrow glass. Thus, the narrow glass would need to be tilted farther before the water will begin to pour.

You may have found that this problem was harder to solve than the five-gear problem. In fact, Daniel Schwartz and Tamara Black (1999) found that when they asked participants for the answer to the water-pouring problem, without giving them time to either reason out the problem or use mental imagery, most of the participants answered incorrectly that both glasses would pour at the same angle (Figure 9.25b). However, when participants were told to close their eyes and imagine the glasses being tilted, almost all of them were able to "see" that the narrow glass would have to be tilted farther than the wide glass (Figure 9.25c).

This result is relevant to the tacit-knowledge explanation that Pylyshyn used to explain people's performance in visual imagery tasks (see page 331). Because most people do not know the answer to the water-pouring problem beforehand, its solution by using imagery cannot depend on tacit knowledge.

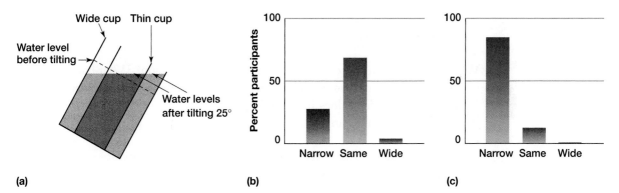

■ **Figure 9.25** (a) The solution to the water-pouring problem, illustrated by superimposing the wide and narrow glasses. This shows that when the glasses are tilted at 25 degrees, the water is close to the edge of the wide glass, but that more tilt is necessary before the water will reach the edge of the narrow glass (Schwartz & Black, 1999). (b) Participants' immediate predictions of the solution to the water-pouring problem, indicating the percentage of participants who predicted which glass would need to be tilted more to pour. (c) Participants' solutions to the water-pouring problem, after closing their eyes and imagining the glasses being tilted (based on data from Schwartz & Black, 1999).

The water-pouring problem, like the five-gear problem, can be solved without using imagery. One way to do this is to use a diagram like the one in Figure 9.25a. Imagery, therefore, is an effective way to solve mechanical problems, but is not the only way. In fact, there is evidence that people solve some mechanical problems by first using mental simulation and then later shift to using rules (Schwartz & Black, 1996).

Another question we can ask, in addition to *when* imagery is used to solve mechanical problems, is *how* is it used? The answer to this question may depend on the specific problem, but Mary Hegarty (1992) found that when asked to solve the pulley problem in Figure 9.24c, participants took longer to determine the motion of the lower pulley than the upper pulley. Based on this result, she concluded that people do not solve the pulley problem by creating an image of the entire system, which they then inspect as they imagine the pulleys moving. Instead, people create images of the part of the system that is most relevant to solving the problem.

We have seen that imagery can be an effective way (and sometimes the most effective way) of solving mechanical problems, and also that there is often more than one way to solve a problem. When we discuss problem solving in Chapter 11, we will return to this idea that there is often more than one way to solve a particular problem, but that some ways are more effective than others.

Test Yourself 9.2

1. Describe how experiments using the following physiological techniques have provided evidence of parallels between imagery and perception: (1) brain imaging; (2) deactivation of part of the brain; (3) neuropsychology; and (4) recording from single neurons.
2. Some of the neuropsychological results demonstrate parallels between imagery and perception, and some results do not. How has Behrmann explained these contradictory results?
3. What are some differences between imagery and perception? What have most psychologists concluded about the connection between imagery and perception?
4. Under what conditions does imagery improve memory? Describe techniques that use imagery as a tool to improve memory. What is the basic principle that underlies these techniques?
5. What is the evidence that solving mechanical problems can involve mental simulation? How is this evidence related to visual imagery?

Chapter Summary

1. Mental imagery is experiencing a sensory impression in the absence of sensory input. Visual imagery is "seeing" in the absence of a visual stimulus. Imagery has played an important role in the creative process and as a way of thinking, in addition to purely verbal techniques.

2. Early ideas about imagery included the imageless-thought debate and Galton's work with visual images, but imagery research stopped during the behaviorist era. Imagery research began again in the 1960s, with the advent of the cognitive revolution.

3. The idea that imagery shares the same mechanisms as perception (that is, creates a depictive representation in the person's mind) was suggested by Kosslyn's mental scanning experiments, but these results and others were challenged by Pylyshyn, who stated that imagery is based on a mechanism related to language (that is, it creates a propositional representation in a person's mind).

4. One of Pylyshyn's arguments against the idea of a depictive representation is the tacit-knowledge explanation, which states that when asked to imagine something, people ask themselves what it would look like to see it, and then they simulate this staged event.

5. Finke and Pinker's "flashed dot" experiment argued against the tacit knowledge explanation. The following experiments also demonstrated parallels between imagery and perception: (1) size in the visual field (visual-walk task); (2) interaction between perception and imagery (Perky's 1910 experiment; Farah's H/T experiment); and (3) physiological experiments.

6. Parallels between perception and imagery have been demonstrated physiologically by the following methods: (1) recording from single neurons (imagery neurons); (2) brain imaging (demonstrating overlapping activation in the brain); (3) transcranial magnetic stimulation experiments (comparing effect of brain inactivation on perception and imagery); and (4) neuropsychological case studies (removal of visual cortex affects image size; unilateral neglect).

7. There is also physiological evidence for differences between imagery and perception. This evidence includes (1) differences in areas of the brain activated and (2) brain damage causing dissociations between perception and imagery.

8. Most psychologists, taking all of the above evidence into account, have concluded that imagery is closely related to perception and shares some (but not all) mechanisms.

9. The action of imagery can improve memory in a number of ways: (1) visualizing interacting images; (2) organization using the method of loci; and (3) associating items with nouns using the pegword technique.

10. Solving problems using mechanical reasoning can be carried out using either mental simulation or rule-based approaches. Experiments with the water-pouring problem show that it is unlikely that tacit knowledge is involved in using imagery to solve this problem. Experiments with the pulley problem indicate that people may direct their attention to imagining specific areas of the problem.

Think About It

1. Look at an object for a minute, and then look away, create a mental image of it, and draw a sketch of the object based on your mental image. Then draw a sketch of the same object while you are looking at it. How do the two sketches differ? What

kinds of information about the object were you able to include in the sketch that was based on your mental image? What information was omitted, compared to the sketch you created by looking at the object?

2. Write a description of an object as you are looking at it. Then compare the difference between the written description and the information you can obtain by looking at the object or at a picture of the object. Is it true that "a picture is worth a thousand words"? How does your comparison of written and visual representations relate to the discussion of propositional versus depictive representations in this chapter?

3. Try using one of the techniques described at the end of this chapter to create images that represent things you have to do later today or during the coming week. Then, after some time passes (anywhere from an hour to a few days), check to see whether you can retrieve the memories for these images and if you can remember what they stand for.

4. Describe the connection between the description of the visual process in Figure 9.20 and the result of Ganis's fMRI experiment shown in ● Color Plate 9.1.

If You Want to Know More

1. Auditory imagery. Auditory imagery occurs when you mentally rehearse a telephone number or when a particular song keeps running through your mind. Recent research has demonstrated a connection between auditory imagery and brain activity.

Kraemer, D. J. M., Macrae, C. N., Green, A. E., & Kelly, W. M. (2005). Sound of silence activates auditory cortex. *Nature, 434,* 158.

Zatorre, R. J., Halpern, A. R., Perry, D. W., Meyer, E., & Evans, A. C. (1996). Hearing in the mind's ear: A PET investigation of musical imagery and perception. *Journal of Cognitive Neuroscience, 8,* 29–46.

2. Visual imagery. Although we have discussed visual imagery extensively in this chapter, it is worth looking at Stephen Kosslyn's books on the topic. His latest one is the following.

Kosslyn, S. M. (2006) *The case for mental imagery.* Oxford: Oxford University Press.

3. Mechanical reasoning and working memory. The relationship between solving mechanical problems, imagery, and working memory has been studied by determining how placing a load on the visuospatial sketch pad component of working memory affects the ability to solve these problems. These experiments are analogous to the ones we described on page 160 of Chapter 5.

Sims, V. K., & Hegarty, M. (1997). Mental animation in the visuospatial sketch pad. Evidence from dual task studies. *Memory & Cognition, 25,* 321–333.

Key Terms

Conceptual-peg hypothesis, 326
Depictive representation, 330
Epiphenomenon, 329
Imageless-thought debate, 325
Imagery debate, 328
Imagery neurons, 338
Mental imagery, 323
Mental scanning, 327
Mental simulation, 350
Mental-walk task, 334
Method of loci, 348

Paired-associate learning, 326
Pegword technique, 349
Propositional representation, 329
Rule-based approach (to mechanical reasoning), 350
Spatial representation, 329
Tacit-knowledge explanation, 331
Transcranial magnetic stimulation (TMS), 340
Unilateral neglect, 342
Visual imagery, 323

CogLab To experience these experiments for yourself, go to http://coglab.wadsworth.com. Be sure to read each experiment's setup instructions before you go to the experiment itself. Otherwise, you won't know which keys to press.

Primary Labs

Mental rotation How a stimulus can be rotated in the mind to determine whether its shape matches another stimulus (p. 326).

Link word A demonstration of how imagery can be used to help learn foreign vocabulary (p. 349).

Language

10

What Is Language?
  The Creativity of Human Language
  The Universality of Language
  Studying Language in Cognitive Psychology

Perceiving and Understanding Words
  Components of Words
  Perceiving Words
  Understanding Words
  ▶ Demonstration: Lexical Decision Task
  ◀▶ Method: Lexical Priming
  Summary: Words Alone and in Sentences

Understanding Sentences
  Semantics and Syntax
  ◀▶ Method: Event-Related Potential
  Parsing a Sentence

Test Yourself 10.1

Understanding Text and Stories
  How Inference Creates Coherence
  Situation Models

Producing Language: Speech Errors
  ◀▶ Method: Identifying Speech Errors
  Speech Errors and Language Mechanisms

Producing Language: Conversations
  Semantic Coordination
  Syntactic Coordination
  ◀▶ Method: Syntactic Priming

Something to Consider: Culture, Language, and Cognition
  ◀▶ Method: Categorical Perception

Test Yourself 10.2

Chapter Summary

Think About It

If You Want to Know More

Key Terms

CogLab: Word Superiority; Lexical Decision; Categorical Perception—Identification; Categorical Perception—Discrimination

Some Questions We Will Consider

- How do we understand individual words, and how are words combined to create sentences? (363)

- How can we understand sentences that have more than one meaning? (370)

- What do speech errors (slips of the tongue) tell us about language? (381)

- Is it true that the language that people use in a particular culture can affect the way they think? (387)

There are ways to communicate that don't involve language, but language is the most powerful tool we have for transmitting ideas, feelings, and knowledge from one person to another. What exactly is language, and what is it about language that makes it so useful?

What Is Language?

We can define **language** as *a system of communication using sounds or symbols that enables us to express our feelings, thoughts, ideas, and experiences.* Although one of the main features of language is communication, it is important to differentiate human language from the communication of nonhuman animals. Cats "meow" when their food dish is empty. Monkeys have a repertoire of "calls" that stand for things such as "danger" or "greeting," and bees signal through a "waggle dance" that they perform at the hive to indicate the location of flowers. Although there is some evidence that monkeys may be able to use language in a way similar to humans (see "If You Want to Know More: Animal Language"), most animal communication lacks the properties that make human language unique.

The Creativity of Human Language

Human language goes far beyond a series of fixed signals that transmit a single message like "feed me," "danger," or "go that way for flowers." Language provides a way of arranging a sequence of signals—sounds for spoken language, letters and written words for written language, and physical signals for sign language—that provide a wide variety of ways to transmit, from one person to another, things ranging from the simple and commonplace ("My car is over there") to things that have perhaps never been previously written or uttered in the entire history of the world ("I'm thinking of getting a new Mustang because I'm quitting my job in February and taking a trip across the country to celebrate Groundhog Day with my cousin Zelda").

Language makes it possible to create new and unique sentences because it has a structure that is (1) hierarchical and (2) governed by rules. Language is hierarchical because it consists of a series of components that can be combined to form larger units. For example, words can be combined to create phrases, which, in turn, can create sentences, which themselves can become components of a story. Language is governed by rules that specify permissible ways for these components to be arranged ("What is my cat saying?" is permissible in English; "Cat my saying is what?" is not). These two properties—a hierarchical structure and rules—endow humans with the ability to go far beyond the fixed calls and signs of animals to communicate whatever they want to express.

The Universality of Language

Although people do "talk" to themselves, as when Hamlet wondered "To be or not to be" or when you daydream in class, the predominant staging ground for language is one person conversing with another. Consider the following:

- People's need to communicate is so powerful that when deaf children find themselves in an environment where there are no people who speak or use sign language, they invent a sign language themselves (Goldwin-Meadow, 1982).
- Everyone with normal capacities develops a language and learns to follow its complex rules, even though they are usually not aware of these rules. Although many people find the study of grammar to be very difficult, they have no trouble using language.
- Language is universal across cultures. There are over 5,000 different languages, and there isn't a single culture that is without language. When European explorers first set forth in New Guinea, the people they discovered, who had been isolated from the rest of the world for eons, had developed over 750 different languages, many of them quite different from one another.
- Language development is similar across cultures. No matter what the culture, children generally begin babbling at about 7 months, a few meaningful words appear by the first birthday, and the first multiword utterances occur at about age 2 (Levelt, 2001).
- Even though a large number of languages are very different from one another, we can describe them as being "unique but the same." They are unique because they use different words and sounds, and they may use different rules of combining these words (although many languages use similar rules). They are the same because all languages have words that serve the function of nouns and verbs, and all languages include a system to make things negative, to ask questions, and to refer to the past and present.

Studying Language in Cognitive Psychology

Wilhelm Wundt, founder of the first laboratory of scientific psychology, wrote about the nature of the sentence in 1900, but as with other areas of cognitive psychology, modern research on language had to await the "cognitive revolution" that began in the 1950s. Two events that occurred during that time stand out. The first was the 1957 publication of a book by B. F. Skinner, the modern champion of behaviorism. In this book, *Verbal Behavior,* Skinner proposed that language is learned through reinforcement. According to this idea, just as children learn appropriate behavior by being rewarded for "good" behavior and punished for "bad" behavior, children learn language by being rewarded for using correct language and punished (or not rewarded) for using incorrect language.

In the same year, the linguist Noam Chomsky published a book titled *Syntactic Structures*. This book, and Chomsky's work that followed, proposed that human language was coded in the genes. According to this idea, just as humans are genetically programmed to walk, they are programmed to acquire and use language. Chomsky concluded that despite the wide variations that exist across languages, the underlying basis of all language is similar. Most important for our purposes, Chomsky saw studying language as a way to study the properties of the mind and therefore disagreed with the behaviorist idea that the mind is not a valid topic of study for psychology.

Chomsky's disagreement with behaviorism led him to publish a scathing review of Skinner's *Verbal Behavior* in 1959. In his review, he presented arguments that effectively destroyed the behaviorist idea that language can be explained in terms of reinforcements and without reference to the mind. One of Chomsky's most persuasive arguments was that as children learn language, they produce sentences that they have never heard and that have therefore never been reinforced. (A classic example of a sentence that has been created by many children, and which is unlikely to have been taught by parents, is "I hate you, Mommy.") Chomsky's criticism of behaviorism was one of the most important events of the cognitive revolution and led to the development of **psycholinguistics**, the field concerned with the psychological study of language.

The goal of psycholinguistics is to discover the psychological processes by which humans acquire and process language (Clark & Van der Wege, 2002; Gleason & Ratner, 1998). The three major concerns of psycholinguistics are as follows:

1. *Comprehension.* How do people understand spoken and written language? This includes how people process language sounds; how they understand words, sentences, and stories, as expressed in writing, speech, or sign language; and how people have conversations with one another.
2. *Speech production.* How do people produce language? This includes the physical processes of speech production and the mental processes that occur as a person creates speech.
3. *Acquisition.* How do people learn language? This includes not only how children learn language, but also how people learn additional languages, either as children or later in life.

Because of the vast scope of psycholinguistics, we are going to restrict our attention to the first two of these concerns by describing research on how we understand language and how we produce it. (See "If You Want to Know More: Language Acquisition" for suggestions for readings about language acquisition.) We begin by considering each of the components of language, beginning with small components such as *sounds* and *words* (Figure 10.1), then combinations of words that form *sentences*, and finally "texts"—*stories* that are created by combining a number of sentences. At the end of the chapter, we de-

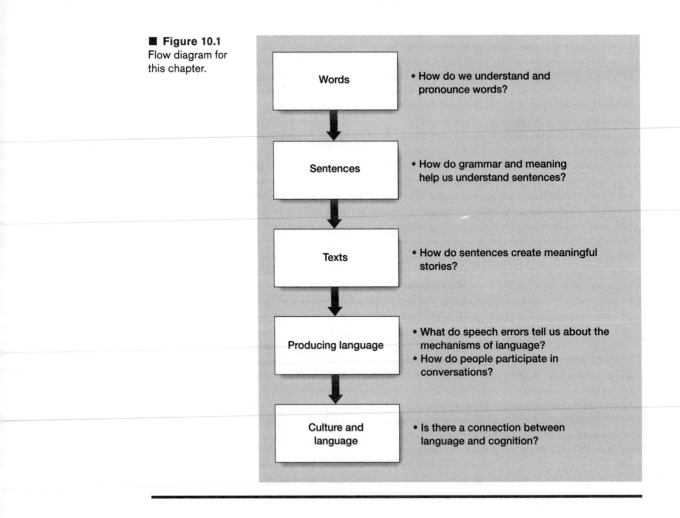

■ **Figure 10.1**
Flow diagram for this chapter.

Words	• How do we understand and pronounce words?
Sentences	• How do grammar and meaning help us understand sentences?
Texts	• How do sentences create meaningful stories?
Producing language	• What do speech errors tell us about the mechanisms of language? • How do people participate in conversations?
Culture and language	• Is there a connection between language and cognition?

scribe some of the factors involved in producing language, considering both the errors people make while speaking and how people participate in and understand conversations. Finally, we look at cross-cultural research on language that considers the role of language in thinking.

▚▚▚ Perceiving and Understanding Words

One of the most amazing things about words is how many we know and how rapidly we acquire them. Infants produce their first words during their second year (sometimes a little earlier, sometimes later), and after a slow start, begin adding words rapidly until, by the time they have become adults, they can understand over 50,000 different words (Altmann, 2001; Dell, 1995). All of the words a person understands are called person's **lexicon**.

Components of Words

The two smallest units of language are phonemes, which refer to sounds, and morphemes, which refer to meanings.

Phonemes Each word you are reading is made up of letters. If you were to read these words out loud, you would produce sounds called phonemes, where a **phoneme** is the shortest segment of speech that, if changed, changes the meaning of a word. Thus, the word *bit* contains the phonemes /b/, /i/, and /t/ (phonemes are indicated by phonetic symbols that are set off with slashes), because we can change *bit* into *pit* by replacing /b/ with /p/, to *bat* by replacing /i/ with /ae/, or to *bid* by replacing /t/ with /d/.

Note that because phonemes refer to sounds, they are not the same as letters, which can have a number of different sounds (consider the "e" sound in "we" and "wet"), and which can be silent in certain situations (the "e" in "some"). Because different languages use different sounds, the number of phonemes varies in different languages. There are only 11 phonemes in Hawaiian, about 47 in English, and as many as 60 in some African dialects.

Morphemes **Morphemes** are the smallest units of language that have a definable meaning or a grammatical function. "Truck" consists of a single morpheme, and even though "table" has two syllables, it also consists of a single morpheme, because the syllables alone have no meaning. In contrast "bedroom" has two syllables and two morphemes, "bed" and "room." Endings such as "s" and "ed," which contribute to the meaning of a word, are morphemes. Thus even though "trucks" has just one syllable, it consists of two morphemes, "truck" and "s."

Perceiving Words

Word Superiority

How we perceive the letters that make up written words and the sounds that create spoken words is a huge topic. We know from our discussion of the word superiority effect in Chapter 3 that a word's meaning helps a person perceive the letters that make up the word (see page 64). The meanings associated with words create a context that makes perception of the word's components easier. The meaning of words also helps us hear a word's phonemes, even when these phonemes are obscured by another sound.

Phonemic Restoration Effect Richard Warren (1970) demonstrated the effect of meaning on the perception of phonemes. Warren had participants listen to a recording of the sentence "The state governors met with their respective legislatures convening in the capital city." Warren replaced the first /s/ in "legislatures" with the sound of a cough and told his participants that they should indicate where in the sentence the cough occurred. No participant identified the correct position of the cough, and, even more significantly, none of them noticed that the /s/ in "legislatures" was missing. This effect, which Warren called the **phonemic restoration effect**, was experienced even by students and staff in the psychology department who knew that the /s/ was missing. Participants "filled in" the missing phoneme based on the context produced by the sentence and the portion of the word that was presented.

Warren also showed that the phonemic restoration effect can be influenced by the meaning of the words that *follow* the missing phoneme. For example, the last word of the phrase "There was time to *ave . . ." (where the * indicates the presence of a cough or some other sound) could be *shave, save, wave,* or *rave,* but participants heard the word *wave* when the remainder of the sentence had to do with saying good-bye to a departing friend. Thus, our perception of speech is influenced by top-down processing—our knowledge of the meanings of words that we bring to the situation. The effect of top-down processing has also been demonstrated by finding that more restoration occurs for a real word like prOgress (where the capital letter indicates the masked phoneme) than for a similar "pseudoword" like crOgress (Samuel, 1990). We will now consider another example of how our knowledge of the meanings of words helps us to perceive them.

Speech Segmentation The words on this page are easy to recognize. Each word is separated by a space, so it's easy to tell one word from another. However, when people hear words in a conversation, these words are not separated by spaces, or pauses, even though it may sound like they are.

When we look at a record of the physical energy produced by conversational speech, we see that the speech signal is continuous, with either no physical breaks in the signal or breaks that don't correspond to the breaks we perceive between words (Figure 10.2). The fact that there are usually no spaces between words becomes obvious when you listen to someone speaking a foreign language. To someone who is unfamiliar with that language, the words seem to speed by in an unbroken string. However, to a speaker of

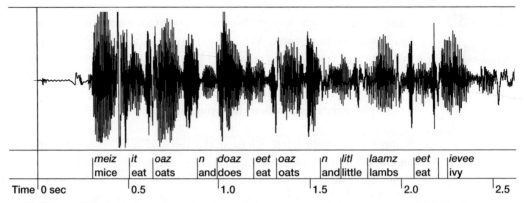

| *meiz* | *it* | *oaz* | *n* | *doaz* | *eet* | *oaz* | *n* | *litl* | *laamz* | *eet* | *ievee* |
| mice | eat | oats | and | does | eat | oats | and | little | lambs | eat | ivy |

Time 0 sec · 0.5 · 1.0 · 1.5 · 2.0 · 2.5

■ **Figure 10.2** Sound energy for the phrase "Mice eat oats and does eat oats and little lambs eat ivy." The italicized words just below the sound record indicate how this phrase was pronounced by the speaker. The vertical lines next to the words indicate where each word begins. Note that it is difficult or impossible to tell from the sound record where one word ends and the other begins. (Speech signal courtesy of Peter Howell.)

that language, the words seem separated, just as the words of languages you know seem separated to you. The process of perceiving individual words from the continuous flow of the speech signal is called **speech segmentation** (see Chapter 3, page 82).

Our ability to achieve speech segmentation is made more complex by the fact that not everyone produces words in the same way. People talk with different accents and at different speeds, and most important, people often take a relaxed approach to pronouncing words when they are speaking naturally. For example, how would you say "Did you go to class today," if you were talking to a friend? Would you say "Did you" or "Dijoo"? You have your own ways of producing various words and phonemes, and other people have theirs. For example, analysis of how people actually speak has determined that there are 50 different ways to pronounce the word *the* (Waldrop, 1988).

The way people pronounce words in conversational speech makes about half of the words unintelligible when taken from their fluent context and presented alone. Irwin Pollack and J. M. Pickett (1964) demonstrated this by recording the conversations of participants who sat in a room, waiting for the experiment to begin. When the participants were then presented with recordings of single words taken out of their own conversations, they could identify only half the words, even though they were listening to their own voices!

There are a number of types of information that listeners can use to deal with the problems posed by words in spoken sentences. One of these is the context, or the meaning, of a conversation. The importance of context is illustrated by the results of the Pollack and Pickett experiment, because it showed that when words are taken out of the context provided by other words in a conversation, understanding the words becomes much more difficult.

Our understanding of meaning also helps solve the problem of speech segmentation. An unfamiliar language that sounds like an unbroken string of sounds becomes segmented into individual words once you learn the language. When you learn the language, you not only learn meanings but you also learn that certain sounds are more likely to occur at the ends or beginnings of words. For example, in English, words can end in *rk* (*work*, *fork*), but not *kr*. However, words can begin with *kr* (*krypton*, *krill*), but not *rk*. There is evidence that people learn these rules about permissible beginnings and endings of words as young children (Gomez & Gerkin, 1999, 2000; Saffran et al., 1999). As we saw in Chapter 3, infants as young as 8 months of age can achieve speech segmentation through a process called *statistical learning*. We now move from *perceiving* letters and words to factors that influence our ability to *understand* words.

Understanding Words

Our ability to understand words is influenced by a number of factors, including how common the word is and the other words that surround it in a sentence.

Word Frequency An adult's lexicon may contain over 50,000 words, but some of these words can be more easily accessed than others. One factor that contributes to these differences in accessibility is **word frequency**—the relative usage of a word in a particular language. For example, in English, *home* occurs 547 times per million words, and *hike* occurs only 4 times per million words. The **word-frequency effect** refers to the fact that we respond more rapidly to high-frequency words like *home* than to low-frequency words like *hike*. One way this has been demonstrated is through the *lexical decision task* (see Method: Lexical Decision Task, page 303).

 ## Demonstration

Lexical Decision Task

CogLab

**Lexical
Decision**

In the **lexical decision task**, a participant reads a list that consists of words and nonwords. Your task is to indicate as quickly as possible whether each entry in the lists below is a word. Try this yourself by silently reading List 1 below and saying "yes" each time you encounter a word. Either time yourself to determine how long it takes to get through the list or just notice how difficult the task is.

List 1

Gambastya, revery, voitle, chard, wefe, cratily, decoy, puldow, faflot, oriole, voluble, boovle, chalt, awry, signet, trave, crock, cryptic, ewe, himpola.

Now try the same thing for List 2:

List 2

Mulvow, governor, bless, tuglety, gare, relief, ruftily, history, pindle, develop, grdot, norve, busy, effort, garvola, match, sard, pleasant, coin, maisle.

The task you have just completed (which is taken from D. W. Carroll, 1999; also see Hirsh-Pasek et al., 1993) is called a lexical decision task because you had to decide whether each group of letters was a word in your lexicon. ❧

When researchers presented this task under controlled conditions, they found that people read high-frequency words faster than low-frequency words (Savin, 1963). Thus, it is likely that you were able to carry out the lexical decision task more rapidly for List 2 compared to List 1.

This slower response for less-frequent words has also been demonstrated by measuring people's eye movements as they are reading (see Method: Measuring Eye Movements, page 120). The eye movements that occur during reading consist of fixations, during which the eye stops on a word for about a quarter of a second (250 ms), and movements, which propel the eye to the next fixation.

In a recent eye-movement study, Keith Rayner and coworkers (2003) had participants read sentences that contained either a high- or a low-frequency target word. For example, the sentence "Sam wore the horrid coat though his pretty girlfriend complained," contains the high-frequency target word *pretty*. The other version of the sentence was exactly the same, but with the high-frequency word *pretty* replaced by the

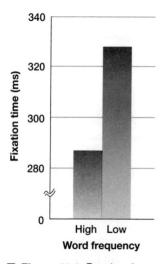

Figure 10.3 Results of Rayner et al.'s (2003) experiment. The bars indicate how long participants looked at target words like *pretty* and *demure*. These results show that participants fixated low-frequency words longer than high-frequency words.

low-frequency word *demure*. The results, shown in Figure 10.3, indicate that readers looked at the low-frequency words about 40 ms longer than the high-frequency words.

Context Effects Our ability to access words in a sentence is affected not only by frequency, but also by the meaning of the rest of the sentence. As we will see when we consider how we understand sentences, we are constantly attempting to figure out what a sentence means as we are reading it. This process involves both understanding individual words and understanding how these words fit into the overall meaning of the sentence. For example, it takes less time to understand *The Eskimos were frightened by the walrus* than to understand *The bankers were frightened by the walrus*, because words that are expected within the context of the sentence (like *walrus* appearing with *Eskimos*) are understood more rapidly than words that are not expected (like *walrus* appearing with *bankers*; Marslen-Wilson, 1990).

Lexical Ambiguity Words can often have more than one meaning, a situation called **lexical ambiguity**. For example, the word *bug* can refer to insects, or hidden listening devices, or being annoyed, among other things. When ambiguous words appear in a sentence, we usually use the context of the sentence to determine which definition applies. For example, if Susan says "My mother is bugging me," we can be pretty sure that *bugging* refers to the fact that Susan's mother is annoying her, as opposed to sprinkling insects on her or installing a hidden listening device in her room (although we might need further context to totally rule out this last possibility).

Context often clears up ambiguity so rapidly that we are not aware of its existence. However, David Swinney (1979) showed that people briefly access multiple meanings of ambiguous words before the effect of context takes over. He did this by presenting participants with a tape recording of sentences such as the following:

> Rumor had it that, for years, the government building had been plagued with problems. The man was not surprised when he found several spiders, roaches, and other bugs in the corner of the room.

If you had to predict which meaning listeners would use for *bugs* in this sentence, *insect* would be the logical choice because the sentence mentions spiders and roaches. However, using a technique called *lexical priming*, Swinney found that right after the word *bug* was presented, his listeners had accessed two meanings.

◄► Method

Lexical Priming

Remember from Chapter 5 that priming occurs when seeing a stimulus makes it easier to respond to that stimulus when it is presented again (See Method: Repetition Priming, page 192). The basic principle behind priming is that the first presentation of a stimulus activates a representation of the stimulus, and a person can respond more rapidly to the stimulus if this activation is still present when the stimulus is presented again.

Priming involving the naming of words is called **lexical priming**. Because lexical priming involves the *meaning* of words, priming effects can occur when a word is followed by another word with a similar meaning. For example, presenting the word *ant* before presenting the word *bug* can cause a person to respond faster to the word *bug* than if *ant* had not preceded it. The presence of a lexical priming effect would, therefore, indicate whether two words, like *ant* and *bug,* have similar meanings in a person's mind. ◆

Swinney used lexical priming by presenting the passage about the government building to participants and, as they were hearing the word *bug,* presenting a word or a nonword on a screen (Figure 10.4a). The words he presented were either related to the "insect" meaning of *bug* (*ant*), or to the "hidden listening device" meaning (*spy*), or were not related at all (*sky*). The participant was told to indicate as quickly as possible whether the item flashed on the screen was a word or a nonword. (See Method: Lexical Decision Task, page 364.)

Swinney's result, shown in Figure 10.4b, was that participants responded with nearly the same speed to both *ant* and *spy* (the small difference between them is not significant), and the response to both of these words was significantly faster than the response to *sky.* This faster responding to words associated with two of the meanings of *bug* means that even though there is information in the sentence indicating that *bug* is an insect, listeners accessed both meanings of *bug* as it was being presented. This effect was, however, short-lived, because when Swinney repeated the same test but waited for two or three

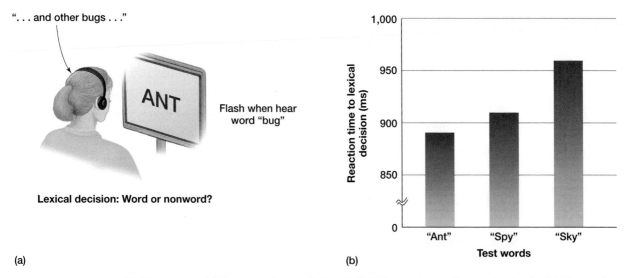

(a)

(b)

■ **Figure 10.4** (a) The procedure for Swinney's (1979) experiment. See text for details. (b) The results of Swinney's experiment. The fact that the reaction times to *ant* and *spy* were not significantly different showed that people briefly accessed both meanings of the word *bugs* as they read this word in a sentence.

syllables before presenting the test words, the effect had vanished. Thus, within about 200 ms after hearing *bug*, the *insect* meaning had been selected from the ones initially activated. Context does, therefore, have an effect on the activation of word meaning, but it exerts its influence after all meanings of a word have been briefly accessed.

Summary: Words Alone and in Sentences

Figure 10.5 summarizes the results we have described for perceiving letters and words, and Figure 10.6 summarizes the results for accessing words. Note that for all of the effects we discussed (except for the word-frequency effect), the meanings of words fa-

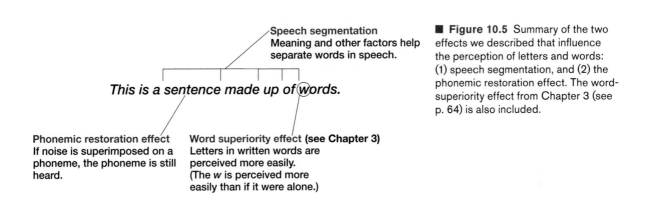

Speech segmentation
Meaning and other factors help separate words in speech.

■ **Figure 10.5** Summary of the two effects we described that influence the perception of letters and words: (1) speech segmentation, and (2) the phonemic restoration effect. The word-superiority effect from Chapter 3 (see p. 64) is also included.

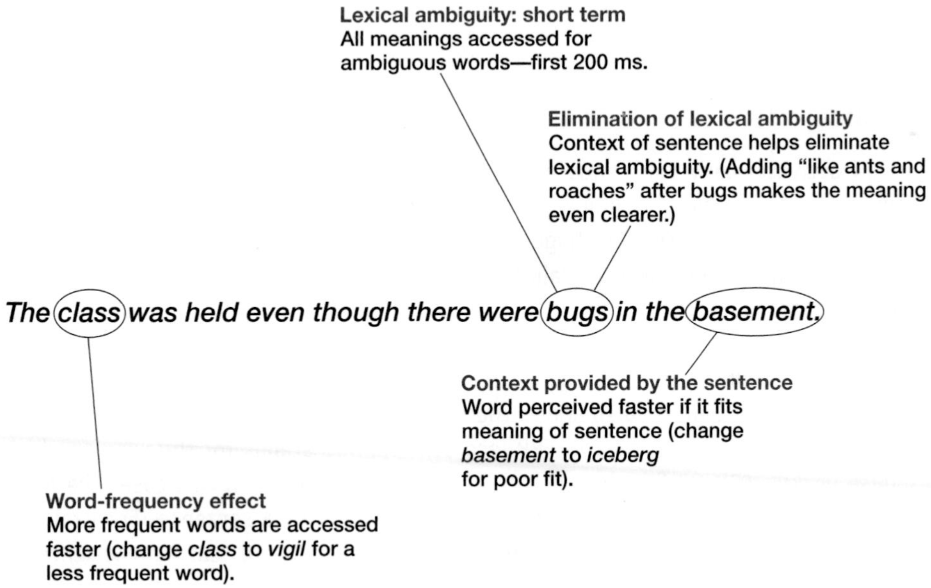

This is a sentence made up of words.

Phonemic restoration effect
If noise is superimposed on a phoneme, the phoneme is still heard.

Word superiority effect **(see Chapter 3)**
Letters in written words are perceived more easily.
(The *w* is perceived more easily than if it were alone.)

Lexical ambiguity: short term
All meanings accessed for ambiguous words—first 200 ms.

Elimination of lexical ambiguity
Context of sentence helps eliminate lexical ambiguity. (Adding "like ants and roaches" after bugs makes the meaning even clearer.)

■ **Figure 10.6** Summary of the four effects we described in connection with accessing words: (1) short-term lexical ambiguity, (2) elimination of lexical ambiguity, (3) how the context of a sentence can cause words to be perceived faster, and (4) the word-frequency effect.

The class was held even though there were bugs in the basement.

Context provided by the sentence
Word perceived faster if it fits meaning of sentence (change *basement* to *iceberg* for poor fit).

Word-frequency effect
More frequent words are accessed faster (change *class* to *vigil* for a less frequent word).

cilitated perceiving letters and phonemes, and the meaning of sentences facilitated understanding words. These results are important because they illustrate one of the main messages of this chapter: Although the study of language is often described in terms of its individual components—such as letters, words, and sentences—these components are not processed in isolation. As we discuss how we understand sentences, we will see more examples of how each of these components interacts with and influences one another.

◆◆◆ Understanding Sentences

Although the last section was about words, we ended up discussing sentences as well. This isn't surprising because words rarely appear in isolation. They appear together in sentences, with all of the words combining to create the meaning of the sentence. To understand how words work together to create the meaning of the sentence, we first need to distinguish between two properties of sentences: semantics and syntax.

Semantics and Syntax

Semantics is the meanings of words and sentences. **Syntax** is the rules for combining words into sentences. Recent experiments have demonstrated a physiological distinction between these two characteristics of words and sentences. For example, semantics and syntax are associated with different components of a physiological response called the *event-related potential (ERP)*.

◆▶ Method

Event-Related Potential

Most stimuli activate many thousands of neurons in the brain. The signals generated by these neurons can be measured in humans by recording the event-related potential with disk electrodes placed on a person's scalp (Figure 10.7a). When a stimulus is presented, the electrodes record voltage changes in the brain that are generated by the thousands of neurons near each electrode.

One thing that makes the ERP a valuable tool for cognitive psychology is that the response consists of a number of different components, which occur at different delays after a stimulus is presented. Figure 10.7b shows the N400 component of the ERP. "N" stands for "negative" (note that negative is up in ERP records), and 400 stands for the time at which the response peaks—400 ms from the presentation of the stimulus in this case. The N400 component is influenced by whether a word fits the meaning of a sentence. For example, the colored line in Figure 10.7b shows the N400 response to the word "eat" in the sentence "The cats won't eat." The gray line shows the response to the word "bake" in "The cats won't

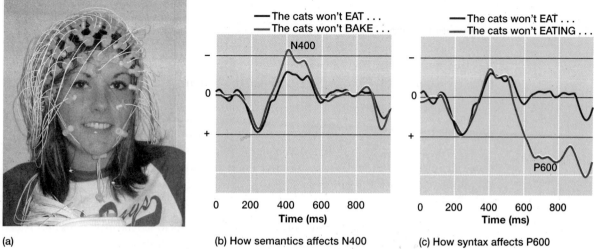

(a)

(b) How semantics affects N400

(c) How syntax affects P600

■ **Figure 10.7** (a) Person wearing electrodes for recording the event-related potential. (b) The N400 wave of the ERP is affected by semantics. It becomes larger (dark gray line) when the meaning of a word does not fit the rest of the sentence. (c) The P600 wave of the ERP is affected by syntax. It becomes larger (dark gray line) when syntax is incorrect. (Parts b and c: Reprinted from *Trends in Cognitive Sciences*, Volume 1, Issue 6, Osterhout et al., "Event-Related Potentials and Language," Figure 1, Copyright © 1997 with permission from Elsevier.)

bake." The N400 response increases to "bake" because the word "bake" doesn't fit in this sentence (Neville et al., 1991; Osterhout et al., 1997; also see Kutas & Federmeier, 2000). ◆

The fact that the N400 response is sensitive to the meaning of a word in a sentence means that this response is associated with semantics. Figure 10.7c shows that the P600 wave is associated with violations of syntax. This wave is small when syntax is correct, but becomes larger when syntax is incorrect. Thus, "The cats won't eating . . ." causes a larger P600 response than "The cats won't eat. . . ." The fact that semantics and syntax are associated with different waves of the ERP supports the idea that they are associated with different mechanisms.

The idea that semantics and syntax are associated with different mechanisms has also been supported by brain imaging studies, which have shown that different areas of the brain are activated by semantics and syntax (Dapretto & Bookheimer, 1999). Also, damage to some areas of the brain causes difficulties in understanding the meanings of words, and damage to other areas causes problems understanding grammar (Breedin & Saffran, 1999).

We will see that semantics and syntax interact with one another as a reader or listener works to determine the meaning of a sentence. One of the central processes for determining meaning is **parsing**, the mental grouping of words in a sentence into phrases.

Parsing a Sentence

The goal of parsing is to determine the message of a sentence. This message is determined by the meanings of the words in the sentence and how these words are grouped together into phrases. As we will see, a number of groupings are often possible for the same string of words. Consider for example, the sentence

The spy saw the man with the binoculars.

As people begin reading a sentence such as this one, they make guesses about how the sentence is going to unfold. Upon reading "The spy saw the man . . . ," it seems as if there is only one meaning—a spy looking at a man. However, as the sentence continues, the phrase ". . . with the binoculars" poses a problem, because now there are two possible meanings:

Meaning 1: The spy was looking through some binoculars to see the man. This meaning groups "the spy" and "the binoculars," like this:

The spy saw the man *with the binoculars.*

or

Meaning 2: The spy was looking at a man, who had some binoculars. This meaning groups "the man" and "the binoculars," like this:

The spy saw *the man with the binoculars.*

This sentence provides an example of **syntactic ambiguity**—the words are the same, but there is more than one possible structure, and so there is more than one meaning. Although there is no way to know the correct meaning of this sentence from the information given, there is a tendency for people to interpret this sentence in terms of the first meaning, with the spy being the one with the binoculars.

What causes us to prefer one way of parsing the sentence over another? Psychologists have proposed that there is a mechanism responsible for determining the meaning of the sentence. This mechanism has been called a number of things, including the *language-analysis device* and the *sentence-analyzing mechanism.* We will simply call it the **parser**. The parser determines the meaning of the sentence, primarily by determining how words are grouped together into phrases. Psychologists are interested in answering the question: "What factors determine how the parsing mechanism works?" Two answers have been proposed to this question; one assigns the central role to syntax, with semantics coming into play later, and the other proposes that syntax and semantics work simultaneously to determine the meaning of a sentence.

The Syntax-First Approach to Parsing As its name implies, the **syntax-first approach to parsing** focuses on how parsing is determined by syntax—the grammatical structure of the sentence. We can appreciate a connection between syntax and sentence understanding by considering the following poem from Lewis Carroll's (1872) *Through the Looking Glass and What Alice Found There:*

> 'Twas brillig, and the slithy toves
> Did gyre and gimble in the wabe:
> All mimsy were the borogoves,
> And the mome raths outgrabe.

Even though the words in this poem are nonsense, we still have a sense of what the poem is about. The first two lines seem to be about creatures called *slithy toves* doing something called *gyring and gimbling* in a place called *the wabe*. We are able to create meaning out of gibberish because we use syntax to infer meaning (Kako & Wagner, 2001).

The syntax-first approach to parsing states that the parsing mechanism groups phrases together based on structural principles. One of these principles is called *late closure*. The principle of **late closure** states that when a person encounters a new word, the parser assumes that this word is part of the current phrase (Frazier, 1987). We can illustrate this by considering the following sentence:

Because he always jogs a mile seems like a short distance to him.

Table 10.1 indicates how you may have read this sentence. At first, this sentence seems to be about a man who jogs a mile (a) and (b), but trouble occurs when you get to *seems*

Table 10.1 The Principle of Late Closure

First Try	
Part of the Sentence	**Probable Reader's Reaction**
(a) Because he always jogs	This is about a man who jogs.
(b) a mile	He jogs a mile.
(c) seems like	This doesn't make sense. How does "seem like" fit in here?
(d) a short distance to him.	OK. I read the sentence incorrectly the first time. I'll try again.
Second Try	
Part of the Sentence	**Probable Reader's Reaction**
Because he always jogs	The man jogs.
a mile seems like a short distance to him.	He is in good shape so a mile doesn't seem like much.

like (c) and after reading *a short distance to him* (d), you realize that there is another way to read the sentence (see "Second Try," Table 10.1). Because this sentence has led the reader "down the garden path" (down a path that seems right, but turns out to be wrong), this sentence is called a **garden-path sentence** (Frazier & Rayner, 1982).

We can see how this sentence illustrates the principle of late closure by focusing on the words *a mile*. According to the late-closure principle, the parser assumes that *a mile* is a continuation of the phrase *because he always jogs*. However, in reality, *a mile* is the beginning of a new phrase. Late closure (so named because it proposes to keep adding new words to the current phrase, so it delays closing off the phrase for as long as possible) leads to the wrong parse—the phrase needed to be closed after *jogs*, so the new phrase can begin. (Note that for this sentence, the correct phrasing could be indicated by inserting a comma after *jogs*. However, there are other garden-path sentences, such as "The student knew the answer to the question was wrong," that cannot be made easier to understand by adding a comma.) Because application of the syntactic rule of late closure results in a garden-path sentence, the syntax-first approach to parsing has also been called the **garden-path model** (Frazier & Rayner, 1982).

A number of experiments show that parsing is determined by late closure and other syntactic principles (Frazier, 1987). Although the garden-path model of parsing focuses on syntax, it doesn't ignore semantics. It states that if analysis in terms of syntax doesn't make sense, then semantics is used to clear up the ambiguity. Thus, according to this approach to parsing, syntax is used first, then semantics is called on, if needed, to make sense of the sentence (as it did in the "Second Try" in Table 10.1).

We can draw a comparison between this process of determining how words in a sentence are grouped into phrases and how parts of a visual scene become perceptually grouped into objects. Remember our example from Chapter 3 of how the Gestalt principles of organization help us guess that the scene shown in Figure 10.8a might be a

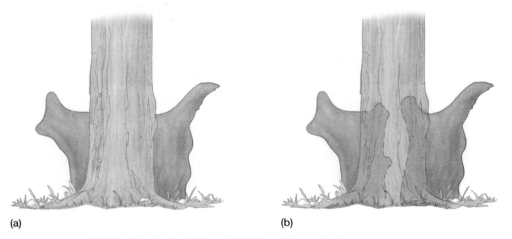

(a)   (b)

■ **Figure 10.8** (a) What lurks behind this tree? (b) It is *not* a creature!

creature hiding behind a tree. As it turns out, further information provided by looking behind the tree proves that guess to be wrong and so we revise our assessment of the situation from "creature hiding behind a tree" to "strange tree trunks behind a tree" (Figure 10.8b).

We used this example in the perception chapter to illustrate the idea that the Gestalt laws of organization are heuristics—rules of thumb that are "best-guess" rules for determining our perceptions. Most of the time, these rules result in perceptions that provide accurate information about what is "out there," and they have the advantage of being fast, which is essential because our very survival depends on quickly reacting to objects and events in the environment.

A similar process occurs when our language system uses a rule such as the principle of late closure to provide a "best guess" about the unfolding meaning of a sentence. Most of the time, this rule leads to the correct conclusion about how the sentence should be parsed. However, in some cases, such as when psychologists create garden-path sentences like the one about the jogger, the rule results in an incorrect parsing, which has to be corrected when more information becomes available at the end of the sentence.

Thus, just as ambiguous visual scenes help perception researchers understand the processes involved in visual perception, garden-path sentences help language researchers determine the processes involved in understanding language. Garden-path sentences accomplish this by showing us what guesses the parser makes, as in the sentence about the jogger (Fodor, 1995).

The Interactionist Approach to Parsing An indication of the role of semantics in understanding sentences is provided by comparing "The spy saw the man with the binoculars" to "The bird saw the man with the binoculars." We have seen that the sentence about the spy has two meanings: The spy could be looking at a man through the binoculars or could be looking at a man who has a pair of binoculars. However, by changing *spy* to *bird*, we create a sentence with only one reasonable meaning because we know the bird wouldn't be looking at the man through binoculars. Thus, in this sentence, our knowledge of birds makes it clear that the man is the one with the binoculars, and not the bird.

According to the **interactionist approach to parsing**, semantics can influence processing as the person is reading the sentence. *All* information, *both syntactic and semantic*, is taken into account as we read a sentence, so any corrections that need to occur in the processing of a sentence take place as the person is reading the sentence (Altmann, 1998; Altmann & Steedman, 1988; MacDonald et al., 1994). Thus, the crucial question in comparing the syntax-first and interactionist approaches is not *whether* semantics is involved, but *when* semantics comes into play. Is semantics activated only after syntax has determined the initial parsing (syntax-first approach), or does semantics come into play as a sentence is being read (interactionist approach)?

Recently, a number of studies in which readers' or listeners' eye movements have been measured while they are reading or listening to a sentence have helped answer this question (see Method: Eye Movements, page 120). In one study, Michael Tanenhaus and coworkers (1995) used eye movements to study how people process the information in sentences. They presented a picture that illustrated the objects mentioned in the sentence and then determined where participants looked while they were trying to understand the sentence. One of the sentences was

Put the apple on the towel in the box.

The beginning of this sentence (*Put the apple on the towel*) sounds like a straightforward request to put an apple on a towel. But after hearing the last part of the sentence (*in the box*), two possible meanings emerge: The sentence could be about *where* to put the apple (put it on the towel that's inside the box; Figure 10.9a), or about *which* apple (pick the apple that is on the towel to put in the box; Figure 10.9b).

Tanenhaus reasoned that in most real-life situations we hear sentences while we are interacting with the environment. Thus, the purpose of this experiment was to see how the environmental context that accompanies a sentence can influence how a person moves their eyes to fixate on particular objects in the environment. Tanenhaus used two pictures. The picture in Figure 10.10a is the "two-apple condition," in which one apple is shown on a towel and the other is on a napkin. Figure 10.10b is the "one-apple condition," in which one apple is shown on a towel.

The eye movements for participants looking at the two-apple condition, indicated by the arrows, shows that when participants heard "Put the apple," they moved their eyes to the apple on the napkin (arrow A). When they heard "on the towel," they moved their eyes to the apple on the towel (B), and when they heard "in the box," they looked at the box (C).

Participants in the one-apple condition responded differently. After hearing "Put the apple," they moved their eyes to the apple (A). After "on the towel," they looked at

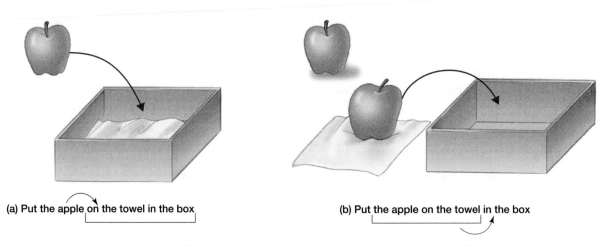

(a) Put the apple on the towel in the box (b) Put the apple on the towel in the box

■ **Figure 10.9** These two pictures indicate two meanings of the sentence "Put the apple on the towel in the box," which was used in Tanenhaus et al.'s (1995) eye-movement study. (a) The apple goes on the towel that's inside the box. (b) The apple on the towel goes in the box.

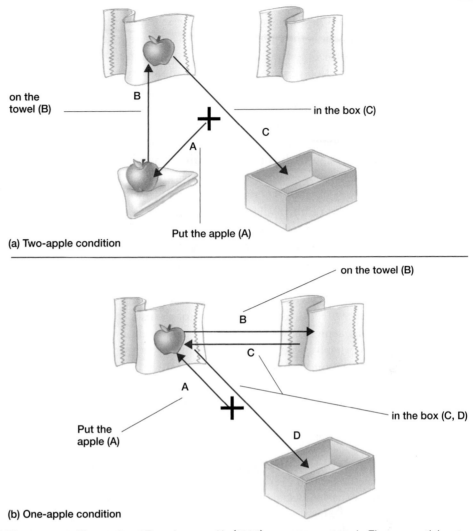

(a) Two-apple condition

on the towel (B)   in the box (C)

Put the apple (A)

(b) One-apple condition

on the towel (B)

in the box (C, D)

Put the apple (A)

■ **Figure 10.10** The results of Tanenhaus et al.'s (1995) eye-movement study. The way participants moved their eyes to different parts of the pictures depended on the information provided by the picture. Note how the eye movements differ in (a) the two-apple condition and (b) the one-apple condition.

the other towel (B). However, upon hearing "in the box," they apparently realized that the sentence was asking them to move the apple not to the other towel, but to the box, so they quickly moved their eyes back to the apple (C) and then to the box (D).

In this experiment, the participants' eye movements provided information about what they were thinking. We can summarize the two conditions as follows: When there were two apples, participants initially thought "*On the towel* means I should pick the apple that is on the towel." (They are thinking *which* apple to pick). But when there was just one apple, participants initially thought "*On the towel* means I should place the apple on the towel." (They are thinking *where* to place the apple). The important result of this experiment is that in the one-apple condition, participants' eye movements changed as soon as they received information that indicated that they needed to revise their initial interpretation of the sentence. This immediate responding supports the interactionist idea that the reader or listener takes both syntactic and semantic information into account simultaneously. (Also see Altmann & Kamide, 1999, for another demonstration of how the eyes rapidly respond to the meaning of a sentence.)

Although the controversy regarding whether the syntax-first approach or the interactionist approach is correct is still not resolved (Bever et al., 1998; Rayner & Clifton, 2002), evidence such as the results of the eye-movement study indicates that semantics can be taken into account earlier than proposed by the syntax-first approach. Furthermore, the result of the "apple in the box" experiment also shows that information in addition to the words in the sentence help determine what a sentence means. This is important, because in real life we rarely encounter sentences in isolation. Rather, we encounter sentences while we are in specific environments, or as we are listening to conversations or reading a story.

That sentences occur within a context is particularly important for reading, because sentences are typically part of a larger text or story. Thus, when we read a particular sentence, we already know a great deal of information about what is happening from what we read before. This brings us to the next level of the study of language—the study of how we understand text and stories (commonly called *discourse processing* or *text processing*). As we will see, most research in text processing is concerned with how readers' understanding of a story is determined by information provided by many sentences taken together.

Test Yourself 10.1

1. What is special about human language? Consider why human language is unique and what it is used for.
2. What events are associated with the beginning of the modern study of language in the 1950s?
3. What is psycholinguistics? What are its concerns, and what part of psycholinguistics does this chapter focus on?
4. What evidence supports the statement that "meaning makes it easier to perceive letters in words, and words in spoken sentences"?
5. How do the frequency of words and the context of a sentence aid in accessing words? How does Swinney's experiment about "bugs" indicate that the meanings of ambiguous words can take precedence over context, at least for a short time?
6. Why do we say that there is more to understanding sentences than simply adding up the meanings of the words that make up the sentence?

7. Describe the syntax-first explanation of parsing and the interactionist explanation. What are the roles of syntax and semantics in each explanation? What evidence supports the interactionist approach?

Understanding Text and Stories

Just as sentences are more than the sum of the meanings of individual words, stories are more than the sum of the meanings of individual sentences. In a well-written story, sentences in one part of the story are related to sentences in other parts of the story. Thus, the reader's task is to use these relationships between sentences to create a coherent, understandable story.

The materials used in research on text processing are usually excerpts from narrative texts. *Narrative* refers to texts in which there is a story that progresses from one event to another, although stories can also include flashbacks of events that happened earlier. An important property of any narrative is **coherence**—the representation of the text in a person's mind so that information in one part of the text is related to information in another part of the text. Texts with coherence are usually easier to understand than texts without coherence.

How Inference Creates Coherence

Most of the coherence in texts is created by inference. **Inference** refers to the process by which readers create information during reading that is not explicitly stated in the text. We have had a great deal of experience with inference from our study of memory in Chapter 7. For example, on page 255 we described an experiment in which participants read the passage "John was trying to fix the bird house. He was pounding the nail when his father came out to watch him do the work." We saw that after reading that passage, participants were likely to say that they had previously seen the following passage: "John was using a hammer to fix the birdhouse. He was looking for the nail when his father came out to watch him." The fact that they thought they had seen this passage, even though they had never read that John was using a hammer, occurred because they had inferred that John was using a hammer from the information that he was *pounding the nail* (Bransford & Johnson, 1973). People use a similar creative process to make a number of different types of inferences as they are reading a text.

Anaphoric Inference Inferences that connect an object or person in one sentence to an object or person in another sentence are called **anaphoric inferences**. For example, consider the following.

Riffifi, the famous poodle, won the dog show. She has now won the last three shows she has entered.

Anaphoric inference occurs when we infer that *She* at the beginning of the second sentence and the other *she* near the end both refer to Riffifi. In the previous "John and the birdhouse" example, knowing that *He* in the second sentence refers to *John* is another example of anaphoric inference.

We usually have little trouble making anaphoric inferences because of the way information is presented in sentences and our ability to make use of knowledge we bring to the situation. But here is an example of a quote from a *New York Times* interview with former heavyweight champion George Foreman (who has recently been known for lending his name to a popular line of grills), which puts our ability to create anaphoric inference to the test.

> What we really love to do on our vacation time is go down to our ranch in Marshall, Texas. We have close to 500 acres. There are lots of ponds and I take the kids out and we fish. And then, of course, we grill them. (Stevens, 2000)

Based just on the structure of the sentence, we might conclude that the kids were grilled, but we know that the chances are pretty good that the fish were grilled, not George Foreman's children! Readers are capable of creating anaphoric inferences even under adverse conditions because they add information from their knowledge of the world to the information provided in the text.

Instrumental Inference Inferences about tools or methods are **instrumental inferences**. For example, when we read the sentence "William Shakespeare wrote Hamlet while he was sitting at his desk," we infer from what we know about the time during which Shakespeare lived that he was probably using a quill pen (not a laptop computer!) and that his desk was made of wood. Similarly, inferring from the passage about John that he is using a hammer to pound the nails would be an instrumental inference.

Causal Inference Inferences that result in the conclusion that the events described in one clause or sentence were caused by events that occurred in a previous sentence are **causal inferences** (Goldman et al., 1999; Graesser et al., 1994; van den Broek, 1994). For example, when we read the sentences

> Sharon took an aspirin. Her headache went away.

we infer that the aspirin caused the headache to go away (Singer et al., 1992). This is an example of a fairly obvious inference that most people in our culture would make based on their knowledge about headaches and aspirin.

Other causal inferences are not so obvious and may be more difficult to figure out. For example, what do you conclude from reading the following sentences?

> Sharon took a shower. Her headache went away.

You might conclude, from the fact that the headache sentence directly follows the shower sentence, that the shower had something to do with eliminating Sharon's headache. However, the causal connection between the shower and the headache is weaker than the connection between the aspirin and the headache in the first pair of sentences. Making the shower–headache connection requires more work for the reader. You might infer that the shower relaxed Sharon, or perhaps her habit of singing in the shower was therapeutic. Or you might decide there actually isn't much of a connection between the two sentences.

Causal inferences create connections that are essential for creating coherence in texts, and making these inferences can involve creativity by the reader. Thus, reading a text involves more than just understanding words or sentences. It is a dynamic process that involves transformation of the words, sentences, and sequences of sentences into a meaningful story (Goldman et al., 1999; Graesser et al., 1994; van den Broek, 1994). Sometimes this is easy, sometimes harder, depending on the skill and intention of the both the reader and writer.

We have, so far, been describing the process of text comprehension in terms of connecting the meanings of sentences to create a story. Another approach to understanding text comprehension is to look directly at the nature of the mental representation that people form as they read a story. This is called the *situation model* approach to text comprehension.

Situation Models

A **situation model** is a mental representation of what a text is about. This approach proposes that the mental representation people form as they read a story does not indicate information about phrases, sentences, or paragraphs, but, instead, includes a representation of the situation in terms of the people, objects, locations, and events that are being described in the story (Graesser & Wiemer-Hastings, 1999; Zwaan, 1999). The situation-model approach also proposes that readers vicariously experience events that are being described in a story and that this experience is often from the point of view of the protagonist—the main character in the story or the character being described at a particular point in the story.

For example, in a story about a man walking through a building, the reader would create a map of the space through which the protagonist is walking and keep track of the protagonist's location in the building. According to the idea of situation models, if specific objects are described in the story, then the reader will have better access to information about objects that are near to the protagonist or are more visible to the protagonist (Morrow et al., 1987).

This way of looking at how readers process stories predicts that information about objects or events that are difficult for the protagonist to access will also be difficult for the reader to access. An experiment by William Horton and David Rapp (2003) tested this idea using short passages like the following:

1. Melanie ran downstairs and threw herself onto the couch.
2. An exciting horror movie was on television.
3. She opened a bag of chips and dug right in.
4. She watched a vampire stalk the helpless victim.
5. She had never seen this movie before.

Participants are then presented with one of the following endings:

Blocked story continuation (Figure 10.11a):

> 6a. Melanie's mother appeared in front of the TV.
> 7a. She told Melanie not to forget about her homework.

or

Unblocked story continuation (Figure 10.11b):

> 6b. Melanie's mother appeared behind the TV.
> 7b. She told Melanie not to forget about her homework.

Participants read the story line by line from a computer screen. After sentence 7, a warning tone sounded, which indicated that the target question was going to be presented. The target question for the story above was "Was the victim being stalked by a vampire?" The participant's task was to answer "yes" or "no" as quickly as possible by pressing the correct key on the computer keyboard.

The situation-model prediction is that participants who read the blocked story continuation should react more slowly to the test question because the TV screen, which

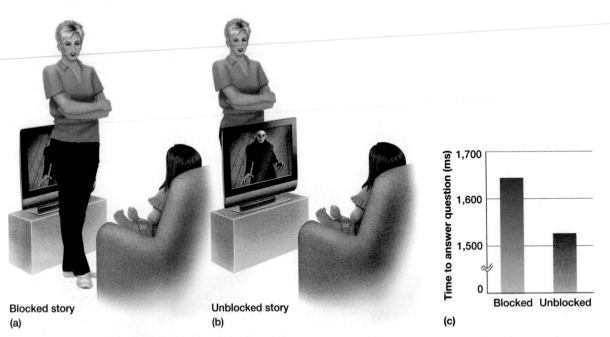

Blocked story
(a)

Unblocked story
(b)

(c)

■ **Figure 10.11** Horton and Rapp's (2003) experiment. (a) In the blocked condition, the story describes Melanie's mother as being in front of the TV. (b) In the unblocked condition, the story describes Melanie's mother as being behind the TV. (c) The results indicate that the reaction time to answer a question about something happening on the screen is slower for the blocked condition.

contained the answer, was blocked, so Mary couldn't see it. The result, shown in Figure 10.11c, confirms this prediction—responding was slower in the blocked condition. This supports the idea that readers represent story events in a manner similar to actual perception. That is, they experience a story as if they are experiencing the situation described in the text.

Producing Language: Speech Errors

Up until now our emphasis has been on comprehending language—either reading text or listening to another person speak. But speech is usually not a one-way street; we are both listeners and speakers. This means we need to broaden our discussion to include not only how listeners understand the meaning of what others are saying, but also how speakers create meaning for others to understand.

Producing language is another one of those cognitive processes we achieve rapidly and easily, but which is actually extremely complex. This complexity becomes apparent when we consider that the act of speaking involves assembling strings of words that have been retrieved from memory. This retrieval is rapid—more than 3 words per second for normal conversation—and is drawn from a lexicon of more than 50,000 words. Not only are the correct words rapidly retrieved, but they are produced in the correct order and combined with other words to create a grammatically correct sentence (Dell, 1995; Levelt, 2001).

One technique for determining how we achieve this feat is to use a technique that has proven valuable in understanding other cognitive processes—analyzing the types of errors that people make. **Speech errors**, which are also called "slips of the tongue," were made famous by Sigmund Freud, who suggested that slips of the tongue reflected the speaker's unconscious motivations (Freud, 1901). According to this idea, introducing a guest at a party by saying "It gives me great pleasure to prevent . . . ," when the speaker means to say "It gives me great pleasure to present . . . ," might be revealing the speaker's distaste for the guest.

Although slips of this kind, which have been called **Freudian slips**, do occur, there is little to support Freud's idea that all slips are caused by unconscious motivation. For one thing, of all the slips that occur in everyday speech, only a small fraction can be linked to a person's unconscious motivations. In addition, this kind of explanation not only involves guessing as to what the unconscious motivation might be, but it is difficult or impossible to make predictions of how a particular person's unconscious motivations might become translated into speech errors. Thus, stories such as the one about introducing the guest, or the man who explained his excellent memory by saying, "I have a pornographic memory" can be "explained" in terms of unconscious motivation, but only after the fact (Dell, 1995).

Rather than focusing on unconscious motivation, speech researchers have used speech errors to provide insights into basic mechanisms of language (Bock, 1995; Dell, 1995; Garrett, 1975, 1980). However, studying speech errors is complicated by the fact that they are very rare, occurring only about 1 or 2 times out of every 1,000 words in normal conversation (Dell, 1995). Thus, one of the challenges of studying speech errors is to identify them. Researchers have used a number of methods to do this.

◄► Method

Identifying Speech Errors

One way to identify speech errors is to note them as they happen in everyday speech. This requires great vigilance by the researcher, who must always be ready to write down an error when it occurs, and also a great deal of patience, because errors happen so infrequently. Another problem with this method is that it may result in a biased sample because errors that are funny or bizarre (for example, switching first letters to create "Hissing his mystery lecture") are more likely to be noticed. One way to avoid this sampling problem is to tape-record samples of speech and then carefully analyze the tapes for speech errors. When Garnham and coworkers (1981) did this, they identified 200 errors in 200,000 words.

Speech errors have also been created in the laboratory by rapidly presenting word pairs and using a tone to instruct participants to repeat the pair they just heard (Baars et al., 1975). This technique has the advantage of increasing the error rate to about 10 percent and also makes it possible to ask some specific questions about the conditions that result in speech errors. For example, using this technique, Baars and coworkers (1975) found that slips that create nonwords, like "beal dack" (when "deal back" was intended) are three times less likely than ones that create meaningful words, like "real dead" (when "deal red" was intended). A disadvantage of this laboratory technique is that it creates errors artificially. It is therefore important to collect both laboratory-produced errors and errors that occur naturally. ◆

Speech Errors and Language Mechanisms

What do speech errors tell us about the basic mechanisms of language? To answer this question, language researchers focus on two aspects of speech errors:

1. *Frequency of different types of errors.* The most common errors indicate the basic units of language production. For example, two of the most common exchanges, which we will describe below, involve phonemes and words. The high frequency of these types of slips, plus other evidence, have led to the conclusion that phonemes and words are basic units of language (Dell, 1995).
2. *Patterns of errors.* Speech errors do not occur randomly. In many cases, researchers have identified rules that govern speech errors. These rules provide insights into mechanisms of normal language production. *Phoneme exchanges* and *word exchanges* illustrate two rules of speech errors.

Phoneme Exchanges **Phoneme exchanges,** such as saying "fleaky squoor" instead of "squeaky floor" (Fromkin, 1973), illustrate the **consonant-vowel rule:** Phonemes of the same type replace one another. Consonants replace consonants and vowels replace vowels. (This particular example involves the exchange of consonant clusters "sq" and "fl.")

Word Exchanges The following are two examples of **word exchanges**:

1. "I have to fill up my *gas* with *car*" instead of "I have to fill up my *car* with *gas*" (noun exchange).
2. "Once I *stop* I can't *start*" instead of "Once I *start* I can't *stop*" (verb exchange).

Word exchanges such as these follow the **syntactic category rule**: When one word replaces another, the same syntactic categories are used. Nouns slip with nouns (example 1), and verbs slip with verbs (example 2).

These examples indicate that speech errors are far from random. Speech errors follow rules that reflect the importance of specific sound units (consonants and vowels) and parts of speech (nouns and verbs). Our final example of speech errors, *word substitution*, illustrates how speech can be influenced by knowledge that a speaker brings to the situation.

Word Substitutions An example of **word substitution** is when someone says "Liszt's second Hungarian restaurant" instead of "Liszt's second Hungarian rhapsody." This type of error is probably caused by the fact that both "restaurant" and "rhapsody" are associated with Hungarian. This is therefore an example of an error based on the speaker's knowledge of classical music and ethnic restaurants. This is also an example of the syntactic category rule, because both restaurant and rhapsody are nouns. It also illustrates substitution of one three-syllable word beginning with "r" with another three-syllable word beginning with "r." Clearly, speech errors are influenced by numerous factors, related both to the basic structure of language and to a person's prior knowledge.

Producing Language: Conversations

Although language can be produced by a single person talking alone, as when a person recites a monologue or gives a speech, the most common form of language production is conversation—two or more people talking with one another. Conversation, or dialogue, provides another example of a cognitive skill that seems easy but contains underlying complexities.

In a conversation, other people are involved, so each person needs to take what the other people are saying into account (Pickering & Garrod, 2004). This is an impressive accomplishment because we often do not know what the other person is going to say. Nonetheless, we are usually able to respond to their statements almost immediately. One way that people deal with these difficulties is that they coordinate their conversations on both semantic and syntactic levels.

Semantic Coordination

When people are talking about a topic, each person brings his or her own knowledge to the conversation, and conversations go more smoothly when the participants bring *shared* knowledge to a conversation. Thus, when people are talking about current events, it helps when everyone has been keeping up with the news, and is more difficult when one of the people has just returned from 6 months of meditation in an isolated monastery.

But even when everyone brings similar knowledge to a conversation, it helps when speakers take steps to guide their listeners through the conversation. One way this can be achieved is by following the *given–new contract*. The **given–new contract** states that the speaker should construct sentences so they include two kinds of information: (1) *given information*—information that the listener already knows; and (2) *new information*—information that the listener is hearing for the first time (Haviland & Clark, 1974). For example, consider the following two sentences.

1. Ed was given an alligator for his birthday.
   Given information (from previous conversation): Ed had a birthday.
   New information: He got an alligator.
2. The alligator was his favorite present.
   Given information (from sentence 1): Ed got an alligator.
   New information: It was his favorite present.

Notice how the new information in the first sentence becomes the given information in the second sentence. Susan Haviland and Herbert Clark (1974) demonstrated the consequences of not following the given–new contract by presenting pairs of sentences and asking participants to press a button when they felt they understood the second sentence in each pair. They found that it took longer for the participants to comprehend the second sentence in pairs like this one:

> We checked the picnic supplies.
> The beer was warm.

than it took to comprehend the second sentence in pairs like this one:

> We got some beer out of the trunk.
> The beer was warm.

The reason comprehending the second sentence in the first pair takes longer is that the given information, *that there were picnic supplies,* does not mention beer. Thus, the reader or listener needs to make an inference in the first case that beer was among the picnic supplies. In contrast, this inference is not required in the second pair because the first sentence includes the information that beer is in the trunk.

Syntactic Coordination

When two people exchange statements in a conversation, it is common for them to use similar grammatical constructions. Kathryn Bock (1990) provides the following example, taken from a recorded conversation between a bank robber and his lookout, which was intercepted by a ham radio operator as the robber was removing the equivalent of a million dollars from a bank vault in England.

Robber: "... *you've got to hear* and witness it *to realize how bad it is.*"
Lookout: "You *have got to experience exactly* the same position as me, mate, *to understand how I feel.*" (from Schenkein, 1980, p. 22)

Bock has added italics to the statements to illustrate how the lookout has copied the form of the robber's statement. This copying of form reflects a phenomenon called **syntactic priming**—hearing a statement with a particular syntactic construction increases the chances that a sentence will be produced with the same construction. Syntactic priming is important because it can lead people to coordinate the grammatical form of their statements during a conversation. Holly Branigan and coworkers (2000) illustrated syntactic priming by using the following procedure to set up a give-and-take between two people.

◀▶ Method

Syntactic Priming

In a syntactic priming experiment two people engage in a conversation, and the experimenter determines whether production of a specific grammatical construction by one person increases the chances that the same construction will be used by the other person.

Participants in Branigan's experiment were told that the experiment was about how people communicate when they can't see each other. They thought they were working with another participant who was on the other side of a screen (the left person in Figure 10.12a). In reality, the person on the other side of the screen was a confederate who was working with the experimenter.

The confederate began the experiment by making a *priming statement,* as shown on the left of Figure 10.12a. This statement was in one of the following two forms:

1. "The girl gave the book to the boy."
2. "The girl gave the boy the book."

The participant had two tasks: (1) find the *matching card* on the table that corresponded to the confederate's statement, as shown on the right of Figure 10.12a; and (2) describe one of the *response cards* to the confederate, as shown in Figure 10.12b. We can conclude that syntactic priming has occurred if the form of the participant's statement to the confederate matches the form of the confederate's original statement. ◆

Branigan found that on 78 percent of the trials, the form of the participant's statement matched the form of the confederate's priming statement. Thus, if the participant heard the confederate say "The girl gave the boy the book," this increased the chances that the participant would describe a response card like the one shown in Figure 10.12b as "The father brought his daughter a present" (instead of "The father brought a present for his daughter" or some other construction). This supports the idea that speakers are sensitive to the linguistic behavior of other speakers and adjust their behaviors to match. This coordination of syntactic form between speakers reduces the computational load involved in creating a conversation because it is easier to copy the form of someone else's sentence than it is to create your own form from scratch.

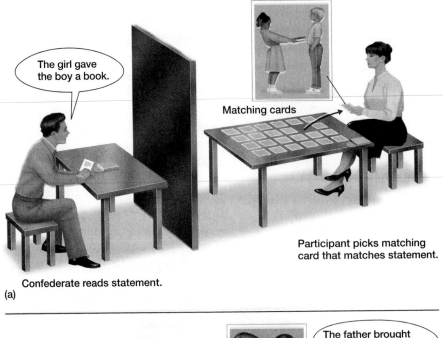

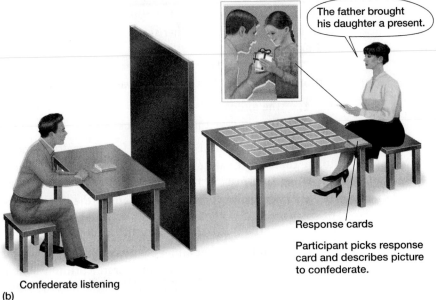

■ **Figure 10.12** The Branigan et al. (2000) experiment. (a) The participant, on the right, picks from the matching cards on the table a card with a picture that matches the statement read by the confederate. (b) The participant then picks a card from the pile of response cards and describes the picture on the response card to the confederate.

Let's summarize what we have said about conversations: Conversations are dynamic and rapid, but a number of processes make them easier. On the semantic side, people take other people's knowledge into account (if they don't, confusion can result). On the syntactic side, people coordinate or align the syntactic form of their statements. This makes speaking easier and frees up resources to deal with the tasks of alternating between understanding and producing messages that is the hallmark of successful conversations.

Something to Consider

Culture, Language, and Cognition

According to the **Sapir-Whorf hypothesis**, which was proposed by anthropologist Edward Sapir and linguist Benjamin Whorf, the nature of a culture's language can affect the way people think (Whorf, 1956). Although there was little evidence to support this when Whorf made his proposal, recent research has provided evidence that favors the idea that language can influence cognition. Debi Roberson and coworkers (2000; also see Davidoff, 2001) demonstrated that language can affect the way people perceive colors, by comparing color perception in British participants and participants from a culture called the Berinmo from New Guinea.

Roberson had the British and Berinmo participants name the colors of 160 Munsell color chips (small color chips similar to those found in paint stores, but scientifically color-calibrated to be used in research). The results for the British and Berinmo are shown in ● Color Plate 10.1. These diagrams indicate the color names that each group assigned to each of the chips. For example, chip 5B-9, indicated by the dot in the diagrams, was called *blue* by the British participants and *wap* by the Berinmo participants.

One difference in the results for the two cultures was that the British used eight different color names (blue, green, yellow, pink, red, brown, orange, and purple) and the Berinmo used just five (wap, wor, mehi, kel, and nol). Another difference was that the borders between the colors were different. For example, look at the area marked *yellow* for the British, and compare this to *wor* for the Berinmo. The Berinmo gave one name (wor) to many of the chips that the British called yellow, orange, green, and brown.

Having demonstrated differences in how participants in the two cultures *assigned names* to the color chips, Roberson and coworkers did an additional experiment to determine whether the two *perceive* colors differently. They accomplished this by doing a categorical perception experiment.

◄► Method

Categorical Perception

In a categorical perception experiment, participants are presented with pairs of stimuli and are asked to indicate whether they are the same or different. For example, would you say chips A and B in ● Color Plate 10.2 are the same or different? How about chips B and C?

It was probably easier to make the judgment "different" for chips B and C. This is because most English speakers place chips A and B in the same category (green), but place B and C in different categories (green and blue). **Categorical perception** occurs when stimuli that are in the same categories (like A and B) are more difficult to discriminate from one another than are stimuli that are in different categories (like B and C). ◆

When Roberson and coworkers presented the British and Berinmo participants with pairs of colors and asked them to indicate whether they were the same or different, British participants discriminated more easily between blue and green chips than the Berinmo, but the Berinmo discriminated more easily between *nol* and *wor* than the British. This means that differences in the way names were assigned to colors (indicated by the diagrams in ● Color Plate 10.1) affected the ability to tell the difference between colors. The fact that language has an effect on behavior supports the Sapir-Whorf hypothesis (see also Gentner & Goldwin-Meadow, 2003).

Although Roberson's experiments show that language can affect color perception, there is also evidence for similarities in color perception across different languages. Terry Regier and coworkers (2005) provided this evidence by tabulating the color naming data from speakers of over 100 different languages. Each participant was presented with the chips in ● Color Plate 10.3 and was asked to name the color of each chip. This is what Roberson did, but in addition participants were asked to pick the *best* example of each color. For example, English speakers would pick the best red, the best green, and so on. Regier's results, shown in ● Color Plate 10.1c, indicate that the "best" colors tend to cluster around the areas that English speakers call red, yellow, green, and blue. Notice that there is some variation, but that there are four distinct "islands" that correspond to the best examples of each color.

What do these results mean? Apparently, language can affect color perception, as Roberson showed, but there are also limits to the effects of language, as Regier showed. Other experiments have demonstrated differences in how Westerners and East Asians think about objects (Iwao & Gentner, 1997), numbers (Lucy & Gaskins, 1997), and space (Levinson, 1996). See If You Want to Know More on page 392 for more references on the connection between language and thinking.

✎ Test Yourself 10.2

1. Why do we say that understanding a story involves more than adding up the meanings of the sentences that make up the story?
2. What is coherence? Inference? What are the different types of inference, and what is their relation to coherence?
3. What are the assumptions behind the situation model, and what predictions does this model make?

4. What are speech errors? Describe Freud's ideas about speech errors and why modern language researchers do not consider these ideas to be that important.

5. What aspects of speech errors provide information about language mechanisms? What do phoneme exchanges and word exchanges tell us about language? What does the example of word substitution that involves Hungarian restaurants indicate about language mechanisms?

6. Describe how semantic coordination and syntactic coordination facilitate conversations. Be sure you understand syntactic priming and what it demonstrates about language production.

7. What is the Sapir-Whorf hypothesis? Describe experiments on color perception that support this hypothesis. Also describe the evidence that indicates that some aspects of color perception are the same across different languages.

Chapter Summary

1. Language is a system of communication that uses sounds or symbols that enables us to express our feelings, thoughts, ideas, and experiences. Human language can be distinguished from animal communication by its creativity, hierarchical structure, governing rules, and universality.

2. Modern research in the psychology of language blossomed in the 1950s and 1960s, with the advent of the cognitive revolution. One of the central events in the cognitive revolution was Chomsky's critique of Skinner's behavioristic analysis of language.

3. All the words a person knows are his or her lexicon. Phonemes and morphemes are two basic units of words.

4. The effect of meaning on the perception of phonemes is illustrated by the phonemic restoration effect. Meaning, as well as a person's experience with other aspects of language, are important for achieving speech segmentation.

5. The ability to understand words is influenced by word frequency and the context provided by the sentence.

6. Lexical ambiguity refers to the fact that a word can have more than one meaning and that the word's meaning in a sentence may not be clear. Lexical priming experiments show that all meanings of a word are activated immediately after the word is presented, but then context determines the eventual meaning of the word.

7. The meaning of a sentence is determined by both semantics (the meanings of words) and syntax (rules for using words in sentences).

8. Parsing is the process by which words in a sentence are grouped into phrases. Grouping into phrases is a major determinant of the meaning of a sentence. This process has been studied by using ambiguous sentences.

9. Two mechanisms proposed to explain parsing are (1) the syntax-first approach and (2) the interactionist approach. The syntax-first approach emphasizes how syntactic principles such as late closure determine how a sentence is parsed. The interaction-

ist approach states that both semantics and syntax operate simultaneously to determine parsing. This approach is supported by eye-movement studies.

10. Coherence enables us to understand stories. Coherence is largely determined by inference. Three major types of inference are anaphoric, instrumental, and causal.

11. The situation model approach to text comprehension states that people represent the situation in a story in terms of the people, objects, locations, and events that are being described in the story. Experiments support the idea that a reader often takes the protagonist's point of view in the story.

12. One of the major tools in the study of speech production is the determination and interpretation of speech errors (slips of the tongue). Research showing that some speech errors are more common than others and that speech errors often follow rules have provided insights into the mechanisms of normal language production.

13. Conversations, which involve give and take between two or more people, are made easier by two mechanisms of cooperation between participants in a conversation—semantic coordination and syntactic coordination. Syntactic priming experiments provide evidence for syntactic coordination.

14. There is evidence that a culture's language can influence the way people perceive and think. Experiments comparing color perception in Westerners and people in the Berinmo culture have revealed differences in color perception related to language. However, there is also evidence for some consistency in color perception across different languages.

Think About It

1. How do the ideas of coherence and connection apply to some of the movies you have seen lately? Have you found that some movies are easy to understand whereas others are more difficult? In the movies that are easy to understand, does one thing appear to follow from another, whereas in the more difficult ones, some things seem to be left out? What is the difference in the "mental work" needed to determine what is going on in these two kinds of movies? (You can also apply this kind of analysis to books you have read.)

2. Next time you are able to eavesdrop on a conversation, notice how the give-and-take among participants follows (or does not follow) the given–new contract. Also, notice how people change topics and how that affects the flow of the conversation. Finally, see if you can find any evidence of syntactic priming. One way to "eavesdrop" is to be part of a conversation that includes at least two other people. But don't forget to say something every so often!

3. One of the interesting things about languages is the use of "figures of speech," which people who know the language understand but which nonnative speakers often find baffling. One example is the sentence "He brought everything but the kitchen sink." Can you think of other examples? If you speak a language other than

English, can you identify figures of speech in that language that might be baffling to English speakers?

4. Newspaper headlines are often good sources of ambiguous phrases. For example, consider the following, which were actual headlines: "Milk drinkers are turning to powder," "Iraqi head seeks arms," "Farm bill dies in house," and "Squad helps dog bite victim." See if you can find examples of ambiguous headlines in the newspaper, and try to figure out what it is that makes the headlines ambiguous.

5. People often say things in an indirect way, but listeners can often still understand what they mean. See if you can detect these indirect statements in normal conversation. (Examples: "Do you want to turn left here?" to mean "I think you should turn left here"; "Is it cold in here?" to mean "Please close the window.")

If You Want to Know More

1. Animal language. Can monkeys use language in a way similar to humans? This is a controversial question, with some psychologists answering "yes" and others "no."

Savage-Rumbaugh, S., & Lewin, R. (1994). *Kanzi, the ape at the brink of the human mind.* New York: Wiley.

2. Indirect statements. People use indirect statements all the time (see preceding Think About It). There is evidence that indirect statements are more prevalent in some cultures than in others.

Holtgraves, T. (1998). Interpreting indirect replies. *Cognitive Psychology, 37,* 1–27.

3. Bilingualism. When people speak two or more languages, are these languages stored together or separately? This question, as well as other questions about the mechanisms involved in bilingualism, has been studied both behaviorally and physiologically.

Kroll, J. F., & Tokowicz, N. (2005). Models of bilingual representation and processing: Looking back and to the future. In J. F. Kroll & A. M. B. De Groot (Eds.), *Handbook of bilingualism: Psycholinguistic approaches* (pp. 531–553). New York: Oxford University Press.

Perani, D., & Abutalebi, J. (2005). The neural basis of first and second language processing. *Current Opinion in Neurobiology, 15,* 202–206.

Petitto, L. A., Katerelos, M., Levy, B. G., Gauna, K., Tétreault, K., & Ferraro, V. (2001). Bilingual signed and spoken language acquisition from birth: Implications for the mechanisms underlying early bilingual language acquisition. *Journal of Child Language, 28,* 453–496.

Snow, C. E. (1998). Bilingualism and second language acquisition. In J. B. Gleason & N. B. Ratner (Eds.) *Psycholinguistics* (2nd ed., pp. 453–481). Ft. Worth, TX: Harcourt.

4. Psychology of reading. Much of our use of language involves reading. This involves vision or touch (in the case of Braille) and demands on memory that are different than for spoken language.

Price, C. J., & Mechelli, A. (2005). Reading and reading disturbance. *Current Opinion in Neurobiology, 15,* 231–238.

Starr, M. S., & Rayner, K. (2001). Eye movements during reading: Some current controversies. *Trends in Cognitive Sciences, 5,* 156–163.

5. Language, culture, and the representation of space. Figure 10.13 indicates three ways of expressing spatial relationships. Different cultures favor different systems, and there is evidence that language plays an important role in this.

Majid, M., Bowerman, M., Kita, S., Haun, D. B. M., & Levinson, S. C. (2004). Can language restructure cognition? *Trends in Cognitive Sciences, 8,* 108–114.

6. Culture and categories. Which two objects in Figure 10.14 would you place together? Which two of the following words would you place together? Panda, Monkey, Banana. Research has shown that Chinese and Americans sort these items differently and that these differences may be related to language.

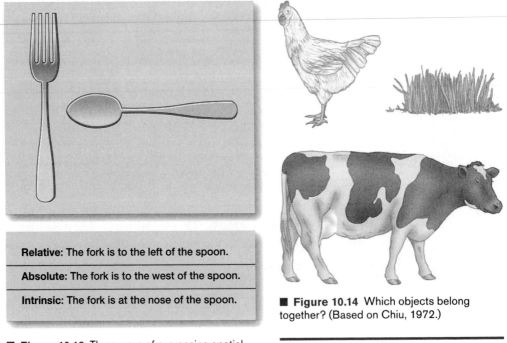

Relative: The fork is to the left of the spoon.

Absolute: The fork is to the west of the spoon.

Intrinsic: The fork is at the nose of the spoon.

■ **Figure 10.13** Three ways of expressing spatial relationships (Majid et al., 2004).

■ **Figure 10.14** Which objects belong together? (Based on Chiu, 1972.)

Chiu, L-H. (1972). A cross-cultural comparison of cognitive styles in Chinese and American children. *International Journal of Psychology, 7,* 235–242.

Ji, L., Peng, K., & Nisbett, R. E. (2000). Culture, control, and perception of relationships in the environment. *Journal of Personality and Social Psychology, 78,* 943–955.

7. Effect of brain damage on language. In the 1800s Paul Broca and Karl Wernicke identified areas in the frontal and temporal lobes of the brain that when damaged cause aphasia—disorders of language. Modern researchers have identified many types of aphasia.

Farah, M. J., & Feinberg, T. E. (2000). *Patient-based approaches to cognitive neuroscience* (pp. 165–271). Cambridge, MA: MIT Press.

8. Language acquisition. Children usually begin learning language before they can speak, produce their first words at about a year, and have mastered the basic linguistic structures of language by about 3 years of age.

Carroll, D. W. (2004). *Psychology of language* (4th ed.). Belmont, CA: Wadsworth.

Gleason, J. B., & Ratner, N. B. (1998). Language acquisition. In J. B. Gleason & N. B. Ratner (Eds.), *Psycholinguistics* (2nd ed., pp. 347–407). Fort Worth, TX: Harcourt.

Key Terms

Anaphoric inference, 377
Categorical perception, 388
Causal inference, 378
Coherence, 377
Consonant-vowel rule, 382
Freudian slip, 381
Garden-path model, 372
Garden-path sentence, 372
Given–new contract, 384
Inference, 377
Instrumental inference, 378
Interactionist approach to parsing, 373
Language, 357
Late closure, 371
Lexical ambiguity, 365
Lexical decision task, 364
Lexical priming, 366
Lexicon, 360
Morpheme, 361
Parser, 370

Parsing, 369
Phoneme, 361
Phoneme exchange, 382
Phonemic restoration effect, 361
Psycholinguistics, 359
Sapir-Whorf hypothesis, 387
Semantics, 368
Situation model, 379
Speech error, 381
Speech segmentation, 363
Syntactic ambiguity, 370
Syntactic category rule, 383
Syntactic priming, 385
Syntax, 368
Syntax-first approach to parsing, 371
Word exchange, 383
Word frequency, 363
Word-frequency effect, 364
Word substitution, 383

CogLab

To experience these experiments for yourself, go to http://coglab.wadsworth.com. Be sure to read each experiment's setup instructions before you go to the experiment itself. Otherwise, you won't know which keys to press.

Primary Labs

Word superiority How speed of identifying a letter compares when the letter is isolated or in a word (p. 361).

Lexical decision Demonstration of the lexical decision task, which has been used to provide evidence for the concept of spreading activation (p. 364).

Categorical perception—identification Demonstration of categorical perception based on the identification of different sound categories (p. 388).

Categorical perception—discrimination Demonstration of categorical perception based on the ability to discriminate between sounds (p. 388).

Problem Solving

11

What Is a Problem?

The Gestalt Approach: Problem Solving
as Representation and Restructuring
  Representing a Problem in the Mind
  Insight in Problem Solving
    Demonstration: Two Insight Problems
  Obstacles to Problem Solving
    Demonstration: The Candle Problem

Modern Research on Problem Solving: The Information-
Processing Approach
  Newell and Simon's Approach
    Demonstration: Tower of Hanoi Problem
  The Importance of How a Problem Is Stated
    Demonstration: The Mutilated-Checkerboard Problem
    Method: Think-Aloud Protocol

Test Yourself 11.1

Using Analogies to Solve Problems
  Method: Analogical Transfer
  Analogical Problem Solving and the Duncker Radiation
    Problem
    Demonstration: Duncker's Radiation Problem
  Analogical Encoding
  Analogy in the Real World
    Method: In-vivo Problem-Solving Research

How Experts Solve Problems
  Some Differences Between How Experts and Novices
    Solve Problems

Creative Problem Solving
    Demonstration: Creating an Object

Something to Consider: Sleep Inspires Insight

Test Yourself 11.2

Chapter Summary

Think About It

If You Want to Know More

Key Terms

Some Questions We Will Consider

- How does the ability to solve a problem depend on how the problem is represented in the mind? (397)
- Is there anything special about "insight" problems? (398)
- How can analogies be used to help solve problems? (413)
- What is the difference between how experts in a field solve problems and how nonexperts solve problems? (421)

The following is a story about physicist Richard Feynman, who received the Nobel Prize in Physics for his work in nuclear fission and quantum dynamics, and who had a reputation as a scientific genius.

> A physicist working at the California Institute of Technology in the 1950s is having trouble deciphering some of Feynman's notes. He asks Murray Gell-Mann, a Nobel Laureate and occasional collaborator of Feynman, "What are Feynman's methods?" Gell-Mann leans coyly against the blackboard and says—"Dick's method is this. You write down the problem. You think very hard." [Gell-Mann shuts his eyes and presses his knuckles periodically to his forehead.] "Then you write down the answer." (adapted from Gleick, 1992, p. 315)

This is an amusing way of describing Feynman's genius, but leaves unanswered the question of what was really going on inside his head while he was thinking "very hard." Although we may not know the answer to this question for Feynman, research on problem solving has provided some answers for people in general. In this chapter we will describe some of the ways cognitive psychologists have described the mental processes that occur as people work toward determining the solution to a problem.

Throughout this chapter, we will focus on research designed to determine the cognitive processes that occur as people try to solve problems for which the solution is not immediately obvious. We will do this by describing the two dominant approaches to studying problem solving: (1) the Gestalt approach, which describes problem solving as involving a process called *restructuring* (Figure 11.1); and (2) the information-processing approach, which describes problem solving as involving *search*. We will then consider how analogies can be used to solve problems, a method that combines elements of both restructuring and search. We will also consider differences between the way experts and nonexperts solve problems, and some of the processes involved in creative thinking.

◆◆◆ What Is a Problem?

When I ask students in my cognitive psychology class to indicate some problems they have solved or are currently working on, I get answers such as the following: problems for math, chemistry, or physics courses; getting writing assignments in on time; dealing with roommates, friends, and relationships in general; deciding what courses to take, what career to go into; whether to go to graduate school or look for a job; how to pay for a new car. Many of these things fit the following definition: A **problem** occurs when there is an obstacle between a present state and a goal, and it is not immediately obvious how to get around the obstacle (Lovett, 2002). Thus *problem*, as defined by psychologists, is difficult, and the solution is not immediately obvious.

You may notice, however, that my students' list includes two different types of problems. One type, such as solving a math or physics problem, is called a well-defined problem. **Well-defined problems** usually have a correct answer, and there are certain procedures that, when applied correctly, will lead to a solution. Another type of problem, like dealing with relationships or picking a career, is called an ill-defined problem. **Ill-defined problems**, which occur frequently in everyday life, do not necessarily have one "correct"

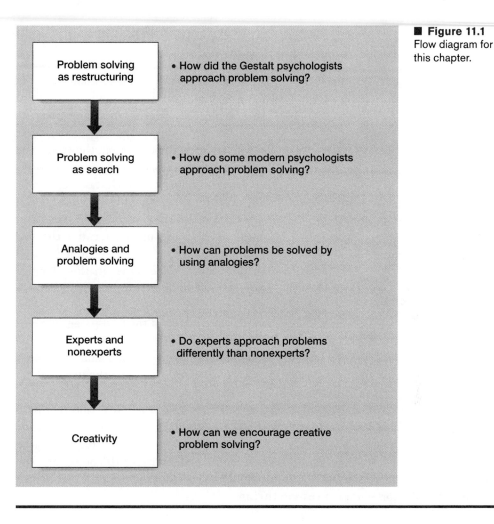

■ **Figure 11.1**
Flow diagram for
this chapter.

answer, and the path to their solution is often unclear (Pretz et al., 2003). We will consider ill-defined problems at the end of the chapter when we discuss creative problem solving. Our main concern will be well-defined problems, because psychological research has focused on this type of problem. We begin by considering the approach of the Gestalt psychologists, who introduced the study of problem solving to psychology in the 1920s.

❧❧❧ The Gestalt Approach: Problem Solving as Representation and Restructuring

The Gestalt psychologists realized that one way to approach problem solving was to ask how problems are represented in a person's mind. Problem solving, for the Gestalt psychologists, was about (1) how people represent a problem in their mind, and (2) how solving a problem involves a *reorganization* or *restructuring* of this representation.

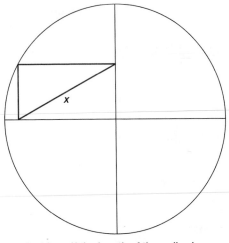

Problem: If the length of the radius is *r*, what is the length of line *x*?

■ **Figure 11.2** The circle problem. See Figure 11.23 on page 433 for the solution.

Representing a Problem in the Mind

We introduced the Gestalt psychologists in Chapter 3 by describing their laws of perceptual organization. The Gestalt psychologists were interested not only in perception, but also in learning, problem solving, and even attitudes and beliefs (Koffka, 1935). But, even as they considered areas of psychology in addition to perception, they took a perceptual approach to these other areas.

We can illustrate the Gestalt idea of representation and restructuring in problem solving by considering Figure 11.2. This problem, which was posed by Gestalt psychologist Wolfgang Kohler (1929), asks us to determine the length of the segment marked *x*, if the radius of the circle has a length *r*. (A number of problems will be posed in this chapter. The answers appear at the end of the chapter. See Figure 11.23 (page 433) for the answer to the "circle" problem. For this problem, the answer is also stated in the next paragraph, so don't read any further if you want to try solve it.)

The key to solving this problem is to create the mental representation of *x* as being a diagonal of the small rectangle. Representing *x* as the diagonal enables us to reorganize the representation by creating the rectangle's other diagonal (Figure 11.23). Once we realize that this diagonal is the radius of the circle, and that both diagonals are the same length, we can conclude that the length of *x* equals the length of the radius, *r*. What is important about this solution is that it doesn't require mathematical equations. Instead, the solution is obtained by first *perceiving* the object and then *representing* it in a different way. The Gestalt psychologists called the process of changing the problem's representation **restructuring**.

Insight in Problem Solving

The Gestalt psychologists also introduced the idea that restructuring is associated with **insight**—a sudden realization of a problem's solution. Gestalt psychologists' emphasis on insight is reflected in the types of problems they posed. The solution to most of their problems involves discovering a crucial element that leads to solution of the problem (Dunbar, 1998).

The Gestalt psychologists assumed that people solving their problems were experiencing insight because the solutions usually seemed to come to them all of a sudden. Modern researchers have debated whether insight actually exists, with some pointing to the fact that people often experience problem solving as an "Aha!" experience—at one point they don't have the answer, and then next minute they have solved the problem—which is one of the characteristics associated with insight problems. However, other researchers have emphasized the lack of evidence, other than anecdotal reports, to support the specialness of the insight experience (Weisberg, 1995; Weisberg & Alba, 1981, 1982).

Janet Metcalfe and David Wiebe (1987) did an experiment designed to distinguish between insight problems and noninsight problems. Their starting point was the idea that there should be a basic difference between how participants feel they are progressing toward a solution as they are working on an insight problem, and how they feel as they are working on a noninsight problem. They predicted that participants working on an insight problem, in which the answer appears suddenly, should not be very good at predicting how near they are to a solution, but that participants working on a noninsight problem, which involves a more methodical process, would have some knowledge that they are getting closer to the solution.

To test this hypothesis, Metcalfe and Wiebe gave participants insight problems, like the ones in the demonstration below, and noninsight problems and had them make "warmth" judgments every 15 seconds, as they were working on the problems. Ratings closer to "hot" (7 on a 7-point scale) were used when they felt they were getting close to a solution, and ratings closer to "cold" (1 on the scale) were used when they felt that they were far from a solution. Here are some examples of insight problems.

Demonstration

Two Insight Problems

Triangle Problem The triangle shown in Figure 11.3a points to the top of the page. Show how you can move three of the circles to get the triangle to point to the bottom of the page. (For the answer, see Figure 11.24 on page 433.)

Chain Problem A woman has four pieces of chain. Each piece is made up of three links, as shown in Figure 11.3b. She wants to join the pieces into a single closed loop of chain. To open a link costs 2 cents and to close a link costs 3 cents. She only has 15 cents. How does she do it? (For the answer, see Figure 11.25 on page 433.)

As you work on these problems, see whether you can monitor your progress. Do you feel as though you are making steady progress toward a solution, until eventually it all adds up

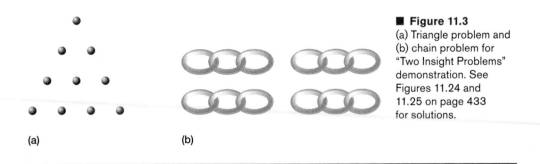

(a)   (b)

■ **Figure 11.3**
(a) Triangle problem and (b) chain problem for "Two Insight Problems" demonstration. See Figures 11.24 and 11.25 on page 433 for solutions.

to the answer, or as though you were not really making much progress, but, if you did solve the problem, you experienced the solution all of a sudden, like an "Aha!" experience?

For noninsight problems, Metcalfe and Wiebe used algebra problems like the following, which were taken from a high school mathematics text.

- Solve for x: $(1/5)x + 10 = 25$
- Factor $16y^2 - 40yz + 25z^2$

The results of their experiment are shown in Figure 11.4, which indicates the median warmth ratings for all of the participants for the minute just before the participants solved the two kinds of problems.

For the insight problems (solid line), warmth ratings remain low at 2 or 3 until just before the problem is solved. Notice that 15 seconds before the solution, the medium rating is a relatively cold 3. In contrast, for the algebra problems (dashed line), the ratings gradually increased until the problem was solved. Thus, Metcalfe and Wiebe demonstrated a difference between insight and noninsight problems. The solution for problems that have been called insight problems does, in fact, occur suddenly, as measured by people's reports of how close they feel they are to a solution.

The Gestalt psychologists felt that restructuring was usually involved in solving insight problems, so they focused on these types of problems. Their research strategy was to devise problems and situations that made it difficult for people to achieve the restructuring needed to solve the problem. They hoped to learn about processes involved in problem solving by studying *obstacles* to problem solving.

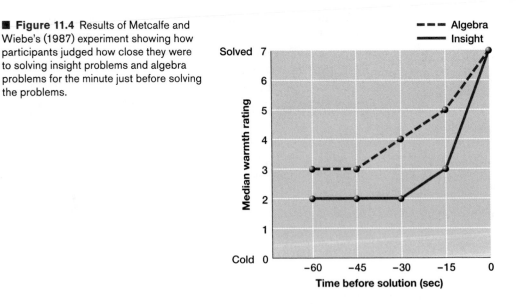

■ **Figure 11.4** Results of Metcalfe and Wiebe's (1987) experiment showing how participants judged how close they were to solving insight problems and algebra problems for the minute just before solving the problems.

Obstacles to Problem Solving

One of the major obstacles to problem solving, according to the Gestalt psychologists, is **fixation**—people's tendency to focus on a specific characteristic of the problem that keeps them from arriving at a solution.

One type of fixation that can work against solving a problem is focusing on familiar uses of an object. Restricting the use of an object to its familiar functions is called **functional fixedness** (Jansson & Smith, 1991). The **candle problem**, first described by Karl Duncker (1945), illustrates how functional fixedness can hinder problem solving. In his experiment, he asked participants to use various objects to complete a task. The following demonstration asks you to try to solve Duncker's problem by imagining that you have the specified objects.

Demonstration

The Candle Problem

You are in a room with a corkboard on the wall. You are given the materials in Figure 11.5— some candles, matches in a matchbox, and some tacks. Your task is to mount a candle on the corkboard so it will burn without dripping wax on the floor. Try to figure out how you would solve this problem before reading further, and then check your answer in Figure 11.26 (page 433) at the end of the chapter. ➷

The solution to the problem occurs when the person realizes that the matchbox can be used as a support rather than as a container. When Duncker did this experiment, he presented one group of participants with small cardboard boxes containing the materials (candles, tacks, and matches) and presented another group with the same materials, but outside the boxes, so the boxes were empty. When he compared the performance of the two groups, he found that the group that had been presented with the boxes as containers found the problem more difficult than did the group that was presented with empty boxes. Robert Adamson (1952) repeated Duncker's experiment and obtained the same result: Participants who were presented with empty boxes were twice as likely to solve the

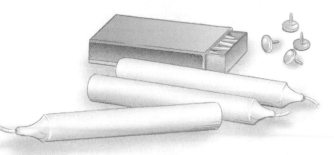

■ **Figure 11.5** Objects for Duncker's (1945) candle problem. See Figure 11.26 on page 433 for the solution.

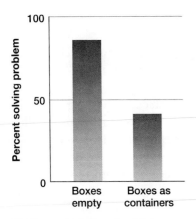

■ **Figure 11.6** Results of Adamson's (1952) replication of Duncker's candle problem.

problem as participants who were presented with boxes that were used as containers (Figure 11.6).

The fact that seeing the boxes as containers inhibited using them as supports is an example of functional fixedness. Another demonstration of functional fixedness is provided by Maier's (1931) **two-string problem**, in which the participants' task was to tie together two strings that were hanging from the ceiling. This is difficult because the strings are separated, so it is impossible to reach one of them while holding the other (Figure 11.7). Other objects available for solving this problem were a chair and a pair of pliers.

To solve this problem, participants needed to tie the pliers to one of the strings to create a pendulum, which could be swung to within the person's reach. There are two things that are particularly significant about this problem. First, 60 percent of the participants did not solve the problem because they focused on the usual function of pliers and did not think of using them as a weight. Second, when Maier set the string into motion by "accidentally" brushing against it, 23 of 37 participants who hadn't solved the problem after 10 minutes proceeded to solve it within 60 seconds. Seeing the string swinging from side to side apparently triggered the insight that the pliers could be used as a weight to create a pendulum. In Gestalt terms, the solution to the problem occurred once the participants restructured their representation of how to

■ **Figure 11.7** Maier's (1931) two-string problem. As hard as Sebastian tries, he can't grab the second string. How can he tie the two strings together?

achieve the solution (get the strings to swing from side to side) and their representation of the function of the pliers (they can be used as a weight to create a pendulum).

Both the candle problem and the two-string problem were difficult because of people's preconceptions about the uses of objects. The Gestalt psychologists also created problems in which the fixation was created by what a person experienced as he or she tried to solve the problem. When a person encounters a situation that influences his or her approach to a problem, this is called **situationally produced mental set**.

A. S. Luchins (1942) demonstrated situationally produced mental set by using the **water-jug problem**, in which participants were given three jugs of different capacities and were required to use these jugs to measure out a specific quantity of water, as shown in Figure 11.8. Problem 1 is solved by first filling the 127-cup jug (B) and then pouring the water from B into A once and into C two times, thereby subtracting 27 cups and leaving 100 in jug B. This solution, which can be stated by the formula Desired quantity = B − A − 2C, works for all of the problems in Figure 11.8. However, problems 7 and 8

	Capacities (cups)			
Problem	Jug A	Jug B	Jug C	Desired quantity
1	21	127	3	100
2	14	163	25	99
3	18	43	10	5
4	9	42	6	21
5	20	59	4	31
6	23	49	3	20
7	15	39	3	18
8	28	59	3	25

■ **Figure 11.8** Luchins's (1942) water-jug problem. Each problem specifies the capacities of jugs A, B, and C, and a final desired quantity. The task is to use the jugs to measure out the final quantity. The solution to problem 1 is shown. All of the other problems can be solved using the same pattern of pourings, indicated by the equation, but there are more efficient ways to solve 7 and 8.

Solution to Problem 1: Desired quantity = B − A − 2C

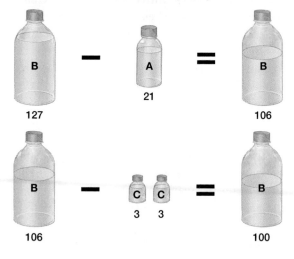

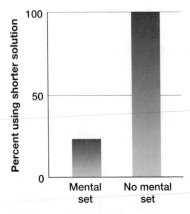

can be solved in fewer steps by using jugs A and C. For problem 7: Pour A (15) and C (3) into a container to arrive at 18 (Desired quantity = A + C). For problem 8: Fill jug A (28) and then pour from A into C (3), to leave 25 in A (Desired quantity = A − C).

Luchins had some participants begin with problem 1 and do each problem in sequence (the mental set group), and had other participants begin with problem 7 (the no mental set group). Figure 11.9 compares the performance of the two groups. All of the participants in the *no mental set group* used the shorter solution for problems 7 and 8, whereas only 23 percent in the *mental set group* used this solution for these problems. Clearly, participants in the mental set group learned the procedure described by the formula B − A − 2C as they solved problems 1 to 7 and simply continued to apply that procedure to solve problems 8 and 9. The situationally produced mental set created by solving problems 1 to 7 inhibited them from using the simpler solution for 8 and 9.

The Gestalt psychologists were the pioneers of problem-solving research. Between about 1920 and 1950 they described problems and solutions illustrating that solving a problem often involves creating a new representation. This idea that problem solving depends on how the problem is represented in the mind is one of the enduring contributions of Gestalt psychology. Modern research has taken this idea as a starting point for the information-processing approach to the study of problem solving.

■ Figure 11.9 All of the participants who began the Luchins's water-jug problem with problem 7 used the shorter solution (right bar), but less than a quarter who had established a mental set by beginning with problem 1 used the shorter solution to solve problem 7 (left bar).

Modern Research on Problem Solving: The Information-Processing Approach

In our description of the history of cognitive psychology in Chapter 1, we noted that in 1956 there were two important conferences, one at the Massachusetts Institute of Technology and one at Dartmouth University, that brought together researchers from many disciplines to discuss new ways to study the mind. At both of these conferences, Alan Newell and Herbert Simon described their "logic theorist" computer program that was designed to simulate human problem solving. This marked the beginning of a research program that described problem solving as a process that involves *search*. That is, instead of just considering the initial structure of a problem and then the new structure achieved when the problem is solved, Newell and Simon described problem solving as a search that occurs between the posing of the problem and its solution.

The idea of problem solving as a search is part of our language. People commonly talk about problems in terms of "searching for a way to reach a goal," "getting around roadblocks," "hitting a dead end," and "approaching a problem from a different angle" (Lakoff & Turner, 1989). We will introduce Newell and Simon's approach by describing a problem called the *Tower of Hanoi problem*.

Newell and Simon's Approach

Newell and Simon (1972) saw problems in terms of an **initial state**—conditions at the beginning of the problem—and a **goal state**—the solution of the problem. Figure 11.10a shows the initial state of the **Tower of Hanoi problem** as three discs stacked on the left peg, and the goal state as these discs stacked on the right peg. Try solving this problem by following the instructions in the demonstration.

 Demonstration

Tower of Hanoi Problem

In addition to specifying initial and goal states of a problem, Newell and Simon also introduced the idea of **operators**—rules that specify which moves are allowed and which are not. The operators for the Tower of Hanoi problem are as follows (see Figure 11.10b):

1. Discs are moved one at a time from one peg to another.
2. A disc can be moved only when there are no discs on top of it.
3. A large disc can never be placed on top of a smaller disc.

As you try solving this problem count the number of moves it takes to get from the initial to the goal state.

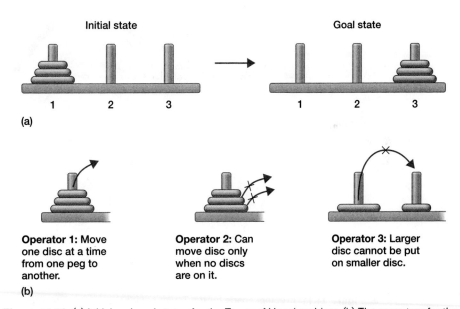

Figure 11.10 (a) Initial and goal states for the Tower of Hanoi problem. (b) The operators for the Tower of Hanoi problem.

This problem is called the Tower of Hanoi problem because of a legend that states that there are monks in a monastery near Hanoi who are working on this problem. Their version of it is, however, vastly more complex than ours, with 64 discs on peg 1. According to the legend, the world will end when the problem is solved. Luckily, this will take close to a trillion years to accomplish even if the monks make one move every second and every move is correct (Raphael, 1976).

As you tried solving the problem, you may have realized that there were a number of possible ways to move the discs as you tried to reach the goal state. Newell and Simon conceived of problem solving as moving through a number of steps, with each step creating an **intermediate state**. Thus, a problem starts with an initial state, continues through a number of intermediate states, and finally reaches the goal state. The initial state, goal state, and all the *possible* intermediate states for a particular problem is called the **problem space**.

The problem space for the Tower of Hanoi problem is shown in Figure 11.11. The initial and goal states are highlighted. All of the other configurations of discs on pegs

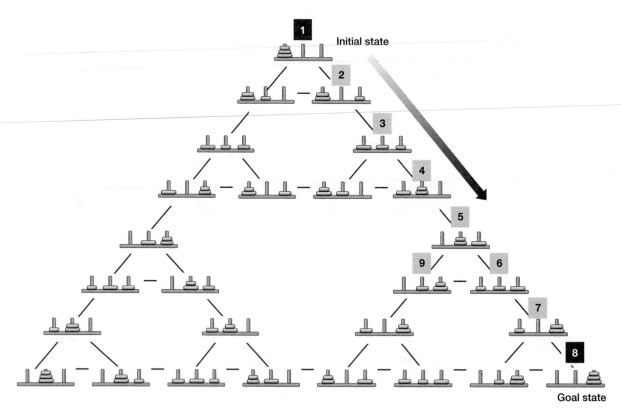

■ **Figure 11.11** Problem space for the Tower of Hanoi problem. The arrow on the right indicates that the most efficient solution involves reaching the goal state (8) by traversing intermediate states 2–7 (Dunbar, 1998).

are intermediate states. From the diagram, you can see that by choosing the path along the right side of the problem space, as indicated by the arrow, it is possible to solve the problem by making just seven moves.

Given all of the possible ways to reach the goal, how can we decide which moves to make, especially when starting out? It is important to realize that the problem-solver does not have a picture of the problem space, like the one in Figure 11.11, when trying to solve the problem. The person therefore has to search the problem space to find a solution. Newell and Simon proposed that one way to direct the search is to use a strategy called **means-end analysis**. The primary goal of means-end analysis is to reduce the difference between the initial and goal states. This is achieved by creating **subgoals**—goals that create intermediate states that are closer to the goal.

Our overall goal in applying means-end analysis to the tower of Hanoi problem is to reduce the size of this difference between initial and goal states. However, if we are to obey the operators, we can't accomplish this in just one step (we can move only one disc at a time). Thus, our first subgoal is to free up the large disc so we can move it onto peg 3. To accomplish this, we remove the small disc and place it on the third peg (Figure 11.12a; see intermediate state 2 in Figure 11.11). Then we remove the medium disc and place it on the second peg (Figure 11.12b; state 3, Figure 11.11). This completes the subgoal of freeing up the large disc. Our second subgoal is to free up the third peg so we can move the large disc onto it. We do this by moving the small disc onto the medium one (Figure 11.12c; state 4). We can now achieve subgoal 3, which is to move the large disc onto peg 3 (Figure 11.12d; state 5).

Now that we have reached state 5 in the problem space, let's stop and decide how to achieve the next subgoal, freeing up the medium-sized disc. We can move the small disc either onto peg 3 (to state 9) or onto peg 1 (to state 6). These two possible choices illustrate that to find the shortest path to the goal, we need to look slightly ahead. When we do this, we can see that we should not move the small disc to peg 3, because that blocks moving the medium disc there, which would be our next subgoal. Thus, we move the disc back to peg 1, which makes it possible to move the medium disc to peg 3 (state 7), and we have almost solved the problem! This procedure of setting subgoals and looking slightly ahead often results in an efficient solution to a problem.

One of the main contributions of Newell and Simon's approach to problem solving is that it provided a way to specify the possible pathways from the initial to goal states. But the idea that we can understand problem solving just by analyzing

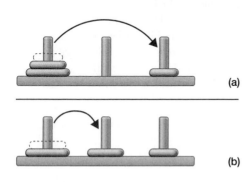

Subgoal 1: Free up large disc.

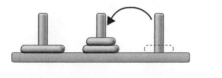

Subgoal 2: Free up third peg.

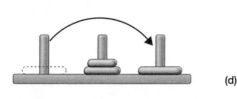

Subgoal 3: Move large disc onto third peg.

■ **Figure 11.12** Initial steps in solving the Tower of Hanoi problem, showing how the problem can be broken down into subgoals.

the structure of the problem space was called into question by research using problems that are stated in different ways, but which have the same number of intermediate states and therefore have the same problem space. As we will see in the next section, this research showed that two problems with the same problem space can vary greatly in difficulty.

The Importance of How a Problem Is Stated

How a problem is stated can affect its difficulty. We can appreciate this by considering two similar problems—the **acrobat problem** and the **reverse acrobat problem**.

The Acrobat Problem

Three circus acrobats developed an amazing routine in which they jumped to and from each other's shoulders to form human towers (Figure 11.13). The routine was quite spectacular because it was performed atop three very tall flagpoles. It was made even more impressive because the acrobats were very different in size: The large acrobat weighed 400 pounds; the medium acrobat, 200 pounds; and the small acrobat, a mere 40 pounds. These differences forced them to follow these safety rules:

1. Only one acrobat may jump at a time.
2. Whenever two acrobats are on the same flagpole, one must be standing on the shoulders of the other.

(a)   (b)

■ **Figure 11.13** (a) Initial and (b) goal states of the acrobat problem. See text for details.

3. An acrobat may not jump when someone is standing on his or her shoulders.

4. A bigger acrobat may not stand on the shoulders of a smaller acrobat.

At the beginning of their act, the medium acrobat was on the left, the large acrobat in the middle, and the small acrobat was on the right (Figure 11.13a). At the end of the act, they were arranged small, medium, and large from left to right (Figure 11.13b). How did they manage to do this while obeying the safety rules?

K. Kotovsky and coworkers (1985) found that it took their participants an average of 5.63 minutes to solve this problem. However, when they made one small change in the problem, it became much more difficult.

The Reverse Acrobat Problem

The reverse acrobat problem is the same as the acrobat problem, except that rule 4 above was changed to state that a smaller acrobat could not stand on a larger one.

Kotovsky's participants took an average of 9.51 minutes to solve the reverse acrobat problem. There are a number of possible reasons that the reverse acrobat problem is more difficult. One possibility is that the idea of a 400-pound acrobat standing on the shoulders of a 40-pound acrobat is not consistent with our knowledge of the real world, in which it would be highly unlikely that the small acrobat could support the large one. In addition, it may be harder to visualize larger acrobats on top of smaller ones, which would make the problem more difficult by increasing the load on the problem-solver's memory. Whatever the reason for the difficulty of the reverse acrobat problem, these results show that to understand problem solving, we need to go beyond analyzing the structure of the problem space.

We will now consider the **mutilated-checkerboard problem**, which has been used to show how the way a problem is stated can influence its difficulty.

Demonstration

The Mutilated-Checkerboard Problem

A checkerboard consists of 64 squares. These 64 squares can be completely covered by placing 32 dominos on the board so each domino covers two squares. If we eliminate two corners of the checkerboard, as shown in Figure 11.14, can we now cover the remaining squares with 31 dominos?

See whether you can solve this problem. A solution would be either a "yes" or "no" answer plus a statement of the rationale behind your answer.

Craig Kaplan and Herbert Simon (1990) used this problem and variations of it to study how the way a problem is stated affects its difficulty. There were four conditions in their experiment. Each group received a different version of the problem. The

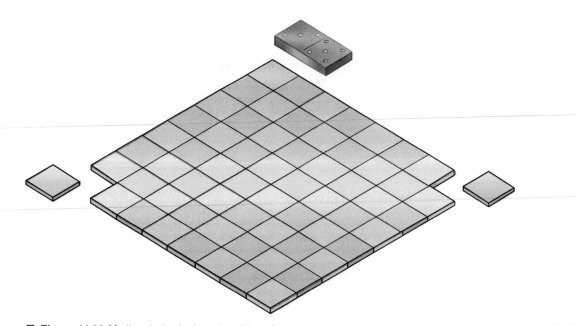

■ **Figure 11.14** Mutilated-checkerboard problem. See demonstration for instructions.

four conditions, shown in Figure 11.15, were (1) *blank:* a board with all blank squares; (2) *color:* alternating black and pink squares as might appear on a regular checkerboard; (3) *black and pink:* the words *black* and *pink* on the board; and (4) *bread and butter:* the words *bread* and *butter* on the board.

The key to solving the problem is to realize that when a domino is placed on the board so it covers just two squares, it is always covering two squares that are different (pink and black, for example). There is no way to place a domino so it covers two pink squares or two black squares. Therefore, for 31 dominos to cover the board there must be 31 pink squares and 31 black squares. However, this isn't the case, because two pink squares were removed. Thus, the board can't be covered by 31 dominos.

All four versions of the checkerboard problem have the same board layout and the same solution. What is different is the information on the squares (or lack of information on the blank board) that can be used to provide participants with the insight that a domino covers two squares and that these squares must be different colors. Not surprisingly, participants who were presented with representations of the board that emphasized the difference between adjoining squares found the problem to be easier. The bread-and-butter condition emphasized the difference the most, because bread and butter are very different but are also associated with each other. The blank board had no information about the difference, because all squares were the same.

Participants in the bread-and-butter group solved the problem twice as fast as those in the blank group and required fewer hints, which the experimenter provided when

The four conditions:

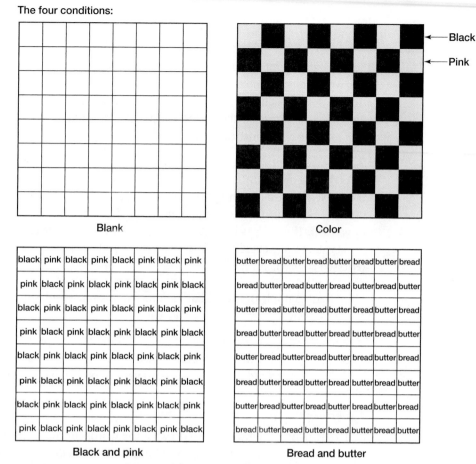

(Note: Boards not drawn to actual size.)

■ **Figure 11.15** Conditions in Kaplan and Simon's (1990) study of the mutilated-checkerboard problem. (Reprinted from *Cognitive Psychology,* Volume 22, C. A. Kaplan & H. A. Simon, "In Search of Insight," pp. 374–419, Figure 2. Copyright © 1990, with permission from Elsevier.)

participants appeared to be at a "dead end." The bread-and-butter group required an average of 1 hint, and the blank group required an average of 3.14 hints. The performance of the color and the black-and-pink groups fell between these two. This shows that solving a problem becomes easier when information is provided that helps point people toward the correct representation of the problem.

To achieve a better understanding of participants' thought processes as they were solving the problem, Kaplan and Simon used a technique introduced by Simon called **think-aloud protocols**.

◄► Method

Think-Aloud Protocol

For the think-aloud protocol procedure, participants are asked to say out loud what they are thinking while doing a problem. They are instructed not to describe what they are doing, but to verbalize new thoughts as they enter attention. One goal of think-aloud protocols is to determine what information the person is attending to while solving a problem. The following is an example of the instructions given to a participant:

> In this experiment we are interested in what you say to yourself as you perform some tasks that we give you. In order to do this we will ask you to talk aloud as you work on the problems. What I mean by talk aloud is that I want you to say out loud everything that you say to yourself silently. Just act as if you are alone in the room speaking to yourself. If you are silent for any length of time, I will remind you to keep talking aloud. . . . Any questions? Please talk aloud while you solve the following problem. (Ericsson & Simon, 1993) ◆

Here is an example of the verbalizations from Kaplan and Simon's experiment. This participant was in the bread-and-butter condition.

Participant: Just by trial and error I can only find 31 places. . . . I dunno, maybe someone else would have counted the spaces and just said that you could fit 31, but if you try it out on the paper, you can only fit 30. (Pause)

Experimenter: Keep trying.

Participant: Maybe it has to do with the words on the page? I haven't tried anything with that. Maybe that's it. OK, dominos, umm, the dominos can only fit . . . alright, the dominos can fit over two squares, and no matter which way you put it because it cannot go diagonally, it has to fit over a butter and a bread. And because you crossed out two breads, it has to leave two butters left over so it doesn't . . . only 30, so it won't fit. Is that the answer?

Notice that the person was stuck at first, and then suddenly got the answer after realizing that the words *bread* and *butter* were important. The results of think-aloud protocols support the idea that one of the processes that occurs during problem solving is a shift in how problem-solvers perceive elements of a problem. This idea is very similar to what the Gestalt psychologists were proposing. For example, remember the circle problem in Figure 11.2. The key to solving that problem was realizing that the line x was the same length as the radius of the circle. Similarly, the key to solving the mutilated-checkerboard problem is realizing that adjoining squares are paired, because a domino always covers two different-colored squares in a normal checkerboard.

Kaplan and Simon used two different colors to help their participants realize that pairing of adjacent squares is important. But this has also been achieved in another way—by telling the following story, which has parallels to the checkerboard problem.

The Russian Marriage Problem

In a small Russian village, there were 32 bachelors and 32 unmarried women. Through tireless efforts, the village matchmaker succeeded in arranging 32 highly satisfactory marriages. The village was proud and happy. Then one drunken night, two bachelors, in a test of strength, stuffed each other with pirogies and died. Can the matchmaker, through some quick arrangements, come up with 31 heterosexual marriages among the 62 survivors? (adapted from Hayes, 1978, p. 180)

The answer to this problem is obvious. Losing two males makes it impossible to arrange 31 heterosexual marriages. Of course, this is exactly the situation in the mutilated-checkerboard problem, except instead of males and females being paired up, light and dark squares are. People who read this story are usually able to solve the mutilated-checkerboard problem if they realize the connection between the couples in the story and the black and pink squares in the checkerboard. This process of noticing connections between similar problems and applying the solution for one problem to other ones is called the method of **analogy**. In the next section we will look more closely at how analogy has been used in problem solving.

Test Yourself 11.1

1. What is the psychological definition of a problem? Distinguish between well-defined and ill-defined problems.
2. What is the basic principle behind the Gestalt approach to problem solving? Describe how the following problems illustrate this principle, and also what else these problems demonstrate about problem solving: the circle (radius) problem; the candle problem; the two-string problem; the water-jug problem.
3. What is insight, and what is the evidence that insight does, in fact, occur as people are solving a problem?
4. Describe Newell and Simon's approach to problem solving, in which "search" plays a central role. How does means-end analysis as applied to the Tower of Hanoi problem illustrate this approach?
5. How do the acrobat problem and Kaplan and Simon's mutilated-checkerboard experiment illustrate that the way a problem is stated can affect a person's ability to solve the problem? What are the implications of this research for Newell and Simon's "problem space" approach?

Using Analogies to Solve Problems

A person is faced with a problem and wonders how to proceed. Questions such as "What move should I make?" or "How should I begin thinking about this problem?" arise. One tactic that is sometimes helpful is to pose questions like the following: "How did I solve that other problem?" or "Can I apply the same methods to solving this new problem?" and then to use the previously solved problem to help arrive at a solution to a new problem. This technique of using the solution to a similar problem to guide solution of a new problem is called **analogical problem solving**.

Using the Russian marriage problem to help solve the mutilated-checkerboard problem is an example of an effective use of analogy to solve a problem. Research on analogical problem solving has considered some of the conditions in which using analogies to solve problems is and is not effective.

Method

Analogical Transfer

The starting point for much of the research on analogical problem solving has been to first determine how well people can transfer their experience from solving one problem to solving another, similar, problem. To do this, a group of participants is presented with either a **source problem** or a **source story**, which is similar to the **target problem**—the problem to be solved. The Russian marriage problem is an example of a source problem for the mutilated-checkerboard test problem. Evidence that analogical problem solving has occurred is provided when presentation of the source problem or story enhances the ability to solve the target problem compared to a control group in which the target problem is presented alone. ◆

Analogical Problem Solving and the Duncker Radiation Problem

A problem that has been widely used in research on analogical problem solving is Karl Duncker's **radiation problem**.

Demonstration

Duncker's Radiation Problem

Try solving the following problem:

Radiation Problem Suppose you are a doctor faced with a patient who has a malignant tumor in his stomach. It is impossible to operate on the patient, but unless the tumor is destroyed the patient will die. There is a kind of ray that can be used to destroy the tumor. If the ray reaches the tumor at a sufficiently high intensity, the tumor will be destroyed. Unfortunately, at this intensity the healthy tissue that the ray passes through on the way to the tumor will also be destroyed. At lower intensities the ray is harmless to healthy tissue, but it will not affect the tumor either. What type of procedure might be used to destroy the tumor with the rays and at the same time avoid destroying the healthy tissue? (Gick & Holyoak, 1980) 🌑

If after thinking about this problem for a while, you haven't come up with a suitable answer, you are not alone. When Duncker (1945) originally posed this problem, most of this participants could not solve it, and Mary Gick and Keith Holyoak (1980, 1983) found that only 10 percent of their participants arrived at the correct solution, shown in Figure 11.16a. The solution is to bombard the tumor with a number of low-intensity rays from different directions, which destroys the tumor without damaging the tissue the rays are passing through. The solution to this problem is actually the procedure used in a modern procedure called radiosurgery, in which a tumor is bombarded with 201 gamma ray beams that intersect at the tumor (Tarkan, 2003; Figure 11.16b).

Notice how the radiation problem and its solution fit with the Gestalt idea of representation and restructuring. The initial representation of the problem is a single ray that destroys the tumor but also destroys healthy tissue. The restructured solution involves dividing the single ray into many smaller rays.

After confirming Duncker's finding that the radiation problem is extremely difficult, Gick and Holyoak (1980, 1983) had another group of participants read and memorize "The Fortress" story below, giving them the impression that the purpose was to test their memory for the story.

Fortress Story

A small country was ruled from a strong fortress by a dictator. The fortress was situated in the middle of the country, surrounded by farms and villages. Many roads led to the fortress through the countryside. A rebel general vowed to capture the fortress. The general knew that an attack by his entire army would capture the fortress. He gathered his army at the head of one of the roads, ready to launch a full-scale direct attack. However, the general then learned that the dictator had planted mines on each of the roads. The mines were set so that small bodies of men could pass over them safely, since the dictator needed to move his troops and workers to and from the fortress. However, any large force would detonate the mines. Not only would this blow up the road, but it would also destroy many neighboring villages. It therefore seemed impossible to capture the fortress.

However, the general devised a simple plan. He divided his army into small groups and dispatched each group to the head of a different road. When all was ready he gave the signal and each group marched down a different road. Each group continued down its road to the fortress so that the entire army arrived together at the fortress at the same time. In this way, the general captured the fortress and overthrew the dictator. (See Figure 11.16c.)

The fortress story is analogous to the radiation problem because the dictator's fortress corresponds to the tumor and the small groups of soldiers sent down different roads correspond to the of low-intensity rays that can be directed at the tumor. After Gick and Holyoak's participants read the story, they were told to begin work on the radiation problem. Thirty percent of the people in this group were able to solve the radiation problem, an improvement over the 10 percent who solved the problem when it was presented alone. However, what is significant about this experiment is that 70 percent of the participants were still unable to solve the problem, even after reading an analogous source story. This result highlights one of the major findings of research on using analogies as an aid to problem solving: Even when exposed to analogous source prob-

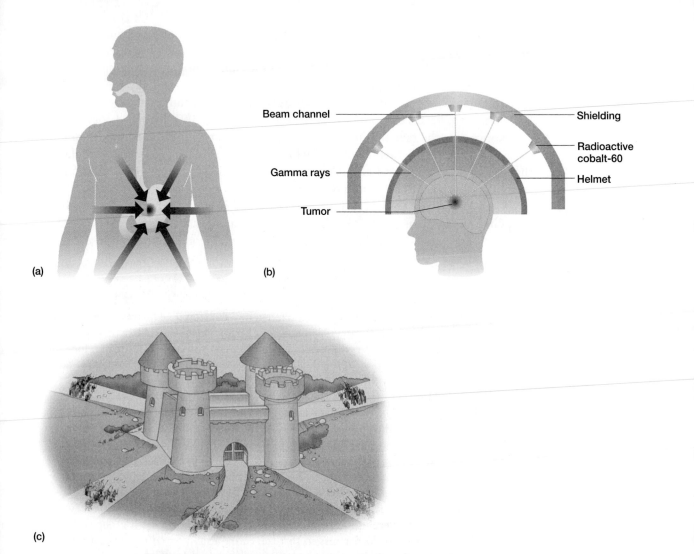

Figure 11.16 (a) Solution to the radiation problem. Bombarding the tumor, in the center, with a number of low-intensity rays from different directions destroys the tumor without damaging the tissue it passes through. (b) Radiosurgery, a modern medical technique for irradiating brain tumors with a number of beams of gamma rays, uses the same principle. The actual technique uses 201 gamma ray beams. (c) The general's plan from the fortress problem.

lems, most people do not make the connection between the source problem and the target problem.

However, when Gick and Holyoak's participants were given a hint to make them aware that they could use the fortress story to help solve the radiation problem, 75 percent were able to solve the problem. These results led Gick and Holyoak to propose that the process of analogical problem solving involves the following three steps:

1. *Noticing* that there is an analogous relationship between the source story and the target problem. This step is obviously crucial in order for analogical problem solving to work. However, as we have seen, most participants need some prompting before they notice the connection between the source problem and the target problem. Gick and Holyoak consider this *noticing* step to be the most difficult of the three steps to achieve. A number of experiments have shown that the most effective source stories are those that are most similar to the target problems (Catrambone & Holyoak, 1989; Holyoak & Thagard, 1995). This similarity could make it easier to notice the analogical relationship between the source story and the target problem, and could also help achieve the next step—mapping.

2. *Mapping* the correspondence between the source story and the target problem. To use the story to solve the problem, the participant has to map corresponding parts of the story onto the test problem by connecting elements in one story (for example, the dictator's fortress) to elements in the target problem (the tumor).

3. *Applying* the mapping to generate a parallel solution to the target problem. This would involve, for example, generalizing from the many small groups of soldiers approaching the fortress from different directions to the idea of using many weaker rays that would approach the tumor from different directions.

Once they determined that analogies can help with problem solving, but that hints are required to help participants notice the presence of the source problem, Gick and Holyoak (1983) proceeded to look for factors that help facilitate the *noticing* and *mapping* steps. One thing that makes noticing difficult is that people often focus on **surface features**, specific elements that make up the problem, such as the rays and the tumor. Surface features of the source problem and the target problem can be very different. For example, there is a big difference between a tumor and a fortress, and between rays and marching soldiers. To use the information in the fortress problem to solve the radiation problem, participants have to ignore surface features and focus instead on **structural features**, the underlying principle that the problems have in common.

To test the idea that people are more likely to realize structural similarities between problems when surface features are more similar, Keith Holyoak and Kyunghee Koh (1987) created a problem that had surface features similar to the radiation problem. The following is a shortened version of this problem.

Lightbulb Problem

In a physics lab at a major university, a very expensive lightbulb, which would emit precisely controlled quantities of light, was being used in some experiments. One morning Ruth, the research assistant, came into the lab and found that the lightbulb no longer worked. She noticed that the filament inside the bulb had broken into two parts. The surrounding glass bulb was completely sealed, so there was no way to open it. Ruth knew that the lightbulb could be repaired if a brief, high-intensity laser beam could be used to fuse the two parts of the filament into one.

However, a high-intensity laser beam would also break the fragile glass surrounding the filament. At lower intensities the laser would not break the glass, but neither would it fuse the filament. What type of procedure might be used to fuse the filament with the laser and at the same time avoid breaking the glass? (Adapted from Holyoak & Koh, 1987)

Holyoak and Koh (1987) used the lightbulb problem as the test problem and the radiation problem as the source problem. Participants in one group were taught about the radiation problem and its solution in an introductory psychology class, just prior to being given the lightbulb problem. Participants in the control group did not know about the radiation problem. The result was that 81 percent of participants who knew about the radiation problem solved the lightbulb problem, but only 10 percent of the participants in the control group solved it. Holyoak and Koh hypothesized that this excellent transfer from the radiation problem to the lightbulb problem occurred because of the high surface similarity between lasers (lightbulb problem) and rays (radiation problem).

Having determined that similar *surface features* enhance analogical transfer, Holyoak and Koh did another experiment in which they investigated the effect of varying the *structure* of the problem. In this experiment they used the lightbulb problem as the source problem and the radiation problem as the target problem. They presented two versions of a lightbulb story. Both versions began with a first paragraph of the lightbulb problem above, and then the two versions were created by adding one of the following endings:

Fragile-Glass Version

(Begins with the first paragraph of the lightbulb problem above.)

However, a high-intensity laser beam would also break the fragile glass surrounding the filament. At lower intensities the laser would not break the glass, but neither would it fuse the filament. So it seemed that the lightbulb could not be repaired.

Ruth was about to give up when she had an idea. She placed several lasers in a circle around the lightbulb and administered low-intensity laser beams from several directions all at once. The beams all converged on the filament, where their combined effect was enough to fuse it. Because each spot on the surrounding glass received only a low-intensity beam from each laser, the glass was left intact.

Insufficient-Intensity Version

(Begins with the first paragraph of the lightbulb problem.)

However, the laser generated only low-intensity beams that were not strong enough to fuse the filament. She needed a much more intense laser beam. So it seemed that the lightbulb could not be repaired.

Ruth was about to give up when she had an idea. She placed several lasers in a circle around the lightbulb and administered low-intensity laser beams from several directions all at once. The beams all converged on the filament, where their combined effect was enough to fuse it.

One group of participants read the fragile-glass version of the story, and another group read the insufficient-intensity version, and then both groups were presented with the radiation problem to solve. The result was that 69 percent of participants in the fragile-glass group solved the radiation problem, but only 33 percent in the insufficient-intensity group solved the problem. In this experiment the crucial surface features of both stories was the same (a light bulb with a broken filament). However, the structure of the fragile-glass version of the story was similar to the structure of the radiation problem (both involved the principle of needing high-intensity radiation to fix something that was surrounded by material that could be damaged by a high-intensity beam). In contrast, the structure of the insufficient-intensity version was different, and therefore participants were less likely to make the connection between the lightbulb story and radiation problem.

All of these experiments taken together show that transfer is aided by making surface features more similar and by making structural features more obvious. But what about situations in which structural similarities are not as obvious as in the lightbulb and radiation problems? One way to help people notice structural similarities is by a training procedure called *analogical encoding*.

Analogical Encoding

Dedre Gentner and coworkers (2003) have shown that it is possible to get people to discover similar structural features, by using a technique called **analogical encoding** in which participants compare two cases that illustrate a principle. The idea behind analogical encoding is that when learners compare cases, they become more likely to see the underlying structure.

Gentner's experiment involved a problem in negotiation. In the first part of the experiment participants were taught about the negotiation strategies of *trade-off* and *contingency*. The strategy of trade-off is illustrated by a story about two sisters quarreling over an orange. Eventually they decide to compromise by cutting the orange in half. However, later they realize that one wanted just the juice and the other wanted just the peel, so another solution would be for one sister to receive the juice, and the other the peel. The trade-off between juice and peel is a better solution than the compromise solution because both sisters get what they wanted. (Story attributed to management consultant Mary Parker Follet in Gentner et al., 2003).

The strategy of contingency is illustrated by a situation in which an author wants 18 percent royalties, but the publisher wants to pay only 12 percent. The compromise solution would be halfway between, at 15 percent. The contingent solution would be to tie royalties to sales, so that the rate would be 12 percent if sales are low, but would increase if sales rise to higher levels.

After familiarizing participants with these negotiating strategies, one group of participants received two sample cases, both of which described trade-off solutions to the two different problems. The participants' task was to compare the two examples involving the trade-off principle to arrive at a successful negotiation. Another group did the

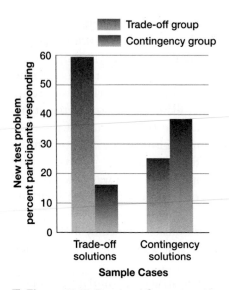

Legend:
- Trade-off group
- Contingency group

New test problem percent participants responding (y-axis: 0, 10, 20, 30, 40, 50, 60)

Sample Cases (x-axis): Trade-off solutions, Contingency solutions

■ **Figure 11.17** Results of Gentner et al.'s (2003) study of negotiating strategies. In the sample case, participants who had compared trade-off examples were more apt to find trade-off solutions, whereas those who had compared contingency examples were more apt to find contingency solutions. (Based on data in Gentner et al., 2003.)

same thing, but their examples involved comparing two examples involving the contingency principle. Then both groups were given a new case, which potentially could be solved by either negotiating principle.

The results of this experiment are shown in Figure 11.17. When presented with the new test problem, participants who had compared the sample cases tended to use the negotiating strategy that was emphasized in the sample cases. Gentner concluded from these results that having people compare source stories is an effective way to get them to pay attention to structural features that enhance their ability to solve other problems.

Analogy in the Real World

So far, our examples of analogy problems have involved laboratory research. But what about the use of analogy in the real world? Based on comparisons of analogical reasoning in the real world and in laboratory experiments, Kevin Dunbar (2001) has posed the **analogical paradox**—participants in psychological experiments tend to focus on surface features in analogy problems, whereas people in the real world frequently use deeper, more structural features. Dunbar reached his conclusion that people in real-world situations use analogy effectively, by using a technique called in-vivo research.

◆◇ Method

In-vivo Problem-Solving Research

In-vivo problem-solving research is a method in which people are observed to determine how they solve problems in real-world situations. This technique has been used to study the use of analogy in a number of different settings, such as laboratory meetings of a university research group, and design brainstorming sessions in an industrial research and development department. Discussions recorded during these meetings are analyzed for statements indicating that analogy is being used to help solve a problem. The advantage of the in-vivo approach is that it captures thinking in naturalistic settings. A disadvantage is that it is time-consuming and, like most observational research, it is difficult to isolate and control specific variables. ◆

When Dunbar and coworkers (Dunbar, 1999; Dunbar & Blanchette, 2001) videotaped molecular biologists and immunologists during their lab meetings, they found that researchers used analogies from 3 to 15 times in a 1-hour laboratory meeting. An example of an analogy from these laboratory meetings is the statement, "If *E. coli* works like this, maybe your gene is doing the same thing." Similarly, when Bo Christensen and Christian Schunn (2007) used the in-vivo method to record meetings of design engineers who were creating new plastic products for medical applications, they found that the engineers proposed an analogy about every 5 minutes. Thus, analogies play an important role in both solving scientific problems and in designing new products. When we discuss creativity later in this chapter, we will describe a famous example of how analogical thinking led to the development of a well-known product.

Although we understand some of the mental processes that occur as a person works toward the solution to a problem, what actually happens is still somewhat mysterious. We do know, however, that one factor that can sometimes make problem solving easier is practice or training. Some people can become very good at solving certain kinds of problems because they become experts in an area. We will now consider what it means to be an expert and how being an expert affects problem solving.

How Experts Solve Problems

Experts are people who, by devoting a large amount of time to learning about a field and practicing the application of that learning, have become acknowledged as being extremely knowledgeable or skilled in the particular field. For example, by spending 10,000–20,000 hours playing and studying chess, some chess players have reached the rank of grand master (Chase & Simon, 1973a, 1973b). Not surprisingly, experts tend to be better than nonexperts at solving problems in their field. Research on the nature of expertise has focused on determining differences between the way experts and nonexperts go about solving problems.

Some Differences Between How Experts and Novices Solve Problems

Experts in a particular field usually solve problems faster with a higher success rate than do novices (people who are beginners or who have not had the extensive training of experts; Chi et al., 1982; Larkin et al., 1980). But what is behind this faster speed and greater success? Are experts smarter than novices? Are they better at reasoning in general? Do they approach problems in a different way? Cognitive psychologists have answered these questions by comparing the performance and methods of experts and novices, and have reached the following conclusions.

Experts Possess More Knowledge About Their Fields In Chapter 5 we discussed Chase and Simon's (1973a, 1973b) research on how well chess masters and novices can reproduce positions on a chessboard that they have seen briefly. The results showed that experts excelled at this task when the chess pieces were arranged in actual game positions, but were no better than novices when the pieces were arranged randomly (see Figure 5.9). The reason for the experts' good performance for actual positions is that the chess masters were able to recognize specific arrangements of pieces from actual game positions. A chess master has about 50,000 patterns in his or her memory, compared to 1,000 patterns for a good player and few or none for a poor player (Bedard & Chi, 1992). But what is important for the purposes of problem solving is not just that the expert's mind contains lots of knowledge, but that this knowledge is *organized* so it can be accessed when needed to work on a problem.

Experts' Knowledge Is Organized Differently From Novices' The difference in organization between experts and novices is illustrated by an experiment by Michelene Chi and coworkers (1982; also see Chi et al., 1981). They presented 24 physics problems to a group of experts (physics professors) and a group of novices (students with one semester of physics) and asked them to sort the problems into groups based on their similarities. Figure 11.18 shows diagrams of problems that were grouped together by an expert and by a novice.

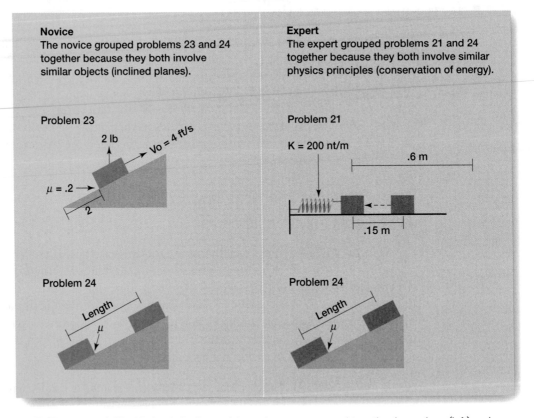

■ **Figure 11.18** The kinds of physics problems that were grouped together by novices (left) and experts (right; Chi et al., 1981).

We don't need a statement of the actual problems to see from the diagrams that the novice sorted the problems based on surface characteristics such as how similar the *objects* in the problem were. Thus, two problems that included inclined planes were grouped together, even though the physical principles involved in the problems were quite different.

The expert, in contrast, sorted problems based on structural features, such as general principles of physics. The expert perceived two problems as similar because they both involved the principle of conservation of energy, even though the diagrams indicate that one problem involved a spring and another an inclined plane. Thus, novices categorized problems based on their *surface features* (what the objects looked like) and the experts categorized them based on their *deep structure* (the underlying principles involved). Experts' ability to organize knowledge has been found to be important not only for chess masters and physics experts, but for experts in many other fields as well (Egan & Schwartz, 1979; Reitman, 1976).

Experts Spend More Time Analyzing Problems Experts often get off to what appears to be a slow start on a problem because they spend time trying to understand the problem, rather than immediately trying to solve it (Lesgold, 1988). Although this may slow them down at the beginning, this strategy usually pays off in a more effective approach to the problem.

Experts Are Often No Better Than Novices When Given Problems Outside of Their Field When James Voss and coworkers (1983) posed a real-world problem involving Soviet agriculture to expert political scientists, expert chemists, and novice political scientists, they found that the expert political scientists performed best and that the expert chemists performed as poorly as the novice political scientists. In general, experts are experts only within their own field and perform like anyone else outside of their field (Bedard & Chi, 1992). This makes sense when we remember that the superior performance of experts occurs largely because they possess a larger and better organized store of knowledge about their specific field.

Before leaving our discussion of expertise, we should note that being an expert is not always an advantage. One disadvantage to being an expert is that knowing about the established facts and theories in a field may make experts less likely to be open to new ways of looking at problems. This may be why younger and less experienced scientists in a field are often the ones responsible for revolutionary discoveries (Kuhn, 1970; Simonton, 1984). In line with this, it has been suggested that one situation in which being an expert would be a disadvantage is when solving a problem that involves flexible thinking, that might involve rejecting the usual procedures for solving the problem in favor of other procedures that might not normally be used (Frensch & Sternberg, 1989).

Creative Problem Solving

There's a story about a physics student who, in answer to the exam question "Describe how the height of a building can be measured using a barometer," wrote "attach the barometer to a string and lower it from the top of the building. The length of string needed to lower the barometer to the ground indicates the height of the building." The professor was looking for an answer that involved measuring barometric pressure on the ground and on top of the building, using principles learned in class. He therefore gave the student a zero for his answer.

The student protested the grade, so the case was given to another professor, who asked the student to provide an answer that would demonstrate his knowledge of physics. The student's answer was that the barometer could be dropped from the roof measuring how long it took to hit the ground. Using a formula involving the gravitational constant it would be possible to determine how far the barometer fell. The student was awarded full credit for that answer, and then, with a little prompting from the appeals professor, provided these additional answers:

- Put the barometer in the sun and measure the length of its shadow and the length of the building's shadow. The height of the building could be determined using proportions.
- Give the building superintendent the barometer in exchange for information about the height of the building.

Upon hearing these answers, the appeals professor was amazed, and asked the student whether he had known the right answer all along. The student replied that he did, but was tired of just repeating back information to get a good grade (Lubart & Mouchiroud, 2003).

There are a number of points to this story, one of which is that sometimes being too creative can get you into trouble. But the main point is that most people would agree that this student's answers to the professor's question, although perhaps not what the professor was looking for, surely qualified as being creative. The definition of creativity is hard to pin down because many different definitions have been offered, but one aspect of creativity is that it involves innovative thinking, generating novel ideas, or making new connections between existing ideas to create something new (Csikszentmihalyi, 1996; Ward et al., 1995, 1997).

Creativity is often associated with **divergent thinking**—thinking that is open-ended and for which there are a large number of potential "solutions" and no "correct" answer (although some proposals might work better than others; see Guilford, 1956; Ward et al., 1997). Divergent thinking can be contrasted with **convergent thinking**, which is thinking that works toward finding a solution to a specific problem that usually has a correct answer. In this case, thinking *converges* onto the correct answer. Divergent thinking is most closely associated with ill-defined problems and convergent thinking with well-defined problems (see page 396).

Although creativity is highly valued in our society and has been responsible for many inventions and scientific discoveries, we have only a limited understanding of the processes involved in creativity. We do know, however, that some of the principles we have discussed with regard to problem solving in general also operate during the creative process.

In our earlier discussion of Gestalt psychologists' research on obstacles to problem solving, we discussed fixation. An example of how fixation almost derailed a promising project occurred when Sony temporarily abandoned work on music CDs in the mid-1970s because 18 hours of music on a CD was not considered commercially viable. Their problem was that they were fixated on the current way of recording music by taking as their starting point the 12-inch LP record. Once they overcame that fixation and decided that CDs could be smaller, they returned to the project and revolutionized the music industry (Ward, 2004).

David Jansson and Steven Smith (1991) studied the effect of fixation on creative design by presenting engineering design students with design problems and telling them to generate as many designs as possible in 45 minutes. One of the problems was to design an inexpensive, spill-proof coffee cup. It was specified that the design could not include a straw or mouthpiece. Half the students were assigned to the "fixation group" and were presented with a sample design like the one in Figure 11.19a, which they were told illustrated what *not* to do. Notice that this sample design includes a mouthpiece and straw—two features specifically forbidden by the design specifications. Another group of students, the control group, was given the same task and specification, but did not see a sample design.

The average number of designs per person was approximately the same for the two groups, but the fixation group's designs included many more instances of cups with straws and mouthpieces (Figure 11.19b). Apparently, they were influenced by the sample design, even though they were told not to include straws or mouthpieces. This effect, which Jansson and Smith call **design fixation**, is analogous to the Gestalt psychologists' demonstrations of how fixation can inhibit problem solving (see page 401).

Another carryover from our discussion of problem solving to creativity is the process of analogical thinking. A famous example is the story of George de Mestral, who in 1948 went for a nature hike with his dog and returned home with burrs covering his pants and the dog's fur. To discover why the burrs were clinging so tenaciously, de Mestral inspected the burrs under a microscope. What he saw was many tiny hooklike structures, which led him to design a fabric fastener with many small hooks on one side and soft loops on the other side. In 1955 he patented his design and called it Velcro!

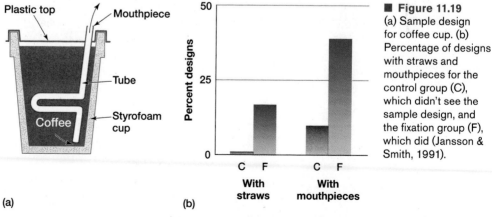

■ Figure 11.19 (a) Sample design for coffee cup. (b) Percentage of designs with straws and mouthpieces for the control group (C), which didn't see the sample design, and the fixation group (F), which did (Jansson & Smith, 1991).

This story illustrates not only how analogy stimulated a new invention but that coming up with the initial idea is often just the beginning of the creative process. It took de Mestral 7 years of trial and error to transform his innovative insight into a marketable product. Creativity therefore involves having unique insights and also being able to follow through to transform that insight into a product—be it a work of art, an idea for a scientific experiment, or a commercially viable invention.

Although de Mestral was a particularly creative individual, you don't have to be a famous inventor to be creative. Cognitive psychologist Ronald Finke developed **creative cognition**, which is a technique to train people to think creatively. The following demonstration illustrates Finke's technique.

Demonstration

Creating an Object

Figure 11.20 shows 15 object parts and their names. Close your eyes and touch the page three times, in order to randomly pick three of these object parts. After reading these instructions, take 1 minute to construct a new object using these three parts. The object

■ **Figure 11.20** Objects used by Finke (1990, 1995). See text for instructions. (Reprinted from R. A. Finke, "Creative Insight and Preinventive Forms," from *The Nature of Insight*, by R. J. Sternberg & J. E. Davidson, Eds., pp. 255–280, Figure 8.1. Copyright © 1995 with permission from the MIT Press.)

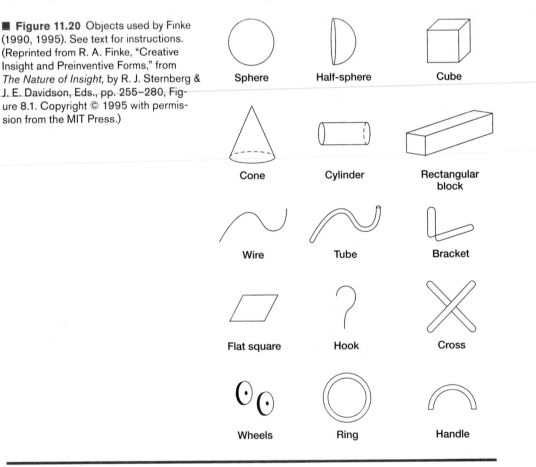

should be interesting-looking and possibly useful, but try to avoid making your object correspond to a familiar object, and don't worry what it might be used for. You can vary the size, position, orientation, and material of the parts, as long as you don't alter the basic shape (except for the wire and the tube, which can be bent). Once you come up with something in your mind, draw a picture of it. ❧

This exercise is patterned after one devised by Ronald Finke (1990, 1995), who randomly selected three of the object parts from Figure 11.20 for his participants. After the participants had created an object, they were provided with the name of one of the object categories from Table 11.1 and were given 1 minute to interpret their object. For example, if the category was tools and utensils, the person had to interpret their form as a screwdriver, a spoon, or some other tool or utensil. To do this for your form, pick a category, and then decide what your object could be used for and describe how it functions. Figure 11.21 shows how a single form that was constructed from the half-sphere, wire, and handle could be interpreted in terms of each of the eight categories in Table 11.1.

Finke called these "inventions" *preinventive forms* because they are ideas that precede the creation of a finished creative product. Just as it took de Mestral years to develop Velcro after his initial insight, preinventive forms need to be developed further before becoming useful "inventions."

In an experiment in which participants created 360 objects, a panel of judges rated 120 of these objects as being "practical inventions" (the objects received high ratings for "practicality") and rated 65 as "creative inventions" (they received high ratings for both practicality and originality; Finke, 1990, 1995). Remarkably, Finke's participants had received no training or practice, were not preselected for "creativity," and were not even told that they were expected to be creative.

Finke demonstrated not only that you don't have to be an "inventor" to be creative, but also that many of the processes that occur during creative cognition are similar to

Table 11.1 Object Categories in Preinventive Form Studies

Category	Examples
(a) Furniture	Chairs, tables, lamps
(b) Personal items	Jewelry, glasses
(c) Scientific instruments	Measuring devices
(d) Appliances	Washing machines, toasters
(e) Transportation	Cars, boats
(f) Tools and utensils	Screwdrivers, spoons
(g) Toys and games	Baseball bats, dolls
(h) Weapons	Guns, missiles

Adapted from Finke, 1995.

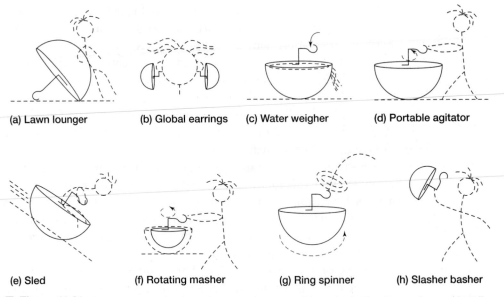

(a) Lawn lounger   (b) Global earrings   (c) Water weigher   (d) Portable agitator

(e) Sled   (f) Rotating masher   (g) Ring spinner   (h) Slasher basher

■ **Figure 11.21** How a preinventive form that was constructed from the half-sphere, wire, and handle can be interpreted in terms of each of the eight categories in Table 11.1. (Reprinted from R. A. Finke, "Creative Insight and Preinventive Forms," from *The Nature of Insight,* by R. J. Sternberg & J. E. Davidson, Eds., pp. 255–280, Figure 8.6. Copyright © 1995 with permission from the MIT Press.)

cognitive process from other areas of cognitive psychology. For example, Finke found that people were more likely to come up with creative uses for preinventive objects that they had created themselves than for objects created by other people. This occurred even though participants were instructed not to consider uses for the forms as they were creating them. This result is similar to the generation effect we discussed in Chapter 6—people remember material better when they generate it themselves (page 204). This advantage for self-generated material also occurs for retrieval cues (page 217).

Another relevant cognitive principle is the idea that fixations can inhibit problem solving. Having participants combine objects rapidly and without reference to uses lessens the chance that fixations, caused by prior experience, will inhibit creativity. Although there is certainly something special about creativity, it appears we can understand some aspects of creativity in terms of general cognitive principles.

Something to Consider

Sleep Inspires Insight

Solving a problem can often involve insight. In fact, there is a great deal of anecdotal evidence for insight occurring after a night's sleep: A person thinks about a problem during the day without solving it, then "sleeps on it" and wakes up the next morning and solves the problem. Along with these reports of insightful solutions after a night's sleep are the re-

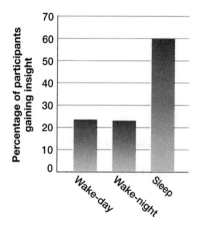

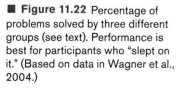

■ **Figure 11.22** Percentage of problems solved by three different groups (see text). Performance is best for participants who "slept on it." (Based on data in Wagner et al., 2004.)

sults of animal studies that show that neural representations of stimulus-response connections, which were acquired during training when the animal was awake, are reactivated when the animal is sleeping (Pavlides & Winston, 1989; Wilson & McNaughton, 1994).

To test the idea that sleep can enhance the possibility of insight, Ullrich Wagner and coworkers (2004) presented a problem to participants that involved discovering a rule that governed the way strings of numbers, which changed from trial to trial, were constructed. During the initial training, participants were familiarized with the problem and were given practice trials, but never became aware of the rule. After the training period participants were divided into three groups. Each group took a break from working on the problem, with the breaks being structured as follows: (1) sleep group, slept for 8 hours; (2) night wakefulness group, remained awake at night for 8 hours; (3) daytime wakefulness group, remained awake during the day for 8 hours.

The result of this experiment, shown in Figure 11.22, is that participants benefited from an 8-hour interval only when the interval was spent sleeping. Wagner concluded from this result that sleep facilitates discovering the hidden structure needed to solve the problem.

We can understand how this might occur by returning to the principle of reactivation we considered in Chapter 6 (see page 211). Remember that reactivation occurs when information in the hippocampus is played back to the cortex during the process of consolidation. This process of replaying hippocampal-cortical activation strengthens memory and also triggers mental restructuring, which could lead to insight. We don't know whether this is what was occurring in Wagner's experiment, but because both consolidation and insight are enhanced by sleep, that raises the possibility that both may involve similar mechanisms.

Whatever the mechanism is behind Wagner's result, the fact that "sleep inspires insight" is yet another piece of evidence supporting the idea that one of the most effective breaks you can take from studying involves going to sleep. Not only does sleep have a restorative effect that improves your ability to concentrate and pay attention, but it helps consolidate what you were studying before you went to sleep.

Test Yourself 11.2

1. What is the basic idea behind analogical problem solving? How effective is it to present a source problem and then the target problem, without indicating that the source problem is related to the target problem?

2. What are the three steps in the process of analogical problem solving? Which of the steps appears to be the most difficult to achieve?

3. How do the surface features and structural features of problems influence a person's ability to make effective use of analogies in problem solving? Describe experiments

relevant to this question, and also techniques that have been used to improve analogical problem solving.

4. What is the analogical paradox? How has analogical problem solving been studied in the real world?

5. What is an expert? What are some differences between the way experts and nonexperts go about solving problems? How good are experts at solving problems outside of their field?

6. What is convergent thinking? What is divergent thinking? How are these two types of thinking related to creativity? Describe experiments that have shown (a) how fixation can affect creativity; (b) de Mestral's use of analogy to invent Velcro; and (c) Finke's "creative cognition" procedure.

7. What is the evidence that "sleep inspires insight"?

Chapter Summary

1. A problem occurs when there is an obstacle between a present state and a goal, and it is not immediately obvious how to get around the obstacle.

2. The Gestalt psychologists focused on how people represent a problem in their mind. They devised a number of problems to illustrate how solving a problem involves a restructuring of this representation and to demonstrate factors that pose obstacles to problem solving.

3. The Gestalt psychologists introduced the idea that reorganization is associated with insight—a sudden realization of a problem's solution. Insight has been demonstrated experimentally by tracking how close people feel they are to solving "insight" and "noninsight" problems.

4. Functional fixedness is an obstacle to problem solving that is illustrated by Duncker's candle problem and Maier's two-string problem. Situationally produced mental set is illustrated by Luchins's water-jug problem.

5. Alan Newell and Herbert Simon were early proponents of the information-processing approach to problem solving. They saw problem solving as the searching of a problem space to find the path between the statement of the problem (the initial state) and the solution to the problem (the goal state). This search is governed by operators and is usually accomplished by setting subgoals. The Tower of Hanoi problem has been used to illustrate this process.

6. The acrobat problem and the reverse acrobat problem illustrate that how the problem is stated can influence problem difficulty. Research on the mutilated-checkerboard problem also illustrates the importance of how a problem is stated.

7. Newell and Simon developed the technique of think-aloud protocols to study participants' thought process as they are solving a problem.

8. Analogical problem solving occurs when experience with a previously solved source problem or a source story is used to help solve a new target problem. Research involving Duncker's radiation problem has shown that even when people are exposed

to analogous source problems or stories, most people do not make the connection between the source problem or story and the target problem.

9. Analogical problem solving is facilitated by hints regarding the relevance of the source problem, when the source and target problems have similar surface features, and when structural features are made more obvious. Analogical encoding is a process that helps people discover similar structural features.

10. The analogical paradox is that participants in psychological experiments tend to focus on surface features in analogy problems, whereas people in the real world frequently focus on deeper, more structural features. In-vivo problem-solving research has shown that analogical problem solving is often used in real-world settings.

11. Experts are better than novices at solving problems in their field of expertise. They have more knowledge of the field, organize this knowledge based more on deep structure than on surface features, and spend more time analyzing a problem when it is first presented.

12. Creative problem solving is associated with divergent thinking rather than with convergent thinking. We have only a limited knowledge of the processes involved in creative problem solving and creativity in general. There is evidence that fixation can inhibit creative problem solving, and that using analogical thinking can enhance it. A technique called creative cognition has been used to train people to think creatively.

13. There is evidence that sleep enhances insightful problem solving. This probably involves mental restructuring triggered by a reactivation process like the one involved in memory consolidation.

Think About It

1. Pick a problem you have had to deal with, and analyze the process of solving it into subgoals, as is done in means-end analysis.

2. Have you ever experienced a situation in which you were trying to solve a problem, but stopped working on it because you couldn't come up with the answer? Then, after a while, when you returned to the problem, you got the answer right away? What do you think might be behind this process?

3. On August 14, 2003, a power failure caused millions of people in the northeast and midwest United States and in eastern Canada to lose their electricity. A few days later, after most people had their electricity restored, experts still did not know why the power failure occurred and said it would take weeks to determine the cause. Imagine that you are a member of a special commission that has the task of solving this problem, or some other major problem. How could the processes described in this chapter be applied to finding a solution? What would the shortcomings of these processes be for solving this kind of problem?

4. Think of some examples of situations in which you overcame functional fixedness by finding a new use for an object.

1. Incubation and creative problem solving. People often report that they are able to solve a problem by taking a break from working on it and then coming back to it later. This effect, which is called incubation, can play a role in creative problem solving.

Dodds, R. A., Smith, S. M., & Ward, T. B. (2002). The use of environmental cues during incubation. *Creativity Research Journal, 14,* 287–304.

2. Cognition, creativity, and entrepreneurship. How do entrepreneurs come up with novel and useful ideas for business ventures? Some answers to this question can be found in the results of cognitive research.

Ward, T. B. (2004). Cognition, creativity and entrepreneurship. *Journal of Business Venturing, 19,* 173–188.

Baron, R. A., & Ward, T. B. (2004). Expanding entrepreneurial cognition's toolbox: Potential contributions from the field of cognitive science. *Entrepreneurship Theory and Practice, 28,* 553–573.

Key Terms

Acrobat problem, 408
Analogical encoding, 419
Analogical paradox, 420
Analogical problem solving, 414
Analogy, 413
Candle problem, 401
Convergent thinking, 424
Creative cognition, 426
Design fixation, 425
Divergent thinking, 424
Experts, 421
Fixation, 401
Functional fixedness, 401
Goal state, 405
Ill-defined problem, 396
Initial state, 405
Insight, 398
Intermediate state, 406
In-vivo problem-solving research, 420

Means-end analysis, 407
Mutilated-checkerboard problem, 409
Operators, 405
Problem, 396
Problem space, 406
Radiation problem, 414
Restructuring, 398
Reverse acrobat problem, 408
Situationally produced mental set, 403
Source problem (or source story), 414
Structural features, 417
Subgoal, 407
Surface features, 417
Target problem, 414
Think-aloud protocol, 411
Tower of Hanoi problem, 405
Two-string problem, 402
Water-jug problem, 403
Well-defined problem, 396

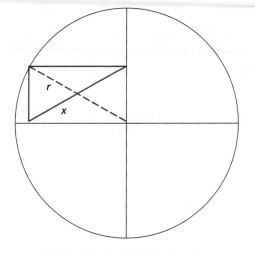

Solution: The length of the line x is r.

■ **Figure 11.23** Solution to the circle problem. Note that the length of x is the same as the radius, r, because x and r are both diagonals of the rectangle.

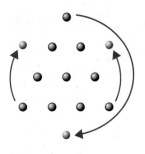

■ **Figure 11.24** Solution to the triangle problem. Arrows indicate movement; colored circles indicate new positions.

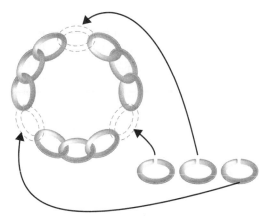

■ **Figure 11.25** Solution to the chain problem. All the links in one chain are cut and separated (3 cuts @ 2 cents = 6 cents). Then each separated link is used to connect the other three pieces and are then closed (3 closings @ 3 cents = 9 cents). Total = 15 cents.

■ **Figure 11.26** Solution to candle problem.

Reasoning and Decision Making

12

Deductive Reasoning: Thinking Categorically
Validity and Truth in Syllogisms
How Well Can People Judge Validity?
Mental Models of Deductive Reasoning

Deductive Reasoning: Thinking Conditionally
Forms of Conditional Syllogisms
Why People Make Errors in Conditional Reasoning:
The Wason Four-Card Problem
Demonstration: Wason Four-Card Problem

Test Yourself 12.1

Inductive Reasoning: Reaching Conclusions
From Evidence
The Nature of Inductive Reasoning
The Availability Heuristic
Demonstration: Which Is More Prevalent?
The Representativeness Heuristic
Demonstration: Judging Occupations
Demonstration: Description of a Person
Demonstration: Male and Female Births
The Confirmation Bias

Culture, Cognition, and Inductive Reasoning
Demonstration: Questions About Animals

Decision Making: Choosing Among Alternatives
The Utility Approach to Decisions
Decisions Can Depend on How Choices Are Presented
Demonstration: What Would You Do?
Justification in Decision Making

The Physiology of Thinking
The Prefrontal Cortex
Neuroeconomics: The Neural Basis of Decision Making

Something to Consider: Is What Is Good
for You Also Good for Me?
Demonstration: A Personal Health Decision

Test Yourself 12.2

Chapter Summary

Think About It

If You Want to Know More

Key Terms

CogLab: Wason Selection Task; Typical Reasoning;
Risky Decisions; Decision Making: Monty Hall

Some Questions We Will Consider

- Do people reason logically, or do they make errors in reasoning? (438)

- How does reasoning operate in the discoveries made by scientists? (454)

- What kinds of reasoning "traps" do people get into when reasoning and when making decisions? (456)

- How does the fact that people sometimes feel a need to justify their decisions affect the process by which they make these decisions? (471)

hat is **reasoning**? One definition is *the process of drawing conclusions* (Leighton, 2004). Another, more specific, definition is *cognitive processes by which people start with information and come to conclusions that go beyond that information* (Kurtz et al., 1999). Whatever definition we use, there is no question that reasoning is relevant to material in most of the chapters in this book. For example, in Chapter 3, on perception, we saw that perceiving an object can involve inference from incomplete information (Figure 12.1); in

COGNITION	REASONING
Chapter 3: Perception "That's an animal lurking."	Animal is inferred from ambiguous shapes.
Chapter 6: Long-Term Memory "I remember, on the first day of class. . . ."	Memories are constructed from what we remember, plus perhaps other information.
Chapter 10: Language "To be or not to be . . ." "I understand what he is saying."	Meaning is created by using knowledge we obtained earlier to help interpret Hamlet's statement.

■ **Figure 12.1** Some examples of processes that fit the definition of "reasoning" that we have encountered in previous chapters.

Chapter 6, on long-term memory, we saw that our memories of events from the past are created by a process of construction, also from incomplete information; and in Chapter 10, on language, we saw how understanding one part of a story can depend on inferences based on what you know has happened before.

As these examples show, reasoning is involved in a large portion of what we study in cognitive psychology. In this chapter we are going to focus on how cognitive psychologists have studied reasoning by focusing on two specific types: deductive reasoning and inductive reasoning. We first consider **deductive reasoning**, which involves sequences of statements called **syllogisms** (Figure 12.2). For example, if we know that at least a C average is required to graduate from State U., and that Josie is graduating from State U., we can logically conclude that Josie had at least a C average.

We then consider **inductive reasoning**, in which we arrive at conclusions about what is *probably* true, based on evidence. Thus, if we know that Richard attended State U. for 4 years and that he is now the vice president of a bank, we might conclude that it is likely that he graduated. Notice, however, that in this example, we cannot say that he *definitely* graduated (maybe he never completed all the requirements, and his father, who is president of the bank, made him a vice president). Thus, we can make *definite* conclusions based on deductive reasoning and *probable* conclusions based on inductive reasoning. Studying both kinds of reasoning provides insights both about how the mind works and about everyday thinking.

■ **Figure 12.2**
Flow diagram for this chapter.

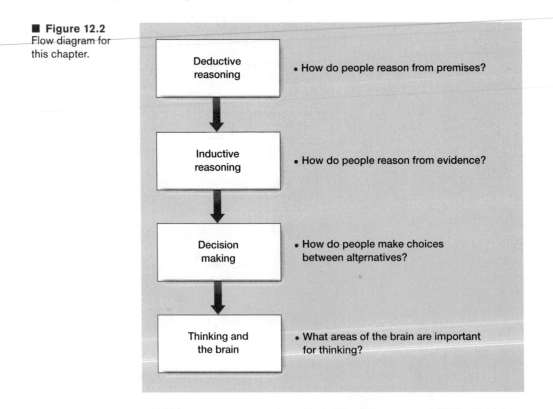

We will also consider **decisions**, which usually involve making choices between alternatives, and which can involve both inductive and deductive reasoning. Finally, we will describe how the brain is involved in thinking.

Deductive Reasoning: Thinking Categorically

Aristotle is considered the father of deductive reasoning because he introduced the basic form of deductive reasoning called the *syllogism*. A syllogism includes two statements, called **premises**, followed by a third statement, called the **conclusion**. We will first consider **categorical syllogisms**, in which the premises and conclusion describe the relation between two categories by using statements that begin with *all*, *no*, or *some*. An example of a categorical syllogism is:

Syllogism (1)	Premise 1:	All birds are animals.
	Premise 2:	All animals eat food.
	Conclusion:	Therefore, all birds eat food.

We will refer to categorical syllogisms as simply *syllogisms* in the discussion that follows.

Validity and Truth in Syllogisms

The word "valid" is often used in everyday conversation to mean something is true or might be true. For example, saying "Susan has a valid point" could mean that what Susan is saying is true, or possibly that it should be considered further. However, when used in conjunction with categorical syllogisms, the term *validity* has a very specific meaning: A syllogism is valid when its conclusion follows *logically* from its two premises. Conversely, the syllogism is invalid when the conclusion does not follow from the premises.

Determining whether a particular syllogism is valid or invalid is not always easy because there are many different combinations of premises and conclusions. Instead of considering all of the possibilities (which would be more appropriate for a course in logic), we will consider a few examples of valid and invalid syllogisms. The syllogism below is the classic example of a valid syllogism. It is called Aristotle's "perfect" syllogism because it was introduced by Aristotle, and it is almost immediately obvious that the conclusion follows from the two premises.

Syllogism (2)	Premise 1:	All A are B.
	Premise 2:	All B are C.
	Conclusion:	Therefore, all A are C.

The conclusion begins with "therefore" to indicate that it follows from the two premises. For brevity, we will omit the *therefore* in the rest of the syllogisms, with the understanding that in valid syllogisms the conclusion always follows from the premises.

Syllogisms can be stated abstractly, in terms of A, B, and C, as in syllogism 2, or more concretely, using meaningful terms, as in syllogism 1. Notice that syllogism 1 has exactly the same form as syllogism 2, with A becoming "bird," B becoming "animals," and C becoming "eat food."

Although syllogisms may seem like an artificial way of studying thinking, the advantage of using them is that we can construct syllogisms that are either **valid** (like syllogisms 1 and 2, in which the conclusion follows logically from the two premises), or not valid (the conclusion does not follow from the premises). These syllogisms can then be used to determine how well people evaluate validity.

A basic principle of deductive reasoning states that if the two premises of a valid syllogism are true, the syllogism's conclusion must be true. Syllogism 1 illustrates this principle because both premises are true, and the syllogism is logically valid. But what happens when one or more of the premises are not true? Consider the following syllogism:

Syllogism (3)   All birds are animals.
                All animals have four legs.
                All birds have four legs.

In this case, the second premise is not true, and the conclusion is not true. Nonetheless, the syllogism is still *valid* because validity depends on the *form* of the syllogism, not its *content*. This apparent conflict between "validity" and "truth" is often confusing, because "valid" is sometimes used interchangeably with "true" in everyday conversation. But remember that with regard to syllogisms, validity refers only to the *logical progression* of the premises and conclusions. As we will see, it is often difficult to separate validity and truth, and this sometimes leads to errors in reasoning. Here is an example of an invalid syllogism that contains premises and a conclusion that could be true.

Syllogism (4)   All of the students are tired.
                Some tired people are irritable.
                Some of the students are irritable.

If you think this syllogism is valid, consider what happens when we replace "students" with "men" and "irritable" with "women."

Syllogism (5)   All of the men are tired.
                Some tired people are women.
                Some of the men are women.

Now it is clear that this syllogism is not valid because even though two premises could be true, it is clear that the conclusion is not. Thus, sometimes it is easy to see that a syllogism is valid, as in syllogism 1, but sometime it isn't easy, as in syllogism 4.

How Well Can People Judge Validity?

Why are psychologists interested in whether people can judge the validity of a syllogism? One reason is to help answer the question, "Do people think logically?" One approach to this question was taken by early philosophers, who said that people's minds work logically, and so if they do make errors in judging validity it means that they were being careless or were not paying attention.

Another approach, which has been adopted by most cognitive psychologists, is that logic is not necessarily built into the human mind, and so if people do make errors, these errors tell us something about how the mind operates. Psychologists are interested in determining what errors occur and what contributes to these errors.

People's performance in judging syllogisms has been determined using two methods: (1) *evaluation:* Present two premises and a conclusion, and ask people to indicate whether the conclusion logically follows from the premises; (2) *production:* Present two premises and ask people to indicate what conclusion logically follows from the premises, or if no conclusion logically follows. We will focus our attention on the evaluation task because researchers have studied deductive reasoning extensively using this method.

When people are tested using the evaluation method, they make errors for all syllogisms except for syllogism 2, and for some syllogisms the error rate can be as high as 70–80 percent (Gilhooly, 1988). The exact error rate depends on a number of factors, including whether the syllogism is stated abstractly (in terms of A's, B's, and C's) or in real-world terms (for example, in terms of birds and animals).

There are many reasons that people make errors in syllogisms. We will focus on two that have been widely studied, the *atmosphere effect* and the *belief bias.* The **atmosphere effect** states that the words *All*, *Some*, and *No* in the premises creates an overall "mood" or "atmosphere" that can influence the evaluation of the conclusion. According to the atmosphere effect, two *All*'s generally suggests an *All* conclusion. One or two *No*'s suggest a *No* conclusion; and one or two *Some*'s suggest a *Some* conclusion. If you look back at the syllogisms we have considered so far, you can see that application of these ideas can lead to a correct evaluation. For example, syllogism 1, which has two *All* premises and an *All* conclusion, is valid. However, for syllogism 4, which has a *Some* premise and a *Some* conclusion, the atmosphere effect would lead to the incorrect conclusion that this invalid syllogism is valid. Thus, just considering the initial terms of premises sometimes leads to correct evaluations of validity, but also leads to errors.

According to the **belief bias**, if a syllogism's conclusion is true or agrees with a person's beliefs, this increases the likelihood that the syllogism will be judged as valid. In addition, if the conclusion is false, this increases the likelihood that the syllogism will be judged as invalid. The belief bias could lead to the erroneous conclusion that syllogism 4 is valid because it seems possible that "Some of the students are irritable" could be true. Here is an example of two invalid syllogisms—both of which have the same form, but which have conclusions that differ in believability.

Syllogism (6)   No police dogs are vicious.
                Some highly trained dogs are vicious.
                Some police dogs are not highly trained.
Syllogism (7)   No addictive drugs are inexpensive.
                Some cigarettes are inexpensive.
                Some addictive drugs are not cigarettes.

When people are presented with these two syllogisms, they are more likely to indicate that syllogism 6 is invalid because they doubt the truth of the conclusion, but will

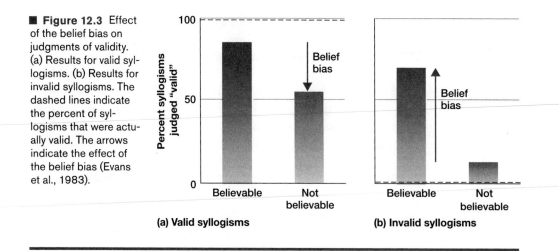

■ **Figure 12.3** Effect of the belief bias on judgments of validity. (a) Results for valid syllogisms. (b) Results for invalid syllogisms. The dashed lines indicate the percent of syllogisms that were actually valid. The arrows indicate the effect of the belief bias (Evans et al., 1983).

often indicate that syllogism 7 is valid because the conclusion is believable (Evans & Feeney, 2004).

The results of a study in which people were presented with valid and invalid syllogisms with both believable and not-believable conclusions are shown in Figure 12.3 (Evans et al., 1983). Figure 12.3a shows the results for valid syllogisms, which, if people judge validity correctly, should result in 100 percent "valid" responses, as indicated by the dashed line. It is no surprise that when the conclusion is believable, 86 percent of the judgments were "valid." However, when the conclusion was not believable, the rates of "valid" responses dropped to 55 percent. This decrease in "valid" responses due to the unbelievability of the conclusion is an example of the belief bias.

Figure 12.3b shows the results for invalid syllogisms (Evans et al., 1983). In this case the belief bias has a huge effect. Even though the syllogism is invalid (so the percent of "valid" responses should be 0, as shown by the dashed line at the bottom of the graph), 70 percent of the responses with believable conclusions were judged to be "valid."

The data in Figure 12.3 indicate that people are influenced by the believability of the conclusion, and therefore they do not always follow the rules of logic.

Mental Models of Deductive Reasoning

We have presented some data on deductive reasoning, but we still haven't considered how people might go about determining whether a syllogism is valid or invalid. One way is to use diagrams, such as Venn diagrams or Euler circles (see If You Want To Know More on page 481 for more about using diagrams to determine syllogism validity). But Phillip Johnson-Laird (1999a) wonders whether people would use these diagram methods if they hadn't been taught about them, and also points out that some of these methods don't work for some of the more complex syllogisms.

So what could people be doing? To begin a discussion of this question, Johnson-Laird (1995) posed a problem similar to this one (try it):

On a pool table there is a black ball directly above the cue ball. The green ball is on the right side of the cue ball, and there is a red ball between them. If I move so the red ball is between me and the black ball, the cue ball is to the _____ of my line of sight.

How did you go about solving this problem? Johnson-Laird points out that the problem can be solved by applying logical rules, but that most people solve it by imagining the way the balls are arranged on the pool table (see Figure 12.21 on page 484). This idea, that people will imagine situations, is the basis of Johnson-Laird's proposal that people use mental models to solve deductive reasoning problems.

A **mental model** is a specific situation that is represented in a person's mind that can be used to help determine the validity of syllogisms in deductive reasoning. The basic principle behind mental models is that people create a model, or representation of the situation, for a reasoning problem. They generate a tentative conclusion based on this model, and then look for exceptions that might falsify the model. If they do find an exception, they modify the model. Eventually, when they can find no more exceptions, they accept their final model.

We can illustrate how this would work for a categorical syllogism by using the following example (from Johnson-Laird, 1999a):

None of the artists are beekeepers.
All of the beekeepers are chemists.
Some of the chemists are not artists.

We will imagine that we are visiting a meeting of the Artists, Beekeepers, and Chemists Society (the ABC Society, for short). We know that everyone who is eligible to be a member must be an artist, a beekeeper, or a chemist, and that they must also abide by the following rules, which correspond to the first two premises of the syllogism above:

No artists can be beekeepers.
All of the beekeepers must be chemists.

Our task is made easier because we can tell what professions people have by what they are wearing. As shown in Figure 12.4, artists are wearing berets, beekeepers are

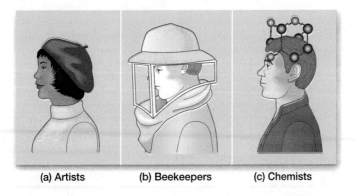

■ **Figure 12.4** Costumes of the Artists, Beekeepers, and Chemists Society (see text).

(a) Artists   (b) Beekeepers   (c) Chemists

wearing protective beekeeper's veils, and chemists are wearing molecule hats. According to the rules, no artists can be beekeepers, so people wearing berets can never wear beekeeper's veils. Also the fact that all beekeepers must be chemists means that everyone wearing a beekeeper's veil must also be wearing a molecule hat. When we meet Alice, we know she is an artist because of her beret, and we notice she is following the rule of not being a beekeeper (Figure 12.5a). Then we meet Beechem, who is wearing a combination beekeeper-molecule getup, in line with the rule that all beekeepers must be chemists (Figure 12.5b). Remember that the conclusion that has been proposed has to do with artists and chemists. Based on what we have seen so far, we can formulate our first model: *No artists are chemists.*

Remember, however, that once we have proposed our first model, we need to look for possible exceptions that would falsify this model. We do this by milling around in the crowd until we meet Cyart, who is wearing a beret and a molecule hat (Figure 12.5c). We note that he is not violating the rules, so we now know that *No artists are chemists* cannot be true, and, thinking back to Beechem, the beekeeper-chemist, we revise our model to *Some of the chemists are not artists.*

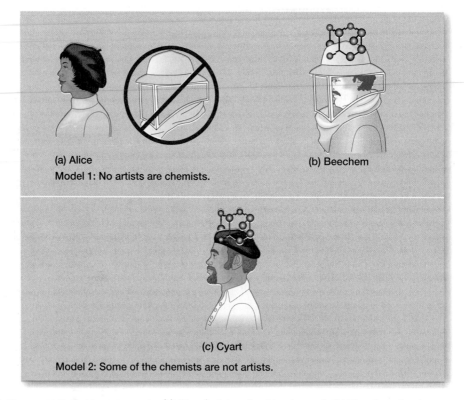

(a) Alice
Model 1: No artists are chemists.

(b) Beechem

(c) Cyart
Model 2: Some of the chemists are not artists.

■ **Figure 12.5** Costumes worn by (a) Alice (artist and not beekeeper); (b) Beechem (beekeeper and chemist); (c) Cyart (artist and chemist).

We keep looking for an exception to this rule, but find only Clara, who is a chemist, which is also allowed by the membership regulations. But this case does not refute our new model, and after more searching, we can't find anyone else in the room whose existence would refute this syllogism's conclusion, so we accept it. This example illustrates the basic principle behind the mental model theory: A conclusion is valid only if it cannot be refuted by any model of the premises.

The mental model theory is attractive because it can be applied without training in the rules of logic, and because it makes predictions that can be tested. For example, the theory predicts that syllogisms that require more models will be more difficult to solve, and this prediction has been confirmed in experiments (Buciarelli & Johnson-Laird, 1999).

There are other proposals about how people might test syllogisms (see Rips, 1995, 2002), but there isn't agreement among researchers regarding the correct approach. We have presented the mental model theory because it is supported by the results of a number of experiments and because it is one of the models that is easiest to apply and explain. However, a number of challenges face researchers who are trying to determine how people evaluate syllogisms. These problems include the fact that people use a variety of different strategies in reasoning, and that some people are much better at solving syllogisms than others (Buciarelli & Johnson-Laird, 1999). Thus, the question of how people go about solving syllogisms remains to be answered.

The categorical syllogisms we have been considering so far have premises and conclusions that begin with *All*, *Some*, or *No*. We will now consider another type of syllogism called *conditional* syllogisms, in which the first premise has the form "If . . . then. . . ."

Deductive Reasoning: Thinking Conditionally

Conditional syllogisms have two premises and a conclusion, like the ones we have been discussing, but the first premise has the form "If . . . then. . . ." This kind of deductive reasoning is common in everyday life. For example, let's say that you lent your friend Steve $20, but he has never paid you back. Knowing Steve, you might say to yourself that you knew this would happen. Stated in the form of a syllogism, your reasoning might look like this: If I lend Steve $20, then I won't get it back. I lent Steve $20. Therefore, I won't get my $20 back.

Forms of Conditional Syllogisms

There are four major types of conditional syllogisms. Each of them is listed in Table 12.1. They are presented in abstract form (p and q) on the left, and in concrete "everyday" form on the right. For conditional syllogisms, the notations p and q are typically used instead of A and B. P is the first, or "If," term, called the **antecedent**, and q is the second, or "then," term, called the **consequent**.

Table 12.1 Four Syllogisms That Begin With the Same First Premise

First premise of all syllogisms:
If *p*, then *q* (abstract version), or
If I study, then I'll get a good grade (concrete example)

Syllogism	Second Premise	Conclusion	Is it Valid?	Performance
Syllogism 1: Affirming the antecedent	*p* (Abstract) I studied (Concrete)	Therefore, *q* Therefore, I'll get a good grade	 Yes	 97%
Syllogism 2: Denying the consequent	Not *q* I didn't get a good grade	Therefore, not *p* Therefore, I didn't study	 Yes	 60%
Syllogism 3: Affirming the consequent	*q* I got a good grade	Therefore, *p* Therefore, I studied	 No	 40%
Syllogism 4: Denying the antecedent	Not *p* I didn't study	Therefore, not *q* Therefore, I didn't get a good grade	 No	 40%

Source: Performance daa from Evans et al. (1993).

Syllogisms 1 and 2 are valid. Syllogism 1 is called **affirming the antecedent** because the antecedent, *p*, or *studying*, in the second premise is affirmed. Syllogism 2 is called **denying the consequent** because the consequent, *q*, or g*etting a good grade*, in the second premise is negated.

Syllogism 3 is called **affirming the consequent**, because *q* is affirmed in the second premise. This conclusion is invalid, because even though you didn't study, it is still possible that you could have received a good grade. Perhaps the exam was easy, or maybe you knew the material because it was about your job experience. If that explanation is not convincing, consider the following syllogism, which has the same form as syllogism 3, with "studying" replaced by "robin" and "good grade" replaced by "bird."

If it's a robin, then it's a bird.
It's a bird.
Therefore, it's a robin.

When stated in this way, it becomes more obvious that the affirming the consequent form of the syllogism is invalid.

Syllogism 4 is called **denying the antecedent**, because *p* is negated (not *p*) in the second premise. As in syllogism 3, you can probably think of situations that would contradict the conclusion, in which a good grade was received even though the person didn't study. Again, this fact that this syllogism is invalid becomes more obvious when restated in terms of birds and robins:

If it is a robin, then it's a bird.
It's not a robin.
Therefore, it's not a bird.

How well can people judge the validity of these syllogisms? The results of many experiments, shown in the far right column of Table 12.1, indicate that most people (close to 100 percent in most experiments) correctly judge that syllogism 1 is valid, but that performance is lower on syllogism 2, which is also valid, and 3 and 4, which are not valid. These percentages are the average results from many studies in which the letters p and q were used for the antecedent and the consequent. We have already seen that the ease of determining the validity of conditional syllogisms can be greatly affected by whether the task is stated abstractly (in terms of p's and q's) or concretely (studying and grades; robins and birds). In the next section we will describe a reasoning problem that has been studied using an abstract task and many different forms of real-world tasks.

Why People Make Errors in Conditional Reasoning: The Wason Four-Card Problem

CogLab

Wason Selection Task

If reasoning from conditional syllogisms depended only on applying rules of formal logic, then it wouldn't matter whether the syllogism was stated in terms of abstract symbols, such as p's and q's, or in terms of real-world items, such as studying or robins. However, we know that people are often better at judging the validity of syllogisms when real-world items are substituted for abstract symbols, and we also know that real-world items can sometimes lead to errors, as when people are influenced by the belief bias. Evidence for the effect of using real-world items in a conditional-reasoning problem is provided by a series of experiments involving the **Wason four-card problem**. Try this task in the following demonstration.

Demonstration

Wason Four-Card Problem

Four cards are shown in Figure 12.6. There is a letter on one side of each card and a number on the other side. Your task is to indicate the *minimum* number of cards you would need to turn over to test the following rule: *If there is a vowel on one side, then there is an even number on the other side.*

■ **Figure 12.6** The Wason four-card problem (Wason, 1966). Follow the directions in the demonstration and try this problem.

If vowel, then even number.

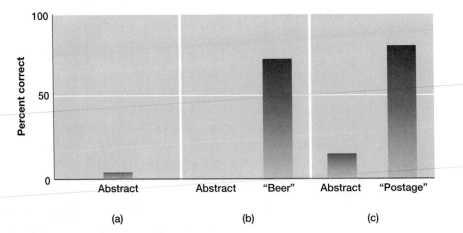

■ **Figure 12.7** Performance on different versions of the four-card problem. (a) Abstract version in Figure 12.6. (b) Abstract version and the beer/drinking-age version in Figure 12.8. (c) Abstract version and the postage version in Figure 12.9. Performance is better on concrete versions of the problem.

When Wason (1966) posed this task (which we will call the abstract task from now on), 53 percent of his participants indicated that the E must be turned over. This is correct because turning over the E directly tests the rule. (If there is an E, then there must be an even number, so if there is an odd number on the other side, this would prove the rule to be false.) However, another card needs to be turned over to fully test the rule. Forty-six percent of Wason's participants indicated that in addition to the E, the 4 would need to be turned over. The problem with this answer is that if a vowel is on the other side of the card, this is consistent with the rule, but if a consonant is on the other side, turning over the 4 tells us nothing about the rule, because having a consonant on one side and a vowel on the other does not violate the rule. As shown in Figure 12.7a, only 4 percent of Wason's participants came up with the correct answer that the card with the 7 also needs to be turned over. Turning over the 7 is important because revealing a vowel would disconfirm the rule.

The key to solving the card problem is to be aware of the **falsification principle**: *To test a rule, it is necessary to look for situations that falsify the rule.* As you can see from Table 12.2, the only two cards that have the potential to achieve this are the E and the 7. Thus, these are the only two cards that need to be turned over to test the rule.

The Role of "Regulations" in the Wason Task The Wason task has generated a great deal of research. One reason for the degree of interest in this problem is because it is a conditional-reasoning task. (Note that the problem is stated as an "If . . . then . . ." statement.) But the main reason researchers are interested in this problem is that they want to know why participants make so many errors.

One way researchers have gone about answering this question is to determine how participants perform when the problem is restated in real-world terms. In one of these

Table 12.2 Outcomes of Turning Over Each Card in the Wason Task

The Rule: If there is a vowel on one side, then there is an even number on the other side.

If turn over . . .	And the result is . . .	Then this _____ the rule.
E	Even	confirms
E	Odd	**falsifies**
K	Even	is irrelevant to*
K	Odd	is irrelevant to
4	Vowel	confirms
4	Consonant	is irrelevant to
7	Vowel	**falsifies**
7	Consonant	is irrelevant to

*This outcome of turning over the card is irrelevant because the rule does not say anything about what should be on the card if a consonant is on one side. Similar reasoning holds for all of the other irrelevant cases.

experiments Richard Griggs and James Cox (1982) used the following version of the problem:

> Four cards are shown in Figure 12.8. Each card has an age on one side and the name of a beverage on the other side. Imagine you are a police officer who is applying the rule "If a person is drinking beer, then he or she must be over 19 years old." (The participants in this experiment were from Florida, where the drinking age was 19 at the time.) Which of the cards in Figure 12.8 must be turned over to determine whether the rule is being followed?

This beer/drinking-age version of Wason's problem is identical to the abstract version except that concrete everyday terms (beer, soda, and ages) are substituted for the letters and numbers. Griggs and Cox found that for this version of the problem, 73 percent of their participants provided the correct response: It is necessary to turn over the "beer" and the "16 years" cards. In contrast, none of their participants answered the ab-

If drinking beer, then over 19 years old.

■ **Figure 12.8** The beer/drinking-age version of the four-card problem (Griggs & Cox, 1982).

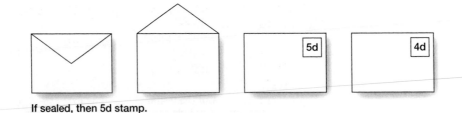

If sealed, then 5d stamp.

■ **Figure 12.9** Postage version of the four-card problem (Johnson-Laird et al., 1972).

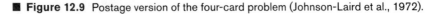

stract task correctly (Figure 12.7b). Why is the concrete task easier than the abstract task? Apparently, being able to relate the beer task to regulations about drinking makes it easier to realize that the "16 years" card must be turned over.

The idea that knowing about regulations helps solve the Wason task has also been demonstrated using the cards in Figure 12.9 and the following instructions:

> Pretend you are a postal worker sorting letters. According to postal regulations, if a letter is sealed, it must have a 5d stamp on it (*d* is pence in Great Britain). Which of the four envelopes in Figure 12.9 would you have to turn over to determine whether the rule is being obeyed?

The answer to the English postal version of the problem is that the sealed envelope and the one with a 4d stamp on it must be turned over to check the rule. When Philip Johnson-Laird and coworkers (1972) presented this problem to English participants who were familiar with an actual postal regulation similar to the one stated in the problem, performance was 81 percent correct, compared to 15 percent for the abstract task (Figure 12.7c). When Griggs and Cox (1982) tested American participants on the postal regulation task, they did not observe the large improvement in performance observed for the English participants. The reason for this result appears to be that the American participants were not familiar with postal regulations that specified different postage for opened and sealed envelopes.

The Role of "Permissions" in the Wason Task Patricia Cheng and Keith Holyoak (1985) took the Wason task a step further by proposing the concept of *pragmatic reasoning schemas*. A **pragmatic reasoning schema** is a way of thinking about cause and effect in the world that is learned as part of experiencing everyday life. One schema that people learn is the **permission schema**, which states that if a person satisfies condition A (such as being the legal age for drinking), then they get to carry out action B (being served alcohol). The permission schema for the drinking problem "If you are 19, then you got to drink beer" is something that most of the participants in this experiment had learned, so they were able to apply that schema to the card task.

This idea that people apply a real-life schema like the permissions schema to the card task makes it easier to understand the difference between the abstract version of the card task and the "drinking beer" or "postal regulation" versions. The abstract task

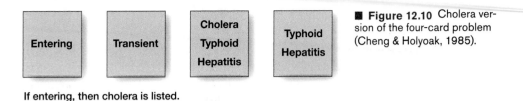

If entering, then cholera is listed.

is set up so that participants approach it as a problem in which their goal is to indicate whether an abstract statement about letters and numbers is true. But the drinking-beer task and postal-regulation tasks are set up so participants approach it as problems in which their goal is to be sure that a person has permission to drink alcohol or mail a letter. Apparently, activating the permission schema helps people to focus attention on the far right card, which participants often ignore for the abstract task.

To test this idea that a permissions schema may be involved in reasoning about the card task, Cheng and Holyoak ran an experiment with two groups of participants who both saw the cards in Figure 12.10. One of the groups was read the following directions:

> You are an immigration officer at the International Airport in Manila, capital of the Philippines. Among the documents you have to check is a sheet called Form H. One side of this form indicates whether the passenger is entering the country or in transit, and the other side of the form lists names of tropical diseases. You have to make sure that if the form says "Entering" on one side, that the other side includes cholera among the list of diseases.* Which of the following forms would you have to turn over to check? Indicate only those that you need to check to be sure. [*The asterisk is explained in the text that follows.]

Sixty-two percent of the participants in this group chose the correct cards ("Entering" and "Typhoid, Hepatitis"). Participants in the other group saw the same cards and heard the same instructions as the first group, but with the following changes: Instead of saying that the form listed tropical diseases, it said that the form listed *inoculations the travelers had received in the past 6 months*. In addition, the following sentence was added where indicated by the asterisk (*): *This is to ensure that entering passengers are protected against the disease*.

The changes in the instructions were calculated to achieve a very important effect: Instead of checking just to see whether the correct diseases are listed on the form, the immigration officer is checking to see whether the travelers have the inoculations necessary to *give them permission* to enter the country. These instructions were intended to activate the participants' permissions schema, and apparently this happened, because 91 percent of the participants in this condition picked the correct cards (Figure 12.11).

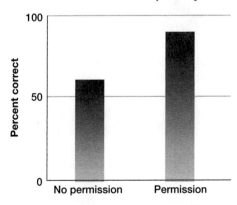

■ **Figure 12.11** Results of Cheng and Holyoak's (1985) experiment that used two versions of the cholera problem. When "permissions" are implied by the instructions, performance is better.

An Evolutionary Approach to the Four-Card Problem One of the things we have learned from our descriptions of cognitive psychology research is that one set of data can be interpreted in different ways by different investigators. We saw this in the case of the misinformation effect in Chapter 7, in which memory errors were caused by presenting misleading postevent information (MPI) after a person witnessed an event. We saw that one group of researchers explained these errors by stating that the MPI distorted existing memories (Loftus, 1993), but that other researchers offered explanations based on the effect of retroactive interference and source monitoring errors (Lindsay, 1990).

Our consideration of the Wason four-card problem now leads us to another controversy, in which different explanations have been offered to explain the results of various experiments. For example, one proposed alternative to a permissions schema is that performance on the Wason task is governed by a built-in cognitive program for detecting cheating. Let's consider the rationale behind this idea.

Leda Cosmides and John Tooby (1992) are among psychologists who have an **evolutionary perspective on cognition**. They argue that we can trace many properties of our minds to the evolutionary principles of natural selection. According to natural selection, adaptive characteristics—characteristics that help a person or animal survive to pass their genes to the next generation—will, over time, become basic characteristics of humans. Charles Darwin originally proposed this theory based on observations of physical characteristics. For example, Darwin observed that birds in a specific area had beaks with shapes adapted to enable them to obtain the food that was available.

Applying this idea to cognition, it follows that a highly adaptive feature of the mind would, through a similar evolutionary process, become a basic characteristic of the mind. One such characteristic, according to the evolutionary approach, is related to **social-exchange theory**, which states that an important aspect of human behavior is the ability for two people to cooperate in a way that is beneficial to both people. Thus, when caveman Morg lends caveman Eng his carving tool in exchange for some food that Eng has brought back from the hunt, both people benefit from the exchange.

Everything works well in social exchange as long as each person is receiving a benefit for whatever he or she is giving up. However, problems arise when someone cheats. Thus, if Morg gives up his carving tool, but Eng fails to give him the food, this does not bode well for Morg. It is essential, therefore, that people be able to detect cheating behavior so they can avoid it. According to the evolutionary approach, people who can do this will have a better chance of surviving, so "detecting cheating" has become a part of the brain's cognitive makeup.

The evolutionary approach proposes that the Wason problem can be understood in terms of cheating. Thus, people do well in the postal version of the four-card problem (Figure 12.9) because they can detect cheaters—someone who mails a letter with incorrect postage. Similarly, people do well in the cholera task (Figure 12.10) because they can detect someone who cheats by entering the country without a cholera shot.

To test the idea that cheating (and not permissions) is the important variable in the four-card problem, Cosmides and Tooby (1992) devised a number of four-card scenarios involving unfamiliar situations. Remember that one idea behind the permissions schema is that people perform well because they are familiar with various rules.

To create unfamiliar situations, Cosmides and Tooby created a number of experiments that took place in a hypothetical culture called the Kulwane. Participants in these experiments read a story about this culture, which led to the conditional statement, "If a man eats cassava root, then he must have a tattoo on his face." Participants saw the following four cards: (1) eats cassava roots; (2) eats molo nuts; (3) tattoo; and (4) no tattoo. Their task was to determine which cards they needed to turn over to determine whether the conditional statement above was being adhered to. This is a situation unfamiliar to the participants, and one in which cheating could occur, because a man who eats the cassava root without a tattoo would be cheating.

Cosmides and Tooby found that participants' performance was high on this task, even though it was unfamiliar. They also ran other experiments in which participants did better for statements that involved cheating than for other statements that could not be interpreted in this way (Cosmides, 1989; also see Gigerenzer & Hug, 1992).

However, in response to this proposal, other researchers have created scenarios that involve unfamiliar permission rules. For example, Ken Manktelow and David Over (1990) tested people using a rule that said, "If you clean up spilt blood, you must wear gloves." Note that this is a "permission" statement that most people have not heard before, and which does not involve cheating. However, stating the problem in this way caused an increase in performance, just like many of the other examples of the Wason task that we have described.

The controversy continues among those who feel permissions are important, those who focus on cheating, and researchers who have proposed other explanations for the results of the Wason task. This is mainly because evidence has been presented for and against every proposed mechanism (Johnson-Laird, 1999b; Manktelow, 1999).

We are left with the important finding that the context within which conditional reasoning occurs makes a big difference. Stating the four-card problem in terms of familiar situations can often generate better reasoning than abstract statements or statements that people cannot relate to. However, familiarity is not always necessary for conditional reasoning (as in the tattoo problem), and situations have also been devised in which people's performance is not improved, even in familiar situations (Evans & Feeney, 2004; Griggs, 1983; Manktelow & Evans, 1979).

Sometimes controversies such as this one are frustrating to read about because, after all, aren't we looking for "answers"? But another way to look at controversies is that they illustrate the complexity of the human mind and the challenge facing cognitive psychologists. Remember that at the beginning of this book, we described an experiment by Donders that involved simply indicating when a light was presented or whether the light was presented on the right or on the left (see Chapter 1, page 6). We described Donders' experiment to illustrate the basic principle that cognitive psychologists must infer the workings of the mind from behavioral observations. It is fitting, therefore, that in this, the last chapter of the book, we are now describing a task that involves mental processes far more complex than judging whether a light has flashed, but which illustrates exactly the same principle—the workings of the mind must be inferred from behavioral observations.

We see in this controversy, about how people deal with the Wason task, how a number of different hypotheses about what is happening in the mind can be plausibly inferred from the same behavioral evidence. Perhaps, in the end, the actual mechanism will be something that has yet to be proposed, or perhaps the mind, in its complexity, has a number of different ways of approaching the Wason task, depending on the situation.

Test Yourself 12.1

1. What is deductive reasoning? What does it mean to say that the conclusion to a syllogism is "valid"? How can a conclusion be valid but not true? True but not valid?
2. How well can people judge the validity of syllogisms? Why are psychologists interested in the errors that people make in judging validity?
3. What is a categorical syllogism, and how do the atmosphere effect and belief bias influence evaluation of categorical syllogisms?
4. What is a mental model for reasoning? Explain how this model can be applied to the Artists, Beekeepers, and Chemists syllogism on page 441.
5. What is a conditional syllogism? Which of the four types of syllogisms described in the chapter are valid, which are not valid, and how well can people judge the validity of each type?
6. What is the Wason four-card problem, and what do the results of experiments that have used abstract and concrete versions of the problem indicate about the roles of (a) concreteness; (b) knowledge of regulations; and (c) permissions schemas in solving this problem?
7. How has the evolutionary approach to cognition been applied to the Wason four-card problem? What can we conclude from all of the experiments on the Wason problem?

Inductive Reasoning: Reaching Conclusions From Evidence

In deductive reasoning, premises are stated as a fact, such as "All robins are birds." However, in inductive reasoning, premises are based on observation of one or more specific cases, and we generalize from these cases to a more general conclusion.

The Nature of Inductive Reasoning

For inductive reasoning, conclusions do not *definitely* follow from premises, and conclusions are *suggested*, with varying degrees of certainty. This is illustrated by these two inductive arguments:

| Observation: | All the crows I've seen in Pittsburgh are black. When I visited my brother in Washington, DC, the crows I saw there were black too. |
| Conclusion: | I think it is a pretty good bet that all crows are black. |

| Observation: | Here in Nashville, the sun has risen every morning. |
| Conclusion: | The sun is going to rise in Nashville tomorrow. |

Notice there is a certain logic to each argument, but the second argument is more convincing than the first. Let's consider some of the things that influence the strength of an inductive argument.

Determining the Strength of an Inductive Argument In evaluating inductive arguments, we do not consider validity, as we did for deductive arguments, but instead we decide how strong the argument is. Strong arguments are more likely to result in conclusions that are true, and weak arguments to result in conclusions that are not as likely to be true. Remember that for inductive arguments we are dealing with what is *probably* true, not what is *definitely* true.

There are a number of factors that can contribute to the strength of an inductive argument. Among them are the following:

- *Representativeness of observations:* How well do the observations about a particular category represent all of the members of that category? Clearly, the crows example suffers from a lack of representativeness because it does not consider crows from other parts of the country. If there are rare blue crows in California, then the conclusion is not true.
- *Number of observations:* The argument about the crows is made stronger by adding the Washington, DC, observations to the Pittsburgh observations. Adding more observations would strengthen it further. The conclusion about the sun rising in Nashville is extremely strong because it is supported by a very large number of observations.
- *Quality of the evidence:* Stronger evidence results in stronger conclusions. For example, although the conclusion that "The sun will rise in Nashville" is extremely strong because of the number of observations, it becomes even stronger when we consider scientific descriptions of how the earth rotates on its axis and revolves around the sun. Thus, adding the observation that "scientific measurements of the rotation of the earth indicate that every time the earth rotates the sun will appear to rise" strengthens the conclusion even further.

Bringing in scientific evidence to support an inductive argument illustrates the connection between inductive and deductive reasoning because the scientific observation about the rotation of the earth can be stated as the following *deductive* syllogism:

If the earth rotates around its axis, then the place where Nashville is located will experience sunrise for each rotation.

The earth rotates on its axis.

Therefore, Nashville will experience sunrise for each rotation.

The possibility of using scientific evidence in both inductive and deductive arguments illustrates that although it is important to distinguish between the two types of reasoning, the borderline between them can sometimes become fuzzy. We will describe the link between inductive and deductive reasoning further as we consider how inductive reasoning is used in science.

Inductive Reasoning in Science   Inductive reasoning is the basic procedure used to make scientific discoveries. The goal in science is to discover something new. To achieve this, scientists often make systematic observations. These observations can include taking a poll about political attitudes, observing social behavior in a shopping mall, or doing a laboratory experiment on the Wason four-card problem. If these observations yield interesting data, these observations can be generalized to a larger population and perhaps be used to create a theory that goes beyond the specific observations.

In most scientific research, and especially in psychology, we base our conclusions on more than one observation. We test a large number of participants and may run an experiment in a number of different ways. Added participants and obtaining similar results in variations of an experiment all strengthen our conclusions. The strength of scientific conclusions also depends on the representativeness of our observations.

An obvious example of the importance of representative observations is determining attitudes by polling. Predicting the presidential election by taking a poll of students in your cognitive psychology class might tell you something about the cognitive psychology class, but would not necessarily provide an accurate prediction of the election results. To make a statement about attitudes in the United States it is necessary to elicit opinions from a representative cross-section of people in the United States. Similarly, conclusions from laboratory experiments in cognitive psychology can be safely generalized only to the population represented in the sample of people who participate in the experiment. Thus, it would be a mistake to say that the results for the beer/drinking-age version of the Wason four-card experiment will necessarily generalize to people in a society in which there are no laws regulating drinking.

Inductive reasoning is used not only to make the jump from specific observations to more general conclusions, but to create hypotheses for further experiments. An example of how inductive reasoning has been used to devise scientific experiments is provided by the way Cheng and Holyoak devised the cholera experiment we described on page 449 (Holyoak, 2003). The first step was to observe that people's performance on the Wason task improves when the task is stated in terms of receiving "permission" to do something, as is the case in the beer/drinking-age and stamp/sealed-envelope versions of the task.

Based on this observation, Cheng and Holyoak reasoned that making people more aware that permissions are involved when they are trying to solve the Wason task should improve their performance. They devised a way to test this idea by creating the scenario for the cholera problem, which included one condition in which permissions were not emphasized and another condition in which they were. We can state the reasoning behind their thinking about this experiment (which, as we have described above, was created using inductive reasoning), by the following *deductive* syllogism:

> If a permissions schema is activated, then performance on the Wason task should improve.
> In this experiment, one of the groups will read a sentence that will activate a permissions schema.
> Therefore, the performance of this group will improve.

As we saw when we described the "cholera" experiment, adding a sentence that was designed to activate a permissions schema did, in fact, increase performance, thereby confirming the "If . . . then . . ." premise of the conditional argument. Thus, inductive reasoning can be used to generate a hypothesis about what might be going on, and deductive reasoning sets forth the rationale of the experiment that is designed to test this hypothesis.

Inductive Reasoning in Everyday Life Inductive reasoning is used not just for creating scientific experiments, but for determining many of the choices we make in everyday life. For example, Sarah has observed, from a course she took with Professor X, that he asked a lot of questions about experimental procedures on his exams. Based on this observation, Sarah concludes that the exam she is about to take in another of Professor X's courses will probably be similar. In another example, Sam has bought merchandise from mail-order company Y before and got good service, so he places another order based on the assumption that he will continue to get good service. Thus, anytime we make a prediction about *what will happen* based on our observations about *what has happened in the past*, we are using inductive reasoning.

It makes sense that we make predictions and choices based on past experience, especially when predictions are based on familiar situations such as studying for an exam or buying merchandise by mail. However, we make so many assumptions about the world, based on past experience, that we are using inductive reasoning constantly, often without even realizing it. For example, did you run a stress test on the chair you are sitting in to be sure it wouldn't collapse when you sat down? Probably not. You assumed, based on your past experience with chairs, that it would not collapse. This kind of inductive reasoning is so automatic that you are not aware that any kind of "reasoning" is happening at all. Think about how time consuming it would be if you had to approach every experience as if you were having it for the first time. Inductive reasoning provides the mechanism for using past experience to guide present behavior.

When people use past experience to guide present behavior, they often use shortcuts to help them reach conclusions rapidly. After all, we don't have the time or energy to stop and gather every bit of information that we need to be 100 percent certain that every conclusion we reach is correct. These shortcuts take the form of heuristics, which are "rules of thumb" that are likely to provide the correct answer to a problem, but which are not foolproof.

Using heuristics may sound familiar because we saw that people use heuristics to help them understand what they are seeing (Chapter 3, page 79) and what a sentence means (Chapter 10, page 373). There are a number of heuristics that people use in reasoning that often lead to the correct conclusion, but that sometimes do not. We will now describe two of these heuristics, the *availability heuristic* and the *representative heuristic*.

The Availability Heuristic

The following demonstration introduces the availability heuristic.

 **Demonstration**

Which Is More Prevalent?

Answer these questions.

- Which is more prevalent, words that begin with the letter *r*, or words in which *r* is the third letter?
- Each item in the following list consists of two different possible causes of death. Your task is to judge, for each pair of cases, which cause of death you consider more likely for people in the United States. Think about this question in this way: Imagine you randomly picked someone in the United States. Will that person be more likely to die next year from cause A or cause B?

Cause A	Cause B	Most likely?
Homicide	Appendicitis	
Auto-train collision	Drowning	
Measles	Smallpox	
Botulism	Asthma	
Asthma	Tornado	
Appendicitis	Pregnancy	

When faced with a choice, we are often guided by what we remember from the past. The **availability heuristic** states that events that are more easily remembered are judged as being more probable than events that are less easily remembered (Tversky & Kahneman, 1973). Consider, for example, the problems we posed in the demonstration. When participants were asked to judge whether there are more words with *r* in the first position or the third, 70 percent stated that there are more words that begin with *r*, even though in reality there are three times more words that have *r* in the third position (Tversky & Kahneman, 1973; but see also Gigerenzer & Todd, 1999).

Figure 12.12 shows the results of experiments in which participants were asked to judge the relative prevalence of various causes of death (Lichtenstein et al., 1978). The height of the bars indicates the percentage of participants who picked the least likely al-

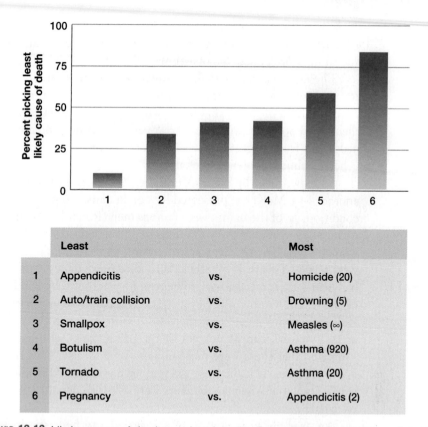

	Least		Most
1	Appendicitis	vs.	Homicide (20)
2	Auto/train collision	vs.	Drowning (5)
3	Smallpox	vs.	Measles (∞)
4	Botulism	vs.	Asthma (920)
5	Tornado	vs.	Asthma (20)
6	Pregnancy	vs.	Appendicitis (2)

■ **Figure 12.12** Likely-causes-of-death experiment results. Pairs of "causes of death" are listed below the graph, with the least likely cause on the left. The number in parentheses on the right indicates how many more times more people were actually killed by the cause on the right. The bars in the graph indicate the number of people who judged the *least likely* alternative in each pair as causing the most deaths. (Adapted from Lichtenstein et al., 1978.)

ternative. The key below the graph indicates the pairs for each bar, with the least likely cause indicated first, followed by the more likely cause. The number in parentheses indicates the relative frequency of the more likely cause compared to the less likely cause. For example, the far left bar indicates that 9 percent of the participants thought it was more likely that a person would die from appendicitis compared to homicide. However, actual mortality data indicate that 20 times more people die from homicide than from appendicitis. Thus, in this case, 9 percent of the participants made an incorrect judgment, but most of the participants made an accurate judgment regarding the most likely cause of death.

For the other causes of death, a substantial proportion of the participants misjudged which cause is more likely. In these cases, large numbers of errors were associated with causes that were publicized by the media. For example, 58 percent thought that more deaths were caused by tornados than by asthma, when in reality, 20 times more people die from asthma than from tornados. Particularly striking is that fact that 41 percent of the participants thought that botulism caused more deaths than asthma, even though 920 times more people die of asthma.

The explanation for these misjudgments appears linked to availability. When you try to think of words that begin with *r* or that have *r* in the third position, it is much easier to think of words that begin with *r* (run, rain, real . . .) than words that have *r* in their third position (word, car, arranged . . .). When someone dies of botulism or tornados it is front-page news, whereas deaths from asthma go virtually unnoticed by the general public (Lichtenstein et al., 1978).

An experiment by Stuart McKelvie (1997) demonstrates the availability heuristic in another way. McKelvie presented lists of 26 names to participants. In the "famous men" condition, 12 of the names were famous men (Ronald Reagan, Mick Jagger) and 14 were nonfamous women. In the "famous women" condition, 12 of the names were famous women (Tina Turner, Beatrix Potter) and 14 were nonfamous men. When participants were asked to estimate whether there were more males or more females in the list they had heard, their answer was influenced by whether they had heard the male-famous list or the female-famous list. Seventy-seven percent of the participants who had heard the male-famous list stated that there were more males in their list (notice that there were actually fewer), and 81 percent of the participants who had heard the female-famous list stated that there were more females in their list. This result is consistent with the availability heuristic, because the famous names would be more easily remembered and would stand out when participants were asked to decide whether there were more male or female names.

An example of operation of the availability heuristic in everyday life is the drop in the number of people flying on commercial airlines that occurred during the year following the 9/11 terrorist attacks. The persistent images of airplanes smashing into the World Trade Center have led many people to avoid air travel in favor of driving even though, according to the National Transportation Safety Board, the fatality rate is about 500 times greater for driving than for flying in a commercial airplane. Although factors other than thinking about safety are undoubtedly involved in the drop in air travel, it is likely that the ready availability of images and descriptions of this disaster is one of the factors involved.

Another example of the availability heuristic is provided by how people's judgments are based on correlations they observe between events. For example, you might know from past observations that when it is cloudy and there is a certain smell in the air, it is likely to rain later in the day. Being aware of correlations can be extremely useful. If you have observed that your boss is more likely to grant your requests when he or she is in a good mood, you can use this knowledge to determine the best time to ask for a raise.

Although knowledge of correlations between events can be useful, sometimes people fall into the trap of creating illusory correlations. **Illusory correlations** occur when a correlation between two events appears to exist, but in reality doesn't exist or is much weaker than it is assumed to be.

Illusory correlations can occur when we expect two things to be related, and so we fool ourselves into thinking they are related even when they are not. These expectations often take the form of **stereotypes**—an oversimplified generalization about a group or class of people that often focuses on the negative. Often, people's stereotype about the characteristics of a particular group leads them to pay particular attention to behaviors associated with that stereotype, and this attention creates an illusory correlation, which reinforces the stereotype. This is related to the availability heuristic because selective attention to the stereotypical behaviors makes these behaviors more "available" (Chapman & Chapman, 1969; Hamilton, 1981).

We can appreciate how illusory correlations reinforce stereotypes by considering the stereotype that gay males are effeminate. A person who believes this stereotype might pay particular attention to effeminate gay characters on TV programs or in movies, and to situations in which they see a person who they know is gay acting effeminate. Although these observations support a correlation between being gay and being effeminate, the person has ignored the large number of cases in which gay males are not effeminate. This may be because these cases do not stand out or because the person chooses not to pay attention to them. Whatever the reason, selectively taking into account only the situations that support the person's preconceptions can create the illusion that a correlation exists, when there may be only a weak correlation or none at all.

CogLab

Typical
Reasoning

The Representativeness Heuristic

The representativeness heuristic is based on the idea that people often make judgments based on how much one event resembles another event.

Making Judgments Based on Resemblances The **representativeness heuristic** states that the probability that an event A comes from class B can be determined by how well A resembles the properties of class B. To put this in more concrete terms, consider the following demonstration.

 Demonstration

Judging Occupations

We randomly pick one male from the population of the United States. That male, Robert, wears glasses, speaks quietly, and reads a lot. Is it more likely that Robert is a librarian or a farmer?

When Amos Tversky and Daniel Kahneman (1974) presented this question in an experiment, more people guessed that Robert was a librarian. Apparently the description of Robert as wearing glasses, speaking quietly, and reading a lot matched these people's image of a typical librarian (see "illusory conjunctions" above). Thus, they were influenced by the representativeness heuristic into basing their judgment on how closely they think Robert's characteristics (which correspond to "A" in our definition of the representativeness heuristic) match those of a "typical" librarian ("B"). However, in doing this they were ignoring another important source of information—the base rates of farmers and librarians in the population. The **base rate** is the relative proportion of different classes in the population. In 1972, when this experiment was carried out, there were many more male farmers than male librarians in the United States, and this base rate leads to the conclusion that it is much more likely that Robert is a farmer (remember that he was randomly chosen from the population).

One reaction to the farmer–librarian problem might be that the participants might not have been aware of the base rates for farmers and librarians, and so didn't have the information they needed to make a correct judgment. The effect of knowing the base rate has been demonstrated by presenting participants with the following problem:

> In a group of 100 people, there are 70 lawyers and 30 engineers. What is the chance that if we pick one person from the group at random that the person will be an engineer?

Participants given this problem correctly guessed that there would be a 30 percent chance of picking an engineer. However, for some participants the following description of the person who was picked was added:

> Jack is a 45-year-old man. He is married and has four children. He is generally conservative, careful, and ambitious. He shows no interest in political and social issues and spends most of his free time on his many hobbies, which include home carpentry, sailing, and mathematical puzzles.

Adding this description caused participants to greatly increase their estimate of the chances that the randomly picked person (Jack, in this case) was an engineer. Apparently, when only base-rate information is available, people use that information to make their estimates. However, when any descriptive information is available, people disregard the base-rate information, and this often causes errors in reasoning.

Making Judgments Without Considering the Conjunction Rule The following demonstration illustrates another characteristic of the representativeness heuristic.

Demonstration

Description of a Person

Linda is 31 years old, single, outspoken, and very bright. She majored in philosophy. As a student, she was deeply concerned with issues of discrimination and social justice, and also participated in antinuclear demonstrations. Which of the following alternatives is more probable?

1. Linda is a bank teller.
2. Linda is a bank teller and is active in the feminist movement.

The correct answer to this problem is that it is more likely that Linda is a bank teller, but when Tversky and Kahneman (1983) posed this problem to their participants, 85 percent picked statement 2. It is easy to see why they did this. They were influenced by the representativeness heuristic, because the description of Linda fits people's idea of

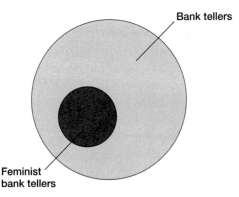

Bank tellers

Feminist bank tellers

■ **Figure 12.13** Because feminist bank tellers are a subset of bank tellers, it is always more likely that someone is a bank teller than a feminist bank teller.

a typical feminist. However, in doing this they violated the **conjunction rule**, which states that the probability of a conjunction of two events (A and B) cannot be higher than the probability of the single constituents (A alone or B alone). For example, the probability that Anne has a red Corvette cannot be greater than the probability that she has a Corvette, because the two constituents together (Corvette *and* red) define a smaller number of cars than one constituent (Corvette) alone. Similarly, there are fewer feminist bank tellers than bank tellers, so stating that Linda is a bank teller *includes* the possibility that she is a *feminist* bank teller (Figure 12.13).

People tend to violate the conjunction rule even when it is clear that they understand it. The culprit is the representativeness heuristic; in the example just cited, the participants saw Linda's characteristics as more representative of *feminist bank teller* than *bank teller*.

Incorrectly Assuming That Small Samples Are Representative People also make errors in reasoning by ignoring the importance of the size of the sample on which observations are based. The following demonstration illustrates the effect of sample size.

 Demonstration

Male and Female Births

A certain town is served by two hospitals. In the larger hospital about 45 babies are born each day, and in the smaller hospital about 15 babies are born each day. As you know, about 50 percent of all babies are boys. However, the exact percentage varies from day to day. Sometimes it may be higher than 50 percent, sometimes lower.

For a period of 1 year, each hospital recorded the days on which more than 60 percent of the babies born were boys. Which hospital do you think recorded more such days?

- The larger hospital?
- The smaller hospital?
- About the same (that is, within 5 percent of each other)?

When participants were asked this question in an experiment (Tversky & Kahneman, 1974), 22 percent picked the larger hospital, 22 percent picked the smaller hospital, and 56 percent stated that there would be no difference. The group that thought there would be no difference was presumably assuming that the birthrate for males and females in both hospitals would be representative of the overall birthrate for males and females. However, the correct answer is that there would be more days with over 60 percent male births in the small hospital.

We can understand why this result would occur by considering a statistical rule called the **law of large numbers**, which states that the larger the number of individuals that are randomly drawn from a population, the more representative the resulting group will be of the entire population. Conversely, samples of small numbers of individuals will be less representative of the population. Thus, in the hospital problem it is more likely that the percentage of boys born on any given day will be near 50 percent in the large hospital and farther from 50 percent in the small hospital. To make this conclusion clear, imagine that there is a very small hospital that records only one birth each day. Over a period of a year there will be 365 births, with about 50 percent being boys and 50 percent being girls. However, on any given day, there will be either 100 percent boys or 100 percent girls—clearly percentages that are not representative of the overall population. The problem for reasoning, however, is that people often assume representativeness holds for small samples, and this results in errors in reasoning. (See Gigerenzer & Hoffrage, 1995; Gigerenzer & Todd, 1999, for additional perspectives on how statistical thinking and heuristics operate in reasoning.)

The Confirmation Bias

One of the major roadblocks to accurate reasoning is the **confirmation bias**, our tendency to selectively look for information that conforms to our hypothesis and to overlook information that argues against it. This effect was demonstrated by Wason (1960), who presented participants with the following instructions:

> You will be given three numbers which conform to a simple rule that I have in mind. . . . Your aim is to discover this rule by writing down sets of three numbers together with your reasons for your choice of them. . . . After you have written down each set, I shall tell you whether your numbers conform to the rule or not. . . . When you feel highly confident that you have discovered the rule, you are to write it down and tell me what it is. (p. 131)

After Wason presented the first set of numbers, *2, 4,* and *6,* the participants began creating their own sets of three numbers and receiving feedback from Wason. Note that Wason told participants only whether their numbers fit *his* rule. The participants did not find out whether *their* rationale was correct until they felt confident enough to actually announce their rule. The most common initial hypothesis was "increasing intervals of two." Because the actual rule was "three numbers in increasing order of magnitude," the rule "increasing intervals of two" is incorrect even though it creates sequences that satisfy Wason's rule.

The secret to determining the correct rule is to try to create sequences that *don't* satisfy the person's current hypothesis, but which *do* satisfy Wason's rule. Thus, determining that the sequence 2, 4, 5 is correct, allows us to reject our "increasing intervals of two" hypothesis and formulate a new one. The few participants whose rule was correct on their first guess followed the strategy of testing a number of hypotheses by creating sequences that were designed to *disconfirm* their current hypothesis. In contrast, participants who didn't guess the rule correctly on their first try tended to keep creating sequences that confirmed their current hypothesis.

The confirmation bias acts like a pair of blinders—we see the world according to rules we think are correct and are never dissuaded from this view because we seek out only evidence that confirms our rule. The confirmation bias is so strong that it can affect people's reasoning by causing them to ignore relevant information. Charles Lord and coworkers (1979) demonstrated this in an experiment that tested how people's attitudes are affected by exposure to evidence that contradicts the attitudes.

By means of a questionnaire, Lord identified one group of participants in favor of capital punishment and another group against it. Each participant was then presented with descriptions of research studies on capital punishment. Some of the studies provided evidence that capital punishment had a deterrent effect on murder; others provided evidence that capital punishment had no deterrent effect. When the participants reacted to the studies, their responses reflected the attitudes they had at the beginning of the experiment. For example, an article presenting evidence that supported the deterrence effect of capital punishment was rated as "convincing" by proponents of capital punishment and "unconvincing" by those against capital punishment. This is the confirmation bias at work—people's prior beliefs caused them to focus only on information that agreed with their beliefs and to disregard information that didn't.

Culture, Cognition, and Inductive Reasoning

When we discussed categories in Chapter 8, we described research comparing the way Itza and American participants think about categories (see Chapter 8, page 315, for a description of the Itza). We saw that Itza and American participants have different ideas about which level of categories is "basic," with Itza focusing on the level "sparrow, oak" and Americans focusing on the level "bird, tree." We also saw that there are similarities, with both American and Itza using categories similarly for an inductive-reasoning task.

We now return to these two groups to consider some further comparisons of how they use categories in reasoning. Let's start with a demonstration.

 Demonstration

Questions About Animals

The following two questions are about animals that live on an island.

> Question 1:
> Porcupines have a disease.
> Squirrels have another disease.
> Do you think all other mammals on the island have the disease of *porcupines* or the disease of *squirrels?*

Question 2:

> Wolves and deer have a disease.
> Wolves and coyotes have another disease.
> Do you think all other mammals on the island have the disease of *wolves and deer* or of *wolves and coyotes*? 🐾

The preceding questions both involve induction, because they require reasoning from specific observations to more general conclusions, and because the answer is a "probably" answer rather than a "definitely" answer. These items are based on a model of reasoning about categories called the **similarity-coverage model** (Osherson et al., 1990). The goal of this model is to explain how people's conceptions of different categories influence the strength of inductive arguments. We will discuss this model by posing a few more problems, and will then return to the questions from the demonstration. One principle of the model, called the **typicality principle**, is illustrated by asking which of the following is most likely to be true.

Premise: Robins have a higher potassium concentration in their blood than humans.

Conclusion 1: Therefore, all birds have a higher potassium concentration in their blood than humans.

Premise: Penguins have a higher potassium concentration in their blood than humans.

Conclusion 2: Therefore, all birds have a higher potassium concentration in their blood than humans.

According to the typicality principle, the argument with the most typical example of a category in the premise is the strongest argument. Thus, if people think robins are more typical of birds than penguins, they will pick conclusion 1 as more likely to be true.

Here is an example that illustrates another principle. Which of the following arguments are more likely to be true?

Premise: Hippopotamuses have an ulnar artery.
Hamsters have an ulnar artery.

Conclusion 1: All mammals have an ulnar artery.

Premise: Hippopotamuses have an ulnar artery.
Rhinoceroses have an ulnar artery.

Conclusion 2: All mammals have an ulnar artery.

According to the **diversity principle**, the argument with the greatest coverage of a category is stronger. Because hippopotamus and hamster taken together are more diverse than hippopotamus and rhinoceros, they have higher coverage of the category *mammal*. Therefore, according to the principle of diversity, conclusion 1 is stronger.

Now return to the demonstration "Questions About Animals," and decide which argument illustrates typicality and which illustrates diversity. (Note that the questions in the demonstration are stated differently from the examples we have just considered, but it is still possible to determine which principles apply. Stop and decide, before reading further.)

When Alejandro Lopez and coworkers (1997) presented problems like question 1 in the demonstration to Itza and U.S. participants, they found that the overall responses of both groups agreed with the principle of typicality (Figure 12.14a; picking *squirrel* rather than *porcupine*). Thus, both groups' answers reflected the animals in the premises that they thought were more typical.

Although the results for typicality were similar for both groups, the results for diversity were different. Thus, when the two groups were presented with problems like question 2 in the demonstration, almost all of the U.S. participants (96 percent) gave an answer that corresponded to the principle of diversity (picking *wolves and deer*), whereas only 38 percent of the Itza participants gave an answer that corresponded to this principle (Figure 12.14b).

What does this result mean? Why do Itza ignore diversity in making their choices? One reason is that the Itza, but not the U.S. participants, are influenced by ecological considerations. For example, one Itza participant was presented with the following problem.

> Rats and pocket mice have a disease. Tapirs and squirrels have a disease. Do you think all other mammals on the island would have the disease of rats and pocket mice or the disease of tapirs and squirrels?

The person chose "rats and pocket mice," even though the principle of diversity predicts that tapirs and squirrels, which are more different, would be chosen. The person explained that tapirs and squirrels are less likely to pass on the disease because they probably got it from another agent, such as a bat biting them, whereas rats and pocket mice are similar enough so they don't need an agent like a bat biting them to both get the disease. Thus, the Itza participant was not being illogical. Rather, she was using logic that was based on her knowledge of the animals in their environment.

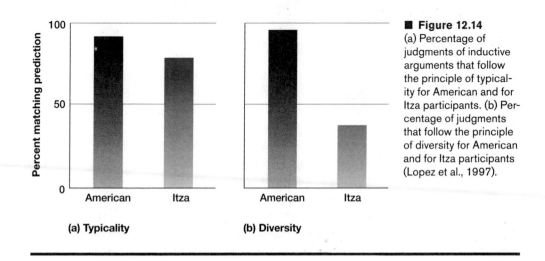

■ **Figure 12.14**
(a) Percentage of judgments of inductive arguments that follow the principle of typicality for American and for Itza participants. (b) Percentage of judgments that follow the principle of diversity for American and for Itza participants (Lopez et al., 1997).

Interestingly, similar effects of knowledge on reasoning about categories have been observed for different groups of U.S. participants. For example, when asked to sort trees into different categories, taxonomists (who are schooled in scientific biology) sorted the trees by their scientific biological category, whereas park maintenance workers (who are responsible for maintaining the trees) sorted the trees based on their experience in taking care of trees. When tested, the park maintenance workers rejected the diversity principle in favor of ecologically based reasoning—just like the Itza (Medin et al., 1997)!

These cross-cultural and cross-occupational studies emphasize that in studying cognition, we can't assume that people always think in exactly the same way or use the same information to support their thinking.

Decision Making: Choosing Among Alternatives

We make decisions every day, from relatively unimportant ones (what clothes to wear, what movie to see) to those that can have great impact on our lives (what college to attend, whom to marry, what job to choose). The process of decision making can involve both inductive and deductive reasoning, so we have already considered some of the principles that apply to the study of how people make decisions.

When we discussed the availability and representativeness heuristics we used examples in which people were asked to make judgments about things like causes of death or people's occupations. As we discuss decision making, our emphasis will be on how people make judgments that involve choices between different courses of action. These choices can be concerned with personal decisions, such as deciding what school to attend or whether to fly or drive to a destination, or they can be concerned with decisions that a person might make in conjunction with their profession, such as "Which advertising campaign should my company run?" or "What is the best economic policy for the United States?" We begin by considering one of the basic properties of decision making: Decisions involve both benefits and costs.

The Utility Approach to Decisions

Much of the early theorizing on decision making was influenced by **economic utility theory**, which is based on the assumption that people are basically rational, so if they have all of the relevant information, they will make a decision which results in the maximum expected utility. **Utility** refers to outcomes that are desirable because they are in the person's best interest (Manktelow, 1999; Reber, 1995). The economists who studied decision making thought about utility in terms of monetary value, with the goal of good decision making being to make choices that resulted in the maximum monetary payoff.

One of the advantages of the utility approach is that it specifies procedures that make it possible to determine which choice would result in the highest monetary value. For example, if we know the odds of winning when playing a slot machine in a casino, and also know the cost of playing and the size of the payoff, it is possible to determine that, in the long run, playing slot machines is a losing proposition. Thus, in terms of monetary payoff, it would be unwise to play the slots.

A Problem for the Utility Approach: People Do Not Necessarily Act to Maximize Monetary Value Even though most people realize that in the long run the casino wins, the huge popularity of casinos indicates that many people have decided to patronize casinos anyway. Observations such as this, as well as the results of many experiments, have led psychologists to conclude that people do not always make decisions that maximize their monetary outcome. This does not necessarily mean that people are irrational, but that they find value in things other than money. Thus, for some people the fun of gambling might outweigh the probable loss of some money, and, of course, there's the thrill of thinking about the possibility of "beating the odds" and being the one who hits the jackpot.

Another problem with the utility approach is that many decisions do not involve payoffs that can be calculated. As the popular television advertisement for a credit card says, *Tickets to the ball game, $60; Hot dogs, $10; Your team's baseball cap, $20; Seeing the game with your son or daughter, "priceless."* Thus, utility is not always reducible to dollars and cents, but is often in the mind of the person.

The idea that utility can be in the person's mind brings up another potential problem with the utility approach. When people have to make decisions that will affect their lives, they often create mental simulations, which can sometimes be misleading (Kahneman & Tversky, 1982; Dunning & Parpal, 1989). **Mental simulations** are models that people create about what will happen following different decisions. For example, if Roberta is trying to decide whether to go to "University A" or "University B," she may imagine what it would be like attending each school. In doing this she may imagine life at University A to be intellectual and the atmosphere at University B to be more socially oriented.

Although the procedure of creating mental simulations can be useful, there is a danger that it may not lead to accurate predictions. After all, Roberta hasn't actually attended either school and has no experience with college, so she is just guessing what each school would be like. In fact, people often make inaccurate predictions about what will happen in a particular situation. For example, when people win the lottery, they may initially see nothing but positive outcomes, such as being able to quit their job, buy a new house, and finance their children's college educations. Later, however, they become aware of negative aspects, such as being hounded by other people who want a piece of the action, lack of privacy, losing friends, and worries about what's happening to their investments in the stock market. Events that people imagine will occur are often different from the events that actually do occur (T. D. Wilson et al., 2000).

People Are Often Not Good at Predicting Their Emotional Reactions T. D. Wilson and coworkers (2000) point out that even if people were able to accurately predict what would happen, they are often poor at predicting how happy or unhappy the event will cause them to feel. One of the things responsible for this lack of accuracy in predicting their emotions is called the **focusing illusion**, which occurs when people focus their attention on just one aspect of a situation and ignore other aspects of a situation that may be important. For example, when college students were asked the questions "How happy are you?" and "How many dates did you have last month?" their answers depended on the order in which the questions were asked. When the happiness question was asked first, the correlation between the answers to the two questions was 0.12, but when the dating question was asked first, the correlation rose to 0.66. Apparently, asking the dating question first caused participants to focus on dating as being an important determinant of happiness, and so they rated themselves as happier if they had a large number of dates (Strack et al., 1988).

The focusing illusion has also been demonstrated in a study that considered people's perceptions of how satisfied a target person would be if they lived in different locations. The participants for this study were students at two Midwestern universities (the University of Michigan and the University of Ohio) and at two California universities (the University of California at Irvine and UCLA).

There were two groups, the *self* group and the *other* group. The self group rated *themselves* on overall life satisfaction. The *other* group predicted how a hypothetical *target person* who was similar to themselves would rate their life satisfaction if they lived in California and if they lived in the Midwest. (Both groups also rated other things as well, but for our purposes we will focus on overall life satisfaction.)

The results of this study showed that there was no difference in how the California and Midwest students in the *self* group rated their own overall life satisfaction, but both California and Midwest students in the *other* group predicted that their hypothetical target person would be happier in California (Table 12.3; Schkade & Kahneman, 1998).

Why did both California and Midwest students in the *other* group predict that their target person would be happier in California? The experimenters suggest that the higher ratings for California were probably caused by the participants' tendency to focus on the most easily observed and distinctive differences between the two locations, such as good weather and natural beauty (which people generally associate with California), and to ignore other factors, such as job prospects, academic opportunities, and financial situation. The message here is that before you decide that moving to California will make you happier, it is important to consider a wide range of outcomes from this decision—not just that the weather will be better.

All of the evidence above shows that people often make decisions that do not result in maximizing monetary value. In addition, they may not be able to accurately predict

Table 12.3 Focusing Illusion Experiment

Group	Question Asked	Answer
Self	How would you rate your life satisfaction?	No difference in self-ratings for California and Midwest students.
Other	Would a person be happier living in California or the Midwest?	Both California and Midwest students answered that the hypothetical person would have higher life satisfaction in California.

what outcome a particular decision will bring or how they will feel about the outcome when it happens. We will now consider research on decision making that has shown that people's evaluation of different choices can depend on the way these choices are presented.

Decisions Can Depend on How Choices Are Presented

Our discussion of deductive and inductive reasoning has shown that reasoning is affected by more than just the facts of the situation. This also happens in decision making, when a person's judgments are affected by the way choices are stated. For example, take the decision about whether to become a potential organ donor. Although a poll has found that 85 percent of Americans approve of organ donation, only 28 percent have granted permission by signing a donor card. This signing of the card is called the **opt-in procedure**, because it involves the person taking an active step (Johnson & Goldstein, 2003).

The low American consent rate for organ donation also occurs in other countries, such as Denmark (4 percent), the United Kingdom (27 percent), and Germany (12 percent). One thing that these countries have in common is that they all use the opt-in procedure. However, in France and Belgium the consent rate is over 99 percent. These countries use the **opt-out procedure**, in which the person is a potential organ donor unless he or she requests not to be.

Besides having important ramifications for public health (in 1995 more than 45,000 people in the United States died waiting for a suitable donor organ), the difference between opt-in and opt-out procedures has important implications for the theory of decision making, because according to the utility approach, people make their decisions based on expected utility value. According to this approach, people's decisions shouldn't depend on how the potential choices are stated. However, the opt-in versus opt-out results indicates that the procedure used to identify people's willingness to be organ donors does have an effect.

But what about when people are confronted with hypothetical situations in which they are forced to choose between two alternatives? The following demonstration provides an example of such a situation.

 Demonstration

What Would You Do?

Risky Decisions

Imagine that the United States is preparing for the outbreak of an unusual Asian disease that is expected to kill 600 people. Two alternative programs to combat the disease have been proposed. Assume that the exact scientific estimates of the consequences of the programs are as follows:

Decision Making

- If Program A is adopted, 200 people will be saved.
- If Program B is adopted, there is a 1/3 probability that 600 people will be saved, and a 2/3 probability that no people will be saved.

Which of the two programs would you favor?

Now consider the following additional proposals for combating the same disease:

- If Program C is adopted, 400 people will die.
- If Program D is adopted, there is a 1/3 probability that nobody will die, and a 2/3 probability that 600 people will die.

Which of these two programs would you pick?

For the first pair of proposals, Program A was chosen by 72 percent of the students in an experiment by Tversky and Kahneman (1981) and the rest picked Program B (Figure 12.15). The choice of Program A represents a **risk-aversion strategy**. The idea of saving 200 lives with certainty is more attractive than the risk that no one will be saved. However, when Tversky and Kahneman presented the descriptions of Programs C and D to another group of students, 22 percent picked Program C and 78 percent picked Program D. This represents a **risk-taking strategy**. The certain death of 400 people is less acceptable than a 2 in 3 chance that 600 people will die.

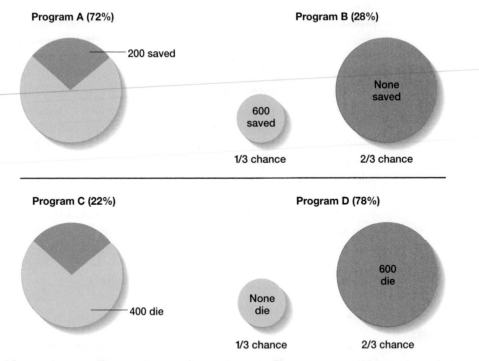

■ **Figure 12.15** How framing affects decision making. These pie charts diagram the conditions set forth for Programs A, B, C, and D in the text. Note that the number of deaths and probabilities for programs A and B are exactly the same as for programs C and D. The percentages indicate the percentage of participants who picked each program when given choices between A and B or between C and D (Tversky & Kahneman, 1981).

Tversky and Kahneman concluded that, in general, when a choice is framed in terms of gains (as in the first problem, which is stated in terms of saving lives) people use a risk-aversion strategy, and when a choice is framed in terms of losses (as in the second problem, which is stated in terms of losing lives), people use a risk-taking strategy.

But if we look at the four programs closely, we can see that they are identical pairs (Figure 12.15). Programs A and C both result in 200 people living and 400 people dying. Yet 72 percent of the participants picked program A and only 22 percent picked program C. A similar situation occurs if we compare programs B and D. Both lead to the same number of deaths, yet one was picked by 28 percent of the participants and the other by 78 percent. These results illustrate the **framing effect**—decisions are influenced by how a decision is stated, or *framed*.

One reason people's decisions are affected by framing is that the way a problem is stated can highlight some feature of the situation (for example, that people will die) while deemphasizing other features (Kahneman, 2003). It should not be a surprise that the way a choice is stated can influence cognitive processes, because this is similar to what happens when the way a syllogism is stated influences a person's ability to determine whether the syllogism is valid (page 438). We also saw, in the chapter on problem solving, that the way a problem is stated can influence our ability to solve the problem (page 408).

Justification in Decision Making

To end our consideration of decision making, we will consider yet another factor that influences how people make decisions. This factor is the need to justify the decision. We can illustrate this by considering an experiment by Tversky and Eldar Shafir (1992), in which they presented the following problem to two groups of students. The "pass" group read the words that are underlined, and the "fail" group had these words replaced by the words in italics (which the pass group did not see).

> Imagine that you have just taken a tough qualifying examination. It is the end of the semester, you feel tired and run-down, and you find out that you passed the exam/ *[failed the exam. You will have to take it again in a couple of months—after the Christmas holidays]*. You now have the opportunity to buy a very attractive 5-day Christmas vacation package to Hawaii at an exceptionally low price. The special offer expires tomorrow. Would you
>
> • buy the vacation package?
> • not buy the vacation package?
> • pay a $5 nonrefundable fee in order to retain the rights to buy the vacation package at the same exceptional price the day after tomorrow?

The results for the two groups are shown in the columns headed "passed" and "failed" in Table 12.4. Notice that there is no difference between the two groups. Fifty-four percent of the participants in the "pass" group opt to buy the vacation package, and 57 percent of the participants in the "fail" group opt for the package. The interesting

Table 12.4 Choice Behavior and Knowledge of Exam Outcome

	Passed Test	Failed Test	Test Results Not Available for 2 Days
Buy vacation package	54%	57%	32%
Don't buy	16	12	7
$5 to keep open option to buy later	30	31	61

result happened when a third group received the same problem as above, except these participants were told that the outcome of the exam wouldn't be available for 2 more days. Notice that only 32 percent of these participants opted for the package and that 61 percent decided they would pay the $5 so they could put off making the decision until they knew whether they had passed or failed the exam.

Apparently what happened in this experiment is that 61 percent of the participants in the "no result" group did not want to make a decision about the trip until they found out whether they passed or failed, even though the results for the other two groups indicates that passing or failing actually made no difference in the decision about the vacation packages.

To explain this result, Tversky and Shafir suggest that once the students know the outcome they can then assign a reason for deciding to buy the vacation. Participants who passed could see the vacation as a reward; participants who failed could see the vacation as a consolation that would provide time to recuperate before taking the exam again.

Although there are other possible interpretations for these results, there is a great deal of other evidence that the decision-making process often includes looking for justification so the person can state a rationale for his or her decision. This is why doctors may carry out medical tests that might not lead to different treatments but that provide additional evidence for the treatment they have recommended, thereby making it easier to justify the treatment to themselves, their patients, and, if necessary, to the courts (Tversky & Shafir, 1992).

The Physiology of Thinking

In this section we will consider the types of thinking we have discussed in this chapter and the previous one. We begin by asking the question, "How is the brain involved in problem solving, reasoning, and making decisions?" Because all of these forms of thinking involve a number of different cognitive capacities—including perception, memory, and the ability to focus and maintain attention—it isn't surprising that a number of different areas of the brain are involved. However, we will focus on one area in particular, the prefrontal cortex, because it plays such a major role in thinking.

The Prefrontal Cortex

The prefrontal cortex (PFC; Figure 12.16) is activated by stimuli from all of the senses, by the retrieval of memories and the anticipation of future events, and can be affected by a person's emotional state (Wallis et al., 2001). It is not surprising, therefore, that the PFC plays a central role in determining complex behaviors that are involved in thinking.

One of the earliest reports of the effect of frontal lobe damage on functioning was the case of a young homemaker who had a tumor in her frontal lobe that made it impossible for her to plan a family meal, even though she was capable of cooking the individual dishes (Penfield & Evans, 1935). Results such as this led to the conclusion that the PFC plays an important role planning future activities (Owen et al., 1990).

The prefrontal cortex has been linked to problem solving in a number of ways. Damage to the PFC interferes with people's ability to act with flexibility, a key requirement for solving problems. One symptom of PFC damage is a behavior called **perseveration**, in which patients have difficulty in switching from one pattern of behavior to another (Hauser, 1999; Munakata et al., 2003). For example, patients with damage to the PFC have difficulty when the rules change in a card-sorting task. Thus, if they begin by successfully separating out the blue cards from a pack, they continue picking the blue cards even after the experimenter tells them to shift to separating out the brown cards. Clearly, perseveration would play havoc with attempts to solve complex problems for which it is necessary to consider one possible solution and then shift to another possibility if the first one doesn't work.

Because damage to the PFC results in perseveration and poor planning ability, it is not surprising that PFC damage decreases performance on tasks such as the Tower of London problem (a task similar to the Tower of Hanoi problem that involves moving colored beads between two vertical rods; Carlin et al., 2000; Owen et al., 1990),

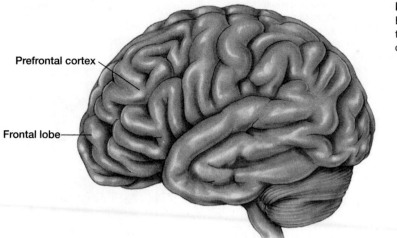

Prefrontal cortex

Frontal lobe

■ **Figure 12.16**
Brain showing location of the prefrontal cortex (PFC).

the Tower of Hanoi problem (Morris et al., 1997), and the Luchins water-jug problem (Colvin et al., 2001). Brain imaging has also shown that problem solving activates the PFC in normal participants (Rowe et al., 2001).

Other research has shown that the PFC is important for a number of cognitive tasks involving planning, reasoning, and making connections among different parts of a problem or a story. For example, when Tiziana Zalla and coworkers (2002) tested patients with PFC damage, she found that these patients were able to understand individual words and could identify events described in stories. However, they were unable to follow the order of events in the story or to make inferences that connected different parts of the story.

There is also a large amount of evidence that the PFC is important for reasoning. This has been demonstrated by presenting a deductive-reasoning task to people with PFC damage. Participants were presented with relationships such as the following: *Sam is taller than Nate; Nate is taller than Roger*, and their task was to arrange the names in order of the people's heights. When James Waltz and coworkers (1999) presented these tasks to patients with PFC damage and control groups of participants without brain damage and patients with temporal lobe damage, they found that all of these groups did well when the task was easy, like the previous one about Sam, Nate, and Roger (Figure 12.17a). However, when the task was made more difficult by scrambling the order of presentation (example: *Beth is taller than Tina; Amy is taller than Beth*), then the people without brain damage and the patients with temporal lobe damage still did well, but the PFC patients performed poorly (Figure 12.17b). This result confirms the conclusion of

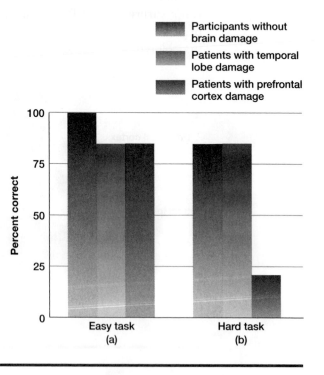

■ **Figure 12.17** Effect of damage to the PFC on performance on a reasoning task. Participants without brain damage, participants with temporal lobe damage, and participants with PFC damage can all solve the easy task (left bars), but the PFC group's performance drops to a low level when the task is made more difficult (Waltz et al., 1999).

Legend:
■ Participants without brain damage
■ Patients with temporal lobe damage
■ Patients with prefrontal cortex damage

brain imaging studies, which show that as reasoning problems become more complex, reasoning activates larger areas of the PFC (Kroger et al., 2002). (Also see "If You Want to Know More: Neurons That Respond to Abstract Rules," on page 483.)

Neuroeconomics: The Neural Basis of Decision Making

A new approach to studying decision making, called **neuroeconomics**, combines approaches from the fields of psychology, neuroscience, and economics (Lee, 2006; Sanfey et al., 2006). One outcome of this approach has been research that has identified areas of the brain that are activated as people make decisions while playing economic games. This research shows that decisions are often influenced by emotions, and that these emotions are associated with activity in specific areas of the brain.

To illustrate the neuroeconomic approach, we will describe an experiment by Alan Sanfey and coworkers (2003) in which people's brain activity was measured as they played the ultimatum game. The **ultimatum game** is very simple. Two people play: One is designated as the *proposer* and one as the *responder*. The proposer is given a sum of money, say $10, and makes an offer to the responder as to how this money should be split between them. If the responder accepts the offer, then the money is split according to the proposal. If the responder rejects the offer, neither player receives anything. Either way, the game is over after the responder makes his or her decision.

According to utility theory, the responder should accept the proposer's offer, no matter what it is. This is the rational response, because if you accept the offer you get something, but if you refuse, you get nothing (remember that the game is only one-trial long, so there is no second chance).

In Sanfey's experiment, participants played 20 separate games as responder: 10 with 10 different human partners and 10 with a computer partner. The offers made by both the human and computer partners were determined by the experimenters, with some being "fair" (evenly split, so the responder received $5) and some "unfair" (the responder received $1, $2, or $3). The results of responders' interactions with their human partners (gray bars in Figure 12.18) match the results of other research on the ultimatum game—all responders accept an offer of $5, most accept the $3 offer, and half or more reject the $1 or $2 offers.

Why do people reject low offers? When Sanfey and coworkers asked participants, many explained that they were angry because they felt the offers were unfair. Consistent with this explanation, when participants received exactly the same offers from their computer partner, more accepted "unfair" proposals (blue bars in Figure 12.18). Apparently, people are less likely to get angry with an unfair computer than with an unfair person.

In addition to testing people's behavior, Sanfey and coworkers measured brain activity in the responders as they were making their decisions. The results showed that the right anterior insula, an area located deep within the brain between the parietal and temporal lobes, was activated about three times more strongly when responders rejected an offer than when they accepted it (Figure 12.19a). Also, participants with higher activation to unfair offers rejected a higher proportion of the offers. The fact that the insula responded during rejection is not surprising when we consider that this area of

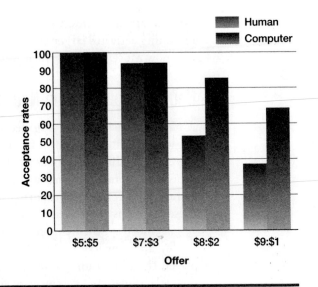

■ **Figure 12.18** Behavioral results of Sanfey and coworkers' (2003) experiment, showing responders' acceptance rates in response to different offers made by human partners and computer partners.

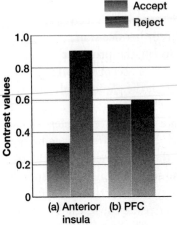

■ **Figure 12.19** Response of the insula and PFC to "fair" and "unfair" offers (Sanfey et al., 2006).

the brain is connected with negative emotional states, including pain, distress, hunger, anger, and disgust.

What about the prefrontal cortex, which plays such a large role in complex cognitive behaviors? The PFC is also activated by the decision task, but this activation is the same for offers that are rejected and offers that are accepted (Figure 12.19b). Sanfey hypothesizes that the function of the PFC may be to deal with the cognitive demands of the task, which involves the goal of accumulating as much money as possible. Looked at in this way, each of these brain areas represents a different goal of the ultimatum game—the emotional goal of resenting unfairness is handled by the anterior insula, and the cognitive goal of accumulating money is handled by the PFC.

The results of this experiment support the idea that it is important to take emotional factors into account when considering decision making. It also illustrates the value of combining both physiological and behavioral approaches to the study of decision making.

Something to Consider

Is What Is Good for You Also Good for Me?

When we discussed how framing affects decision making, we saw that people's decisions regarding programs to deal with the outbreak of a hypothetical Asian disease depended on how the problem was stated (pages 469–470). We now pose a similar type of medical problem, but in a more personal way, because the hypothetical decision you are asked to make could affect you personally.

 **Demonstration**

A Personal Health Decision

Imagine that there will be a deadly flu going around your area next winter. Your doctor says that you have a 10 percent chance (10 out of 100) of dying from this flu. A new flu vaccine has been developed and tested. If administered, the vaccine will prevent you from catching the deadly flu. However, there is one serious risk involved: The vaccine is made from a somewhat weaker type of flu virus, so there is a 5 percent risk (5 out of 100) that the vaccine could kill you. Considering this information, decide between the following two alternatives:

- I will not take the vaccine, and I accept the 10 percent chance of dying from this flu.
- I will take the vaccine, and I accept the 5 percent chance of dying from the weaker flu in the vaccine. (Adapted from Zikmund-Fisher et al., 2006)

When Brian Zikmund-Fisher and coworkers (2006) gave this choice to their participants, 48 percent said they would take the vaccine. This is an interesting result, because it means that 52 percent of the participants decided to do nothing, even though statistically this doubled their chances of dying.

This result is an example of the **omission bias**—the tendency to do nothing to avoid having to make a decision that could be interpreted as causing harm. However, Zikmund-Fisher's experiment asked participants not only to imagine that they were making a decision for themselves, as in the demonstration, but to make the decision while imagining themselves in the following three roles: (1) as a physician recommending a treatment for a patient; (2) as a hospital medical director setting treatment guidelines for all patients in the hospital; and (3) as a parent of a child who might receive the treatment. The results of this experiment, shown in Figure 12.20, indicate that people

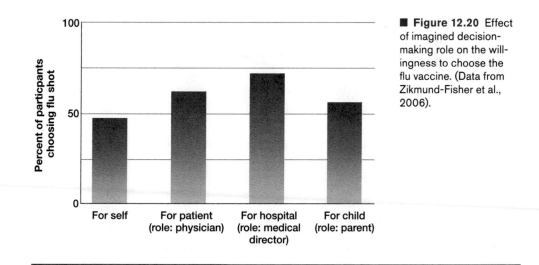

■ **Figure 12.20** Effect of imagined decision-making role on the willingness to choose the flu vaccine. (Data from Zikmund-Fisher et al., 2006).

are more likely to recommend that others receive the shot than they are to choose the shot for themselves.

Apparently, the decision a person makes can be influenced by the person or group for whom they are making the decision. But why does this occur? Zikmund-Fisher and coworkers propose that when making decisions for others, people take into account the possibility that they will be held responsible if something bad happens. Looked at from this point of view, it is easy to understand why a medical director would be prone to recommend that hospital patients receive the vaccine, because it is easy to justify a decision that maximizes survival chances for a group of people.

The most important implication of these results may be what it suggests about how physicians should present choices to their patients. Physicians often feel that they should simply present the information and let their patients deal with making the decision. But perhaps physicians should be sensitive to some of the emotional factors facing patients who are being asked to make decisions about their own treatment. Zikmund-Fisher and coworkers suggest that physicians should consider asking patients to "reframe" their decision by thinking about it as if it were a decision they were making for someone else. The idea behind doing this would be to help the patient gain a better understanding of the trade-offs they face.

Test Yourself 12.2

1. What is inductive reasoning, and how is it different from deductive reasoning?
2. How is inductive reasoning involved in the practice of science? How do inductive and deductive reasoning work together in scientific research?
3. How is inductive reasoning involved in everyday experience?
4. How do the following cause errors in reasoning: availability heuristic; illusory correlations; representativeness heuristic; confirmation bias?
5. How can failure to take into account base rates and small sample sizes cause errors in reasoning?
6. What is the cross-cultural evidence regarding how U.S. and Itza participants use typicality and diversity when making inferences about categories? How are the behaviors of these two groups similar? Different? What is an explanation for the differences?
7. What is the utility approach to decisions? What are some problems with the utility approach? As you consider this, take into account mental simulations and the focusing illusion.
8. How does the way a problem is stated and the need to justify decisions affect the decisions people make?
9. How is the prefrontal cortex involved in problem solving and reasoning? Cite evidence from both neuropsychology and brain imaging experiments to support your answer.
10. What is neuroeconomics? Describe Sanfey and coworkers' (2003) experiment, and indicate what it adds to our understanding of decision making.

11. How are people's decisions about treatment options influenced by the person or group for whom they are making the decision?

Chapter Summary

1. Reasoning is a cognitive process by which people start with information and come to conclusions that go beyond that information. Deductive reasoning involves syllogisms and can result in definite conclusions. Inductive reasoning is based on evidence and results in conclusions that are *probably* true.

2. Categorical syllogisms have two premises and a conclusion that describe the relation between two categories by using statements that begin with *All, No,* or *Some.*

3. A syllogism is valid if its conclusion follows logically from its premises. If the premises of a valid syllogism are true, then the conclusion must be true. People are able to correctly judge the validity of Aristotle's "perfect" syllogism, but make errors in all other forms of categorical syllogisms. Two reasons for errors are the atmosphere effect and the belief bias.

4. One way to determine whether a categorical syllogism is valid or invalid is to use diagrams. Another method is to create mental models representing the premises.

5. Conditional syllogisms have two premises and a conclusion, like categorical syllogisms, but the first premise has the form "If . . . then. . . ." The four basic types of conditional syllogism are (a) affirming the antecedent and (b) denying the consequent (both valid), and (c) affirming the consequent and (d) denying the antecedent (both invalid).

6. The Wason four-card problem has been used to study how people think when evaluating conditional syllogisms. People make errors in the abstract version, but perform better for versions of the problem that are restated in real-world terms, such as the "drinking age" and "postal" versions. The key to solving the problem is to apply the falsification principle.

7. Based on experiments using different versions of the Wason problem, a number of mechanisms have been proposed to explain people's performance. These mechanisms include using permission schemas, and the evolutionary approach, which explains performance in terms of social-exchange theory. Many experiments have provided evidence for and against these explanations, leaving the controversy about how to explain the Wason problem still unresolved.

8. In inductive reasoning, conclusions follow not from logically constructed syllogisms, but from evidence. Conclusions are *suggested* in inductive reasoning, with varying degrees of certainty. The strength of an inductive argument depends on the representativeness, number, and quality of observations on which the argument is based.

9. Inductive reasoning is one of the basic mechanisms for developing scientific theories and evaluating scientific evidence. It also plays a major role in everyday life because we often make predictions about what we think will happen based on our observations about what has happened in the past.

10. The availability heuristic states that events that are more easily remembered are judged as being more probable than events that are less easily remembered. This heuristic can sometimes lead to correct judgments, and sometimes not. Errors due to the availability heuristic have been demonstrated by having people estimate the relative prevalence of various causes of death.

11. Illusory correlations and stereotypes, which can lead to incorrect conclusions about relationships between things, are related to the availability heuristic, because they draw attention to specific relationships and therefore make them more "available."

12. The representativeness heuristic is based on the idea that people often make judgments based on how much one event resembles another event. Errors due to this heuristic have been demonstrated by asking participants to judge a person's occupation based on descriptive information. Errors occur when the representativeness heuristic leads people to ignore base-rate information. In other situations, judgment errors occur when people ignore the conjunction rule and the law of large numbers.

13. The confirmation bias is the tendency to selectively look for information that conforms to a hypothesis and to overlook information that argues against it. Operation of this bias was demonstrated by Wason's number-sequence task. This bias also operates in real life when people's attitudes influence the way they evaluate evidence.

14. Cultural differences in inductive reasoning have been demonstrated by comparing how Itza and American participants apply the similarity-coverage model and the associated typicality and diversity principles to their conceptions of different categories. Experiments have demonstrated that these groups apply the typicality principle similarly but differ in their application of the diversity principle.

15. The utility approach to decision making states that people are basically rational, so when they have all of the relevant information, they will make a decision that results in outcomes that are in their best interest. Evidence that people do not always act in accordance with this approach includes failure to act in a way to maximize monetary value, errors caused by application of mental simulations, and errors caused by the focusing illusion.

16. Decisions can depend on how choices are presented, or *framed*. For example, when a choice is framed in terms of gains, people use a risk-aversion strategy, and when a choice is framed in terms of losses, people use a risk-taking strategy. Decision making is also influenced by people's tendency to want to justify their decision and state a rationale for the decision.

17. The prefrontal cortex (PFC) is one of the major areas of the brain involved in thinking. Damage to the PFC can cause perseveration and poor planning ability, which results in poor performance on everyday tasks, problems such as the Tower of Hanoi and water-jug problem, and some basic problems in reasoning.

18. Neuroeconomics studies decision making by combining approaches from psychology, neuroscience, and economics. The results of a neuroeconomics experiment using the ultimatum game have shown that people's emotions can interfere with their ability to make rational decisions. Brain imaging indicates that the anterior insula is

associated with the emotions that occur during the ultimatum game and also suggests that the PFC may be involved in the cognitive demands of the task.

19. An experiment that involved asking people to make a risky decision about being vaccinated against a deadly disease has shown that people are more likely to recommend that others receive the vaccination than they are to choose to receive the vaccination themselves. This result has implications about how physicians talk about treatment options with their patients.

Think About It

1. Astrology is popular with many people because they perceive a close connection between astrological predictions and events in their lives. Explain factors that might lead to this perception, even if a close connection does not, in fact, exist.

2. Think about a decision you have made recently. It can be a minor one, such as deciding which restaurant to go to on Saturday evening, or a more major one, such as picking an apartment or deciding which college to attend. Analyze this decision, taking into account the processes you went through to arrive at it, and how you justified it in your mind as being a good decision.

3. Create deductive syllogisms and inductive arguments that apply to the decision you analyzed in the previous question.

4. Johanna has a reputation for being extremely good at justifying her behavior by a process that is often called "rationalization." For example, she justifies the fact that she eats anything she wants by saying "Ten years ago this food was supposed to be bad for you, and now they are saying it may even have some beneficial effects, so what's the point of listening to the so-called health experts?" or "That movie actor who was really into red meat lived to be 95." Analyze Johanna's arguments by stating them as inductive or deductive arguments or, better yet, do that for one of your own rationalizations.

5. From watching the news or reading the paper, what can you conclude about how the availability heuristic can influence our conceptions of the nature of the lives of different groups of people (for example, movie stars, rich people, various racial, ethnic, or cultural groups) and how accurate these conceptions might actually be?

6. Describe cases in which you made a poor decision because your judgment was clouded by emotion or some other factor.

If You Want to Know More

1. Using diagrams to determine the validity of syllogisms. There are a number of ways to use diagrams to determine whether syllogisms are valid. One method uses Venn diagrams; another uses Euler circles.

Edwards, A. W. F. (2004). *Cogwheels of the mind: The story of Venn diagrams.* Baltimore: Johns Hopkins University Press.

Shin, S-J. (1994). *The logical status of diagrams.* Cambridge, UK: Cambridge University Press.

2. Culture and cognition. We have seen that culture can affect inductive reasoning (see page 463 in this text). Other studies in which reasoning has been tested in different cultural groups (and usually compared with a sample of participants from the United States) have investigated how people from different cultures solve syllogisms, reason inductively, and solve math problems.

Dehaene, S., Izard, V., Pica, P., & Spelke, E. (2006). Core knowledge of geometry in an Amazonian indigene group. *Science, 311,* 381–384.

Nisbett, R. E. (2003). *The geography of thought.* New York: Free Press.

Scribner, S. (1977). Modes of thinking and ways of speaking: Culture and logic reconsidered. In P. N. Johnson-Laird & P. C. Wason (Eds.), *Thinking: Readings in cognitive science* (pp. 483–500). Cambridge: Cambridge University Press.

Tang, Y., Zhang, W., Chen, K., Feng, S., Ji, Y., Shen, J., Reiman, E. M., & Liu, Y. (2006). Arithmetic processing in the brain shaped by cultures. *Proceedings of the National Academy of Sciences, 103,* 10775–10780.

3. Making decisions rapidly. The deliberation-without-attention effect states that under certain conditions, people make better decisions when they act quickly than when they consciously deliberate over the decisions.

Dijksterhuis, A., Bos, M. W., Nordgren, L. F., & van Baaren, R. B. (2006). On making the right choice: The deliberation-without-attention effect. *Science, 311,* 1005–1007.

4. Reasoning and the law. Juries are asked to come to a conclusion by evaluating evidence. New research indicates that a person's beliefs can affect his or her decision making. Also, the brain's response depends on whether the evidence is consistent or inconsistent with the person's beliefs.

Fugelsang, J. A., & Dunbar, K. N. (2004). A cognitive neuroscience framework for understanding causal reasoning and the law. *Philosophical Transactions of the Royal Society of London, B: Biological Sciences, 359,* 1749–1754.

5. Regret and decision making. The results of the ultimatum game experiments show that human decision making can be influenced by emotions. Other experiments have shown that people's decision making is influenced by a desire to avoid the regret they would experience if they made the wrong decision.

Coricelli, G., Critchley, H. D., Joffily, M., O'Doherty, J. P., Sirigu, A., & Dolan, R. J. (2005). Regret and its avoidance: A neuroimaging study of choice behavior. *Nature Neuroscience, 8,* 1255–1262.

6. Another view of rationality. We described the idea that people's reasoning and decision making can be negatively affected by bias and the use of heuristics. Some researchers have proposed another approach that sees people as behaving more rationally than this view gives them credit for.

Chase, V. M., Hertwig, R., & Gigerenzer, G. (1998). Views of rationality. *Trends in Cognitive Sciences, 2,* 206–214.

7. Embodied cognition. Some cognitive psychologists propose that to understand cognition, we need to take into account how a person's body interacts with the environment. This idea has implications for understanding problem solving, reasoning, and language.

Wilson, M. (2002). Six views of embodied cognition. *Psychonomic Bulletin and Review, 9,* 625–636.

8. Neurons that respond to abstract rules. There are neurons in the monkey PFC that respond to abstract rules. This adds to the evidence that the PFC is important for problem solving.

Wallis, J. D., Anderson, K. C., & Miller, E. K. (2001). Single neurons in prefrontal cortex encode abstract rules. *Nature, 411,* 953–956.

Key Terms

Affirming the antecedent, 444
Affirming the consequent, 444
Antecedent, 443
Atmosphere effect, 439
Availability heuristic, 456
Base rate, 460
Belief bias, 439
Categorical syllogism, 437
Conclusion, 437
Conditional syllogism, 443
Confirmation bias, 462
Conjunction rule, 461
Consequent, 443
Decisions, 437
Deductive reasoning, 436
Denying the antecedent, 444
Denying the consequent, 444
Diversity principle, 464
Economic utility theory, 466
Evolutionary perspective on cognition, 450

Falsification principle, 446
Focusing illusion, 467
Framing effect, 471
Illusory correlation, 458
Inductive reasoning, 436
Law of large numbers, 462
Mental model, 441
Mental simulation, 467
Neuroeconomics, 475
Omission bias, 477
Opt-in procedure, 469
Opt-out procedure, 469
Permission schema, 448
Perseveration, 473
Pragmatic reasoning schema, 448
Premise, 437
Reasoning, 435
Representativeness heuristic, 459
Risk-aversion strategy, 470
Risk-taking strategy, 470

Similarity-coverage model, 464
Social-exchange theory, 450
Stereotype, 459
Syllogism, 436
Typicality principle, 464

Ultimatum game, 475
Utility, 466
Valid, 438
Wason four-card problem, 445

CogLab

To experience these experiments for yourself, go to http://coglab.wadsworth.com. Be sure to read each experiment's setup instructions before you go to the experiment itself. Otherwise, you won't know which keys to press.

Primary Labs

Wason selection task Two versions of the Wason four-card problem (p. 445).

Typical reasoning How the representativeness heuristic can lead to errors of judgment (p. 459).

Risky decisions How decision making is influenced by framing effects (p. 469).

Decision making An experiment that demonstrates how decisions can be affected by the context within which the decision is made (p. 469).

Related Lab

Monty Hall A simulation of the Monty Hall three-door problem, which involves an understanding of probability.

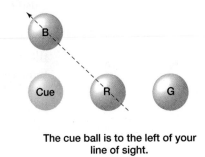

The cue ball is to the left of your
line of sight.

■ **Figure 12.21** Result of visualization of pool balls (see page 441).

Glossary

(Number in parentheses is the chapter in which the term first appears.)

Acrobat problem A problem involving acrobats that is similar to the Tower of Hanoi problem. Used to illustrate how the way a problem is stated can influence its difficulty. See also **Reverse acrobat problem.** (11)

Action potential Electrical potential that travels down a neuron's axon. (2)

Affirming the antecedent Occurs in a conditional syllogism of the following form: *If* p, *then* q; p *occurs; therefore* q *occurs.* The antecedent, *p*, is affirmed in the second premise. This is a valid form of syllogism. See Table 12.1. See also **Denying the consequent.** (12)

Affirming the consequent Occurs in a conditional syllogism of the following form: *If* p, *then* q; the second premise is q *occurs;* and the third is *therefore*, p *occurs.* This is an invalid form of conditional syllogism. See also **Denying the antecedent.** (12)

Algorithm A procedure that is guaranteed to solve a problem. (3)

American Sign Language (ASL) A language based on hand and arm gestures that is used by deaf people in the United States and parts of Canada. (5)

Amygdala A subcortical structure that is involved in processing emotional aspects of experience, including memory for emotional events. (2)

Analogical encoding A technique in which people compare two problems that illustrate a principle. This technique is designed to help people discover similar structural features of cases or problems. (11)

Analogical paradox Participants in psychological experiments tend to focus on surface features in analogy problems, whereas people in the real world frequently use deeper, more structural features. (11)

Analogical problem solving The use of analogies as an aid to solving problems. Typically, a solution to one problem, the source problem, is presented that is analogous to the solution to another problem, the target problem. (11)

Analogy Drawing a comparison in order to show a similarity between two different things. (11)

Analytic introspection A procedure used by early psychologists in which trained participants described their experiences and thought processes elicited by stimuli presented under controlled conditions. (1)

Anaphoric inference An inference that connects an object or person in one sentence to an object or person in another sentence. See also **Causal inference; Instrumental inference.** (10)

Antecedent In a conditional syllogism, the term *p* in the conditional premise *If* p, *then q.* See also **Consequent.** (12)

Anterograde amnesia Amnesia for events that occur after an injury—that is, the inability to form new memories. Compare to **retrograde amnesia**—the inability to remember information from the past. (6)

Articulatory suppression Interference with operation of the phonological loop that occurs when a person repeats an irrelevant word such as "the" as he or she is carrying out a task that requires the phonological loop. (5)

Atmosphere effect The idea that the words *All*, *Some*, and *No* in the premises of a syllogism create an overall "mood" or "atmosphere" that can influence the evaluation of the validity of the conclusion. According to this idea, two *All*'s suggest an *all* conclusion, one or two *No*'s suggests a *no* conclusion, and one or two *Some*'s suggests a *some* conclusion. (12)

Attention Focusing on specific features of the environment or on certain thoughts or activities. (4)

Attenuation theory of attention Anne Treisman's model of selective attention that proposes that selection occurs in two stages. In the first stage, an attenuator analyzes the incoming message and lets through the attended message—and also the unattended message, but at a lower (attenuated) strength. (4)

Attenuator In Treisman's model of selective attention, the attenuator analyzes the incoming message in terms of physical characteristics, language, and meaning. Attended messages pass through the attenuator at full strength, and unattended messages pass though with reduced strength. (4)

Auditory coding Representation of the sound of a stimulus in the mind. (5)

Autism A developmental disorder in which one of the major symptoms is the withdrawal of contact from other people. People with autism often direct their attention differently from people without autism. (4)

Autobiographical memory Memory for dated events in a person's life. Autobiographical memory is usually considered to be a type of episodic memory, but has also been defined as including personal semantic memories. (7)

Automatic processing Processing that occurs automatically without the person intending to do it, and which also uses few cognitive resources. Automatic processing is associated with easy or well-practiced tasks. (4)

Availability heuristic We base our judgments of the frequency of events on what events come to mind. (12)

Axon Part of the neuron that transmits signals from the cell body to the synapse at the end of the axon. (2)

Back propagation A process by which learning can occur in a connectionist network, in which an error signal is transmitted backward through the network. This backward-transmitted error signal provides the information needed to adjust the weights in the network to achieve the correct output signal for a stimulus. (8)

Balint's syndrome A condition caused by brain damage that causes a person to have difficulty focusing attention on individual objects. (3)

Base rate The relative proportions of different classes in a population. Failure to consider base rates can often lead to errors of reasoning. (12)

Basic level In Rosch's categorization scheme, the level below the superordinate level that would correspond to *table* or *chair* for the superordinate category of *furniture*. According to Rosch, the basic level is psychologically special because it is the level above which much information is lost and below which little is gained. See also **Subordinate level; Superordinate level.** (8)

Behavioral approach to the study of the mind When the mind is studied by measuring a person's behavior and by explaining this behavior in behavioral terms. (1)

Behaviorism The approach to psychology, founded by John B. Watson, which stated that observable behavior is the only valid data for psychology. A consequence of this idea is that consciousness and unobservable mental processes were considered not worthy of study by psychologists. (1)

Belief bias The idea that if a syllogism's conclusion is true or agrees with a person's beliefs, this increases the likelihood that the syllogism will be judged to be valid. Also, if the conclusion is viewed as false, this increases the likelihood that the syllogism will be judged as invalid. (12)

Bottom-up processing Processing that starts with information received by the receptors. This type of processing can also be called data-based processing. (3)

Brain imaging Techniques such as functional magnetic resonance imaging (fMRI) and positron emission tomography (PET) that result in images of the brain that represent the brain activity. In cognitive psychology, activity is measured in response to specific cognitive tasks. (2)

Candle problem A problem first described by Duncker in which a person is given a number of objects and is given the task of mounting a candle on a wall so it can burn without dripping wax on the floor. This problem was used to study functional fixedness. (11)

Categorical perception It is difficult to discriminate between two stimuli that are within a category, and it is easier to discriminate between two stimuli that are in different categories. (10)

Categorical syllogism A syllogism in which the premises and conclusion describe the relationship between two categories by using statements that begin with *All*, *No*, or *Some*. (12)

Categorization The process by which objects are placed in categories. (8)

Category Groups of objects that belong together because they belong to the same class of objects, such as "houses," "furniture," or "schools." (8)

Category-specific neurons Neurons in the temporal lobe that respond best to objects in a specific category. (8)

Causal inference An inference that results in the conclusion that the events described in one clause or sentence were caused by events that occurred in a previous sentence. See also **Anaphoric inference; Instrumental inference.** (10)

Cell body Part of a cell that contains mechanisms that keep the cell alive. In some neurons the cell bodies, and the dendrites associated with it, receive information from other neurons. (2)

Central executive The part of working memory that coordinates the activity of the phonological loop and the visuospatial sketch pad. (5)

Cerebral cortex The 3-mm-thick outer layer of the brain that contains the mechanisms responsible for higher mental functions such as perception, language, thinking, and problem solving. (2)

Change blindness Difficulty in detecting changes in similar, but slightly different, scenes that are presented one after another. The changes are often easy to see once attention is directed to them, but are usually undetected in the absence of appropriate attention. (3)

Change blindness blindness Occurs when, after being informed of the kinds of changes that occur in a change blindness experiment, a person believes that he or she would be able to detect these changes. The person is "blind" to the fact that change blindness does, in fact, occur. (3)

Choice reaction time Reacting to one of two or more stimuli. For example, in Donders' experiment (see Chapter 1), participants had to make one response to one stimulus, and a different response to another stimulus. (1)

Chunk Used in connection with the idea of chunking in memory. A chunk is a collection of elements that are strongly associated with each other, but are weakly associated with elements in other chunks. (5)

Chunking Combining small units into larger ones, such as when individual words are combined into a meaningful sentence. Chunking can be used to increase the capacity of memory. (5)

Cocktail party phenomenon The ability to focus attention on one message and ignore others. The name is taken from the ability to pay attention to one conversation at a crowded party without attending to other conversations that are happening at the same time. (4)

Coding The form in which stimuli are represented in the mind. For example, information can be represented in visual, semantic, and phonological forms. See also **Neural code,** which refers to how stimuli are represented in the firing of neurons. (5)

Cognition The mental processes involved in perception, attention, memory, language, problem solving, reasoning, and making decisions. (1)

Cognitive economy A feature of some semantic network models in which properties of a category that are shared by many members of a category are stored at a higher-level node in the network.

For example, the property *can fly* would be stored at the node for *bird* rather than at the node for *canary*. (8)

Cognitive hypothesis An explanation for the reminiscence bump, which states that memories are better for adolescence and early adulthood because encoding is better during periods of rapid change that are followed by stability. (7)

Cognitive interview A procedure used for interviewing crime-scene witnesses that involves letting witnesses talk with a minimum of interruption, and also uses techniques that help witnesses recreate the situation present at the crime scene by having them place themselves back in the scene and recreate things like emotions they were feeling, where they were looking, and how the scene may have appeared when viewed from different perspectives. (7)

Cognitive psychology The branch of psychology concerned with the scientific study of the mental processes involved in perception, attention, memory, language, problem solving, reasoning, and decision making. In short, cognitive psychology is concerned with the scientific study of the mind and mental processes. (1)

Cognitive revolution A shift in psychology, that began in the 1950s, from the behaviorist approach to an approach in which the main thrust was to explain behavior in terms of the mind. One of the outcomes of the cognitive revolution was the introduction of the information-processing approach to studying the mind. (1)

Cognitive science The interdisciplinary approach to the study of the mind. Cognitive science includes a wide net of disciplines including computer science, linguistics, neuroscience, artificial intelligence, philosophy, and psychology. (1)

Coherence The representation of a text or story in a reader's mind so that information in one part of the text or story is related to information in another part. (10)

Common fate, law of Law of perceptual organization that states that things moving in the same direction appear to be grouped together. (3)

Complex cells A type of neuron in the visual cortex that responds best to a moving, oriented bar of light. Responding often occurs to a specific direction of movement. (2)

Concept A mental representation used for a variety of cognitive functions, including memory, reasoning, and using and understanding language. An example of a concept would be the way a person mentally represents "cat" or "house." (8)

Conceptual-peg hypothesis A hypothesis associated with Paivio's dual coding theory that states that concrete nouns create images that other words can hang onto, and that this enhances memory for these words. (9)

Conclusion The final statement in a syllogism, which follows from the two premises. (12)

Conditional syllogism Syllogisms with two premises and a conclusion, like categorical syllogisms, but the first premise is an "If . . . then . . ." statement. (12)

Conditioning A procedure in which pairing a neutral stimulus with a stimulus that elicits a response causes the neutral stimulus to elicit that response. (6)

Confirmation bias The tendency to selectively look for information that conforms to our hypothesis and to overlook information that argues against it. (12)

Conjunction rule The probability of the conjunction of two events (such as feminist and bank teller) cannot be higher than the probability of the single constituents (feminist alone or bank teller alone). (12)

Connectionism A network model of mental operation that proposes that concepts are represented in networks that are modeled after neural networks. This approach to describing the mental representation of concepts is also called the *parallel distributed processing approach*. See also **Connectionist network**. (8)

Connectionist network The type of network proposed by the connectionist approach to the representation of concepts. Connectionist networks are based on neural networks, but are not necessarily identical to them. One of the key properties of a connectionist network is that a specific category is represented by activity that is distributed over many units in the network. This contrasts with semantic networks, in which specific categories are represented at individual nodes. (8)

Consequent In a conditional syllogism, the term *q* in the conditional premise *If* p, *then* q. See also **Antecedent.** (12)

Consolidation The process that transforms new memories into a state in which they are more resistant to disruption. See also **Standard model of consolidation.** (6)

Consonant-vowel rule When people make speech errors in which phonemes of the same type replace one another, so consonants replace consonants and vowels replace vowels. (10)

Constructive approach to memory The idea that what people report as memories are constructed based on what actually happened plus additional factors, such as expectations, other knowledge, and other life experiences. (7)

Control processes In Atkinson and Shiffrin's modal model of memory, active processes that can be controlled by the person and may differ from one task to another. Rehearsal is an example of a control process. (5)

Controlled processing Processing that involves close attention. This term is especially associated with Schneider and Shiffrin's (1977) experiment, which showed that controlled processing was needed in the difficult, varied mapping condition of their experiment, even after extensive practice. (4)

Convergence Synapsing of a number of neurons onto one neuron. (2)

Convergent thinking Thinking that works toward finding a solution to a specific problem that usually has a correct answer. Can be contrasted with **Divergent thinking.** (11)

Creative cognition A technique developed by Finke to train people to think creatively. (11)

Cued recall A procedure for testing memory in which a participant is presented with cues such as words or phrases to aid recall of previously experienced stimuli. See also **Free recall.** (6)

Cultural life script Life events that commonly occur in a particular culture. (7)

Cultural life script hypothesis The idea that events in a person's life story become easier to recall when they fit the cultural life script for that person's culture. (7)

Decisions Making choices between alternatives. (12)

Declarative memory Memory that involves conscious recollections of events or facts that we have learned in the past. (6)

Deductive reasoning Reasoning that involves syllogisms in which a conclusion logically follows from premises. See also **Inductive reasoning.** (12)

Deep processing Processing that involves attention to meaning and relating an item to something else. Deep processing is usually associated with elaborative rehearsal. See also **Depth of processing; Shallow processing.** (6)

Definitional approach to categorization The idea that we can decide whether something is a member of a category by determining whether the object meets the definition of the category. See also **Family resemblance.** (8)

Delayed partial report method A procedure used in Sperling's experiment in which he was studying the properties of the visual icon. His participants were instructed to report only some of the stimuli in a briefly presented display. A cue tone that was delayed for a fraction of a second after the display was extinguished indicated which part of the display to report. See also **Partial report method; Whole report method.** (5)

Delayed-response task A task in which information is provided, a delay is imposed, and then memory is tested. This task has been used to study short-term memory by testing monkeys' ability to hold information about the location of a food reward during a delay. (5)

Dendrites Structures that branch out from the cell body to receive electrical signals from other neurons. (2)

Denying the antecedent Occurs in a conditional syllogism of the following form: *If* p, *then* q; p *does not occur; Therefore* q *does not occur.* This is an invalid form of conditional syllogism. See also **Affirming the consequent; Denying the consequent.** (12)

Denying the consequent Occurs in a conditional syllogism of the following form: *If* p, *then* q; q *does not occur; Therefore* p *does not occur.* The consequent, *q*, is denied in the second premise. This is a valid form of syllogism. See Table 12.1. See also **Affirming the antecedent.** (12)

Depictive representation Corresponds to spatial representation. So called because a spatial representation can be depicted by a picture. (9)

Depth of processing The idea that the processing that occurs as an item is being encoded into memory can be deep or shallow. Deep processing involves attention to meaning and is associated with elaborative rehearsal. Shallow processing involves repetition with little attention to meaning and is associated with maintenance rehearsal. See also **Levels of processing.** (6)

Design fixation When presenting a sample, design influences the creation of new designs. (11)

Dichotic listening The procedure of presenting one message to the left ear and a different message to the right ear. (4)

Dictionary unit A component of Treisman's attenuation theory of attention. This processing unit contains stored words and thresholds for activating the words. The dictionary unit helps explain why we can sometimes hear a familiar word, such as our name, in an unattended message. See also **Attenuation theory of attention.** (4)

Digit span The number of digits a person can remember. Digit span is used as a measure of the capacity of short-term memory. (5)

Discriminability In recognition-by-components theory, the property that geons can be distinguished from each other from almost all viewpoints. (3)

Dissociations A situation in cases of brain damage, in which the damage causes a problem in one function while not affecting other functions. See also **Double dissociation; Single dissociation.** (2)

Distributed coding Representation of an object or experience by the firing of a number of neurons. (2)

Distributed versus massed practice effect Memory is better when learning occurs in a number of short study sessions, with breaks in-between, than when learning occurs in one long session. (6)

Divergent thinking Thinking that is open-ended and for which there are a large number of potential solutions. Can be contrasted with **Convergent thinking.** (11)

Diversity principle The inductive argument with the greatest coverage of a category is stronger. See also **Similarity-coverage model; Typicality principle.** (12)

Divided attention The ability to pay attention to, or carry out, two or more different tasks simultaneously. (4)

Double dissociation A situation in which a single dissociation can be demonstrated in one person, and the opposite type of single dissociation can be demonstrated in another person (i.e., Person 1: function A is present; function B is damaged; Person 2: function A is damaged; function B is present). (2)

Early-selection model Model of attention that explains selective attention by early filtering-out of the unattended message. In Broadbent's early-selection model, the filtering step occurs before the message is analyzed to determine its meaning. (4)

Echoic memory Brief sensory memory for auditory stimuli that lasts for a few seconds after a stimulus is extinguished. (5)

Economic utility theory The idea that people are basically rational, so if they have all of the relevant information, they will make a decision that results in the maximum expected utility. (12)

Elaborative rehearsal Rehearsal that involves thinking about the meaning of an item to be remembered or making connections between that item and prior knowledge. Compare to **Maintenance rehearsal.** (6)

Encoding The process of acquiring information and transferring it into memory. (6)

Encoding specificity The principle that we learn information together with its context. This means that presence of context can lead to enhanced memory for the information. (6)

End-stopped cells A type of neuron in the visual cortex that responds best to an oriented bar of light of a particular length moving in a particular direction. (2)

Epiphenomenon A phenomenon that accompanies a mechanism, but is not actually part of the mechanism. An example of an epiphenomenon is lights that flash on a mainframe computer as it operates. (9)

Episodic buffer An additional component added to Baddeley's original working memory model that serves as a "backup" store that communicates with both LTM and the components of working memory. Holds information longer and has greater capacity than the phonological loop or visuospatial sketch pad. (5)

Episodic memory Memory for specific events that have happened to the person having the memory. These events are usually remembered as a personal experience that occurred at a particular time and place. Episodic and semantic memory, together, make up declarative memory. (6)

Error signal During learning in a connectionist network, the difference between the output signal generated by a particular stimulus and the output that actually represents that stimulus. (8)

Evolutionary perspective on cognition Based on the idea that many properties of our minds can be traced to the evolutionary principles of natural selection. See also **Social-exchange theory.** (12)

Excitation An effect caused by excitatory neurotransmitter that increases the rate of nerve firing or the likelihood of nerve firing. (2)

Excitatory neurotransmitter Neurotransmitter that causes an excitatory effect on a membrane. This excitatory effect causes an increase in firing or in the likelihood of firing. (2)

Exemplar In categorization, members of a category that a person has experienced in the past. (8)

Exemplar approach to categorization The approach to categorization in which members of a category are judged against exemplars, which are examples of members of the category that the person has encountered in the past. (8)

Experience-dependent plasticity A mechanism that causes neurons to develop so they respond best to the type of stimulation that they experience. (2)

Expert Person who, by devoting a large amount of time to learning about a field and practicing application of that learning, has become acknowledged as being extremely skilled or knowledgeable about that field. (11)

Extrastriate body area (EBA) An area in the temporal cortex that is activated by pictures of bodies and parts of bodies, but not by faces or other objects. (3)

Eye tracker A device for measuring where people look (fixate) in a scene and how they move their eyes from one fixation point to another. (4)

Eyewitness testimony Testimony by eyewitnesses to a crime about what they saw during commission of the crime. (7)

Falsification principle The reasoning principle that to test a rule, it is necessary to look for situations that falsify the rule. (12)

Familiarity, law of Law of perceptual organization that states that things are more likely to form groups if the groups appear familiar or meaningful. (3)

Family resemblance In considering the process of categorization, the idea that things in a particular category resemble each other in a number of ways. This approach can be contrasted with the definitional approach, which states that an object belongs to a category only when it meets a definite set of criteria. (8)

Fear conditioning A procedure in which pairing a neutral stimulus with a stimulus that elicits fear or avoidance causes the neutral stimulus to elicit fear or avoidance. (6)

Feature detectors Neurons that respond to specific visual features, such as orientation or size or the more complex features that make up environmental stimuli. (2)

Feature integration theory (FIT) An approach to object perception developed by Anne Treisman that proposes that object perception occurs in a sequence of stages in which features are first analyzed and then combined to result in perception of an object. (3)

Feature level Part of the interactive activation model of word recognition that contains feature units. These units receive inputs from stimuli in the environment and respond to specific features such as straight lines, curved lines, or lines with a specific orientation. See also **Letter level; Word level.** (3)

Feature units Units in the interactive activation model of word recognition that respond to specific features. See also **Letter units; Word units.** (3)

Feedback activation In the interactive activation model of word recognition, activation that is sent from word units back to each of the letter units for that word. (3)

Field perspective Remembering an event as though you are seeing it. Compare to **Observer perspective,** in which the person remembering the event is seen as part of the event. (7)

Filter model of attention A model of attention that proposes that selective attention is achieved by a filtering out of unattended messages. An early filter model of attention was proposed by Donald Broadbent. (4)

Fixation In perception and attention, a pausing of the eyes on places of interest while observing a scene. (4)

Fixation In problem solving, people's tendency to focus on a specific characteristic of the problem that keeps them from arriving at a solution. See also **Design fixation; Functional fixedness.** (11)

Flanker-compatibility task A procedure in which participants are instructed to respond to a target stimulus that is flanked, or surrounded, by distractor stimuli that they are supposed to ignore. The degree to which the distractor interferes with responding to the target is taken as an indication of whether the distractor stimuli are being processed. (4)

Flashbulb memories Memories of emotionally charged or especially memorable events that have been claimed to be particularly vivid and accurate. See **Narrative rehearsal hypothesis** for another viewpoint. (7)

Focused attention stage The second stage of Treisman's feature integration theory. According to the theory, attention causes the combination of features into perception of an object. (3)

Focusing illusion When people focus their attention on just one aspect of a situation and ignore other aspects of a situation that may be important, this can lead to lack of accuracy in predicting emotional reactions to events. (12)

Framing effect Occurs when decisions are influenced by how a decision is stated. (12)

Free recall A procedure for testing memory in which the participant is asked to remember stimuli that were originally presented. See also **Cued recall.** (6)

Freudian slip Speech errors that, according to Freud, are caused by unconscious motivations. (10)

Frontal lobe The lobe in the front of the brain that serves higher functions such as language, thought, memory, and motor functioning. (2)

Functional fixedness An effect that occurs when the ideas a person has about an object's function inhibit the person's ability to use the object for a different function. See also **Fixation** (in problem solving). (11)

Functional magnetic resonance imaging (fMRI) A brain-imaging technique involving the measurement of how blood flow changes in response to cognitive activity. Unlike positron emission tomography, this technique does not involve the injection of a radioactive tracer. (2)

Fusiform face area (FFA) An area in the temporal lobe that contains many neurons that respond selectively to faces. (2)

Garden-path model See **Syntax-first approach to parsing.** (10)

Garden-path sentence A sentence in which the meaning that seems to be implied at the beginning of the sentence turns out to be incorrect, based on information that is presented later in the sentence. (10)

Generation effect Memory for material is better when a person generates the material him- or herself, rather than passively receiving it. (6)

Geon The basic feature unit of the recognition-by-components approach to object perception. Geons are basic three-dimensional volumes. (3)

Gestalt psychologists A group of psychologists who disagreed with the structuralist approach to perception. In the area of perception, they proposed the laws of perceptual organization and were concerned with how figure is separated from ground. In problem solving, they were concerned with mechanisms such as fixation that inhibit problem solving. (3)

Given–new contract A speaker should construct sentences so that they contain both given information (information that the listener already knows) and new information (information that the listener is hearing for the first time). (10)

Goal state In problem solving, the condition at the end of a problem. (11)

Good continuation, law of Law of perceptual organization stating that points that, when connected, result in straight or smoothly curving lines, are seen as belonging together. In addition, lines tend to be seen as following the smoothest path. (3)

Good figure, law of See **Pragnanz, law of.** (3)

Graceful degradation Disruption of performance due to damage to a system that occurs only gradually as parts of the system are damaged. This occurs in some cases of brain damage and also when parts of a connectionist network are damaged. (8)

Graded amnesia When amnesia is most severe for events that occurred just prior to an injury and becomes less severe for earlier, more remote events. (6)

Grandmother cell A neuron that responds only to a highly specific stimulus. This stimulus could be a specific image, such as a picture of a person's grandmother, or a concept, such as the idea of grandmothers in general, or a person's real-life grandmother. (2)

Heuristic A "rule of thumb" that provides a best-guess solution to a problem. (3)

Hidden units Units in a connectionist network that are located between input units and output units. See also **Connectionist network; Input units; Output units.** (8)

Hierarchical organization Organization of categories in which larger, more general categories are divided into smaller, more specific categories. These smaller categories can, in turn, be divided into even more specific categories to create a number of levels. (8)

High prototypicality A category member that closely resembles the category prototype. See also **Prototypicality.** (8)

High-load task A task that uses most or all of a person's resources and so leaves little capacity to handle other tasks. (4)

Hippocampus A subcortical structure that is important in forming memories. There is also evidence that the hippocampus may be involved in retrieving older episodic memories. (2)

Iconic memory Brief sensory memory for visual stimuli that lasts for a fraction of a second after a stimulus is extinguished. This corresponds to the sensory memory stage of the modal model of memory. (5)

Ill-defined problem A problem in which it is difficult to specify a clear goal state or specific operators. Many real-life problems are ill-defined problems. (11)

Illusory conjunctions A situation that has been demonstrated in experiments by Anne Treisman, in which features from different objects are inappropriately combined. (3)

Illusory correlation A correlation between two events that appears to exist, when in reality there is no correlation or it is weaker than it is assumed to be. (12)

Imageless-thought debate The debate about whether thought is possible in the absence of images. (9)

Imagery debate The debate about whether imagery is based on spatial mechanisms such as those involved in perception, or on propositional mechanisms that are related to language. (9)

Imagery neuron A type of category-specific neuron that is activated by imagery. (9)

Implicit (nondeclarative) memory Memory that occurs when an experience affects a person's behavior, even though the person is not aware that he or she had the experience. Also called *nondeclarative memory*. (6)

Inattentional blindness Not noticing something even though it is in clear view, usually caused by failure to pay attention to the object or the place where the object is located. Also see **Change blindness.** (4)

Inductive reasoning Reasoning in which a conclusion follows from a consideration of evidence. This conclusion is stated as being probably true, rather than definitely true, as can be the case for the conclusions from deductive reasoning. (12)

Inference The process by which readers create information during reading that is not explicitly stated in the text. (10)

Information-processing approach The approach to psychology, developed beginning in the 1950s, in which the mind is described as processing information through a sequence of stages. (1)

Inhibition An effect caused by an inhibitory neurotransmitter that decreases the rate of nerve firing or the likelihood of nerve firing. (2)

Inhibitory neurotransmitter Neurotransmitter that causes an inhibitory effect on a membrane. This inhibitory effect causes a decrease in firing or in the likelihood of firing. (2)

Initial state In problem solving, the conditions at the beginning of a problem. (11)

Input units Units in a connectionist network that are activated by stimulation from the environment. See also **Connectionist network; Hidden units; Output units.** (8)

Insight Sudden realization of a problem's solution. (11)

Instrumental inference An inference about tools or methods that occurs during reading or listening to speech. See also **Anaphoric inference; Causal inference.** (10)

Interactionist approach to parsing The approach to parsing that takes into account all information—both semantic and syntactic—to determine parsing as a person reads a sentence. This approach to parsing assigns more weight to semantics than does the syntax-first approach to parsing. (10)

Interactive activation model McClelland and Rumelhart's model of word recognition that proposes that word recognition is based on activation, sent through three levels: the feature level, the letter level, and the word level. (3)

Intermediate states In problem solving, the various conditions that exist along the pathways between the initial and goal states. (11)

Inverse projection problem The ambiguity of the retinal image caused by the fact that a particular image could be caused by an infinite number of objects, with different sizes, shapes, orientations, and located at different distances from the eye. (3)

In-vivo problem-solving approach A method in which people are observed to determine how they solve problems in real-world situations. This technique has been used to study the use of analogy in a number of different settings, such as laboratory meetings of a university research group, and design brainstorming sessions in an industrial research and development department. (11)

Knowing Used by Tulving to describe the experience of semantic memory. Contrast with **Self-knowing** or **Remembering,** which he used to describe the experience of episodic memory. See also **Non-knowing,** used to describe implicit memory. (6)

Korsakoff's syndrome A condition caused by prolonged vitamin B1 deficiency that leads to destruction of areas on the frontal and temporal lobes that causes severe impairments in memory. (6)

Language A system of communication through which we code and express our feelings, thoughts, ideas, and experiences. (10)

Late closure When a person encounters a new word, the parser assumes that this word is part of the current phrase. (10)

Late-selection model A model of selective attention that proposes that selection of stimuli for final processing does not occur until after the information in the message has been analyzed for its meaning. (4)

Law of large numbers The larger the number of individuals that are randomly drawn from a population, the more representative the resulting group will be of the entire population. (12)

Law(s) of common fate, familiarity, good continuation, good figure, nearness, Pragnanz, proximity, similarity, simplicity See inverted entries (e.g., **Common fate, law of**).

Laws of perceptual organization Rules proposed by the Gestalt psychologists to explain how small elements of a scene or a display become perceptually grouped to form larger units. These "laws" are described as being "heuristics" in this book. (3)

Letter level Part of the interactive activation model of word recognition that contains letter units, which respond to specific letters. Letter units receive inputs from feature units. See also **Feature level; Word level.** (3)

Letter units Units in the interactive activation model of word recognition that respond to specific letters. See also **Feature units; Word units.** (3)

Levels of processing (LOP) Part of levels-of-processing theory that states that there are different depths of processing that can be achieved as information is being encoded. See also **Depth of processing; Levels-of-processing theory.** (6)

Levels-of-processing theory The idea that memory depends on how information is encoded, with better memory being achieved when processing is deep than when processing is shallow. Deep processing involves attention to meaning and is associated with elaborative rehearsal. Shallow processing involves repetition with little attention to meaning and is associated with maintenance rehearsal. (6)

Lexical ambiguity When a word can have more than one meaning. For example, *bug* can mean *insect*, *listening device*, or *annoy*. (10)

Lexical decision task A procedure in which a person is asked to decide as quickly as possible whether a particular stimulus is a word or a nonword. (8, 10)

Lexical priming Priming that involves the meaning of words. Typically occurs when a word is followed by another word with a similar meaning. For example, when presenting the word *ant* before the word *bug* causes a person to respond faster to the word *bug* than if *ant* had not preceded it. (10)

Lexicon All of the words that a person understands—the person's vocabulary. (10)

Life-narrative hypothesis An explanation for the reminiscence bump, which states that memories are better for adolescence and early adulthood because people assume their life identities during that time. (7)

Light-from-above heuristic The assumption that light is coming from above. This heuristic can influence how we perceive three-dimensional objects that are illuminated by light. (3)

Localization of function Location of specific functions in specific areas of the brain. For example, areas have been identified that are specialized to process information involved in the perception of movement, form, speech, and different aspects of memory. (2)

Location-based attention Models of attention that propose that attention operates on whatever stimuli are at a particular location. This contrasts with object-based attention, in which attention is focused on a particular object. (4)

Long-term memory A memory mechanism that can hold large amounts of information for long periods of time. Long-term memory is one of the stages in the modal model of memory. (1, 5)

Long-term potentiation (LTP) The increased firing that occurs in a neuron due to prior activity at the synapse. (6)

Low-load task A task that uses few resources, leaving some capacity to handle other tasks. (4)

Low prototypicality A category member that does not resemble the category prototype. See also **Prototypicality.** (8)

Maintenance rehearsal Rehearsal that involves repetition without any consideration of meaning or making connections to other information. Compare to **Elaborative rehearsal.** (6)

Means-end analysis A problem-solving strategy in which the goal is to reduce the difference between the initial and goal state. This is achieved by working to achieve subgoals that move the process of solution closer to the goal. (11)

Medial temporal lobe (MTL) An area in the temporal lobe that consists of the hippocampus and a number of surrounding structures. Damage to the MTL causes problems in forming new long-term memories. (6)

Memory The processes involved in retaining, retrieving, and using information about stimuli, images, events, ideas, and skills, after the original information is no longer present. (5)

Memory-trace replacement hypothesis The idea that misleading postevent information impairs or replaces memories that were formed during the original experiencing of an event. (7)

Mental approach to coding Determining how a stimulus or experience is represented in the mind. (5)

Mental chronometry Measuring the time-course of mental processes. (1)

Mental imagery Experiencing a sensory impression in the absence of sensory input. (9)

Mental model In reasoning, a mental model is a specific situation that is represented in a person's mind that can be used to help determine the validity of syllogisms in deductive reasoning. (12)

Mental rotation Rotating an image of an object in the mind. Shepard and Metzler's experiment provided evidence that people use this method when asked to determine whether two depictions are of the same object viewed from different angles or are two different objects. (1, 9)

Mental scanning A process of mental imagery in which a person scans a mental image in his or her mind. (9)

Mental simulation Models that people create about what will happen following different decisions. (9, 12)

Mental time travel According to Tulving, the defining property of the *experience* of episodic memory, in which a person travels back in time in his or her mind to reexperience events that happened in the past. See also **Self-knowing.** (6)

Mental-walk task A task used in imagery experiments in which participants are asked to form a mental image of an object and to imagine that they are walking toward this mental image. (9)

Method of loci A method for remembering things in which things to be remembered are placed at different locations in a mental image of a spatial layout. See also **Pegword technique.** (9)

Microelectrodes Small wires that are used to record electrical signals from the axons of neurons. (2)

Misinformation effect Occurs when misleading information presented after a person witnesses an event can change how that person describes the event later. (7)

Misleading postevent information (MPI) The misleading information that causes the misinformation effect. (7)

Modal model of memory The model proposed by Atkinson and Shiffrin describing memory as a mechanism that involves processing information through a series of stages, which include short-term memory and long-term memory. It is called the *modal model* because of the great influence it has had on memory research. (1, 5)

Model A model in cognitive psychology is a representation of the workings of the mind. There are many different kinds of models, but many are presented as interconnected boxes that each represent the operation of specific mental functions. (1)

Mutilated-checkerboard problem A problem that has been used to study how the statement of a problem influences a person's ability to reach a solution. (11)

Narrative rehearsal hypothesis The idea that we remember some life events better because we rehearse them. This idea was proposed by Neisser as an explanation for "flashbulb" memories. (7)

Nearness, law of Law of perceptual organization that states that things that are near to each other appear to be grouped together. (3)

Nerve fiber See **Axon.** (2)

Neural circuit Group of interconnected neurons that are responsible for neural processing. (2)

Neural code The representation of specific stimuli or experiences by the firing of neurons. (2)

Neural processing Interactions between neurons that cause a target neuron or group of neurons to respond to specific stimuli. (2)

Neuron Cell that is specialized to receive and transmit information in the nervous system. (2)

Neuropsychology The study of the behavioral effects of brain damage in humans. (2)

Neurotransmitter Chemical that is released at the synapse in response to incoming action potentials. (2)

Nonknowing A term used by Tulving to describe implicit memory. Refers to the fact that the defining characteristic of implicit memory is that a person is unaware that it is being used. See also **Knowing.** (6)

Object-based attention Model of attention proposing that the enhancing effects of attention can be located on a particular object. This contrasts with *location-based attention*, in which attention is focused on a location. (4)

Observer perspective Remembering an event as observed from the outside, so the person observes him- or herself experiencing the event. See also **Field perspective.** (7)

Occipital lobe The lobe at the back of the brain that is devoted primarily to analyzing incoming visual information. (2)

Occlusion heuristic When a large object is occluded by a smaller one, we perceive the large object as continuing behind the smaller one. (3)

Omission bias The tendency to do nothing to avoid having to make a decision that could be interpreted as causing harm. (12)

Operators In problem solving, permissible moves that can be made toward a problem's solution. (11)

Optic nerve The bundle of about 1 million nerve fibers (in the human) that leaves the back of the eye. These fibers carry signals that were generated and processed in the retina. (2)

Opt-in procedure Procedure in which a person must take an active step to *choose* a course of action. For example, choosing to be an organ donor. (12)

Opt-out procedure Procedure in which a person must take steps to *avoid* taking a particular course of action. For example, choosing not to be an organ donor. (12)

Output units Units in a connectionist network that contain the final output of the network. See also **Connectionist network; Hidden units; Input units.** (8)

Paired-associate learning Learning that occurs when a participant is presented with pairs of words during a study period and then is tested when one of the words is presented, and the task is to recall the other word. (9)

Parahippocampal place area An area in the temporal lobe that contains neurons that are selectively activated by pictures of indoor and outdoor scenes. (3)

Parallel distributed processing approach (PDP) See **Connectionism;** see also **Connectionist network.** (8)

Parietal lobe The lobe at the top of the brain that contains mechanisms responsible for sensations caused by stimulation of the skin, and also some aspects of visual information. (2)

Parser The mechanism for determining the meaning of a sentence. The parser has also been called the *language-analysis device* and the *sentence-analyzing mechanism.* (10)

Parsing The mental grouping of words in a sentence into phrases. The way a sentence is parsed determines its meaning. (10)

Partial-report method The procedure used in Sperling's experiment in which he was studying the properties of the visual icon. His participants were instructed to report only some of the stimuli in a briefly presented display. See also **Delayed partial-report method; Sensory memory; Whole-report procedure.** (5)

Pegword technique A method for remembering things in which the things to be remembered are associated with concrete words. See also **Method of loci.** (9)

Perception Conscious experience that results from stimulation of the senses. (3)

Perceptual organization The process of organizing elements of the environment into separate objects. (3)

Permission schema A pragmatic reasoning schema that states that if a person satisfies condition A, then they get to carry out action B. The permission schema has been used to explain the results of the Wason four-card problem. (12)

Perseveration Difficulty in switching from one behavior to another, which can hinder a person's ability to solve problems that require flexible thinking. Perseveration is observed in cases in which the prefrontal cortex has been damaged. (12)

Persistence of vision The continued perception of light for a fraction of a second after the original light stimulus has been extinguished. Perceiving a trail of light from a moving sparkler is caused by the persistence of vision. See also **Iconic memory.** (5)

Personal semantic memory Semantic memories that have personal significance. These are often easier to remember than semantic memories that are not personally significant. (6, 7)

Phoneme The shortest segment of speech that, if changed, changes the meaning of a word. (10)

Phoneme exchange A type of speech error that involves exchanging phonemes between words, such as saying "fleaky squoor" instead of "squeaky floor." (10)

Phonemic restoration effect When a phoneme in a word is heard, even though it is obscured by a noise, such as a cough. This typically occurs when the word is part of a sentence. (10)

Phonological loop The part of working memory that holds and processes verbal and auditory informa-

tion. See also **Central executive; Visuospatial sketch pad; Working memory.** (5)

Phonological similarity effect An effect that occurs when letters or words that sound similar are confused. For example, *T* and *P* are examples of two similar-sounding letters that could be confused. (5)

Physiological approach to coding Determining how a stimulus or experience is represented by the firing of neurons. (5)

Physiological approach to the study of the mind When the mind is studied by measuring physiological and behavioral responses, and when behavior is explained in physiological terms. (1)

Positron emission tomography (PET) A brain-imaging technique involving the injection of a radioactive tracer. (2)

Pragmatic inference Inference that occurs when reading or hearing a statement leads a person to expect something that is not explicitly stated or necessarily implied by the statement. (7)

Pragmatic reasoning schema A way of thinking about cause and effect in the world that is learned as part of experiencing everyday life. See also **Permission schema.** (12)

Pragnanz, law of Law of perceptual organization that states that every stimulus pattern is seen in such a way that the resulting structure is as simple as possible. Also called the *law of good figure* and the *law of simplicity.* (3)

Preattentive stage The first stage of Treisman's feature integration theory, in which an object is analyzed into its features. (3)

Precueing A procedure in which participants are given a cue which will, usually, help them carry out a subsequent task. This procedure has been used in visual attention experiments in which participants are presented with a cue that tells them where to direct their attention. (4)

Premise The first two statements in a syllogism. (12)

Primacy effect In a memory experiment in which a list of words is presented, enhanced memory for words presented at the beginning of the list. See also **Recency effect.** (6)

Priming stimulus The initial stimulus presented in the repetition priming procedure. If priming occurs, the presentation of this stimulus affects a participant's response to a test stimulus, which is presented later. See also **Repetition priming.** (6)

Proactive interference (PI) When information learned previously interferes with learning new information. See also **Retroactive interference.** (5)

Problem A situation that occurs when there is an obstacle between a present state and a goal state and it is not immediately obvious how to get around the obstacle. (11)

Problem space The initial state, goal state, and all the possible intermediate states for a particular problem. (11)

Procedural memory Memory for how to carry out highly practiced skills. Procedural memory is a type of implicit memory because although people can carry out a skilled behavior, they often cannot explain exactly how they are able to carry out this behavior. (6)

Propaganda effect When people are more likely to rate statements they have read or heard before as being true, just because of prior exposure to the statements. (6)

Propagated A property of action potentials. Once they are generated, they travel unchanged down the length of an axon. (2)

Propositional representation A representation in which relationships are represented by symbols, as when the words of language represent objects and the relationships between objects. (9)

Prospective memory Remembering to perform intended actions. (7)

Prototype A standard used in categorization that is formed by averaging the category members a person has encountered in the past. (8)

Prototype approach to categorization The idea that we decide whether something is a member of a category by determining whether it is similar to a standard representation of the category, called a prototype. (8)

Prototypicality The degree to which a particular member of a category matches the prototype for that category. See also **High prototypicality; Low prototypicality.** (8)

Proximity, law of Law of perceptual organization that states that things that are near to each other appear to be grouped together. (3)

Psycholinguistics The field concerned with the psychological study of language. (10)

Radiation problem A problem posed by Duncker that involves finding a way to destroy a tumor by radiation, without damaging other organs in the body. This problem has been widely used to study the role of analogy in problem solving. (11)

Rat–man demonstration Demonstration in which presentation of a "ratlike" or "manlike" stimulus picture can bias perception of another picture that is presented immediately afterward, so that it is more likely to be perceived as a rat or as a man. This is an example of the technique of priming. (3)

Reaction time The time it takes for a person to react to a stimulus. This is usually determined by measuring the time between presentation of a stimulus and the person's response to the stimulus. Examples of responses are pushing a button, saying a word, moving the eyes, and appearance of a particular brain wave. (1)

Reactivation A process that occurs during memory consolidation, in which the hippocampus replays the neural activity associated with a memory. During reactivation, activity occurs in the network connecting the hippocampus and the cortex. This activity results in the formation of connections between the cortical areas. (6)

Reasoning Cognitive processes by which people start with information and come to conclusions that go beyond that information. See also **Deductive reasoning; Inductive reasoning.** (12)

Recall test A test in which participants are presented with stimuli and then, after a delay, are asked to remember as many of the stimuli as possible. See also **Cued recall; Free recall.** (6)

Recency effect In a memory experiment in which a list of words is presented, enhanced memory for words presented at the end of the list. See also **Primacy effect.** (6)

Recognition test A procedure for testing memory in which stimuli are presented during a study period and then, later, the same stimuli plus other, new stimuli are presented. The participants' task is to pick the stimuli that were originally presented. (6)

Recognition-by-components (RBC) theory A feature-based approach to object perception that proposes that the recognition of objects is based on three-dimensional features called geons. See also **Geons.** (3)

Reconsolidation A process proposed by Nader and others that occurs when a memory is reactivated. This process is similar to the consolidation that occurs after initial learning, although it apparently occurs more rapidly. (6)

Rehearsal The process of repeating a stimulus over and over, usually for the purpose of remembering it, that keeps the stimulus active in short-term memory. (5)

Release from proactive interference A situation in which conditions occur that eliminate or reduce the decrease in performance caused by proactive interference. See Wickens' experiment described in Chapter 5. (5)

Remembering Used by Tulving as equivalent to the self-knowing characteristic of episodic memory. See also **Mental time travel; Self-knowing.** (6)

Reminiscence bump The empirical finding that people over 40 years old have enhanced memory for events from adolescence and early adulthood, compared to other periods of their lives. (7)

Remote memory Memory for events that occurred long ago. (6)

Repeated recall Recall that is tested immediately after an event and then is retested at various times after the event. (7)

Repeated reproduction A method of measuring memory in which a person reproduces a stimulus on repeated occasions so his or her memory is tested at longer and longer intervals after the original presentation of the material to be remembered. (7)

Repetition priming When an initial presentation of a stimulus affects the person's response to the same stimulus when it is presented later. See also **Priming stimulus.** (6)

Representativeness heuristic The probability that an event A comes from class B can be determined by how well A resembles the properties of class B. (12)

Resistance to visual noise In recognition-by-components theory, the property that geons can be perceived under "noisy" conditions that obscure part of the geon. (3)

Restructuring The process of changing a problem's representation. According to the Gestalt psychologists, restructuring is the key mechanism of problem solving. (11)

Retina A network of neurons that lines the back of the eye. Transduction and the initial processing of visual information occur in the retina. (2)

Retrieval The process of remembering information that has been stored in long-term memory. (6)

Retrieval cues Cues that help a person remember information that is stored in memory. (6)

Retroactive interference When more recent learning interferes with memory for something that happened the past. See also **Proactive interference.** (7)

Retrograde amnesia Loss of memory for something that happened prior to an injury or traumatic event such as a concussion. See also **Anterograde amnesia.** (6)

Reverse acrobat problem A modification of the acrobat problem that is used to show how the way a problem is stated can influence its difficulty. (11)

Risk-aversion strategy A decision-making strategy that is governed by the idea of avoiding risk. Often used when a problem is stated in terms of gains. See also **Risk-taking strategy.** (12)

Risk-taking strategy A decision-making strategy that is governed by the idea of taking risks. Often used when a problem is stated in terms of losses. See also **Risk-aversion strategy.** (12)

Rule-based approach (to mechanical reasoning) Applying a rule to solve a mechanical reasoning problem. Contrasts with approaches that involve mental imagery. (9)

Saccades Eye movements from one fixation point to another. See also **Fixation** (in perception and attention). (4)

Saliency map A map calculated by Parkhurst and co-workers based on stimulus salience, which indicates the how observers will fixate different areas of a scene. See also **Stimulus salience.** (4)

Sapir-Whorf hypothesis The idea that the nature of language in a particular culture can affect the way people in that culture think. (10)

Savings method Method used to measure retention in Ebbinghaus's memory experiments. He read lists of nonsense syllables and determined how many repetitions it took to repeat the lists with no errors. He then repeated this procedure after various intervals following initial learning and compared the number of repetitions needed to achieve no errors. (1)

Scene schema A person's knowledge about what is likely to be contained in a particular scene. This knowledge can help guide attention to different areas of the scene. For example, knowledge of what is usually in an office may cause a person to look toward the desk to see the computer. (4)

Schema A person's knowledge about what is involved in a particular experience. See also **Script.** (7)

Script A type of schema. The conception of the sequence of actions that describe a particular activity. For example, the sequence of events that are associated with going to class would be a "going to class" script. See also **Schema.** (7)

Selective attention The ability to focus on one message and ignore all others. (4)

Self-knowing The experience of mental time travel that occurs when experiencing an episodic memory. See also **Mental time travel; Remembering.** (6)

Self-reference effect Memory for a word is improved by relating the word to the self. (6)

Semantic coding Coding in the mind in the form of meaning. An example of semantic coding would be remembering the meaning of something you have read, as opposed to what the letters or words looked like (visual coding) or sounded like (auditory coding). (5)

Semantic memory Memory for knowledge about the world that is not tied to any specific personal experience. Semantic and episodic memory, together, make up declarative memory. (6)

Semantic network approach The approach to concepts in which concepts are arranged in networks that represent the way concepts are organized in the mind. (8)

Semantics The meanings of words and sentences. Distinguished from **Syntax.** (10)

Sensations The small elementary units that, according to the structuralists, are added together to create perceptions. (3)

Sensory memory A brief stage of memory that holds information for seconds or fractions of a second. It is the first stage in the modal model of memory. See also **Iconic memory; Persistence of vision.** (1, 5)

Sensory receptors Specialized neural structures that respond to environmental stimuli such as light, mechanical stimulation, or chemical stimuli. (2)

Sentence verification technique A technique in which the participant is asked to indicate whether a particular sentence is true or false. For example, sentences like "an apple is a fruit" have been used in studies on categorization. (8)

Serial-position curve In a memory experiment in which a number of participants are presented with a list of words, the serial position curve is a plot of the percentage of participants remembering each word, versus the position of that word in the list. See also **Primacy effect; Recency effect.** (6)

Shadowing The procedure of repeating a message out loud as it is heard. Shadowing is commonly used in conjunction with studies of selective attention that use the dichotic-listening procedure. (4)

Shallow processing Processing that involves repetition with little attention to meaning. Shallow processing is usually associated with maintenance rehearsal. See also **Deep processing; Depth of processing.** (6)

Short-term memory A memory mechanism that can hold a limited amount of information for a brief period of time, usually around 30 seconds, unless there is rehearsal (such as repeating a telephone number) that can maintain information in long-term memory. Short-term memory is one of the stages in the modal model of memory. (1, 5)

Similarity, law of Law of perceptual organization that states that similar things appear to be grouped together. (3)

Similarity-coverage model A model designed to explain how people's conceptions of different categories influences the strength of inductive arguments. Two basic principles of the model are **typicality** (the argument with the most typical example of a category in the premise is the strongest argument) and **diversity** (the argument with the greatest coverage of a category is stronger). (12)

Simple cells A type of neuron in the visual cortex that responds best to presentation of an oriented bar of light. (2)

Simple reaction time Reacting to the presence or absence of a single stimulus (as opposed to having to choose between a number of stimuli before making a response). See also **Choice reaction time.** (1)

Simplicity, law of See **Pragnanz, law of.** (3)

Single dissociation A situation that occurs in cases of brain damage, in which the damage causes a problem in one function while not affecting other functions. A single dissociation occurs when one function is present and another is absent. See also **Double dissociation.** (2)

Situation model A mental representation of what a text is about. (10)

Situationally produced mental set Mental set that occurs because of what a person experiences while trying to solve a problem. (11)

Social-exchange theory An important aspect of human behavior is the ability for two people to cooperate in a way that is beneficial to both people. According to the evolutionary perspective on cognition, application of this theory can lead to the conclusion that detecting cheating is an important part of the brain's cognitive makeup. This idea has been used to explain the results of the Wason four-card problem. (12)

Source memory Knowledge of the *origins* of our memories, knowledge, or beliefs. For example, knowing that the source of a person's memory for a particular event was seeing it reported on television. (7)

Source misattribution Occurs when the source of a memory is misidentified. Equivalent to source monitoring error. See also **Source memory.** (7)

Source monitoring The process by which people determine the origins of memories, knowledge, or beliefs. Remembering that you heard about something from a particular person would be an example of source monitoring. See also **Source memory.** (7)

Source monitoring error Misidentifying the source of a memory. Equivalent to source misattribution. (7)

Source problem (or story) A problem or story that is analogous to the target problem and which therefore provides information that can lead to a solution to the target problem. See also **Target problem.** (11)

Spatial representation A representation in which different parts of an image can be described as corresponding to specific locations in space. See also **Depictive representation.** (9)

Specificity coding The representation of a specific stimulus by the firing of neurons that respond to only that stimulus. An example would be the signaling of a person's face by the firing of a neuron that responds only to that person's face. See also **Grandmother cell.** (2)

Speech error Error made while speaking, often involving exchanging sounds of words in a sentence or using incorrect sounds or words. Sometimes called "slip of the tongue." (10)

Speech segmentation The process of perceiving individual words from the continuous flow of the speech signal. (3, 10)

Spreading activation Activity that spreads out along any link in a network that is connected to an activated node. (8)

Standard model of consolidation Proposes that memory retrieval depends on the hippocampus during consolidation, and then once consolidation is complete, retrieval no longer depends on the hippocampus. (6)

State-dependent learning The principle that memory is best when a person is in the same state for encoding and retrieval. This principle is related to encoding specificity. (6)

Statistical learning The process of learning about transitional probabilities and other characteristics of the environment. Statistical learning for properties of language has been demonstrated in 8-week-old infants. See also **Transitional probabilities.** (3)

Stereotype An oversimplified generalization about a group or class of people that often focuses on negative characteristics. See also **Illusory correlation.** (12)

Stimulus salience Bottom-up factors that determine attention to elements of a scene. Examples are color, contrast, and orientation. The meaningfulness of the images, which is a top-down factor, does not contribute to stimulus salience. See also **Salience map.** (4)

Stroop effect An effect originally studied by J. R. Stroop, using a task in which a person is instructed to respond to one aspect of a stimulus, such as the color of ink that a word is printed in, and ignore another aspect, such as what the word spells. The Stroop effect refers to the fact that people find this task difficult when the ink color differs from what the word spells. (4)

Structural features The underlying principle of a problem. For example, in the radiation problem, needing high intensity to fix something surrounded by material that could be damaged by high intensity. Contrast with **Surface features.** (5, 11)

Structuralism An approach to psychology that explained perception as the adding up of small elementary units called sensations. (1, 3)

Subcortical structures Brain structures located beneath the cerebral cortex. Subcortical structures that are important for cognition are the amygdala, hippocampus, and thalamus. (2)

Subgoal In the means-end analysis approach to problem solving, subgoals are goals that create intermediate states that move the process of solution closer to the goal. (11)

Subordinate level The level in Rosch's categorization scheme that is a level below the basic level, and so would correspond to *kitchen table* for the basic category of *table*. See also **Basic level; Superordinate level.** (8)

Subtraction technique The technique used in brain imaging in which baseline activity is subtracted from the activity generated by a specific task. The result is the activity due only to the task that is being studied. (2)

Superordinate level The highest level in Rosch's categorization scheme that corresponds to general categories such as *furniture* or *vehicles*. See also **Basic level; Subordinate level.** (8)

Supervised learning A learning process in which mistakes are corrected. This mechanism is a property of some types of connectionist networks. (8)

Surface features Specific elements that make up a problem. For example, in the radiation problem, the rays and the tumor are surface features. Contrast with **Structural features.** (11)

Syllogism A series of three statements: two premises followed by a conclusion. The conclusion can follow from the premises based on the rules of logic. See also **Categorical syllogism; Conditional syllogism.** (12)

Synapse Space between the end of an axon and the cell body or dendrite of the next axon. (2)

Synaptic consolidation A process of consolidation that involves structural changes at synapses that happen rapidly, over a period of minutes. See also **Consolidation; Systems consolidation.** (6)

Syntactic ambiguity Sentences that are ambiguous because they can be parsed in more than one way. (10)

Syntactic category rule When one word replaces another to cause a speech error, the same syntactic categories are used. Nouns replace nouns, and verbs replace verbs. (10)

Syntactic priming Occurs when hearing a statement with a particular syntactic construction increases the chances that a statement that follows will be produced with the same construction. (10)

Syntax The rules for combining words into sentences. Distinguished from semantics. (10)

Syntax-first approach to parsing The approach to parsing that emphasizes the role of syntax in determining parsing. See also **Interactionist approach to parsing.** (10)

Systems consolidation A consolidation process that involves the gradual reorganization of circuits within brain regions and takes place on a long time scale, lasting weeks, months, or even years. See also **Consolidation; Synaptic consolidation.** (6)

Tacit-knowledge explanation An explanation proposed to account for the results of some imagery experiments that states that participants unconsciously use knowledge about the world in making their judgments. This explanation has been used as one of the arguments against describing imagery as a depictive or spatial representation. (9)

Target problem A problem to be solved. In analogical problem-solving, solution of this problem can become easier when the problem solver is exposed to an analogous source problem or story. See also **Source problem.** (11)

Task load How much of a person's cognitive resources are used to accomplish a task. The idea of task load is important for some explanations of selective attention and also for explanations of how people process information in working memory. (4)

Template matching A model of object recognition that proposes that recognition occurs when a stimulus matches a specific template. (3)

Temporal lobe The lobe on the side of the brain that contains mechanisms responsible for language, memory, hearing, and vision. (2)

Thalamus A subcortical structure that is important for processing information from the senses of vision, hearing, and touch. (2)

Think-aloud protocol A procedure in which participants are asked to say out loud what they are thinking while doing a problem. This procedure is used to help determine a person's thought processes as they are solving a problem. (11)

Top-down processing Processing that involves a person's knowledge or expectations. This type of processing has also been called knowledge-based processing. (3)

Tower of Hanoi problem A problem involving moving discs from one set of pegs to another set. It has been used to illustrate the process involved in means-end analysis. (11)

Transcranial magnetic stimulation (TMS) A procedure in which magnetic pulses are applied to the skull in order to temporarily disrupt the functioning of part of the brain. (9)

Transduction The transformation of one form of energy into another. In the nervous system, environmental energy is transformed into electrical energy. (2)

Transfer-appropriate processing When the type of task that occurs during encoding matches the type of task that occurs during retrieval. This type of processing can result in enhanced memory. (6)

Transitional probabilities In language, the chances that one sound will follow another sound. Every language has transitional probabilities for different sounds. Part of learning a language involves learning about the transitional probabilities in that language. See also **Statistical learning.** (3)

Two-string problem A problem first described by Maier in which a person is given the task of attaching two strings together that are too far apart to be reached at the same time. This task was devised to illustrate the operation of functional fixedness. (11)

Typicality effect The ability to judge the truth or falsity of sentences involving high-prototypical members of a category more rapidly than sentences involving low-prototypical members of a category. See also **Sentence verification technique.** (8)

Typicality principle The inductive argument with the most typical example of a category in the premise is the strongest argument. See also **Diversity principle; Similarity-coverage model.** (12)

Ultimatum game A game in which a *proposer* is given a sum of money and makes an offer to a *responder* as to how this money should be split between them. The responder must choose to accept or reject the offer. This game has been used to study people's decision-making strategies. (12)

Unconscious inference Helmholtz's idea that some of our perceptions are the result of unconscious assumptions that we make about the environment. (1)

Unilateral neglect A problem caused by brain damage, usually to the right parietal lobes, in which the patient ignores objects in the left half of his or her visual field. (9)

Units "Neuronlike processing units" in a connectionist network. See also **Hidden units; Input units; Output units.** (8)

Utility An approach to decision making that states that optimal decision making occurs when the outcome of the decision causes the maximum expected utility, where utility refers to outcomes that are desirable. (12)

Valid A situation that occurs in syllogisms when the conclusion follows logically from the premises. (12)

View invariance In recognition-by-components theory, the idea that geons can be identified when viewed from many different angles. (3)

View invariant properties In recognition-by-components theory, properties that give geons the property of view invariance. (3)

Visual agnosia A condition associated with brain damage in which a person can see an object but cannot name the object. (8)

Visual coding Coding in the mind in the form of a visual image. An example of visual coding would be remembering something by conjuring up an image of it in your mind. Also see **Semantic coding.** (5)

Visual icon See **Iconic memory.** (5)

Visual imagery A type of mental imagery involving vision, in which an image is experienced in the absence of a visual stimulus. (9)

Visuospatial sketch pad The part of working memory that holds and processes visual and spatial information. See also **Central executive; Phonological loop; Working memory.** (5)

Wason four-card problem A conditional-reasoning task involving four cards that was developed by Wason. Various versions of this problem have been used to determine the mechanisms that determine the outcomes of conditional-reasoning tasks. (12)

Water-jug problem A problem first described by Luchins that illustrates how mental set can influence the strategies that people use to solve a problem. (11)

Weapons focus A situation that occurs in which eyewitnesses to a crime tend to focus attention on a weapon, which causes poorer memory for other things that are happening. (7)

Weight The strength of a connection between units in a connectionist network. (8)

Well-defined problem A problem that has a correct answer. There are usually procedures that, when applied correctly, will lead to a solution. See also **Ill-defined problem.** (11)

Whole-report procedure The procedure used in Sperling's experiment in which he was studying the properties of the visual icon. His participants were instructed to report all of the stimuli they saw in a brief presentation. See also **Partial-report method; Sensory memory.** (5)

Word exchange Speech error in which one word in a sentence is exchanged with another word in the sentence. (10)

Word frequency The relative usage of words in a particular language. For example, in English, *home* has higher word frequency than *hike*. (10)

Word-frequency effect The phenomenon of faster reading time for high-frequency words compared to low-frequency words. (10)

Word-length effect The notion that it is more difficult to remember a list of long words than a list of short words. (5)

Word level Part of the interactive activation model of word recognition that contains word units, which are all of the words that a person knows. Word units receive input from letter units. See also **Feature level; Letter level.** (3)

Word substitution A speech error in which an incorrect word is substituted for the correct word in a sentence. Often related to knowledge that a speaker brings to a situation. (10)

Word-superiority effect The idea that letters are easier to identify when they are part of a word than when they are seen in isolation or in a string of letters that do not form a word. (3)

Word units Units in the interactive activation model of word recognition that respond to specific words. See also **Feature units; Letter units.** (3)

Working memory A limited-capacity system for temporary storage and manipulation of information for complex tasks such as comprehension, learning, and reasoning. (5)

References

Abel, T., & Lattal, K. M. (2001). Molecular mechanisms of memory acquisition, consolidation, and retrieval. *Current Opinion in Neurobiology, 11,* 180–187.

Adamson, R. E. (1952). Functional fixedness as related to problem solving. *Journal of Experimental Psychology, 44,* 288–291.

Aguirre, G. K., Zarahn, E., & D'Esposito, M. (1998). An area within human ventral cortex sensitive to "building" stimuli: Evidence and implications. *Neuron, 21,* 373–383.

Allende, I. (2001). *Portrait in sepia.* New York: HarperCollins.

Altmann, G. T. (1998). Ambiguity in sentence processing. *Trends in Cognitive Sciences, 2,* 146–152.

Altmann, G. T. M. (2001). The language machine: Psycholinguistics in review. *British Journal of Psychology, 92,* 129–170.

Altmann, G. T. M., & Kamide, Y. (1999). Incremental interpretation at verbs: Restricting the domain of subsequent reference. *Cognition, 73,* 247–264.

Altmann, G. T. M., & Steedman, M. J. (1988). Interaction with context during human sentence parsing. *Cognition, 30,* 191–238.

Amedi, A., Malach, R., & Pascual-Leone, A. (2005). Negative BOLD differentiates visual imagery and perception. *Neuron, 48,* 859–872.

American Psychological Association. (1996). Interim report of the working group on investigation of memories of childhood abuse. In K. Pezelek & W. P. Banks (Eds.), *The recovered memory/false memory debate* (pp. 371–392). San Diego: Academic Press.

Anderson, C. A., & Bushman, B. J. (2001). Effect of violent video games on aggressive behavior, aggressive cognitions, aggressive affect, physiological arousal, and prosocial behavior: A meta-analytic review of the literature. *Psychological Science, 12,* 353–359.

Anderson, J. R. (1978). Arguments concerning representation for mental imagery. *Psychological Review, 85,* 249–277.

Anderson, J. R., & Bower, G. H. (1973). *Human associative memory.* Washington, DC: V. H. Winston.

Anderson, J. R., & Schooler, L. J. (1991). Reflections of the environment in memory. *Psychological Science, 2,* 396–408.

Andrade, J. (Ed.). (2002). *Working memory in perspective.* Philadelphia: Psychology Press.

Annenberg/CPB Project/WNET-TV. (2000). *The mind* (2nd ed.) [Video]. F. J. Vattano, T. L. Bennett, & M. Butler (Eds.), Module 11: Clive Wearing, part 2: Living without memory.

Arkes, H. R., & Freedman, M. R. (1984). A demonstration of the costs and benefits of expertise in recognition memory. *Memory & Cognition, 12,* 84–89.

Assefi, S. L., & Garry, M. (2003). Absolut® memory distortions: Alcohol placebos influence the misinformation effect. *Psychological Science, 14,* 77–80.

Atkinson, R. C., & Shiffrin, R. M. (1968). Human memory: A proposed system and its control processes. In K. W. Spence & J. T. Spence (Eds.), *The psychology of learning and motivation.* New York: Academic Press.

Baars, B. J., Motley, M. T., & MacKay, D. G. (1975). Output editing for lexical status in artificially elicited slips of the tongue. *Journal of Verbal Learning and Verbal Behavior, 14,* 382–391.

Baddeley, A. D. (1996). Exploring the central executive. *Quarterly Journal of Experimental Psychology, 49A,* 5–28.

Baddeley, A. D. (2000a). The episodic buffer: A new component of working memory? *Trends in Cognitive Sciences, 4,* 417–423.

Baddeley, A. D. (2000b). Short-term and working memory. In E. Tulving & F. I. M. Craik (Eds.), *The Oxford handbook of memory* (pp. 77–92). New York: Oxford University Press.

Baddeley, A. D., & Hitch, G. J. (1974). Working memory. In G. A. Bower (Ed.), *The psychology of learning and motivation* (pp. 47–89). New York: Academic Press.

Baddeley, A. D., Lewis, V. F. J., & Vallar, G. (1984). Exploring the articulatory loop. *Quarterly Journal of Experimental Psychology, 36,* 233–252.

Baddeley, A. D., Thomson, N., & Buchanan, M. (1975). Word length and the structure of short-term memory. *Journal of Verbal Learning and Verbal Behavior, 14,* 575–589.

Bahrick, H. P., Hall, L. L., & Berger, S. A. (1996). Accuracy and distortion in memory for high school grades. *Psychological Science, 7,* 265–271.

Bailenson, J. N., Shum, M. S., Atran, S., Medin, D. L., & Coley, J. D. (2002). A bird's-eye view: Biological categorization and reasoning within and across cultures. *Cognition, 84,* 1–53.

Barlow, H. B. (1995). The neuron in perception. In M. S. Gazzaniga (Ed.), *The cognitive neurosciences* (pp. 415–434). Cambridge, MA: MIT Press.

Baron, R. A., & Ward, T. B. (2004). Expanding entrepreneurial cognition's toolbox: Potential contributions from the field of cognitive science. *Entrepreneurship Theory and Practice, 28,* 553–573.

Barrow, H. G., & Tannenbaum, J. M. (1986). Computational approaches to vision. In K. R. Boff, L. Kaufman, & J. P. Thomas (Eds.), *Handbook of perception and human performance* (Chapter 35). New York: Wiley.

Bartlett, F. C. (1932). *Remembering: A study in experimental and social psychology.* Cambridge, UK: Cambridge University Press.

Bavelier, D., Newport, E., Hall, M., Supalla, T., & Boutla, M. (in press). Persistent difference in short-term memory span between sign and speech: Implications for cross-linguistic comparisons. *Psychological Science.*

Bayley, P. J., Gold, J. J., Hopkins, R. O., & Squire, L. R. (2005). The neuroanatomy of remote memory. *Neuron, 46,* 799–810.

Baylis, G. C., & Driver, J. (1993). Visual attention and objects: Evidence for hierarchical coding of location. *Journal of Experimental Psychology: Human Perception and Performance, 19,* 451–470.

Bayliss, D. M., Jarrold, C., Baddeley, A. D., & Leigh, E. (2005). Differential constraints on the working memory and reading abilities of individuals with learning difficulties and typically developing children. *Journal of Experimental Child Psychology, 92,* 76–99.

Bechtel, W., Abrahamsen, A., & Graham, G. (1998). The life of cognitive science. In W. Bechtel & G. Graham (Eds.), *A companion to cognitive science* (pp. 2–104). Oxford, UK: Blackwell.

Beck, J. (1982). Textural segmentation. In J. Beck (Ed.), *Organization and representation in perception.* Hillsdale, NJ: Erlbaum.

Beck, J., Hope, B., & Rosenfeld, A. (Eds.). (1983). *Human and machine vision.* New York: Academic Press.

Bedard, J., & Chi, M. T. H. (1992). Expertise. *Current Directions in Psychological Science, 1,* 135–139.

Begg, I. (1972). Recall of meaningful phrases. *Journal of Verbal Learning and Verbal Behavior, 11,* 431–439.

Begg, I., Anas, A., & Farinacci, S. (1992). Dissociation of processes in belief: Source recollection, statement familiarity, and the illusion of truth. *Journal of Experimental Psychology: General, 121,* 446–458.

Behrmann, M., Moscovitch, M., & Winocur, G. (1994). Intact visual imagery and impaired visual perception in a patient with visual agnosia. *Journal of Experimental Psychology: Human Perception and Performance, 30,* 1068–1087.

Behrmann, M., & Tipper, S. P. (1994). Object-based attentional mechanisms: Evidence from patients with unilateral neglect. In C. Umilta & M. Moscovitch (Eds.), *Attention and performance XV: Conscious and nonconscious information processing* (pp. 351–375). Cambridge, MA: MIT Press.

Behrmann, M., & Tipper, S. P. (1999). Attention accesses multiple reference frames: Evidence from visual neglect. *Journal of Experimental Psychology: Human Perception and Performance, 25,* 83–101.

Bensley, L., & VanEewyk, J. (2001). Video games and real life aggression: Review of the literature. *Journal of Adolescent Health, 29,* 244–257.

Berntsen, D., & Rubin, C. (2004). Cultural life scripts structure recall from autobiographical memory. *Memory & Cognition, 32,* 427–442.

Bever, T. G., Sanz, M., & Townsend, D. J. (1998). The emperor's psycholinguistics. *Journal of Psycholinguistic Research, 27,* 261–284.

Biederman, I. (1981). On the semantics of a glance at a scene. In M. Kubovy & J. Pomerantz (Eds.), *Perceptual organization.* Hillsdale, NJ: Erlbaum.

Biederman, I. (1987). Recognition-by-components: A theory of human image understanding. *Psychological Review, 94,* 115–147.

Biederman, I. (2001). Recognizing depth-rotated objects: A review of results of research and theory. *Spatial Vision, 13,* 241–253.

Biederman, I., & Cooper, E. E. (1991). Priming contour deleted images: Evidence for intermediate representations in visual object recognition. *Cognitive Psychology, 23,* 393–419.

Biederman, I., Cooper, E. E., Hummel, J. E., & Fiser, J. (1993). Geon theory as an account of shape recognition in mind, brain, and machine. In J. Illingworth (Ed.), *Proceedings of the Fourth British Machine Vision Conference* (pp. 175–186). Guildford, Surrey, UK: BMVA Press.

Biegler, R., McGregor, A., Krebs, J. R., & Healy, S. D. (2001). A larger hippocampus is associated with longer-lasting spatial memory. *Proceedings of the National Academy of Sciences, USA, 98,* 6941–6944.

Bisiach, E., & Luzzatti, G. (1978). Unilateral neglect of representational space. *Cortex, 14,* 129–133.

Blakemore, C., & Cooper, G. G. (1970). Development of the brain depends on the visual environment. *Nature, 228,* 477–478.

Bliss, T. V. P., Collingridge, G. L., & Morris, R. G. M. (2003). Introduction. *Philosophical Transactions of the Royal Society, Series B: Biological Sciences, 358,* 607–611.

Bliss, T. V. P., & Lomo, T. (1973). Long-lasting potentiation of synaptic transmission in the dentate area of the anaesthetized rabbit following stimulation of the perforant path. *Journal of Physiology (Lond.), 232,* 331–336.

Blume, E. S. (1990). *Secret survivors: Uncovering incest and its aftereffects in women.* New York: Ballantine.

Bock, K. (1990). Structure in language. *American Psychologist, 45,* 1221–1236.

Bock, K. (1995). Sentence production: from mind to mouth. In J. C. Miller & P. D. Eimas (Eds.), *Speech, language, and communication* (pp. 181–216). San Diego: Academic Press.

Boring, E. G. (1942). *Sensation and perception in the history of experimental psychology.* New York: Appleton-Century-Crofts.

Boutla, M., Supalla, T., Newport, E. L., & Bavelier, D. (2004). Short-term memory span: Insights from sign language. *Nature Neuroscience, 7,* 997–1002.

Bower, G. H., Black, J. B., & Turner, T. J. (1979). Scripts in memory for text. *Cognitive Psychology, 11,* 177–220.

Bower, G. H., Clark, M. C., Lesgold, A. M., & Winzenz, D. (1969). Hierarchical retrieval schemes in recall of categorized word lists. *Journal of Verbal Learning and Verbal Behavior, 8,* 323–343.

Bower, G. H., & Winzenz, D. (1970). Comparison of associative learning strategies. *Psychonomic Science, 20,* 119–120.

Brandimonte, M. A., Hitch, G. J., & Bishop, D. V. M. (1992). Influence of short-term memory codes on visual image processing: Evidence from image transformation tasks. *Journal of Experimental Psychology: Learning, Memory, and Cognition, 18,* 157–165.

Branigan, H. P., Pickering, M. J., & Cleland, A. A. (2000). Syntactic co-ordination in dialogue. *Cognition, 75,* B13–B25.

Bransford, J. D., & Johnson, M. K. (1972). Contextual prerequisites for understanding: Some investigations of comprehension and recall. *Journal of Verbal Learning and Verbal Behavior, 11,* 717–726.

Bransford, J. D., & Johnson, M. K. (1973). Consideration of some problems of comprehension. In W. C. Chase (Ed.), *Visual information processing* (pp. 383–438). New York: Academic Press.

Breedin, S. D., & Saffran, E. M. (1999). Sentence processing in the face of semantic loss: A case study. *Journal of Experimental Psychology: General, 128,* 547–562.

Bregman, A. (1981). Asking the "what for" question in auditory perception. In M. Kubovy & J. R. Pomerantz (Eds.), *Perceptual organization* (pp. 99–119). Hillsdale, NJ: Erlbaum.

Breland, K., & Breland, M. (1961). The misbehavior of organisms. *American Psychologist, 16,* 631–684.

Brewer, J. G., Zhao, Z., Desmond, J. E., Glover, G. H., & Gabrieli, J. D. E. (1998). Making memories: Brain activity that predicts whether visual experience will be remembered or forgotten. *Science, 281,* 1185–1187.

Brewer, W. F. (1977). Memory for the pragmatic implication of sentences. *Memory & Cognition, 5,* 673–678.

Brewer, W. F., & Treyens, J. C. (1981). Role of schemata in memory for places. *Cognitive Psychology, 13,* 207–230.

Broadbent, D. E. (1958). *Perception and communication.* London: Pergammon.

Brooks, L. (1968). Spatial and verbal components of the act of recall. *Canadian Journal of Psychology, 22,* 349–368.

Brown, C. M. (1984). Computer vision and natural constraints. *Science, 224,* 1299–1305.

Brown, J. (1958). Some tests of the decay theory of immediate memory. *Quarterly Journal of Experimental Psychology, 10,* 12–21.

Brown, R., & Kulik, J. (1977). Flashbulb memories. *Cognition, 5,* 73–99.

Brown, R., & McNeil, D. (1966). The "tip of the tongue" phenomenon. *Journal of Verbal Learning and Verbal Behavior, 5,* 325–337.

Brown, S. C., & Craik, F. I. M. (2000). Encoding and retrieval of information. In E. Tulving & F. I. M. Craik (Eds.), *The Oxford handbook of memory* (pp. 93–107). New York: Oxford University Press.

Bruck, M., Ceci, S. J., & Hembrooke, H. (2002). The nature of children's true and false narratives. *Developmental Review, 22,* 520–554.

Buciarelli, M., & Johnson-Laird, P. N. (1999). Strategies in syllogistic reasoning. *Cognitive Science, 23,* 247–303.

Buckner, R. L., & Wheeler, M. E. (2001). The cognitive neuroscience of remembering. *Nature Reviews, 2,* 624–634.

Bugelski, B. R., & Alampay, D. A. (1961). The role of frequency in developing perceptual sets. *Canadian Journal of Psychology, 15,* 205–211.

Burton, A. M., Young, A. W., Bruce, J., Johnston, R. A., & Ellis, A. W. (1991). Understanding covert recognition. *Cognition, 39,* 129–166.

Butler, L. T., & Berry, D. C. (2001). Implicit memory: Intention and awareness revisited. *Trends in Cognitive Sciences, 5,* 192–197.

Butterworth, B., Shallice, T., & Watson, F. L. (1990). Short-term retention without short-term memory. In G. Vallar & T. Shallice (Eds.), *Neuropsychological impairments of short term memory* (pp. 187–213). Cambridge, UK: Cambridge University Press.

Cabeza, R., Anderson, N. D., Locantore, J. K., & McIntosh, A. R. (2002). Aging gracefully: Compensatory brain activity in high-performing older adults. *Neuroimage, 17,* 1394–1402.

Cabeza, R., & Nyberg, L. (2000). Imaging cognition II: An empirical review of 275 PET and fMRI studies. *Journal of Cognitive Neuroscience, 12,* 1–47.

Cabeza, R., Prince, S. E., Daselaar, S. M., Greenberg, D. L., Budde, M., Dolcos, F., LaBar, K. S., & Rubin, D. C. (2004). Brain activity during episodic retrieval of autobiographical and laboratory events: An fMRI study using novel photo paradigm. *Journal of Cognitive Neuroscience, 16,* 1583–1594.

Cahill, L., Babinsky, R., Markowitsch, H. J., & McGaugh, J. L. (1995). The amygdala and emotional memory. *Nature, 377,* 295–296.

Cahill, L., Haier, R. J., Fallon, J., Alkire, M. T., Tang, C., Keator, D., Wu, J., & McGaugh, J. L. (1996). Amygdala activity at encoding correlated with long-term free recall of emotional information. *Proceedings of the National Academy of Sciences, USA, 93,* 8016–8021.

Cahill, L., & McGaugh, J. L. (1998). Mechanisms of emotional arousal and lasting declarative memory. *Trends in Neurosciences, 21,* 294–299.

Caramazza, A. (2000). The organization of conceptual knowledge in the brain. In M. S. Gazzaniga (Ed.), *The cognitive neurosciences* (2nd ed., pp. 1037–1046). Cambridge, MA: MIT Press.

Caramazza, A., & Shelton, J. R. (1998). Domain-specific knowledge systems in the brain: The animate-inanimate distinction. *Journal of Cognitive Neuroscience, 10,* 1–34.

Carlin, D., Bonerba, J., Phipps, M., Alexander, G., Shapiro, M., & Grafman, J. (2000). Planning impairments in frontal lobe dementia and frontal lobe lesion patients. *Neuropsychologia, 38,* 655–665.

Carroll, D. W. (2004). *Psychology of language* (4th ed.). Belmont, CA: Wadsworth.

Carroll, L. (1872). *Through the looking glass and what Alice found there.* New York: Macmillan.

Catrambone, R., & Holyoak, K. J. (1989). Overcoming contextual limitations on problem-solving transfer. *Journal of Experimental Psychology: Learning, Memory, and Cognition, 15,* 1147–1156.

Chalmers, D., & Reisberg, D. (1985). Can mental images be ambiguous? *Journal of Experimental Psychology: Human Perception and Performance, 11,* 317–328.

Chan, J. C. K., & McDermott, K. B., (2006). Remembering pragmatic inferences. *Applied Cognitive Psychology, 20,* 633–639.

Chao, L. L., Haxby, J. V., & Martin, A. (1999). Attribute-based neural substrates in temporal cortex for perceiving and knowing about objects. *Nature Neuroscience, 2,* 913–919.

Chapman, L. J., & Chapman, J. P. (1969). Genesis of popular but erroneous psychodiagnostic observations. *Journal of Abnormal Psychology, 74,* 272–280.

Chase, V. M., Hertwig, R., & Gigerenzer, G. (1998). Views of rationality. *Trends in Cognitive Sciences, 2,* 206–214.

Chase, W. G., & Simon, H. A. (1973a). Perception in chess. *Cognitive Psychology, 4,* 55–81.

Chase, W. G., & Simon, H. A. (1973b). The mind's eye in chess. In W. G. Chase (Ed.), *Visual information processing.* New York: Academic Press.

Cheng, P. W., & Holyoak, K. J. (1985). Pragmatic reasoning schemas. *Cognitive Psychology, 17,* 391–416.

Cherry, E. C. (1953). Some experiments on the recognition of speech, with one and with two ears. *Journal of the Acoustical Society of America, 25,* 975–979.

Chi, M. T. H., Feltovich, P. J., & Glaser, R. (1981). Categorization and representation of physics problems by experts and novices. *Cognitive Science, 5,* 121–152.

Chi, M. T. H., Glaser, R., & Rees, E. (1982). Expertise in problem solving. In R. J. Sternberg (Ed.), *Advances in the psychology of human intelligence.* Hillsdale, NJ: Erlbaum.

Chino, Y., Smith, E., Hatta, S., & Cheng, H. (1997). Postnatal development of binocular disparity sensitivity in neurons of the primate visual cortex. *Journal of Neuroscience, 17,* 296–307.

Chiu, L.-H. (1972). A cross-cultural comparison of cognitive styles in Chinese and American children. *International Journal of Psychology, 7,* 235–242.

Chklovskii, D. B., Mel, B. W., & Svoboda, K. (2004). Cortical rewiring and information storage. *Nature, 431,* 782–788.

Chomsky, N. (1957). *Syntactic structures.* The Hague, Netherlands: Mouton.

Chomsky, N. (1959). A review of Skinner's *Verbal Behavior. Language, 35,* 26–58.

Christensen, B. T., & Schunn, C. D. (in press). The relationship of analogical distance to analogical function and pre-inventive structure: The case of engineering design. *Memory & Cognition.*

Chun, M. M., & Wolfe, J. M. (2001). Visual attention. In E. B. Goldstein (Ed.), *Blackwell's handbook of perception* (pp. 272–310). Oxford, UK: Blackwell.

Clark, H. H., & Van der Wege, M. M. (2002). Psycholinguistics. In H. Pashler & S. Yantis (Eds.), *Stevens' handbook of experimental psychology* (3rd ed., pp. 209–259). New York: Wiley.

Colby, C. L., Duhamel, J.-R., & Goldberg, M. E. (1995). Oculocentric spatial representation in parietal cortex. *Cerebral Cortex, 5,* 470–481.

Coley, J. D., Medin, D. L., & Atran, S. (1997). Does rank have its privilege? Inductive inferences within folkbiological taxonomies. *Cognition, 64,* 73–112.

Collins, A. M., & Loftus, E. F. (1975). A spreading-activation theory of semantic processing. *Psychological Review, 82,* 407–428.

Collins, A. M., & Quillian, M. R. (1969). Retrieval time from semantic memory. *Journal of Verbal Learning and Verbal Behavior, 8,* 240–247.

Colman, A. W. (2001). *Dictionary of psychology.* Oxford, UK: Oxford University Press.

Colvin, M. K., Dunbar, K., & Grafman, J. (2001). The effects of frontal lobe lesions on goal achievement in the water jug task. *Journal of Cognitive Neuroscience, 13,* 1129–1147.

Conrad, C. (1972). Cognitive economy in semantic memory. *Journal of Experimental Psychology, 92,* 149–154.

Conrad, R. (1964). Acoustic confusion in immediate memory. *British Journal of Psychology, 55,* 75–84.

Conway, A. R. A., Kane, M. J., & Engle, R. W. (2003). Working memory capacity and its relation to general intelligence. *Trends in Cognitive Sciences, 7,* 547–552.

Conway, M. A. (1996). Autobiographical memory. In E. L. Bjork & R. A. Bjork (Eds.), *Handbook of perception and cognition* (2nd ed., pp. 165–194). *Volume 10: Memory.* New York: Academic Press.

Conway, M. A., Anderson, S. J., Larsen, S. F., Donnelly, C. M., McDaniel, M. A., McClelland, A. G. R., Rawles, R. E., & Logie, R. H. (1994). The formation of flashbulb memories. *Memory and Cognition, 22,* 326–343.

Conway, M. A., & Ross, M. (1984). Getting what you want by revising what you had. *Journal of Personality and Social Psychology, 47,* 738–748.

Coppola, D. M., White, L. E., Fitzpatrick, D., & Purves, D. (1998). Unequal distribution of cardinal and oblique contours in ferret visual cortex. *Proceedings of the National Academy of Sciences, 95,* 2621–2623.

Coricelli, G., Critchley, H. D., Joffily, M., O'Doherty, J. P., Sirigu, A., & Dolan, R. J. (2005). Regret and its avoidance: A neuroimaging study of choice behavior. *Nature Neuroscience, 8,* 1255–1262.

Cosmides, L. (1989). The logic of social exchange: Has natural selection shaped how humans reason? Studies with the Wason selection task. *Cognition, 31,* 187–226.

Cosmides, L., & Tooby, J. (1992). Cognitive adaptations for social exchange. In J. H. Barkow, L. Cosmides, & J. Tooby (Eds.), *The adapted mind* (pp. 179–228). Oxford, UK: Oxford University Press.

Courtney, S. M., Petit, L., Maisog, J. M., Ungerleider, L. G., & Haxby, J. V. (1998). An area specialized for spatial working memory in human frontal cortex. *Science, 279,* 1347–1351.

Cowan, N. (2001). The magical number 4 in short-term memory: A reconsideration of mental storage capacity. *Behavioral Brain Sciences, 24,* 87–185.

Cowan, N., & Morey, C. C. (2006). Visual working memory depends on attentional filtering. *Trends in Cognitive Sciences, 10,* 139–141.

Craik, F. I. M., & Lockhart, R. S. (1972). Levels of processing: A framework for memory research. *Journal of Verbal Learning and Verbal Behavior, 11,* 671–684.

Craik, F. I. M., & Tulving, E. (1975). Depth of processing and retention of words in episodic memory. *Journal of Experimental Psychology: General, 104,* 268–294.

Craver-Lemley, C., & Reeves, A. (1992). How visual imagery interferes with vision. *Psychological Review, 99,* 633–649.

Crook, T. H., & Adderly, B. (1998). *The memory cure.* New York: Simon & Schuster.

Csikszentmihalyi, M. (1996). *Creativity: Flow and the psychology of discovery and invention.* New York: HarperCollins.

Cutler, B. L., Pernod, S. D., & Dexter, H. R. (1990). Juror sensitivity to eyewitness identification evidence. *Law and Human Behavior, 14,* 185–191.

Dapretto, M., & Bookheimer, S. Y. (1999). Form and content: Dissociating syntax and semantics in sentence comprehension. *Neuron, 24,* 427–432.

Darwin, C. J., Turvey, M. T., & Crowder, R. G. (1972). An auditory analogue of the Sperling partial report procedure: Evidence for brief auditory storage. *Cognitive Psychology, 3,* 255–267.

Davachi, L., Mitchell, J. P., & Wagner, A. C. (2003). Multiple routes to memory: Distinct medial temporal lobe processes build item and source memories. *Proceedings of the National Academy of Sciences, 100,* 2157–2162.

Davachi, L., & Wagner, A. D. (2002). Hippocampal contributions to episodic encoding: Insights from relational and item-based learning. *Journal of Neurophysiology, 88,* 982–990.

Davidoff, J. (2001). Language and perceptual categorization. *Trends in Cognitive Sciences, 5,* 382–387.

Davidson, P. S. R., Cook, S. P., & Glisky, E. L. (2006). *Aging, Neuropsychology, and Cognition, 13,* 196–206.

Davidson, P. S. R., & Glisky, E. L. (2002). Is flashbulb

memory a special instance of source memory? Evidence from older adults. *Memory, 10,* 99–111.

Deese, J. (1959). On the prediction of occurrence of particular verbal intrusions in immediate recall. *Journal of Experimental Psychology, 58,* 17–22.

DeGroot, A. (1965). *Thought and choice in chess.* The Hague, Netherlands: Mouton.

Dehaene, S., Izard, V., Pica, P., & Spelke, E. (2006). Core knowledge of geometry in an Amazonian indigene group. *Science, 311,* 381–384.

Dell, G. S. (1995). Speaking and misspeaking. In L. Gleitman & M. Liberman (Eds.), *An invitation to cognitive science* (Vol. 1, pp. 183–208). Cambridge, MA: MIT Press.

DeRenzi, E., Liotti, M., & Nichelli, P. (1987). Semantic amnesia with preservation of autobiographic memory: A case report. *Cortex, 23,* 575–597.

DeRenzi, E., & Spinnler, H. (1967). Impaired performance on color tasks inpatients with hemispheric lesions. *Cortex, 3,* 194–217.

Desimone, R., Miller, E. K., Chelazzi, L., & Lueschow, A. (1995). Multiple memory systems in the visual cortex. In M. Gazzaniga (Ed.), *The cognitive neurosciences* (pp. 475–486). Cambridge, MA: MIT Press.

Deutsch, D. (1996). The perception of auditory patterns. In W. Prinz & B. Bridgeman (Eds.), *Handbook of perception and action* (Vol. 1, pp. 253–296). San Diego, CA: Academic Press.

Deutsch, J. A., & Deutsch, D. (1963). Attention: Some theoretical considerations. *Psychological Review, 70,* 80–90.

DeVreese, L. P. (1991). Two systems for colour-naming defects: Verbal disconnection vs. colour imagery disorder. *Neuropsychologia, 29,* 1–18.

Dijksterhuis, A., Bos, M. W., Nordgren, L. F., & van Baaren, R. B. (2006). On making the right choice: The deliberation-without-attention effect. *Science, 311,* 1005–1007.

Dodds, R. A., Smith, S. M., & Ward, T. B. (2002). The use of environmental cues during incubation. *Creativity Research Journal, 14,* 287–304.

Dolcos, F., LaBar, K. S., & Cabeza, R. (2005). Remembering one year later: Role of the amygdala and the medial temporal lobe memory system in retrieving emotional memories. *Proceedings of the National Academy of Sciences, 102,* 2626–2631.

Donders, F. C. (1868/1969). Over de snelheid van psychische processen [Speed of mental processes]. Onderzoekingen gedann in het Psyciologish Laboratorium der Utrechtsche Hoogeschool (W. G. Koster, Trans.). In W. G. Koster (Ed.), Attention and performance II. *Acta Psychologica, 30,* 412–431.

Dougherty, R. F., Koch, V. M., Brewer, A. A., Fischer, B., Modersitzki, J., & Wandell, B. A. (2003). Visual field representations and locations of visual areas V1/2/3 in human visual cortex. *Journal of Vision, 3,* 586–598.

Downing, P. E., Jiang, Y., Shuman, M., & Kanwisher, N. (2001). A cortical area selective for visual processing of the human body. *Science, 293,* 2470–2473.

Driver, J., & Baylis, G. C. (1989). Movement and visual attention: The spotlight metaphor breaks down. *Journal of Experimental Psychology: Human Perception and Performance, 15,* 448–456.

Driver, J., & Baylis, G. C. (1998). Attention and visual object segmentation. In R. Parasuraman (Ed.), *The attentive brain* (pp. 299–325). Cambridge, MA: MIT Press.

DuBreuil, S. C., Garry, M., & Loftus, E. F. (1998). Tales from the crib. In S. J. Lynn & K. M. McConkie (Eds.), *Truth in memory* (pp.137–160). New York: Guilford.

Dudai, Y. (2006). Reconsolidation: The advantage of being refocused. *Current Opinion in Neurobiology, 16,* 174–178.

Dudai, Y., & Eisenberg, M. (2004). Rites of passage of the engram: Reconsolidation and the lingering consolidation hypothesis. *Neuron, 44,* 93–100.

Dunbar, K. (1998). Problem solving. In W. Bechtel & G. Graham (Eds.), *A companion to cognitive science* (pp. 289–298). London: Blackwell.

Dunbar, K. (1999). How scientists build models: Invivo science as a window on the scientific mind. In L. Magnani, N. Nersessian, & P. Thagard (Eds.), *Model-based reasoning in scientific discovery* (pp. 89–98). New York: Plenum.

Dunbar, K. (2001). The analogical paradox: Why analogy is so easy in naturalistic settings yet so difficult in the psychological laboratory. In D. Gentner, K. J. Holyoak, & B. Kokinov (Eds.), *Analogy: Perspectives form cognitive science.* Cambridge, MA: MIT Press.

Dunbar, K., & Blanchette, I. (2001). The *in vivo/in vitro* approach to cognition: The case of analogy. *Trends in Cognitive Sciences, 5,* 334–339.

Duncker, K. (1945). On problem solving. *Psychological Monographs 58*(5, Whole No. 270).

Dunning, D., & Parpal, M. (1989). Mental addition versus subtraction in counterfactual reasoning: On assessing the impact of personal actions and life events. *Journal of Personality and Social Psychology, 57,* 5–15.

Duzel, E., Cabeza, R., Picton, T. W., Yonelinas, A. P., Scheich, H., Heinze, H.-J., & Tulving, E. (1999). Task-related and item-related brain processes of memory retrieval. *Proceedings of the National Academy of Sciences, USA, 96,* 1794–1799.

Easterbrook, J. (1959). The effect of emotion on cue utilization and the organization of behavior. *Psychological Review, 66,* 183–201.

Ebbinghaus, H. (1913/1885). *Memory: A contribution to experimental psychology* (Henry A. Ruger & Clara E. Bussenius, Trans.). New York: Teachers College, Columbia University. (Original German: *Über das Gedächtnis*, published 1885.)

Edwards, A. W. F. (2004). *Cogwheels of the mind: The story of Venn diagrams.* Baltimore: Johns Hopkins University Press.

Egan, D. E., & Schwartz, B. J. (1979). Chunking in recall of symbolic drawings. *Memory and Cognition, 7,* 149–158.

Egly, R., Driver, J., & Rafal, R. D. (1994). Shifting visual attention between objects and locations: Evidence from normal and parietal lesion subjects. *Journal of Experimental Psychology: General, 123,* 161–177.

Eich, E. (1995). Searching for mood dependent memory. *Psychological Science, 6,* 67–75.

Eich, E., & Metcalfe, J. (1989). Mood dependent memory for internal vs. external events. *Journal of Experimental Psychology: Learning, Memory and Cognition, 15,* 443–455.

Einstein, G. O., & McDaniel, M. A. (1990). Normal aging and prospective memory. *Journal of Experimental Psychology: Learning, Memory, and Cognition, 16,* 717–726.

Einstein, G. O., & McDaniel, M. A. (2005). Prospective memory: Multiple retrieval processes. *American Psychological Society, 14,* 286–290.

Einstein, G. O., McDaniel, M. A., Thomas, R., Mayfield, S., Shank, H., & Morisette, N. (2005). Multiple processes in prospective memory retrieval: Factors determining monitoring versus spontaneous retrieval. *Journal of Experimental Psychology: General, 134,* 327–342.

Ellis, N., & Hennelly, R. A. (1980). A bilingual word-length effect: Implications for intelligence testing and the relative ease of mental calculation in Welsh and English. *British Journal of Psychology, 71,* 43–52.

Emmorey, K., & Wilson, M. (2004). The puzzle of working memory for sign language. *Trends in Cognitive Sciences, 8,* 521–523.

Epstein, R., Harris, A., Stanley, D., & Kanwisher, N. (1999). The parahippocampal place area: Recognition, navigation, or encoding? *Neuron, 23,* 115–125.

Epstein, R., & Kanwisher, N. (1998). A cortical representation of the local visual environment, *Nature, 392,* 598–601.

Ericsson, K. A., Chase, W. G., & Falloon, F. (1980). Acquisition of a memory skill. *Science, 208,* 1181–1182.

Ericsson, K. A., & Kintsch, W. (1995). Long-term working memory. *Psychological Review, 102,* 211–245.

Ericsson, K. A., & Simon, H. A. (1993). *Protocol analysis.* Cambridge, MA: MIT Press.

Eriksen, B. A., & Eriksen, C. W. (1974). Effects of noise letters upon the identification of a target letter in a nonsearch task. *Perception and Psychophysics, 16,* 143–149.

Eriksen, C. W., & St. James, J. D. (1986). Visual attention within and around the field of focal attention: A zoom lens model. *Perception and Psychophysics, 40,* 225–240.

Eriksen, C. W., & Yeh, Y.-Y. (1985). Allocation of attention in the visual field. *Journal of Experimental Psychology: Human Perception and Performance, 11,* 583–597.

Evans, J. St. B. T., Barston, J. L., & Pollard, P. (1983). On the conflict between logic and belief in syllogistic reasoning. *Memory and Cognition, 11,* 295–306.

Evans, J. St. B. T., & Feeney, A. (2004). In J. P. Leighton & R. J. Steinberg (Eds.), *The nature of reasoning* (pp. 78–102). Cambridge, UK: Cambridge University Press.

Evans, J. St. B. T., Newstead, S. E., & Byrne, R. M. J. (1993). *Human reasoning: The psychology of deduction*. Hove, UK: Erlbaum.

Farah, M. J. (1985). Psychophysical evidence for a shared representational medium for mental images and percepts. *Journal of Experimental Psychology: General, 114*, 91–103.

Farah, M. J. (1988). Is visual imagery really visual? Overlooked evidence from neuropsychology. *Psychological Review, 95*, 307–317.

Farah, M. J. (2000). The neural basis of mental imagery. In M. Gazzaniga (Ed.), *The cognitive neurosciences* (2nd ed., pp. 965–974). Cambridge, MA: MIT Press.

Farah, M. J., & Feinberg, T. E. (2000). *Patient-based approaches to cognitive neuroscience* (pp. 165–271). Cambridge, MA: MIT Press.

Farah, M. J., & Feinberg, T. E. (2003). *Behavioral neurology and neuropsychology* (2nd ed.). New York: McGraw-Hill.

Farah, M. J., Levine, D. N., & Calvanio, R. (1988). A case study of mental imagery deficit. *Brain and Cognition, 8*, 147–164.

Farah, M. J., O'Reilly, R. C., & Vecera, S. P. (1993). Dissociated overt and covert recognition as an emergent property of a lesioned neural network. *Psychological Review, 100*, 571–588.

Farah, M. J., Peronnet, F., Gonon, M. A., & Girard, M. H. (1988). Electrophysiological evidence for a shared representational medium for visual images and percepts. *Journal of Experimental Psychology, 117*, 248–257.

Farah, M. J., Peronnet, F., Weisberg, L. L., & Monheit, M. A. (1989). Brain activity underlying mental images: Event-related potentials during image generation. *Journal of Cognitive Neuroscience, 1*, 302–316.

Farah, M. J., Soso, M. J., & Dasheiff, R. M. (1992). The visual angle of the mind's eye before and after unilateral occipital lobectomy. *Journal of Experimental Psychology: Human Perception and Performance, 18*, 241–246.

Farah, M. J., & Wallace, M. A. (1992). Semantically bound amnesia: Implications for the neural implementation of naming. *Neuropsychologia, 30*, 609–621.

Fiez, J. A. (2001). Bridging the gap between neuroimaging and neuropsychology: Using working memory as a case study. *Journal of Clinical and Experimental Neuropsychology, 23*, 19–31.

Finke, R. A. (1990). *Creative imagery: Discoveries and inventions in visualization*. Hillsdale, NJ: Erlbaum.

Finke, R. A. (1995). Creative insight and preinventive forms. In R. J. Sternberg & J. E. Davidson (Eds.), *The nature of insight* (pp. 255–280). Cambridge, MA: MIT Press.

Finke, R. A., & Pinker, S. (1982). Spontaneous imagery scanning in mental exploration. *Journal of Experimental Psychology: Learning, Memory and Cognition, 8*, 142–147.

Finke, R. A., Pinker, S., & Farah, M. J. (1989). Reinterpreting visual patterns in visual imagery. *Cognitive Science, 13*, 51–78.

Fisher, R. P., Geiselman, R. E., Amador, M. (1989). Field test of the cognitive interview: Enhancing the recollection of actual victims and witnesses of crime. *Journal of Applied Psychology, 74*, 722–727.

Fleischman, D. A., & Gabrieli, J. (1999). Long-term memory in Alzheimer's disease. *Current Opinion in Neurobiology, 9, 240–244.*

Fleischman, D. A., Wilson, R. S., Gabrieli, J. D. E., Schneider, J. A., Bienias, J. L., Bennett, D. A. (2005). Implicit memory and Alzheimer's disease: Neuropathology. *Brain, 128*, 2006–2015.

Fodor, J. D. (1995). Comprehending sentence structure. In L. R. Gleitman & M. Liberman (Eds.), *An invitation to cognitive science* (Vol. 1, pp. 209–246). Cambridge, MA. MIT Press.

Frankland, P. W., & Bontempi, B. (2005). The organization of recent and remote memories. *Neuroscience, 6*, 119–130.

Frase, L. T. (1975). Prose processing. In G. H. Bower (Ed.), *The psychology of learning and motivation* (Vol. 9). New York: Academic Press.

Frazier, L. (1987). Sentence processing: A tutorial review. In M. Coltheart (Ed.), *Attention and performance: Vol. XII. The psychology of reading* (pp. 559–586). Hove, UK: Erlbaum.

Frazier, L., & Rayner, K. (1982). Making and correcting errors during sentence comprehension: Eye movements in the analysis of structurally ambiguous sentences. *Cognitive Psychology, 14*, 178–210.

Fredrickson, R. (1992). *Repressed memories: A journey*

to recovery from sexual abuse. New York: Simon & Schuster.

Freedman, D. J., Riesenhuber, M., Poggio, T., Miller, E. K. (2001). Categorical representations of visual stimuli in the primate prefrontal cortex. *Science, 291*, 312–316.

Freedman, M. L., & Martin, R. C. (2001). Dissociable components of short-term memory and their relation to long-term learning. *Cognitive Neuropsychology, 18*, 193–226.

Frensch, P. A., & Sternberg, R. J. (1989). Expertise and intelligent thinking: When is it worse to know better? In R. J. Sternberg (Ed.), *Advances in the psychology of human intelligence, Vol. 5.* Hillsdale, NJ: Erlbaum.

Freud, S. (1901). *The psychopathology of everyday life.* New York: Norton.

Friedman-Hill, S. R., Robertson, L. C., & Treisman, A. (1995). Parietal contributions to visual feature binding: Evidence from a patient with bilateral lesions. *Science, 269*, 853–855.

Fromkin, V. A. (Ed.). (1973). *Speech errors as linguistic evidence.* The Hague, Netherlands: Mouton.

Fugelsang, J. A., & Dunbar, K. N. (2004). A cognitive neuroscience framework for understanding causal reasoning and the law. *Philosophical Transactions of the Royal Society of London, Series B: Biological Sciences, 359*, 1749–1754.

Funahashi, S. (2006). Prefrontal cortex and working memory processes. *Neuroscience, 139*, 251–261.

Funahashi, S., Bruce, C. J., & Goldman-Rakic, P. S. (1989). Mnemonic coding of visual space in the primate dorsolateral prefrontal cortex. *Journal of Neurophysiology, 61*, 331–349.

Furmanski, C. S., & Engel, S. A. (2000). An oblique effect in human primary visual cortex. *Nature Neuroscience, 3*, 535–536.

Galton, F. (1883). *Inquiries into human faculty and its development.* London: Macmillan.

Ganis, G., Thompson, W. L., Kosslyn, S. M. (2004). Brain areas underlying visual mental imagery and visual perception: An fMRI study. *Cognitive Brain Research, 20*, 226–241.

Gardiner, J. M. (2001). Episodic memory and autonoetic consciousness: A first-person approach. *Philosophical Transactions of the Royal Society of London B., 356*, 1351–1361.

Garnham, A., Shillcock, R. C., Brown, G. D. A., Mill, A. I. D., & Cutler, A. (1981). Slips of the tongue in the London-Lund corpus of spontaneous conversation. *Linguistics, 19*, 805–817.

Garrett, M. F. (1975). The analysis of sentence production. In G. H. Bower (Ed.), *The psychology of learning and motivation* (Vol. 9, pp. 133–177). San Diego, CA: Academic Press.

Garrett, M. F. (1980). Levels of processing in sentence production. In B. Butterworth (Ed.), *Language production* (Vol. 1, pp. 177–220). San Diego, CA: Academic Press.

Garrod, S., & Pickering, M. J. (2004). Why is conversation so easy? *Trends in Cognitive Sciences, 8*, 8–11.

Gauthier, I., Skudlarski, P., Gore, J. C., & Anderson, A. W. (2000). Expertise for cars and birds recruits brain areas involved in face recognition. *Nature Neuroscience, 3*, 191–197.

Gauthier, I., Tarr, M. J., Anderson, A. W., Skudlarski, P., & Gore, J. C. (1999). Activation of the middle fusiform "face area" increases with expertise in recognizing novel objects. *Nature Neuroscience, 2*, 568–573.

Gazzaley, A., Cooney, J. W., Rissman, J., & D'Esposito, M. (2005). Top-down suppression deficit underlies working memory impairment in normal aging. *Nature Neuroscience, 8*, 1298–1300.

Gazzaniga, M. S. (2000). In E. Tulving & F. I. M. Craik (Eds.), *The Oxford handbook of memory* (back cover quotation). New York: Oxford University Press.

Geiselman, R. E., Fisher, R. P., MacKinnon, D. P., & Holland, H. L. (1985). Eyewitness memory enhancement in the police interview: Cognitive retrieval mnemonics versus hypnosis. *Journal of Applied Psychology, 70*, 401–412.

Geiselman, R. E., Fisher, R. P., MacKinnon, D. P., & Holland, H. L. (1986). Enhancement of eyewitness memory with the cognitive interview. *American Journal of Psychology, 99*, 385–401.

Gentner, D., & Goldin-Meadow, S. (Eds.). (2003). *Language in mind.* Cambridge, MA: MIT Press.

Gentner, D., Lowenstein, J., & Thompson, L. (2003). Learning and transfer: A general role for analogical encoding. *Journal of Educational Psychology, 95*, 393–408.

Gick, M. L., & Holyoak, K. J. (1980). Analogical problem solving. *Cognitive Psychology, 12*, 306–355.

Gick, M. L., & Holyoak, K. J. (1983). Schema induction and analogical transfer. *Cognitive Psychology, 15*, 1–38.

Gigerenzer, G., & Hoffrage, U. (1995). How to improve Bayesian reasoning without instruction: Frequency formats. *Psychological Review, 98*, 506–528.

Gigerenzer, G., & Hug, K. (1992). Domain-specific reasoning: Social contracts, cheating, and perspective change. *Cognition, 43*, 127–171.

Gigerenzer, G., & Todd, P. M. (1999). *Simple heuristics that make us smart.* Oxford, UK: Oxford University Press.

Gilboa, A., Ramirez, J., Kohler, S., Westmacott, R., Black, S. E., & Moscovitch, M. (2005). Retrieval of autobiographical memory in Alzheimer's disease: Relation to volumes of medial temporal lobe and other structures. *Hippocampus, 15*, 535–550.

Gilboa, A., Winocur, G., Grady, C. L., Hevenor, S. J., & Moscovitch, M. (2004). Remembering our past: Functional neuroanatomy of recollection of recent and very remote personal events. *Cerebral Cortex, 14*, 1214–1225.

Gilhooly, K. J. (Ed.). (1988). *Thinking: Directed, undirected and creative* (2nd ed.). San Diego, CA: Academic Press.

Glanzer, M., & Cunitz, A. R. (1966). Two storage mechanisms in free recall. *Journal of Verbal Learning and Verbal Behavior, 5*, 351–360.

Glass, A. L., & Holyoak, K. J. (1975). Alternative conceptions of semantic memory. *Cognition, 3*, 313–339.

Gleason, J. B., & Ratner, N. B. (1998). Language acquisition. In J. B. Gleason & N. B. Ratner (Eds.), *Psycholinguistics* (2nd ed., pp. 347–407). Fort Worth, TX: Harcourt.

Gleick, J. (1992). *Genius: The life and science of Richard Feynman.* New York: Pantheon.

Gobet, F., Land, P. C. R., Croker, S., Cheng, P. C.-H., Jones, G., Oliver, I., & Pine, J. M. (2001). Chunking mechanisms in human learning. *Trends in Cognitive Science, 5*, 236–243.

Godden, D. R., & Baddeley, A. D. (1975). Context-dependent memory in two natural environments: On land and underwater. *British Journal of Psychology, 66*, 325–331.

Goldberg, N. (1993). *Long quiet highway.* New York: Bantam.

Goldenberg, G., Podreka, I., Steiner, M., Willmes, K., Suess, E., & Deecke, L. (1989). Regional cerebral blood flow patterns in visual imagery. *Neuropsychologia, 27*, 641–664.

Goldman, S. R., Graesser, A. C., & Van den Broek, P. (Eds.). (1999). *Narrative comprehension, causality, and coherence.* Mahwah, NJ: Erlbaum.

Goldman-Rakic, P. S. (1992, September). Working memory and the mind. *Scientific American*, 111–117.

Goldstein, A. G., Chance, J. E., & Schneller, G. R. (1989). Frequency of eyewitness identification in criminal cases: A survey of prosecutors. *Bulletin of the Psychonomic Society, 27*, 71–74.

Goldstein, E. B., & Fink, S. I. (1981). Selective attention in vision: Recognition memory for superimposed line drawings. *Journal of Experimental Psychology: Human Perception and Performance, 7*, 954–967.

Goldwin-Meadow, S. (1982). The resilience of recursion: A study of a communication system developed without a conventional language model. In E. Wanner & L. R. Gleitman (Eds.), *Language acquisition: The state of the art* (pp. 51–77). Cambridge, UK: Cambridge University Press.

Gollin, E. S. (1960). Developmental studies of visual recognition of incomplete objects. *Perceptual and Motor Skills, 11*, 289–298.

Gomez, R. L., & Gerken, L. A. (1999). Artificial grammar learning by one-year-olds leads to specific and abstract knowledge. *Cognition, 70*, 109–135.

Gomez, R. L., & Gerken, L. A. (2000). Infant artificial language learning and language acquisition. *Trends in Cognitive Sciences, 4*, 178–186.

Graesser, A. C., Singer, M., & Trabasso, T. (1994). Constructing inferences during narrative text comprehension. *Psychological Review, 101*, 371–395.

Graesser, A. C., & Wiemer-Hastings, K. (1999). Situation models and concepts in story comprehension. In S. R. Goldman, A. C. Graesser, & P. Van den Broek (Eds.), *Narrative comprehension, causality, and coherence* (pp. 77–92). Mahwah, NJ: Erlbaum.

Grant, H., Bredahl, L. S., Clay, J., Ferrie, J., Goves, J. E., Mcdorman, T. A., & Dark, V. J. (1998). Context-dependent memory for meaningful material: Information for students. *Applied Cognitive Psychology, 12*, 617–623.

Gray, J. A., & Wedderburn, A. I. (1960). Grouping strategies with simultaneous stimuli. *Quarterly Journal of Experimental Psychology, 12*, 180–184.

Green, C. S., & Bavelier, D. (2003). Action video game modifies visual selective attention. *Nature, 423*, 534–537.

Green, C. S., & Bavelier, D. (in press). Effect of action video games on the spatial distribution of visuospatial attention. *Journal of Experimental Psychology: Human Perception & Performance.*

Greenberg, D. L., & Rubin, D. C. (2003). The neuropsychology of autobiographical memory. *Cortex, 39*, 687–728.

Grelotti, D. J., Gauthier, I., & Schultz, R. T. (2002). Social interest and the development of cortical face specialization: What autism teaches us about face processing. *Developmental Psychobiology, 40*, 213–225.

Griggs, R. A. (1983). The role of problem content in the selection task and in the THOG problem. In J. St. B. T. Evans (Ed.), *Thinking and reasoning: Psychological approaches.* London: Routledge & Kegan Paul.

Griggs, R. A., & Cox, J. R. (1982). The elusive thematic-materials effect in Wason's abstract selection task. *British Journal of Psychology, 73*, 407–420.

Gross, C. G. (2002). Genealogy of the "grandmother cell." *Neuroscientist, 8*, 84.

Guariglia, C., Padovani, A., Pantano, P., & Pizzamiglio, L. (1993). Unilateral neglect restricted to visual imagery. *Nature, 364*, 235–237.

Guilford, J. (1956). The structure of intellect. *Psychological Bulletin, 53*, 267–293.

Haber, R. N. (1983). The impending demise of the icon: A critique of the concept of iconic storage in visual information processing. *The Behavioral and Brain Sciences, 6*, 1–11.

Hafner, K. (1999, July 29). Road daze: A hand on the wheel and an ear to the phone. *New York Times*, p. G8.

Haigney, D., & Westerman, S. J. (2001). Mobile (cellular) phone use and driving: A critical review of research methodology. *Ergonomics, 44*, 132–143.

Haist, F., Gore, J. B., & Mao, H. (2001). Consolidation of human memory over decades revealed by functional magnetic resonance imaging. *Nature Neuroscience, 4*, 1139–1145.

Halligan, P. W., Fink, G. R., Marshall, J. C., & Vallar, G. (2003). Spatial cognition: Evidence from visual neglect. *Trends in Cognitive Science, 7*, 125–133.

Hamann, S. B., Ely, T. D., Grafton, S. T., & Kilts, C. D. (1999). Amygdala activity related to enhanced memory for pleasant and aversive stimuli. *Nature Neuroscience, 2*, 289–293.

Hamilton, D. L. (1981). Illusory correlation as a basis for stereotyping. In D. L. Hamilton (Ed.), *Cognitive processes in stereotyping and intergroup behavior.* Hillsdale, NJ: Erlbaum.

Hart, J., Berndt, R. S., & Caramazza, A. (1985). Category-specific naming deficit following cerebral infarction. *Nature, 316*, 439–440.

Hart, J., & Gordon, B. (1992). Neural subsystems for object knowledge. *Nature, 359*, 60–64.

Hauser, M. D. (1999). Perseveration, inhibition and the prefrontal cortex: A new look. *Current Opinion in Neurobiology, 9*, 214–222.

Haviland, S. E., & Clark, H. H. (1974). What's new? Acquiring new information as a process in comprehension. *Journal of Verbal Learning and Verbal Behavior, 13*, 512–521.

Hays, J. R. (1978). *Cognitive psychology.* Homewood, IL: Dorsey Press.

Hebb, D. O. (1948). *Organization of behavior.* New York: Wiley.

Hecaen, H., & Angelerques, R. (1962). Agnosia for faces (prospagnosia). *Archives of Neurology, 7*, 92–100.

Hedden, T., & Gabrieli, J. D. E. (2004). Insights into the ageing mind: A view from cognitive neuroscience. *Nature Reviews Neuroscience, 5*, 87–97.

Hegarty, M. (1992). Mental animation: Inferring motion from static displays of mechanical systems. *Journal of Experimental Psychology: Learning, Memory, and Cognition, 18*, 1084–1102.

Hegarty, M. (2004). Mechanical reasoning by mental simulation. *Trends in Cognitive Sciences, 8*, 280–285.

Helmholtz, H. von. (1866). *Treatise on physiological optics.* Leipzig, Germany: Voss.

Helson, H. (1933). The fundamental propositions of Gestalt psychology. *Psychological Review, 40*, 13–32.

Henderson, A., Bruce, V., & Burton, A. M. (2001). Matching the faces of robbers captured on video. *Applied Cognitive Psychology, 15*, 445–464.

Henderson, J. M. (2003). Human gaze control during

real-world scene perception. *Trends in Cognitive Sciences, 7,* 498–503.

Henderson, J. M., & Hollingworth, A. (2003). Global transsaccadic change blindness during scene perception. *Psychological Science, 14,* 493–497.

Hills, A. E., & Caramazza, A. (1991). Category-specific naming and comprehension impairment: A double-dissociation. *Brain, 114,* 2081–2094.

Hillyard, S. A., & Anllo-Vento, L. (1998). Event-related brain potentials in the study of visual selective attention. *Proceedings of the National Academy of Sciences, USA, 95,* 781–787.

Hillyard, S. A., Hink, R. F., Schwent, V. L., & Picton, T. W. (1973). Electrical signs of selective attention in the human brain. *Science, 182,* 177–180.

Hinton, G. E., & Shallice, T. (1991). Lesioning an attractor network: Investigations of acquired dyslexia. *Psychological Review, 98,* 74–95.

Hirsh-Pasek, K., Reeves, L. M., & Golinkoff, R., (1993). Words and meaning: From primitives to complex organization. In J. B. Gleason & N. B. Ratner (Eds.), *Psycholinguistics* (p. 138). Fort Worth, TX: Harcourt Brace Jovanovich.

Hochberg, J. E. (1971). Perception. In J. W. Kling & L. A. Riggs (Eds.), *Experimental psychology* (3rd ed., pp. 396–450). New York: Holt, Rinehart and Winston.

Hoffman, E. J., Phelps, M. E., Mullani, N. A., Higgins, C. S., & Ter-Pogossian, M. M. (1976). Design and performance characteristics of a whole-body positron transaxial tomography. *Journal of Nuclear Medicine, 17,* 493–502.

Hoffman, H. G., Granhag, P. A., See, S. T. K., & Loftus, E. F. (2001). Social influences on reality-monitoring decisions. *Memory and Cognition, 29,* 394–404.

Holtgraves, T. (1998). Interpreting indirect replies. *Cognitive Psychology, 37,* 1–27.

Holyoak, K. J. (2003). Personal communication to the author.

Holyoak, K. J., & Koh, K. (1987). Surface and structural similarity in analogical transfer. *Memory and Cognition, 15,* 332–340.

Holyoak, K. J., & Thagard, P. (1995). Analogical mapping by constraint satisfaction. *Cognitive Science, 13,* 295–355.

Horton, W. S., & Rapp, D. N. (2003). *Psychonomic Bulletin & Review, 10,* 104–110.

Hubel, D. H. (1995). *Eye, brain and vision.* New York: Scientific American Books.

Hubel D. H., & Wiesel, T. N. (1965). Receptive fields and functional architecture in two non-striate visual areas (18 and 19) of the cat. *Journal of Neurophysiology, 28,* 229–289.

Huber, R., Ghilardi, M. F., Massimini, M., & Tononi, G. (2004). Local sleep and learning. *Nature 430,* 78–81.

Huesmann, L. R., Moise, T. J., Podolski, C. L., & Eron, L. D. (2003). Longitudinal relations between children's exposure to TV violence and their aggressive and violent behavior in young adulthood: 1977–1992. *Developmental Psychology, 39,* 201–222.

Huitema, J. S., Dopkins, S., Klin, C. M., & Myers, J. L. (1993). Connecting goals and actions during reading. *Journal of Experimental Psychology: Learning, Memory and Cognition, 19,* 1053–1060.

Hyde, T. S., & Jenkins, J. J. (1969). Differential effects of incidental tasks on the organization of a list of highly associated words. *Journal of Experimental Psychology, 82,* 472–481.

Hyman, I. E., Jr., Husband, T. H., & Billings, J. F. (1995). False memories of childhood experiences. *Applied Cognitive Psychology, 9,* 181–197.

Intons-Peterson, M. J. (1983). Imagery paradigms: How vulnerable are they to experimenters' expectations? *Journal of Experimental Psychology: Human Perception and Performance, 9,* 394–412.

Intons-Peterson, M. J. (1993). Imagery's role in creativity and discovery. In B. Roskos-Ewoldson, M. J. Intons-Peterson & R. E. Anderson (Eds.), *Imagery, creativity, and discovery: A cognitive perspective* (pp. 1–37). New York: Elsevier.

Ishai, A., Ungerleider, L. G., Martin, A., & Haxby, J. V. (2000). The representation of objects in the human occipital and temporal cortex. *Journal of Cognitive Neuroscience, 12,* 35–51.

Iwao, M., & Gentner, D. (1997). A cross-linguistic study of early word meaning: Universal ontology and linguistic influence. *Cognition, 62,* 169–200.

Jacoby, L. L., Kelley, C. M., Brown, J., & Jaseckko, J. (1989). Becoming famous overnight: Limits on the ability to avoid unconscious inferences of the past. *Journal of Personality and Social Psychology, 56,* 326–338.

James, W. (1890). *The principles of psychology* (Vol. 1). New York: Henry Holt & Co. (Reprinted 1981, Harvard University Press)

Jansson, D. G., & Smith, S. M. (1991). Design fixation. *Design Studies, 12,* 3–11.

Jenkins, J. J., & Russell, W. A. (1952). Associative clustering during recall. *Journal of Abnormal and Social Psychology, 47,* 818–821.

Ji, L., Peng, K., & Nisbett, R. E. (2000). Culture, control, and perception of relationships in the environment. *Journal of Personality and Social Psychology, 78,* 943–955.

Johnson, E. J., & Goldstein, D. (2003). Do defaults save lives? *Science, 302,* 1338–1339.

Johnson, K. E., & Mervis, C. B. (1997). Effects of varying levels of expertise on the basic level of categorization. *Journal of Experimental Psychology: General, 126,* 248–277.

Johnson, M. K., Hashtroudi, S., & Lindsay, D. S. (1993). Source monitoring. *Psychological Bulletin, 114,* 3–28.

Johnson-Laird, P. N. (1995). Inference and mental models. In S. E. Newstead & J. St. B. T. Evans (Eds.), *Perspectives on thinking and reasoning. Essays in honour of Peter Wason.* Hove, UK: Erlbaum.

Johnson-Laird, P. N. (1999a). Formal rules versus mental models in reasoning. In R. Sternberg (Ed.), *The nature of cognition* (pp. 587–624). Cambridge, MA: MIT Press.

Johnson-Laird, P. N. (1999b). Deductive reasoning. *Annual Review of Psychology, 50,* 109–135.

Johnson-Laird, P. N., Herrmann, D. J., & Chaffin, R. (1984). Only connections: A critique of semantic networks. *Psychological Bulletin, 96,* 292–315.

Johnson-Laird, P. N., Legrenzi, P., & Legrenzi, M. S. (1972). Reasoning and a sense of reality. *British Journal of Psychology, 63,* 395–400.

Jones, M. R., & Yee, W. (1993). Attending to auditory events: The role of temporal organization. In S. McAdams & E. Bigand (Eds.), *Thinking in sound: The cognitive psychology of human audition* (pp. 69–112). Oxford, England: Oxford University Press.

Julesz, B. (1984). A brief outline of the text on theory of human vision. *Trends in Neuroscience, 7,* 41–45.

Junkin, T. (2004). *Bloodsworth: The true story of the first death row inmate exonerated by DNA.* Chapel Hill, NC: Algonquin.

Kahneman, D. (1973). *Attention and effort.* Englewood Cliffs, NJ: Prentice-Hall.

Kahneman, D. (2003). A perspective on judgment and choice. *American Psychologist, 58,* 697–720.

Kahneman, D., & Tversky, A. (1982). The simulation heuristic. In D. Kahneman, P. Slovic, & A. Tversky (Eds.), *Judgment under uncertainty: Heuristics and biases* (pp. 201–208). New York: Cambridge University Press.

Kako, E., & Wagner, L. (2001). The semantics of syntactic structures. *Trends in Cognitive Sciences, 5,* 102–108.

Kandel, E. R. (2001). A molecular biology of memory storage: A dialogue between genes and synapses. *Science, 294,* 1030–1038.

Kanwisher, N. (2003). The ventral visual object pathway in humans: Evidence from fMRI. In L. M. Chalupa & J. S. Werner (Eds.), *The visual neurosciences* (pp. 1179–1190). Cambridge, MA: MIT Press.

Kaplan, C. A., & Simon, H. A. (1990). In search of insight. *Cognitive Psychology, 22,* 374–419.

Keppel, G., & Underwood, B. J. (1962). Proactive inhibition in short-term retention of single items. *Journal of Verbal Learning and Verbal Behavior, 1,* 153–161.

Keri, S., Janka, Z., Benedek, G., Aszalos, P., Szatmary, B., Szirtes, G., & Lorincz, A. (2002). Categories, prototypes and memory systems in Alzheimer's disease. *Trends in Cognitive Sciences, 6,* 132–136.

Keysers, C., Xiao, D. K., Foeldiak, P., & Perrett, D. I. (2001). The speed of sight. *Journal of Cognitive Neuroscience, 13,* 90–101.

Kida, S., Josselyn, S. A., Peña de Oritz, S., Kogan, J. H., Chevere, I., Masushige, S., & Silva, A. J. (2002). CREB required for the stability of new and reactivated fear memories. *Nature Neuroscience, 5,* 348–355.

Kleffner, D. A., & Ramachandran, V. S. (1992). On the perception of shape from shading. *Perception and Psychophysics, 52,* 18–36.

Kliegel, M., Martin, M., McDaniel, M. A., & Einstein,

G. O. (2004). Importance effects on performance in event-based prospective memory tasks. *Memory, 12*, 553–561.

Klin, A., Jones, W., Schultz, R., & Volkmar, F. (2003). The enactive mind, or from actions to cognition: Lessons from autism. *Philosophical Transactions of the Royal Society of London B, 345–360.*

Kneller, W., Memon, A., & Stevenage, S. (2001). Simultaneous and sequential lineups: Decision processes of accurate and inaccurate eye witnesses. *Applied Cognitive Psychology, 15*, 659–671.

Koffka, K. (1935). *Principles of Gestalt psychology.* New York: Harcourt Brace & World.

Kohler, E., Keysers, C., Umilta, M. A., Fogassi, L., Gallese, V., Rizzolatti, G. (2002). Hearing sounds, understanding actions: Action representation in mirror neurons. *Science, 297*, 846–848.

Kohler, W. (1929). *Gestalt psychology.* New York: Liveright.

Kolb, B., & Wishaw, I. Q. (1990). *Fundamentals of human neuropsychology* (3rd ed.). New York: Freeman.

Konorski, J. (1967). *Integrative activity of the brain: An interdisciplinary approach.* Chicago: University of Chicago Press.

Kosslyn, S. M. (1973). Scanning visual images: Some structural implications. *Perception & Psychophysics, 14*, 90–94.

Kosslyn, S. M. (1978). Measuring the visual angle of the mind's eye. *Cognitive Psychology, 10*, 356–389.

Kosslyn, S. M. (1980). *Image and mind.* Cambridge, MA: Harvard University Press.

Kosslyn, S. M. (1994). *Image and brain: The resolution of the imagery debate.* Cambridge, MA: MIT Press.

Kosslyn, S. M. (2006). *The case for mental imagery.* Oxford, UK: Oxford University Press.

Kosslyn, S. M., Alpert, N. M., Thompson, W. L., Maljkovic, V., Weise, S. B., Chabris, C. F., Hamilton, E., Rauch, S. L., & Buonanno, F. S. (1993). Visual mental imagery activates topographically organized/visual cortex: PET investigations. *Journal of Cognitive Neuroscience, 5*, 263–287.

Kosslyn, S. M., Ball, T., & Reiser, B. J. (1978). Visual images preserve metric spatial information: Evidence from studies of image scanning. *Journal of Experimental Psychology: Human Perception and Performance, 4*, 47–60.

Kosslyn, S. M., & Osherson, D. N. (1995). Mental imagery. In S. M. Kosslyn (Ed.), *An invitation to cognitive science. Volume 2: Visual cognition* (2nd ed., pp. 267–296). Cambridge, MA: MIT Press.

Kosslyn, S. M., Pascual-Leone, A., Felician, O., Camposano, S., Keenan, J. P., Thompson, W. L., Ganis, G., Sukel, K. E., & Alpert, N. M. (1999). The role of area 17 in visual imagery: Convergent evidence form PET and rTMS. *Science, 284*, 167–170.

Kosslyn, S. M., & Thompson, W. L. (2000). Shared mechanisms in visual imagery and visual perception: Insights from cognitive neuroscience. In M. Gazzanaga (Ed.), *The cognitive neurosciences* (2nd ed., pp. 975–985). Cambridge, MA: MIT Press.

Kosslyn, S. M., Thompson, W. L., Kim, I. J., & Alpert, N. M. (1995). Topographical representations of mental images in primary visual cortex. *Nature, 378*, 496–498.

Kotovsky, K., Hayes, J. R., and Simon, H. A. (1985). Why are some problems hard? Evidence from Tower of Hanoi. *Cognitive Psychology, 17*, 248–294.

Kraemer, D. J. M., Macrae, C. N., Green, A. E., & Kelley, W. M. (2005). Sound of silence activates auditory cortex. *Nature, 434*, 158.

Kreiman, G., Koch, C., & Fried, I. (2000a). Category-specific visual responses of single neurons in the human medial temporal lobe. *Nature Neuroscience, 3*, 946–953.

Kreiman, G., Koch, C., & Fried, I. (2000b). Imagery neurons in the human brain. *Nature, 408*, 357–361.

Kroger, J. K., Sabb, F. W., Fales, C. L., Bookheimer, S. Y., Cohen, M. S., & Holyoak, K. J. (2002). Recruitment of anterior dorsolateral prefrontal cortex in human reasoning: A parametric study of relational complexity. *Cerebral Cortex, 12*, 477–485.

Kroll, J. F., & Tokowicz, N. (2005). Models of bilingual representation and processing: Looking back and to the future. In J. F. Kroll & A. M. B. De Groot (Eds.), *Handbook of bilingualism: Psycholinguistic approaches* (pp. 531–553). New York: Oxford University Press.

Kroll, N. (1970). Short-term memory while shadowing: Recall of visually and aurally presented letters. *Journal of Experimental Psychology, 85*, 220–224.

Kuhn, T. (1970). *The structure of scientific revolution* (2nd ed.). Chicago: University of Chicago Press.

Kurtz, K. J., Gentner, D., & Gunn, V. (1999). Reasoning. In B. M. Bly & D. E. Rumelhart (Eds.), *Cognitive science: Handbook of perception and cognition* (2nd ed., pp. 145–200). San Diego, CA: Academic Press.

Kutas, M., & Federmeier, K. D. (2000). Electrophysiology reveals semantic memory use in language comprehension. *Trends in Cognitive Sciences, 4,* 463–470.

LaBar, K. S., & Cabeza, R. (2006). Cognitive neuroscience of emotional memory. *Neuroscience, 7,* 54–64.

LaBar, K. S., & Phelps, E. A. (1998). Arousal-mediated memory consolidation: Role of the medial temporal lobe in humans. *Psychological Science, 9,* 490–493.

Lakoff, G., & Turner, M. (1989). *More than cool reason: The power of poetic metaphor.* Chicago: Chicago University Press.

Lamble, D., Kauranen, T., Laakso, M., & Summala, H. (1999). Cognitive load and detection thresholds in car following situations: Safety implications for using mobile (cellular) telephones while driving. *Accident Analysis and Prevention, 31,* 617–623.

Lamprecht, R., & LeDoux, J. (2004). Structural plasticity and memory. *Nature Reviews Neuroscience, 5,* 45–54.

Land, M. F., & Hayhoe, M. (2001). In what ways do eye movements contribute to everyday activities? *Vision Research, 41,* 3559–3565.

Land, M. F., Mennie, N., & Rusted, J. (1999). The roles of vision and eye movements in the control of activities of daily living. *Perception, 28,* 1311–1328.

Larkin, J. H., McDermott, J., Simon, D. P., & Simon, H. A. (1980). Expert and novice performance in solving physics problems. *Science, 208,* 1335–1342.

Lavie, N. (1995). Perceptual load as a necessary condition for selective attention. *Journal of Experimental Psychology: Human Perception and Performance, 21,* 451–486.

Lavie, N. (2005). Distracted and confused? Selective attention under load. *Trends in Cognitive Sciences, 5,* 75–82.

Lavie, N., & Driver, J. (1996). On the spatial extent of attention in object-based visual selection. *Perception & Psychophysics, 58,* 1238–1251.

Lavie, N., Ro, T., & Russell, C. (2003). The role of perceptual load in processing distractor faces. *Psychological Science, 15,* 510–515.

Lea, G. (1975). Chronometric analysis of the method of loci. *Journal of Experimental Psychology: Human Perception and Performance, 2,* 95–104.

LeBihan, D., Turner, R., Zeffiro, T. A., Cuenod, A., Jezzard, P., & Bonnerdot, V. (1993). Activation of human primary visual cortex during visual recall: A magnetic resonance imaging study. *Proceedings of the National Academy of Sciences, USA, 90,* 11802–11805.

Lee, D. (2006). Neural basis of quasi-rational decision making. *Current Opinion in Neurobiology, 16,* 191–198.

Lee, J. L. C., DiCiano, P., Thomas, K. L., & Everitt, B. J. (2005). Disrupting reconsolidation of drug memories reduces cocaine-seeking behavior. *Neuron, 47,* 795–801.

Lehman, J. F., Laird, J. E., & Rosenbloom, P. (1998). A gentle introduction to Soar: An architecture for human cognition. In D. Scarborough & S. Sternberg (Eds.), *An invitation to cognitive science* (Vol. 4, 2nd ed., pp. 212–249). Cambridge, MA: MIT Press.

Leighton, J. P. (2004). Defining and describing reasoning. In J. P. Leighton & R. J. Steinberg (Eds.), *The nature of reasoning* (pp. 3–11). Cambridge, UK: Cambridge University Press.

Lesgold, A. M. (1988). Problem solving. In R. J. Sternberg & E. E. Smith (Eds.), *The psychology of human thoughts.* New York: Cambridge University Press.

Levelt, W. J. M. (2001). Spoken word production: A theory of lexical access. *Proceedings of the National Academy of Sciences, 98,* 13464–13471.

Levin, D. T., Momen, N., & Drivdahl, S. B. (2000). Change blindness blindness: The metacognitive error of overestimating change-detection ability. *Visual Cognition, 7,* 397–412.

Levin, D. T., & Simons, D. (1997). Failure to detect changes in attended objects in motion pictures. *Psychonomic Bulletin and Review, 4,* 501–506.

Levine, B., Turner, G. R., Tisserand, D., Hevenor, S. J., Graham, S. J., & McIntosh, A. R. (2004). The functional neuroanatomy of episodic and semantic autobiographical remembering: A prospective functional MRI study. *Journal of Cognitive Neuroscience, 16,* 1633–1646.

Levinson, S. C. (1996). Language and space. *Annual Review of Anthropology, 25,* 353–382.

Lewis, D. J., & Maher, B. A. (1965). Neural consolidation and electroconvulsive shock. *Psychological Review, 72,* 225–239.

Li, F. F., VanRullen, R., Koch, C., & Perona, P. (2002). Rapid natural scene categorization in the near absence of attention. *Proceedings of the National Academy of Sciences, USA, 99,* 9596–9601.

Lichtenstein, S., Slovic, P., Fischoff, B., Layman, M., & Combs, B. (1978). Judged frequency of lethal events. *Journal of Experimental Psychology: Human Learning and Memory, 4,* 551–578.

Lindsay, D. S. (1990). Misleading suggestions can impair eyewitnesses' ability to remember event details. *Journal of Experimental Psychology: Learning, Memory, and Cognition, 16,* 1077–1083.

Lindsay, D. S. (1993). Eyewitness suggestibility. *Current Directions in Psychological Science, 2,* 86–89.

Lindsay, D. S, Hagen, L., Read, J. D., Wade, K. A., & Garry, M. (2004). True photographs and false memories. *Psychological Science, 15,* 149–154.

Lindsay, R. C. L., & Wells, G. L. (1980). What price justice? Exploring the relationship of lineup fairness to identification accuracy. *Law and Human Behavior, 4,* 303–313.

Lindsay, R. C. L., & Wells, G. L. (1985). Improving eyewitness identifications from lineups: Simultaneous versus sequential lineup presentation. *Journal of Applied Psychology, 70,* 556–564.

Loftus, E. F. (1979). *Eyewitness testimony.* Cambridge, MA: Harvard University Press.

Loftus, E. F. (1982). Memory and its distortions. In Kraut, A. G. (Ed.), *The G. Stanley Hall lecture series* (Vol. 2, pp. 123–154). Washington, DC: American Psychological Association.

Loftus, E. F. (1993). Made in memory: Distortions in recollection after misleading information. In D. L. Medin (Ed.), *The psychology of learning and motivation: Advances in theory and research* (pp. 187–215). New York: Academic Press.

Loftus, E. F. (1998). Imaginary memories. In M. A. Conway, S. E. Gathercole, & C. Cornoldi (Eds.), *Theories of memory II* (pp. 135–145). Hove, UK: Psychology Press.

Loftus, E. F., Garry, M., & Feldman, J. (1994). Forgetting sexual trauma: What does it mean when 38% forget? *Journal of Consulting and Clinical Psychology, 62,* 1177–1181.

Loftus, E. F., Miller, D. G., & Burns, H. J. (1978). Semantic integration of verbal information into visual memory. *Journal of Experimental Psychology: Human Learning and Memory, 4,* 19–31.

Loftus, E. F., & Palmer, J. C. (1974). Reconstruction of an automobile destruction: An example of the interaction between language and memory. *Journal of Verbal Learning and Verbal Behavior, 13,* 585–589.

Loftus, E. F., & Pickerel, J. E. (1995). The formation of false memories. *Psychiatric Annals, 25,* 720–725.

Logie, R. H. (1995). *Visuo-spatial working memory.* Hove, UK: Erlbaum.

Lopez, A., Atran, S., Coley, J. D., Medin, D. L., & Smith, E. E. (1997). The tree of life: Universal and cultural features of folkbiological taxonomies and inductions. *Cognitive Psychology, 32,* 251–295.

Lorayne, H., & Lucas, J. (1996). *The memory book.* New York: Ballantine Books.

Lord, C. G., Ross, L., & Lepper, M. (1979). Biased assimilation and attitude polarization: The effects of prior theories on subsequently considered evidence. *Journal of Personality and Social Psychology, 46,* 1254–1266.

Lovatt, P., Avons, S. E., & Masterson, J. (2000). The word-length effect and disyllabic words. *The Quarterly Journal of Experimental Psychology, 53A,* 1–22.

Lovatt, P., Avons, S. E., & Masterson, J. (2002). Output decay in immediate serial recall: Speech time revisited. *Journal of Memory and Language, 46,* 227–243.

Lovett, M. C. (2002). Problem solving. In D. L. Medin (Ed.), *Stevens' handbook of experimental psychology* (3rd ed., pp. 317–362). New York: Wiley.

Low, A., Bentin, S., Rockstroh, B., Silberman, Y., Gomolla, A., Cohen, R., & Elbert, T. (2003). Semantic categorization in the human brain: Spatiotemporal dynamics revealed by magnetoencephalography. *Psychological Science, 14,* 367–372.

Lubart, T. I., & Mouchiroud, C. (2003). Creativity: A source of difficulty in problem solving. In J. E. Davidson and R. J. Sternberg (Eds.), *The psychology of problem solving* (pp. 127–148). New York: Cambridge University Press.

Luchins, A. S. (1942). Mechanization in problem solving—the effect of Einstellung. *Psychological Monographs, 54*(6), 195.

Luck, S. J., Chelazzi, L., Hillyard, S. A., & Desimone, R. (1997). Neural mechanisms of spatial selective attention in areas V1, V2, and V4 of macaque visual cortex. *Journal of Neurophysiology, 77,* 24–42.

Luck, S. J., & Vecera, S. P. (2002). Attention. In H. Pashler & S. Yantis (Eds.), *Stevens' handbook of experimental psychology* (3rd ed., pp. 235–286). New York: Wiley.

Lucy, J. A., & Gaskins, S. (1997). Grammatical categories and the development of classification preferences: A comparative approach. In S. C. Levinson & M. Bowerman (Eds.), *Language acquisition and conceptual development.* Cambridge, UK: Cambridge University Press.

Luria, A. R. (1968). *The mind of a mnemonist* (L. Solotaroff, Trans.). New York: Basic Books.

MacDonald, M. C., Pearlmutter, N. J., & Seidenberg, M. S. (1994). Lexical nature of syntactic ambiguity resolution. *Psychological Review, 101,* 676–703.

Mack, A., & Rock, I. (1998). *Inattentional blindness.* Cambridge, MA: MIT Press.

MacKay, D. G. (1973). Aspects of the theory of comprehension, memory and attention. *Quarterly Journal of Experimental Psychology, 25,* 22–40.

Maguire, E. A., Gadian, D. G., Johnsrude, I. S., Good, C. D., Ashburer, J., Frackowiak, R. S. J., & Frith, C. D. (2000). Navigation-related structural change in the hippocampi of taxi drivers. *Proceedings of the National Academy of Sciences, 97,* 4398–4403.

Maguire, E. A., Valentine, E. R., Wilding, J. M., & Kapur, N. (2003). Routes to remembering: The brains behind superior memory. *Nature Neuroscience, 6,* 90–95.

Maier, N. R. F. (1931). Reasoning in humans: II. The solution of a problem and its appearance in consciousness. *Journal of Comparative Psychology, 12,* 181–194.

Majid, A., Bowerman, M., Kita, S., Haun, D. B. M., & Levinson, S. C. (2004). Can language restructure cognition? The case of space. *Trends in Cognitive Sciences, 8*(3), 108–114.

Malenka, R. C., & Nicoll, R. A. (1999). Long-term potentiation—A decade of progress? *Science, 285,* 1870–1874.

Malpass, R. S., & Devine, P. G. (1981). Eyewitness identification: Lineup instructions and absence of the offender. *Journal of Applied Psychology, 66,* 482–489.

Malt, B. C. (1989). An on-line investigation of prototype and exemplar strategies in classification. *Journal of Experimental Psychology: Learning, Memory and Cognition, 4,* 539–555.

Manktelow, K. I. (1999). *Reasoning and thinking.* Hove, UK: Psychology Press.

Manktelow, K. I., & Evans, J. St. B. T. (1979). Facilitation of reasoning by realism: Effect or non-effect? *British Journal of Psychology, 70,* 477–488.

Manketelow, K. I., & Over, D. E. (1990). Deontic thought and the selection task. In K. J. Gilhooly, M. T. G. Keane, R. H. Logie, & G. Erdos (Eds.), *Lines of thinking: Reflections on the psychology of thought* (Vol. 1). Chichester, UK: Wiley.

Mansfield, R. J. (1974). Neural basis of orientation perception in primate vision. *Science, 186,* 1133–1135.

Mantyla, T. (1986). Optimizing cue effectiveness: Recall of 500 and 600 incidentally learned words. *Journal of Experimental Psychology: Learning Memory, and Cognition, 12,* 66–71.

Marcus, G. B. (1986). Stability and change in political attitudes: "Observe, recall, and explain." *Political Behavior, 8,* 21–44.

Marslen-Wilson, W. (1990). Activation, competition, and frequency in lexical access. In G. T. M. Altmann (Ed.), *Cognitive models of speech processing: Psycholinguistic and computational perspectives.* Cambridge, MA: MIT Press.

Martin, A., & Chao, L. L. (2001). Semantic memory and the brain: Structure and processes. *Current Opinion in Neurology, 11,* 194–201.

Martinez-Conde, S., Macknik, S. L., & Hubel, D. H. (2004). The role of fixational eye movements in visual perception. *Nature Neuroscience, 5,* 229–240.

Mast, F. W., & Kosslyn, S. M. (2002). Visual mental images can be ambiguous: Insights from individual differences in spatial transformation abilities. *Cognition, 86,* 57–70.

McArthur, D. J. (1982). Computer vision and perceptual psychology. *Psychological Bulletin, 92,* 283–309.

McClelland, J. L. (1988). Connectionist models and psychological evidence. *Journal of Memory and Language, 27,* 107–123.

McClelland, J. L. (1995a). Constructive memory and memory distortions: A parallel-distributed processing approach. In D. L. Schacter (Ed.), *Memory distortion* (pp. 69–90). Cambridge, MA: Harvard University Press.

McClelland, J. L. (1995b). Why there are complementary learning systems in the hippocampus and neocortex: Insights from the successes and failures of connectionist models of learning and memory. *Psychological Review, 102,* 419–457.

McClelland, J. L. (1999). Cognitive modeling, connectionist. In R. W. Engel (Ed.), *The MIT encyclopedia of cognitive science* (pp. 137–141). Cambridge, MA: MIT Press.

McClelland, J. L. (2003, November 17). *Why is it hard to learn? Insights from models of how learning occurs in the brain.* Lecture at Carnegie-Mellon University, Pittsburgh, PA.

McClelland, J. L., McNaughton, B. L., & O'Reilly, R. C. (1995). Why there are complementary learning systems in the hippocampus and neocortex: Insights from the successes and failures of connectionist models of learning and memory. *Psychological Review, 102,* 419–457.

McClelland, J. L., & Rogers, T. T. (2003). The parallel-distributed processing approach to semantic cognition. *Nature Reviews Neuroscience, 4,* 310–322.

McClelland, J. L., & Rumelhart, D. E. (1981). An interactive activation model of context effects in letter perception, Part 1: An account of basic findings. *Psychological Review, 88,* 375–405.

McClelland, J. L., & Rumelhart, D. E. (1986). *Parallel distributed processing: Explorations in the microstructure of cognition.* Cambridge, MA: MIT Press.

McCloskey, M., & Zaragoza, Z. (1985). Misleading postevent information and memory for events: Arguments and evidence against memory impairment hypothesis. *Journal of Experimental Psychology: General, 114,* 3–18.

McDermott, K. B., & Chan, J. C. K. (in press). Effects of repetition on memory for pragmatic inferences. *Memory & Cognition.*

McElroy, S. L., & Keck, P. E. (1995). Recovered memory therapy: False memory syndrome and other complications. *Psychiatric Annals, 25,* 731–735.

McKelvie, S. L. (1997). The availability heuristic: Effects of fame and gender on the estimated frequency of male and female names. *Journal of Social Psychology, 137,* 63–78.

McKoon, G., & Ratcliff, R. (1992). Inference during reading. *Psychological Review, 99,* 440–466.

Mecklinger, A., Gruenwald, C., Besson, M., Magnie, M., & Von Cramon, D. Y. (2002). Separable neuronal circuitries for manipulable and nonmanipulable objects in working memory. *Cerebral Cortex, 12,* 1115–1123.

Medin, D. L., Altom, M. W., Edelson, S. M., & Freko, D. (1982). Correlated symptoms and simulated medical classification. *Journal of Experimental Psychology: Learning, Memory, and Cognition, 8,* 37–50.

Medin, D. L., & Atran, S. (2004). The native mind: Biological categorization and reasoning in development and across cultures. *Psychological Review, 111,* 960–983.

Medin, D. L., Lynch, E., Coley, J., & Atran, S. (1997). Categorization and reasoning among tree experts: Do all roads lead to Rome? *Cognitive Psychology, 32,* 49–96.

Medin, D. L., Ross, N. O., Atran, S., Cox, D., Coley, J., Proffitt, J. B., Blok, S. (2006). Folkbiology of freshwater fish. *Cognition, 99,* 237–273.

Mellett, E., Tzourino, N., Denis, M., & Mazoyer, B. (1998). Cortical anatomy of mental imagery of concrete nouns based on their dictionary definition. *Neuroreport, 9,* 803–808.

Mervis, C. B., Catlin, J., & Rosch, E. (1976). Relationships among goodness-of-example, category norms and word frequency. *Bulletin of the Psychonomic Society, 7,* 268–284.

Merzenich, M. M., Recanzone, G., Jenkins, W. M., Allard, T. T., & Nudo, R. J. (1988). Cortical representational plasticity. In P. Rakic & W. Singer (Eds.), *Neurobiology of neocortex* (pp. 42–67). Berlin: Wiley.

Metcalfe, J., & Wiebe, D. (1987). Intuition in insight

and noninsight problem solving. *Memory and Cognition, 15,* 238–246.

Meyer, D. E., & Schvaneveldt, R. W. (1971). Facilitation in recognizing pairs of words: Evidence of a dependence between retrieval operations. *Journal of Experimental Psychology, 90,* 227–234.

Miller, G. A. (1956). The magical number seven, plus or minus two: Some limits on our capacity for processing information. *Psychological Review, 63,* 81–97.

Miller, G. A. (2003). The cognitive revolution: A historical perspective. *Trends in Cognitive Sciences, 7,* 141–144.

Milner, A. D., & Goodale, M. A. (1995). *The visual brain in action.* New York: Oxford University Press.

Milner, B. (1966). Amnesia following operation on the temporal lobe. In C. W. M. Whitty & O. L. Zangwill (Eds.), *Amnesia* (pp. 109–133). London: Butterworth.

Milner, B., Corkin, S., & Teuber, H-L. (1968). Further analysis of hippocampal amnesic syndrome: 14-year follow-up study of H. M. *Neuropsychologia, 6,* 215–234.

Minda, J. P., & Smith, J. D. (2001). Prototypes in category learning: The effect of category size, category structure, and stimulus complexity. *Journal of Experimental Psychology: Learning, Memory, and Cognition, 27,* 775–799.

Misiak, H., & Sexton, V. (1966). History of psychology: An overview. New York: Grune & Stratton.

Mitchell, K. J., & Johnson, M. K. (2000). Source monitoring. In E. Tulving and F. I. M. Craik (Eds.), *The Oxford handbook of memory* (pp. 179–195). New York: Oxford University Press.

Moore, C. M., Yantis, S., & Vaughan, B. (1998). Object-based visual selection: Evidence from perceptual completion. *Psychological Science, 9,* 104–110.

Moray, N. (1959). Attention in dichotic listening: Affective cues and the influence of instructions. *Quarterly Journal of Experimental Psychology, 11,* 56–60.

Morimoto, C. H., & Mimica, M. R. M. (2005). Eye gaze tracking techniques for interactive applications. *Computer Vision and Image Understanding, 98,* 4–24.

Morris, C. D., Bransford, J. D., & Franks, J. J. (1977). Levels of processing versus transfer appropriate processing. *Journal of Verbal Learning and Verbal Behavior, 16,* 519–533.

Morris, R. G., Miotto, E. C., Feigenbaum, J. D., Bullock, P., & Polkey, C. E. (1997). Planning ability after frontal and temporal lobe lesions in humans: The effects of selection equivocation and working memory load. *Cognitive Neuropsychology, 14,* 1007–1027.

Morrow, D. G., Greenspan, S. L., & Bower, G. H. (1987). Accessibility and situation models in narrative comprehension. *Journal of Memory and Language, 26,* 165–187.

Moscovitch, M. (1995). Confabulation. In D. L. Schacter (Ed.), *Memory distortion* (pp. 226–251). Cambridge, MA: Harvard University Press.

Moscovitch, M., Rosenbaum, R. S., Gilboa, A., Addis, D. R., Westmacott, R., Grady, C., McAndrews, M. P., Levine, B., Black, S., Winocur, G., & Nadel, L. (2005). Functional neuroanatomy of remote episodic, semantic and spatial memory: A unified account based on multiple trace theory. *Journal of Anatomy, 207,* 35–66.

Mowbray, G. H. (1953). Simultaneous vision and audition: The comprehension of prose passages with varying levels of difficulty. *Journal of Experimental Psychology, 46,* 365–372.

Munakata, Y., Morton, J. B., & Stedron, J. M. (2003). The role of prefrontal cortex in perseveration: Developmental and computational explorations. In P. Quinlan (Ed.), *Connectionist models of development.* East Sussex, UK: Psychology Press.

Munakata, Y., Morton, J. B., & Yerys, B. E. (2003). Children's perseveration: Attentional inertia and alternative accounts. *Developmental Science, 6,* 471–473.

Murdoch, B. B., Jr. (1962). The serial position effect in free recall. *Journal of Experimental Psychology, 64,* 482–488.

Murphy, G. (2004). *The big book of concepts.* Cambridge, MA: MIT Press.

Murray, D. J. (1968). Articulating and acoustic confusability in short-term memory. *Journal of Experimental Psychology, 78,* 679–684.

Nadel, L., & Land, C. (2000). Memory traces revisited. *Neuroscience, 1,* 209–212.

Nadel, L., & Moscovitch, M. (1997). Memory consolidation, retrograde amnesia and the hippocampal complex. *Current Opinion in Neurobiology, 7,* 217–227.

Nader, K. (2003). Memory traces unbound. *Trends in Neurosciences. 26,* 65–72.

Nader, K., Schafe, G. E., & Le Doux, J. E. (2000a). Fear memories require protein synthesis in the amygdala for reconsolidation after retrieval. *Nature, 406,* 722–726.

Nader, K., Schafe, G. E., & Le Doux, J. E. (2000b). The labile nature of consolidation theory. *Nature, 1,* 216–219.

National Highway Traffic Safety Administration. (2006). The impact of driver inattention on near-crash/crash risk: An analysis using the 100-car naturalistic driving study data (Report No. DOT HS 810–594). Washington, DC: U.S. Department of Transportation.

Neath, I., & Suprenant, A. (2003). *Human memory.* Pacific Grove, CA: Brooks-Cole.

Neath, I., Surprenant, A. M., & Crowder, R. G. (1993). The context-dependent stimulus suffix effect. *Journal of Experimental Psychology: Learning, Memory and Cognition, 19,* 698–703.

Neisser, U. (1964). Visual search. *Scientific American, 210,* 94–107.

Neisser, U. (1967). *Cognitive psychology.* New York: Appleton-Century-Crofts.

Neisser, U. (1988). New vistas in the study of memory. In U. Neisser & E. Winograd (Eds.), *Remembering reconsidered: Ecological and traditional approaches to the study of memory* (pp. 1–10). Cambridge, UK: Cambridge University Press.

Neisser, U., & Becklen, R. (1975). Selective looking: Attending to visually-specified events. *Cognitive Psychology, 7,* 480–494.

Neisser, U., & Harsch, N. (1992). Phantom flashbulbs: False recollections of hearing the news about *Challenger.* In E. Winograd & U. Neisser (Eds.), *Affect and accuracy in recall: Studies of "flashbulb" memories* (pp. 9–31). New York: Cambridge University Press.

Neville, H. J., Nicol, J. L., Barss, A., Forster, K. I., & Garrett, M. F. (1991). Syntactically based sentence processing classes: Evidence from event-related brain potentials. *Journal of Cognitive Neuroscience, 3,* 151–165.

Newell, A., & Simon, H. A. (1956). The logic theory machine: A complex information processing system. *Transactions on information theory* (Institute of Radio Engineers), *IT-2,* No. 3, 61–79.

Newell, A., & Simon, H. A. (1972). *Human problem solving.* Englewood Cliffs, NJ: Prentice-Hall.

Newman, L. S., & Baumeister, R. F. (1998). Abducted by aliens. In S. J. Lynn & K. M. McConkie (Eds.), *Truth in memory* (pp. 284–303). New York: Guilford Press.

Nicoletta, B., Pizzourusso, T., Gian-Michele, R., & Maffei, L. (2003). Molecular basis of plasticity in the visual cortex. *Trends in Neurosciences, 26,* 369–378.

Nigro, G., & Neisser, U. (1983). Point of view in personal memories. *Cognitive Psychology, 15,* 467–482.

Nisbett, R. E. (2003). *The geography of thought.* New York: Free Press.

Norman, D. (1968). Toward a theory of memory and attention. *Psychological Review, 75,* 522–536.

Nyberg, L., McIntosh, A. R., Cabeaa, R., Habib, R., Houle, S., & Tulving, E. (1996). General and specific brain regions involved in encoding and retrieval of events: What, where and when. *Proceedings of the National Academy of Sciences, USA, 93,* 11280–11285.

Olesen, P. J., Westerberg, H., & Klingberg, T. (2004). Increased prefrontal and parietal activity after training of working memory. *Nature Neuroscience, 7,* 75–79.

Olson, A. C., & Humphreys, G. W. (1997). Connectionist models of neuropsychological disorders. *Trends in Cognitive Sciences, 1,* 222–228.

Orban, G. A., Vandenbussche, E., & Vogels, R. (1984). Human orientation discrimination tested with long stimuli. *Vision Research, 24,* 121–128.

Osherson, D. N., Smith, E. E., Wilkie, O., Lopez, A., & Shafir, E. (1990). Category-based induction. *Psychological Review, 97,* 185–200.

Osterhout, L., McLaughlin, J., & Bersick, M. (1997). Event-related brain potentials and human language. *Trends in Cognitive Sciences, 1,* 203–209.

Owen, A. M., Downes, J. J., Sahakian, B. J., Polkey, C. E., & Robbins, T. W. (1990). Planning and spatial working memory following frontal lobe lesions in man. *Neuropsychologica, 28,* 1021–1034.

Paivio, A. (1963). Learning of adjective-noun paired associates as a function of adjective-noun word order and noun abstractness. *Canadian Journal of Psychology, 17,* 370–379.

Paivio, A. (1965). Abstractness, imagery, and meaningfulness in paired-associate learning. *Journal of Verbal Learning and Verbal Behavior, 4,* 32–38.

Paivio, A. (1986). *Mental representations: A dual coding approach.* New York: Oxford University Press.

Paivio, A. (2006). *Mind and its evolution: A dual coding theoretical approach.* Hillsdale, NJ: Erlbaum.

Palmer, S. E. (1975). The effects of contextual scenes on the identification of objects. *Memory and Cognition, 3,* 519–526.

Park, H., & Reder, L. M. (2004). Moses illusion: Implications for human cognition. In R. F. Pohl (Ed.), *Cognitive illusions* (pp. 275–291). Hove, UK: Psychology Press.

Parkhurst, D., Law, K., & Niebur, E. (2002). Modeling the role of salience in the allocation of overt visual attention. *Vision Research, 42,* 107–123.

Parkin, A. J. (1996). *Explorations in cognitive neuropsychology.* Oxford, UK: Blackwell.

Pavlides, C., & Winston, J. (1989). Influences of hippocampal place cell firing in the awake state on the activity of these cells during subsequent sleep episodes. *Journal of Neuroscience, 9,* 2907–2918.

Pavlov, I. (1927). *Conditioned reflexes.* New York: Oxford University Press.

Peigneux, P., Laureys, S., Fuchs, S., Gollette, F., Perrin, F., Reggers, J., Phillips, C., Degueldre, C., Del Piore, G., Aerts, J., Luxen, A., & Maquet, P. (2004). Are spatial memories strengthened in the human hippocampus during slow wave sleep? *Neuron, 44,* 535–545.

Penfield, W., & Evans, J. (1935). The frontal lobe in man: A clinical study of maximum removals. *Brain, 58,* 115–133.

Penningroth, S. L. (2005). Free recall of everyday retrospective and prospective memories: The intention-superiority effect is moderated by action versus state orientation and by gender. *Memory, 13,* 711–724.

Perani, D. (2005). The neural basis of language talent in bilinguals. *Trends in Cognitive Sciences, 9,* 211–213.

Perani, D., & Abutalebi, J. (2005). The neural basis of first and second language processing. *Current Opinion in Neurobiology, 15,* 202–206.

Perfect, T. J., & Askew, C. (1994). Print adverts: Not remembered but memorable. *Applied Cognitive Psychology, 8,* 693–703.

Perky, C. W. (1910). An experimental study of imagination. *American Journal of Psychology, 21,* 422–452.

Perret, D. I., Hietanen, J. K., Oram, M. W., & Benson, P. J. (1992). Organization and function of cells responsive to faces in the temporal cortex. *Transactions of the Royal Society of London, B225,* 23–30.

Peters, J. (2004, November 26). "Hi, I'm your car. Don't let me distract you." *New York Times,* p. C1.

Petersen, S. E., Fox, P. T., Posner, M. I., Minturn, M., & Raichle, M. E. (1988). Positron emission tomographic studies of the cortical anatomy of single-word processing. *Nature, 331,* 585–589.

Peterson, L. R., & Peterson, M. J. (1959). Short-term retention of individual verbal items. *Journal of Experimental Psychology, 58,* 193–198.

Peterson, M. A. (1994). Object recognition processes can and do operate before figure-ground organization. *Current Directions in Psychological Science, 3,* 105–111.

Peterson, S. W. (1992). The cognitive functions of underlining as a study technique. *Reading Research and Instrumentation, 31,* 49–56.

Petitto, L. A., Katerelos, M., Levy, B. G., Gauna, K., Tetreault, K., & Ferraro, V. (2001). Bilingual signed and spoken language acquisition from birth: Implications for the mechanisms underlying early bilingual language acquisition. *Journal of Child Language, 28,* 453–496.

Pickering, M. J., & Garrod, S. (2004). Toward a mechanistic psychology of dialogue. *Behavioral and Brain Sciences, 27,* 169–226.

Pillemer, D. B. (1998). *Momentous events, vivid memories.* Cambridge, MA: Harvard University Press.

Pillemer, D. B., Picariello, M. L., Law, A. B., & Reichman, J. S. (1996). Memories of college: The importance of specific educational episodes. In D. C. Rubin (Ed.), *Remembering our past: Studies in autobiographical memory* (pp. 318–337). Cambridge, UK: Cambridge University Press.

Poggio, T. (1984, April). Vision by man and machine. *Scientific American,* 106–116.

Pollack, I., & Pickett, J. M. (1964). Intelligibility of excerpts from fluent speech: Auditory vs. structural context. *Journal of Verbal Learning and Verbal Behavior, 3,* 79–84.

Posner, M. I., & Keele, S. W. (1967). Decay of visual information from a single letter. *Science, 158,* 137–139.

Posner, M. I., Snyder, C. R. R., & Davidson, B. J. (1980). Attention and the detection of signals. *Journal of Experimental Psychology: General, 109,* 160–174.

Pretz, J. E., Naples, A. J., & Sternberg, R. J. (2003). Recognizing, defining, and representing problems. In J. E. Davidson & R. J. Sternberg (Eds.), *The psychology of problem solving* (pp. 3–30). Cambridge, UK: Cambridge University Press.

Price, C. J., & Mechelli, A. (2005). Reading and reading disturbance. *Current Opinion in Neurobiology, 15,* 231–238.

Principe, G. F., Kanaya, T., Ceci, S. J., & Singh, M. (2006). Believing is seeing: How rumors can engender false memories in preschoolers. *Psychological Science, 17,* 243–248.

Proffitt, J. B., Coley, J. D., Medin, D. L. (2000). Expertise and category-based induction. *Journal of Experimental Psychology: Learning, Memory and Cognition, 26,* 811–828.

Proksch, J., & Bavelier, D. (2002). Changes in the spatial distribution of visual attention after early deafness. *Journal of Cognitive Neuroscience, 14,* 687–701.

Pylyshyn, Z. W. (1973). What the mind's eye tells the mind's brain: A critique of mental imagery. *Psychological Bulletin, 80,* 1–24.

Pylyshyn, Z. W. (2001). Is the imagery debate over? If so, what was it about? In E. Dupoux (Ed.), *Language, brain, and cognitive development* (pp. 59–83). Cambridge, MA: MIT Press.

Pylyshyn, Z. W. (2003). Return of the mental image: Are there really pictures in the brain? *Trends in Cognitive Sciences, 7,* 113–118.

Quillian, M. R. (1967). Word concepts: A theory and simulation of some basic semantic capabilities. *Behavioral Science, 12,* 410–430.

Quillian, M. R. (1969). The Teachable Language Comprehender: A simulation program and theory of language. *Communications of the ACM, 12,* 459–476.

Quiroga, R. Q., Reddy, L., Kreiman, G., Kotch, C., & Fried, I. (2005). Invariant visual representation by single neurons in the human brain. *Nature, 435,* 1102–1107.

Ramachandran, V. S., & Anstis, S. M. (1986, May). The perception of apparent motion. *Scientific American,* 102–109.

Ramachandran, V. S., & Blakeslee, S. (1998). *Phantoms of the mind: Probing the mysteries of the human mind.* New York: HarperCollins.

Raphael, B. (1976). *The thinking computer.* New York: Freeman.

Ratcliff, R. (1990). Connectionist models of recognition memory: Constraints imposed by learning and forgetting functions. *Psychological Review, 97,* 285–308.

Rayner, K., & Clifton, C. (2002). Language processing. In H. Pashler & S. Yantis (Eds.), *Stevens' handbook of experimental psychology* (3rd ed., pp. 261–316). New York: Wiley.

Rayner, K., Liersedge, S. P., White, S. J., & Vergilino-Perez, D. (2003). Reading disappearing text: Cognitive control of eye movements. *Psychological Science, 14,* 385–388.

Reber, A. S. (1995). *Penguin dictionary of psychology* (2nd ed.). New York: Penguin.

Redelmeier, D. A., & Tibshirani, R. J. (1997). Association between cellular-telephone calls and motor vehicle collisions. *New England Journal of Medicine, 336,* 453–458.

Reder, L. M., & Anderson, J. R. (1982). Effects of spacing and embellishment for the main points of a text. *Memory and Cognition, 10,* 97–102.

Regier, T., Kay, P., & Cook, R. S. (2005). Focal colors are universal after all. *Proceedings of the National Academy of Sciences, 102,* 8386–8391.

Reicher, G. M. (1969). Perceptual recognition as a function of meaningfulness of stimulus material. *Journal of Experimental Psychology, 81,* 275–280.

Reitman, J. (1976). Skilled perception in Go: Deducing memory structures from inter-response times. *Cognitive Psychology, 8,* 336–356.

Rensink, R. A. (2000). The dynamic representation of scenes. *Visual Cognition, 7,* 17–42.

Rensink, R. A. (2002). Change detection. *Annual Review of Psychology, 53,* 245–277.

Rensink, R. A., O'Regan, J. K., & Clark, J. J. (1997). To see or not to see: The need for attention to perceive changes in scenes. *Psychological Science, 8,* 368–373.

Repovs, G., & Baddeley, A. (2006). The multi-component model of working memory: Explorations in experimental cognitive psychology. *Neuroscience, 139,* 5–21.

Richardson, A. (1994). *Individual differences in imaging: Their measurement, origins, and consequences.* Amityville, NY: Baywood.

Rips, L. J. (1995). Deduction and cognition. In E. Smith & D. N. Osherson (Eds.), *An invitation to cognitive science* (Vol. 2, pp. 297–343). Cambridge, MA: MIT Press.

Rips, L. J. (2002). Reasoning. In D. L. Medin (Ed.), *Stevens' handbook of experimental psychology* (3rd ed., pp. 363–411). New York: Wiley.

Rips, L. J., Shoben, E. J., & Smith, E. E. (1973). Semantic distance and the verification of semantic relations. *Journal of Verbal Learning and Verbal Behavior, 12,* 1–20.

Roberson, D., Davies, I., & Davidoff, J. (2000). Color categories are not universal: Replications and new evidence from a stone-age culture. *Journal of Experimental Psychology: General, 129,* 369–398.

Robertson, L. C., & Rafal, R. (2000). Disorders of visual attention. In M. Gazzaniga (Ed.), *The cognitive neurosciences* (2nd ed., pp. 633–649). Cambridge, MA: MIT Press.

Robertson, L. C, Treisman, A., Freidman-Hill, S., Grabowecky, M. (1997). The interaction of spatial and object pathways: Evidence from Balint's syndrome. *Journal of Cognitive Neuroscience, 9,* 295–317.

Rock, I. (1983). *The logic of perception.* Cambridge, MA: MIT Press.

Roediger, H. L. (1990). Implicit memory: Retention without remembering. *American Psychologist, 45,* 1043–1056.

Roediger, H. L., Guynn, M. J., & Jones, T. C. (1994). Implicit memory: A tutorial review. In G. d'Ydewalle, P. Eallen, & P. Bertelson (Eds.), *International perspectives on cognitive science* (Vol. 2, pp. 67–94). Hillsdale, NJ: Erlbaum.

Roediger, H. L., & McDermott, K. B. (1995). Creating false memories: Remembering words not presented in lists. *Journal of Experimental Psychology: Learning, Memory, and Cognition, 21,* 803–814.

Rogers, T. B., Kuiper, N. A., & Kirker, W. S. (1979). Self-reference and the encoding of personal information. *Journal of Personality and Social Psychology, 35,* 677–688.

Rogers, T. T., & McClelland, J. L. (2004). *Semantic cognition: A parallel distributed processing approach.* Cambridge, MA: MIT Press.

Rosch, E. H. (1973). On the internal structure of perceptual and semantic categories. In T. E. Moore (Ed.), *Cognitive development and the acquisition of language* (pp. 111–144). New York: Academic Press.

Rosch, E. H. (1975a). Cognitive representations of semantic categories. *Journal of Experimental Psychology: General, 104,* 192–233.

Rosch, E. H. (1975b). The nature of mental codes for color categories. *Journal of Experimental Psychology: Human Perception and Performance, 1,* 303–322.

Rosch, E. H., & Mervis, C. B. (1975). Family resemblances: Studies in the internal structures of categories. *Cognitive Psychology, 7,* 573–605.

Rosch, E. H., Mervis, C. B., Gray, W. D., Johnson, D. M., & Boyes-Braem, P. (1976). Basic objects in natural categories. *Cognitive Psychology, 8,* 382–439.

Rosch, E. H., Simpson, C., & Miller, R. S. (1976). Structural bases of typicality effects. *Journal of Experimental Psychology: Human Perception and Performance, 2,* 491–502.

Rosch Heider, E. (1972). Universals in color naming and memory. *Journal of Experimental Psychology, 93,* 10–20.

Rosch Heider, E., & Olivier, D. C. (1972). The structure of color space in naming and memory for two languages. *Cognitive Psychology, 3,* 337–354.

Rose, D. (1996). Guest editorial: Reflections on (or by?) grandmother cells. *Perception, 25,* 881–886.

Rosenbaum, R. S., Köhler, S., Schacter, D. L., Moscovitch, M., Westmacott, R., Black, S. E., Gao, F., Tulving, E. (2005). The case of K.C.: Contributions of a memory-impaired person to memory theory. *Neuropsychologia, 43,* 989–1021.

Ross, D. F., Ceci, S. J., Dunning, D., & Toglia, M. P. (1994). Unconscious transference and mistaken identity: When a witness misidentifies a familiar but innocent person. *Journal of Applied Psychology, 79,* 918–930.

Ross, M., & Buehler, R. (1994). Creative remembering. In U. Neisser and R. Fivish (Eds.), *The remembering self: Construction and accuracy in the self-narrative* (pp. 205–235). New York: Cambridge University Press.

Ross, M., & Makin, V. S. (1999). Prototype versus exemplar models in cognition. In R. J. Sternberg (Ed.), *The nature of cognition* (pp. 205–241). Cambridge, MA: MIT Press.

Rowe, J. B., Owen, A. M., Johnsrude, I. S., & Passingham, R. E. (2001). Imaging the mental components of a planning task. *Neuropsychologia, 39,* 315–327.

Rubin, D. C. (2005). A basic-systems approach to autobiographical memory. *Current Directions in Psychological Science, 14,* 79–83.

Rubin, D. C., Rahhal, T. A., & Poon, L. W. (1998). Things learned in early adulthood are remembered best. *Memory and Cognition, 26,* 3–19.

Rumelhart, D. E., & McClelland, J. L. (1982). An interactive activation model of context effects in letter perception: Part 2. The contextual enhancement effect and some tests and extensions of the model. *Psychological Review, 89,* 60–94.

Rumelhart, D. E., & McClelland, J. L. (1986). *Parallel distributed processing: Explorations in the microstructure of cognition.* Cambridge, MA: MIT Press.

Ryan, L., Nadel, L., Keil, K., Putnam, K., Schnyer, D., Trouard, T., & Moscovitch, M. (2001). Hippocampal complex and retrieval of recent and very remote autobiographical memories: Evidence from functional magnetic resonance imaging in neurologically intact people. *Hippocampus, 11,* 707–714.

Sachs, J. (1967). Recognition memory for syntactic and semantic aspects of a connected discourse. *Perception & Psychophysics, 2,* 437–442.

Sacks, O. W. (1985). *The man who mistook his wife for a hat and other clinical tales.* New York: Summit Books.

Saffran, J. R., Aslin, R. N., & Newport, E. L. (1996). Statistical learning by 8-month-old infants. *Science, 274,* 1926–1928.

Saffran, J. R., Aslin, R. N., & Newport, E. L. (1999). Statistical learning of tone sequences by human infants and adults. *Cognition, 70,* 27–52.

Samuel, A. G. (1990). Using perceptual-restoration effects to explore the architecture of perception. In G. T. M. Altmann (Ed.), *Cognitive models of speech processing* (pp. 295–314). Cambridge, MA: MIT Press.

Sanfey, A. G., Lowenstein, G., McClure, S. M., & Cohen, J. D. (2006). Neuroeconomics: Crosscurrents in research on decision-making. *Trends in Cognitive Sciences, 10,* 106–116.

Sanfey, A. G., Rilling, J. K., Aronson, J. A., Nystrom, L. E., & Cohen, J. D. (2003). The neural basis of economic decision making in the Ultimatum Game. *Science, 300,* 1755–1758.

Sanitioso, R., Kunda, Z., & Fong, G. T. (1990). Motivated recruitment of autobiographical memories. *Journal of Personality and Social Psychology, 59,* 229–241.

Sara, J. J., & Hars, B. (2006). In memory of consolidation. *Learning & Memory, 13,* 515–521.

Sara, S. J. (2000). Strengthening the shaky trace through retrieval. *Neuroscience, 1,* 212–213.

Savage-Rumbaugh, S., & Lewin, R. (1994). *Kanzi, the ape at the brink of the human mind.* New York: Wiley.

Savin, H. B. (1963). Word-frequency effects and errors in the perception of speech. *Journal of the Acoustical Society of America, 35,* 200–206.

Schacter, D. L. (1987). Implicit memory. History and current status. *Journal of Experimental Psychology: Learning, Memory and Cognition, 13,* 501–518.

Schacter, D. L. (1996). *Searching for memory: The brain, the mind, and the past.* New York: Basic Books.

Schacter, D. L. (2001). *The seven sins of memory.* New York: Houghton Mifflin.

Schacter, D. L., Norman, K. A., & Koutstaal, W. (1998). The cognitive neuroscience of constructive memory. *Annual Review of Psychology, 49,* 289–318.

Schacter, D. L., & Slotnick, S. D. (2004). The cognitive neuroscience of memory distortion. *Neuron, 44,* 149–160.

Schenkein, J. (1980). A taxonomy for repeating action sequences in natural conversation. In B. Butterworth (Ed.), *Language production* (Vol. 1, pp. 21–47). San Diego, CA: Academic Press.

Schkade, D. A., & Kahneman, D. (1998). Does living in California make people happy? *Psychological Science, 9*, 340–346.

Schmolck, H., Buffalo, E. A., & Squire, L. R. (2000). Memory distortions develop over time: Recollections of the O. J. Simpson trial verdict after 15 and 32 months. *Psychological Science, 11*, 39–45.

Schneider, W., & Shiffrin, R. M. (1977). Controlled and automatic human information processing: I. Detection, search, and attention. *Psychological Review, 84*, 1–66.

Schrauf, R. W., & Rubin, D. C. (1998). Bilingual autobiographical memory in older adult immigrants: A test of cognitive explanations of the reminiscence bump and the linguistic encoding of memories. *Journal of Memory and Language, 39*, 437–457.

Schwartz, B. I., Travis, D. M., Castro, A. M., & Smith, S. S. (2000). The phenomenology of real and illusory tip-of-the-tongue states. *Memory & Cognition, 28*, 18–27.

Schwartz, D. L., & Black, J. B. (1996). Analog imagery in mental model reasoning: Depictive models. *Cognitive Psychology, 30*, 154–219.

Schwartz, D. L., & Black, T. (1999). Inferences through imagined actions: Knowing by simulated doing. *Journal of Experimental Psychology: Learning, Memory, and Cognition, 25*, 116–136.

Schweickert, R., & Boruff, B. (1986). Short-term memory capacity: Magic number or magic spell? *Journal of Experimental Psychology: Learning, Memory and Cognition, 12*, 419–425.

Scoville, W. B., & Milner, B. (1957). Loss of recent memory after bilateral hippocampal lesions. *Journal of Neurology, Neurosurgery, and Psychiatry, 20*, 11–21.

Scribner, S. (1977). Modes of thinking and ways of speaking: Culture and logic reconsidered. In P. N. Johnson-Laird & P. C. Wason (Eds.), *Thinking: Readings in cognitive science* (pp. 483–500). Cambridge, UK: Cambridge University Press.

Segal, S. J., & Fusella, V. (1970). Influence of imaged pictures and sounds on detection of visual and auditory signals. *Journal of Experimental Psychology, 83*, 458–464.

Seidenberg, M. S., & Zevin, J. D. (2006). Connectionist models in developmental cognitive neuroscience: Critical periods and the paradox of success. In Y. Munakata & M. Johnson (Eds.), *Processes of change in brain and cognitive development: Attention and performance XXI.* Oxford, UK: Oxford University Press.

Shallice, T., & Warrington, E. K. (1970). Independent functioning of verbal memory stores: A neuropsychological study. *Quarterly Journal of Experimental Psychology, 22*, 261–273.

Shaw, J. S. (1996). Increases in eyewitness confidence resulting from postevent questioning. *Journal of Experimental Psychology: Applied, 2*, 126–146.

Shepard, R. N., & Metzler, J. (1971). Mental rotation of three-dimensional objects. *Science, 171*, 701–703.

Sheridan, J., & Humphreys, G. W. (1993). A verbal-semantic category-specific recognition impairment. *Cognitive Neuropsychology, 10*, 143–184.

Sherry, J. L. (2001). The effects of violent video games on aggression: A meta-analysis. *Human Communication Research, 27*, 409–431.

Shiffrin, R. M., & Schneider, W. (1977). Controlled and automatic human information processing: II. Perceptual learning, automatic attending, and a general theory. *Psychological Review, 84*, 127–190.

Shin, S.-J. (1994). *The logical status of diagrams.* Cambridge, UK: Cambridge University Press.

Shomstein, S., & Behrmann, M. (2006). Cortical systems mediating visual attention to both objects and spatial locations. *Proceedings of the National Academy of Sciences, 103*(30), 11387–11392.

Silveri, M. C., & Gainotti, G. (1988). Interaction between vision and language in category-specific impairment. *Cognitive Neuropsychology, 5*, 677–709.

Simons, D. J., & Chabris, C. F. (1999). Gorillas in our midst: Sustained inattentional blindness for dynamic events. *Perception, 28*, 1059–1074.

Simonton, D. K. (1984). Creative productivity and age: A mathematical model based on a two-step cognitive process. *Developmental Review, 4*, 77–111.

Sims, V. K., & Hegarty, M. (1997). Mental animation in the visuospatial sketch pad. Evidence from dual task studies. *Memory & Cognition, 25*, 321–333.

Singer, M., Andrusiak, P., Reisdorf, P., & Black, N. L. (1992). Individual differences in bridging inference processes. *Memory & Cognition, 20,* 539–548.

Sinha, P. (2002). Recognizing complex patterns. *Nature Neuroscience Supplement, 5,* 1094–1097.

Skinner, B. F. (1938). *The behavior of organisms.* New York: Appleton Century.

Skinner, B. F. (1957). *Verbal behavior.* New York: Appleton-Century Crofts.

Slameka, N. J., & Graf, P. (1978). The generation effect: Delineation of a phenomenon. *Journal of Experimental Psychology: Human Learning and Memory, 4,* 592–604.

Slobin, D. I. (1966). Grammatical transformations and sentence comprehension in childhood and adulthood. *Journal of Verbal Learning and Verbal Behavior, 5,* 219–227.

Slotnick, S. D., Thompson, W. L., & Kosslyn, S. M. (2005). Visual mental imagery induces retinotopically organized activation of early visual areas. *Cerebral Cortex, 15,* 1570–1583.

Smith, E. E., Schoben, E. J., & Rips, L. J. (1974). Structure and process in semantic memory. *Psychological Review, 81,* 214–241.

Smith, J. D., & Minda, J. P. (1998). Prototypes in the mist: The early epochs of category learning. *Journal of Experimental Psychology: Learning, Memory, and Cognition, 24,* 1411–1436.

Smith, J. D., & Minda, J. P. (2000). Thirty categorization results in search of a model. *Journal of Experimental Psychology: Learning, Memory, and Cognition, 26,* 3–27.

Smith, S. M., Glenberg, A. M., & Bjork, R. A. (1978). Environmental context and human memory. *Memory & Cognition, 6,* 342–353.

Smith, S. M., & Rothkopf, E. Z. (1984). Contextual enhancement and distribution of practice in the classroom. *Cognition and Instruction, 1,* 341–358.

Snow, C. E. (1998). Bilingualism and second language acquisition. In J. B. Gleason & N. B. Ratner (Eds.), *Psycholinguistics* (2nd ed., pp. 453–481). Fort Worth, TX: Harcourt Brace.

Solomon, K. O., Medin, D. L., & Lynch, E. (1999). Concepts do more than categorize. *Trends in Cognitive Science, 3,* 99–105.

Spalding, T. L., & Murphy, G. L. (1996). Effects of background knowledge on category construction. *Journal of Experimental Psychology: Learning, Memory and Cognition, 22,* 525–538.

Spelke, E., Hirst, W., & Neisser, U. (1976). Skills of divided attention. *Cognition, 4,* 215–230.

Spence, C., & Read, L. (2003). Speech shadowing while driving: On the difficulty of splitting attention between eye and ear. *Psychological Science, 14,* 251–256.

Sperling, G. (1960). The information available in brief visual presentations. *Psychological Monographs, 74*(11, Whole No. 498), 1–29.

Sporer, S. L., Penrod, S., Read, D., & Cutler, B. (1995). Choosing, confidence, and accuracy: A meta-analysis of the confidence-accuracy relation in eyewitness identification studies. *Psychological Bulletin, 118,* 315–327.

Sprecher, S. (1999). "I love you more today than yesterday": Romantic partners' perceptions of changes in love and related affect over time. *Journal of Personality and Social Psychology, 76,* 46–53.

Squire, L. R. (1986). Mechanisms of memory. *Science, 232,* 1612–1619.

Squire, L. R., & Cohen, N. (1979). Memory and amnesia: Resistance to disruption develops for years after learning. *Behavioral and Neural Biology. 25,* 115–125.

Squire, L. R., Slater, D. C., & Chace, P. M., (1975). Retrograde amnesia: Temporal gradient in very long term memory following electro-convulsive therapy. *Science, 187,* 77–79.

Squire, L. R., & Zola-Morgan, S. (1996). Structure and functioning of declarative and nondeclarative memory systems. *Proceedings of the National Academy of Sciences, 93,* 13515–13522.

Squire, L. R., & Zola-Morgan, S. (1998). Episodic memory, semantic memory, and amnesia. *Hippocampus, 8,* 205–211.

Srinivasan, M. V., & Ventatesh, S. (Eds.). (1997). *From living eyes to seeing machines.* New York: Oxford University Press.

Stanny, C. J., & Johnson, T. C. (2000). Effects of stress induced by a simulated shooting on recall by police and citizen witnesses. *American Journal of Psychology, 113,* 359–386.

Starr, M. S., & Rayner, K. (2001). Eye movements during reading: Some current controversies. *Trends in Cognitive Sciences, 5,* 156–163.

Stevens, K. (2002, May 7). Out of the kitchen, and other getaways. *New York Times.*

Strack, F., Martin, L. L., & Schwarz, N. (1988). Priming and communication: Social determinants of information use in judgments of life satisfaction. *European Journal of Social Psychology, 18,* 429–442.

Strayer, D. L., & Johnston, W. A. (2001). Driven to distraction: Dual-task studies of simulated driving and conversing on a cellular telephone. *Psychological Science, 12,* 462–466.

Stroop, J. R. (1935). Studies of interference in serial verbal reactions. *Journal of Experimental Psychology, 18,* 643–662.

Styles, E. A. (1997). *The psychology of attention.* Hove, UK: Psychology Press.

Super, H., Spekreijse, H., & Lamme, V. A. F. (2001). A neural correlate of working memory in the monkey primary visual cortex. *Science, 293,* 120–124.

Swinney, D. A. (1979). Lexical access during sentence comprehension: (Re)considerations of context effects. *Journal of Verbal Learning and Verbal Behavior, 18,* 645–659.

Talarico, J. M., & Rubin, D. C. (2003). Confidence, not consistency, characterizes flashbulb memories. *Psychological Science, 14,* 455–461.

Tanaka, J. W., & Taylor, M. (1991). Object categories and expertise: Is the basic level in the eye of the beholder? *Cognitive Psychology, 23,* 457–482.

Tanaka, K. (1993). Neuronal mechanisms of object recognition. *Science, 262,* 684–688.

Tanenhaus, M. K., Spivey-Knowlton, M. J., Beerhard, K. M., & Sedivy, J. C. (1995). Integration of visual and linguistic information in spoken language comprehension. *Science, 268,* 1632–1634.

Tang, Y. (2006). Arithmetic processing in the brain shaped by cultures. *Proceedings of the National Academy of Sciences, 103,* 10775–10780.

Tang, Y., Zhang, W., Chen, K., Feng, S., Ji, Y., Shen, J., Reiman, E. M., & Liu, Y. (2006). Arithmetic processing in the brain shaped by cultures. *Proceedings of the National Academy of Sciences, 103*(28), 10775–10780.

Tarkan, L. (2003, April 29). Brain surgery, without knife or blood, gains favor. *New York Times,* p. F5.

Ter-Pogossian, M. M., Phelps, M. E., Hoffman, E. J., & Mullani, N. A. (1975). A positron-emission tomography for nuclear imaging (PET). *Radiology, 114,* 89–98.

Terr, L. C. (1994). *Unchained memories: The stories of traumatic memories lost and found.* New York: Basic Books.

Tipper, S. P., & Behrmann, M. (1996). Object-centered not scene-based visual neglect. *Journal of Experimental Psychology: Human Perception and Performance, 22,* 1261–1278.

Todd, J. J., & Marois, R. (2004). Capacity limit of visual short-term memory in human posterior parietal cortex. *Nature, 428,* 751–754.

Toni, N., Buchs, P.-A., Nikonenko, I., Bron, C. R., & Muller, D. (1999). LTP promotes formation of multiple spine synapses between a single axon terminal and a dendrite. *Nature 402,* 421–425.

Tooley, V., Bringham, J. C., Maass, A., & Bothwell, R. K. (1987). Facial recognition: Weapon effect and attentional focus. *Journal of Applied Social Psychology, 17,* 845–859.

Treadeau, K. (1997). *Mega memory.* New York: William Morrow.

Treisman, A. M. (1964a). Selective attention in man. *British Medical Bulletin, 20,* 12–16.

Treisman, A. M. (1964b). Contextual cues in selective listening. *Quarterly Journal of Experimental Psychology, 12,* 242–245.

Treisman, A. M. (1986). Features and objects in visual processing. *Scientific American, 225,* 114–125.

Treisman, A. M. (1998). The perception of features and objects. In R. D. Wright (Ed.), *Visual attention* (pp. 26–54). New York: Oxford University Press.

Treisman, A. M. (1999). Solutions to the binding problem: Progress through controversy and convergence. *Neuron, 24,* 105–110.

Treisman, A. M., & Schmidt, H. (1982). Illusory conjunctions in the perception of objects. *Cognitive Psychology, 14,* 107–141.

Trueswell, J. C., Tannehaus, M. K., & Garnsey, S. M. (1994). Semantic influences on parsing: Use of thematic role information in syntactic ambiguity resolution. *Journal of Memory and Language, 33,* 285–318.

Tulving, E. (1962). Subjective organization in free recall of "unrelated" words. *Psychological Review, 69,* 344–354.

Tulving, E. (1972). Episodic and semantic memory. In E. Tulving & W. Donaldson (Eds.), *Organization of memory* (pp. 381–403). New York: Academic Press.

Tulving, E. (1985). How many memory systems are there? *American Psychologist, 40,* 385–398.

Tulving, E. (2001). Episodic memory and common sense: How far apart? *Philosophical Transactions of the Royal Society of London B, 356,* 1501–1515.

Tulving, E., & Markowitsch, H. J. (1998). Episodic and declarative memory: Role of the hippocampus. *Hippocampus, 8,* 198–204.

Tulving, E., & Pearlstone, Z. (1966). Availability versus accessibility of information in memory for words. *Journal of Verbal Learning and Verbal Behavior, 5,* 381–391.

Tulving, E., Schacter, D. L., & Stark, H. A. (1982). Priming effects in word-fragment completion are independent of recognition memory. *Journal of Experimental Psychology: Learning Memory, and Cognition, 8,* 336–342.

Tversky, A., & Kahneman, D. (1973). Availability: A heuristic for judging frequency and probability. *Cognitive Psychology, 5,* 207–232.

Tversky, A., & Kahneman, D. (1974). Judgment under uncertainty: Heuristics and biases. *Science, 185,* 1124–1131.

Tversky, A., & Kahneman, D. (1981). The framing of decisions and the psychology of choice. *Science, 211,* 453–458.

Tversky, A., & Kahneman, D. (1983). Extensional versus intuitive reasoning: The conjunction fallacy in probability judgment. *Psychological Review, 90,* 293–315.

Tversky, A., & Shafir, E. (1992). Choice under conflict: The dynamics of deferred decision. *Psychological Science, 3,* 358–361.

Tyler, S. W., Hertel, P. T., McCallum, M. C., & Ellis, H. C. (1979). *Journal of Experimental Psychology: Human Learning and Memory, 6,* 607–617.

Underwood, G., & Batt, V. (1996). *Reading and understanding.* Oxford, UK: Blackwell.

Vallar, G., & Baddeley, A. D. (1984). Fractionation of working memory: Neuropsychological evidence for a phonological short-term store. *Journal of Verbal Learning and Verbal Behavior, 23,* 151–161.

Van den Broek, P. (1994). Comprehension and memory of narrative texts. In M. A. Gernsbacher (Ed.), *Handbook of psycholinguistics* (pp. 539–588). San Diego: Academic Press.

Van Rullen, R., & Thorpe, S. J. (2001). The time course of visual processing: From early perception to decision-making. *Journal of Cognitive Neuroscience, 13,* 454–461.

Vargha-Khadem, F., Gadian, D. G., Watkins, K. E., Connolly, A., Van Paesschen, W., & Mishkin, M. (1997). Differential effects of early hippocampal pathology on episodic and semantic memory. *Science, 277,* 376–380.

Vecera, S. P., & O'Reilly, R. C. (2000). Graded effects in hierarchical figure-ground organization: Reply to Peterson (1999). *Journal of Experimental Psychology: Human Perception and Performance, 26,* 1221–1231.

Violanti, J. M. (1998). Cellular phones and fatal traffic collisions. *Accident Analysis and Prevention, 28,* 265–270.

Vogel, E. K., McCollough, A. W., & Machizawa, M. G. (2005). *Nature, 438,* 500–503.

Voss, J. F., Greene, T. R., Post, T., & Penner, B. C. (1983). Problem-solving skill in the social sciences. In G. Bower (Ed.), *The psychology of learning and motivation.* New York: Academic Press.

Wagenaar, W. A. (1986). My memory: A study of autobiographical memory over six years. *Cognitive Psychology, 18,* 225–252.

Wagner, A. D., Schacter, D. L., Rotte, M., Koutstaal, W., Maril, A., Dale, A. M., Rosen, B. R., & Buckner, R. L. (1998). Building memories: Remembering and forgetting of verbal experiences as predicted by brain activity. *Science, 281,* 1188–1191.

Wagner, U., Gais, S., Haider, H., Verleger, R., & Born, J. (2004). Sleep inspires insight. *Nature, 427,* 352–355.

Waldrop, M. M. (1988). A landmark in speech recognition. *Science, 240,* 1615.

Walker, M. P., & Stickgold, R. (2004). Sleep-dependent learning and memory consolidation. *Neuron, 44,* 121–133.

Wallis, J. D., Anderson, K. C., & Miller, E. K. (2001). Single neurons in prefrontal cortex encode abstract rules. *Nature, 411,* 953–956.

Waltz, J. A., Knowlton, B. J., Holyoak, K. J., Boone, K. B., Mishkin, F. S., de Menezes Santos, M., Thomas, C. R., & Miller, B. L. (1999). A system for relational reasoning in human prefrontal cortex. *Psychological Science, 10,* 119–124.

Ward, T. B. (2004). Cognition, creativity and entrepreneurship. *Journal of Business Venturing, 19,* 173–188.

Ward, T. B., Finke, R. A., & Smith, S. M. (1995). *Creativity and the mind: discovering the genius within.* New York: Plenum.

Ward, T. B., Smith, S. M., & Vaid, J. (Eds.). (1997). *Creative thought: An investigation of conceptual structures and processes.* Washington, DC: American Psychological Association.

Warren, R. M. (1970). Perceptual restoration of missing speech sounds. *Science, 167,* 392–393.

Warrington, E. K., & McCarthy, R. (1983). Category specific access dysphasia. *Brain, 106,* 859–878.

Warrington, E. K., & Shallice, T. (1969). The selective impairment of auditory verbal short-term memory. *Brain, 92,* 885–896.

Warrington, E. K., & Shallice, T. (1984). Category specific semantic impairments. *Brain, 107,* 829–854.

Warrington, E. K., & Weiskrantz, L. (1968). New method of testing long-term retention with special reference to amnesic patients. *Nature, 217,* 972–974.

Wason, P. C. (1960). On the failure to eliminate hypotheses in a conceptual task. *Quarterly Journal of Experimental Psychology, 12,* 129–140.

Wason, P. C. (1966). Reasoning. In B. Foss (Ed.), *New horizons in psychology* (pp. 135–151). Harmonsworth, UK: Penguin.

Watson, J. B. (1913). Psychology as the behaviorist views it. *Psychological Review, 20,* 158–177.

Watson, J. B. (1928). *The ways of behaviorism.* New York: Harper and Brothers.

Watson, J. B., & Rayner, R. (1920). Conditioned emotional reactions. *Journal of Experimental Psychology, 3,* 1–14.

Waugh, N. C., & Norman, D. A. (1965). Primary memory. *Psychological Review, 72,* 69–104.

Wearing, D. (2005). *Forever today.* London, UK: Doubleday.

Weisberg, R. W. (1995). Prolegomena to theories of insight in problem solving: A taxonomy of problems. In R. J. Sternberg & J. E. Davidson (Eds.), *The nature of insight.* (pp. 157–196). Cambridge, MA: MIT Press.

Weisberg, R. W., & Alba, J. W. (1981). An examination of the alleged role of "fixation" in the solution of several "insight" problems. *Journal of Experimental Psychology: General, 110,* 169–192.

Weisberg, R. W., & Alba, J. W. (1982). Problem solving is not like perception: More on Gestalt theory. *Journal of Experimental Psychology: General, 111,* 326–330.

Wells, G. L. (1985). Verbal descriptions of faces from memory: Are they diagnostic of identification accuracy? *Journal of Applied Social Psychology, 14,* 89–103.

Wells, G. L., & Bradfield, A. L. (1998). "Good, you identified the suspect": Feedback to eyewitnesses distorts their reports of the witnessing experience. *Journal of Applied Psychology, 83,* 360–376.

Wells, G. L., Malpass, R. S., Lindsay, R. C. L., Fisher, R. P., Turtle, J. W., & Fulero, S. M. (2000). From the lab to the police station. *American Psychologist, 55,* 581–598.

Westmacott, R., & Moscovitch, M. (2003). The contribution of autobiographical significance to semantic memory. *Memory and Cognition, 31,* 761–774.

Wheeler, D. D. (1970). Processes in word recognition. *Cognitive Psychology, 1,* 59–85.

Wheeler, M. E., & Buckner, R. L. (2004). Functional-anatomic correlates of remembering and knowing. *NeuroImage, 21,* 1337–1349.

Wheeler, M. E., Petersen, S. E., & Buckner, R. L. (2000). Memory's echo: Vivid remembering reactivates sensory-specific cortex. *Proceedings of the National Academy of Sciences, 97,* 11125–11129.

Wheeler, M. E., Stuss, D. T., & Tulving, E. (1997). Toward a theory of episodic memory: The frontal lobes and autonoetic consciousness. *Psychological Bulletin, 121,* 331–354.

Whitaker, B. (2003, June 10). California may restrict vehicle cellphone use. *New York Times,* p. A25.

Whorf, B. J. (1956). The relation of habitual thought and behavior to language. In J. B. Carroll (Ed.), *Language, thought and reality: Essays by B. L. Whorf* (pp. 35–270). Cambridge, MA: MIT Press.

Wickelgren, W. A. (1965). Acoustic similarity and retroactive interference in short-term memory. *Journal of Verbal Learning and Verbal Behavior, 4,* 53–61.

Wickens, D. D., Dalezman, R. E., & Eggemeier, F. T. (1976). Multiple encoding of word attributes in memory. *Memory & Cognition, 4,* 307–310.

Wilding, J., & Valentine, E. R. (1997). *Superior memory.* Hove, UK: Psychology Press.

Williams, L. M. (1994). Recall of childhood trauma: A prospective study of women's memories of child sexual abuse. *Journal of Consulting and Clinical Psychology, 62,* 1167–1176.

Wilson, B., & Baddeley, A. (1988). Semantic, episodic, and autobiographical memory in a postmeningitic amnesic patient. *Brain and Cognition, 8,* 31–46.

Wilson, M. (2002). Six views of embodied cognition. *Psychonomic Bulletin and Review, 9,* 625–636.

Wilson, M., & Emmorey, K. (1997). Working memory for sign language: A window into the architecture of the working memory system. *Journal of Deaf Studies and Deaf Education, 2,* 120–130.

Wilson, M., & Emmorey, K. (2006). Comparing sign language and speech reveals a universal limit on short-term memory capacity. *Psychological Science, 17,* 682–683.

Wilson, M., & Emmorey, K. (in press). No difference in short-term memory span between sign and speech. *Psychological Science.*

Wilson, M. A., & McNaughton, B. L. (1994). Reactivation of hippocampal ensemble memories during sleep. *Science, 265,* 676–679.

Wilson, T. D., Wheatley, T., Meyers, J. M., Gilbert, D. T., & Axsom, D. (2000). Focalism: A source of durability bias in affective forecasting. *Journal of Personality and Social Psychology, 78,* 821–836.

Wiltgen, B. J., Brown, R. A. M., Talton, L. E., & Silva, A. J. (2004). New circuits for old memories: The role of the neocortex in consolidation. *Neuron, 44,* 101–108.

Wiseman, S., & Neisser, U. (1974). Perceptual organization as a determinant of visual recognition memory. *American Journal of Psychology, 87,* 675–681.

Wittgenstein, L. (1953). *Philosophical investigations* (G. E. M. Amnscombe, Trans.). Oxford, UK: Blackwell.

Wollen, K. A., Weber, A., & Lowry, D. H. (1972). Bizarreness versus interaction of mental images as determinants of learning. *Cognitive Psychology, 3,* 518–523.

Wood, N., & Cowan, N. (1995). The cocktail party phenomenon revisited: How frequent are attention shifts to one's name in an irrelevant auditory channel? *Journal of Experimental Psychology: Human Perception and Performance, 21,* 255–260.

Wright, D. B., Loftus, E. F., & Hall, M. (2001). Now you see it; now you don't: Inhibiting recall and recognition of scenes. *Applied Cognitive Psychology, 15,* 471–482.

Yamauchi, T., and Markman, A. B. (2000). Inference using categories. *Journal of Experimental Psychology: Learning, Memory and Cognition, 26,* 776–795.

Yarbus, A. (1967). *Eye movements and vision.* New York: Plenum.

Yost, W. A., & Sheft, S. (1993). Auditory processing. In W. A. Yost, A. N. Popper, & R. R. Fay (Eds.), *Handbook of auditory research* (Vol. 3). New York: Springer-Verlag.

Zalla, T., Phipps, M., & Grafman, J. (2002). Story processing in patients with damage to the prefrontal cortex. *Cortex, 38,* 215–231.

Zaragoza, M. S., & McCloskey, M. (1989). Misleading postevent information and the memory impairment hypothesis: Comment on Belli and reply to Tversky and Tuchin. *Journal of Experimental Psychology: General, 118,* 92–99.

Zatorre, R. J., Halpern, A. R., Perry, D. W., Meyer, E., & Evans, A. C. (1996). Hearing in the mind's ear: A PET investigation of musical imagery and perception. *Journal of Cognitive Neuroscience, 8,* 29–46.

Zhang, G., & Simon, H. A. (1985). STM capacity for Chinese words and idioms: Chunking and acoustical loop hypotheses. *Memory and Cognition, 13,* 193–201.

Zihl, J., von Cramon, D., & Mai, N. (1983). Selective disturbance of movement vision after bilateral brain damage. *Brain, 106,* 313–340.

Zihl, J., von Cramon, D., Mai, N., & Schmid, C. (1991). Disturbance of movement vision after bilateral posterior brain damage. *Brain, 114,* 2235–2252.

Zikmund-Fisher, B. J., Sarr, B., Fagerlin, A., Ubel, P. A. (2006). A matter of perspective: Choosing for others differs from choosing for yourself when making treatment decisions. *Journal of General Internal Medicine, 21,* 618–622.

Zola-Morgan, S., Squire, L., & Amaral, D. G. (1986). Human amnesia and the medial temporal region: Enduring memory impairment following a bilateral lesion limited to field CA1 of the hippocampus. *Journal of Neuroscience, 6,* 2950–2967.

Zwaan, R. A. (1999). Situation models: The mental leap into imagined worlds. *Current Directions in Psychological Science, 8,* 15–18.

Name Index

Abutalebi, J., 391
Adamson, R. E., 401, 402
Adderly, B., 349
Aguirre, G. K., 90
Alampay, D. A., 59, 60
Alba, J. W., 399
Altmann, G. T. M., 360, 373, 376
Amedi, A., 340
Anderson, J. R., 223, 260, 307, 336
Anderson, K. C., 483
Anderson, N. D., 232
Aniston, J., 51
Anstis, S. M., 96
Aristotle, 437
Arkes, H. R., 256
Askew, C., 196
Assefi, S. L., 280
Atkinson, R. C., 20, 138, 139
Atran, S., 316, 317

Baars, B. J., 382
Baddeley, A. D., 154, 155, 157, 158, 159, 163, 164, 173, 218, 219
Bahrick, H. P., 251
Bailenson, J. N., 317
Ball, T., 329
Bannister, R., 252
Barlow, H. B., 41
Baron, R. A., 432
Barrymore, D., 178
Bartlett, F. C., 250
Bavelier, D., 111, 112, 113, 132, 133, 170
Bayley, P. J., 213
Baylis, G. C., 126
Bayliss, D. M., 173
Bechtel, W., 15
Becklen, R., 92
Bedard, J., 422, 423
Begg, I., 196
Behrmann, M., 127, 133, 344, 345
Berntsen, D., 241
Berry, D. C., 193
Berry, H., 51
Besson, M., 173
Bever, T. G., 376
Biederman, I., 69, 71
Bisiach, E., 343
Black, J. B., 352
Black, T., 351
Blakemore, C., 48, 49
Blakeslee, S., 53
Blanchette, I., 420

Bliss, T. V. P., 208
Bloodworth, K., 267
Blume, E. S., 275
Bock, K., 381, 384
Bontempi, B., 210, 211
Bookheimer, S. Y., 369
Boring, E. G., 142
Boruff, B., 158
Bos, M. W., 482
Boutla, M., 170
Bower, G. H., 202, 203, 205, 258, 307
Bowerman, M., 392
Bradfield, A. L., 268, 271, 272
Branigan, H. P., 385, 386
Bransford, J. D., 206, 255, 377
Breedin, S. D., 369
Bregman, A., 85
Breland, K., 13
Breland, M., 13
Bresjanac, M., 173
Brewer, J. G., 47
Brewer, W. F., 254, 255, 257
Bridgeman, B., 96
Broadbent, D. E., 14, 103–106
Broca, P., 393
Brooks, L., 159, 160, 161
Brown, J., 146
Brown, R., 233, 243–244
Bruck, M., 280
Buciarelli, M., 443
Buckner, R. L., 224, 280
Bugelski, B. R., 59, 60, 63
Burton, R., 128
Butler, L. T., 193
Butterworth, B., 149

Cabeza, R., 189, 232, 239
Cahill, L., 214
Caramazza, A., 44, 45, 314
Carlin, D., 473
Carroll, D. W., 364, 393
Carroll, L., 371
Castro, A. M., 233
Catrambone, R., 417
Ceci, S. J., 280, 281
Chabris, C. F., 91, 92
Chalmers, D., 346
Chalupa, L. M., 91
Chan, J. C. K., 254, 256
Chao, L. L., 314
Chapman, J. P., 459

Chapman, L. J., 459
Chase, V. M., 483
Chase, W. G., 149, 421
Chen, K., 482
Cheng, P. W., 448, 449, 454
Cherry, E. C., 14, 102, 113
Chi, M. T. H., 421, 422, 423
Chiu, L-H., 393
Chklovskii, D. B., 208
Chomsky, N., 12, 359
Christensen, B. T., 421
Clark, C., 267
Clark, H. H., 359, 384
Clifton, C., 376
Colby, C. L., 124, 125
Coley, J. D., 297, 316, 317
Collins, A. M., 299, 300, 301, 302, 305, 306
Colman, A. W., 100
Colvin, M. K., 474
Conrad, C., 304
Conrad, R., 150
Conway, A. R. A., 173
Conway, M. A., 240
Cooper, E. E., 71
Cooper, G. G., 48, 49
Coricelli, G., 482
Cosmides, L., 450, 451
Courtney, S. M., 47, 167
Cowan, N., 106, 173
Cox, J. R., 447, 448
Craik, F. I. M., 197, 199, 202, 203
Craver-Lemley, C., 335
Critchley, H. D., 482
Crook, T. H., 349
Crowder, R. G., 232
Csikszentmihalyi, M., 424
Cunitz, A. R., 183, 184
Cutler, B. L., 267

Dapretto, M., 369
Darwin, C., 48, 450
Darwin, C. J., 144
Davachi, L., 19
Davidoff, J., 387
Davidson, J. E., 426, 428
Davidson, P. S. R., 247, 248, 249
Deese, J., 258
DeGroot, A., 150
Dehaene, S., 482
Dell, G. S., 360, 381, 382
De Mestral, G., 425–426

Dennis, S., 128
DeRenzi, E., 188, 342
Desimone, R., 167
Deutsch, D., 96, 109
Deutsch, J. A., 109
Devine, P. G., 273
DeVreese, L. P., 342
DiCiano, P., 232
Dijksterhuis, A., 482
Dodds, R. A., 432
Dolan, R. J., 482
Dolcos, F., 214
Donders, F. C., 5–7, 10, 16
Downing, P. E., 90
Driver, J., 126, 127
DuBreuil, S. C., 266
Dudai, Y., 226
Dunbar, K., 398, 406, 420, 482
Duncker, K., 401, 414
Dunning, D., 467
Duzel, E., 189

Easterbrook, J., 268
Ebbinghaus, H., 8–9, 10
Edwards, A. W. F., 482
Egan, D. E., 423
Egly, R., 125, 126
Eich, E., 220, 221
Einstein, A., 323
Einstein, G. O., 237, 238
Eisenberg, M., 226
Ellis, N., 158
Emmorey, K., 168, 169, 170
Engle, R. W., 173
Epstein, R., 90
Ericsson, K. A., 149, 412
Evans, A. C., 354
Evans, J., 473
Evans, J. St. B. T., 440, 451
Everitt, B. J., 232

Farah, M. J., 43, 44, 53, 313, 314, 335,
  336, 342, 344, 393
Federmeier, K. D., 369
Feeney, A., 440, 451
Feinberg, T. E., 43, 53, 393
Feng, S., 482
Ferraro, V., 391
Feynman, R., 396
Fiez, J. A., 47, 168
Fink, G. R., 133
Fink, S. I., 92
Finke, R. A., 331, 346, 426, 427, 428
Fisher, R. P., 274
Fleischman, D. A., 232
Fodor, J. D., 373

Fogassi, L., 53
Follet, M. P., 419
Foreman, G., 378
Frankland, P. W., 210, 211
Franklin, G., 275
Frase, L. T., 222
Frazier, L., 371, 372
Fredrickson, R., 275
Freedman, D. J., 48, 338
Freedman, M. R., 256
Frensch, P. A., 423
Freud, S., 381
Fried, I., 315, 337
Friedman-Hill, S. R., 68
Fromkin, V. A., 382
Fugelsang, J. A., 482
Funahashi, S., 166, 167
Fusella, V., 335

Gabrieli, J. D. E., 232
Gainotti, G., 44, 314
Gallese, V., 53
Galton, F., 325
Ganis, G., 339
Gardiner, J. M., 187
Garnham, A., 382
Garrett, M. F., 381
Garrod, S., 383
Garry, M., 266, 280
Gaskins, S., 388
Gauna, K., 391
Gauthier, I., 48, 49, 50
Gazzaley, A., 162, 163
Gazzaniga, M. S., 136, 342
Geiselman, R. E., 274
Gell-Mann, M., 396
Gentner, D., 388, 419, 420
Gerken, L. A., 363
Gertner, L., 267
Gick, M. L., 414, 416, 417
Gigerenzer, G., 451, 456, 462, 483
Gilboa, A., 212, 232
Gilhooly, K. J., 439
Glanzer, M., 183, 184
Glass, A. L., 307
Gleason, J. B., 359, 391, 393
Gleick, J., 396
Glisky, E. L., 249
Gobet, F., 149, 150
Godden, D. R., 218, 219
Goldenberg, G., 339
Goldman, S. R., 378, 379
Goldman-Rakic, P. S., 166
Goldstein, A. G., 267
Goldstein, D., 469
Goldstein, E. B., 92

Goldwin-Meadow, S., 358, 388
Golgi, C., 30
Gollin, E. S., 194
Gomez, R. L., 363
Gordon, B., 44, 314
Graesser, A. C., 378, 379
Graf, P., 204
Granhag, P. A., 280
Grant, H., 218, 219
Gray, J. A., 106, 107
Green, A. E., 354
Green, G. S., 111, 112, 113, 133
Greenberg, D. L., 239
Grelotti, D. J., 128
Griggs, R. A., 447, 448, 451
Gross, C. G., 41, 42
Gruenwald, C., 173
Guariglia, C., 344
Guilford, J. P., 424

Haber, R. N., 145
Hagen, L., 266
Haigney, D., 119
Haist, F., 212
Halligan, P. W., 133
Halpern, A. R., 354
Hamann, S. B., 47, 214
Hamilton, D. L., 459
Hars, B., 225
Harsch, N., 244, 245
Hart, J., 44, 314
Haun, D. B. M., 392
Hauser, M. D., 473
Haviland, S. E., 384
Hayhoe, M., 122
Hays, J. R., 413
Hebb, D. O., 208
Hedden, T., 232
Hegarty, M., 350, 352, 354
Helmholtz, H. von, 7–8, 10
Hembrooke, H., 280
Henderson, A., 268
Henderson, J. M., 93, 120, 121, 133
Hennelly, R. A., 158
Hertwig, R., 483
Hills, A. E., 44, 314
Hinton, G. E., 313
Hitch, G. J., 154, 155
Hitchcock, A., 178
Hochberg, J. E., 78
Hoffman, E. J., 45
Hoffman, H. G., 280
Hoffrage, U., 462
Hollingworth, A., 93
Holtgraves, T., 391

Holyoak, K. J., 307, 414, 416, 417, 418, 448, 449, 454
Horton, W. S., 379, 380
Howell, P., 362
Hubel, D. H., 38, 39, 62, 97
Huber, R., 211
Hug, K., 451
Humphreys, G. W., 44, 313, 314
Hyman, I. E., Jr., 264

Intons-Peterson, M. J., 324, 332
Iwao, M., 388
Izard, V., 482

Jacoby, L. L., 252, 253
James, W., 30, 100
Jansson, D. G., 401, 425
Jarrold, C., 173
Jenkins, J. J., 205
Ji, L., 393
Ji, Y., 482
Joffily, M., 482
Johnson, E. J., 469
Johnson, K. E., 252, 298
Johnson, M. K., 206, 252, 255, 377
Johnson, T. C., 268, 269
Johnson-Laird, P. N., 307, 440, 441, 443, 448, 451
Johnston, W. A., 119
Jones, W., 128, 129
Junkin, T., 267

Kahneman, D., 109, 456, 459, 460, 461, 467, 468, 470, 471
Kako, E., 371
Kamide, Y., 376
Kanaya, T., 281
Kandel, E. R., 208
Kane, M. J., 173
Kanwisher, N., 90, 91
Kaplan, C. A., 409, 411, 412
Kapur, N., 232
Katerelos, M., 391
Keele, S. W., 151
Kekule, F. A., 323
Kelly, W. M., 354
Kennedy, J. F., 243, 244
Keppel, G., 147
Keri, S., 294
Keysers, C., 53
Kida, S., 208
King, M. L., Jr., 244
Kita, S., 392
Kleffner, D. A., 86
Kliegel, M., 238
Klin, A., 128, 129

Kneller, W., 268
Koch, C., 315, 337
Koffka, K., 398
Koh, K., 417, 418
Kohler, E., 53
Kohler, W., 96, 398
Kolb, B., 36
Konorski, J., 41
Kosslyn, S. M., 327, 328, 329, 330, 332, 333, 336, 340, 341, 346, 354
Kotovsky, K., 409
Kraemer, D. J. M., 354
Kreiman, G., 314, 315, 337
Kroger, J. K., 475
Kroll, J. F., 391
Kroll, N., 151
Kubovy, M., 85
Kuhn, T., 423
Kulik, J., 243–244
Kurtz, K. J., 435
Kutas, M., 369

LaBar, K. S., 214
Lakoff, G., 404
Lamble, D., 119
Land, C., 225, 226
Land, M. F., 122
Larkin, J. H., 421
Lavie, N., 110, 113, 127, 132
Lea, G., 328
LeBihan, D., 338
Lee, D., 475
Lee, J. L. C., 232
Leigh, E., 173
Leighton, J. P., 435
Lesgold, A. M., 423
Lettvin, J., 41
Levelt, W. J. M., 358, 381
Levin, D. T., 93, 94
Levine, B., 189
Levinson, S. C., 388, 392
Levy, B. G., 391
Lewin, R., 391
Lewis, D. J., 225
Lichtenstein, S., 456, 457, 458
Lindsay, D. S., 263, 265, 266, 275, 450
Lindsay, R. C. L., 273, 274
Lipsker, E., 275
Liu, Y., 482
Locantore, J. K., 232
Lockhart, R. S., 197
Loftus, E. F., 251, 261, 262, 267, 275, 280, 305, 306, 450
Lopez, A., 317, 465
Lorayne, H., 349
Lord, C. G., 463

Lovatt, P., 158
Lovett, M. C., 396
Low, A., 314
Lubart, T. I., 424
Lucas, J., 349
Luchins, A. S., 403, 404
Luck, S. J., 127
Lucy, J. A., 388
Luria, A. R., 259
Luzzatti, G., 343

MacDonald, M. C., 373
Mack, A., 123
MacKay, D. G., 109
Macknick, S. L., 97
Macrae, C. N., 354
Magnie, M., 173
Maguire, E. A., 49, 232
Maher, B. A., 225
Maier, N. R. F., 402
Majid, M., 392
Malpass, R. S., 273
Malt, B. C., 294
Manktelow, K. I., 451, 466
Mantyla, T., 216, 217, 248
Marios, R., 173
Markman, A. B., 284
Markowitsch, H. J., 189
Marlsen-Wilson, W., 365
Marshall, J. C., 133
Martin, A., 314
Martinez-Conde, S., 97
Mast, F. W., 346
McCarthy, R., 44, 314
McCartney, P., 323
McClelland, J. L., 62, 307, 308, 312, 313
McCloskey, M., 280
McDaniel, M. A., 237, 238
McDermott, K. B., 254, 256, 259
McIntosh, A. R., 232
McKelvie, S. L., 458
McNaughton, B. L., 429
McNeil, D., 233
Mechelli, A., 392
Mecklinger, A., 173
Medin, D. L., 316, 317, 466
Meltzer, J., 326
Mervis, C. B., 289, 290, 291, 296, 297, 298
Merzenich, M. M., 48
Metcalfe, J., 220, 399, 400
Metzler, J., 17, 18, 151
Meyer, D. E., 303, 304
Meyer, E., 354
Miller, E. K., 483
Miller, G. A., 15, 21, 148

Milner, B., 185
Mimica, M. R. M., 120
Minda, J. P., 295
Misiak, H., 15
Mitchell, K. J., 252
Moore, C. M., 125, 126
Moray, N., 103, 106
Morey, C. C., 173
Morimoto, C. H., 120
Morris, C. D., 200, 201
Morris, R. G., 474
Morrow, D. G., 379
Moscovitch, M., 190, 210, 211, 213, 280
Mouchiroud, C., 424
Munakata, Y., 473
Murdoch, B. B., Jr., 181, 182
Murphy, G., 320
Murphy, G. L., 284
Murray, D. J., 158

Nadel, L., 210, 211, 213, 225
Nader, K., 225, 226, 227, 228, 232
Neath, I., 184, 232
Neisser, U., 15, 24–25, 92, 223, 239, 244, 245, 249
Neville, H. J., 369
Newell, A., 15, 404, 405–408
Nicklaus, J., 324
Nigro, G., 239
Nisbett, R. E., 393, 482
Nordgren, L. F., 482
Norman, D. A., 109
Nyberg, L., 189

O'Doherty, J. P., 482
Olesen, P. J., 168
Olson, A. C., 313
Osherson, D. N., 330, 464
Osterhout, L., 369
Over, D. E., 451
Owen, A. M., 473

Paidousis, A., 4, 216
Paivio, A., 325, 326
Palmer, J. C., 261
Palmer, S. E., 60
Park, H., 281
Parkhurst, D., 121
Parpal, M., 467
Pavlides, C., 429
Pavlov, I., 11, 225
Pearce, G., 178
Pearl, M., 252
Pearlstone, Z., 216, 217
Peck, G., 178
Peigneux, P., 211

Penfield, W., 473
Peng, K., 393
Penningroth, S. L., 238
Perani, D., 173, 391
Perfect, T. J., 196
Perky, C. W., 334
Perret, D. I., 39
Perry, D. W., 354
Peters, J., 119
Peterson, L. R., 146, 147
Peterson, M. J., 146, 147
Peterson, S. E., 280
Peterson, S. W., 222
Petitto, L. A., 391
Phelps, E. A., 214
Pica, P., 482
Pickering, M. J., 383
Pickett, J. M., 363
Pillemer, D. B., 240
Pinker, S., 331
Pollack, I., 363
Pomerantz, J. R., 85
Posner, M. I., 123, 124, 151
Pretz, J. E., 397
Price, C. J., 392
Principe, G. F., 281
Prinz, W., 96
Proffitt, J. B., 317
Proksch, J., 132
Pylyshyn, Z. W., 328, 329, 331, 340, 346

Quillian, M. R., 299, 300, 301, 302
Quiroga, R. Q., 50, 51

Ramachandran, V. S., 53, 86, 96
Raphael, B., 406
Rapp, D. N., 379, 380
Ratner, N. B., 359, 391, 393
Rayner, K., 364, 365, 372, 376, 392
Rayner, R., 11
Read, J. D., 266
Read, L., 119
Reber, A. S., 100, 466
Redelmeier, D. A., 119
Reder, L. M., 223, 281
Reeves, A., 335
Regier, T., 388
Reicher, G. M., 64
Reiman, E. M., 482
Reisberg, D., 346
Reiser, B. J., 329
Reitman, J., 423
Rensink, R. A., 92, 93, 94
Repovs, G., 164, 173
Richardson, A., 325
Rips, L. J., 304, 443

Rizzolatti, G., 53
Roberson, D., 387, 388
Robertson, L. C., 68
Rock, I., 96, 123
Roediger, H. L., 191, 259
Rogers, T. B., 203
Rogers, T. T., 308, 312, 313
Rosch, E. H., 288, 289, 290, 292, 293, 295–297
Rose, D., 41
Rosenbaum, R. S., 188
Ross, D. F., 269, 270
Rothkopf, E. Z., 223
Rowe, J. B., 473
Rubin, D. C., 238, 239, 240, 241, 242, 246, 247, 248
Rumelhart, D. E., 62, 307
Russell, W. A., 205
Ryan, L., 212, 213

Sachs, J., 186, 193
Sacks, O. W., 53, 177
Saffran, J. R., 88, 89, 363, 369
Samuel, A. G., 362
Sandler, A., 178
Sanfey, A. G., 475, 476
Sapir, E., 387
Sara, J. J., 225, 226
Saunders, L., 82
Savage-Rumbaugh, S., 391
Savin, H. B., 364
Schacter, D. L., 191, 238, 250n, 269, 279, 280, 349
Schenkein, J., 385
Schkade, D. A., 468
Schmidt, H., 67
Schmolck, H., 246
Schneider, W., 115, 116, 117, 118
Schooler, L. J., 260
Schrauf, R. W., 241, 242
Schultz, R., 128, 129
Schunn, C. D., 421
Schvaneveldt, R. W., 303, 304
Schwartz, B. I., 233
Schwartz, B. J., 423
Schwartz, D. L., 351, 352
Schweickert, R., 158
Scoville, W. B., 185
Scribner, S., 482
Segal, G., 128
Segal, S. J., 335
Seidenberg, M. S., 313
Sexton, V., 15
Shafir, E., 471, 472
Shakespeare, W., 378
Shallice, T., 44, 185, 313, 314

Shaw, J. S., 271, 273
Shelton, J. R., 44, 314
Shen, J., 482
Shepard, R. N., 17, 18, 151, 326
Shereshevskii, 259
Sheridan, J., 44, 314
Shiffrin, R. M., 20, 115, 116, 117, 118, 138, 139
Shin, S.-J., 482
Shomstein, S., 127
Silveri, M. C., 44, 314
Simon, H. A., 15, 149, 151, 404, 405–408, 409, 411, 412, 421
Simonides, 348
Simons, D. J., 91, 92, 93
Simonton, D. K., 423
Simpson, C., 297
Simpson, O. J., 246
Sims, V. K., 354
Singer, M., 378
Singh, M., 281
Sinha, P., 56, 83
Sirigu, A., 482
Skinner, B. F., 12, 13, 358
Slameka, N. J., 204
Slotnick, S. D., 279, 340
Smith, E. E., 291
Smith, J. D., 295
Smith, S. M., 223, 224, 401, 425, 432
Smith, S. S., 233
Snow, C. E., 391
Solomon, K. O., 284, 285
Spalding, T. L., 284
Spelke, E., 114–115, 482
Spence, C., 119
Sperling, G., 142–145
Spinnler, H., 342
Sporer, S. L., 267
Squire, L. R., 189, 210
Stanny, C. J., 268, 269
Starr, M. S., 392
Steedman, M. J., 373
Sternberg, R. J., 423, 426, 428
Stevens, K., 378
Strack, F., 468
Strayer, D. L., 119
Strickgold, R., 211
Stroop, J. R., 117
Super, H., 167
Surprenant, A. M., 184, 232
Swinney, D. A., 365, 366

Talarico, J. M., 246, 247, 248
Tanaka, J. W., 298

Tanaka, K., 39
Tanenhaus, M. K., 373, 374, 375
Tang, C., 317
Tang, Y., 482
Tarkan, L., 415
Tavakkoli, M., 222
Taylor, M., 298
Ter-Pogossian, M. M., 45
Terr, L. C., 275
Tétreault, K., 391
Thagard, P., 417
Thomas, K. L., 232
Thompson, D., 268
Thompson, W. L., 336
Tibshirani, R. J., 119
Tipper, S. P., 127, 133
Todd, J. J., 173
Todd, P. M., 456, 462
Tokowicz, N., 391
Tooby, J., 450, 451
Tooley, V., 268
Travis, D. M., 233
Treadeau, K., 349
Treisman, A. M., 66, 67, 96, 106, 107, 108–109
Treyens, J. C., 257
Tulving, E., 3, 187, 188, 189, 191, 192, 193, 194, 199, 202, 203, 216, 217
Turner, M., 404
Tversky, A., 456, 459, 460, 461, 467, 470, 471, 472

Umita, M. A., 53
Underwood, B. J., 147

Valentine, E. R., 232, 259
Vallar, G., 133, 163
Van Baaren, R. B., 482
Van den Broek, P., 378, 379
Van der Wege, M. M., 359
Vecera, S. P., 127
Violanti, J. M., 119
Volkmar, F., 128, 129
Von Cramon, D. Y., 173
Voss, J. F., 423

Wade, K. A., 266
Wagenaar, W. A., 218
Wagner, A. D., 47
Wagner, L., 371
Wagner, U., 429
Waldrop, M. M., 363
Walker, M. P., 211
Wallace, M. A., 44, 314

Wallis, J. D., 473, 483
Waltz, J. A., 474
Ward, T. B., 424, 425, 432
Warren, R. M., 361
Warrington, E. K., 44, 185, 193, 194, 195, 314
Wason, P. C., 445, 446, 462
Watson, J. B., 11–12, 325
Wearing, C., 137, 178, 184, 185, 196
Wearing, D., 137
Webb, D., 267
Wedderburn, A. I., 106, 107
Weisberg, R. W., 399
Weiskrantz, L., 193, 194, 195
Wells, G. L., 267, 268, 271, 272, 273, 274
Werner, J. S., 91
Wernicke, C., 393
Westerman, S. J., 119
Westmacott, R., 190
Wheeler, M. E., 187, 224, 280
Whorf, B. J., 387
Wickelgren, W. A., 151
Wickens, D. D., 152, 153
Wiebe, D., 399, 400
Wiemer-Hastings, K., 379
Wiesel, T. N., 38, 39, 62
Wilding, J. M., 232, 259
Wilson, B., 163
Wilson, M., 168, 169, 170, 483
Wilson, M. A., 429
Wilson, T. D., 467
Wiltgen, B. J., 212
Winston, J., 429
Winzenz, D., 202, 203
Wiseman, S., 223
Wishaw, I. Q., 36
Wittgenstein, L., 288
Wollen, K. A., 347
Wood, N., 106
Wundt, W., 9–10, 325, 358

Yamauchi, T., 284
Yarbus, A., 120

Zalla, T., 474
Zaragoza, M., 280
Zatorre, R. J., 354
Zevin, J. D., 313
Zhang, G., 151
Zhang, W., 482
Zikmund-Fisher, B. J., 477
Zola-Morgan, S., 189
Zwaan, R. A., 379

Subject Index

Acrobat problem, 408–409
Action potentials, 32–34
Advertisements, 196
Affirming the antecedent, 444
Affirming the consequent, 444
Aging and cognition, 232
Algebra problems, 400
Algorithms, 79
Alzheimer's disease, 232
Ambiguity
  lexical, 365
  perceptual stimulus and, 81
  syntactic, 370
American Sign Language (ASL),
    168–170
Amnesia
  anterograde, 209, 210
  retrograde, 209–210
Amygdala, 43
  emotions and, 214
  long-term memory and, 214
Analogical encoding, 419–420
Analogical paradox, 420
Analogical problem solving, 414
  analogical encoding and, 419–420
  creative thinking and, 425–426
  in-vivo research on, 420–421
  radiation problem and, 414–419
Analogical transfer, 414
Analogies, 413–421
Analytic introspection, 10
Anaphoric inference, 377–378
Animal language, 357, 391
Anisomycin, 225–227
Antecedents, 443–445
Anterograde amnesia, 210
Apparent motion, 98, 174
Articulatory suppression, 158–159
Association techniques, 223
Atmosphere effect, 439
Attention, 99–134
  attenuation theory of, 106–109
  autism and, 127–129
  automatic processing and, 116–117
  CogLab experiments on, 134
  controlled processing and, 118
  divided, 114–119
  early experiments on, 14
  eyewitness testimony and, 268
  filter model of, 103–106
  late-selection models of, 109–110
  location-based, 125, 127

object-based, 125–127
perception and, 91–94
physiology of, 124–125
resources related to, 132–133
review questions on, 113–114, 130,
    131–132
selective, 101–113
social situations and, 127–129
summary points about, 130–131
task load and, 110–113
visual processing and, 120–127
Attentional blink, 134
Attenuation theory of attention, 106–109
Attenuator, 106, 108
Auditory coding, 150–151, 185
Auditory imagery, 323, 354
Autism, 127–129
Autobiographical memory, 238–249
  definition of, 238
  emotional stimuli and, 248–249
  flashbulb memories and, 242–249
  life events and, 240–242
  multidimensional nature of, 239–240
  review questions on, 253–254, 279
  summary points about, 277
Automatic processing, 116–117
Availability heuristic, 456–459
Axons, 30

Back propagation, 311
Balint's syndrome, 68
Base rate, 460
Basic level of categories, 296
Behavioral approach to cognition, 16–19
Behaviorism, 11
  decline of, 12–13
  rise of, 11–12
Behavior of Organisms, The (Skinner), 13
Belief bias, 439–440
Berinmo culture, 387–388
Bias
  belief, 439–440
  confirmation, 462–463
  memory and, 280
  omission, 477
  reasoning and, 439–440, 462–463
Bilingualism, 391
Blindness
  change, 92–94
  inattentional, 123
Blind spot, 98
Blurred objects, 83

Bottom-up processing, 58–59, 66, 345
Brain
  categorization in, 314–315
  CogLab experiments on, 54
  cognitive processes and, 42–47
  decision making and, 475–476
  experience-dependent plasticity of,
    48–50
  localization of function in, 43–45
  measuring activity in, 45–47
  memory storage in, 207–214
  neurons and neural circuits in, 30–42
  physical layout of areas in, 43
  problem solving and, 473–474
  reasoning and, 474–475
  resources related to, 53
  review questions on, 40, 51, 52–53
  summary points about, 52
  thinking processes and, 472–476
  visual imagery and, 337–347
  working memory and, 164–168, 173
  See also Neurons; Physiology
Brain asymmetry, 54
Brain damage
  behavior affected by, 53
  imagery problems and, 342–344
  language problems and, 393
  memory impairment and, 137,
    177–179, 184–185, 188–189
Brain imaging, 19, 45–46
  categorization and, 314
  cognitive processes and, 45–47
  imagery and, 338–340
  memory and, 19, 47, 167–168, 189
  techniques used for, 45–46
  working memory and, 167–168

Candle problem, 401–402, 433
Car accidents, 118–119
Categorical perception, 387–388, 394
Categorical syllogisms, 437–443
  mental models and, 440–443
  validity of, 437–440
Categories, 284–288
Categorization, 284–318
  CogLab experiments on, 321
  connectionist approach to, 307–313
  culture and, 315–317, 392–393, 463,
    465
  definitional approach to, 286–288
  effect of culture on, 315–317
  exemplar approach to, 293–295

hierarchical organization and, 295
inductive reasoning and, 463–466
knowledge and, 297–298
language and, 392–393
levels related to, 295–298
physiology of, 314–315
prototype approach to, 288–293,
294–295
review questions on, 298–299,
318, 320
semantic networks and, 299–307
summary points about, 318–320
usefulness of, 284–286
Category-specific neurons, 314–315
Causal inference, 378–379
Cell body, 30
Cell phone experiment, 118–119
Central executive, 156, 162–163
Cerebral cortex, 43
Chain problem, 399–400, 433
Change blindness, 92–94
Change blindness blindness, 94
Change detection, 97, 134
Children
sexual abuse of, 275–276
suggestibility of, 280
Choice reaction time, 6, 7
Chunk, 149
Chunking, 149–150, 223
Circle problem, 398, 433
Classical conditioning, 11–12
Cocktail party phenomenon, 103
Coding, 150–153
auditory, 150–151
distributed, 42
long-term memory, 185–186
semantic, 150, 152–153, 185–186
short-term memory, 150–153
specificity, 41
visual, 150, 151–152
See also Encoding
CogLab experiments
on attention, 134
on brain physiology, 54
on categorization, 321
on decision making, 484
on imagery, 25, 355
on language, 394
on memory, 174–175, 233–234, 281
on perception, 97–98
on reasoning, 484
Cognition, 2
age-related changes in, 232
behavioral approach to, 16–19
complexity of, 3–4
creative, 426–428

evolutionary perspective on, 450–451
examples of, 2, 3–4
interdisciplinary study of, 21–22
physiological approach to, 16–17, 19
Cognitive anthropology, 22
Cognitive economy, 301
Cognitive hypothesis, 241
Cognitive interviews, 274
Cognitive neuroscience, 173
Cognitive psychology, 2
computer use and, 13–14
decline and rebirth of, 10–15
first modern textbook on, 24–25
historical origins of, 5–10
models used in, 19–21
Cognitive Psychology (Neisser), 24–25
Cognitive revolution, 13–15, 325–327
Cognitive science, 21–22
Coherence, 377–379
Color perception, 387–388
Common fate, law of, 77
Comparing objects, 17, 18
Complex cells, 39
Comprehension of language, 359
Computers
cognitive psychology and, 13–14
connectionist networks and, 313
"logic theorist" program for, 15
perception and, 56, 80–84, 91
Computer science, 22
Concepts, 284
connectionism and, 307–313
information resource on, 320
semantic networks and, 299–307
Conceptual-peg hypothesis, 326
Conclusions, 437
Conditional syllogisms, 443–452
four major types of, 443–445
Wason four-card problem and,
445–452
Conditioning, 225
classical, 11–12
fear, 225–227
operant, 12
Confabulation, 280
Confirmation bias, 462–463
Conjunction rule, 461
Connectionism, 307
Connectionist networks, 66, 307–313
characteristics of, 308–309
computer models of, 313
graceful degradation in, 313
supervised learning in, 309–313
Consequents, 443–445
Consistent mapping condition, 115
Consolidation, 210–213

Consonant-vowel rule, 382
Constructive nature of memory, 249–260
advantages/disadvantages of, 259–260
false memories and, 258–259
high school grades study, 251–252
inferences and, 254–256
review questions on, 254
schemas and scripts related to,
256–258
source monitoring errors and, 252–253
summary points about, 277–278
"War of the Ghosts" experiment,
250–251
Context
perception and, 60–61
word comprehension and, 365
Contingency strategy, 419–420
Controlled processing, 118
Control processes of modal model,
139–141
Convergence, 36–37
Convergent thinking, 424
Conversational speech, 383–387
perception of words in, 87–90
semantic coordination in, 383–384
syntactic coordination in, 384–387
Creative cognition, 426–428
Creative problem solving, 423–428, 432
Crime scene memories, 268–272
Cued recall, 216, 217
Cues, retrieval, 141, 197, 215–218
Cultural life script, 241
Cultural life script hypothesis, 241–242
Culture
categorization and, 315–317, 392–393,
463, 465
color perception and, 387–388
inductive reasoning and, 463, 465,
482
language and, 358, 387–388, 392

"Dear Aunt Jane" experiment, 106, 107
Decision making, 24, 466–472
CogLab experiment on, 484
emotions and, 475–476, 482
focusing illusion and, 467–468
framing of choices and, 469–471,
476–478
justification in, 471–472
mental simulations and, 467
neuroeconomics and, 475–476
omission bias and, 477
physiology of, 475–476
reasoning and, 437, 466
resources related to, 482
review questions on, 478, 481

Decision making (*continued*)
summary points about, 480–481
utility approach to, 466–469
Decisions, 437
Declarative memory, 186, 187–191
Deductive reasoning, 436, 437–452
categorical syllogisms and, 437–443
conditional syllogisms and, 443–452
mental models of, 440–443
review questions on, 452
Deep processing, 199
Deep structure, 423
Definitional approach to categorization, 286–288
Delayed partial report method, 144
Delayed-response task, 165–166
Delayed test, 253
Dendrites, 30
Denying the antecedent, 444
Denying the consequent, 444
Depictive representations, 330
Depth of processing, 198–200
Design fixation, 425
Dichotic listening, 102–103
Dictionary unit, 108
Digit span, 148, 169
Discriminability, 70
Dissociations, 43
of imagery and perception, 343–344
of memory functions, 184–185, 188–189
Distributed coding, 42
Distributed vs. massed practice effect, 223–224
Divergent thinking, 424
Diversity principle, 464
Divided attention, 114–119
practice and, 114–117
task difficulty and, 117–118
traffic accidents and, 118–119
Diving experiment, 218, 219
Double dissociation, 43, 44
Driver inattention, 118–119

Early-selection models, 104, 109
Echoic memory, 144
Economic utility theory, 466, 475
Elaboration, 221–222
Elaborative rehearsal, 197, 221
Electroconvulsive therapy (ECT), 210
Embodied cognition, 483
Emotions
decision making and, 475–476, 482
eyewitness testimony and, 268
flashbulb memories and, 248–249
long-term memory and, 213–214

state-dependent learning and, 220–221
Encoding, 196–207
connections and, 202–204
factors that aid, 202–207
generation effect and, 204
information retrieval and, 224
levels-of-processing theory and, 197–200
organization and, 204–207
rehearsal and, 197
self-reference effect and, 203–204
transfer-appropriate processing and, 200–202
See also Coding
Encoding specificity, 218–220, 234
End-stopped cells, 39
Entrepreneurship, 432
Epiphenomenon, 329
Episodic buffer, 163–164
Episodic memory, 187–191, 239
Error signal, 311
Event-based tasks, 237–238
Event-related potential (ERP), 368–369
Evolutionary perspective on cognition, 450–451
Excitation, 35
Excitatory neurotransmitters, 35
Exemplar approach to categorization, 293–295
Exemplars, 294
Experience-dependent plasticity, 48–50
Experiments
cognitive revolution and, 14
generated by good theories, 306
See also CogLab experiments
Expertise in problem solving, 421–423
Experts, 421
Explanatory power, 306
Extrastriate body area (EBA), 90, 91
Eye movements
measurement of, 120
sentence information and, 373–376
visual attention and, 120–122, 133
word-frequency effect and, 364–365
Eye tracker, 120, 121
Eyewitness Evidence: A Guide for Law Enforcement (U.S. Justice Department), 275
Eyewitness testimony, 266–275
correcting problems with, 272–275
errors associated with, 268–272, 273
misidentifying people in, 267–268
review questions on, 276, 279
summary points about, 278–279

Face perception, 41–42
False memories, 258–259, 264–266, 275, 278
Falsifiability, 306
Falsification principle, 446
Familiarity
eyewitness testimony and, 268–270
law of, 78
Family resemblance, 288, 289–291
Fear conditioning, 225–227
Feature detectors, 39
Feature integration theory (FIT), 66–69, 72
Feature level, 62
Feature units, 62
Feedback activation, 65
Field perspective, 238–239
50 First Dates (film), 178
Film images
persistence of vision and, 142
See also Movie themes
Filter model of attention, 103–106
Five-gear problem, 350
Fixations
eye movement and, 120
problem solving and, 401–403, 424–425, 428
Flanker-compatibility task, 111–113
Flashbulb memories, 242–249
emotional events and, 248–249
narrative rehearsal and, 249
repeated recall and, 244
review questions on, 254, 279
summary points about, 277
Flow diagrams, 14
Focused attention stage, 68
Focusing illusion, 467–468
Forgetting curve, 9
Fortress story, 415–417
Framing effect, 471
Free recall, 216, 217
Freudian slips, 381
Frontal lobe, 43
Functional fixedness, 401–403
Functional magnetic resonance imaging (fMRI), 45–46. *See also* Brain imaging
Fusiform face area (FFA), 43

Garden-path model, 372
Garden-path sentences, 372, 373
Generation effect, 204, 222
Geons, 69
Gestalt approach
perception and, 74–80
problem solving and, 397–404

Gestalt laws of perceptual organization, 74–80
Gestalt psychologists, 72, 74, 96
Given–new contract, 384
Goal state, 405
Golgi stain, 30, 31
Good continuation, law of, 76, 78, 79
Good figure, law of, 74
Graceful degradation, 313
Graded amnesia, 210
Grandmother cell, 41–42, 50–51
Greeble experiment, 48–49, 50, 90

Heuristics
    availability, 456–459
    inductive reasoning and, 455–462
    language and, 373
    perception and, 79, 84–87
    representativeness, 459–462
Hidden objects, 82–83
Hidden units, 308
Hierarchical organization, 295
High-load task, 110
High prototypicality, 289
Hippocampus, 43, 211–212, 213, 429

Iconic memory, 144
Ill-defined problems, 396–397
Illusory conjunctions, 67–68
Illusory correlations, 458–459
Imageless-thought debate, 325
Imagery, 322–355
    brain damage and, 342–344
    brain imaging experiments on, 338–340
    CogLab experiment on, 355
    dissociations of perception and, 343–344
    history of psychological study of, 325–327
    interactions of perception and, 334–336
    memory improvement using, 347–349
    mental scanning and, 327–328, 329
    method of loci and, 348–349
    neurons related to, 337–338
    neuropsychological case studies on, 341–346
    object interactions in, 347–348
    organizational function of, 348–349
    pegword technique using, 349
    perception and, 327–337, 342–347
    physiology of, 337–347
    resources related to, 354
    review questions on, 336–337, 352, 353–354

scientific debate about, 328–332, 336, 346–347
    sizing in the visual field, 332–334, 342
    solving mechanical problems with, 350–352, 354
    summary points about, 352–353
    TMS experiments on, 340–341
    uses of, 323–324
Imagery debate, 328–332, 336, 346–347
Imagery neurons, 337–338
Immediate test, 252–253
Implicit learning, 233
Implicit memory, 186, 187, 191–196
    advertisements and, 196
    procedural memory as, 191, 195–196
    repetition priming as, 191, 192–195
Inattentional blindness, 123
Incubation, 432
Indirect statements, 391
Inductive reasoning, 436, 452–466
    availability heuristic and, 456–459
    categorization and, 463–466
    confirmation bias and, 462–463
    cultural influences on, 463, 465, 482
    everyday life use of, 455–456
    general explanation of, 452–453
    heuristics used in, 455–462
    representativeness heuristic and, 459–462
    review questions on, 478
    scientific discoveries and, 454–455
    strength of arguments in, 453–454
Inference
    anaphoric, 377–378
    causal, 378–379
    coherence and, 377–379
    instrumental, 378
    memory and, 254–256
    pragmatic, 255
Inferior temporal (IT) lobe, 314
Information-processing approach, 13, 404
Information resources
    on attention, 132–133
    on the brain, 53
    on concepts, 320
    on decision making, 482
    on imagery, 354
    on language, 391–393
    on memory, 173, 231–233, 279–281, 354
    on perception, 96–97
    on problem solving, 432
    on reasoning, 481–483
Inhibition, 35, 37
Inhibitory neurotransmitters, 35

Initial state, 405
Input units, 308
Insight
    inspired by sleep, 428–429
    problem solving and, 398–400
Instrumental inference, 378
Intelligence, working memory and, 173
Interacting images, 347–348
Interactionist approach to parsing, 373–376
Interactive activation model, 62–66
Interference
    proactive, 147–148, 152–153
    retroactive, 263, 264
Intermediate-selection models, 109
Intermediate state, 406
Interviews, cognitive, 274
Inverse projection problem, 81
In-vivo problem-solving research, 420–421
Irrelevant speech effect, 174
Itza culture
    categorization in, 316–317, 463, 465
    inductive reasoning in, 465

Knowing, 188
Knowledge, 283–321
    categorization and, 284–318
    concepts and, 284, 320
    effect of culture on, 315–317
    perception and, 57–61, 84–91
Korsakoff's syndrome, 177–178

Laboratory memories, 239–240
Language, 356–394
    brain damage and, 393
    categorization and, 392–393
    CogLab experiments on, 394
    color perception and, 387–388
    conversational speech and, 383–387
    creativity of, 357
    culture and, 358, 387–388, 392
    definition of, 357
    physiology of, 368–369
    psychological study of, 358–360
    reasoning and, 435, 436
    resources related to, 391–393
    review questions on, 376–377, 388–389, 390–391
    sentences in, 368–376
    speech errors in, 381–383
    summary points about, 389–390
    text processing in, 377–381
    universality of, 358
    words in, 360–368
    working memory and, 173

Language acquisition, 359, 393
Large numbers, law of, 462
Late closure, principle of, 371–372, 373
Late-selection models, 109–110
Law of large numbers, 462
Laws of perceptual organization, 74–80
    common fate, 77
    familiarity, 78
    good continuation, 76
    Pragnanz, 74–75
    proximity or nearness, 77
    similarity, 75
Learning
    implicit, 233
    paired-associate, 326
    state-dependent, 220–221
    statistical, 88–90, 363
    study techniques and, 221–224
    supervised, 309
    testing conditions and, 224
Letter level, 62
Letter recognition, 63
Letter units, 62
Levels of processing (LOP), 197, 233
Levels-of-processing theory, 197–200
Lexical ambiguity, 365, 367
Lexical decision task, 303–304, 321,
    364, 394
Lexical priming, 365–367
Lexicon, 360
Life-narrative hypothesis, 241
Lightbulb problem, 417–419
Light-from-above heuristic, 86–87
Linguistics, 22
Listening, dichotic, 102
"Little Albert" experiment, 11–12
Localization of function, 43–45
Location-based attention, 125, 127
Logical progression, 438
Logical thinking, 438–439
"Logic theorist" computer program, 15,
    20, 404
Long-term memory (LTM), 20, 139,
    176–234
    amnesia and, 209–210
    coding in, 185–186
    CogLab experiments on, 233–234
    consolidation of, 210–213
    declarative, 186, 187–191
    emotional stimuli and, 213–214,
        248–249
    encoding process for, 196–207
    general explanation of, 179–181
    impairments of, 177–179, 184–185,
        188–189, 208–210
    implicit, 186, 187, 191–196

information storage in, 196–214
physiology of, 207–214
reasoning and, 435, 436
reconsolidation of, 226–228
resources related to, 231–233
retrieving information from, 197,
    215–221
review questions on, 207, 228, 231
short-term memory vs., 181–186
study methods and, 221–224
summary points about, 229–231
types of, 186–196
Long-term potentiation (LTP), 208
Low-load task, 110
Low prototypicality, 289

Maintenance rehearsal, 197, 221
Mapping, 417
Meaning
    perceptual organization and, 78
    selective attention and, 109–110
    semantics and, 373–376
    speech segmentation and, 82, 363
Means-end analysis, 407
Mechanical reasoning, 350–352, 354
Medial temporal lobe (MTL), 212, 213
Memento (film), 178
Memory
    amnesia and, 209–210
    autobiographical, 238–249
    brain imaging and, 19, 47, 167–168,
        189
    childhood sexual abuse and, 275–276
    CogLab experiments on, 174–175,
        233–234, 281
    consolidation of, 210–213
    constructive approach to, 249–260
    declarative, 186, 187–191
    definition of, 136
    Ebbinghaus's experiments on, 8–9
    emotional stimuli and, 213–214
    episodic, 187–191
    eyewitness testimony and, 266–275
    false, 258–259, 264–266, 275
    flashbulb, 242–249
    iconic and echoic, 144
    impairments of, 137, 177–179,
        184–185, 188–189, 208–210
    implicit, 186, 187, 191–196
    improving using imagery, 347–349
    inferences and, 254–256
    long-term, 20, 139, 176–234
    modal model of, 20, 138–141
    physiology of, 19, 164–168, 173,
        184–185, 207–214
    procedural, 191, 195–196

prospective, 237–238
purposes of, 136–137
reconsolidation of, 226–228
resources related to, 173, 231–233,
    279–281
retrieving information from, 197,
    215–221
review questions on, 172–173, 231,
    253–254, 276, 279
schemas and scripts and, 256–258
semantic, 187–191
sensory, 20, 103, 139, 141–145
short-term, 20, 104, 139, 145–153,
    181–186
source, 252
study methods and, 221–224
suggestion and, 260–266, 275
summary points about, 171–172,
    229–231, 276–279
working, 154–171
Memory span, 174
Memory-trace replacement hypothesis,
    262, 264
Mental approach to coding, 150
Mental chronometry, 5, 326
Mental imagery, 323. See also Imagery
Mental models, 441
Mental rotation, 17–19, 25, 326–327, 355
Mental scanning, 327–328, 329
Mental set, 403–404
Mental simulations
    decision making and, 467
    problem solving and, 350–351
Mental time travel, 187
Mental-walk task, 334, 342
Metacontrast masking, 98
Method of loci, 348–349
Microelectrodes, 32
Mind, use of word, 24
Mirror neurons, 53
"Misbehavior of Organisms, The"
    (Breland and Breland), 13
Misinformation effect, 261–264, 280
Misleading postevent information
    (MPI), 261–264, 450
Modality effect, 175
Modal model of memory, 20, 138–141,
    171
Models in cognitive psychology, 19–21
Monty Hall three-door problem, 484
Morpheme, 361
Moses illusion, 281
Movie themes
    memory loss, 178, 231
    See also Film images
Muller-Lyer illusion, 98

Mutilated-checkerboard problem, 409–412

Narrative rehearsal hypothesis, 249
Narratives, 377
Nearness, law of, 77
Neglect
    unilateral, 342–343
    visual, 133
Nerve fibers, 30
Networks
    connectionist, 66, 307–313
    semantic, 299–307
Neural circuits, 36–38
Neural code, 40–42
Neural processing, 36–40
Neuroeconomics, 475–476
Neurons, 30–42
    basic components of, 31
    category-specific, 314–315
    communication between, 34–35
    imagery, 337–338
    information processing by, 36–40
    response to specific stimuli by, 38–40
    stimuli represented by firing of, 40–42
    transformation of energy in, 30–34
    working memory and, 166–167
    See also Brain
Neuropsychology, 43
    categorization and, 314–315
    imagery and, 341–346
    long-term memory and, 184–185, 188–189
Neuroscience, 22, 173
Neurotransmitters, 34–35
News stories, 2, 24
Nondeclarative memory. See Implicit memory
Nonknowing, 191
Noticing, 417

Object-based attention, 125–127
Observer perspective, 238–239
Occipital lobe, 43
Occlusion heuristic, 84, 85
Omission bias, 477
Operant conditioning, 12
Operators, 405
Optic nerve, 32
Opt-in procedure, 469
Opt-out procedure, 469
Organization
    imagery and, 348–349
    long-term memory and, 204–207, 222–223
    perceptual, 72–80

problem solving and, 422–423
    studying and, 222–223
Output units, 308

Paired-associate learning, 326
Parahippocampal place area (PPA), 90, 91
Parallel distributed processing (PDP) approach, 309
Parallel Distributed Processing: Explorations in the Microstructure of Cognition (McClelland and Rumelhart), 307
Parietal lobe, 43
Parser, 370
Parsing, 369, 370–376
    interactionist approach to, 373–376
    syntax-first approach to, 371–373
Partial report method, 144, 174
Pegword technique, 349
Perception, 55–98
    attention and, 91–94
    bottom-up processing in, 58–59, 66
    categorical, 387–388
    CogLab experiments on, 97–98
    computers and, 56, 80–84, 91
    context used in, 60–61
    feature integration theory of, 66–69, 72
    heuristics and, 79, 84–87
    hidden/blurred objects and, 82–83
    imagery and, 327–337, 342–347
    interactive activation model of, 62–66
    inverse projection problem in, 81
    knowledge and, 57–61, 84–91
    language and, 387–388
    lightness/darkness changes and, 83–84
    neural code and, 41–42, 90–91
    organization of elements in, 72–80
    physiology of, 28, 29, 41–42
    recognition-by-components theory of, 69–72
    resources related to, 96–97
    review questions on, 72, 94, 95–96
    speech segmentation and, 82, 87–90, 362–363
    summary points about, 94–95
    template matching and, 61–62
    top-down processing in, 58–61, 66, 78
    of words, 361–363
Perceptual intelligence, 56, 57, 84–91
    conversational speech and, 87–90
    heuristics and, 84–87
    neurons and, 90–91
Perceptual load, 132

Perceptual organization, 72–80
    effect of meaning on, 78
    Gestalt laws of, 74–80
    hearing and, 96
    structuralist approach to, 72, 73, 74
Permission schema, 448–449
Perseveration, 473
Persistence of vision, 142
Personal semantic memories, 190, 239
Philosophy, 22
Phoneme, 361
Phoneme exchanges, 382
Phonemic restoration effect, 361–362, 367
Phonological loop, 155, 156–159, 169
Phonological similarity effect, 156–157, 168–169, 174
Physiological approach to coding, 150
Physiological approach to cognition, 16–17, 19
Physiology
    of attention, 124–125
    of categorization, 314–315
    of decision making, 475–476
    of imagery, 337–347
    of language, 368–369
    of memory, 19, 164–168, 173, 184–185
    of neurons and the brain, 30–51
    of perception, 28, 29, 41–42
    of problem solving, 473–474, 483
    of reasoning, 474–475
    of thinking, 472–476
    of working memory, 164–168, 173
    See also Brain
Positron emission tomography (PET), 45. See also Brain imaging
Pragmatic inference, 255
Pragmatic reasoning schemas, 448
Pragnanz, law of, 74–75
Preattentive stage, 66
Precueing, 123–124
Predictive power, 306
Prefrontal cortex (PFC)
    decision making and, 476
    memory consolidation and, 211–212
    reasoning tasks and, 474–475
    thinking processes and, 473–475
    working memory and, 164–168
Preinventive forms, 427–428
Premises, 437
Primacy effect, 182–183, 184
Priming
    lexical, 365–367
    prototypical objects and, 292–293
    repetition, 191, 192–195
    syntactic, 385

Priming stimulus, 192
Principles of Physiology (James), 100
Proactive interference (PI), 147–148
  release from, 152–153
Problems
  definition of, 396
  types of, 396–397
Problem solving, 395–433
  analogical, 413–421, 425–426
  creative, 423–428, 432
  expertise in, 421–423
  fixations and, 401–404, 424–425, 428
  Gestalt approach to, 397–404
  imagery used in, 350–352, 354
  insight and, 398–400, 428–429
  mental set and, 403–404
  modern research on, 404–413
  Newell and Simon's approach to,
    405–408
  obstacles to, 401–404
  perception and, 96
  physiology of, 473–474, 483
  problem statement and, 408–413
  resources related to, 432
  restructuring and, 398, 400
  review questions on, 413, 429–430, 431
  sleep and, 428–429
  solutions to sample problems, 433
  summary points about, 430–431
  think-aloud protocols in, 411–412
Problem space, 406
Procedural memory, 191, 195–196
Propaganda effect, 196
Propagated action potentials, 33
Propositional mechanisms, 328
Propositional representations, 329–331,
  351
Prospective memory, 237–238, 277
Prototype, 288–289
Prototype approach to categorization,
  288–293, 294–295
Prototypicality, 289, 294
  family resemblance and, 289–291
  naming order and, 291
  priming and, 292–293
  typicality effect and, 291
Proximity, law of, 77
Psycholinguistics, 359
Psychology, 22
  early laboratories of, 9–10
  See also Cognitive psychology;
    Neuropsychology
Pulley problem, 350, 352

Radiation problem, 414–419
Rationality, 483

Rat–man demonstration, 60, 63
Reaction time, 6
  Donders' experiment on, 5–7
  simple vs. choice, 6, 7
Reactivation, 211
Reading, psychology of, 392
Reasoning, 435–466
  CogLab experiment on, 484
  culture and, 463, 465, 482
  decision making and, 437, 466
  deductive, 436, 437–452
  definition of, 435
  inductive, 436, 452–466
  language and, 435, 436
  long-term memory and, 435, 436
  perception and, 435
  physiology of, 474–475
  resources related to, 481–483
  review questions on, 452, 478, 481
  summary points about, 479–480
Recall test, 193
Recency effect, 183, 184
Receptive fields, 54
Recognition-by-components (RBC)
  theory, 69–72
Recognition test, 193
Reconsolidation, 226–228, 232
Reconstructive memory, 250n
Regret avoidance, 482
Rehearsal, 139
  elaborative, 197, 221
  flashbulb memories and, 249
  maintenance, 197, 221
Release from proactive interference,
  152–153
Remembering, 187
Reminiscence bump, 240–242
Remote memories, 212
Repeated recall, 244
Repeated reproduction, 250–251
Repetition priming, 191, 192–195
Representativeness heuristic, 459–462
  conjunction rule and, 460–461
  sample size and, 461–462
Resistance to visual noise, 70
Resources. *See* Information resources
Restructuring, 398
Retina, 32
Retrieval, 141, 197, 215–221
  cues used for, 204, 215–218
  encoding specificity and, 218–220
  state-dependent learning and,
    220–221
Retrieval cues, 204, 215–218
Retroactive interference, 262–263, 264
Retrograde amnesia, 209–210

Reverse acrobat problem, 408, 409
Review questions
  on attention, 113–114, 130, 131–132
  on brain physiology, 40, 51, 52–53
  on categorization, 298–299, 318, 320
  on decision making, 478, 481
  on imagery, 336–337, 352, 353–354
  on language, 376–377, 388–389,
    390–391
  on memory, 172–173, 231, 253–254,
    276, 279
  on perception, 72, 94, 95–96
  on problem solving, 413, 429–430,
    431
  on reasoning, 452, 478, 481
Risk-aversion strategy, 470
Risk-taking strategy, 470
Rule-based approach, 350, 351
Russian marriage problem, 413

Saccades, 120
Saliency map, 121
Sample size, 461–462
Sapir-Whorf hypothesis, 387, 388
Savings method, 8–9
Scene schema, 121
Schemas
  memory and, 256–257
  permission, 448–449
  pragmatic reasoning, 448
  scene, 121
Science, reasoning in, 454–455
Scripts, 257–258
Selective attention, 101–113
  attenuation theory of, 106–109
  dichotic listening and, 102–103
  filter model of, 103–106
  late-selection models of, 109–110
  task load and, 110–113
Self-knowing, 187
Self-reference effect, 203–204
Semantic coding, 150, 152–153, 185–186
Semantic memory, 187–191, 239
Semantic network approach, 299–307
  assessment and critique of, 306–307
  Collins and Loftus model, 305–306
  Collins and Quillian model, 299–305
Semantics, 368–369
  conversational speech and, 383–384
  sentence parsing and, 373–376
Sensations, 73
Sensory memory, 20, 139, 141–145, 171
  persistence of vision and, 142
  selective attention and, 103
  Sperling's experiment on, 142–144
Sensory reactivation hypothesis, 279

Sensory receptors, 30
Sentences, 368–376
    garden-path, 372, 373
    parsing of, 369, 370–376
    semantics of, 368–369, 373–376
    syntax of, 368–369, 371–373
    See also Words
Sentence verification technique, 291
Serial-position curve, 182–184
Sexual abuse, 275–276
Shadowing, 102
Shallow processing, 198–199
Short-term memory (STM), 20, 139,
        145–153
    capacity of, 148–150
    chunking and, 149–150
    coding in, 150–153
    duration of, 146–148
    impairments of, 185
    long-term memory vs., 181–186
    review questions on, 153
    selective attention and, 104
    summary points about, 171
    working memory vs., 154
    See also Working memory
Signal detection, 98
Sign language, 168–170
Similarity, law of, 75, 78
Similarity-coverage model, 464
Simon effect, 134
Simple cells, 39
Simple reaction time, 6, 7
Simplicity, law of, 74–75
Single dissociation, 43, 44
Situationally produced mental set,
        403–404
Situation models, 379–381
Sleep and insight, 428–429
Social-exchange theory, 450
Social situations, attention in, 127–129
Source memory, 252
Source misattributions, 252
Source monitoring, 252, 280
Source monitoring errors, 252–253,
        263–264
Source problem, 414
Source story, 414
Spatial cueing, 134
Spatial representations, 329, 351, 392
Specificity coding, 41
Speech
    errors in producing, 381–383
    perception of words in, 82, 87–90,
        362–363
    sign language compared to, 168–170
    studying the production of, 359

Speech errors, 381–383
    identification of, 382
    language mechanisms and, 382–383
Speech segmentation, 82, 87–90,
        362–363, 367
Spellbound (film), 178
Sperling's experiment, 142–144
"Split-scan" experiment, 104–106
Spreading activation, 302–303
Standard model of consolidation, 210,
        211
State-dependent learning, 220–221
Statistical learning, 88–90, 363
Stereotypes, 459
Stimulus salience, 120–121
Stories, 377–381
Stroop effect, 117, 134
Structural features
    of modal model, 139–141
    of problems, 417
Structuralism, 9–10, 73
Studying
    encoding specificity and, 218,
        219, 220
    state-dependent learning and,
        220–221
    techniques for improving, 221–224
Subcortical structures, 43
Subgoals, 407
Subordinate level of categories, 296
Subtraction technique, 45, 46
Suffix effect, 231, 234
Suggestion, 260–266
    eyewitness testimony and, 270–271,
        272
    false memories and, 264–266, 275
    misinformation effect and, 261–264
Superordinate level of categories, 296
Supervised learning, 309
Surface features, 417, 418, 423
Syllogisms, 436, 437–452
    categorical, 437–443
    conditional, 443–452
    validity of, 437–440, 481
Synapse, 34–35, 208, 209
Synaptic consolidation, 210
Syntactic ambiguity, 370
Syntactic category rule, 383
Syntactic priming, 385
Syntactic Structures (Chomsky), 359
Syntax, 368–369
    conversational speech and, 384–386
    sentence parsing and, 371–373
Syntax-first approach to parsing,
        371–373
Systems consolidation, 210

Tacit-knowledge explanation, 331–332,
        351
Target problem, 414
Task load, 110–113
Template matching, 61–62
Temporal lobe, 43
Testing conditions, 224
Text processing, 377–381
    inferences in, 377–379
    situation models in, 379–381
Thalamus, 43
Think-aloud protocols, 411–412
Thinking
    convergent, 424
    creative, 425–426
    divergent, 424
    logical, 438–439
    physiology of, 472–476
Through the Looking Glass (Carroll), 371
Time-based tasks, 237–238
Tip-of-the-tongue phenomenon,
        232–233
Top-down processing, 58–61, 66, 78,
        345
Tower of Hanoi problem, 405–407
Trade-off strategy, 419–420
Traffic accidents, 118–119
Transcranial magnetic stimulation
        (TMS), 340–341
Transduction, 31–32
Transfer-appropriate processing,
        200–202
Transitional probabilities, 88–90
Trauma-memory oriented therapists,
        275
Triangle problem, 399, 433
Two-string problem, 402–403
Typicality effect, 291
Typicality principle, 464

Ultimatum game, 475
Unconscious inference, 7–8
Unilateral neglect, 342–343
Units, 308
Utility, 466
Utility theory, 466, 475

Validity of syllogisms, 437–440
Varied mapping condition, 117
Venn diagrams, 440, 481
Verbal Behavior (Skinner), 12, 358, 359
Video games, 133
View invariance, 69
View-invariant properties, 69–70
Vision, persistence of, 142
Visual agnosia, 314

Visual attention, 120–127
  autism and, 127–129
  eye movements and, 120–122, 133
  inattentional blindness and, 123
  object-based, 125–127
  precueing procedure and, 123–124
Visual coding, 150, 151–152, 185
Visual cortex, 345
Visual icon, 144
Visual imagery, 323, 354. *See also*
    Imagery
Visual neglect, 133
Visual perception. *See* Perception
Visual search, 96, 98
Visual working memory, 173
Visuospatial sketch pad, 156, 159–161

"War of the Ghosts" experiment,
    250–251
Wason four-card problem, 445–452
  evolutionary approach to, 450–452

falsification principle and, 446
  permissions schema and, 448–449
  regulations and, 446–448
Water-jug problem, 403–404
Water-pouring problem, 350, 351–352
Weapons focus, 268, 269
Weights, 309
Well-defined problems, 396
Whole report method, 143
Word exchanges, 383
Word frequency, 363–365
Word-frequency effect, 364, 367
Word-length effect, 157–158, 169–170
Word level, 62
Word recognition, 63–64
Words, 360–368
  components of, 361
  images associated with, 349
  perception of, 82, 87–90, 361–363
  understanding of, 363–367
  See also Sentences

Word substitution, 383
Word superiority effect, 64, 367, 394
Word units, 62
Working memory, 154–171
  American Sign Language and,
    168–170
  central executive in, 156, 162–163
  definition of, 154
  episodic buffer in, 163–164
  overview of components, 155–156
  phonological loop in, 155, 156–159
  physiology of, 164–168
  resources related to, 173, 354
  review questions on, 170–171
  short-term memory vs., 154
  summary points about, 172
  visuospatial sketch pad in, 156,
    159–161
  See also Short-term memory